THOMAS HARDY

A BIOGRAPHY
REVISITED

THOMAS HARDY

A BIOGRAPHY REVISITED

MICHAEL MILLGATE

OXFORD

UNIVERSITY PRESS

OXFORD
UNIVERSITY PRESS

Great Clarendon Street, Oxford OX2 6DP

Oxford University Press is a department of the University of Oxford.
It furthers the University's objective of excellence in research, scholarship,
and education by publishing worldwide in

Oxford New York

Auckland Bangkok Buenos Aires Cape Town Chennai
Dar es Salaam Delhi Hong Kong Istanbul Karachi Kolkata
Kuala Lumpur Madrid Melbourne Mexico City Mumbai Nairobi
São Paulo Shanghai Taipei Tokyo Toronto

Oxford is a registered trade mark of Oxford University Press
in the UK and in certain other countries

Published in the United States
by Oxford University Press Inc., New York

British Library Cataloguing in Publication Data
Data available

Library of Congress Cataloging in Publication Data
Data applied for

ISBN 0-19-927565-3

1 3 5 7 9 10 8 6 4 2

Typeset by Regent Typesetting, London
Printed in Great Britain
on acid-free paper by
Biddles Ltd,
King's Lynn, Norfolk

In Memoriam

RICHARD LITTLE PURDY

and

CATHARINE CARVER

CONTENTS

LIST OF ILLUSTRATIONS

ILLUSTRATIONS IN THE TEXT

SOURCES

Illustrations are reproduced by kind permission of: Mr Frederick B. Adams, 41, 57; Mr John Antell, 6, 13; the Beinecke Rare Book and Manuscript Library, Yale University, 14, 15, 16, 45, 53; the Henry W. and Albert A. Berg Collection, the New York Public Library, Astor, Lenox and Tilden Foundations, 23, 25, 43; Mrs Gertrude Bugler, 27; University Library, University of California at Riverside, 52, 56; the Syndics of Cambridge University Library, 33, 60; W. & R. Chambers, Ltd., 20; the Trustees of the Thomas Hardy Memorial Collection in the Dorset County Museum, Dorchester, 2, 8, 9, 17, 21, 22, 24, 28, 29, 30, 32, 34, 39, 44, 47, 51, 54, 55, 58; Professor Leslie Greenhill, 61; Harold Hoffman papers, Miami University of Ohio, 10; Mr David Holmes, 49; Mr T. W. Jesty, 46; Mr Henry Lock, for the H. E. F. Lock Collection, on loan to the Dorset County Museum, 3, 4, 5, 7, 11, 12; Mrs Elfrida Manning, 38; Michael Millgate, 31, 61; Princeton University Library, the Morris H. Parrish Collection, 40, the Robert H. Taylor Collection, 59; the Harry Ransom Humanities Research Center, University of Texas at Austin, 26; Mrs Daphne Wood, 50. Copyright illustrations reproduced with permission: Simmons Aerofilms, 19; Pitkin Pictorials Ltd., 1; Tate Gallery (© Tate London 2004), 48.

PROLOGUE

To undertake the revision of a biography is scarcely less risky—less of a venture over potentially dangerous waters—than embarking on it in the first place. However much the biographer knows, that knowledge can never account for more than a fraction of the life actually lived. No sources are entirely unproblematic, and they may in any case remain permanently deficient for those periods or aspects of a life commonly considered to be of particular significance: early childhood, for example, sexual relationships, and those supremely elusive processes of literary and artistic creativity. In returning, however, to *Thomas Hardy: A Biography* some two decades after its original appearance, I do at least have the confidence of knowing that much material of interest and importance has been published during the intervening years.

The collective edition of Hardy's letters is now complete, editions of his interviews, his public writings, and the letters written by his wives have all appeared, and the editing of his surviving notebooks continues. Genealogical researchers, local historians, and writers on Wessex have turned up important new pieces of information. Scholarly research has revised and sometimes revolutionized earlier assumptions about such issues as the precise nature of Hardy's open literary collaboration with Florence Henniker, his secret assistance to Florence Dugdale, and his participation in the writing of the official biography published shortly after his death. And Hardy's stature continues to grow. His poetry, admirably edited, is now altogether more widely and sympathetically read than it was fifty or even twenty years ago. Film and television productions have helped to keep his novels and stories alive in the popular imagination, and although a comprehensive scholarly edition of the fiction is still lacking there are excellent editions and textual studies of individual works and of the previously uncollected stories. Useful editorial work has also been incorporated into some of the numerous paperback editions that collectively testify to Hardy's continuing presence in school and university syllabuses on both sides of the Atlantic and, indeed, around the world.

Because of my own role in the editing of Hardy's letters, his wives' letters, his ghosted biography, and some of the other new resources for the study of his life and work, the twentieth birthday of *Thomas Hardy: A Biography* in 2002 became an occasion for looking back not just to 1982 but to the early 1960s when I began working towards my first book in the field, *Thomas Hardy: His Career as a Novelist*, published in 1971. That retrospective stocktaking led to the projection and now the completion of this new, expanded, and extensively revised edition of *Thomas Hardy: A Biography* that draws on all the additional information that has recently become available and, more broadly, on the full range of materials and insights that I have accumulated in the process of working on Hardy over a period of some forty years. I believe this to be the most useful contribution to Hardy studies I can now make. I also think of it, more self-indulgently, as in some sense an acknowledgement and even a justification of the unrepeatable opportunities I have enjoyed of talking with people who encountered Hardy at first hand, among them E. M. Forster, Harold Macmillan, Edmund Blunden, Gertrude Bugler, Norman Atkins (another of the 'Hardy Players'), May O'Rourke (Hardy's part-time secretary), Alice Harvey (Emma Hardy's personal maid), and Charles Gale (Tryphena Sparks's son), and of profiting from the friendship and cooperation of others, such as Irene Cooper Willis, Richard Little Purdy, Frederick Baldwin Adams, and the poet Henry Reed, who had known Florence Hardy during her widowhood and visited Max Gate at a time when Hardy's study remained very much as he had left it.

When I reread the original edition of *Thomas Hardy: A Biography* I was reassured to discover that it stood up well and contained very little—other than a numerical miscalculation in an important footnote—by which I needed to feel embarrassed. At the same time it did not at all fully reflect what I felt that I now knew. There were issues and episodes that had been left untreated, others whose treatment seemed in need of sophistication and renarration, and some major aspects of Hardy's life that demanded to be more solidly and specifically established. I recognized above all the possibility of arriving at better informed and more sympathetic understandings of Emma Lavinia Gifford and Florence Emily Dugdale and of their relationships to each other—both before and, in a sense, after Emma's death—and to the man they successively married. Not only had I now read all of their discoverable letters in preparation for the editing of *Letters of Emma and Florence Hardy*, but I had also learned much from working on the annotations to that volume, revisiting St Juliot and other relevant locations, tracking down previously unknown photographs, documents, and first-hand records, and devoting intensive study to Florence Hardy's crucial roles in assisting Hardy's composition of his own official biography and in carrying out the provisions of his disastrous will.

But the fundamental problems of confronting Hardy as a biographical subject have proved no less recalcitrant the second time around. It is at once accurate and commonplace to speak of his birth as obscure, but from a biographical standpoint that obscurity had implications going much beyond his having been conceived out of wedlock by an impecunious rural couple and brought with difficulty to birth in a lonely lane's-end cottage adjacent to what Shakespeare might have characterized as a blasted heath. People of the time, class, and background of Hardy's parents and their families typically wrote very few letters, if indeed they could write at all; nor, unless they fell foul of the law, were their names likely to appear in local newspapers or in any public records other than the most basic registrations of births, marriages, and deaths. It is true that Hardy's parents rather remarkably succeeded in propelling their children into the middle class. But direct and unmediated evidence of Hardy's early years remains extremely sparse, and he made even in young adulthood so little impact on the world that fewer than ten of his letters are known to have survived from the years prior to his thirtieth birthday.

Hardy became over time an intensely private man who always managed to protect the privacy of his parents and siblings and seems genuinely to have dreaded for himself the kind of posthumous exposure he so poignantly imagined for Susan Henchard in *The Mayor of Casterbridge*: 'And all her shining keys will be took from her, and her cupboards opened; and little things a' didn't wish seen, anybody will see; and her wishes and ways will all be as nothing!' He learned caution from the strongly and personally hostile reviews he sometimes received and from his encounters with journalistic interviewers and occasional brushes with would-be biographers. In his famous later years, settling into a still creative old age as into a role for which his earlier life had been simply a preparation, he sought quite systematically to exercise control over everything that risked becoming material for others to use. He destroyed many letters, notebooks, and other documents during his lifetime, mandated the destruction of others immediately following his death, and did everything he could to establish and protect the unique authority of the third-person narrative of his own life, written for posthumous publication over his wife's name, by which he hoped to pre-empt other and potentially more intrusive biographies.

Included in the later chapters of this book are accounts of how that narrative was written and revised in secret by Hardy himself, typed and extensively retyped in secret by Florence Hardy, reviewed and revised by Florence and others in the wake of Hardy's death, published in 1928 and 1930 as *The Early Life of Thomas Hardy 1840–91* and *The Later Years of Thomas Hardy 1892–1928*, and subsequently republished as a single volume entitled *The Life of Thomas Hardy*. Both of the original volumes carried the name of Florence Emily Hardy as author, and the *Life*, as it came to be called, was initially accepted as a work that she had herself written, if with considerable assistance from Hardy himself. Subsequent revelation of Hardy's central role in the composition of the *Life* resulted in its being widely categorized as his autobiography, although its claim to that status had been seriously compromised by the well-intentioned omissions, alterations, and insertions made by Florence Hardy after her husband's death. The text now accepted as 'standard'—and frequently invoked in the following pages—restores Hardy's original title, *The Life and Work of Thomas Hardy*, and substitutes for the published *Early Life* and *Later Years* a reconstruction, derived from Florence Hardy's undestroyed typescripts, of the text as Hardy himself finally left it.

Intensive engagement with that reconstruction has convinced me that Hardy's autobiographical evasions consisted for the most part of mild distortions and outright omissions rather than of actual misstatements. But the uncertainties remain. What was omitted must sometimes have been of major significance, what was emphasised may not in fact have been of the foremost importance, and there is sufficient evidence to show that when incorporating the text of a letter or notebook entry Hardy—like many a Victorian biographer—saw nothing wrong in cutting, expanding, or rewriting the original in accordance with his hindsighted judgement as to how it should ideally read. *Life and Work*, in short, like Hallam Tennyson's account of his father's life, is both an indispensable biographical source and a formidable and sometimes absolute barrier to further and deeper knowledge.

Hardy, of course, could and did determine the fate of his own personal papers and of most of the letters he received from other people. He also gave his approval, within his lifetime, to the distribution of his major literary manuscripts. His outgoing correspondence, on the other hand, was beyond his control, and he seems to have had no knowledge of the contents of the numerous and often complaint-filled letters so indiscreetly written by both his wives. It is on the evidence of such letters, reinforced by the recollections of the journalists, admirers, friends, and fellow writers who encountered Hardy in London or over tea at Max Gate, that the narrative of *Life and Work* can for the most part be amplified, corroborated, and, on rarer occasions, corrected.

What cannot be so readily verified or challenged are the elderly Hardy's accounts of his childhood, youth, and early adulthood. These are, of course, periods for which biographers are often thrown back upon their subject's own reminiscences, but that dependence has in Hardy's case been rendered especially questionable both by the scarcity of evidence from other sources and by a widespread suspicion—sharpened by knowledge of how the *Life* was written—that he exaggerated his family's social and economic status in order to conceal its actual poverty and obscurity. The most one can say is that the available fragments of independent evidence tend to endorse or only mildly qualify what Hardy says about his Higher Bockhampton childhood, if not the romantic aura thrown by his memory over the entire place and period.

Revisiting, revising, and expanding *Thomas Hardy: A Biography* has proved to be an absorbing and exhilarating experience, rich in arrivals at fresh interconnections and new or at least firmer conclusions. Though I have excised numerous passages that seemed superfluous and made detailed revisions even to passages whose narrative content remained largely unchanged, my principal and pleasantest task has been the incorporation of new or substantially reconsidered material: *Thomas Hardy: A Biography Revisited* is in consequence somewhat longer than its predecessor. No biography, of course, is ever 'definitive', in the sense of being absolutely the last word. Discoveries will continue to be made, additional letters will come to light, fresh or differently angled interpretations can always be offered. But this is a biography now twice grounded in a forty-year devotion and exposure to Hardy studies, and I must—and do—hope and expect that it will serve a wide spectrum of both general and specialist readers for many years to come.

1

Hardys and Hands

Thomas Hardy is unique among English writers in achieving recognition both as a major novelist and as a major poet. He is also exceptional in his combination of a self-consciously 'modern' cast of thought with an intense, apparently paradoxical, preoccupation with the personal, local, and national past. Born in 1840 to humble parents in an out of the way corner of the English countryside, he lived and wrote into his eighty-eighth year, registering with extraordinary sensitivity and precision, in both prose and verse, the historic changes that swept over England, and especially over his native Dorset, during the course of the nineteenth century and the beginning of the twentieth. At the end of a life that had spanned the Crimean War, the Indian Mutiny, the South African War, and the First World War, it was still the Napoleonic period, prior to his own birth, that chiefly haunted his imagination. In 1919 he saw time as stretching back into the past 'like a railway line covered with a blue haze, and it goes uphill till 1900 and then it goes over the hill and disappears till about the middle of the century, and then it rises again up to about 1800, and then it disappears altogether'.[1] Four years later T. E. Lawrence, writing to Robert Graves, described Hardy as being 'so far-away. Napoleon is a real man to him, and the country of Dorsetshire echoes that name everywhere in Hardy's ears. He lives in his period, and thinks of it as the great war.'[2]

But Hardy was no less fascinated by the obscure and private lives lived by his own parents and grandparents, their relatives and acquaintances, by the cottages they called home, the customs they observed, the songs they sang, and the social and economic realities with which they had to deal. His novels, stories, and poems are heavily dependent for their settings, their details, and often their plots upon things heard and seen in his childhood: told and retold stories of smuggling and invasion alarms, local scandals and public punishments; personal memories of mail coaches and tinderboxes, Corn Law and anti-popery demonstrations, and marks left on Dorset barns by the musket balls of a vanished soldiery. He drew above all on the vivid taletelling of his parents and, as time went by, on his own researches into old newspapers and records, on the breadth of his reading, and on his active and wide-ranging observation of the world into which he had himself been born.

Nothing in Hardy's immediate ancestry offered the remotest hint of what he would become, and he retained to the very last a wry fascination, compounded of an artist's vanity and a child's sense of wonder, with those quirks of heredity, human affection, social history, and the class system that had combined, or collided, in the conception and birth of a man who could come from rural obscurity and live to be celebrated as the most famous man of letters of his day. In the historical distance, beyond reach of certainty, it was possible to discern, or to project, the outlines of family connections of a moderately distinguished kind. Among the several works of genealogy in Hardy's library at the time of his death was an anonymous account of the ancient le Hardy family of Jersey, in the Channel Islands, and he liked to think that it was from a late fifteenth-century Clement le Hardy and his son John that 'the Dorset Hardys' were all derived, including the Thomas Hardye of Frampton who endowed the Dorchester Grammar School in 1579 and the Thomas Masterman Hardy of Portisham who was Nelson's flag-captain at Trafalgar. Various landowning Hardys figure in the pages of John Hutchins's *The History and Antiquities of the County of Dorset*, originally compiled in the eighteenth century, and Hardy's markings in his own much-prized copy show that he was well aware of those families and of the possible links between them and his own 'branch', the Hardys of Owermoigne, Bockhampton, and other places in or near the valley of the river Frome.[3]

Such links, however vague, were important to Hardy in that they fed his sense of belonging to a family that had come down in the world. To have a family crest but not to use it was intricately pleasurable in itself; it also validated the scornful deflation of family pretensions in such novels as *The Hand of Ethelberta* and *Tess of the d'Urbervilles*. Complaining in his early seventies that there were still people in Dorchester who thought themselves too grand to speak to him, Hardy exclaimed: 'Ours was also a county family if they only knew!'[4] But the name Hardy is by no means uncommon in Dorset. There is scarcely a parish in the entire county whose churchyards and registers would fail to yield one or more pockets of Hardys, and in drawing up a family tree, rather portentously headed 'The Hardy Pedigree', towards the end of his life, Hardy wisely chose to advance only a general-ized claim to be descended from the le Hardys and the landowning Hardys memorialized by Hutchins.[5]

Gently suggesting that 'the less people know of a writer's antecedents (till he is dead) the better', Hardy was nevertheless willing to tell Charles Kegan Paul in 1881: 'From time immemorial—I can speak from certain knowledge of four generations—my direct ancestors have all been master-masons, with a set of journeymen masons under them: though they have never risen above this level, they have *never* sunk below it—i.e. they have never been journeymen themselves.'[6] If there is exaggeration here it is of the mildest kind. Although Hardy's paternal forebears may not always have been employers, they were certainly masons and for the most part self-employed and independent—much like Michael Henchard at the beginning of *The Mayor of Casterbridge*. And the acknowledged uncertainty about the remoter reaches of the ancestral line allows for a family tradition that a John Hardy, his mason's tools in a basket over his shoulder, simply appeared (like Henchard again) one day in the late eighteenth century from nobody knew where.[7]

That particular John Hardy, Hardy's great-grandfather, appears in the 'pedigree' as John Hardy of Puddletown—to use the modern name of the village, five miles north-east of Dorchester, that was often less decorously known as Piddletown—and assigned the birth-date of 1755 and the death-date of 1821. The latter date is certain enough, but intensive genealogical research has failed—such is the plethora of Dorset Hardys—to determine with absolute confidence either the date of that John Hardy's birth or even the names of his parents. The probability, however, is that he was not, as has been asserted,[8] one of the sons of a John Hardy of Owermoigne and his wife Elizabeth Swire, but rather the only son, baptized (and probably born) in 1756, of a John and Martha Hardy of Tolpuddle. Tolpuddle is not far from Puddletown, but since the younger John Hardy, trained as a mason, seems to have made that transition unaccompanied by parents or siblings, it is likely enough that his new neighbours would have viewed him as a somewhat mysterious figure. In either case, the 'pure Irish' great-great-grandmother to whom Hardy once laid claim in a letter to Lady Gregory remains unidentified and unguessed-at: virtually nothing is known of Martha Hardy, and whether or not Elizabeth Swire was related to Hardy, she was evidently not related to anybody Irish.[9]

What is known is that in 1777 a John Hardy, then living in the Dorchester parish of Fordington, was married at Woodsford, in the Frome valley, to Jane Knight of that parish, several of whose possible relatives her great-

The Family of Thomas Hardy, Sen.

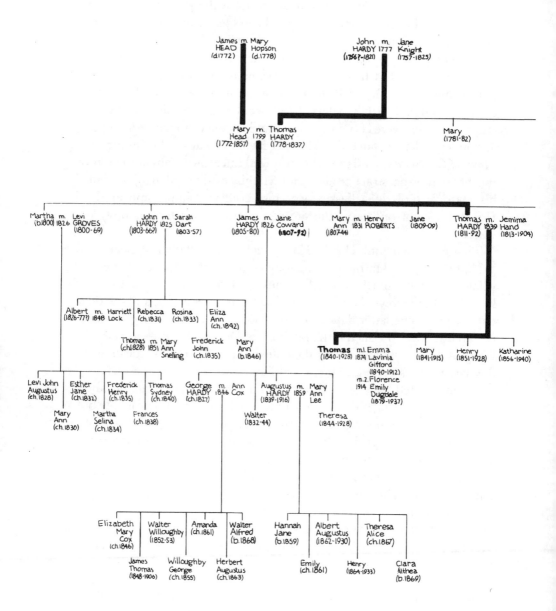

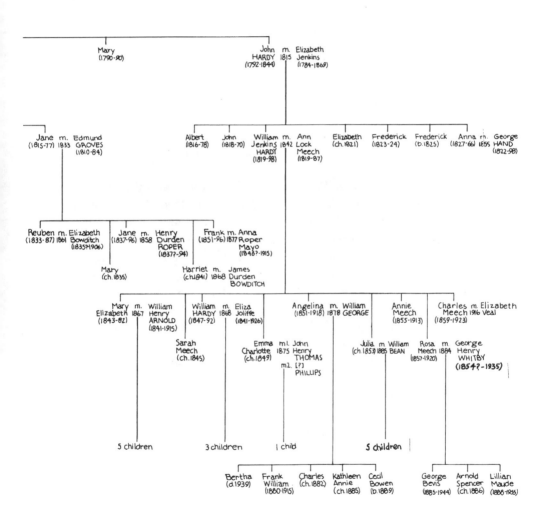

grandson took the trouble to track down in the Stinsford church registers nearly 150 years later. It was in Athelhampton, close to Puddletown, that their first child, Thomas, was born in 1778, but in Puddletown itself that John subsequently practised his trade as a bricklayer and mason. Near the century's end, Thomas, become a mason in his turn, somehow met Mary Head, the orphaned daughter of James and Mary Head of the distant Berkshire village of Fawley, and married her in Puddletown Church in December 1799. Just seven months after that, in July 1800, and still in Puddletown, Mary gave birth to a daughter, and in the following year the family now of three went to live in the comfortable cottage that John Hardy had built for them across the heath in what later became the tiny hamlet of Higher or Upper Bockhampton. The land on which the cottage stood belonged to the extensive Kingston Maurward estate, and although it was an extremely isolated spot John Hardy, setting his son up in business for the first time, presumably thought of it as being within reasonable distance of Kingston Maurward House, the village of Bockhampton, and the parish church at Stinsford, for which he himself had already done some work.[10] The distancing of potential competition could also have been a factor.

The cottage into which Thomas and Mary Hardy and their daughter Martha had moved was, in fact, only three miles from Dorchester, the principal town of Dorset, but it stood at the end of a narrow lane, solitary, deep among trees, and on the very edge of what was then open heathland, stretching almost uninterruptedly across south Dorset and into Hampshire. The building itself stands still at the edge of Thorncombe Wood, famously picturesque and, as a National Trust property, accessible to public view, and the adjacent heathland remains uncultivated, though thick in many places with interloping rhododendrons and encroached upon by the dark plantations of the Forestry Commission. Some sense, indeed, can still be recovered of the commercially unpromising location in which Hardy's paternal grandfather thenceforward carried on the trade of bricklayer and mason that he had learned from his father and would pass on in turn to his three sons, John (born 1803), James (born 1805), and Thomas (born 1811). There were also four daughters, three of whom lived into adulthood and departed for other Dorset villages as the wives of, respectively, a butcher, a shopman, and a thatcher. During the Hardys' early years in the cottage, the isolation that handicapped legitimate business interests was perceived as a distinct advantage by the smugglers then active along the nearby Dorset coast, and Hardy's grandfather allowed them to use the building as a staging post from 1801 to 1805 or thereabouts, when his wife put a stop to it:

'He sometimes', Hardy once noted, 'had as many as eighty "tubs" in a dark closet . . . each tub containing 4 gallons. The spirits often smelt all over the house, being proof, & had to be lowered for drinking. The tubs, or little elongated barrels, were of thin staves with wooden hoops: I remember one of them which had been turned into a bucket by knocking out one head, & putting a handle.'[11]

Over the years the Hardys did indeed do a good deal of the building work for Kingston Maurward House, the principal property in the parish, but they were also tenants of the estate, and in both capacities found themselves in a position inferior to that of another Thomas Hardy, no relation, who held the post of estate steward and the status of gentleman until (as Hardy would have heard as a child) he fell into the river Frome and, having lost an arm in an earlier accident, was unable to save himself from drowning. It had been in 1832, while the steward was still alive, that the death of an elderly woman automatically terminated the 'lifehold' lease of the cottage in which John Hardy, eldest of the Hardy sons, was living, and a new lease was drawn upon the lives of the steward's own son and daughters.[12] Effectively expelled from the hamlet by this apparent exercise of social privilege, John Hardy moved with his growing family (he was to have seven children in all) to the Dorchester suburb of Fordington, where he became increasingly isolated from his Bockhampton relatives.[13]

In October 1835 a new lease on the cottage of Thomas and Mary Hardy was executed upon the lives of Thomas himself and his two younger sons. Two years later the father died, leaving an estate consisting of the leasehold of the cottage itself, valued at £180, together with £60 in cash and a further £61 in uncollected debts. After funeral and other expenses had been met the youngest son, Thomas, was allowed a substantial portion of the residue in recognition of wages left unpaid over the past eight years: these were reckoned at fourteen shillings a week, less what he was deemed to have received in the form of his keep, clothes, and pocket money. The other son, James, as a married man with children, had been receiving his wages on a regular basis.[14] Hardy always insisted upon the lack of commercial ambition shown by his father and grandfather, and the casualness of the financial arrangements between them lends support to such a view. So, too, does their failure, over a period of several years, to collect the payments due to them from the Kingston Maurward estate, although it must always have been difficult to bring pressure to bear on their own landlord.[15] For several years after their father's death the two brothers, James and Thomas, ran the business together under their mother's name, but by the late 1840s they had decided to divide the 'goodwill' and go their separate ways. One account has it that the division took the form of physical combat, out on the heath, but the determining factors seem rather to have been Mary Hardy's partiality for her youngest son and his responsive willingness to take care of his mother in her old age. Her will left all her property 'to my Son, Thomas Hardy, for his kindness and affection towards me'. That will was dated 24 January 1841, thirteen months after her son's marriage to Jemima Hand in December 1839, and slightly less than seven months after the birth of her famous grandson.[16]

Hardy's mother's family, the Hands, came from the tiny village of Melbury Osmond in north-west Dorset. Jemima Hand herself was born in 1813, the fifth child of George Hand and his wife Elizabeth, or Betty, Swetman. George Hand was the eldest of the nine children of a Puddletown couple, William and Betty Hand. Betty Swetman's mother, however, was a Childs, a long-established Melbury family several of whom in Hardy's own time were professional people, active in medicine and publishing.[17] Her father's family, the Swetmans, had been small landowners—or, as Hardy was fond of saying, 'yeomen'—for generations, farming land subsequently absorbed into the Melbury House estates of the earls of Ilchester: the fields had been theirs, Hardy once told a friend, 'when the Ilchesters were at plow'.[18] Swetman family anecdotes had come down from the late seventeenth century, when the family was said to have been 'ruined' as a consequence of its sympathy with the Monmouth rebellion, and Hardy later drew upon such stories in his own short story 'The Duke's Reappearance'.[19] His grandmother Betty herself he seems to have remembered only vaguely from a very few childhood encounters. From her daughters, however, his mother and his aunts, he built up an image of her that was probably accurate as to her exceptional courage, intelligence, and independence, but exaggerated in respect of her medical wisdom and breadth of reading.[20]

George Hand and Betty Swetman were married in Melbury Osmond Church on 27 December 1804, just eight days ahead of the birth of Betty's first child, Maria. Hardy's family 'pedigree', echoed in *Life and Work*, rather mysteriously describes the marriage as 'clandestine'; the church records, on the other hand, show that it did indeed take place on that day in that place. That the banns had been duly called on each of the three preceding Sundays rather reduces the possibility of Hardy's meaning that the bride's condition had required the ceremony to be performed with the maximum of obtainable privacy.[21] It seems more likely that he had simply repeated the word his mother had used to describe a marriage of which she knew little other than that it had taken place in defiance of the wishes of Betty's father

and without his participation or consent, John Swetman having so disapproved of his daughter's pregnancy and marital choice that he refused to
have anything further to do with her. According to one account, she was
allowed to take her clothes and her books—such as they can have been—
and then disowned. This decree of Betty's 'stern father', as he is called in *Life
and Work*, reinforced by her omission from his will, was the principal cause
of the family's subsequent poverty, and it seems likely that in addition to
despising the lowly social and economic status of his daughter's husband he
also knew something of those darker aspects of George Hand's personality
that all too soon revealed themselves.[22]

Described in his marriage certificate as a 'servant', George Hand seems
to have worked chiefly as a gardener, or as a shepherd. Though he was only
briefly in receipt of poor relief, his always meagre wages appear to have
been largely consumed in drinking, a propensity for which his sons were
also to be notorious, and Hardy's mother's recollections of her violent,
drunken, unregenerate father—said to have died of consumption, sitting
up by the fire—contributed significantly to the creation of such characters
as Michael Henchard and Jude Fawley. Driven by fierce anti-religious
prejudices, further inflamed by resentment of his wife's claims to social and
educational superiority, Hand refused to have his children christened in
church, and on the very day in 1822 when their father was buried—even,
according to one account, while his coffin sat in the church awaiting
burial—the two youngest children were 'received into the congregation',
after having been 'privately' baptized several years earlier. Some of the
elder children, including Jemima herself, had also received private
baptisms, although formally registered after a briefer interval and within
their father's lifetime.[23] When Hardy in *Life and Work* referred to the 'very
stressful experiences' of his mother's youth that cost her such pain to speak
of in later years, he not only had in mind her father's brutality and the
family's poverty but also her harrowing memories of those secret and con-
spiratorial baptisms. Her stories later stimulated his own imagination of
the midnight baptism in *Tess of the d'Urbervilles*, even as the poem 'Her
Late Husband' sprang from Jemima's account of her mother's insistence on
having George Hand buried alongside the woman who had been his
mistress.[24]

Widowed, disinherited, and with almost all her children still at home,
Betty Hand was frequently obliged to seek poor relief, to 'go on the parish',
and a letter she wrote to her daughter Mary in January 1842 is eloquent of
her difficulties and her unyielding sense of personal injustice:

The Family of Jemima Hand

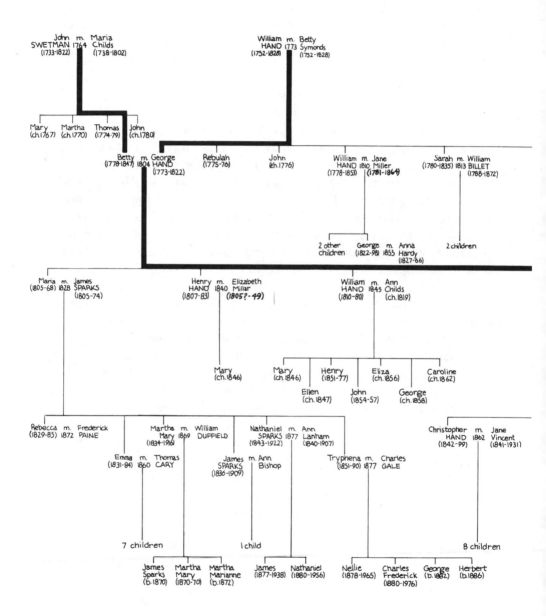

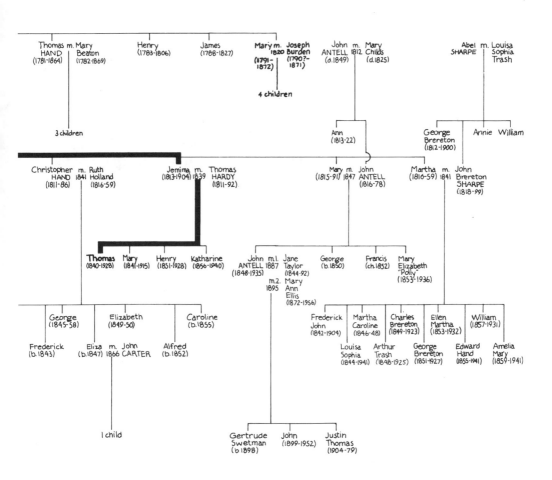

Thomas m. Mary
HAND | Beaton
(1781-1864) | (1782-1869)

Henry
(1783-1806)

James
(1788-1827)

Mary m. Joseph
1820 Burden
(1791- | (1790?-
1872) | 1871)

John m. Mary
ANTELL 1812 Childs
(d.1849) | (d.1825)

Abel m. Louisa
SHARPE | Sophia
Trash

4 children

3 children

Ann
(1813-22)

George
Brereton
(1812-1900)

Annie   William

Christopher m. Ruth
HAND 1841 Holland
(1811-86) | (1816-59)

Jemima m. Thomas
(1813-1904) 1839 HARDY
(1811-92)

Mary m. John
(1815-91) 1847 ANTELL
(1816-78)

Martha m. John
(1816-59) 1841 Brereton
SHARPE
(1818-99)

Thomas
(1840-1928)

Mary
(1841-1915)

Henry
(1851-1928)

Katharine
(1856-1940)

John m.1. Jane
ANTELL 1887 Taylor
(1848-1935) (1844-92)
m.2. Mary
1895 Ann
Ellis
(1872-1956)

George
(b.1850)

Francis
(ch.1852)

Mary
Elizabeth
"Polly"
(1853-1936)

George
(1845-58)

Elizabeth
(1849-50)

Caroline
(b.1855)

Frederick
John
(1842-1904)

Martha
Caroline
(1846-48)

Charles
Brereton
(1849-1923)

Ellen
Martha
(1853-1932)

William
(1857-1931)

Frederick
(b.1843)

Eliza m. John
(b.1847) 1866 CARTER

Alfred
(b.1852)

Louisa
Sophia
(1844-1941)

Arthur
Trash
(1848-1925)

George
Brereton
(1851-1927)

Edward
Hand
(1855-1941)

Amelia
Mary
(1859-1941)

1 child

Gertrude
Swetman
(b.1898)

John
(1899-1952)

Justin
Thomas
(1904-79)

[I]t is a true saying that poverty seperates chiefest friends—and I should not have been poor if right had took its place—you wished me to let you know what beef I had att Christmas it was a small bit of lean cut of the leg or shene—it would have been quite dear att. 3d. Chrises was worth 20. of it because his was good.[25]

The 'Chris' of this letter was her youngest son Christopher who followed his brother Henry (sometimes spelled Henery) to Puddletown, where they both worked in the building trade and drank more than was altogether wise. William, the middle son, seems also to have spent some time in Puddletown before returning permanently to Melbury. The four daughters, all of them important to Hardy in their different ways, also left their native village. For unknown reasons possibly related to the inconvenient timing of her arrival, Maria, the eldest, was given into the care of her paternal grandparents and brought up in relative comfort in Puddletown, where, on Christmas Day 1828, she married a local cabinetmaker named James Sparks. Mary, the third daughter, married John Antell, the Puddletown town shoemaker, in 1847, while Martha, the youngest and prettiest, moved still further away from the family, first to Hertfordshire and then to Canada, as the wife of the dashing but persistently unsuccessful John Brereton Sharpe.

Jemima, the second daughter, would a century or so later be described by her admiring son as possessing 'unusual ability and judgement, and an energy that might have carried her to incalculable issues'. In the actual circumstances of her childhood, she inherited through Maria's absence the position of eldest daughter, called upon as such to assume more than her share of domestic responsibilities. Because of the family's poverty, she was sent out into the world at an early age, went into service under the patronage of the third Earl of Ilchester of nearby Melbury House, by far the largest landowner in the area, and worked initially for his uncle, the Revd Charles Redlynch Fox-Strangways, the rector of Maiden Newton in central Dorset. She was accustomed to accompany the family when it went up to London for the 'season', and many years later her son would often attend St James's Church, Piccadilly, because his mother had gone there 'when as a young woman she was living for some months in London'.[26] Following the rector's death in November 1836, she took her now developed culinary skills to the household of Lord Ilchester's brother-in-law the Revd Edward Murray, the vicar of Stinsford. Not, however, to the vicarage itself, Murray having chosen to live, more grandly, at nearby Stinsford House, owned by the Strangways family since the sixteenth century and the home until her death in 1827 of Lady Susan Fox-Strangways, in whose runaway marriage to William O'Brien, the actor, Hardy would always take a romantic interest.[27]

· · ·

It was at Stinsford that Jemima met her future husband. Stinsford House was, and is, immediately adjacent to the west door of Stinsford Church, and Murray, a keen musician, was an active supporter of the Stinsford choir, the little group of singers and instrumentalists that provided the music for the church services in the manner so affectionately recreated in the pages of *Under the Greenwood Tree*. Hardy's grandfather became the choir's leading spirit soon after his arrival in the parish, achieving as a performer something of the local reputation assigned to Clym's late father in the fifth chapter of *The Return of the Native*. His own instrument was the bass viol, predecessor of the modern cello, and by the early 1830s—as Hardy's reconstruction of the west gallery's seating arrangements plainly shows—he was regularly assisted each Sunday by the violins of his sons James and Thomas and his neighbour James Dart.[28]

The younger Thomas Hardy was no less passionately devoted to music, but it increasingly interfered with his business, so that regret was mingled with relief when the Stinsford choir, weakened in 1837 by the death of the elder Hardy and the replacement of Murray by a new vicar who did not share his musical enthusiasms, was finally disbanded in the early 1840s. Its ultimate demise was signalled by the decision of the Stinsford churchwardens in 1843 that any future payments to choir members should be made by public subscription and not from the regular parish revenues.[29] Though excluded from the church, the surviving members of the choir continued for some time to perform for local dances, weddings, and christenings, and to keep up the old custom of Christmas carolling from house to house. Hardy perhaps did not discover until after he had written his idyllic account in *Under the Greenwood Tree* that the choir's past fulfilment of secular engagements under the name of the Bockhampton Band had led in the 1820s to a violent confrontation with a group of rival musicians from Fordington.[30]

Edward Murray's association with the choir and its players, who often practised at Stinsford House, evidently provided the context, if not the specific occasion, for Jemima Hand's first meeting with the younger Thomas Hardy, and the poem 'A Church Romance' evokes, romantically enough, an early moment in their courtship:

> She turned in the high pew, until her sight
> Swept the west gallery, and caught its row
> Of music-men with viol, book, and bow
> Against the sinking sad tower-window light.

> She turned again; and in her pride's despite
> One strenuous viol's inspirer seemed to throw
> A message from his string to her below,
> Which said: 'I claim thee as my own forthright!'[31]

Family tradition, characteristically emphasizing earthier aspects of the affair, has the young mason catching sight of the young servant woman while working on a nearby building and promptly seducing her under the bushes by the river Frome. Whatever the precise circumstances of that first meeting, it must have taken place not later than 1837. Jemima knew her future husband's father, who died in that year, and could vividly recall in old age the spectacle of 'the three Hardys' arriving at church on a Sunday morning, wearing 'top hats, stick-up shirt-collars, dark blue coats with great collars and gilt buttons, deep cuffs and black silk "stocks" or neckerchiefs'.[32] It was not until late in 1839, however, that she found herself pregnant. The marriage then arranged—rather against the inclinations, so it is said, of both the contracting parties—took place at Melbury Osmond on 22 December 1839, Jemima's younger sister Mary and her brother-in-law James Sparks acting as the two witnesses. Hardy's story 'Interlopers at the Knap' is partly based upon his father's journey to Melbury Osmond on the eve of the wedding, but while family tradition endorses the bridegroom's hesitancy and the ascent of the signpost in order to read it in the dark, it also holds that James Sparks had been assigned the responsibility of getting his man to the church, that the two of them walked together from Puddletown to Melbury, arriving somewhat tipsily in the early hours of the wedding morning, and that the whole party then sat up drinking until the time came for the actual ceremony.[33]

Jemima set up house in the cottage at Higher Bockhampton, sharing it with her widowed mother-in-law, and it was there on 2 June 1840, less than five and a half months after the marriage, that her first child was born—at about eight o'clock on a Tuesday morning, as that child himself, with his customary precision, later determined and recorded.[34] On 5 July, at Stinsford Church, the baby was christened Thomas after his father and grandfather, although his mother had wanted him called Christopher, after the Childses and other members of her family. Hardy would himself have preferred Christopher: there were 'so many Thomas Hardys', he once complained, inventiveness as to names having been 'as lacking in all branches of the Hardy family as with Dandie Dinmont in the christening of his dogs: they are Thomases & Johns everywhere'.[35] Doubts have sometimes been raised as to the authenticity of the familiar account of Jemima's difficult delivery, requiring the presence of a surgeon, and of the newborn

baby's being been cast aside as dead, only to be rescued ('"Dead! Stop a
minute: he's alive enough, sure!"') by the watchfulness of the midwife. But
while that passage was certainly a late insertion into the opening chapter of
Florence Hardy's *Early Life of Thomas Hardy*, it was always present elsewhere
in the typescript—as part of Hardy's heartfelt expression of gratitude to
Elizabeth, or Lizzy, Downton, the local nurse who had cared for him at his
(perhaps premature) birth—and only moved to the earlier position at the
suggestion of Sir James Barrie.[36]

Lizzy Downton was for Hardy a woman 'of infinite kind-heartedness,
humour, and quaintness' on whom he continued to depend during his
feeble and sometimes sickly childhood. His very survival into adulthood
was long in doubt—his parents once said in his hearing, thinking him
asleep, that they did not expect to rear him[37]—and he retained into extreme
old age a vivid sense of his early experiences of sickness and weakness. The
poem 'In Tenebris. III' pictures him sitting in the chimney corner of the
cottage, 'the smallest and feeblest of folk there, | Weak from my baptism of
pain', and as late as October 1925 he was reported as saying that 'he felt so
unwell, & just as he used to when he was a little boy & very delicate'.[38] The
story that Hardy was for some time after his birth little better than a 'vege-
table', pitifully lacking in motion or discernible intelligence, may well be
doubted, but an early unresponsiveness does seem to have caused some
parental concern and even impatience: 'I hope the little girl will not be so
tiresome as Tomey,' wrote Betty Hand shortly after the birth of Hardy's
sister in December 1841.[39] The arrival of the healthier and more naturally
active Mary was an important moment for Hardy himself, serving to ani-
mate the family circle and centre it more persistently and attentively on
both the children: the doll's tea service and tiny china house with which
'Tomey' played had presumably been at first his sister's toys.[40] A degree of
initial passivity would square well enough with the early anecdote of
Hardy's being found asleep in his crib with a snake curled up beside him
and with his later habits of quiet observation and physical withdrawal, but
any quasi-catatonic phase, if it existed at all, can scarcely have been of long
duration. The claim that Hardy could read almost before he could walk
may be rendered less impressive by the suspicion that he was a late walker,
but there remains his sister's assertion—and indeed his own—that he could
read by the age of 3.[41]

No more than hints can be gathered of the precise nature of Hardy's
deeply affectionate relationship with his sister Mary, much closer to him in
age and in interests, enthusiasms, and sympathies than either Henry, born
when Hardy was 10, or Katharine, born when he was 16. Mary cared about

music, literature, and art, and displayed a modest talent for drawing and portrait-painting. Hardy depended heavily upon her in childhood and youth, and even in early manhood, when they were much less often together, he continued to think of her as his 'chief confidante'. Like him, she was private and introspective, and shy to a degree which made her eventual career as a schoolteacher something of a perpetual burden: 'I shall never forget the misery of first taking a school,' she once said.[42] She seems also to have been sexually timid—perhaps inevitably so, given her temperament and lack of any particular charm of face or manner—and may have contributed something to the creation of Sue Bridehead.

The poems about Mary that Hardy wrote after her death in 1915 reflect only in general terms his devotion to 'the country girl', as she is called in one of the titles, and offer only occasional glimpses of the child who climbed with him the apple trees in the Bockhampton garden, 'her foot near mine on the bending limb, | Laughing, her young brown hand awave'.[43] Their closeness, however, is beyond question, intensified as it was by the cramped conditions of life in the cottage itself: it is likely that they shared a bedroom in infancy and even beyond, and that their grandmother slept in the same room as well. They may also have been somewhat isolated from the other children in Higher Bockhampton, including those of their uncle James, partly because the cottage was at the far end of the hamlet, right next to the heath, but also because Jemima wanted to keep them from mixing with those she considered socially inferior.

The widowed Mary Hardy—'granny', as Hardy called her—lived on in the Bockhampton cottage until her death in 1857. Of her orphaned and desperately unhappy childhood she would say little, nor can anything much better than guesses now be made as to the causes of that unhappiness or the sequence of events that brought her from Berkshire to Dorset at the end of the eighteenth century. She is known to have spent some time in Reading, and it is possible, though by no means certain, that she was the Mary Head who gave birth to an illegitimate daughter there in 1796. But there is no substance to the speculation that she was the Mary Head charged at Newbury Quarter Session in April 1797 with the theft of a copper kettle: that Mary Head died in 1816 in the very parish in which the alleged theft occurred and was of precisely the age specified in the April 1797 Calendar of Prisoners.[44] The Mary Head who became Hardy's grandmother had certainly been in Dorset at least since 1799 and at Higher Bockhampton since the cottage was first built in 1801, and she was an important daily presence during his early years and the source of many of the stories and songs with which he grew up.

In the poem 'One We Knew' it is Hardy and Mary who sit at their grand-mother's knee as—like Elspeth Mucklebackit in Scott's *The Antiquary*—she gazes into the fire and talks of the past 'not as one who remembers, | But rather as one who sees'. Hardy would always remember, and sometimes invoke, her early Berkshire memories of 'the gibbet creaking | As it swayed in the lightning flash' and 'a small child's shrieking | At the cart-tail under the lash',[45] as well as her slightly later Dorset recollections of a threatened Napoleonic invasion and Hardy's grandfather's mustering as a private with the Puddletown Volunteer Light Infantry. It was she, as the early poem 'Domicilium' makes clear, who brought alive for the boy the extraordinary isolation of the cottage as she had first known it:

> 'Our house stood quite alone, and those tall firs
> And beeches were not planted. Snakes and efts
> Swarmed in the summer days, and nightly bats
> Would fly about our bedrooms. Heathcroppers
> Lived on the hills, and were our only friends;
> So wild it was when first we settled here.'[46]

Later on she would become the model for Mrs Martin, Swithin St Cleeve's grandmother in *Two on a Tower*, introduced as 'quietly re-enacting in her brain certain of the long chain of episodes, pathetic, tragical, and humor-ous, which had constituted the parish history for the last sixty years'.[47]

Hardy's other grandmother, Betty Hand, moved from Melbury Osmond to Puddletown shortly before her death. Hardy was not quite 7 when she died, but was able to identify her, from report if not from memory, as the singer of the songs associated with 'G. Melbury'—i.e. 'Granny [from] Melbury' rather than the fictional Grace Melbury of *The Woodlanders*—in his annotated copy of John Hullah's *The Song Book*, among them 'Black-Eyed Susan', 'Poor Tom Bowling', and 'Shepherds, I Have Lost my Love'.[48] There is a story of Jemima's having made off, for her son's sake, with more than her fair share of Betty Hand's books, but Betty's letter of January 1842 anticipates the disposition of only a few household items, none of them books, and Hardy had on his own shelves only the *Companion to the Bible: Intended for Bible Classes, Families, and Young Persons in General*, published by The Religious Tract Society in 1836, purchased in 1838, and subsequently passed on with the inscription 'T. Hardy The gift of his dear Grandmother B. Hand'.[49]

Important as these and other family presences were to the young Hardy, they inevitably loomed less large than the sharply contrasted figures of his parents—Jemima hard-driving, her husband easygoing to the point of indolence. Hardy's affection for his father emerges movingly from the description in *Life and Work* of his fondness for going alone to the woods or the heath to gaze at the landscape through his telescope or, 'in the hot weather, lying on a bank of thyme or camomile with the grasshoppers leaping over him'. The son, however, may have exaggerated the father's lack of practicality. The family business survived and eventually prospered, as Thomas senior's will would show, and there is a story of his paying a fine levied against one of his workmen in order to keep him out of jail and adding a corresponding amount to the bill for the job then in progress—which happened to be on the estate of the sentencing magistrate.[50] In person, Hardy vividly wrote, his father was a man

who in his prime could be, and was, called handsome. To the courtesy of his manners there was much testimony among the local county-ladies with whom he came in contact as a builder. . . . He was about five feet nine in height, of good figure, with dark Vandyke-brown hair, and a beard which he wore cut back all round in the custom of his date; with teeth that were white and regular to nearly the last years of his life, and blue eyes that never faded grey; a quick step and a habit of bearing his head a little to one side as he walked. He carried no stick or umbrella till past middle-life, and was altogether an open-air liver, and a great walker always.[51]

Women other than the 'local county-ladies' are said to have found his manners charming and his person attractive. As a young man he had a reputation as a womanizer and an occupation which provided ample opportunities—taken or not—for sexual adventure. When a job took him beyond convenient walking distance from Higher Bockhampton he would often lodge in the vicinity during the working week: in 1911 a farmer at Owermoigne—the 'original' of the village in Hardy's short story 'The Distracted Young Preacher'—was able to point out the cottage in which Thomas Hardy senior 'used to lodge as a young man, when he was engaged in the building of Galton Farmhouse near by. I've often heard my mother speak of him. She knew him well, and a very charming fellow he must have been.'[52]

Such excursions were perhaps terminated, or severely curtailed, following his marriage, in which Jemima's was by all accounts the dominant personality. Hardy almost invariably refers to the Bockhampton cottage as his mother's rather than as his father's house, and she certainly played the more decisive role in the lives of their children. Like her mother and her sisters, she was short, with a head a little too large for her body, and a Roman nose and strong chin that approached each other, Punch- or nutcracker-like, in old age. Hardy's recollections stress that she had 'wonderful vitality', remaining slim and active, with a 'buoyant' walk, at least into her late sixties.[53] He spoke, too, of her natural cheerfulness and sense of humour,[54] but the humour could sometimes be harshly expressive of the sterner, more abrasive side of her personality that is said to have emerged as a consequence of a serious illness precipitated by a dangerous miscarriage suffered during the period 1843–6.[55] Her sister, the as yet unmarried Mary Hand, moved into the cottage at that time as nurse to her sister and housekeeper to the family, and Hardy once mentioned (apropos of the controversy over the Deceased Wife's Sister legislation) his mother's distress at her husband's refusal to promise to marry Mary for the children's sake if she herself should die.[56] Since Jemima did not die, she referred sardonically to the experience as a 'wasted' illness, a phrase her son was to take up when writing about a serious illness of his own some thirty-five years later.[57]

As Hardy himself acknowledged, Mrs Yeobright in *The Return of the Native* was closely based upon Jemima as she was in early middle age—a woman 'who, possessing two distinct moods in close contiguity, a gentle mood and an angry, flew from one to the other without the least warning'.[58] Although she seems always to have commanded the unquestioning devotion of her children, Jemima could be cold in her manner, intolerant in her views, and tyrannical in her governance. She had inherited in full measure the ancient pessimism of the rural poor, their perpetual imagination of disaster, and she kept it alive with a diet of sensational tales—as when, in 1849, she puzzled her son by declaring of the murderer James Rush that 'the governess hanged him'.[59] Satan played an active role in Jemima's morality—Hardy once confessed to having in his childhood 'devoutly believed in the devil's pitchfork'—and her vision of fate as standing with hand uplifted 'to knock us back from any pleasant prospect we indulge in as probable' was shared by Hardy himself and found its counterpart in Sue Bridehead's conception of the 'something external to us which says, "You shan't!"'[60]

Somewhat illogically coexisting with Jemima's fatalism was a fierce determination to move her family forward in the world, to prevent it at all costs from slipping back into the kind of destitution and self-destruction she had known as a child. She inculcated an intense clannishness that went far beyond the countryman's instinctive localism and distrust of outsiders, teaching her children to be above all things loyal to their parents and to each other, to seek always to be well spoken of, to defend the family's reputation and their own, and to present at all costs a united front to out-siders. She wanted them never to marry but to live together in pairs, a son with a daughter, Hardy with Mary, Henry with Kate, and thus maintain throughout life the unity and interdependence of their childhood.[61] In her terror of poverty she preached solidarity in financial matters, instilling the principle that money amassed by any member of the family should be kept within the family, and urged her husband to a commercial aggressiveness that went against the grain of his whole personality. She also kept her children unyieldingly to the marks she had set for them, not only putting a stop to their learning dance steps no longer deemed 'genteel' but sometimes forcing them to go to school even when they were unwell.[62]

As has often been noticed, Jemima's ambitions for her eldest son—and for herself through her son—are strikingly similar to Mrs Morel's ambitions for Paul in *Sons and Lovers*, and some of the other tensions so powerfully dramatized in Lawrence's novel had their milder counterparts within the Hardy household. A glimpse of the psychological battles being fought, within himself as well as between his parents, can be caught from Hardy's childhood memory—echoed in the poem 'Childhood among the Ferns' and in a famous passage in *Jude the Obscure*—of lying on his back in the sun, gazing up through the interstices of a straw hat, and deciding that he did not want to grow up, become a man, or take on adult responsibilities.[63] Implicit but unmistakable here is the instinctive identification with his father's passivity and the corresponding resistance to his mother's drive, her constant planning and projecting on his behalf. Understandably enough, Jemima showed distress when her son told her of his conclusions, and she never let him forget the incident in the years of his literary success.[64] Hardy well knew, and correctly asserted, that if he had lost his mother in early childhood his 'whole life would have been different'. In the poem 'In Tenebris. III' he recalls his childhood dependence upon her as 'matchless in might and with measureless scope endued', and in *The Return of the Native* Clym Yeobright's overt conflict with his mother occurs within the context of a love so sure as to need no expression: he is 'a part of her', their conversations are 'as if carried on between the right and left hands of the same body'.[65]

Hardy was undoubtedly strengthened by the absolute security of such a relationship. It was his mother's strong-willed impulsion alone that enabled him, for good or ill, to resist his father's infinitely attractive example, defy his own native instincts, and break away from the traditional patterns of families grounded, generations deep, in the almost inert conservatism of the Dorset countryside. But he was at the same time damaged, like Clym Yeobright, by so extreme an emotional dependence upon his mother, as by his early and perhaps inevitable surrender to her all-encompassing influence and direction. The tenacity of that maternal hold was to hamper him at all stages of his first marriage, and become the principal cause, along with his early ill health, of that prolonged immaturity which left him, in his own estimation, 'a child till he was sixteen, a youth till he was five-and-twenty, and a young man till he was nearly fifty'.[66]

2

Bockhampton

B Y 1840, when Hardy was born, there were seven or eight cottages scattered along Cherry Lane at Higher or, as it was often called, Upper Bockhampton, and some fifty people crowded into them. The hamlet had earlier been nicknamed 'Veterans' Valley' on account of the military men who had retired to live along its single street,[1] and although Hardy himself would have known only one of these, a Lieutenant Thomas Drane who had fought at Trafalgar, his father told him highly coloured tales of an army officer, Captain Meggs, who had lived in the 'house by the well'. This was in Hardy's childhood the home of John Cox, the local relieving officer and registrar, and a note on his sketch plan of its ground floor indicates that he had it in mind when describing the house occupied by Clym and Eustacia in *The Return of the Native*.[2]

At the far end of the lane, right next to the heath, stood the Hardys' cottage, 'standing alone, mud walls and thatched', as it was described in an insurance policy of 1829, which put a value of £100 on all the furniture, linen, wearing apparel, and 'liquors in private use therein'.[3] The cottage next nearest to the heath was similar in size, but, like several of the other cottages, it had two sets of occupants, Hardy's uncle James and his family living in one half and William Keates (the 'tranter' of *Under the Greenwood Tree*) and his family in the other. The Hardy cottage, on the other hand, was occupied by a single family and boasted extensive outbuildings and nearly two acres of attached land. Hardy has routinely been criticized for exaggerating the size and importance of his birthplace, and its description in *Life and Work* as a 'seven-roomed rambling house' is certainly distorted both by the substitution of 'house' for 'cottage' and by the subtly spacious implications of 'rambling'. In nineteenth-century Dorset, on the other hand, 'cottage' often meant 'hovel', and the building was, and is, far from being that. In 1853, indeed, when the Kingston Maurward estate was put up for auction by Francis Pitney Brouncker Martin, the Hardy homestead was separately described in the sale prospectus as 'A Neat Cottage, next Piddletown

Heath, forming a Lodge to the Wood Drives, with large garden, &c.',
currently 'Granted on Lease for Two Lives, aged 41 and 48'. Though the
description of the property is disappointingly incomplete, the accompanying map of the estate clearly shows the presence of a second building,
evidently comprising the 'stabling and like buildings since removed' mentioned in *Life and Work*.[4]

Those 'mud walls' of the cottage were in fact composed of what is more
commonly referred to as 'cob', locally dug chalk, clay, gravel, and sand
mixed with straw and water and shovelled and worked into what Hardy
himself once described as a 'dough-pudding'. This would have been thrown
up into walls two-feet thick that were trodden down and then left to settle
and harden for a day or two, the process being repeated until the wall had
reached its required height of roughly fourteen feet. Strong tree branches
were used as rafters, the roof itself was thatched with wheat straw, and on
the ground floor large Portland flagstones were laid directly on the earth. It
was only at a later date that the building was faced with brick and the end
walls strengthened with cement. The cottage seems originally to have had
only one room on each of its two floors, the lower with a large open fireplace
at one end, the upper divided by curtains into distinct sleeping areas. At
some later date—perhaps to provide separate living space for his widowed
mother—Hardy's father added new rooms at the south end. The slightly
lower roof line of the extension remains clearly visible, although it may have
existed from the first, as a storage space or workroom of some kind, and
been simply taken into the main building later on. At about the same time,
partitions were built between the bedrooms upstairs, the single room on the
ground floor was divided into two, and the front door of the cottage moved
further to the south and thus kept more or less central. An accompanying
relocation of the original staircase destroyed that intense impact of sunset
upon its red-painted walls in which Hardy had so delighted as a child.[5]
Thus improved and enlarged, the building had some claims to be called a
'house', but its photogenic picturesqueness has doomed it to remain a
cottage and even to become something of a stock image of the 'traditional'
English thatched cottage, much reproduced as such on postcards and book
jackets and in tourist brochures.

The outbuildings were used chiefly for the family business, which continued over the years to survive and even to enjoy a modest expansion. In
the 1851 census Thomas Hardy senior was described as a 'bricklayer'
employing only two men; by 1861 the number of his employees had risen to
six; by 1871 there were eight men and a boy; and in a directory for 1880 he
is described as a 'builder'. Later on, after his younger son had taken over

the business, it prospered still further: in the 1890s the work done for the Kingston Maurward estate alone amounted in some years to well over £1,000.[6] During the early years of his marriage, however, Hardy's father was still operating on only a very small scale, and his prized independence left him dangerously exposed to fluctuations in the local economy. His family often found itself in difficulties—even, at times, in 'bitter poverty'—and great sacrifices are said to have been made for the children's sake.[7]

Hardy's parents could nevertheless think of themselves, and with some justice, as being a cut above most of their neighbours. In the village society of that period there was a sharp and sometimes cruel division between those who worked for themselves and those who laboured for an employer, and it was precisely on the mobility of individuals across that line, in either an upward or a downward direction, that so much of the action of Hardy's novels was later to turn. As he himself put it in 1927:

Down to the middle of the last century, country villagers were divided into two distinct castes, one being the artisans, traders, 'liviers' (owners of freeholds), and the manor-house upper servants; the other the 'work-folk', i.e. farm labourers (these were never called by the latter name by themselves and other country people till about 70 years ago). The two castes rarely intermarried, and did not go to each other's house-gatherings save exceptionally.[8]

Thomas Hardy senior, like his wife, had relatives who clearly belonged to the second and lower of the two castes, but he and his immediate family laid claim to the superior rank by virtue of his position as a master mason, an employer of men (however few), and the lifehold tenant of a substantial dwelling with adjoining land and outbuildings. Such discriminations mattered, and more than simple snobbery underlay Hardy's insistence, in his later years, upon distinctions that had to do not only with his own background but also with the fates of such fictional characters as Stephen Smith, Gabriel Oak, Michael Henchard, and Giles Winterborne.

There were perceptible speech differences, too, at a time when the Dorset dialect was still a distinct linguistic form. In *Under the Greenwood Tree* the ways in which the Dewys conduct themselves towards their social equals (such as Mr Penny and Uncle James) are markedly different from those they adopt towards those inferiors to whom, as loyal members of the choir, they are benevolently extending their hospitality. Hardy of course knew the dialect, but used it only in conversation with dialect speakers. At the same time, his observation that the dialect was 'not spoken in his mother's house, but only when necessary to the cottagers, & by his father to his workmen',[9] rather slides over the fact that both his parents had grown up as dialect speakers and largely remained so—the persistence and broadness of Thomas senior's dialect becoming for his elder son and daughter a shared source of affectionate amusement. Hardy quoted some of their father's words ('he zid a lot of other voke guane up') in a letter to Mary of 1862, and when in 1888 he told a friend that he had heard the Dorset 'Ich' (for 'I') just the previous Sunday, it was almost certainly from his father's lips. Many years later Mary Hardy, sending a holiday postcard from a guest house in Swanage, told her cousin Mary Antell, 'There is a "Father" to this establishment: I heard him say from the yard "Where's the coalbox to".'[10]

Their mother's speech in old age similarly became an occasion of amusement to outsiders, though less because of any dialectal excesses than because of its vigorous outspokenness—what one visitor called its 'salt and savour'.[11] Jemima's concern for her children—perhaps because of her past glimpses of wealthier lifestyles—was always directed towards their acquisition of the linguistic, educational, and social skills that she saw as equipping them to rise out of their background and into the middle class. Mrs Dewy's aspersions in *Under the Greenwood Tree* upon the coarseness of her husband's speech and manners evidently recall, within a humorous context, remarks made by Jemima to her own husband in all sharpness, and *Life and Work* records her disapproval of his passing on to the children his own folk-dancing skills—'all the old movements of leg-crossing and hop'—instead of introducing them to 'the more genteel "country-dance"' that was now in fashion.[12]

The representations of the Dewy family in *Under the Greenwood Tree* and the remarkably similar Smith family in *A Pair of Blue Eyes* are directly reflective of the Hardy household at Higher Bockhampton—what Hardy sometimes referred to as 'the homestead'—and the largely self-supporting simplicity of its daily life. Thomas Hardy senior, though a mason and jobbing builder by trade, was simultaneously a smallholder by necessity. He dug the garden and filled it with vegetables—successive beds of carrots, onions, parsnips, broad beans, peas, and potatoes. Each autumn he gathered in the orchard's several varieties of apple in expectation of the arrival of the cider-maker, with his 'mill, and tubs, and vat, and press'.[13] He fattened a pig for slaughtering and salting down each year and kept a hive or two of bees and, when times were good, a horse for the transportation of building materials and tools. Jemima, for her part, was obliged to add to her maternal responsibilities the roles of cook, housekeeper, nurse, sempstress, and family economist; she helped with the garden and probably kept hens, selling the eggs that were surplus to her own family's needs; she also earned a little extra by glove embroidery, one of several local cottage industries that died out as the century drew on.[14]

Even when the money began to come more easily, the Hardys continued to occupy the Bockhampton cottage—the father dying there in 1892, the mother in 1904—and to lead their lives on a rural pattern that had changed little in several hundred years. When Jemima Hardy sent her younger daughter, Katharine, to a music teacher in 1873, she paid the bill partly in honey; when, in early December 1878, that same daughter was preparing to return home from college for the last time, her father wrote:

Dear Katie—We should wrote to you before But We Have been expecting to Heard from you About your School How it was settled. We are going on much as usale it is very Cold Hear. . . . We are going to kill the Pig about next Thursday so you will be Home to Help make the blackpudding with Mother Monday & just in time for the White Meat.[15]

Beyond the Hardys' garden lay, in one direction, Thorncombe Wood, in another, Snail's Creep, the path leading down to the main London road. To the east it was all heath, a wild and sometimes frightening territory, almost unmarked by human habitation or activity, hence uniquely available for imaginative colonization. Below the heath lay the lush landscape of the Frome valley, best seen from the ancient burial mound known as Rainbarrow, on which, in Napoleonic times, a beacon fire had been kept ready to be lit in the event of an invasion. Dorchester was slightly less than three miles away, and Puddletown somewhat nearer in the opposite direction. It was rather more than a mile across the fields to the Stinsford parish church of St Michael, not quite so far to Lower Bockhampton, the nearest village. Many of the family's numerous relatives lived within feasible walking distance, but still others—Hardys and Hands, uncles, aunts, and cousins—lived beyond easy reach in widely scattered villages and hamlets such as Portland, Upwey, and Melbury Osmond.

Like any nineteenth-century countryman, Hardy learned from childhood to know his own district with an intimacy not now easily imaginable. Travelling everywhere on foot—or at best on a wagon drawn by a slow-paced horse—he became familiar with the occupants of every cottage, the name of every field and every gate, the profile of every tree, the depth and temperament of every pond and stream. He knew, too, the histories of all these, their associations with old crimes or follies or family quarrels, and whatever of legend or folklore might attach to them. So the Hardy children heard at an early age that Rushy Pond on the heath had been dug by fairy shovels, that a drowned traveller had given his name to Heedless William's

Pond, and that no one was ever present to see the first flowing of a 'winter-bourne' after its summer dryness. The brief entries in the diary kept, years afterwards, by Hardy's younger sister Kate are full of the names of relatives and neighbours, of local place names and local gossip.[16] Hardy himself thought of the English landscape as 'scored with prints of perished hands' and wrote in *The Woodlanders* of the conditions necessary to give meaning to life in an isolated rural location:

> They are old association—an almost exhaustive biographical or historical acquain-tance with every object, animate or inanimate, within the observer's horizon. He must know all about those invisible ones of the days gone by, whose feet have tra-versed the fields which look so grey from his windows; recall whose creaking plough has turned those sods from time to time; whose hands planted the trees that form a crest to the opposite hill; whose horses and hounds have torn through that under-wood; what birds affect that particular brake; what bygone domestic dramas of love, jealousy, revenge, or disappointment have been enacted in the cottages, the mansion, the street or on the green.[17]

Through the storytelling and anecdote-swapping of his elders Hardy absorbed just such knowledge of the past and current history of the parish. Through his own childhood games and rambles he attained the kind of topographical familiarity that underlies the reference, in *Jude the Obscure*, to Phillotson's walking unhesitatingly across country in darkness 'as a man goes on, night or day, in a district over which he has played as a boy'.[18] He knew, too, what birds affected which brakes, and possessed an extraordi-nary sensitivity to the sights, the smells, and especially the sounds of the countryside at every hour of the day or night: 'To dwellers in a wood', runs the opening sentence of *Under the Greenwood Tree*, 'almost every species of tree has its voice as well as its feature.' His responsiveness to the natural world was not, however, that of a naturalist. He knew plants and creatures by their country names rather than by their technical designations, but that did not mean that he knew them less well. As he told William Archer: 'The town-bred boy will often appreciate nature more than the country boy, but he does not know it in the same sense. He will rush to pick a flower which the country boy does not seem to notice. But it is part of the country boy's life. It grows in his soul—he does not want it in his buttonhole.'[19]

The Dorset countryside with which Hardy began to become familiar in his childhood was in many respects a pleasanter and more prosperous place than most contemporary accounts would suggest. A guidebook of 1856 describes Dorset as 'a bleak country of chalk downs and sandy heaths,

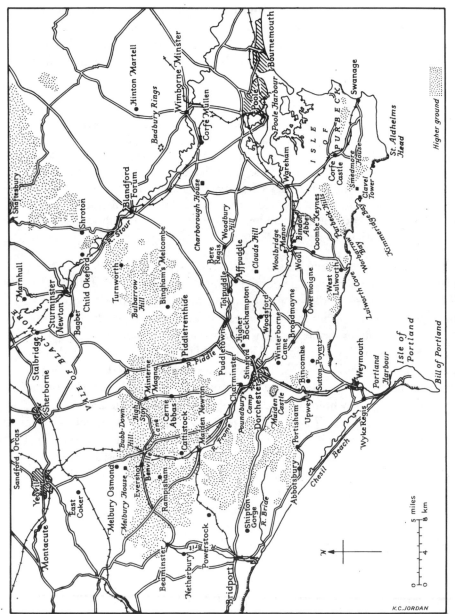

THOMAS HARDY'S DORSET

K.C.JORDAN

Higher ground

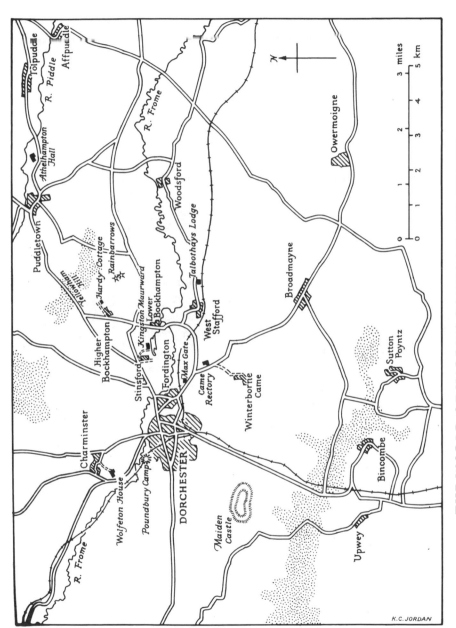

THE WORLD OF HARDY'S BOYHOOD AND YOUTH

Also showing sites of Max Gate (1885) and Talbothays Lodge (1893)

K.C. JORDAN

thinly peopled, and below the average of the English counties in fertility'—though possessing 'a certain charm in its very wildness and the forlorn aspect of its villages'.[20] Topographically speaking, this is to account only for the second and third of the three divisions of Dorset, *Felix*, *Petraea*, and *Deserta*, which nineteenth-century writers were fond of invoking, and to omit such 'happy' vales as those of Blackmore and Frome. It is, however, eloquent of the county's contemporary reputation as a poor, backward, and somewhat uncouth corner of the kingdom. Ten years before Hardy's birth the English countryside had erupted in riots, rick-burnings, and machine-breakings, and while such outbreaks touched only the fringes of the Dorchester area, his father recalled, among the numerous retributive executions which followed, the hanging on little more than suspicion of a youth so light through hunger that weights were attached to his feet to ensure that strangulation would occur. And in 1834 the six 'martyrs' from Tolpuddle, just a few miles across the heath from Bockhampton, were sentenced to transportation for their attempts to organize a primitive trade union.[21]

In the mid–1840s the vicar of Durweston, Lord Sidney Godolphin Osborne ('S.G.O.'), conducted in the columns of *The Times* a vigorous campaign to draw attention to the economic hardships and insanitary living conditions of the Dorset labourer. Examples were cited of men with large families who earned a mere seven shillings a week and were forced, from sheer inability to purchase other food, to take much of their wages in the form of 'grist', poor-quality wheat for which they were liable to be over-charged. In some areas it was the custom to make the labourer an allowance of grist, and sometimes of fuel, on top of his wages, but such relative generosity still left him in a position of total dependence. Because farmers and landowners sought to discourage the rapid expansion of the rural population—with a resulting increase in poor-relief payments—that had begun in the late eighteenth century, they had little if any interest in building or even maintaining cottages on their land, and would often pull them down as leases fell in. Villages decayed and became places of filth and disease, with farmyard drainage running into the streets or beneath the earth floors of the ruinous cottages in which whole families, of both sexes and all ages, were sometimes forced to sleep in a single bedroom.

Twenty and more years later investigators for a Parliamentary Commission found conditions and wages somewhat improved but received ample evidence—including submissions from 'S.G.O.' himself and from such other Dorset notables as the Reverend Henry Moule and the Reverend William Barnes—that the labourer was always on the edge of pauperism, that women were often employed (like Hardy's Tess Durbey-field) on threshing machines and at such heavy tasks as swede-hacking, and that boys typically went into regular employment at the age of 9 or 10. From Stinsford, as from many other districts, came reports of men being hired only on the understanding that all the family—wife and children—would come to work at the farmer's need and call. Charles Kegan Paul, then vicar of the village of Sturminster Marshall, wrote in 1868:

Wages are so low that a man with children above eight years old is glad of the few shillings which may be earned by them, and the employers of labour insist on these boys being sent into the fields, even if the parents would willingly make an effort to keep them at school. The farmer finds it pays him well to get two boys who, under a man, will do a man's work, but whose combined work costs less than an able-bodied man's wages.[22]

In Higher Bockhampton itself, mostly inhabited by tradesmen's families of much the same class as his own, Hardy was in his childhood relatively isolated from such realities, but he could not remain unaware of their implications for the 'workfolk' at nearby farms. Asked by Rider Haggard in 1902 about the lot of the Dorset agricultural labourer, he replied that 'down to 1850 or 1855 his condition was in general one of great hardship', citing as an admittedly extreme case his childhood memory of 'a sheep-keeping boy who, to my horror, shortly afterwards died of want, the contents of his stomach at the autopsy being raw turnip only. His father's wages were 6*s.* a week, with about £2 at harvest, a cottage rent free, and an allowance of thorn faggots from the hedges as fuel.'[23]

Conditions were no less squalid in the semi-rural, semi-urban slums of Fordington, on the outskirts of Dorchester. 'Vice ran freely in and out certain of the doors of the neighbourhood,' wrote Hardy in *The Mayor of Casterbridge* of a Fordington street whose 'original', the pointedly named Cuckold Row, had been the address of his uncle John in the early 1840s.[24] The area was notoriously a breeding ground for the cholera, and Hardy remembered all his life the terrible final epidemic of 1854 when the Reverend Henry Moule, as vicar of Fordington, ignored personal danger to visit the sick, organize the boiling or burning of the clothes of those who had died, and initiate other attempts to prevent the spread of infection. Drunkenness was always prevalent, with market days and hiring fairs readily degenerating into the kind of sexual rowdyism that occurs during and after the Chaseborough dance in chapter 10 of *Tess of the d'Urbervilles*. There was domestic violence within the circle of Hardy's own relatives. In 1842 his grandmother Betty Hand, the recipient of rough treatment from her own husband, responded with anxiety to news of her son Christopher's drunken beatings of his pregnant wife: 'I am afraid there will be something wrong in the child,' she wrote to her daughter Mary, working in Puddletown as a servant to a Mrs Banger, 'as he throws her in such ways sometimes—still he is very kind to her in all respects beside.' When Mary, in turn, encountered similar difficulties in her own marriage, her sisters Maria Sparks and Jemima Hardy are said to have come not just morally but physically to her aid.[25]

In later years Hardy could articulate more clearly what as a child he had observed but only half understood, and in 1888 he jotted down a remarkable reminiscence of life on the Kingston Maurward estate during the late 1840s:

A farm of Labourers, as they appeared to me when a child in Martin's time; in *pink & yellow Valentine hues*:—

Susan Sq———, & Newnt (e.g. leaning & singing at harvest-supper) their simple husbands: Newnt's lovers; Ben B's wife, & her lover, & her hypocrisy; T. Fuller— the schoolmaster, far above his position in education, but a drunkard; also wife— the lech———'s boy T. M....s. Also Walt, Betsy, & Eliza. The school kept by latter, & their chars, sensuous, lewd, & careless, as visible even to me at that time—all incarnadined by passion & youth obscuring the wrinkles, creases, & cracks of life as then lived.

Elsewhere in the same notebook, though not on the same page, is an idea for a possible poem: 'Cf Theocritus & the life at Bockn when I was a boy— in the wheatfield, at the well, cidermaking, wheat weeding, &c.'[26] The conflict implicit in such a juxtaposition remained with Hardy throughout his life and is reflected in the acknowledgement, in a late preface to *Under the Greenwood Tree*, that 'the realities out of which [this novel] was spun were material for another kind of study . . . than is found in the chapters here penned so lightly, even so farcically and flippantly at times'.[27]

Because he remained so sharply aware of the darker as well as the more positive aspects of his early experience, Hardy in his mature years was rarely tempted to indulge in automatic nostalgia for the past. He was always deeply conscious of the process of change itself and of the many good and bad relics of earlier days and ways which were constantly being swept away—including those which had disappeared before he could have known them: the church choir, the smugglers' kegs, the gibbets such as his grandmother recalled with terror from her Berkshire childhood, the public whippings his parents had witnessed in Yeovil and in Dorchester itself. As a child he had himself seen maypoles, mummers, tinderboxes, men in the stocks, and the horse-drawn coaches which—despite the coming of the railway to Dorchester in 1847—continued for some years to depart daily from the Antelope and King's Arms hotels.[28] The eighteenth century had already brought significant changes to the English countryside, but it remains broadly true to say that Hardy was born just in time to catch a last glimpse of a rural world that, especially in so conservative a county, had existed largely undisturbed from medieval times, and that was about to be radically disrupted by the new forces—population expansion, urbanization, railways, cheap printing, cheap food imports, enclosures, agricultural mechanization and depression, improved educational opportunities, and pressures for migration and emigration—that impinged upon it during the course of the nineteenth century. Hardy, looking back, mourned the lost vitality and continuity of the old rural England that had been so largely destroyed during his lifetime. He knew too that his own childhood had been generally happy—and that even the pastoral poets had allowed for the presence of Silenus. But he could not doubt that the changing times had also brought with them many social and economic and even ethical improvements.

When Hardy described his childhood as not only solitary but 'remarkably uneventful', he perhaps meant no more than that the life he knew at Bockhampton—like that invoked in *Under the Greenwood Tree* and *Far from the Madding Crowd*—was still paced by the procession of the seasons, the succession of the generations, and the imperatives of the agricultural and ecclesiastical calendars. Its markers were lambing time, haymaking, and harvest; the first cuckoo, the longest day, the last swallow; Easter, Whitsun, Christmas; births, marriages, and deaths. There were Christmas parties at Mr Cox's house by the well—the 'House of Hospitalities' of the poem, where they 'broached the Christmas barrel, | . . . sang the Christmas carol, | And called in friends[29]—and dances and 'wedding-randies' at other cottages in the neighbourhood. In March 1846 Hardy's cousin George Hardy was married to Anne Cox, also of Higher Bockhampton, and on 14 November 1847 it was from the Hardys' own cottage that Jemima's sister, Mary Hand, was married to John Antell, the well-read and tough-minded Puddletown shoemaker. The 1840s also saw a number of family funerals, including those of Hardy's grandmother Betty Hand in 1847 and of 12-year-old Walter Hardy, another of his Higher Bockhampton cousins, in 1844.

Because the annual festivals and seasonal evolutions were so regular and predictable in their arrival, they were looked forward to long in advance, and Hardy's second wife once said that many of his pleasures, right to the end of his life, were those 'of anticipation'—for example, the coming of spring. Her remark on another occasion that her husband was very superstitious, 'as was natural', serves as a reminder that a world so traditional was inevitably credulous, that the 'fetishistic' outlook of a Mrs Durbeyfield, with 'her fast-perishing lumber of superstitions, folk-lore, dialect, and orally transmitted ballads', was familiar to Hardy from his own childhood, that the witches, weather prophets, and 'planet-rulers' had not yet entirely disappeared,[30] and that he heard at first hand those tales of images burned in slow fires, of blood 'turned' by touching the corpse of a hanged man, and of miller-moths emerging from the mouths of the dying that he drew upon in *The Return of the Native*, 'The Withered Arm', and 'A Few Crusted Characters'.

These early, pre-school years of Hardy's were profoundly significant for his later career as a novelist and poet. He was surrounded by gifted narrators—by the rapt grandmother of 'One We Knew', by a mother who was an inexhaustible source of stories, sayings, and country lore, by a father who could give a 'vivid and captivating' description of an apparently uneventful walk,[31] and by the friends and relations, visiting or visited, who expanded upon their own experiences, repeated tales from the local repertoire, and sang the songs their parents and grandparents had taught them. Hardy was in many respects a child of the oral tradition. He came, too, from a culture in which singing and music-making were natural forms of expression, and from a family in which music was a major preoccupation. An ecstatic musical sensitivity manifested itself from very early on, and although he never saw the Stinsford choir occupying its old place in the church gallery (itself later removed), there was no lack of music in the Bockhampton cottage. The sounds of his father's violin of an evening could move him both to dance and to weep, and in the poem 'Song to an Old Burden' memories of his father's playing are mingled with those of his mother's singing. He is said to have been given a toy concertina at the age of 4; not long afterwards he was introduced to the violin; a little later still he went with his father to local dances and other festivities and even performed himself from time to time with an energy perceived as sorting oddly with the delicacy of his physique at that time.[32]

Hardy always treasured his father's violin and the battered music books that had been laboriously written out by hand for the use of the Stinsford choir. He also preserved some of the books of dance tunes and their steps as performed on more secular occasions, and entered into his copy of Hullah's *The Song Book* the names of people whom he associated with particular songs. From time to time he took the trouble to write out the words of ballads, chiefly from Stinsford and Melbury Osmond, that his mother or another relative had remembered, or that he had himself heard sung at parties, harvest suppers, and the like. Most of them told, conventionally enough, of love disappointed or betrayed. Others turned, like those in *Tess of the d'Urbervilles*, upon sexual innuendo, and Hardy much later wrote out for performance the little 'folk-piece' called 'O Jan, O Jan, O Jan', which he remembered being sung at home when he was about 4 years old. 'Like so many of these old songs & dialogues,' he told a friend, 'it had a rather broad double-entendre in it, quite Shakespearean, at which the men used to laugh, some of the women smirk, others stiffen, & wh. others wd paraphrase for domestic performance.'[33]

In *Tess of the d'Urbervilles* much of Tess's confusion as to her place in the world and in the universe is blamed upon the 'gap of two hundred years' between what she was told by her mother and what she was taught at school.[34] Hardy himself well understood the nature and significance of such a gap, and there is a sense in which some of the central complexities and ambiguities of his own work can be said to derive from the interplay between, on the one hand, the orally transmitted and intensely localized country wisdom of his childhood—combined as it was with an acute emotional susceptibility to the music and rituals of the Church of England— and, on the other, his book-learned intellectual acceptance of some of the more radical and sceptical trends in nineteenth-century thought. Resolution, remarkably enough, took the form less of conflict than of coexistence, so that Hardy, as an agnostic, would always retain his belief in the social function of the Church of England and his love of its services and declare, for instance, in 1901, that while he had been unable to find any evidence whatsoever for the existence of the supernatural he would cheerfully have given ten years of his life to see 'an authentic, indubitable spectre'.[35]

Hardy's introduction to the Church came early, as a natural consequence of his parents' regular attendance at the Stinsford parish church and his father's participation, until so recently, in the performances of the Stinsford choir. The family sympathies were strongly High Church, and the services had for Hardy a dramatic appeal which was soon reflected in his dressing himself in a tablecloth at home in order to play the parson and read the morning service from the altitude of a chair.[36] In Stinsford Church itself he was fascinated by the skull which formed part of the Grey family monument in the north aisle where the Hardys habitually sat, and so thoroughly learned the accompanying inscription (containing the name Angel, used in *Tess of the d'Urbervilles*) that he could repeat it word for word even in old age.[37]

Influenced perhaps by family resentment over the fate of the choir, Hardy seems from the first to have disliked the Stinsford vicar, the well-educated and well-connected Reverend Arthur Shirley, but he attended confirmation classes at the vicarage and later shared with Shirley's sons in the teaching of the Sunday school. Whatever his personal feelings, Hardy could not but recognize that the vicar and even the curate occupied, both in and out of church, positions of dignity and prestige, and although the old choir had gone—replaced by a barrel organ turned by Hardy's uncle James, one of the former players—the church was still a place of music and colour, of satisfying rituals and magnificent language. The church thus answered to Hardy's immediate emotional and aesthetic needs and offered in due course a feasible—though difficult—direction for the social ambitions instilled into him by his mother. 'As a child', declares the auto-biographical *Life and Work*, 'to be a parson had been his dream.'[38]

Once it became clear that her sickly son was destined to survive into adulthood Jemima took an intense interest in his upbringing. She sought the best available education for him, saw that he had books, and indulged his fiddling expeditions with his father as a way of his learning and practising music. Just how much she herself directly contributed to his education is far from certain. Her own mother had the reputation of a literate and knowledgeable woman, a great reader of novels, and Jemima is said, like her mother, to have 'read omnivorously'.[39] Her doctor, indeed, asserted that her favourite book was Dante's *Commedia*, and in an anonymous but obviously Hardy-inspired article published just after her death she was described as 'catholic in her taste for books, enjoying the philosophy of Johnson's *Rasselas* in turn with the frivolities of Combe's *Doctor Syntax*. She preferred *Marmion* to any of Scott's prose works, of the latter liking *Kenilworth* the best. Byron, of course, she admired, influenced possibly by his vogue in her youth.' The further statement that she rated *Vanity Fair* 'above all other novels by deceased writers' neatly sidestepped the question of what she felt about those written by her son.[40]

Jemima, however, seems not to have had any facility with a pen. She certainly put her name (rather than an illiterate's cross) in the church register on the occasion of her own marriage and as a witness to her sister's marriage. But no letters written by her have turned up, and just as her mother was sending messages to her by way of her sister in 1842 so her son was writing and receiving letters on her behalf in 1859.[41] Even the inscription—'Thomas Hardy | the gift of his Mother'—in her remarkable early present of Dryden's translation of Virgil is in the recipient's hand and not her own. The combination of good reading ability with poor—because untaught and unpractised—writing ability was common enough among people of Jemima's class and time, and this legacy of her poverty-stricken childhood contrasts sadly with her obvious strengths of intelligence and character and lends an additional poignancy to the image of her as sighing sadly over a piano she could not play.[42]

It is difficult to establish just what books Hardy had available during his isolated and impecunious childhood. Those that have survived include the *Cries of London*, a little book of words and pictures which he is said to have read before he was 3, and *The Rites and Worship of the Jews*, published by the Religious Tract Society and inscribed 'Thomas Hardy, his book | given by his godfather—A. King. 1847.' If, as seems likely, this was the Abs. (for Absalom) King who worked alongside Mary Hand as a servant in Mrs Banger's Puddletown household, the book was probably presented, without any particular religious implications, on the occasion of Mary Hand's marriage in 1847 to the Puddletown shoemaker John Antell.[43] Also in the Bockhampton cottage were Gifford's *History of the Wars Occasioned by the French Revolution*—an early stimulus to Hardy's fascination with Napoleon —and a translation of Salomon Gessner's *The Death of Abel* that had been signed and dated by his grandmother, Mary Hardy, in 1800.[44] Hardy's lifelong if intermittent habit of annotating bibles and prayer books seems to have begun when he was 9 years old, but there survive from even earlier dates the *Companion to the Bible* presented by his maternal grandmother and *The Psalter, or Psalms of David*, published in 1843. Dated signatures begin to appear in books such as Francis Walkingame's *The Tutor's Assistant; Being a Compendium of Arithmetic* ('Thomas Hardys | Book | 1849') and John M. Moffatt's *The Boy's Book of Science* ('Thomas Hardy | Dec 24th 1849'),[45] while the undated but obviously early signature ('Master Hardy') in Thomas Dilworth's *A New Guide to the English Tongue* lends particular interest to the pencil line drawn firmly alongside the following passage: 'It is a commendable thing for a boy to apply his mind to the study of good letters; they will be always useful to him; they will procure him the favour and love of good men, which those that are wise value more than riches and pleasure.'[46]

Jemima's continuing attempts to keep her son supplied with examples of 'good letters' did not lack ambition: in addition to Dryden's Virgil she gave him *Rasselas* and a little volume containing translations of Bernardin de Saint-Pierre's *Paul and Virginia* and Sophie Cottin's *The Exiles of Siberia*. Though *Paul and Virginia* is a work of impeccable morality, Jemima was perhaps not alert to its quietist message, its preaching of a virtuous obscurity, when she put it into the hands of a son already dangerously sympathetic to the genial unambitiousness of his father. A marker still draws attention to the following passage:

'My son! talents are still more rare than birth or riches, and are, undoubtedly, an inestimable good, of which nothing can deprive us, and which everywhere conciliate public esteem. But they cost dear; they are generally allied to exquisite sensibility, which renders their possessor miserable. But you tell me that you would serve mankind. He who, from the soil which he cultivates, draws forth one additional sheaf of corn, serves mankind more than he who presents them with a book.'[47]

There was a dame school in Lower Bockhampton in Hardy's childhood, kept by Elizabeth Plowman—presumably to be identified with the deplorable 'Eliza' of Hardy's Kingston Maurward memories—but it is not certain that Hardy ever attended it. In any case, it was only with the establishment of a National (i.e. Church of England) School in the parish in 1848 that Hardy first entered a formal classroom, arriving on opening day still wearing a frock and looking 'fresh, | Pink, tiny, crispcurled'. The same poem, 'He Revisits his First School', pictures him sitting at a desk as 'in Walkingame he | Conned the grand Rule-of-Three | With the bent of a bee', and he seems in fact to have progressed well in arithmetic and geography under the direction of the two teachers, Thomas Fuller and his wife—the very 'T. Fuller' later recalled as 'far above his position in education, but a drunkard'.[48]

It was at this first school that Hardy suffered the earliest of those experiences of love, the slighting of the loved one, and subsequent guilt that were to recur throughout his life. He was much attracted to one of his schoolfellows, a girl from Higher Bockhampton called Fanny Hurden, immortalized in 'Voices from Things Growing in a Churchyard' as 'poor Fanny Hurd' who once 'flit-fluttered like a bird | Above the grass'. One winter day, in a moment of childish play or anger, Hardy pushed her back against the schoolroom stove, burning her hands. It was an action, he told Walter de la Mare some seventy years later, for which he could never forgive himself, especially since her early death (in 1861, at the age of 20) had prevented him from making any kind of restitution.[49]

In starting school Hardy encountered for the first time a sizeable group of his own contemporaries and became exposed to their habits, values, and attitudes. He also learned something of their capacity for persecution when they persisted in chanting at him:

> Thomas a-Didymus had a black beard;
> Kissed all the maidens & made 'em afeard.[50]

It is possible that the chanting was a response to the little episode with Fanny Hurden, or to the lady-killing propensities of his father. Otherwise the point of the rhyme—in so far as it had any beyond the mere association of names—presumably lay in some ironic allusion to Hardy's still rather weakly appearance and to his shyness and instinctive reserve. The observation that he disliked being touched by his schoolfellows—or, in adult life, by other men—seems to have had some basis in fact, despite its having been inserted into *Life and Work* after Hardy's death.[51]

That Hardy, until the age of 8, had lived within a world almost exclusively adult and very largely feminine was to be of some importance for his future development. Hardy spoke of Mary as almost his only childhood companion,[52] but even she must often have been absent—attending the dame school, playing with the friends she had made there, or occupied in household tasks. The attitude of uninvolved spectatorship which so often characterizes the narrative voice in his novels seems to be in part a reflection of his early experiences as a sickly, solitary boy accustomed to sitting by, silent and unnoticed, while his parents and their relatives and friends sang, played, joked, and talked together, singing the old songs, retelling the traditional stories of the local past, and trotting out the customary nodules of inherited wisdom and credulity—all in their slow but colourful Dorset speech, with its long-learned fatalisms and self-protective humour. Jemima's canny view of infant baptism—that it could do no harm, and she would not want her children to blame her in another life for failing in some duty in this one[53]—is directly suggestive of the extent to which Hardy's early years of passive but observant listening were subsequently drawn upon in the Wessex novels and stories, most immediately in the portrayal of the Dewy family in *Under the Greenwood Tree* and the Smith family in *A Pair of Blue Eyes*. During the composition of *Far from the Madding Crowd* Hardy specifically acknowledged to Leslie Stephen how advantageous it was to be actually among the people described at the time of describing them.[54]

From Bockhampton it was only a modest walk (for those days) across the heath to Puddletown and the several Puddletown households to which the Hardys were related. It is often said, on flimsy evidence, that Hardy in his years of success became snobbishly indifferent to all but his immediate relatives. But if he and his wife did indeed cycle through Puddletown without looking to left or right, the cumbersomeness of early bicycles and the poor condition of the roads could surely have been a factor. And it was not, in any case, as though they drove through in a coach-and-four or even a pony-and-trap. Hardy seems in fact to have remained cognizant all his life of an extensive network of cousins, second cousins, and even more distant connections on at least three continents, and to have kept in touch—either directly or through his family-centred sisters—at least with the families he had known and visited during his childhood. For reasons perhaps of inherited rather than personal coolness, Hardy seems never to have been particularly intimate with his uncle John's children in Fordington or even his uncle James's smaller family in Higher Bockhampton itself.[55] There was, on the other hand, a close connection with some of the Puddletown Hardys, including Elizabeth, widow of his great-uncle John (his grandfather's younger brother), and some of her children, especially the third son, William Jenkins Hardy, also a mason, and his wife Ann. The nine children of William and Ann Hardy were born over roughly the same period as the four children of Thomas and Jemima, and Hardy seems to have had a particular affection for Charles (always known as Charles Meech Hardy) and Angelina and, later still, for Angelina's son Frank George.

Also at Puddletown were several members of the Hand family, including two and sometimes all three of Jemima's brothers and two of her three sisters; their mother, Hardy's grandmother Betty Hand, was also there for a short period prior to her death in 1847. Jemima depended a good deal for advice and practical assistance on her sister Maria Sparks, and since Maria was the eldest of the siblings, the most solidly established, and the first to have had children of her own, her home provided the family with a natural focus. From his earliest years Hardy was familiar with his uncle and aunt Sparks, with his Sparks cousins—especially Martha, who was six years older than himself, and James, two years her junior—and with their 'cheerful house', as Mary Hardy later called it, 'with the sparkling river in front, and in the near distance the old Church tower with the clock and rambling chimes, around which so many of our people are sleeping'.[56]

In December 1846 Jemima's younger sister Mary (not yet married to John Antell) had written to her mother from Hitchin, Hertfordshire, where she was staying with Martha, the youngest and prettiest of the Hand sisters, and the wife since 1841 of John Brereton Sharpe. Martha's health was never strong, and Mary Hand's visit in 1846 had been timed to coincide with the birth of her sister's third child in November. That child died less than two years later, just four days before the fourth was born, and when Martha again became pregnant in 1849 Jemima Hardy undertook to stay with her as nurse and housekeeper until the crisis should be over. The baby was expected in December and Jemima set off for Hatfield well ahead of time, taking her own 9-year-old son with her.[57]

To Hardy the journey was memorable, not just because it was his first absence from home but because it involved a combination of old and new modes of travel—to London by the railway which had reached Dorchester in 1847, and on to Hatfield by coach. Once there he was enchanted by his 'handsome aunt', who later served as the model for Bathsheba Everdene in *Far from the Madding Crowd*.[58] John Sharpe, the son of a Hertfordshire farmer, seems for his own part to have been in some degree the 'original' of Sergeant Troy. It has generally been assumed that Sharpe, the son of a Hertfordshire farmer, had at one time been a regular soldier who met Martha Sharpe in the course of his military service, perhaps in Dorchester itself, but he seems in fact to have served in the Hertford Yeomanry Cavalry, a part-time auxiliary force functioning only within Hertfordshire. For several years he engaged sporadically and unsuccessfully in various agricultural occupations in the Hatfield area, and in the late 1840s he was perhaps employed as an agricultural bailiff by the Marquess of Salisbury, for whom he certainly wrote, in 1848, some recommendations for improvements to farming methods on the Hatfield House estate.[59]

Sharpe's good looks, educated manner, and military associations made him an altogether more stylish figure than any of the men in Hardy's own family, and the lively letter he wrote to Martha's family soon after the marriage and the gift of storytelling he retained into old age are both suggestive of Troy's verbal facility. Unfortunately, he also had something of Troy's restlessness and improvidence. He left his position on the Hatfield estate in the spring of 1851 and, unable to find permanent employment in England, emigrated to Canada that July with his wife and five children, the youngest just a month old.[60] Wretchedly short of money—dependent even for the cost of the passage on the generosity of Lord Salisbury and of the family with whom his sister was employed as a governess—he set off at short notice with a promise of temporary employment on an estate near Guelph, Ontario, and only the vaguest prospects of eventually obtaining a farm of his own. Within a few years, however, he had found a different and perhaps more appropriate outlet for his talents: when Martha Sharpe died in South Dumfries, Ontario, on 28 August 1859, giving birth to her tenth child, the local newspaper gave her husband's occupation as 'School Teacher'.[61]

Hardy stayed long enough at Hatfield in the late autumn of 1849 to be sent, as a day boy, to the school (now a private house) in Fore Street, Hatfield, that was being run, 'somewhat on the Squeers model', by a Congregationalist minister named Thomas Ray.[62] Martha's child was not born until just before Christmas and it was probably well into the new year before Jemima and her son returned home. Hardy caught glimpses of

various London landmarks as they passed through the city, and once
claimed to have made a tour of the streets described in *Old St Paul's*, the
novel by Harrison Ainsworth, one of his favourite authors at that period. It
seems doubtful that he would have had time or opportunity for such an
expedition, but he certainly retained the horrific impression made upon
him by the sights and sounds of Smithfield meat market, close by the coaching inn, the Cross-Keys, Clerkenwell, where he and his mother stayed the
night—and which he later discovered to have had associations with Shelley
and Mary Godwin.[63] Before going to bed Jemima searched every corner of
the room for a possible intruder. No doubt because of her unhappy childhood, she retained a degree of fearfulness that her otherwise remarkable
energy and spirit could not quite subdue, and had clearly not been
altogether joking when she spoke of taking her young son with her 'for protection'.[64] It was a timidity, a sense of personal vulnerability, that perhaps
communicated itself to her son, who as a child felt nervous when alone on
the heath at night and once hurried home without stopping, like the young
Jude Fawley, when frightened by the portrayal of Apollyon in a copy of *The
Pilgrim's Progress*.[65]

Anxiety about an ongoing cholera epidemic may have deterred Jemima
from sending her own son back to the Bockhampton school in the autumn
of 1849—especially if she was already planning to take him with her to
Hatfield—and it is unclear whether he attended school at all in the months
that followed the return from that expedition. What is clear is that by the
end of the summer of 1850 he was deemed to have the physical strength to
make the daily walk to Dorchester and back in order to attend the new
school that had been chosen for him.[66] This was the Dorchester British
School, an elementary school established by the British and Foreign School
Society, conducted on the same monitorial system as the Bockhampton and
other National Schools but with Nonconformist rather than Anglican
emphases in all religious matters.

Isaac Glandfield Last, the headmaster of the British School, had an
excellent reputation, and the decision to send Hardy there was evidently
made on educational rather than religious grounds. It nevertheless led to a
quarrel between Jemima and Julia Augusta Martin, wife of Francis Pitney
Brouncker Martin, who had purchased the Kingston Maurward estate in
1844, and thus to Hardy's father's losing the estate business.[67] Mrs Martin,
together with the Reverend Arthur Shirley, had been largely responsible
for the building and opening of the Bockhampton National School, and she
took deep offence at what she saw as a desertion both of the school itself
and of the Church of England precepts it sought to instil. But more than

principle was at stake. Mrs Martin had known the Hardys, as people who lived on the estate and occasionally did work for it, ever since her arrival at Kingston Maurward, and perhaps because she had no children of her own, she had (as Hardy himself put it in *Life and Work*) 'grown passionately fond of Tommy almost from his infancy—he is said to have been an attractive little fellow at this time—whom she had been accustomed to take into her lap and kiss until he was quite a big child'.[68] Hardy, unusually small and delicate, could even at the age of 8 scarcely have been called a big child, and Mrs Martin's caresses evidently continued into his first schooldays. She encouraged him to draw and sing for her, and many years later she was to remind him that she had 'taught you yr letters',[69] by which she meant not that she had taught him to read but that she had, in effect, taught him to write. *Life and Work* acknowledges that Hardy's handwriting was 'indifferent' at the time he first started school but does not put a date to his claim to have acted as amanuensis to illiterate local girls whose soldier sweethearts had departed. Hardy in any case flourished under Mrs Martin's supervision, and it is tempting to assign to this period the surviving copybook pages on which he wrote out, several times over, a brief but suggestive series of *sententiae*:

> Passion is a bad counsellor.
> Quit vicious habits.
> Encourage diligence.
> Forget not past favours.[70]

Hardy did not forget, then or ever, the woman who had overwhelmed him not only by her fond and indulgent encouragement but also by a cultivation and elegance, a voluptuousness of dress and person, that were altogether new to his experience. Jemima, however, was deeply resentful of Mrs Martin's influence over her son, and in her determination to break off the relationship she seems to have gone so far as to stop attending Stinsford Church, probably taking the children to Low Church services at Fording-ton St George instead. Hardy, for his part, greatly missed Mrs Martin and her flattering attentions, and it was in the hope of seeing her after a long interval that he went in the early autumn of 1850 to a harvest supper being held in an old barn on the Kingston Maurward estate. The occasion, attended chiefly by local girls and soldiers from the Dorchester barracks—'Red shapes amid the corn'[71]—lingered in his memory for many reasons: because the young woman who brought him was so busy dancing and flirt-ing that she failed to take him home until the early morning hours; because she and the other girls, sitting and leaning together 'in their light gowns', joined in singing 'The Outlandish Knight' and other old ballads they had 'learnt from never a book';[72] and because Mrs Martin did eventually appear and speak briefly, and coquettishly, to him: 'O Tommy, how is this? I thought you had deserted me!'[73]

The interruption of their friendship was deeply painful, and the feeling, 'almost that of a lover', with which he had responded to her attentions was to linger with him for many years. As a young man in London some twelve years later he attempted to re-establish the relationship on something like its old footing, only to recoil when confronted by the brutal fact that Mrs Martin now looked all of her more than fifty years—a visual trauma that he was to recreate imaginatively at the end of *Two on a Tower* and in poems such as 'Amabel' and 'The Revisitation'. Another dozen years on, a letter from her was still capable of reviving 'throbs of tender feeling in him' and memories of 'the thrilling "frou-frou" of her four grey silk flounces when she used to bend over him, and when they brushed against the font as she entered church on Sundays'.[74] No less remarkably, Hardy's rereading of that letter when he was himself in his seventies was enough to stimulate speculations of a wildly romantic kind: 'Thus though their eyes never met again after his call on her in London, nor their lips from the time when she had held him in her arms, who can say that both occurrences might not have been in the order of things, if he had developed their reacquaintance earlier, now that she was in her widowhood, with nothing to hinder her mind from rolling back upon her past.'[75] Like so many of Hardy's attachments, the relationship loomed larger in his imagination than elsewhere, but some at least of the autobiographical intensity informing his first novel, *The Poor Man and the Lady*, derived from his feeling for Mrs Martin and his sense that they had been separated by hostile forces that had had nothing to do with their own emotions but everything to do with conventional attitudes towards religion, age, and social class.

3

Dorchester

IT was in September 1850 that Hardy first walked the three miles in from Higher Bockhampton to present himself at the British School kept by Isaac Glandfield Last in Greyhound Yard, Dorchester. Because of his early physical weakness and slow development, compounded by his late begun and already interrupted schooling, he was a year or two older than most of the other boys—although he looked a good deal younger. Fellow pupils and other contemporaries remembered him as a small, serious, clever, rather solitary child with a large head, who customarily carried a satchel full of books and was always ready to help slower students with their lessons.[1] According to one story he went for his lunch each schoolday to Rebecca and Amelia Sparks, the unmarried sisters of his uncle by marriage James Sparks. They lived in Dorchester, working at home as shoebinders, and are said to have not especially appreciated Hardy's enthusiasm for conjuring tricks—such as tossing buttered bread to the ceiling and making it stick there or throwing the contents of the sugar bowl into the air and catching them in his cupped hands as they descended.[2]

Mid-century Dorchester—so vividly reflected in *The Mayor of Casterbridge* —had as yet scarcely begun to overflow its original Roman fortifications. Its smallness, however, did not prevent it from being in some respects intensely urban. It was the county town, the centre of local government, and it was a garrison town, made colourful by the constant presence of the red-coated and splendidly accoutred soldiery of those days. It had banks and solicitors, markets and hiring fairs, and served as the commercial centre for the whole of southern Dorset. The county court met there, and the Dorset Assizes, presided over by visiting judges who were attended with traditional pageantry and—in a town that had seen Judge Jeffreys at work in the wake of the Monmouth rebellion—with the awe appropriate to men invested with power over life and death. The town, like all towns, did of course have its more sordid and troubled aspects. In January 1856 there was an 'affray' involving seven privates from the 13th Light Dragoons, the regiment currently stationed in the town.[3] In 1857 a young stonemason was fined for being drunk and disorderly and ordered to be 'put in the stocks for six hours' should the fine not be paid, and a tramp sent to prison for vagrancy was said to have slept with another man's wife, 'from which man prisoner had bought the woman'.[4]

Dorchester and Bockhampton were very different from each other, both as societies and as environments, and the future patterns of Hardy's fiction were largely established by that daily walk between a 'world of shepherds and ploughmen', still in touch with the customs and beliefs of past centuries, and 'a county-town of assizes and aldermen, which had advanced to railways and telegraphs and daily London papers'.[5] Hardy had from his earliest years become indirectly aware of major events and outbursts of popular feeling through their impact upon his parents, and in later years he would vividly recall the agitation at the time of Corn Law repeal in 1846 and the 'lurid' scenes of 5 November 1850 when the annual Guy Fawkes celebrations turned into ugly anti-popery demonstrations and the Pope and Cardinal Wiseman were burned in effigy. He would also remember, and invoke in *The Mayor of Casterbridge*, the more decorous passage of the Prince Consort through Dorchester in the summer of 1849, when the mayor was so overwhelmed by finding himself in the royal presence 'that he dropped on *both* knees to read his address'.[6] But a readier access to newspapers and the better informed Dorchester gossip enabled him to grasp more fully the implications of such events as the Great Exhibition of 1851 and the Crimean War and register the anxiety with which news from India was awaited during the Mutiny year of 1857. He shared eagerly in the excitement created by successive parliamentary elections, and took pride in having had a hand on the rope of the carriage in which the Liberal candidate, Richard Brinsley Sheridan, grandson of the dramatist, was drawn around the town after winning one of the Dorchester seats in July 1852.[7]

Hardy's chief preoccupations during the early and middle 1850s were his school work, his reading, and the occasional expeditions made with his father to play 'Haste to the Wedding', 'The New-Rigged Ship', and other country dances at village functions.[8] His mother, who had forbidden him to gamble after he had unexpectedly won a hen by throwing dice at a local raffle, also warned him not to accept payment for his services as a fiddler, but in September 1853 he risked her disapproval and collected a sum sufficient to purchase *The Boy's Own Book: A Complete Encyclopaedia of All the Diversions, Athletic, Scientific, and Recreative, of Boyhood and Youth*, previously seen and lusted after in the window of a Dorchester bookshop.[9] Hardy was eager, then as always, for the kind of miscellaneous information the book offered, but its emphasis upon normal activities and skills of boyhood perhaps had a special appeal at a time when he still felt weak and immature alongside most of his schoolfellows. Nearly seventy years later, responding to a letter in which his friend Edmund Gosse had spoken of spending part of 1853 in Weymouth with his naturalist father, Hardy replied:

Curiously enough I remember my father driving to Weymouth on business one day about that very year (there was no railway further than Dorchester then) & taking me with him as a treat; so that you may certainly have 'brushed up against a boy called T.H.' in the streets there—though not a 'big' boy, for I was small & delicate, & had scarcely started off growing & reaching the robust condition into which I plunged between then & my 21st year.[10]

In 1853 Isaac Last left the British School and set up his own independent 'commercial academy' for older and more advanced pupils. For Hardy, who went with Last to the new school, the years between 1853 and 1856 were a period of rapid intellectual development—and of physical development too, as the daily exercise of walking six and more miles gradually built up his strength. According to one account, Last was a harsh disciplinarian who would 'frequently chase a boy round the room lashing him with his cane until he was white in the face'.[11] But it is the lot of schoolmasters to be caricatured, and Hardy, for one, made good progress under Last's direction. At his mother's instigation—and at a supplementary charge of five shillings per term—he was taking Latin as an additional subject. He had bought a copy of *An Introduction to the Latin Tongue* (the so-called Old Eton Grammar) in 1852, but now redated it September 1853 as a sign and perhaps a celebration of his having begun to use it regularly.[12] The *Breviarum Historiae Romanae* of Eutropius was purchased in 1854, and it was at about this time that he wrote out in his copy of the *King Edward VIth Latin Grammar* a scheme for learning genders, the masculine nouns being coloured red, the feminine white, and the neuter blue, while those of 'Epicene Gender' were distinguished by red diagonal stripes. Another purchase of 1854, Cassell's *Manual of the French Language*, evidently marked the beginning of French lessons from a teacher at the Ladies' School conducted by the Misses Charlotte and Jemima Harvey and now attended by his sister Mary.[13]

In March of the same year he began at Last's Academy a notebook, headed 'Miscellaneous Questions' and kept in a meticulous copperplate hand, in which he worked through a series of mathematical problems related to bricklaying, carpentry, plumbing, and other building trades. That December another notebook, 'Conic Sections and their Solids', was started, and although the problems were now more theoretical they were still framed in down-to-earth terms:

Two porters agreed to drink off a pot of strong beer at two pulls or a draught each; now the first having given it a black eye as it is called or drunk till the surface of the liquor just touched the opposite edge of the bottom, gave the remaining part to the other; what was the difference of their shares, supposing the pot was the frustum of a cone whose top diameter was 3.7, bottom diameter 4.23 and perpendicular depth 5.7 inches?[14]

Last—whose son became director of the Science Museum at South Kensington—evidently believed that education should not be too remote from the world of his students' experience, and while Hardy's parents may have differed in their ambitions for their son, he was performing too well in technical and academic subjects alike to give either of them a reason to think of transferring him to the Grammar School or such other local alternatives as the group of pupils taught by the Reverend Henry Moule at Fordington vicarage, the 'Classical and Mathematical School' over which the Reverend William Barnes, the philologist and dialect poet, had been presiding for a good many years, or the 'Classical, Mathematical and Commercial School' more recently founded by Barnes's former assistant Isaac Hann.

Last, for his part, was sufficiently satisfied with Hardy's progress to present him, at Christmas 1854, with a volume entitled *Scenes & Adventures at Home and Abroad* as a prize for diligence and good behaviour. The choice of book suggests that Hardy was perceived as bright but not excessively bookish and as having the interests normal to his years. At the same time, it was probably not quite up to the mark of his contemporary reading of Harrison Ainsworth, Dumas *père*, James Grant's *The Scottish Cavalier*, and Shakespeare's tragedies 'for the plots only'.[15] In 1855 Hardy made further progress in mathematics and French; at midsummer Last thought his Latin good enough to justify another prize, Theodore Beza's *Novum Testamentum*; and there also survives an exercise book containing specimen commercial letters, receipts, and so forth, written out in copperplate and bearing Hardy's signatures and various dates between April and September 1855. That Christmas he put his name in the first two volumes of *The Popular Educator*, originally published by 'that genius in home-education, John Cassell'; he obtained the third volume five months later, on Whit Monday, 12 May 1856.[16]

At midsummer in 1856, shortly after his sixteenth birthday, Hardy's schooldays came to an end. By this time he had bought (from the

Dorchester shop kept by an upholsterer named William Treves, whose son Frederick was to become a famous surgeon) the leather writing desk that he still owned at the time of his death.[17] He had also ventured upon his first literary exercises. On 19 December 1855 he copied out Charles Swain's poem 'The Old Cottage Clock', glued it to the inside of the door of the family's grandfather clock, and then added his own name, apparently out of comic bravado rather than in a deliberate attempt to deceive.[18] Not long afterwards, according to *Life and Work*, he got into print by tricking a Dorchester paper into publishing 'an anonymous skit . . . on the disappearance of the Alms-House clock, . . . the paragraph being in the form of a plaintive letter from the ghost of the clock'. The clock—still hanging in South Street outside the former almshouse known as Napper's Mite—was certainly mentioned from time to time in the Dorchester newspapers of that period, but exhaustive searches have not resulted in any confident identification of such an item. That Hardy's memory may on this occasion have been somewhat at fault is suggested by the existence of an alternative story, originating with another of Last's former pupils, that he once amused his schoolfellows with 'a little poem' about an occasion when the clock's hands fell off.[19] If, however, Hardy did write some such skit and get it printed, it would not be the only instance in his career of his publishing under a disguise.

On 11 July 1856, shortly after leaving school, Hardy was articled for three years to John Hicks, a Dorchester architect, to receive instruction 'in architectural drawing and surveying', Hicks having been persuaded to accept a cash down-payment of £40 in lieu of the standard premium of £100 payable at mid-term.[20] It was a sufficiently logical step for a boy with a sound technical education, connections in the building trade, and some skill with a pencil, and while it did not require knowledge of Latin it did hold promise of social and economic advancement into the middle class. Hardy asserts in *Life and Work* that he 'cheerfully agreed to go to Mr Hicks's'.[21] What reservations he had at the time can only be guessed at. He seems already to have dreamed of a university education followed by ordination and a useful but leisured life in a country parsonage. But while he knew that Last had given him an unusually good grounding for a youth of his time, place, and class, he also knew that an imperfect knowledge of Latin combined with an almost total ignorance of Greek left him ill prepared for the university admission that would constitute the crucial first step towards his dream's realization. In the meantime architecture offered a by no means uncongenial way of earning a living and left open the possibility of working privately towards more adequate levels of classical education. That process of self-education, determinedly pursued for several years at the cost of long hours of wearisomely invested and ultimately sterile labour, would have a certain long-term value for Hardy as a writer, but its specific goals remained unfulfilled and he never quite lost the sense of inferiority and resentment stemming from the incompleteness of his schooling, especially as signalled by the lack of a university degree. Nor did he ever forget the humiliation of sitting in Stinsford Church at his mother's side in that early summer of 1856 while the Reverend Shirley preached against the presumption shown by one of Hardy's class in seeking to rise, through architecture, into the ranks of professional men.[22]

His introduction to Hicks's office on the ground floor of 39 South Street—next door to William Barnes's school—was in other respects a very agreeable experience. Of the two pupils already in the office, one, Herbert Fippard, was about to leave, while the other, Henry Bastow, nearer to Hardy in age and temperament, stayed on and became one of his earliest and closest friends. Hicks himself, who had come to Dorchester from Bristol a few years earlier, was a genial, well-educated man in his early forties, quite prepared to be indulgent towards his pupils' pursuit of self-improvement even during business hours. The office seems, indeed, to have been altogether an informal place, likely to be invaded at any time by the children of Hicks's brother, the vicar of Piddletrenthide, one of whom Hardy was to remember as 'inconveniently smart sometimes at riddles &c'.[23]

Of Hardy's specifically architectural work at this period little now remains, although he was proud enough of some tracings 'from Paley's Mouldings' to preserve them in a specially made folder.[24] Hicks, a clergyman's son, was primarily an ecclesiastical architect, a specialist in the rebuilding and 'restoration' of Gothic churches, and this became, perforce, Hardy's own speciality. One of his first assignments was to draw—or perhaps only copy—a ground plan of St Peter's, Dorchester, scheduled for further minor 'improvements' in addition to those just completed under Hicks's direction. He was also given the job of identifying and numbering the stones of the church's Easter Sepulchre so that it could be exactly reconstructed after relocation. As an articled pupil Hardy performed only the relatively mechanical tasks appropriate to his position, and because he proved to be an excellent draughtsman, he spent much of his time in the office copying or tracing existing plans. Later on he would have been employed in 'improving' plans, both of churches and of secular buildings, that Hicks had roughly sketched out, and in surveying and measuring churches being considered for restoration. In the opening paragraph of *A*

Laodicean the description of the architect hero measuring and drawing a church tower is clearly based upon Hardy's own memories of such pleasant and peaceful expeditions into the local countryside. The Dorset churches built or restored by Hicks during the years when Hardy was in the South Street office included Athelhampton, Coombe Keynes, Powerstock, Rampisham, Shipton Gorge, and St Mary's, Bridport, and some of the *Dorset County Chronicle*'s reports of the reopenings and rededications of these churches are said to have been drafted by Hardy himself for the newspaper's 'grateful reporter'.[25]

In those days of enthusiastic 'medievalism' and religious revivalism there was much demand for the kind of work in which Hicks was so largely engaged. As the century wore on, however, there was a growing realization, chiefly voiced by the Society for the Protection of Ancient Buildings, of the wholesale destruction that a nominal 'restoration' all too frequently involved. It was clearly necessary to maintain the fabric of old churches so that they could continue to be used for their original purpose but—as Hardy himself acknowledged years later in 'Memories of Church Restoration', a kind of public confession of the part he had himself unwittingly played—disaster too often attended the zealous attempts of incumbents, parishioners, architects, and builders to regularize what for centuries had been irregular, give consistency to what was stylistically various, and modernize in the interests of efficiency what was quaintly inconvenient. What Hardy came especially to deplore was the disruption of ancient continuities: 'Life, after all, is more than art, and that which appealed to us in the (maybe) clumsy outlines of some structure which had been looked at and entered by a dozen generations of ancestors outweighs the more subtle recognition, if any, of architectural qualities.'[26]

Hardy's account of himself as having remained a child until he was 16 suggests that his leaving school and beginning his articles coincided with an equally significant stage in his emotional development. A surviving photograph of this date shows him rather strenuously engaged in asserting and even exaggerating his age and his aspirations towards gentility. The hair is carefully arranged; a shadow of moustache is just visible on the upper lip; a cravat lies loosely tied under the slightly wayward collar; and a smart hat, almost of sombrero proportions, is clutched under the right arm. The pose itself, however, is self-conscious to the point of gaucherie, and suggestive of a shyness and hesitancy that his outward appearance was specifically designed to conceal, especially from the assessing eyes of young women.

Hardy would be susceptible throughout his life to the attractions of women only briefly glimpsed or slightly known, and there were several such episodes during the years when he was growing up, his head already crammed with the romantic conceptions and aspirations accumulated during his lonely but literate childhood. In addition to his extraordinarily charged feelings towards the much older Mrs Martin, he had a ready admiration for the handsomest of the village girls who were just a few years older than himself—the 'bevy now underground' later celebrated in the poem 'At Middle-Field Gate in February'. One of them, Unity Sargent, he would remember as a possible model for a 'Wessex Faustina'; another, Elizabeth Bishop, a gamekeeper's red-headed daughter from Lower Bockhampton, was later poetically addressed as 'Lizbie Browne'.[27] When Hardy was working at Hicks's he did not fail to take notice of William Barnes's daughter Lucy, just two or three years older than himself, as she went in and out of the house next door. As he recalled in the obituary he wrote of her in 1902: 'At that time of her life she was of sweet disposition, but provokingly shy, with plenty of brown hair, a tripping walk, a face pretty rather than handsome, and extremely piquant to a casual observer, having a nose tip-tilted to that slight Tennysonian degree which is indispensable to a contour of such character.'[28]

To roughly this same period belonged his brief infatuation with a girl who once smiled at him from horseback and his longer-lasting devotion to Louisa Harding, a year younger than himself, the daughter of Stephen Toghill Harding of Stinsford Farm. The Hardings, people of some substance, considered themselves much superior to the Hardys, and Stephen Harding had been one of the Stinsford churchwardens at the time of the dissolution of the old choir. The class barrier certainly loomed large so far as Louisa was concerned, but Hardy seems to have persuaded himself that it was his own shyness that prevented the relationship from progressing even to an exchange of words, let alone of vows. In the poem 'The Passer-by', for instance, subtitled '(L.H. Recalls her Romance)', Louisa Harding is imagined as recalling her youthful admirer:

> He used to pass, well-trimmed and brushed,
>   My window every day,
> And when I smiled on him he blushed,
> That youth, quite as a girl might; aye,
>   In the shyest way.[29]

The evidence for the actual nature and duration of the relationship is conflicting and confused—especially since the account in *Early Life* was written and inserted after Hardy's death.[30] But even if this was another romance existing mostly in Hardy's imagination, that did not prevent his affections from being keenly, if naively, engaged. He remembered Louisa Harding always, and when she died, unmarried, in September 1913, and was buried in Stinsford churchyard, he wrote not only the poem 'Louie', associating her death with that of his first wife less than a year previously, but also 'To Louisa in the Lane', a moving expression of regret for a moment and an opportunity lost.[31] When conducting friends around the churchyard in his old age, he would take them to the site of her unmarked grave and lament her family's failure to erect a memorial stone.[32]

Hardy's shyness made his Puddletown cousins especially important to him. Simply because they *were* his cousins, Hardy could approach the older Sparks sisters with an ease and informality impossible to him in his contacts with strangers. But Rebecca, who worked at home as a sempstress, was eleven years Hardy's senior and possessed, unlike Mrs Martin, none of the glamour derived from superior wealth and rank, while Emma, the second sister, went early into service away from home and in 1860 was married, at Hemington in Somerset, to Thomas Cary, with whom she subsequently emigrated to Australia. Martha, the third of the sisters, was acknowledged to be the handsomest: Rebecca once called her 'the flower of our flock',[33] and her experience as a lady's maid in London and, briefly, in Paris had given her both the skill and the means to dress well. Hardy's attraction to her appears to have been genuine but temporary: she was, after all, his cousin and six years his senior, and both sets of parents are said to have voiced their disapproval. He did, however, meet Martha in London on at least one occasion in the early 1860s,[34] and when she too emigrated to Australia after her marriage in 1870 to William Duffield, the butler in the London household in which she was herself employed, she is said to have taken with her at least one volume affectionately inscribed 'to dear Patty' in Hardy's hand. With James and Nathaniel, the two Sparks sons, Hardy seems to have been on good if by no means intimate terms, while Tryphena, the youngest child, born in 1851, he as yet knew only as a small girl just beginning school.[35]

Hardy's home life during these important years was an unfailing source of stability and assurance. He was devoted to both his parents, and they depended absolutely upon each other. That did not, however, prevent them from being often at verbal odds, and much of the sometimes clamorous but fundamentally affectionate tenor of life in the Bockhampton cottage can unquestionably be caught from the exchanges between Reuben Dewy the tranter and his wife in *Under the Greenwood Tree* and between John

Smith the mason and his wife, the closely similar couple in *A Pair of Blue Eyes*. It was Jemima who confronted Mrs Martin, stirred her husband to find sources of business other than the Kingston Maurward estate, insisted that her son should study Latin, and bargained with his teachers for cheaper terms. Her husband, meanwhile, maintained the passivity and patience that had long constituted his best defence. Their shared devotion to their children was always a unifying factor, and what virtually constituted a second and younger family was initiated by the arrival of a second son, Henry, in August 1851, ten years after the birth of Mary. A fourth and last child, Katharine, was born in September 1856, and it was during the brief interval preceding the death of Hardy's grandmother the following year that the cottage was at its most crowded. Jemima's clutch of four children was, even so, small by comparison with the families of her sisters and of most countrywomen at that period, but by 1856 she was already in her forties, and the presence of a doctor rather than a midwife at Katharine's birth, as at Hardy's so many years earlier, would seem to suggest that difficult deliveries were always anticipated.[36]

Hardy, now 16, and Mary, nearly 15, were almost of a different generation from this youngest member of the family, and there was always to be a sharp division in personality and interests as well as in age between Hardy and Mary on the one hand and Henry and Kate (as she was called) on the other. The two elder children were private, anxious, and intellectual, absorbed in themselves, in each other, and in their personal hopes and ambitions. The two younger seem to have had altogether less of their mother in them, more of their father: intelligent and astute, they were at the same time easygoing and self-indulgent, giving little thought to the future or to anything beyond their immediate pleasure and comfort. But the ties of affection and kinship were nevertheless strong and constantly renewed. Firmly instructed by their mother as to the importance of family solidarity, the Hardy children remained devoted to their parents and to each other, and the images of the life of Higher Bockhampton that find their way into Hardy's work are almost without exception positive and warm.

By the late 1850s Hardy was old enough to take a more active part in the festivals and observances of the local community. His father and his uncle James were much in demand as musicians at cottage weddings, christenings, and dances, and Hardy would sometimes go along as second violin to his father's first, with James Hardy playing the cello.[37] The christening of Katharine Hardy on 26 October 1856 would certainly have been celebrated with all due conviviality—even though the rite itself was necessarily performed by the choir's old enemy the Reverend Arthur Shirley—and two months later, on Christmas Day (then a favourite date for Dorset weddings), the Hardy musicians played for their neighbour William Keates, whose daughter Sarah was being married to Thomas Russell, a gardener from Charminster.[38] If this was the occasion Hardy had chiefly in mind when writing the Christmas party and wedding episodes of *Under the Greenwood Tree*, he would have remembered also the marriage of William Keates's elder son to Ann West, also of Higher Bockhampton, on 2 February 1855, not least because of its association with a natural phenomenon of unusual beauty: some twenty years later, entering into a notebook a reference to the Canadian 'silver frost', he added: '(precisely as when Ann West was md)'.[39]

There were also more sombre occasions, among them the death and funeral, in January 1857, of Mary Hardy, the last of his grandparents and the only one whom he had really known. Less than two years later came news from Canada of the death of Martha Sharpe, who in 1851 had made with her husband and children, Hardy's cousins, what must have been recognized as their irrevocable departure for Canada. Little had been heard from the Sharpes, and no reply seems to have been received to a letter that Hardy had written and sent on his mother's behalf in January 1858: as Martha's brother-in-law, George Brereton Sharpe, observed in September 1859, 'My brother was always a very bad correspondent except when quite forced to write & poor Martha with her numerous duties & weak health—no doubt found much to lead her to put aside writing.' It now became clear that the family was still almost destitute, and George Brereton Sharpe acknowledged in that same letter the £3 Jemima had earlier sent to help alleviate their distress.[40] That Jemima had evidently found difficulty in sparing anything at all is a reminder of the heavy expenses with which the Hardys themselves were burdened. The family business was in a moderately healthy state, but the costs of private schooling and professional training for both Hardy and Mary (destined to become a schoolteacher) had to be reckoned in terms not just of fees, books, and lodging but also of the loss to the family exchequer of the incomes that young people of their age would normally have been expected to bring home.

Throughout this period Hardy continued to divide his life between the rural isolation of Higher Bockhampton and the comparative bustle of Dorchester—although by the early 1860s he seems to have been staying in town during the week and returning home only at the weekends.[41] Dorchester, as the social as well as political and commercial centre of its region, could boast concerts, lectures, and public performances of all kinds, and Hardy took particular advantage of opportunities to indulge that life-long love of circuses which so curiously coexisted with his passionate hatred of cruelty to animals.[42] Cooke's Circus was a particular favourite of his youth, and he would vividly remember when writing *Far from the Madding Crowd* the occasion in July 1856 when that 'celebrated equestrian troupe' came to Dorchester with a programme featuring 'The battle of the Alma, and other scenes of the late war, . . . together with the various equestrian feats and exercises peculiar to such establishments'.[43]

Less than two weeks earlier, on 30 June, Dorchester had combined its annual commemoration of Queen Victoria's coronation with a somewhat belated celebration of the Peace which had concluded the Crimean War. On the ancient earthwork called Poundbury, just outside the town, was presented a programme of such sports as 'donkey races, foot races, climbing greasy poles for legs of mutton, &c, jumping in sacks, and many other games of like character'. Later there were wheelbarrow races and a highly popular competition for clambering across the river on a greasy pole, with a pig for a prize. In the town itself tea was served on tables laid out in the West Walks and, as night fell, a 'most enchanting' effect was created by the banners, flags, and the Chinese lanterns suspended from the trees in the South Walks.[44] The scenes thus enthusiastically recorded by one of the local papers were vividly recalled by Hardy himself when writing chapter 16 of *The Mayor of Casterbridge*, and he seems also to have glimpsed—and recreated for the same novel—the scene at the King's Arms Hotel in November 1856 when the retiring Mayor of Dorchester entertained his friends and fellow councillors at what the *Southern Times* called a '*recherché* repast'.[45] Occasionally there was a conjunction, even a collision, of Hardy's two worlds when friends and family members found themselves in court, and consequently in the local newspapers. At the County Petty Sessions held in Dorchester on 14 November 1857 William Keates, the Higher Bockhampton tranter and the Hardys' immediate neighbour, was fined four shillings and costs for recklessly standing on the shafts of a two-horse wagon while driving it downhill. Rather more than four years later, in the County Petty Sessions of February 1862, Hardy's first cousin Christopher Hand, the son of his mother's brother Christopher, successfully defended himself against a charge of having wilfully abandoned his apprenticeship to 'the art of a wheelwright, carpenter, and builder'.[46]

In the summer of 1856, after a sensational trial, occurred the first of the two public hangings in Dorchester that Hardy witnessed and—not surprisingly—remembered to the end of his life. On 9 August, when Martha Brown was executed at Dorchester prison for the murder of her husband,

Hardy stood close to the gallows, among the watching crowd of three or four thousand. As his account of the occasion nearly seventy years later reveals, his reaction had a strong sexual component: 'I remember what a fine figure she showed against the sky as she hung in the misty rain, & how the tight black silk gown set off her shape as she wheeled half-round & back.' As it came on to rain, Hardy recalled on another occasion, 'I saw— they had put a cloth over the face—how, as the cloth got wet, *her features came through it*. That was extraordinary.'[47] The other execution, that of James Seale, almost exactly two years later, Hardy witnessed only at long distance, through the family telescope, from the heath near his home. Even so, the experience was profoundly disturbing: 'He seemed alone on the heath with the hanged man, and crept homeward wishing he had not been so curious.'[48]

By eight o'clock in the morning, the time when Seale's execution took place, Hardy would have been up reading for two or three hours before setting off for Dorchester and Hicks's office: when only candles were available for indoor illumination it was necessary to keep a countryman's hours and take advantage of all the available daylight. He had now added the study of Greek to his continuing study of Latin: the signature in his first copy of the *Iliad* is dated 1858, and he seems to have worked persistently through it until some time in 1860, marking the passages that he had read—and that Jude Fawley, much later, would be described as reading in *Jude the Obscure*.[49]

Hardy's determination to pursue his self-education in this new direction had been largely stimulated by the enthusiasm for the classics evinced both by his office-mate Henry Bastow and by Hicks himself. Bastow, however, was less interested in Homer than in the Greek New Testament. Brought up at Bridport in a Baptist family, he was baptized on his admission to the Dorchester Baptist congregation in September 1858 and became immediately zealous for the conversion of his fellow pupil to his own belief in personal salvation and adult baptism. He was a year older than Hardy and his senior in Hicks's office, and tended to cast himself in the role of an elder brother. He gave Hardy a photograph of himself, inscribing it 'for Tom Hardy.—from *HRB* with *love*', and wrote out for him the words of Charlotte Elliott's hymn, 'Just as I Am', with its refrain 'O Lamb of God, I come'.[50] The two young men were for a time devoted to each other. They had animated religious discussions both in and out of office hours, often meeting by prearrangement in a field on the Kingston Maurward estate about halfway between Dorchester and Higher Bockhampton, and Hardy's hitherto unreflective Anglicanism was severely tested by the argumentative resources brought to bear by Bastow and his allies Alfred and William

Perkins, sons of the local Baptist minister and (though no older than Hardy himself) students at Aberdeen University. Dismayed by the absence of New Testament authority for infant baptism, put at a loss by his opponents' familiarity with the Greek New Testament, Hardy responded as best he could by a laborious perusal of the Griesbach text, purchased for the purpose in February 1860.[51]

What Hardy chiefly retained from the whole experience was a lasting respect for the example of 'plain living and high thinking' set by the Perkins household and especially by the father, the Reverend Frederick Perkins, on whom Mr Woodwell, the Baptist minister of *A Laodicean*, is affectionately based. At the same time he never quite forgot or forgave the occasion when Bastow and the younger Perkinses had persuaded him to attend a Baptist prayer meeting, only to strand him there, alone and embarrassed, while they were seduced by the secular attractions of a circus parade. A note of the middle 1860s on the discovery that one may blame oneself unnecessarily for actions or feelings that prove in fact to be morally superior to those of others ('that what we blamed is not blameable but great') cites as one instance 'going to the P. meeting that eveng & not finding the Perkins's there having been blaming self for wish to stay away'.[52]

Bastow left Hicks's office soon after the expiration of his articles, going first to London and thence to Hobart, Tasmania, where he set up on his own as an architect and surveyor. If it was indeed true, as Bastow claimed, that Hardy 'once professed to love a crucified saviour', such evangelical fervour did not long survive his friend's departure. 'Don't you dear Brother', wrote Bastow on 17 February 1861, soon after his arrival in Tasmania, 'forget our little meetings together at our place of assignation and oh do let Jesus have the very best of all your time & thoughts.' Inferring from the perfunctoriness of Hardy's replies that his interests and enthusiasms were shifting elsewhere, Bastow became still more urgent in his exhortations: 'Dear old Tom dont you let your eye get off Jesus.—I did hear a whisper that *you* had begun to think that *works may do something* in the way of salvation—but dear fellow if you think so—dont oh dont for a moment let it prevent your leaning for *all your* salvation on "Him".'[53] Hardy eventually let the correspondence drop—though he kept Bastow's photograph and at least some of the letters to the end of his life—and continued in those habits of regular churchgoing which Bastow and the Perkins brothers had never quite managed to disrupt. His marked copies of the Bible, the Book of Common Prayer, and Keble's *The Christian Year* show clearly that throughout 1860 and still more intensively in 1861 he was reading his Bible regularly, attending church frequently, and generally conducting himself as a 'churchy' young man who might conceivably—should circumstances prove favourable—offer himself one day as a candidate for the ministry.[54] Nor is this surprising in view of the extent to which he was being exposed to a variety of influences from the remarkable Moule family.

The Reverend Henry Moule was the vicar of the Dorchester 'suburb' of Fordington St George from 1829 until his death in 1880. A strong Evangelical, he became something of a national figure through his writings on a wide range of theological, social, and horticultural topics, and especially as a result of his courageous efforts, both parochial and political, at the time of the 1854 cholera outbreak.[55] He was also an inventor of some ingenuity and won considerable fame, as may well be imagined, by his introduction of the earth-closet. Of his seven sons who survived infancy, most had notable and even distinguished academic or ecclesiastical careers. It is not clear just how Hardy's connection with the Moules began— perhaps because of his father's business dealings with Henry Moule or even of his mother's employment during the late 1830s in the household of the vicar of Stinsford[56]—but its intensification had much to do with the interest in watercolour sketching which he shared with Henry Joseph Moule, the eldest of the 'seven brethren', later to become the first curator of the Dorset County Museum.

Hardy is said to have made watercolour drawings of animals for Mrs Martin at the age of 9 or 10, but most of his surviving sketches are of architectural or topographical subjects. A view 'From Black Heath Corner', annotated 'Thos Hardy's first attempt at sketching from nature', is not dated, but a pencil drawing of an upended cart in a somewhat dilapidated farmyard is signed 'T. Hardy | 1854', and watercolours of both Athelhampton Hall and the Old Manor House on the Kingston Maurward estate were painted in 1859.[57] After Henry Joseph Moule's death in 1904 Hardy wrote: 'His figure emerges from the obscurity of forgotten and half-forgotten things somewhere between 1856 and 1860, when I recall him as he stood beside me while I was attempting a sketch from nature in water colours. He must have been about thirty, and had already become an adept in out-door painting. As I was but a youth, and by no means practised in that art, he criticized my performance freely.'[58]

By the late 1850s Hardy had become friendly not only with this eldest of the Moule brothers but also with the second, George, who gave him a book of European history in December 1857, with the fifth, Charles, just launched on a successful academic career at Cambridge, and with the youngest, Handley, later to become Bishop of Durham, who was exactly the same age as Mary Hardy.[59] Of far greater emotional and intellectual importance than these relationships—it seems safe to say, than any other male relationship throughout his life—was Hardy's intense friendship with the fourth of the brothers, Horatio Mosley Moule, usually known as Horace. They were on close terms at least as early as 1857, when Horace inscribed to Hardy a copy of Jabez Hogg's *Elements of Experimental and Natural Philosophy*, and saw a good deal of each other during the late 1850s and early 1860s—a period when Horace was 'much at home' following his failure to complete a degree either at Oxford, to which he had first gone in 1851, or at Cambridge, to which he had transferred in 1854.[60]

Explanations for these failures are hard to come by. Moule might have run into trouble, as many students did, with the compulsory mathematical component of the Cambridge Tripos, but such a possibility squares neither with his Oxford difficulties nor with his tutoring in mathematics at a later date. Handley Moule remembered him as a much-loved brother, an excellent classical scholar, and a gifted teacher: 'Wonderful was his subtle faculty for imparting, along with all due care for grammatical precision, a living interest in the subject-matter, and for shedding an indefinable glamour of the ideal over all we read.'[61] At home in Fordington, Moule shared in the teaching of the paying pupils that his father's reputation had for some years been attracting to the vicarage. He was chosen as president of the 'Fordington Times Society', a literary gatheringplace for the Moule brothers, their friends, and their father's pupils, and was well represented in *Tempora Mutantur*, a collection of prose and verse by members of the society that was published in 1859. At the same time he was publishing poems in local newspapers and contributing reviews and occasional essays to national periodicals—a poem by his brother Charles portrayed him as 'snatching rest, | Ere his review to "Fraser" goes'[62]—and completing his lengthy dissertation, *Christian Oratory; An Inquiry into its History during the First Five Centuries*, which won the Hulsean Prize at Cambridge in 1858.

Horace Moule's impact upon Hardy was immense. He was handsome, charming, cultivated, scholarly, thoroughly at home in the glamorous worlds of the ancient universities and of literary London. Although only eight years Hardy's senior, he was already an independent thinker, an accomplished musician, and a publishing critic and poet. Hardy thought he showed promise of becoming 'a distinguished English poet'.[63] He gave Hardy advice, helped him with his Greek, and introduced him to new books and ideas—to Walter Bagehot's *Estimates of Some Englishmen and Scotchmen* of 1858, for example, and the controversial *Essays and Reviews* of 1860.[64] Moule seems never to have abandoned at least a formal allegiance to the Church, but his attitude towards a work such as *Essays and Reviews* would certainly have been more open, more 'liberal', than that of his father and his clerical brothers—who were later to serve, perhaps somewhat unfairly, as models for Angel Clare's father and brothers in *Tess of the d'Urbervilles*. Moule's *Christian Oratory* carried an affectionate dedication to his father when it appeared in book form in 1859, but relations between them were sometimes strained. The episode in chapter 18 of *Tess* in which Angel Clare is rebuked by his horrified father for ordering a theologically offensive book from a local bookseller was based on just such a confrontation between Horace Moule and his father—the two volumes of the condemned work, Gideon Algernon Mantell's *The Wonders of Geology*, being passed on from Moule to Hardy in April 1858.[65]

It is not clear that Hardy was a frequent or especially welcome visitor at Fordington vicarage, but if his exposure to the well-educated and variously talented Moule brothers did little to lighten his sense of social inferiority, it certainly incited his ambition to excel. Having discovered in Horace Moule a model of what he now knew he most deeply desired to become, he was especially attentive to the lecture on 'Oxford and the Middle Class Examinations' that Moule delivered before the local Working Men's Mutual Improvement Society on 15 November 1858. Reviewing the history of the university as a preliminary to explaining how recent changes would make its advantages available to a wider middle-class public, Moule invoked the achievements of such Oxford men 'as Sir Robert Peel, Dr. Arnold, Professor Newman, and Mr. Gladstone'—a litany echoed nearly forty years later in *Jude the Obscure* when Jude Fawley hears the ghostly voices of great Christminster men, including Peel, Newman, and Dr Arnold's son, as he walks among the colleges the night of his arrival. Moule's peroration, too, spoke powerfully to the kind of aspiration that was moving Hardy, as it would later move Jude, to labour in solitude at Latin and Greek in the cherished but elusive hope of eventually going to university: 'The lecture was brought to a close by a recapitulation of some of the advantages arising from the study of a foreign literature, particularly that of a remote and ancient people, like the Greeks of the classical period. In enlarging upon this point Mr. Moule warmed into an eloquence which carried his audience away with him, and he sat down amid loud applause.'[66]

Unfortunately Hardy was to encounter all too soon the darker side of his friend's personality. Early in 1860 Moule went to live in the Cathedral Close at Salisbury with two pupils whom he had undertaken to coach in Greek, Latin, and mathematics preparatory to their sitting Oxford and

Cambridge entrance examinations. One of the pupils, Wynne Albert Bankes (of the Bankes family of Corfe Castle and Kingston Lacy), recorded in his diary his early realization that Moule was 'a Dypsomaniac—and that he was suffering from D.T.', a condition originating in his 'taking opium when reviewing books for Macmillan of Cambridge at which he worked for 48 or 72 hours at a stretch'. Moule eventually recovered, and Bankes agreed to continue with the otherwise satisfactory tutorial arrangement if Moule would neither have drink in the house nor go out of the house alone. The little group moved to Devon on 22 April, spent a few days in Oxford (where the second pupil took and failed his examination), and then proceeded to Saint-Germain-en-Laye for the summer. On Saturday, 28 July, Bankes went into Paris, where Moule was to join him in time for church the following morning. Moule failed to arrive, and when on the Tuesday Bankes returned to Saint-Germain he discovered that Moule 'had ordered a bottle of claret on Saturday, that he had cut his whiskers off & had disappeared'. Bankes made daily visits to the Paris morgue; Horace's brothers Henry and Charles came to France to help in the search; on the following Sunday they learned by telegram that the truant had arrived safely back in England.[67]

Hardy is known to have visited Salisbury in 1860—catching (like Jude Fawley) his first glimpse of the cathedral 'through a driving mist that nearly hid the top of the spire'[68]—and if, as seems likely, he was accompanying his sister Mary on her admission to the Salisbury training college on 3 April 1860, he would have seen Moule in the course of recovering from the first of the two collapses recorded by Bankes.[69] A note in one of Hardy's bibles shows that he attended Evensong at Fordington Church on 5 August, the day on which Moule resurfaced after the second episode, and while he was always deeply moved by the lesson from 1 Kings 19 ('after the fire the still small voice') prescribed for the evening service on that Ninth Sunday after Trinity, the choice of Fordington suggests that he hoped to hear some news. Conceivably, though by no means certainly, it was on this occasion that Horace's father preached the sermon on the text 'All the days of my appointed time will I wait, till my change come' that in 1919 Hardy remembered 'just as if it were yesterday'.[70] That Hardy's friendship with Moule survived such revelations of his alcoholism is a testimony to the extraordinary charm that Moule was capable of exercising over all who encountered him.

In the aftermath of his French escapade Moule seems to have made a genuine effort to redeem himself in his parents' eyes. In February 1861 he lectured on temperance at East Fordington, urging total abstinence upon those who lacked the self-discipline to drink in moderation. In January 1862 he gave the first performance on the new organ at West Fordington Church. Two years later he went with his father to a missionary meeting at West Stafford.[71] Moule's participation in such events was not necessarily hypocritical. His desperate search for approval from his austere father was at the heart of his difficulties, and his share in the moral earnestness characteristic of the Moule family evidently served to intensify the sense of guilt and self-contempt that succeeded each episode of failure. What cannot be so precisely pinned down is the part played in his personal tragedy by the ambiguous sexuality that seems to have constituted the obverse, so to speak, of his gifts as a teacher and his devotion to the boys and young men who were his pupils.[72]

Hardy himself was very much aware of the dazzling presence of one of those pupils, a brilliant young contemporary named Hooper Tolbort. Tolbort lived with his mother and his stepfather, a Dorchester ironmonger, and was apprenticed to a local chemist, but his prodigious talent for languages was so effectively encouraged by Horace Moule and by William Barnes, his former schoolmaster, that he took first place, nationally, not only in the Oxford Middle Class (or Local) Examinations of 1859 but also, three years later, in the competitive examinations for entry into the Indian Civil Service.[73] Hardy incorporated aspects of Tolbort's career into his representation of Oswald Winwood, hero of a story called 'Destiny and a Blue Cloak', published in 1874 but probably written earlier. Winwood, product of an 'obscure little academy', looks forward to a successful future in India: ' "Thanks to Macaulay, of honoured memory, I have as good a chance as the best of them!" he said, with ardour. "What a great thing competitive examination is; it will put good men in good places, and make inferior men move lower down; all bureaucratic jobbery will be swept away." '[74] The optimistic note of the mid-nineteenth-century success ethic and, more specifically, of Horace Moule's speech to the Dorchester working men can clearly be heard, although it is characteristic of Hardy that Winwood's enthusiasm should be promptly undercut by his inability to explain what he means by the word 'bureaucratic'.

The wryness in Hardy's story perhaps sprang from the knowledge that he had himself seemed to Moule the less promising of his two protégés— slower intellectually, less gifted linguistically, not so well prepared academically, with less time to spend on his studies and smaller financial resources to fall back upon: 'the easy circumstances' of young Tolbort's situation, Hardy later recalled, 'left him much spare time, which he devoted entirely to study'. At the time when Moule was urging Tolbort on to spectacular examination successes, he was counselling Hardy to aim towards the modest security of an architectural career rather than persist in what would be, for him, the financially unproductive study of Greek drama. Though always loyal to Moule's memory, Hardy seems rather to have resented this discriminatory advice and to have allowed that resentment both to colour his eventual judgement that Tolbort's 'genius' was in fact 'receptive rather than productive'[75] and to resurface in the patronizing manner that Henry Knight adopts towards his protégé Stephen Smith in *A Pair of Blue Eyes* and in the sense of promise denied that provides so much of the emotional impetus of *Jude the Obscure*. In the meantime he remained very much in the shadow of Tolbort's brilliance, making no attempt to publish either the poems he had himself written in 1858 and 1859 or what he later referred to as his 'critical essays on Tennyson, Coleridge, Lamb, etc.'[76] In his hesitancy and lack of self-confidence he perhaps did not show them to anyone: even so close a friend as Bastow had no notion, as he later wrote, that Hardy 'considered the pen as one of the weapons of [his] struggle for life'.[77]

That Hardy's articles with Hicks were extended for a further year 'in consideration of his immaturity' was not, apparently, an acknowledgement of incompetence on his part but rather of a sense, shared by his employer and his parents alike, that he was still 'young' for his years and not yet ready to seek regular employment. When his fourth year was up, in the summer of 1860, Hicks kept him on as a paid assistant at the rate of fifteen shillings a week.[78] He was now for the first time earning money of his own, and could claim seniority over two more recent arrivals in the office. Business both ecclesiastical and secular was flourishing. There survives a front elevation of some houses 'Designed by T. Hardy 1861', but a sketch of Glastonbury Abbey dated March 1861 and a drawing of Stinsford Church done some time in the same year tend to suggest that Hardy, like his employer, was still primarily interested in churches. That his architectural work continued to extend and deepen his familiarity with the Dorset countryside and its villages is suggested by his drawing of the font at the little church of Coombe Keynes, restored by Hicks in 1860–1 and located in the neighbourhood of Wool and Bindon Abbey, later the settings for important episodes in *Tess of the d'Urbervilles*.[79]

In April 1862, however, shortly after the completion of the work at Coombe Keynes,[80] Hardy 'started alone for London, to pursue the art and science of architecture on more advanced lines'.[81] *Life and Work* simply begins a new chapter with this entirely unheralded information, saying nothing as to the reasons for this 'migration' or to its timing, apart from a brief reference to the imminence of the 1862 Exhibition, successor to the Great Exhibition of 1851. Such brevity, reinforced by a plethora of annotations for early 1862 in Hardy's Bible, prayerbook, and *Christian Year*,[82] creates an impression of his departure as having been a somewhat hurried affair, undertaken in response to some immediate pressure or distress. The great majority of the annotations, however, are simply memoranda of services attended or stages reached in a programme of systematic Bible reading, and the few that could possibly relate to more directly personal concerns are too brief and enigmatic to be reliably illuminating. The occasional appearances of the initials 'M.' and 'M.W.' , therefore, cannot confidently be read as lending support to the story of Hardy's having made, early in 1862, an unsuccessful proposal of marriage to Mary Waight, a young woman seven years his senior who was an assistant in one of the more genteel of the Dorchester shops.[83]

What does emerge is that on 8 February 1862, a Saturday, Hardy was in Trinity Church, Dorchester, writing the date in his prayerbook against the last verse of the Tate and Brady version of Psalm 43, one of the psalms for the day:

> Why then cast down, my soul? and why
> So much oppress'd with anxious care?
> On God, thy God, for aid rely,
> Who will thy ruin'd state repair.[84]

Although the verse is one that Hardy's melancholy temperament might at any time have seized upon, his annotation does suggest that it had some timely applicability. His difficulties, however, seem likely to have been professional rather than emotional, and related to an immediate or prospective termination of his current employment. Hicks had kept Hardy on as an apprentice for an extra year and employed him as an assistant thereafter, but was perhaps unwilling or unable to employ him at the higher salary he now felt he needed and deserved. There was, in any case, little more that he could usefully learn from Hicks; few if any alternative positions would have been available in Dorchester itself; and since he lacked the experience, capital, and social position that might have enabled him to go into independent architectural practice, his obvious course, at that period of spectacular urban expansion, was to seek employment in the metropolis. Bastow had already advised him to that effect,[85] and the moment seemed reasonably propitious. He was approaching his twenty-second birthday. He had completed his articles and gained experience as an architect's clerk (so his occupation is given in the 1861 Census). His father was in a bigger way of business than formerly. Although Henry and Kate were still at school, Mary had overcome a period of illness and was now out in the world, qualifying herself as a teacher at the Salisbury training college—the local newspaper, indeed, had just announced her achievement of 'a first-class certificate at the recent inspector's examination'.[86] Whatever dreams of becoming a parson-poet Hardy might himself still cherish, architecture remained his only visible means of employment and advancement, and it was clearly incumbent upon him to take another step along the path his mother had so deliberately marked out for him.

4

London

THE 21-year-old Thomas Hardy who took the train from Dorchester to London on 17 April 1862—a Thursday, as he meticulously recorded—was not an especially prepossessing young man.[1] His moustache had grown in size and dignity, his hair was swept across the top of his head in a slightly crested wave, and the face that looks, faintly smiling, out of photographs taken in 1861 has aspirations towards the kind of conventional Victorian handsomeness exemplified, not to say caricatured, in the figure of Alec d'Urberville. But Hardy was somewhat below the Victorian average in height, and while altogether healthier and stronger than in childhood he remained lightly built and lacking in presence. Wide reading and exposure to the influence and example of the Moule brothers had taught him much that he could otherwise never have learned in Bockhampton or even in Dorchester, but he was still lacking in worldly experience and social assurance, and unmistakably countrified in his manners and his speech—matters of some importance at a time when (as Hardy himself later recalled) Londoners took such a supercilious view of rural newcomers that it was 'the aim of every provincial, from the squire to the rustic, to get rid of his local articulation at the earliest moment'.[2]

Hardy cannot have seemed especially likely to succeed or even to survive in London, and since he appears to have made no prior arrangements for employment or even for accommodation—since, too, he departed with a return railway ticket in his pocket—it is scarcely surprising that Hicks, for one, confidently expected him to return home defeated within a few weeks.[3] Hardy in fact established himself in the city with quite remarkable rapidity and ease. He found lodgings at 3 Clarence Place, Kilburn, on the east side of the Edgware Road just north of the junction with Quex Road. Several families lived in the building and it is not clear with whom Hardy actually lodged—perhaps with the master shoemaker who occupied the shop at street level. Although Kilburn was becoming rapidly absorbed into the vast urban mass to the south, it was in 1862 still largely an area of fields and farms, and the Kilburn Gate from which Hardy took the omnibus 'for London' each day was an actual turnpike gate until 1868. Hardy quickly located the parish church, St Mary's, found it 'rather to my taste', and became a regular worshipper there throughout the remainder of 1862.[4]

His immediate professional future was determined with similar promptness. Of the two letters of introduction he carried, the one to Benjamin Ferrey (the designer of Dorchester Town Hall) proved of little value, but the other, written by Hicks, led indirectly but almost immediately to his employment by Arthur Blomfield, who happened to be in need of 'a young Gothic draughtsman who could restore and design churches and rectory-houses'.[5] Blomfield, then in his early thirties, was the son of a former Bishop of London and already a successful architect with a large ecclesiastical practice. His office was at 9 St Martin's Place, immediately adjacent to St Martin-in-the-Fields, and Hardy soon became 'as familiar with St Martin's bells as one so near well could be, and with the clock face—or rather the half of it visible from our windows'.[6] Hardy found his new employer extremely congenial, while Blomfield, for his part, was sufficiently impressed with his new draughtsman to propose him, as early as October 1862, for membership of the Architectural Association (motto: 'Design with Beauty. Build in Truth'), of which he was himself the current president. Hardy's formal election along with that of John Lee, another of Blomfield's assistants, followed in November.[7]

Clearly, Hicks had given his pupil a good grounding. Clearly, too, Hardy was extremely fortunate in his early London contacts and arrangements. He could manage comfortably, though not lavishly, on the salary of £110 a year he received from Blomfield, especially since he shared his Clarence Place rooms with another young architect named Philip Shaw. The two got on well together, despite the fact that Shaw's background was both socially and financially superior to Hardy's own. A visible sign of this difference was the set of silver cutlery with which Shaw's parents had equipped him. The young men's landlady resented the responsibility of these expensive items and showed her disapproval by noisily rattling them in her basket as she carried them upstairs after dinner each evening—a performance Hardy later alluded to as 'the procession of the plate'.[8] It was Shaw, naturally enough, to whom Hardy turned for the loan of a dress coat in which he could attend the Architectural Association conversazione on 31 October at which his name was to be proposed for membership. Though impressed at the conversazione by the presence of numerous ladies 'in full dress', Hardy in a letter to his sister Mary referred rather scathingly to the proceedings themselves: 'After lots of speechifying by learned professors, there was music &c, and coffee—this last rather in small quantities.'[9]

In February 1863 Blomfield moved his office the short distance to 8 Adelphi Terrace, the fine Adam Brothers block which then stood along the north bank of the Thames just east of Charing Cross. 'The new office is a capital place,' Hardy told his sister. 'It is on the first floor and on a terrace that overlooks the river. We can see from our window right across the Thames, and on a clear day every bridge is visible. Everybody says that we have a beautiful place.'[10] From the window nearest him and from the balcony outside he was able to watch the construction of the Thames Embankment and the Charing Cross railway bridge; on his way to work each day he saw the station itself going up and the Charing Cross Hotel being built on ground previously occupied by the old Hungerford Market. At that period of unprecedented urban expansion both the physical and the social faces of London were undergoing rapid and permanent change, and Hardy always treasured the glimpses he had caught of customs, manners, entertainments, and ways of life that were soon to vanish forever. As he recalled in old age, 'It was quite Dickens's London in those days.'[11]

He attended a reading by Dickens himself in the spring of 1863, went along the Strand to the London School of Phrenology in September 1864 to have his head read by the proprietor, 'Dr' C. Donovan, and in October 1865 attended Palmerston's Westminster Abbey funeral in company with John Lee and Blomfield's colleague Clement Heaton, the glass painter. As he told his sister the next day, he was deeply impressed by the ceremony itself and by Palmerston's having been 'contemporaneous with Pitt, Fox, Sheridan, Burke &c. I mean to say his life overlapped theirs so to speak.'[12] There were also visits to theatres and occasionally to restaurants, including Bertolini's, off Leicester Square, with friends from Benjamin Ferrey's office, but during his first London years Hardy seems for the most part to have kept to a fairly steady routine of work and study. He danced at Willis's Rooms in St James's—the former Almack's—almost, it would seem, for the sake of being able to say that he had done so (as in the poem 'Reminiscences of a Dancing Man'), but he was too religious, too cautious, and, for that matter, too impecunious to venture far or often into the dubious world of the saloons and cider cellars, let alone of such 'gallant resorts' as the Cremorne and the Argyle. With characteristic ambiguity he recorded of these latter that 'he did not dance there much himself, if at all'.[13]

But if he did not seek out the more garish aspects of the city's night life, with its teeming crowds, its casual violence, and its open and even aggressive prostitution, he inevitably encountered during his visits to theatres and building sites and daily walks through Soho and the Seven Dials, along the Strand and past the Adelphi arches, many of those extraordinary juxta-positions of splendour and squalor, of optimism and despair, that London so abundantly offered. Nor was he immune to the excitement caused by the sexual and financial scandals of the day, the annual holidays and sporting occasions, or such sensational events as the public execution of five pirates at Newgate in February 1864. His worst experience of London crowds was on 10 March 1863 when he went out to see the illuminations following the wedding of the Prince of Wales and the Princess of Denmark and was caught in a dense mass in Piccadilly, 'where my waistcoat buttons were torn off and my ribs bent in before I could get into a doorway'.[14]

The 1862 International Exhibition at South Kensington—successor to the Great Exhibition of 1851 and forerunner of the Victoria and Albert Museum—was in progress throughout Hardy's first London summer, and he spent a good deal of time there, drawn chiefly by the displays of materials and artefacts related to architecture but also by the rich collections of European and especially English paintings. The Exhibition's popular appeal, however, was far wider and more various. His sister Mary and other visitors from Dorset were taken there, as was his cousin Martha Sparks, then working in London as a lady's maid, and at least one visit was made in the company of Horace Moule, whose poem, 'Ave Caesar', inspired by Gérôme's *Roman Gladiators*, one of the paintings they saw together, Hardy was to recall to public attention sixty years later.[15]

On 7 August Moule had descended upon him in a state of high excite-ment at the news of Hooper Tolbort's spectacular success in the Indian Civil Service competitive examinations for 1862. Moule—whether out of curiosity, genuine religious inclination, or self-conscious rebellion against his background—was on his way to the Jesuit Chapel in Farm Street to attend the service held each seventh of August to celebrate the anniversary of the Society's restoration in the United Kingdom. Hardy went with him to what proved to be an impressive occasion and then on by cab to Covent Garden and supper at the Hummums Hotel, named for its Turkish baths and known as a favourite haunt of young bachelors. Tolbort himself had come to London in the autumn of 1861 to pursue his linguistic studies, and Hardy's own intellectual interests were broadened by this renewal of their friendship. He said later that he had frequently encountered Tolbort in London in 1862, adding that he was usually to be found, either in his rooms or at the Marylebone Library and Scientific Institution, 'scribbling transla-tions into and from dead and living languages'.[16]

Just before the International Exhibition closed at the end of October 1862, Thomas Hardy senior came to town for a few days and was given into the care, while Hardy himself was at work, of a 'Miss A.'—almost certainly Eliza Amey, the unmarried aunt of the orphaned Eliza Amey of Dorchester, a classmate of Mary Hardy's at the Salisbury training college.[17] Hardy had become an enthusiastic opera-goer—in after years he spoke of the music of *Il trovatore* as always carrying him back to his first year in London when he was 'strong and vigorous and enjoyed his life immensely' —and he took his father and Miss A. to see Vincent Wallace's *Lurline* at Covent Garden.[18] Nothing, however, as he reported to Mary, 'would satisfy Father unless he went to see the Thames Tunnel'. In the same letter Hardy made gentle fun of their father's broad Dorset accent and indulged in a little verbal humour for his sister's amusement: 'I wish you wd tell me how u. r. when u. write. I have a "cowdid by head" so I have stayed in all day to be all right to morrow.'[19] The Hardy family was reunited at Bockhampton that Christmas, Mary enjoying a brief respite between the successful conclusion of her training at Salisbury and the beginning of her first teaching appointment. There had been talk of their being joined by Shaw, and while Hardy indicated that his friend would be considered 'a great gun' in the world of Stinsford he evinced no social qualms about introducing him—as he had already introduced Bastow and the Moules—into the intimacy of his family circle.[20]

Hardy's submission of prizewinning entries for two architectural competitions in the spring of 1863 should have marked a high point in his professional aspirations, but neither success was unqualified. On 19 February 1863 Hardy reported to Mary that he was 'now very busy getting up a design for a Country Mansion for which a small prize is offered—£3 the best & £2 the second best'.[21] Hardy won the competition, named after its instigator, William Tite,[22] and limited to members of the Architectural Association, and duly received his prize—in the form of copies of William Nesfield's *Specimens of Mediaeval Architecture* and Norman Shaw's *Architectural Sketches from the Continent*—at the conversazione of 17 April 1863. But while Professor T. Roger Smith (later Hardy's employer) and the other judges of the competition made no public criticism of Hardy's entry, it became embarrassingly clear that the number of competitors had been extremely small, and perhaps no more than the two prizewinners themselves.[23]

A worse embarrassment lay just ahead. At a General Meeting of the Royal Institute of British Architects on 18 May 1863 he was presented by the president, T. L. Donaldson, with the Institute's Silver Medal for his essay 'On the Application of Colored Bricks and Terra Cotta to Modern Architecture', based largely on researches he had made in the Reading Room at South Kensington. The judges, not disarmed by the Ciceronian motto ('Tentavi quid in eo genere possem') under which the essay had been submitted, had earlier announced that although Hardy's submission was prize-worthy so far as it had gone, it had seriously skimped 'that portion referring to moulded and shaped bricks'; the additional cash prize of £10 would therefore be withheld and offered for an essay on the same subject in the following year.[24] Since moulded and shaped bricks were not part of the topic as originally announced but had been inserted at a later date, Hardy wrote to the RIBA to explain that he had known nothing of the change and to ask that he be allowed to enlarge his essay and thus qualify for the prize in its entirety. The RIBA's response—that he should resubmit the following year[25]—was not unreasonable, but Hardy's anger and resentment at being publicly presented with the prize on such equivocal terms would surface a few years later in the form of an episode in his first but never published novel, *The Poor Man and the Lady*, in which a company publicly retracted an award it had already made. Although Hardy carefully preserved his Silver Medal, the essay itself long ago disappeared, and it is tempting to give credence to the story that shortly after the prize had been awarded Hardy went to the Institute library, asked for the essay, and simply walked off with it.[26]

On 12 May 1863, in a notebook headed 'Schools of Painting', Hardy began to write succinct summaries of factual information about major painters and their works from the Renaissance onwards. Other notes on paintings survive from the same period—in his copy of the *Golden Treasury* the line 'The bloom of young Desire and purple light of Love' from Gray's 'The Progress of Poesy' is annotated 'mem: S.K. Museum. Etty. 1863', evidently a reference to William Etty's *Cupid and Psyche* in the Sheepshanks Collection—and Hardy seems to have considered at one point the possibility of becoming an art critic.[27] Art history, however, was one of the components of the RIBA's Voluntary Architectural Examinations that he was thinking of sitting, and the notebook may chiefly reflect his enrolment in one of the summer classes provided by the Architectural Association for the assistance of prospective candidates. 'You never told me a word about the voluntary examination,' wrote Bastow late in 1863. 'Surely you are the very fellow who would go in for it . . . and get it too.'[28]

Hardy does not seem to have sat the actual examination, however, let alone been successful in it. His work for Blomfield had turned out to be generally—and disappointingly—of a routine kind, concerned with preparing the working drawings necessary for the realization of the designs more broadly outlined by Blomfield himself. Even when annotations in Hardy's hand appear on surviving plans, such as those for All Saints, Windsor, built by Blomfield in 1862–4, it remains unlikely that he was directly responsible for the actual design work, with the possible exception of details here and there.[29] Blomfield, as his own nephew later recalled, was too busy and successful to give much attention to the instruction and supervision of his pupils and assistants, or even to the continuing development of his own architectural style.[30] The compensating factors for Hardy were that he was kept in constant employment and had frequent opportunities to get out of the office and visit buildings under construction.

Hardy much appreciated his employer's wry humour—when one of the pupils rubbed clean a portion of the Adam fireplace at Adelphi Terrace as a broad hint to the charwoman, Blomfield made him wash it all himself—and the unfailing geniality that made the office such an easygoing place, known then and later for its boisterous good fellowship and its practical jokes, some of them played upon what Blomfield's young men regarded as the unnecessarily solemn and dangerously radical members of the Reform League, which had its headquarters on the ground floor of 8 Adelphi Terrace.[31] Hardy shared Blomfield's love of music and joined as best his rather weak voice would allow in Arne's 'Where the bee sucks', Horn's 'I know a bank', and the other songs, glees, and catches with which the office frequently resounded. The office 'choir' lacked an alto, however, and Blomfield would tell Hardy that if ever he met an alto in the Strand he should 'ask him to come in and join us'.[32] Precisely because his own labours were generally of a mechanical kind, Hardy was able to allow his mind to dwell on non-architectural matters even during working hours, and he struck one of his juniors at that time as being quieter than most of his colleagues, 'very regular' in his attendance, gentle in speech and movement, 'rather dreamy' in manner, and much given to talking about literature and the writers of the day.[33]

In November 1863 Hardy went to Windsor with Blomfield to be present at the laying of the memorial stone of All Saints by the Crown Princess of Germany, the Princess's embarrassed uncertainty as to what to do with the mortar-laden trowel subsequently providing him with material for a brief scene in *The Poor Man and the Lady*. Other expeditions outside London appear to have been non-professional, including one to Dover in September 1862 and another to Brighton—where he sketched the crowds on the beach—on Good Friday of 1863.[34] One weekend in late April 1863 he paid a short visit to his sister Mary, now teaching in the little National

School at Denchworth, quite close to Wantage and about fifteen miles from Oxford. As she reported to her brother in late November 1862, just before leaving the college, her salary would be £40 a year together with a garden and a partly furnished house. The drawback, however, was that she had been obliged, much against her will, to undertake the role of church organist, although her previous experience had been confined to the piano and harmonium.[35] Burdened with new responsibilities, isolated from the accustomed society and reassurances of her home, Mary felt lonely and starved of affection, and discouraged by the prospect that lay before her. As she later wrote: 'It was indeed now that I realized what life would be to me and although I felt no disappointment I was not cheered by the prospect.'[36] In that letter to her brother, however, she had already mentioned the possibility of being joined by her 6-year-old sister, and Kate was indeed sent or taken to Denchworth quite early on, chiefly to counter Mary's loneliness but also to get her own early schooling. It was the beginning of an arrangement that lasted, with only occasional interruptions, for the rest of their lives. Jemima's willingness to part with her youngest child at such a tender age suggests a certain lack of maternal warmth; on the other hand, she may simply have done what seemed best for her children at the time. It is certainly indicative of the closeness of the Hardy children, despite their differences in age and temperament, that Kate should have looked back on her time at Denchworth as one of particular happiness.[37]

Visiting Denchworth again, in 1864, Hardy took the opportunity to go over to the village at Fawley, just south of Wantage, where his paternal grandmother had been born, as Mary Head, in 1772. His sister had already been to Fawley and reported that the inhabitants were 'among the most original & hearty set [that] could ever be'. She found no living Heads there but was told of two farmers of that name, brothers, from the nearby hamlet of Chaddleworth, one of whom had married but remained childless, while the other had disappeared the day after his wedding and returned many years later as an old man.[38] Hardy evidently found out more about the Heads of Chaddleworth—from the parish registers if not from personal contact—and made, in Fawley itself, the acquaintance of those who could tell him something of the history of his grandmother's people and thus lay, all unconsciously, some of the foundations of *Jude the Obscure*.

Early in 1863 Hardy for some reason made a temporary move from 3 Clarence Place to 9 Clarence Place, occupied by a plumber named Isaac Bounford. Four months later he took lodgings at 16 Westbourne Park Villas, a street of solid semi-detached houses running close to the Great

Western Railway line just west of the Paddington terminus. So close, in fact, that the entire north side of the street was later removed to allow for expansion of the railway—from which number 16 on the surviving south side may still be glimpsed. A sketch Hardy made of the view from his window shows that he lived at the rear of the house, on the second floor, looking out over gardens and stables to the backs of the buildings on the north side of Westbourne Park Road. Visible in the sketch is the spire of nearby St Stephen's Church, but while the church is still there the spire was taken down after suffering air-raid damage during the Second World War.[39]

The Westbourne Park area was 'better' and more convenient than Clarence Place, but these were not its only attractions from Hardy's point of view. On at least two occasions during his residence at Kilburn he had walked the mile and more to the south-west to attend service at St Stephen's. It is possible that Martha Sparks or one of her brothers was living in the vicinity.[40] It is also possible that Hardy was drawn to St Stephen's by the fact that its vicar was a close friend of the Reverend Reginald Smith, the rector of West Stafford, the parish adjoining Stinsford.[41] What is certain is that at 2 (later renumbered 40) Orsett Terrace, just a few minutes' walk from 16 Westbourne Park Villas, a young woman named Eliza Bright Nicholls was employed as a lady's maid in the family of Charles Richard Hoare, barrister-at-law, the son of the Venerable Charles James Hoare, Archdeacon of Surrey.[42]

Eliza Nicholls was the most important figure in Hardy's early emotional life, and her intense piety had a significant, if complex, impact on his religious life as well. Many details of their relationship remain obscure or conjectural, but between 1863 and 1867 it seems to have amounted to an 'understanding' that Eliza perhaps understood as an engagement and that Hardy perhaps never quite defined, either to her or even to himself.[43] Eliza had a ring she claimed to have been given to her by Hardy, as well as some manuscripts and a photograph, and while the manuscripts have disappeared, and the ring is said to have been stolen, the photograph—an original print dating from 1862 or 1863—does persuasively survive.[44] Born in Sussex in 1839, Eliza spent much of her early life in a coastguard cottage at Kimmeridge Bay, on the south Dorset coast, where her Cornish-born father, George Nicholls, served as a coastguard until some point in the mid–1850s. A serious operation or accident then forced his retirement to his wife's birthplace, the Sussex village of Findon, where he became landlord of the Running Horse inn (now Nepcote House) on the edge of Nepcote Green. There were stables for racehorses close by and the Green itself was the site of an important sheep-fair each year.[45] It is not impossible that

Hardy met Eliza while she was still living at Kimmeridge, but their emotional involvement seems to date only from Hardy's London period. 'I
suppose you have scarcely been and gone and lost your heart yet, young
man,—have you?' wrote Henry Bastow from Tasmania in May 1861, '—
you must let me know when it has come to that and tell me who is the fair
damsel—though I still am of opinion that you are not of a highly inflam-
mable nature—.'[46] The comment says little for Bastow's perspicuity, but
Hardy had evidently not committed himself ahead of Bastow's departure,
and by that point Eliza Nicholls was already in service in London as the
personal attendant of Charles Richard Hoare's wife Emma, the daughter of
Lieutenant-Colonel John Mansel of Smedmore House, situated within a
mile or so of Kimmeridge Bay.

Hardy's memory of Eliza is incorporated into the drawing he inserted
into *Wessex Poems* opposite the poem 'She, to Him. I'. It shows a male and a
female figure walking or standing hand in hand on a path that leads
up towards a building identifiable as Clavel Tower, an early nineteenth-
century 'folly' which still stands (somewhat precariously) on a cliff-top at the
eastern side of Kimmeridge Bay.[47] Hardy naturally associated the spot with
Eliza—the sun in his drawing is setting behind the tower very much as it
would be seen from the nearby coastguard cottages—and he may well have
visited it in her company on 3 September 1863, the date which appears on
his sketches of Gad Cliff and Worbarrow Bay, not far along the coast from
Kimmeridge.[48] Findon itself is quite close to the Sussex coast, and Hardy's
visit to Brighton on Good Friday of 1863 may well have been an incident in
a longer Easter visit to Eliza and her parents;[49] if so, the late summer of 1863
could have marked Eliza's reciprocal introduction to Bockhampton and to
Hardy's parents. Eliza's departure from London for Godstone, Surrey, at
about this time in order to nurse Archdeacon Hoare during his last illness
may have been a factor in bringing matters to a head. The 'She, to Him'
sonnets—dated 1866 by Hardy and said to be fragments of a much longer
sequence—are reflective in part of letters exchanged by Hardy and Eliza
during their periods of separation, but what they for the most part record is
the decline rather than the climax of a relationship to which Hardy's commitment seems always to have been the weaker. Eliza's religiosity—echoed
in Sue Bridehead's in the closing chapters of *Jude the Obscure*—must largely
have determined the terms of that relationship, rendering it from the first
altogether graver and more consequential than Hardy had intended or
anticipated, and it was of her that Hardy was presumably thinking when he
pencilled the words 'Devotion' and 'Stoicism' below the rough sketch of
Clavel Tower he had drawn inside one of the books he was using in 1865.[50]

The mere existence of such a relationship, as a settled and reasonably satisfactory arrangement, may nevertheless have given Hardy a confidence he had hitherto lacked, and it was certainly at 16 Westbourne Park Villas, in that summer of 1863, that his literary career can truly be said to have begun. He was already reading a great deal of Shakespeare, using the ten-volume edition purchased soon after his arrival in the new lodgings, and he also worked his way through much of Samuel Neil's *The Art of Reasoning: A Popular Exposition of the Principles of Logic* and addressed himself to the study of models of argumentative prose.[51] On Horace Moule's recommendation he purchased J. R. M'Culloch's *Principles of Political Economy*, only to be further instructed by Moule, in a letter of 2 July 1863, that he should read M'Culloch and *The Times* and all such exemplars for their content only, not at all for their style: 'you must in the end write *your own* style,' Moule insisted, 'unless you wd be a mere imitator. It always appears to me that a man whose mind is full of a subject, or who can before writing make his mind full of it, has only to pay that attention to method and arrangement which is obvious to any mind of vigorous tone, in order to write well.'[52] In the autumn of that year Hardy began the study of shorthand—the date 1 October 1863 appears in one of several primers, embodying different systems, which he purchased at about this time—and by Christmas he was able to report to Mary that he could do forty words a minute.[53]

These latter preparations were directed towards the possibility of his embarking upon some form of literary journalism. In February 1864, when Moule wrote to explain the proper use of the subjunctive in English, he also raised the possibility of Hardy's becoming the London correspondent of a country newspaper: 'You know the sort of berth I mean—that of a man who sends down a column of condensed London news & talk.' The piece Hardy had now sent him, he added, a 'chatty description of the Law Courts & their denizens', was '*just* in the style that wd go down'.[54] Hardy was by now ready to try almost anything in his search for some kind, any kind, of journalistic work. In that period of print proliferation—of quarterlies, monthlies, weeklies, and dailies—it seemed reasonable to hope that he might find a niche somewhere. Moule, after all, had published articles, reviews, and poems in *Fraser's*, the *Saturday Review*, the *Quarterly Review*, and elsewhere, and Hardy also had before him the example—no less seductive for being cast in fictional terms—of those busy literary men of Thackeray's, George Warrington and Arthur Pendennis. At this stage he was still too unsure of himself, and too inexperienced, to imagine that he might one day make a living as a writer. His hopes were still fixed upon that persistently cherished dream of entering the Church—more specifically, of following the example of his aunt Martha's brother-in-law George Brereton Sharpe, who had abandoned his first profession of medicine, gone through Cambridge, and become a curate in Wales. Hardy had as yet no capital, however, and no source of income other than the architectural career which necessarily claimed the bulk of his time, and literary journalism seemed a feasible and appealing way of financing himself during the many years he would need to devote to his university studies.

Hardy was at home in Dorset for the Christmas festivities of 1864, spending the evening of Boxing Day in Puddletown with his cousin Nathaniel Sparks.[55] On New Year's Day 1865 Horace Moule presented him with a copy of *The Thoughts of the Emperor M. Aurelius Antoninus*, inscribed with the quotation from within the volume that Hardy was to adopt as one of his principal watchwords: 'This is the chief thing: Be not perturbed: for all things are according to the nature of the universal.'[56] It is not clear what specific implications the inscription was intended to carry, either for Hardy or for Moule himself, but 1865 was in any case to be a year in which some of Hardy's central uncertainties about his life and career begin to move towards resolution. In December 1864 he had submitted to the Edinburgh-based *Chambers's Journal* a prose sketch, 'How I Built Myself a House', originally written for the amusement of his colleagues in Blomfield's office as a satirical comment upon the architect–client relationship. The acceptance and publication of the sketch, in March 1865, Hardy once spoke of as having 'determined' his career, and the sale of the copyright certainly brought him his first literary earnings, of £3 15*s*.[57] No less significant, however, was his deliberately setting himself up as a poet in that same year.

Several surviving volumes of 'classical' English poetry—including the poetical works of Milton, Thomson, and Coleridge—are dated 1865 in Hardy's hand. In the same year he bought Henry Reed's *Introduction to English Literature* together with copies of such useful resources as Nuttall's *Standard Pronouncing Dictionary* and John Walker's *Rhyming Dictionary*, supplementing the latter with his own elaborately constructed tables of 'Kindred sounds'. At this time and over the next three or four years, he also made use of a small notebook, headed 'Studies, Specimens &c.', that has survived to provide an extraordinarily detailed insight into his early literary enthusiasms and the dogged determination with which he sought to acquire the skills he believed necessary to the making of poetry. Realizing that he was still deficient even in basic lexical knowledge, Hardy opened the notebook with a series of vocabulary-building exercises, writing out brief quotations taken from a wide range of sources—including the Old Testament, *The*

Golden Treasury, Spenser, Shakespeare, Burns, Byron, Wordsworth (*The Excursion*), Scott (chiefly *The Lord of the Isles* and *Marmion*), Shelley (*Laon and Cythna*), Tennyson (*In Memoriam*), Jean Ingelow, and William Barnes—and underlining individual words that struck him as interesting, effective, or simply unfamiliar. Similar exercises are headed 'Thes.' (for 'Thesaurus') or 'Dic' (for 'Dictionary'), the latter involving the use of the same word in a variety of different structures and contexts—an idea perhaps suggested by Horace Moule's typically abortive experience as collector of entries for letter *H* of the *New English Dictionary*.[58] The exercises as a whole—like Jude Fawley's (or Thomas Hardy's) attempts to teach himself Greek—make for painful reading. Isaac Last's schooling, though sound enough, had been a better preparation for architecture than for poetry, and the sheer ordinariness of so many of the words and images laboriously entered into 'Studies, Specimens &c.' provides a sharp reminder of the distances Hardy had still to travel in pursuit of those goals of self-education, self-development, and self-discovery to which he had already dedicated himself for so long.

Elsewhere in the notebook are extended quotations from Shakespeare, Byron, Swinburne and other poets recognizably important to Hardy's eventual poetic career. Swinburne is a particularly pervasive presence, and the extracts from *Poems and Ballads* identify some of the individual poems—'Ilicet', 'Hermaphroditus', 'Satia te Sanguine', 'Dolores'—to which Hardy so immediately and rapturously responded upon the book's publication in 1866—to the point, so he told Swinburne thirty years later, of reading it while walking along crowded London streets at imminent risk of being knocked down.[59] The notebook contains none of Hardy's own poems, but his occasional memoranda importantly served as directive reminders of the ways in which particular literary effects might best be achieved, a distinctive poetic voice projected. At one point he notes that 'The plu[ral] often makes a common word novel as grasses, dews'. At another he reminds himself to explore the possibilities inherent in the suffix '-less', so distinctive a feature of his later verse. Under the heading 'Inv.', presumably for 'Inventions', Hardy experiments with word coinages on specific patterns, as in: 'a toning—: a shaping—: a curing—: a nerving—: a leafing—: a quenching—: a matching—: a skilling—'.[60] Later on he tries out phrases entirely of his own making, inventing new epithets or fresh uses for old ones—as in '*clanging* thunder, humble bee: *pealing* waves: *whooping* storm: *clicking* twigs: *flapping* of leaves: . . . *undertones* of wind: *hoarse* & *husky* storm'.[61]

Especially remarkable are the long word-lists headed 'Con' or 'Concoc', apparently for 'Concoctions'. Here Hardy worked intensively through passages from a variety of sources—the Old Testament, the Book of

Common Prayer, even a book on the history of architecture—in such a way as to pick up words and phrases from the original and reuse them in modified forms and totally different contexts. In so doing he often moved beyond word-for-word reworkings and ventured—however gropingly— towards the discovery of new continuities of meaning, mood, or imagery. It is almost, at times, as though he were seeking to construct, or uncover, the skeleton of a possible poem. In the course of an extended 'riff' on the first chapter of Habakkuk, for example, the sixth verse ('For, lo, I raise up the Chaldeans, that bitter and hasty nation, which shall march through the breadth of the land, to possess the dwellingplaces that are not theirs') re-emerges as: 'lips my lips' dwelling place : you raised up heats in me—hopes of haste: . . . hasty pants : hasty treads : hasty heart : marches of pleasure, march into death, the grave: march through the years, march through your beauty : . . .'[62] Hardy's objective, clearly, was to generate new expressive phrases from encounters with great models from the past and progressively develop and exercise a literary vocabulary of his own—a conception of working through imitation to originality that he jotted down on a separate scrap of paper at roughly the same period: *'Lyrical Meth* Find a situn from expce. Turn to Lycs for a form of expressn that has been used for a quite difft situn. Use it (Same sitn from experience may be sung in sevl forms.)'[63]

'Studies, Specimens' interestingly reveals that Hardy was in his mid-twenties distinctly squeamish, not to say prudish, about sexual references of a direct or even an indirect character. As demonstrated by several of the textual reworkings, including the example from Habakkuk, the movement of his imagination was strongly in the direction of the erotic; scarcely less strong, apparently, was the impulse to counter or disguise such tendencies when committing them to writing. Hardy's use of shorthand in 'Studies, Specimens' is largely confined to the representation of words such as 'love' and, more rarely, 'breasts', but is also invoked to symbolize 'went to bed to her' in a quotation from *Pericles*, 'he went to bed to her very description'. Dashes are similarly employed to substitute for the letters omitted from 'k— s' and, more remarkably, to render 'sweet *ache* of neck, lip, soul' as 'sweet *ache* of n—k, l—p, s—l'.[64] It is hard to determine whether what now seems an excessive sense of propriety was the result of his upbringing, an inborn shyness, a continuing sexual innocence, or simply a fear of the notebook's being read by someone else—his mother, perhaps, his London landlady, or the pious Eliza. It remains, in any case, a curious feature of the year in which Hardy became 25, and to which he later assigned his transition from youth to young manhood.

Hardy was meanwhile filling his pocketbooks with notes and occasional drawings of whatever struck him from day to day—street scenes, skyscapes, things observed, things read, human encounters seen or heard—and with ideas and outlines for potential stories or poems. Those pocketbooks were all destroyed, the majority by Hardy himself in his lifetime, the remainder following his death. But some evidence of what they were like can be gathered from a surviving half-dozen or so of detached pages, including the leaf which has on one side of it the sketch from the window of 16 Westbourne Park Villas, and from the available text of a composite note-book, headed 'Poetical Matter', into which Hardy, at a much later date, systematically transferred from the doomed pocketbooks whatever ideas, phrases, images, and poem outlines might still prove useable as material for new poems. One such item, written on pocketbook leaves torn out for trans-fer into 'Poetical Matter', begins as follows:

? [1863–7]
July 18. *Poem* (ballad metre) [good]
     rough outline—
1. 'I sat me down in a foreign town,
    And looked across the way: ⌐sitting
      At a window there was a lady { fair
    Far] fairer than the day.   ⌐leaning
     [Rhyme only 2nd & 4th lines]
2. 'Twelve blessed days she won my gaze
    Twelve days She looked at me', &c

Then follows a prose summary of a story about a man and a woman who fall in love by correspondence without ever meeting. The man sees the woman by chance, but she eludes him until, at last, she writes that she will marry him secretly if he will trust her sufficiently to meet him at the church at an agreed hour. Just as the marriage is about to take place it becomes apparent that she is dumb: 'He jumps from her in horror—She falls—He goes away—thinks of her—returns—dead.' The note concludes with another draft stanza:

    'Six times I named a trysting place,
     Six times replièd she:
    'Perhaps I prize thy love likewise
     But to meet—it cannot be!'
[This ballad was never finished][65]

The square brackets are Hardy's, enclosing words and dates he added when inserting the pocketbook pages into 'Poetical Matter', the fusion of these later notations with the original prose and verse fragments providing a rare example of his working methods—of what he meant when describing a poem as being 'from an old draft'.[66]

Although Hardy was becoming poetically active by the summer of 1865, and had received from the editor of *Chambers's* the message that he was capable of writing what magazines were interested in printing, he remained sharply aware of the need for further education if he was to be successful in a literary or indeed in any career. It was in 1865 that he developed the habit of making short daily visits to the National Gallery, each visit devoted exclusively to a single painting or painter,[67] and in October of that year he enrolled in a French extension class at King's College, London, just a short walk from Adelphi Terrace. For the French class he worked his way, under the guidance of Leonce Stiévenard, through much of Stiévenard's own *Lectures françaises* as well as of *Half-Hours of French Translation* compiled by Alphonse Mariette, the Professor of French at King's. Sixty years later Hardy spoke warmly of Stiévenard and clearly remembered the old classroom and its desks, but added, 'I did not do much in class, I fear'—an impression which his heavily worked copies of the two textbooks do not entirely confirm.[68]

Since the King's College French classes were to constitute Hardy's only experience of university education, it is perhaps not surprising that there should survive so little evidence as to his early thinking on the great contemporary issues of science and religion, of social and political change. He liked to say that he was among the earliest readers of *On the Origin of Species*, first published in 1859, but it is possible to document for these London years only his reading of such thinkers as Fourier, Comte, Newman, and Mill. In 1863 he drew a series of elaborate 'Diagrams shewing Human Passion, Mind, & Character', based in all essentials upon the ideas of Fourier. In the summer of 1865 he was reading John Stuart Mill—whose impressive presence he had glimpsed in Covent Garden on 10 July 1865, the occasion of Mill's accepting nomination as a parliamentary candidate for Westminster—and Newman's *Apologia*, on which he made quite extensive notes.[69] Horace Moule, who had urged him to read Newman, also passed on his copy of the 1865 translation of Auguste Comte's *A General View of Positivism*. Some of the numerous marginal markings appear to be Moule's, but others are certainly Hardy's and show that he paid particular attention to the chapters on 'The Intellectual Character of Positivism' and 'The Influence of Positivism on Women'. His outlook at this period seems, in fact, to have been of a quite strenuously idealistic and altruistic cast: in his copy of M'Culloch a reference in purely economic terms to the human urge 'to improve our condition' has been expanded in the margin to include the words 'either socially, morally or intellectually, & that of others'.[70]

Life and Work speaks of Hardy's continuing to 'practise orthodoxy' in that summer of 1865, still preparing himself for Cambridge and the eventual prospect of 'combining poetry and the Church' by means of a curacy in a country village, and cites in evidence his having recently participated in a Communion service in Westminster Abbey. If, however, Hardy's own dating of the service, 'July 5. Sunday', is correct, it must have occurred not in 1865 but two years earlier, in 1863. A decline in his church attendance and private Scripture reading from the early summer of 1864 onwards can in fact be tracked with some precision from the decreasing frequency of dated annotations in his Bible and prayerbook.[71] Something can perhaps be attributed to Eliza Nicholls's departure from London, but Hardy's religious beliefs and practices were already becoming less central to his thought and life. It seems entirely possible, indeed, that he never did experience a 'loss of faith' of the classic Victorian kind—that his convictions disappeared through a process of gradual erosion rather than as the consequence of a single moment of crisis. His most fundamental beliefs, however sophisticated over time by exposure to Marcus Aurelius and many modern thinkers, retained in any case much of the instinctive, inherited fatalism of a Tess Durbeyfield or of a Jemima Hardy, with the result that he found little difficulty in accommodating himself to the prevailing pessimism of the post-Darwinian intellectual world into which he emerged in early manhood.

It seems necessary to ascribe to this period, when he was being pulled in so many directions by conflicting needs, ambitions, and fears, some of those moods of terrible depression to which Hardy occasionally referred in later years: 'As to despondency', he told a friend in 1887, 'I have known the very depths of it—you would be quite shocked if I were to tell you how many weeks & months in byegone years I have gone to bed wishing never to see daylight again.' There were undoubtedly circumstances conducive to depression. He had always found London unhealthy; he felt confined and wearied by the long hours of private reading that he added to his daily labours; and although Eliza's departure may in some respects have been a relief, it seems to have left him without anyone upon whose reassurance and good advice he could constantly rely. Horace Moule, always elusive, was in any case scarcely a reliable source of personal guidance. Thrown back constantly upon his own judgement and resources, Hardy could not always muster sufficient confidence in his own powers and prospects to be able to withstand the pressures that seemed to push him inexorably towards safe and conventional courses of action. As he would later have the narrator of *Two on a Tower* observe: 'Only those persons who are by nature affected with that ready esteem for others' positions which induces an undervaluing of their own, fully experience the deep smart of such convictions against self— the wish for annihilation that is engendered in the moment of despair, at feeling that at length we, our best and firmest friend, cease to believe in our cause.'[72]

There is no indication that Hardy was in any way skimping or actively resenting the tasks assigned by Blomfield. Describing many years later the little literary lectures he had given to the other people in the office—always exalting the merits and reputations of poets far above those of mere novelists such as Dickens—he explained that architecture never taxed the brain as writing did.[73] That he had opportunities at the office not only to talk about literature but do some writing of his own is strongly suggested by the existence of poems dated from 8 Adelphi Terrace as well as from 16 Westbourne Park Villas. Hardy's ascription of a specific date and place to the composition of a particular poem has always to be treated with some caution, but most of the surviving poems assigned dates in 1865 and 1866 do indeed appear to have been first written in those years, though perhaps in a form considerably cruder than that in which they were eventually published thirty and more years later.

Such early poems as 'Amabel' and 'Her Confession' are essentially self-conscious exercises in conventional modes, although this is not necessarily to say that they had no basis in Hardy's own experience: 'Amabel', for instance, almost certainly relates to his disastrous re-encounter with a visibly aged Julia Augusta Martin shortly after his first arrival in London:

> I marked her ruined hues,
> Her custom-straitened views,
> And asked, 'Can there indwell
>   My Amabel?'

Other early poems—at least in their revised form—already speak with a voice that is unmistakably Hardy's, among them the densely narrative 'Her Dilemma', the bitter 'Discouragement', with its allusion to the dependence of 'A whole life's circumstance on hap of birth', and those no less resentful verses which take 'Hap' as their title:

> —Crass Casualty obstructs the sun and rain,
> And dicing Time for gladness casts a moan. . . .
> These purblind Doomsters had as readily strown
> Blisses about my pilgrimage as pain.

Even in poems such as these[74] it is difficult to distinguish literary from personal impulse, although 'A Confession to a Friend in Trouble' was almost certainly prompted by Hardy's anxieties about Horace Moule. In quite another vein, and more indicative of the attitudes and talents that were to produce *The Poor Man and the Lady*, are such comic and satirical pieces as 'The Fire at Tranter Sweatley's' , 'The Ruined Maid', 'The Two Men', and 'Dream of the City Shopwoman'.[75] The early poems about women—poems of love, of loss, of 'revulsion'—range too widely in mood and argument to offer much insight into Hardy's emotions at this period, except in so far as they fit into an overall pattern of ambivalence and lack of confidence, of rapid alternations between romantic enthusiasm and sullen self-reproach.

The comments about women ascribed in *Life and Work* to the spring of 1865 show the same kind of restless uncertainty, while a melancholy reflection recorded on his twenty-fifth birthday—'Feel as if I had lived a long time, and done very little. Walked about by moonlight in the evening. Wondered what woman, if any, I should be thinking about in five years' time'—is strongly suggestive of a marked deterioration in his relationship with Eliza Bright Nicholls. A visit to Findon could well have been the occasion for Hardy's presence in Brighton on an April weekend in 1864, but he and Eliza saw very little of each other while she was at Godstone and he still in London, and at Archdeacon Hoare's death in January 1865 Eliza had not returned to Orsett Place but gone to live with her parents at Findon. Hardy's copy of Keble's *The Christian Year* carries the annotation '65' against the poem for the Twenty-Fourth Sunday after Trinity, which in that year fell on 26 November:

> For if one heart in perfect sympathy
> Beat with another, answering love for love,
> Weak mortals, all entranced, on earth would lie,
> Nor listen for those purer strains above.[76]

The phrasing, however, is conditional, leaving it uncertain whether Hardy felt he had found such 'perfect sympathy' or had lost it or was still in search of it. There is in fact no clear indication as to when he began to transfer his affections elsewhere: the 'H.A.' whom he accompanied to Denchworth over the Christmas holidays of 1865 was not, as has been suggested, a mysterious love interest, but Henrietta Adams, a family friend who seems to have been in service with Jemima Hardy at Stinsford House.[77]

That 26 November 1865 annotation in *The Christian Year* could well have marked a meeting with Eliza, but there is no firm evidence of his revisiting

Findon earlier than the Whitsuntide weekend of 1866, when he sketched the village church in his architectural notebook.[78] The evidence of the 'She, to Him' and related sonnets tends to indicate that the relationship with Eliza, whatever its formal character, was foundering upon Hardy's growing restlessness. The poem 'Her Reproach' suggests a rejection of love for the sake of literary ambition, but 'She, to Him. IV' speaks of a transfer of affections—and in bitter tones probably reflective of Eliza Nicholls's distress at discovering Hardy's preference for her younger, prettier, and less religious sister Mary Jane, whom he had met during his Findon visits:

> This love puts all humanity from me;
> I can but maledict her, pray her dead,
> For giving love and getting love of thee—
> Feeding a heart that else mine own had fed![79]

During the summer of 1866 Hardy was in a volatile mood, reconciling himself to disappointments, entertaining a multitude of fresh hopes and ideas but despairing of their realization. On Saturday, 2 June, his twenty-sixth birthday, he seems to have begun a short holiday, but a retrospective visit to Hatfield the following week only oppressed him further with an awareness of time's passage: 'Pied rabbits in the Park, descendants of those I knew. The once children are quite old inhabitants.' On 22 June, back in his room at Westbourne Park Villas, he made a sketch of the view from the window, recording on it not only the date but also the time, '½ past 8 in evening'.[80] The view itself is exclusively of nearby buildings, but the open books on the window-sill provide a more accurate register of the direction his thoughts were now taking.

It was this year, and probably this summer, that saw the final collapse of his long-cherished, essentially quietist, ambition of a country living. He asked Horace Moule to send him a copy of the Students' Guide to Cambridge and forced himself to face the discomforting realities of his situation. His financial resources were far from adequate, despite his later assertions that his father would have lent him whatever additional funds he needed; he was a good deal less well prepared for university entrance— especially in Greek—than he had been pretending to himself for the past several years; and the time required was depressing to contemplate.[81] As he explained to Mary: 'I find on adding up expenses and taking into consideration the time I should have to wait, that my notion is too far fetched to be worth entertaining any longer.' It seemed absurd, he added, 'to live on now with such a remote object in view'—a judgement promptly echoed in the four lines of 'A Young Man's Epigram on Existence', written that same year:

A senseless school, where we must give
Our lives that we may learn to live!
A dolt is he who memorizes
Lessons that leave no time for prizes.[82]

The decision, though painful, brought in its train a sense of relief and even of release. Hardy's instinctive impulse was towards the life of the mind and the world of books, and if it had first shaped itself as a call to enter the Church, that was largely because the Church had provided him with his earliest awareness of the beauty and excitement of language, whether alone or allied to music, his first overwhelming sense of the magic and sanctity of the word. His more matured ambitions had encompassed both the university education preparatory to an ecclesiastical career and the ultimate prospect of the career itself, optimistically imagined as a dutiful performance of his clerical functions enlivened by the writing, perhaps even the publishing, of poetry. Recognition of his financial limitations and of his doctrinal differences from the Church had now rendered such a programme both practically and morally untenable. At the same time abandonment of Cambridge and the Church threw into sharper relief the possibility, hitherto only dimly glimpsed, of pursuing a literary career for its own sake. But that would mean giving up architecture, and it was easier to forswear long-term hopes than present realities.

Architecture, as represented by the routine tasks he performed for Blomfield, left him bored and unfulfilled, and offered few prospects of advancement. During the late summer and autumn of 1866 it happened also to involve his being sent to Old St Pancras cemetery to check for irregularities during the macabre process of removing graves from the path of the new railway line.[83] When first in London Hardy was still being propelled by the social ambitions instilled in him by his mother, still trying to make a mark for himself by sheer hard work and (like Hooper Tolbort) by success in open competitions. By the mid–1860s it had come home to him that he might be doomed, as an architect, to a Tom Pinch-like future, always improving and finishing other men's projects. It was true that the profession had already brought him a status and security far beyond anything that could reasonably have been predicted for him in his Bockhampton childhood. And an architectural career, more broadly considered, was by no means unattractive in itself: shortly before his death he was to say that his life might have been happier if he had lived it, like Hicks, as an architect in a small country town.[84] But the independent position Hicks enjoyed, as an architect in private practice, seemed wholly beyond the reach of the young Hardy of the 1860s. Not only did he lack the friends, money, and education necessary to set up in practice for himself, he had none of the assertiveness, poise, and personal charm that might supplement professional skill and win him a partnership by ability alone. On the other hand the publication of 'How I Built Myself a House' was scarcely a guarantee of his capacity to earn even the barest of livings from writing alone, and it was therefore necessary to keep both possibilities still in view. An erased but not obliterated note at the back of the 'Studies, Specimens' notebook reads: 'If lit. fails, try Arch. with a view to such a place as Holderns',[85] but while Holderness was and is known for its fine Gothic churches, Hardy's use of the unconfident 'try' suggests his having imagined east Yorkshire as precisely the kind of remote area where little competition from other architects might be expected.

Hardy's last year with Blomfield, from the summer of 1866 onwards, was nevertheless a 'buoyant time' in his creative life.[86] None of his poems was published at that time—it is not certain that any were actually submitted—but his imagination and enthusiasm had been somehow liberated by the final rejection of all thoughts of a clerical career and the consequent polarization of his architectural and literary options. The period would be subsequently recalled as one of extraordinary excitement in which the intoxication of Swinburne's verse merged with a growing sense of his own capacities as a poet and more prudential aspirations and considerations were progressively swept aside: 'A sense of the truth of poetry, of its supreme place in literature, had awakened itself in me. At the risk of ruining all my worldly prospects I dabbled in it. . . . All was of the nature of being led by a mood, without foresight, or regard to whither it led.'[87]

Hardy had known much depression and darkness during these London years. He deplored many aspects of the city's teeming life, and would eventually be driven back to Dorset by the effects upon his own health of its fog, smoke, and dirt, its 'rayless grime'. 'From Her in the Country', one of the sonnets dated from Westbourne Park Villas in 1866, turns upon a contrast between countryside and 'crass clanging town' of which Hardy must have been sharply aware.[88] But he was always to speak with pride of his knowledge of London, and to the very end of his period with Blomfield he continued to take such advantage as his time and means allowed of those opportunities which London uniquely offered.

The opera was an enthusiasm he shared with Horace Moule—one of Moule's few surviving letters to him refers to Patti and Tietjens[89]—but Moule was teaching at Marlborough College from 1865 to the end of 1868 and most of Hardy's concert- and theatre-going was undertaken alone or with office colleagues. W. O. Milne, who arrived at Blomfield's as an assistant in 1866, later remembered Hardy's fondness for music and the theatre and said that the two of them 'used occasionally to indulge in a pit, at Drury Lane especially when a Shakespeare play was on. I remember especially going with him once to see old Phelps in "King John", & we used afterwards to go in for a modest fish supper at one or other of the old places there used to be round about the Strand'.[90] Hardy particularly admired Samuel Phelps's Falstaff, and he could have seen him in that role as early as March 1864. He certainly saw Phelps in *Othello* in 1865 and recalled fifty years later the 'knocking scene' in Phelps's *Macbeth*, adding that he was 'impressionable' at that time and read Shakespeare 'more closely from 23 to 26 than I have ever done since'.[91] There were fewer opportunities for him to have seen Helen Faucit, whom he also recalled from those years, but she appeared with Phelps in *Cymbeline* and *Macbeth* and played Rosalind in *As You Like It* in November 1866—although even if Hardy saw the latter performance he was more completely won over a few months later by the physically attractive Rosalind of Mrs Scott-Siddons, the addressee of the poem 'To an Impersonator of Rosalind'.[92]

Throughout his life Hardy was to be simultaneously beguiled by the excitement of the theatre and repelled by its artifice—as the unfinished poem 'A Victorian Rehearsal' may rather crudely suggest—even as he adapted to his own specific purposes some of the techniques and conventions of both the serious and the popular stage. At the end of 1866 and the beginning of 1867 he is said to have contemplated a scheme for obtaining stage experience as a preparation for the writing of blank-verse plays, and he did at least succeed—through the good offices of a blacksmith who worked both for Blomfield and for the theatres—in obtaining, for just one night, a walking-on part in Gilbert à Beckett's pantomime *Ali-Baba and the Forty Thieves; or, Harlequin and the Genii of the Arabian Nights!*, which opened at Covent Garden on 26 December 1866 and ran for several weeks thereafter. As a 'nondescript' Hardy took some now unimaginable role in the 'Oxford and Cambridge Boat Race', an element in the final Harlequinade that on the first night had drawn applause from the audience and praise from the critic of *The Times* as 'one of the best exhibitions of its kind that has been witnessed for some time'.[93] It must have been an interesting experience, however little relevant to the writing of verse dramas.

Hardy spent the Christmas holiday of 1866 at home at Bockhampton, giving Mary a copy of *The Golden Treasury* and Kate, now 10 years old, Wood's *Illustrated Natural History*.[94] The new year brought with it a series of personal crises, chief among them the end of his engagement or 'understanding' with Eliza Nicholls, its continuation having been rendered impossible by his attraction to her sister Jane. He went to Findon one last time, and had the final interview with Eliza which is recorded in 'Neutral Tones', the poem's overwhelming sense of personal immediacy deriving from the extraordinary imagist precision with which Hardy recreated its setting—quite possibly the pond surrounded by old lime kilns on the ridge overlooking Tolmare Farm, just west of Findon. The note is not now (as it had been in 'She, to Him. IV') one of ordinary sexual betrayal—only the moralizing last stanza alludes to deceit—but rather of a relationship drained of all vitality, colour, and meaning:

> Your eyes on me were as eyes that rove
> Over tedious riddles of years ago;
> And some words played between us to and fro
> On which lost the more by our love.[95]

Eliza herself was comfortless. She never married but became even more intensively religious, and almost fifty years later, after the death of Hardy's first wife, called upon him in the remote hope that her hour had at last arrived. Nor can Hardy have found much compensation in his new infatuation: though Jane Nicholls may have taken some satisfaction in a mischievous flirtation with her sister's fiancé, she evidently did not think of him as a serious marriage prospect and soon bestowed her affections elsewhere.[96]

The experience left Hardy emotionally exhausted, intensifying the physical weakness which forced him to leave Blomfield and London and return to Dorset in July 1867. Too much reading (several hours each evening after work), too little sleep and exercise, the general insalubrity of the city, and the proximity of Adelphi Terrace to the tidal sewer that was the Thames—all these factors contributed to a serious deterioration in his health, until he scarcely had strength in the mornings 'to hold the pencil and square'. Family tradition adds that he was not getting regular meals in London and that his doctor prescribed a daily bottle of milk stout.[97] There is no indication that he was seriously contemplating any early abandonment of his architectural career, and yet the poem 'Heiress and Architect', dated from Adelphi Terrace in 1867, is so hostile to both sides of the grim debate that Blomfield can scarcely have relished the dedication. Hardy's work at the office was suffering meanwhile, and a request from John Hicks, back in Dorchester, for an assistant to help with church-restoration work was welcomed on all sides as providing a happy opportunity for at least a temporary change of scene, atmosphere, and working rhythm.[98]

5

The Poor Man and the Lady

WHEN Hardy returned from London to Dorset in July of 1867 he had to face the scorn of friends and neighbours who interpreted his retreat as a sign that he had been defeated in the attempt to win his way in the larger world.[1] He of course knew that he had developed intellectually, accumulated experiences and memories, and learned how much his writing mattered to him, but it was obvious enough that he had neither made substantial progress in the architectural profession nor gained an alternative foothold in journalism. It was, even so, a situation with which he was for the time being perfectly content. The position at Blomfield's was being kept open for him, but a brief trip to London in October to collect his belongings served only to confirm him in the decision he had made.[2] After his disappointments and indispositions he was ideally receptive to the restorative influences of Dorset in general and of Bockhampton in particular, and soon recovered both health and spirits.

He was working for Hicks again, but on a basis of mutual convenience. There was certainly architectural work to be done: Hicks had several projects in hand or preparation, including new churches in the Dorset villages of Turnworth, West Lulworth, and Hinton Martell and restoration work on another church, as yet unvisited, in the remote Cornish hamlet of St Juliot.[3] But the arrangement allowed Hardy ample opportunity for catching up with friends and relatives, rediscovering his native countryside, and getting down to some serious writing. A Tuesday in September found him making a sketch of Dogbury, just north of Minterne and the tiny local school recently taken over by his sister Mary—seizing the first available opportunity to return to Dorset if not, as yet, to the immediate vicinity of her home.[4] And he began, naturally enough, to enjoy the available companionship of his cousin Tryphena Sparks, now a pupil-teacher in the Puddletown elementary school.[5]

Tryphena at the age of 16 was pretty, lively, and intelligent. She had a strong sense of fun, as surviving letters show,[6] and exhibited both energy and determination in her subsequent career as schoolteacher and head-mistress. The absence of her name from the pages of *Life and Work*—in which so few of Hardy's family are directly mentioned—has in the recent past been highlighted (rather than made good) by suggestions that she had a passionate love affair with Hardy during the summer of 1867, that an illegitimate son was born in 1868, but that there was no marriage because they were in fact not cousins but uncle and niece. For none of these specu-lations, however, is there any evidence capable of withstanding scholarly or even commonsensical scrutiny.[7] It has, of course, long been known—largely on the basis of Hardy's own reference to a 'cousin'—that Tryphena Sparks was the subject of 'Thoughts of Phena: At News of her Death', first published in *Wessex Poems* as 'Thoughts of Ph—a':

> Not a line of her writing have I,
>   Not a thread of her hair,
> No mark of her late time as dame in her dwelling, whereby
>   I may picture her there;
>   And in vain do I urge my unsight
>   To conceive my lost prize
> At her close, whom I knew when her dreams were upbrimming with light,
>   And with laughter her eyes.[8]

That Hardy chose to publish these lines in *Wessex Poems* as early as 1898 is evidence in itself that his memories of his dead cousin were not only affectionate but unclouded by guilt or self-reproach—except in so far as the difficulties of his own marriage had given him cause to regret past failures to claim Tryphena, Louisa Harding, Eliza Nicholls, Jane Nicholls, or any of the other young women whom his idealizing memory had transformed into 'lost prizes'.

For most of the period between the summer of 1867 and the summer of 1869 Hardy was at Bockhampton, Tryphena at Puddletown, and he is said to have undertaken to teach her French. Family tradition tells of some form of understanding or even engagement between them; the second Mrs Hardy spoke of Hardy's having given his first wife a ring originally intended for a local girl; Nathaniel Sparks junior, Tryphena's nephew, ascribed to his father the story that 'Thomas Hardy first wanted to marry Martha! then he tried to marry Tryphena, but grandmother [i.e. Maria Sparks] put a spoke in his wheel on the ground of its being against the laws of the church'.[9] Though some of this evidence seems questionable—Maria Sparks died on 2 November 1868, and the marriage of first cousins was not in fact forbidden by the Church of England's 'Table of Kindred and Affinity'—it is likely enough that Hardy and Tryphena walked out together and that some members of the family, as is the way of families, were not greatly pleased.

Hardy was attracted by Tryphena's good looks and youthful optimism, by the way 'her dreams were upbrimming with light, | And with laughter her eyes', but she was too closely related, and too much of the same class, to have seemed—at least to Jemima's jealous eyes—an especially good match for an up-and-coming young professional man. Tryphena, for her part, was perfectly content to be escorted and mildly courted by her grown-up if not especially handsome cousin, with his metropolitan experience and literary pretensions, but at the age of 16 and 17 she was less interested in marriage than in the prospect—exciting enough for a girl of her background—of a college education and eventual economic independence as a schoolteacher. The two were often alone together, and it cannot be proved that they never made love. Given, however, their cousinship, the strictness of their up-bringings, and the watchfulness of their elders, it is unlikely that there was ever any risk of Tryphena's becoming pregnant. There was certainly no child, probably no engagement, and perhaps not even a dramatic parting but simply a gradual relapse into the amicable cousinly terms of the past.

In January 1870 Tryphena went off to London for a two-year course at the Stockwell Normal College of the British and Foreign School Society. In January 1872, immediately following the completion of her training, she was appointed headmistress of a girls' elementary school in Plymouth. A year later, while still unmarried, she was joined there by her eldest sister Rebecca, left effectively homeless as a result of her mother's death and the rapid collapse of her own marriage to a Puddletown saddler called Frederick Paine.[10] By 1875 Tryphena was being courted by Charles Gale, owner of a public house in Topsham, near Exeter, and in December 1877 the two were married. Hardy could have met Tryphena in London in 1870–2 and kept in touch with her after she went to Plymouth, but there is no evidence that the attachment was prolonged even so far as Hardy's first meeting with Emma Lavinia Gifford in March 1870. Indeed, in the poem 'The Wind's Prophecy', the lover about to be supplanted by the Emma figure has 'ebon loops of hair', more suggestive (as her photograph shows) of Jane Nicholls than of Tryphena Sparks, whose hair is said to have been a dark chestnut.[11]

At the time of her mother's illness and death Tryphena apparently stayed with her (and Hardy's) aunt Mary Antell, wife of John Antell, the Puddletown shoemaker, of whom Hardy saw a good deal during the late

1860s. Mr Penny, the shoemaker of *Under the Greenwood Tree*, was suggested by one Robert Reason, whose former shop in Lower Bockhampton Hardy had known as a boy, but while Antell's shop in Puddletown also served as a natural centre for village life and gossip, he is painted by family tradition as a man of very different stamp, knowledgeable about the life of the countryside, active in local affairs, and—denied the formal education for which he longed—a prodigy of self-education, achieving some competence in Latin, Greek, and even Hebrew. He was clearly of a type not uncommon at that period: a man of the working class who found no adequate outlet for his native abilities in the social conditions then prevailing, and whose frustrated energies erupted in bitterness, alcoholism, and violence.[12] To what extent he was a radical in politics, after the tradition of village shoemakers, it is difficult to say. Not too much can be made of his supporting, along with his brother-in-law James Sparks, an address of 1870 that advocated complete liberty of religious teaching in state elementary schools.[13] But as he grew older and lost business to the new shoe factories, there was a corresponding increase in his bitterness and self-destructive drinking, until Hardy could describe the 'almost brutal—at least fierce' aspect of one of the Turberville profiles in Wool Manor House as being 'like J.A. when drunk at Noah's Ark', a Dorchester public house.[14] In the late 1860s John Antell was only in his forties and had not yet plumbed the depths of his illness and alcoholism, or of his hostility towards the order of the universe. But Hardy, sitting in the workroom at the back of the shop in High Street, Puddletown, listened to many tirades on the fundamental injustice of man's fate, and there can be little doubt that John Antell's deprived, divided, and tragically driven personality was central, many years later, to the entire conception of *Jude the Obscure*.[15] It may also have made a more immediate contribution to the pervasive class hostility of Hardy's first novel, *The Poor Man and the Lady*.

Hardy continued to write verse following his return to Dorset, recalling later that it was only after he had left London that he finally learned to avoid the poetic 'jewelled line', deeming it 'effeminate', and read for the first time Wordsworth's preface to the *Lyrical Ballads*, 'which influenced me much'.[16] 'The Widow Betrothed' was conceived, if not taken further, in 1867, both 'Retty's Phases' and 'Gallant's Song' were drafted in 1868, while the 'outline of a narrative poem on the Battle of the Nile' said to have been written in June of that same year was an indication of both a continuing poetic ambition and an early interest in Napoleonic material and themes.[17] But Hardy had already recognized that poetry offered very few career possibilities, and during the last five months of 1867, drawing freely upon poems and other materials already to hand, he devoted himself to writing the first draft of *The Poor Man and the Lady*, somewhat unpromisingly subtitled 'A Story with no Plot: Containing some original verses'.[18]

Although the novel was never published, and no portion of the manuscript survives, it is possible to reconstruct from various sources the broad outlines of its evidently episodic narrative.[19] Will Strong, a young architect of peasant background, falls in love with the daughter of the squire on whose estate his parents work. The two become betrothed, despite the lady's distress at the poor man's political radicalism, but are eventually separated by the opposition of the squire, who arranges for his daughter to marry the son of a local landowner. On the eve of that wedding the lovers meet and reaffirm their vows, but their own secret marriage is followed immediately by the lady's sudden death in her father's house. The first draft, completed early in 1868, left some of Hardy's narrative difficulties unresolved. In particular, he had not provided medical explanations for the temporary blindness his hero had to suffer at one point or for the death of his heroine without previous warning and while still in full possession of her faculties. In search of expert advice, Hardy wrote to his aunt Martha's clerical brother-in-law, George Brereton Sharpe, who had formerly practised as a physician and surgeon in Hertfordshire. Sharpe agreed that '*continued* study late at night of small print or Greek characters' might well produce loss of sight, especially if the light were poor, and he recommended 'Hemorrage of the lungs' as the best way of disposing of the heroine in the manner Hardy had specified. 'I hope', he went on, 'you are not building much on expectation of certain *profit* from your work. As that is the lot of but few. I do not say it may not be yours.'[20]

The process of writing out a fair copy of *The Poor Man and the Lady* evidently involved expansion as well as revision, and it not surprisingly occupied all of Hardy's spare time between late January and early June of 1868. On 25 July the completed manuscript, totalling 440 pages, was sent off to Alexander Macmillan on the recommendation of Horace Moule, whose connections with the Macmillan firm dated back to his Cambridge days. In his accompanying letter Hardy acknowledged that his main concern was to attack the manners of the upper classes, but insisted that the novelty and subtlety of the book lay in its use of the point of view of 'a comparative outsider' and in the indirection of the satire: whereas upper-class readers might throw down in disgust a book which was openly hostile, 'the very same feelings inserted edgewise so to say; half-concealed beneath ambiguous expressions, or at any rate written as if they were not the chief aims of the book (even though they may be)—become the most attractive remarks of all'.[21]

Alexander Macmillan can hardly have been much moved by so tenuous an argument, but he was sufficiently impressed by *The Poor Man* itself to write, on 10 August, a reply so long and detailed that it represents the clearest surviving indication of what the novel was like. Although he praised Hardy's presentation of 'country life among working men', Macmillan felt that the portraits of upper-class Londoners were too hostile to be convincing:

The utter heartlessness of *all* the conversation you give in drawingrooms and ballrooms about the working-classes, has *some* ground of truth I fear, and might justly be scourged as you aim at doing, but your chastisement would fall harmless from its very excess. Will's speech to the working men is full of wisdom (though by the way would he have told his own story in public, being as you describe him a man of substantially good taste?—) and you there yourself give grounds for condemning very much that is in other parts of the book. Indeed nothing could justify such a wholesale blackening of a class but large & intimate knowledge of it. Thackeray makes them not greatly better in many respects, but he gave many redeeming traits & characters, besides he did it all in a light chaffing way that gave no offence and I fear did little good, and he soothed them by describing the lower class which he knew nothing of & did not care to know, as equally bad when he touched them at all. He meant fair, you *'mean mischief.'*

The story as a whole struck Macmillan as extravagant and implausible— was it 'within the range of likelihood', he asked, 'that *any* gentleman would pursue his wife at midnight & *strike* her?'—but he praised the characterization and style and spoke of one particular scene in Rotten Row as 'full of real power & insight'. 'You see,' he added, 'I am writing to you as to a writer who seems to me of, at least potentially, considerable mark, of power & purpose. If this is your first book I think you ought to go on. May I ask if it is? and— you are not a lady so perhaps you will forgive the question—are you young?'[22]

Accompanying the letter was another remarkable document, the report of the unidentified reader—in fact John Morley, just beginning his illustrious career in letters and politics—to whom Macmillan had first sent the manuscript:

A very curious & original performance: the opening pictures of the Christmas Eve in the tranter's house are really of good quality, much of the writing is strong & fresh. But there crops up in parts a certain rawness of absurdity that is very displeasing, and makes it read like some clever lad's dream: the thing hangs too loosely together. There is real feeling in the writing, though now & then it is commonplace in form as all feeling turning on the insolence and folly of the rich in face of the poor is apt to sound: (e.g. p. 338.) If the man is young, there is stuff and promise in him; but he must study form & composition, in such writers as Balzac & Thackeray who would I think come as natural masters to him.

For queer cleverness & hard sarcasm—e.g p 280—a little before & after: p 333.—p 352—. For cynical description, half worthy of Balzac pp: 358–9.[23]

Morley's repeated references to Balzac and Thackeray emphasize the novel's strong element of social satire. That its assault on upper-class attitudes and privileges was also pressed home in specifically political terms is suggested by the inclusion of such an obvious set-piece as 'Will's speech to the working men'—which perhaps owed something to George Eliot's 'Address to working-men, by Felix Holt', first published in the January 1868 number of *Blackwood's*. *Life and Work* speaks of the 'tendency' of the work as 'socialistic, not to say revolutionary', but with how much justification it is now impossible to say. There is, however, a sense in which the centrality of the *Poor Man*'s specifically political concerns is affirmed by their re-emergence at the very end of Hardy's career as a novelist, when Jude's public narrative of his own life sounds a clear echo of Will's autobiographical speech to the working men and the dealings of the atheistical Sue in Christian images look back to the music-hall dancer in *The Poor Man* who became 'the kept mistress of an architect' and assisted him in his work by designing 'pulpits, altars, reredoses, texts, holy vessels, crucifixes, and other ecclesiastical furniture'.[24] That the novel was emotionally if not narratively autobiographical is in any case beyond doubt, and its inclusion of specifically personal elements can be inferred from the novella 'An Indiscretion in the Life of an Heiress' put together by Hardy in 1878 from still unused portions of the *Poor Man* manuscript. Will Strong the architect, for example, became in 'Indiscretion' Egbert Mayne the schoolmaster, but 'main' is nearly synonymous with 'strong', as both are with 'hardy', and Hardy's second wife once said that Mayne was unmistakably based upon the author himself.[25]

Although Alexander Macmillan, in the opening paragraph of his letter to Hardy of 10 August 1868, spoke of some 'fatal drawbacks' likely to impede the novel's success, he maintained a generally encouraging tone ('if this is your first book I think you ought to go on') and closed by saying that he was seeking the advice of someone more directly familiar with the upper classes as to possible modifications that might render the manuscript acceptable. Hardy apparently wrote an immediate reply, and then awaited further developments, occupying himself meanwhile with his occasional architectural duties, with his poetry—the surviving manuscript draft of 'Retty's Phases' is dated 22 June 1868—and with his other customary activities of walking, sketching, writing, and, of course, reading. *Life and Work* mentions not only volumes of Thackeray and Macaulay, Horace Walpole's Letters, some Shakespeare plays, and portions of the *Aeneid* but also Walt Whitman, indicating that Hardy may have been among the earliest readers of the first English selection of Whitman's poems, edited in 1868 by William Michael Rossetti.[26] In August his sister Mary was at home for her summer holidays, and a record has survived of an outing they made together:

Aug. 26. 1868. To Weymouth with Mary. Found it was Wth Races. To Lulworth by steamboat. A woman on the paddle-box steps: all laughter: then part illness & the remainder laughter. M. & I alighted at Lulth Cove: she did not, but went back Weyth with the steamer. Saw her for the last time standing on deck as the boat moved off. White feather in hat, brown dress, Dorset dialect, Classic features, short upper lip. A woman I wd have married offhand, with probably disastrous results.

The significance of this as yet another instance of Hardy's romantic readiness to fall immediately, if temporarily, in love with women glimpsed in the street, in railway carriages, on the tops of omnibuses, or indeed in any public place, is implicitly acknowledged in the suggestion for a poem that was added to the note at a later date: 'Combine her with the girl from Keinton Mandeville, &c, as "Women seen".'[27]

When, after a month, Hardy had heard nothing further from Macmillan, he sent off on 10 September 1868 a letter eloquent of his professional and emotional vulnerability at this period, his desperate and almost despairing need to find and secure some sort of foothold in the literary world after so many years of laborious aspiration:

Dear Sir,

I have become anxious to hear from you again. As the days go on, & you do not write, & my production begins to assume that small & unimportant shape everything one does assumes as the time & mood in which one did it recedes from the present I almost feel that I don't care what happens to the book, so long as something happens. The earlier fancy, that *Hamlet* without Hamlet would never do turns to a belief that it would be better than closing the house.

I wonder if your friend meant the building up of a story, & not English composition, when he said I must study composition. Since my letter, I have been hunting up matter for another tale, which would consist entirely of rural scenes & humble life; but I have not courage enough to go on with it till something comes of the first.

Faithfully yours
Thomas Hardy.

Would you mind suggesting the sort of story you think I could do best, or any literary work I should do well to go upon.[28]

The initial consequences of this appeal were the return of the manuscript and an attempt on Hardy's part to remove or dilute some of the passages to which objection had been made. Early that December—evidently following a resubmission of the manuscript in November—he went up to London for an interview with Macmillan, at which the latter still declined to publish the novel but did not declare it unpublishable. He gave Hardy a letter of introduction to another publisher, Frederick Chapman, and it was at the offices of Chapman & Hall that Hardy left the manuscript before returning to Bockhampton a few days later.[29]

Restless, deeply uncertain about the future, anxious at not having heard from Chapman & Hall, Hardy went once more to London on 17 January 1869. In his prayerbook he wrote the date and the words 'Leaving for London' against one of the Psalms for the day, number 86, which begins: 'Bow down thine ear, O Lord, and hear me: for I am poor, and in misery'.[30] He saw Macmillan again and met Morley—looking 'quite boyish'—for the first time. Both suggested kinds of magazine work that might produce a little income, but Hardy could always earn extra money from architecture. What he now needed was 'a clear call to him which course in life to take— the course he loved, and which was his natural instinct, that of letters, or the course all practical wisdom dictated—that of architecture'.[31]

That call would still not be unmistakably heard for a few years more. On 8 February 1869 Chapman & Hall reported that their reader, though confident that Hardy would do good work in the future, had advised against acceptance of the present manuscript, chiefly on the grounds 'that you have not got an interesting story to work upon and thus some of your episodic scenes are fatally injured'.[32] Because Hardy was still in London—'studying pictures' and 'reading desultorily'—he was able to call in person at Frederick Chapman's office, where he was distressed to find the aged Thomas Carlyle being attended to by a clerk rather than by the proprietor himself. When Chapman offered to publish *The Poor Man* if given £20 as a guarantee against loss, Hardy agreed, and went back to Dorset in a more cheerful frame of mind.[33] At the end of February, however, he received, instead of the expected proofs of his book, an invitation to meet in London with 'Mr Chapman & the gentleman who read your manuscript'. The latter, encountered when Hardy kept the appointment in early March, turned out to be George Meredith, 'a handsome man with hair and beard not at all grey, and wearing a frock coat buttoned at the waist and loose above'.[34] Meredith, his tone 'trenchant, turning kind', said that publication of *The Poor Man and the Lady* in its present form would doom it to a hostile reception, and recommended either a drastic reduction of its satirical element or its abandonment altogether in favour of an entirely new work with a stronger plot and an artistic rather than a social purpose: 'Don't nail your colours to the mast just yet.'[35]

Hardy returned with his manuscript to Bockhampton. Although impressed by Meredith's advice, he remained reluctant to abandon the results of so much labour and on 15 April sent the manuscript off again to the publishing house of Smith, Elder, expressing the hope that, whether they liked the story or not, they would 'make some remark' upon it. Their rejection came back within two weeks. In June Hardy tried yet another publisher, Tinsley Brothers, who kept the manuscript for three months before communicating—apparently through Horace Moule—an offer to print it in return for a guarantee that Hardy said was beyond his means but, remembering Chapman & Hall's terms, may simply have thought excessive.[36] In September 1869 the manuscript returned finally into its author's reluctant hands, subsequently to be plundered for material that could be used, virtually prefabricated, in the composition of other, more readily publishable works. It was a severe setback, and Hardy, who always believed *The Poor Man and the Lady* to have been the most original work, for its time, that he had ever written, never forgot the bitterness of its successive rejections and ultimate dismemberment. At some later date he wrote '1868–71' in one of his bibles alongside Job 12: 4, 'I am as one mocked of his neighbour', repeated that inscription alongside the same verse in his copy of the Vulgate Bible, and invoked the Vulgate's Latin text, 'Qui deridetur ab amico suo sicut ego', as the epigraph for his poem 'In the Seventies': 'In the seventies those who met me did not know | Of the vision | That immuned me from the chillings of misprision | And the damps that choked my goings to and fro.'[37]

When requesting the return of his manuscript from Tinsley Brothers on 14 September 1869, Hardy specified that it be sent 'by railway, addressed "to be left at Weymouth Station till calld for"'.[38] In the previous April he had been asked by G. R. Crickmay, a prosperous Weymouth architect, to assist with some unfinished church-restoration work that his firm had taken over following the death of John Hicks earlier that same month.[39] Because Hardy was already familiar with the designs in question, he was willing enough to work on them from time to time in Dorchester at the old South Street office. At the end of May, however, much remained to be done, and since his literary prospects continued to look bleak he accepted Crickmay's offer of three months' regular employment in Weymouth itself. His main task was to be the direction of the rebuilding (apart from its west tower) of the church at Turnworth, a village in central Dorset some two miles south of Okeford Fitzpaine. This was a substantial undertaking, and one in which Crickmay, not a specialist in Gothic, allowed Hardy an almost free hand. This was the first time in his architectural career he had been given so much responsibility, and in due course he would take a special pleasure in having the stone capitals of the new nave carved to his own designs.[40] Feeling 'much lightness of heart at having shelved further thought about himself for at least three months', Hardy moved into Weymouth lodgings and proceeded to enjoy the pleasures of a seaside summer.[41]

Weymouth—subsequently the 'Budmouth' of Hardy's fictional Wessex —was a moderately fashionable resort, made newly accessible by the railway but looking back nostalgically to the glamorous years at the beginning of the century when the presence of George III and his court had effectively turned the town into the country's summer capital during some of the worst crises of the Napoleonic period. It had a naval establishment and a prosperous harbour—busy with shipments of Portland stone to London and regular steamship services to Cherbourg and Jersey—and it was still a garrison town. The band of the 51st Regiment could be heard in the ornamental gardens on Thursday afternoons throughout the 1869 season, its programme often including the Strauss 'Morgenblätter' waltz invoked in Hardy's poem 'At a Seaside Town in 1869'; *Lady Audley's Secret* was playing at the Theatre Royal in June; Mr Henry Manley's English Opera Company presented Gounod's *Faust* at the Royal Hotel Assembly Rooms in July; and sedan chairs could still be rented at the rate of sixpence per 200 yards, although the rate doubled after midnight.[42]

On the evidence of 'At a Seaside Town in 1869' it would appear that Hardy took less advantage of these municipal amenities than of the simpler pleasures afforded by seeing 'The boats, the sands, the esplanade, | The laughing crowd' and receiving 'Light-hearted, loud | Greetings from some not ill-endowed'.[43] He was a keen swimmer, and swam in the mornings while the summer continued and rowed in the evenings, occasionally joined by Horace Moule's brother Charles, recently elected to a Cambridge fellowship, whom Hardy later recalled as diving with him 'from a boat on summer mornings into the green water of Weymouth Bay'.[44] Later in the year, and into the new year, he attended a dancing class, evidently undismayed to find that it functioned primarily as 'a gay gathering for dances and love-making by adepts of both sexes'.[45] He was friendly with the three Cozens sisters, Dorcas, Annie, and Eliza, formerly of Lewell Mill in the Frome valley, who were now running a Ladies' School on Portland, saw something of his two cousins, sons of James Hardy of Bockhampton, who were now warders at Portland prison, and showed the still intact manuscript of *The Poor Man and the Lady* to a friend named Harry Patten, then an insurance agent at Fortuneswell, later the manager of the local branch of the Dorsetshire Bank.[46] His own lodgings were at 3 Wooperton Street, part of a short terrace in a narrow street near the inner harbour, and it was there that he kept working away at his poetic exercises and writing down the outlines of possible stories and poems. A characteristically macabre note of 15 June 1869 reads: *'Good tragic ballad.* A woman who has been seduced finds that the man has married. She kills him. Finds then that his wife is her sister (whom he has also seduced?).'[47] It was at this address that he wrote, during the autumn of 1869, the greater part of *Desperate Remedies*.

Determined now to produce something that publishers would accept, and acting all too literally upon Meredith's advice, Hardy made of *Desperate Remedies* a heavily plotted and deliberately sensational novel involving murder, abduction, impersonation, illegitimacy, and a good deal of fairly explicit sexuality. While he seems to have taken Wilkie Collins's *Basil* as the model for several narrative aspects of the book,[48] he also had *The Woman in White* very much in mind as an example of how to combine the revelation of mysteries, especially criminal mysteries, with effects of melodramatic horror, especially as involving physically or psychologically threatened heroines. As Hardy himself acknowledged in a later preface, the methods adopted in writing the book were 'too exclusively those in which mystery, entanglement, surprise, and moral obliquity are depended on for exciting interest'.[49] Yet it was by no means a shoddy performance. The character of Cytherea is arresting in its anguished powerlessness, and Hardy's instinct as a novelist reveals itself in the way she is kept firmly at the centre of the sensation-novel plot. Were it not for the appeal of her helpless innocence the rather modest apparatus of tension and terror would collapse.

In his desire to finish *Desperate Remedies* as quickly and efficiently as possible Hardy initiated the melancholy process of 'cannibalizing' the manuscript of *The Poor Man and the Lady*. The second Mrs Hardy once spoke of the extent to which *Desperate Remedies* had been drawn from *The Poor Man*,[50] and comparisons with 'An Indiscretion in the Life of an Heiress', itself so heavily indebted to *The Poor Man*, yield further evidence to the same effect. The same calendar (for 1864) is used in the two works; the Knapwater House of *Desperate Remedies* closely resembles the Tollamore House of 'Indiscretion'; the power of landlords over their tenants provides a major plot element in both texts; and those social barriers between the lovers that in *Desperate Remedies* seem somewhat contrived are evidently survivals from divisions more trenchantly established in *The Poor Man*—to the extent that the scene in which Edward and Cytherea clasp hands across the stream may well have been an almost unmodified borrowing. That the new novel's dependence upon its abandoned predecessor went far beyond the transposition of particular episodes and settings is confirmed by the profusion of detailed similarities between the two texts, and there can be no doubt that Hardy had the manuscript of *The Poor Man and the Lady* open beside him as he wrote.[51]

Nor did he disdain the convenience of incorporating such characters and scenes as were most readily to hand. Edward Springrove, though said to be based on a new architectural assistant at Crickmay's, seems specifically autobiographical in his 'very humble origin', his love of books, his knowledge of Shakespeare 'to the very dregs of the foot-notes', and his claim to be 'a poet himself in a small way'. And when the terms of a lease had to be cited, Hardy invoked the precise wording of his own family's lease of the Bockhampton cottage.[52] Weymouth figures largely in the novel as a resort called Creston (changed to Budmouth in later editions). There is boating on the bay, and an excursion steamer takes its passengers to those parts of the Dorset coast that Hardy himself had recently visited with Mary—and that George Nicholls had once watched over as a coastguard. Nicholls's daughter Eliza claimed to have been the model for the heroine of Hardy's first novel—by which she presumably meant *Desperate Remedies*—and in the book's single most moving moment, Cytherea's passionate protest to her unresponsive brother against the personal cost extorted by acceptance of her 'duty to society', she would perhaps have recognized an echo of her own voice as earlier captured in the second of the 'She, to Him' sonnets:

> Perhaps, long hence, when I have passed away,
> Some other's feature, accent, thought like mine,
> Will carry you back to what I used to say,
> And bring some memory of your love's decline.
>
> Then you may pause awhile and think, 'Poor jade!'
> And yield a sigh to me—as ample due,
> Not as the tittle of a debt unpaid
> To one who could resign her all to you—
>
> And thus reflecting, you will never see
> That your thin thought, in two small words conveyed,
> Was no such fleeting phantom-thought to me,
> But the Whole Life wherein my part was played;
> And you amid its fitful masquerade
> A Thought—as I in your life seem to be![53]

The poem is one of several 'prosed' in *Desperate Remedies*, where the transposition, structured around the phrase 'Poor girl!' rather than 'Poor jade!', is both verbally and emotionally close, and it presumably figured as one of the 'original verses' incorporated into the first version of *The Poor Man and the Lady*. Many years later, and evidently with some justice, Hardy claimed that *The Poor Man* had shown 'a wonderful insight into female character', adding, 'I don't know how that came about!'[54] There is, however, an interesting moment early in the serial version of *The Well-Beloved* where the distinctly Hardyan central character is engaged in burning some letters preserved from his youth, many of whose sentiments, 'he was ashamed to think, he had availed himself of in some attempts at lyric verse, as having in them that living fire which no lucubration can reach'.[55] The allusion was surely to those letters of Eliza's that lent such authenticity to the 'She, to Him' sonnets and, whether directly or indirectly, to the characterization of the heroines of *The Poor Man* and *Desperate Remedies*.

Of the several Hardy poems specifically associated with Weymouth during those months of late 1869 when *Desperate Remedies* was being written, a few—such as 'Her Father'—probably reflect nothing more than the casual flirtations of the dancing class, but in 'Singing Lovers' it seems to be the poet himself who rows the boat on Weymouth Bay while the two lovers sit happily in the stern. The sour allusion to the beloved ('she of a bygone vow') who has 'gone away,— | Whither, I shunned to say!'[56] is taken up in other verses of the period. In 'At Waking', for instance, the speaker suddenly perceives that his beloved is 'but a sample | Of earth's poor average kind, | Lit up by no ample | Enrichments of mien or mind'. This unidealizing vision controls the poem and is only confirmed by the final stanza's overstrenuous and obviously doomed attempt to dispel it:

> Off: it is not true;
> For it cannot be
> That the prize I drew
> Is a blank to me![57]

Because of the occurrence of 'prize' both here and in 'Thoughts of Phena', the one poem which can confidently be associated with Tryphena Sparks, 'At Waking' has been read as in some sense documenting the breakdown of that relationship. But the word is common enough in Hardy's work and the poem probably refers—as both 'Her Initials', also of 1869, and the slightly later 'The Wind's Prophecy' appear to do—either to his involvement about this time with a young woman named Cassie Pole (of whom later) or to the final renunciation of a vainly cherished loyalty to Jane Nicholls. If the latter, it was a renunciation made necessary by her marriage on 29 July 1869 and made bitter by her choice of a man who, as a widower with an established position as an inspector of waterworks, must have been her senior by a good many years.[58]

6

St Juliot

Hardy stayed on in Weymouth into the early weeks of 1870, but the town's social life proved increasingly distracting and at the beginning of February he withdrew once again to 'the seclusion of his mother's house' at Bockhampton in order to work more quietly, and more cheaply, on his manuscript. His responsibility for the restoration of Turnworth Church would end with its reopening in April 1870, and work on West Lulworth and Hinton Martel, the other churches Crickmay had taken over at Hicks's death, was also well advanced.[1] There remained one Hicks restoration, outside Dorset, that Crickmay had not yet dealt with, and on 11 February he wrote to ask Hardy if he would go to Cornwall and 'take a plan and particulars' of the dilapidated church in the hamlet of St Juliot, a short way inland from Boscastle. Hardy delayed his journey until he was ready, on 5 March, to send off to Alexander Macmillan the nearly completed manuscript of *Desperate Remedies*. Two days later he set off from Bockhampton in the small hours of the morning ('starlight lit my lonesomeness') and reached St Juliot by train and horse-drawn 'conveyance' after nightfall that same evening.[2]

At the door of the rectory he was greeted not by the rector himself, the Reverend Caddell Holder, who was in bed with gout, nor by the rector's wife, who was nursing her husband, but by a 'young lady in brown' who proved to be Miss Emma Lavinia Gifford, the rector's sister-in-law. Miss Gifford herself, as she later recorded, felt 'a curious uneasy embarrassment at receiving anyone, especially so necessary a person as the Architect. I was immediately arrested by his familiar appearance, as if I had seen him in a dream—his slightly different accent, his soft voice; also I noticed a blue paper sticking out of his pocket.'[3]

Emma Gifford's nervousness sprang from much anticipatory speculation 'as to what the Architect would be like'. Tiny and remote, St Juliot offered little in the way of society beyond the occasional clergyman or school inspector, and any visitor was welcome—'even the dentist from Camelford who called regularly & actually dined with us at our mid-day dinner, Mr. Holder having much employment for him'.[4] Following the death of his first wife in 1867, when he was 64, Holder had married Helen Catherine Gifford, daughter of John Attersoll Gifford of Bodmin,[5] formerly a solicitor in Plymouth, and a niece of Canon Edwin Hamilton Gifford, later Archdeacon of London. When the second Mrs Holder, thirty-five years her husband's junior, moved into the rectory in the autumn of 1868 her younger sister Emma Lavinia came with her—chiefly, it would seem, as a way of escaping from the pressures of life at home with an embittered and often drunken father, but perhaps also because John Attersoll Gifford's forced or voluntary abandonment of his professional position had left the family in difficult economic circumstances. Emma herself acknowledged that her father was given to bouts of heavy drinking—'never a wedding, removal, or death occurred in the family but he broke out again'—and a friend wrote sympathetically in 1872 of the 'many sorrows & trials' Emma and her sister had had to endure.[6]

St Juliot rectory, a double-gabled stone house tucked into the hillside on the site of an old quarry, was of recent construction. It was—and remains— a solid and comfortable building with splendid outlooks, a large and densely planted garden, and an efficient greenhouse of ingenious design. The situation within the rectory, however, was less idyllic. The rector, though generally tolerant and humorous in his outlook upon life, was subject to frequent illnesses, and Helen Holder's loyalty to her husband did not alter the fact that marriage to a man so much older than herself had been largely a means of evading the alternative fate of a life as a governess or companion. Just such a fate presumably threatened Emma herself, and while the sisters were often at odds they were ready enough to cooperate in any campaign to find her a husband. Before Hardy's appearance upon the scene a local farmer—probably John Jose, son of the widowed Cordelia Jose of Pennycrocker—had been 'nearly secured' for Emma, but his active pretensions to her hand were no doubt exaggerated for Hardy's benefit, together with those of the dying William Henry Serjeant of St Clether, the apparent 'original' of 'The Face at the Casement', and the young church-warden at nearby Lesnewth who 'scanned | Her and me' and lit the candles with a 'vanquished air'.[7]

Hardy's social and economic pretensions to Emma Gifford's hand cannot have seemed impressive, and his manners—despite the London years—were far from polished. That much is clear from the retrospective glances incorporated into *A Pair of Blue Eyes*. There can be little doubt, even so, that Hardy's engagement and eventual marriage to Emma Gifford were in some measure the calculated outcome of a conspiracy—if only of discretion—that involved the entire rectory household. But if he was in some sense 'caught' by Emma, it is no less true that he was in the early stages of their courtship entirely captivated by her—that he did indeed return from Lyonnesse with 'magic' in his eyes. Although Emma was born on 24 November 1840, less than six months after Hardy himself, he probably believed her to be younger. At the 1871 Census her age was entered as only 25 when it was in fact 30, and it is hard to think that she would have told or authorized so gross an official lie if she had not been anxious to sustain a deception of every day.

At 29, when Hardy first met her, Emma wore her spectacular and as yet unfaded corn-coloured hair in long ringlets down either side of her face— giving her, as a friend wrote, 'the look of the old pictures in Hampton Court Palace'—and she made a striking figure as she rode dashingly about the countryside in her 'soft deep dark coloured brown habit, longer than to [her] heels'.[8] Writing after Emma's death to the then rector of St Juliot, Hardy suggested that some of the old parishioners might yet 'recall her golden curls & rosy colour as she rode about, for she was very attractive at that time'.[9] There was talk of literature during those first days together in March 1870, Emma having discovered that the blue paper protruding from Hardy's pocket was not a plan but a poem. There was also music in the evenings (as recalled in the poem 'A Duettist to her Pianoforte'), and Emma behaved with a bewitching mixture of freedom—as they ran down to the edge of Beeny Cliff together—and of coyness—as she 'provokingly' read while walking along at Hardy's side. And the closeness of the two bedrooms on the rectory's first-floor landing in which they must have slept—or lain awake—can only have exacerbated the social and emotional pressures to which they were equally if differently exposed.[10] Hardy, bookish, reticent, socially and sexually insecure, was overwhelmed by Emma's good looks, by her physical and nervous energy, and by the kind of fey charm—naive yet by no means unselfconscious—later attributed to Elfride Swancourt in *A Pair of Blue Eyes*.

Emma, on the other hand, was by no means overwhelmed by Hardy's personal attractions. He was neither tall nor strongly built, and struck her initially as a man with a 'yellowish' beard, 'a rather shabby great coat', and 'quite a business appearance', who looked 'much older than he was'. That Emma did not keep such reservations strictly to herself is evident from the somewhat later letter written by a friend in response to the news of her engagement. Sending congratulations and thanking Emma for her 'sweet photo: & letter full of romantic ideas', Margaret Hawes comments: 'They say that a poetical mind keeps one young, & I am sure you do not look more than 18.' Apropos of the 'fortunate' Mr Hardy, she reports a discussion with a friend in which they 'both agreed that we did not like handsome *men*! but decided that clever, well read ones were more to our taste—your ideas are the same I find'.[11] Emma painted an alarmingly similar portrait of Hardy in 'The Maid on the Shore', an unpublished novella-length story set in and around Tintagel that she perhaps began at St Juliot, although it was not finished until some time later. The heroine of the story, Rosabelle Carlenthen, jilted by her cousin, transfers her affections to his best friend Alfred During (i.e. Hardy): 'Mr. During's insignificant face and figure and quiet thoughtful manner had an interest for her more matured mind that no merely dashing handsome man like her cousin and some she had been in contact with lately at Truro could have for her again.'[12]

If Emma's isolated geographical and social situation obliged her to make the best of the unprepossessing lover who had happened to come her way, her appeal for Hardy, on the other hand, was much enhanced by the beauty and wildness of the setting in which they first met:

> I found her out there
> On a slope few see,
> That falls westwardly
> To the salt-edged air,
> Where the ocean breaks
> On the purple strand,
> And the hurricane shakes
> The solid land.[13]

St Juliot Church itself, though in ruinous condition, was old and pictur-esque, with a pair of ancient stone crosses in the churchyard. Even its name, pronounced 'Juliet', was charming, despite the local preference for 'jilt'. Beyond the churchyard lay the thickly wooded valley through which the little Valency river tumbled down to the sea at Boscastle, two miles to the west. Somewhat further along the coast stood the ancient ruins of Tintagel Castle, immemorially associated with Arthurian legend. To the north-west, not much more than a mile away, were Pentargan Bay and the stark cliffs running northwards from Beeny to Cambeak. As Emma, 'with bright hair flapping free', rode on her brown mare across this romantic landscape she created for Hardy a vision which seized his imagination at the time and generated after her death the resurgent power that produced the 'Poems of 1912–13':

> Time touches her not,
> But she still rides gaily
> In his rapt thought
> On that shagged and shaly
> Atlantic spot,
> And as when first eyed
> Draws rein and sings to the swing of the tide.[14]

The moments from that first visit to which Hardy returned most obsessively in later years were those of his initial encounter with Emma on Monday, 7 March—the date to which, after Emma's death, his desk calendar was always set—and the parting at dawn on Friday, 11 March, when Emma rose early to call the two servants and see Hardy safely on his way. It was on that occasion, so the poem 'At the Word "Farewell"' suggests, that the two first kissed and spoke specifically of love:

> Even then the scale might have been turned
>   Against love by a feather,
> —But crimson one cheek of hers burned
>   When we came in together.[15]

In the midst of this emotional turbulence Hardy found time to survey and measure St Juliot Church. Soon after his return to Dorset he moved back into lodgings in Weymouth in order to complete the detailed drawings. Hardy later claimed to have done no more than assist in the restoration of the church, and the decision to pull down the whole of the existing tower, north aisle, and north transept had indeed been made as early as 1866, long before he became involved. Deeply as he regretted in later years the ruthlessness of the St Juliot restoration, including the destruction of the original rood screen and handsomely carved pew-ends, Hardy could plead in extenuation that the original structure was so decrepit that it was something of an achievement to have preserved even the old south aisle, which forms the nave of the church as it now stands.[16]

On 4 April 1870, shortly after Hardy's return from St Juliot, Alexander Macmillan rejected *Desperate Remedies*, declaring that while it had 'very decided qualities, & very considerable power' it was 'of far too sensational an order for us to think of publishing'. In so saying he was again endorsing the judgement of John Morley, whose reader's report had objected to the extravagance of much of the novel, especially 'the disgusting and absurd outrage which is the key to its mystery', but recognized nonetheless that 'the book shows *power*—at present of a violent and undisciplined kind'. 'Don't touch this', he had concluded, 'but beg the author to discipline himself to

1. The Hardy cottage, Higher Bockhampton, photographed by Percy Butler

2. South Street, Dorchester; date uncertain. Almshouse clock to right, location of Hicks's office and Barnes's school immediately to left

3. Jemima Hardy, photographed by W. Pouncy
of Dorchester, 1876

4. Thomas Hardy senior, photographed in Bath,
1877

5. Kate Hardy as a young woman

6. Mary Hardy, photographed while teaching
at Denchworth

7. Horace Moule

8. Thomas Hardy, photographed by
W. Pouncy of Dorchester, *c*.1856

9. The Revd Henry Moule and his wife (both seated) and their family outside Fordington Vicarage,
c.1860. Henry J. Moule is third from left, Horace Moule stands in front of the window

10 (*above left*). Louisa Harding

11 (*above right*). Tryphena Sparks

12 (*left*). Believed to Hardy's aunt Martha Sharpe, the 'original' of Bathsheba Everdene

13. John Antell, shoemaker, of Puddletown, 1816-78

14. Thomas Hardy, *c.*1862: the photograph, taken
in London, that he gave to Eliza Nicholls

15. Eliza Bright Nicholls

16. Jane Nicholls

17. Hardy's sketch of Findon Church,
from his architectural notebook

18. Hardy's illustration for 'She, to Him. I' From *Wessex Poems* (1898)

19. Kimmeridge Bay, Dorset, showing Clavel Tower on the headland and the former coastguard cottages among the trees to its right

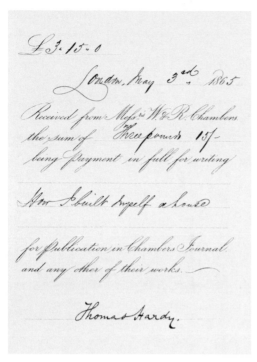

20. Hardy's receipt for his first literary earnings

21. Hardy's sketch of the view from his room at 16 Westbourne Park Villas

22. Turnworth Church, Dorset, restored by Hardy in 1869

keep away from such incidents as violation—and let us see his next story.'[17] Immediately the manuscript returned to his hands Hardy sent it off again, this time to William Tinsley, who had been willing, at a price, to publish *The Poor Man and the Lady*. On 3 May Tinsley forwarded his reader's report and pointed out that there seemed to be 'rather strong reasons why the book should not be published without some alteration'. Two days later, in response to a suggestion of Hardy's, he stated that he would be willing to undertake publication of a revised manuscript on payment of £75 by the author in advance of printing. To this Hardy, however reluctantly, agreed.[18]

Once the St Juliot drawings had been approved and signed by Crickmay on 2 May 1870, Hardy returned briefly to Bockhampton and then went on to London, where he took lodgings at 23 Montpelier Street, a three-storey terrace house about halfway between Montpelier Square and the Brompton Road.[19] Tryphena Sparks was at this time attending a teachers' training college at Stockwell, in south London, but there is no indication and—given his recent Cornish experience—little likelihood of Hardy's having sought her out. Uncertainty about his emotional and professional future seems, indeed, to have left him temporarily lacking in direction or purpose, so that he spent that early London summer 'desultorily and dreamily—mostly visiting museums and picture-galleries'. On the Wednesday following his arrival he was at the Royal Academy, admiring the work of Gérôme; on the Sunday he attended service at St Mary's, Bryanston Square.[20] *Life and Work* mentions that he was reading Auguste Comte, a significant influence on his later thinking, but disappointingly gives no hint of his reaction to the death of Charles Dickens on 9 June. This was only a week after his own thirtieth birthday, on 2 June, and the concatenation of the two events seems to have prompted the unoriginal but nonetheless personal reflection: 'In growing older, the nearer we approach an age which once seemed to us hoar antiquity, the less old does its inherent nature seem to be.'[21] He did a little work for Blomfield at this time, and was employed for a rather longer period by Raphael Brandon, co-author of *An Analysis of Gothick Architecture*, a work he had studied in earlier years. Hardy much admired Brandon's steadfast adherence to English Gothic despite the current fashion—exemplified by Blomfield—for French Gothic, and was sufficiently struck by his office at 17 Clement's Inn to use it as a model for Henry Knight's 'Bede's Inn' chambers in *A Pair of Blue Eyes*.[22]

Horace Moule, whose career was in some respects to be reflected in Knight's, was in London that same summer of 1870. In September 1865 Moule had obtained a post as assistant master at Marlborough College—

on the recommendation, perhaps, of his younger brother Charles, who had taught there from 1858 to 1864—and for more than three years he played an active part in school life, speaking at debates, arranging for William Barnes and other visitors to address the boys, and helping with the school magazine.[23] A few of his letters to the bursar survive, one of them making a fussy complaint about the noise made by the maidservants in the corridors that is reminiscent of his fastidious objection to *Adam Bede* on the grounds that its chronicling of the stages of Hetty Sorel's pregnancy 'read like the rough notes of a man-midwife's conversation with a bride'.[24] In December 1868, however, Moule had left the school, apparently without previous notice, the first issue of the school magazine in 1869 simply stating that 'All Marlburians were sorry to hear of the unexpected retirement of H. M. Moule, Esq., from the Common Room. His services to the *Marlburian* have been very valuable.' No reason is given for his sudden departure, and a letter to the bursar the following May deals so straightforwardly with the settlement of a small account and the examination successes of former students as to give no grounds for assuming that he had left under a visible cloud.[25] Given Moule's previous and subsequent history, however, it seems likely that there had been trouble of some kind—some accusation of homosexual involvement, perhaps, or another alcoholic breakdown. Wynne Albert Bankes speaks in his diary of encountering Moule unexpectedly during a visit to Marlborough some years after the Paris episode, and although Moule behaved 'as if nothing had happened', he may have felt that his past had caught up with him and made his position at the school no longer tenable.[26]

By the time Hardy saw him in London in 1870 Moule seems to have found employment as a coach for the Indian Civil Service competitive examinations in which Hooper Tolbort, now in India, had been so successful. Hardy told Moule of Miss Gifford and wrote the poem 'Ditty (E.L.G.)' about 'the spot | That no spot on earth excels, | —Where she dwells!'[27] A regular correspondence with Emma had been maintained since the previous March, and a note of Hardy's attributed to 25 April 1870 ('Nine-tenths of the letters in which people speak unreservedly of their inmost feelings are written after ten at night')[28] suggests that one or both had written in passionate terms. Throughout this courtship, indeed, repeated separations bridged by correspondence did much to sustain the high pitch of Hardy's feelings. The need and opportunity to recreate again and again the image of the absent beloved and to reassert his own romantic qualifications led Hardy to project for Emma, and to himself, hopes and promises that reality could not in the nature of things fulfil.

On 8 August 1870 he returned to St Juliot and found Emma waiting for him in 'summer blue', the 'original air-blue gown' of later recollection. Hardy stayed in Cornwall for three ecstatic weeks. He and Emma explored the local countryside together, visited Tintagel Castle—where they nearly got locked in for the night—and went down to Boscastle and across to Beeny Cliff on sketching expeditions.[29] On Sundays they attended the services held in the schoolroom at St Juliot, Emma, as usual, playing the harmonium for the hymn-singing, and on the first Sunday, 14 August, they went also to nearby Lesnewth Church for evening service, Hardy recalling years afterwards the sight of the churchwarden—evidently the 'vanquished' one of the poem—lighting the candles for the evening hymn.[30] As the poem 'Quid Hic Agis?' indicates, he also long remembered his exchange of smiles with Emma as they 'heard read out | During August drought' those words from 1 Kings 19: 12, part of the lesson for the Ninth Sunday after Trinity, which had already so established themselves in his imagination: 'and after the fire a still small voice'. It is precisely the lesson Knight is given to read in church in *A Pair of Blue Eyes*.[31]

The Franco-Prussian War had broken out in mid-July 1870, and on 18 August Hardy observed, from the end of the rectory garden, the profoundly undramatic scene that was to inspire many years later the poem 'In Time of "the Breaking of Nations"'. The notes were scribbled in pencil on the endpapers of Lackmann's *Specimens of German Prose. . . with a Literal and Interlineal Translation*, a textbook from which Hardy, perhaps disturbed by the course of European events, was endeavouring to teach himself some German: 'Sc. rusty harrow—behind that rooks—behind them, 2 men hoeing mangel, with bowed backs, behind that a heap of couch smoking, behind these horse & cart doing nothing in field—then the ground rising to plantn.'[32] Some time that same day Emma light-heartedly drew her lover as he sat on a fence with a makeshift flag in his hand. The following day he sketched her as, sleeves pulled up and ringlets falling forward, she groped in the water for a tumbler which had fallen between the rocks of a miniature waterfall by which they had picnicked in the Valency valley. A tiny sketch by Emma showing a tomblike slab beneath a tree carries Hardy's annotation 'Our Stone' and evidently records a spot in the extensive rectory garden where they were accustomed to sit in a shared privacy which neither Mrs Holder nor her husband would have been anxious to disturb.[33] Occasionally it rained—one day on Beeny they remained sketching until the shower passed—but one of Hardy's notebooks records a more sympathetic and (that summer) more typical day of serene sunshine and stillness: 'The smoke from a chimney droops over the roof like the feather in a girl's hat. Clouds, dazzling white, retain their shape by the half-hour, motionless, & so far below the blue that one can almost see round them.'[34]

The exceptional dryness of the summer of 1870 provides a basis for associating with it the poem entitled 'The Place on the Map': 'Weeks and weeks we had loved beneath that blazing blue, | Which had lost the art of raining, as her eyes to-day had too.' The place itself—'a jutting height' with 'a margin of blue sea'[35]—is immediately suggestive of Beeny Cliff, but because the subject of the poem appears to be the harsh interruption of an idyllic love relationship by the woman's discovery of her pregnancy, it has not generally been associated with Hardy and Emma's long-running courtship and childless marriage. However desperate Emma may have been to catch and hold the man who had so fortuitously intruded upon the isolation of St Juliot, it is not easy to imagine her permitting sexual intimacy, announcing a real, imagined, or pretended pregnancy ('the thing we found we had to face before the next year's prime'), waiting until Hardy had publicly committed himself to marriage, and then—like Arabella in *Jude the Obscure*—announcing that she had been mistaken. But the early episodes of *Jude* are intensely autobiographical, the poem's subtitle, 'A Poor Schoolmaster's Story', links it to the schoolmaster hero of 'Indiscretion', said by the second Mrs Hardy to be modelled on Hardy himself,[36] and there is no mistaking the sexual excitement that pervades Hardy's Cornish poems nor the deliberate provocativeness of Emma's appearance and behaviour as they emerge both from those poems and from the pages of *Life and Work*. Emma's mild adventurousness in intellectual matters—Hardy once said she had been an agnostic at the time of their first meeting[37]—may have been accompanied by some degree of sexual freedom, and Hardy's later sense of having been personally cheated in marriage was perhaps founded upon a perceived parallelism between Emma's sexual advances and retreats and her gradual shift from religious doubt to Evangelical orthodoxy. This is to speculate on the basis of inferences, but Hardy's second wife certainly believed, in light of what her husband had told her, that he was trapped into marriage by the scheming of Mrs Holder,[38] and even if nothing precisely corresponding to 'The Place on the Map' occurred, there is no doubt that Emma was eager to marry, that her sister and brother-in-law conspired to render circumstances propitious, and that when Hardy returned to Bockhampton at the end of August 1870 he considered himself betrothed.

That autumn Hardy revised the existing manuscript of *Desperate Remedies* and sent the reworked pages from Bockhampton to St Juliot for Emma

Gifford to write them out again in fair copy, turning his own attention meanwhile to the completion of the 'three or four remaining chapters'.[39] Curiously, the surviving letters from Tinsley nowhere indicate that the original manuscript was incomplete, and it seems in any case improbable that a novel of sensation and criminal detection would have been submitted without a fully worked out denouement. Unfortunately, the non-survival of the manuscript—said to have been destroyed by Hardy himself when he was moving lodgings and found it would not go into his portmanteau— rules out any determination of the successive stages of composition and revision. Hardy did at some point remove the 'violation of a young lady [Miss Aldclyffe] at an evening party' that Morley had castigated as 'a dis- gusting and absurd outrage', but he retained the scene 'between Miss Aldclyffe and her new maid in bed' that Morley had found 'highly extrava- gant'[40]—and that post-Freudian critics, overlooking Miss Aldclyffe's quasi- maternal relationship to Cytherea, have somewhat simplistically categorized as 'lesbian'.

Writing to Hardy in October 1870, Emma spoke of their love as 'This dream of my life—no, not dream, for what is actually going on around me seems a dream rather'. That Hardy had nevertheless been disappointingly undemonstrative in word or deed is signalled by an additional comment that incidentally calls her reputed agnosticism somewhat into question: 'I take him (the reserved man) as I do the Bible; find out what I can, compare one text with another, & believe the rest in a lump of simple faith.' That the writing in these fragments should be so lively and engaging makes all the more regrettable the fact that, together with one other fragment similarly transcribed by Hardy into one of his notebooks, they constitute all that now survives of a correspondence that Hardy, in his old age, ventured to com- pare to the love letters of Robert and Elizabeth Browning.[41]

On 28 October, immediately after receiving the letter just quoted, Hardy wrote Emma's initials in his Bible against verse 2 and part of verse 3 of the fourth chapter of the Song of Solomon: 'Thy teeth are like a flock of sheep that are even shorn, which came up from the washings; whereof everyone bear twins, and none is barren among them. Thy lips are like a thread of scarlet, and thy speech is comely.' But other notations hint at difficulties and forebodings, originating in self-doubt or in family disapproval of the courses, both professional and emotional, that he was now following. The date 22 September 1870, for example, appears in his Bible against Proverbs 14: 22: 'Do they not err that devise evil? but mercy and truth shall be to them that devise good.' That Jemima's influence was strongly reasserting itself, now that he was again in her daily presence, is clear from a profoundly revealing note of 30 October 1870: 'Mother's notion, & also mine: That a figure stands in our van with arm uplifted, to knock us back from any pleasant prospect we indulge in as probable.' A marking on 16 November of Revelation 10: 11—'And he said unto me, Thou must prophesy again before many peoples, and nations, and tongues, and kings'—may be indicative of a resolution to proceed with a literary career, but it is also apparent that Hardy, during these latter months of 1870, was again reading systematically through much of the New Testament. A more precise reflection of his current mood of mingled determination, apprehension, and resignation is provided by the passage from *Hamlet* that he marked on 15 December: 'Thou wouldst not think how ill all's here about my heart: but it is no matter!'[42]

In one of his Milton volumes, alongside the paragraph beginning at line 167 of book III of *Paradise Lost*, Hardy noted: 'The difficulty of reconciling Freewill and Omnipotce very apparent here.'[43] The comment is undated, and not in itself especially remarkable, but in the late 1860s and early 1870s Hardy was clearly attempting to reconcile a whole series of radically opposed philosophies and creeds, his very lack of a formal and traditional education perhaps making the transition from belief to unbelief a good deal smoother for him than for many of his more sophisticated contemporaries. Long experience of having to find his own intellectual way had made him a habitual eclectic, and he found relatively little difficulty in ranging ideas newly derived from Darwin and Huxley alongside the necessitarian views already instilled in him by the peasant fatalism of his upbringing and reinforced by exposure to the tragic patterns of the Greek drama. In his later years he spoke repeatedly of his essentially emotional and non-intellectual approach to life and of his lack of any systematic philosophy. In early adulthood his most persistent search was for philosophical formulations that answered to his own perceptions of the world, his instinctive sense of the way things were. What mattered emotionally, in terms of human experience, was the fact of individual unfreedom; identification of the inscrutable controlling 'Omnipotence' was, by comparison, a matter of intriguing but ultimately irresolvable intellectual debate.

Hardy resubmitted the manuscript of *Desperate Remedies* to Tinsley in early December 1870. Shortly before Christmas he received, at Bockhampton, a firm offer from Tinsley to publish the novel on the terms already agreed, his reader having reported that, as now revised, it would probably sell—though it might still be wise not to insist quite so specifically that Mrs Manston's '*substitute*' was Manston's '*mistress*'. In response to Hardy's request for some further clarification, Tinsley explained that he would not, as he had assumed, receive back his £75 once the proceeds equalled the expenditures, but that publisher and author would divide between them any *surplus* of income over expenditure.[44] Hardy seems to have felt that the terms had been changed for the worse, but while Tinsley may indeed have been guilty of allowing an inexperienced author to persist in a misapprehension, the final balance sheet, which includes only actual printing and advertising costs and not Tinsley's office expenses, shows plainly enough that the arrangement Hardy had in mind would not, on a printing of 500 copies, have been a worthwhile undertaking from a publisher's standpoint. Though still resentful of what he considered Tinsley's sharp practice, Hardy paid over the money in cash—and in person—in January 1871, when he was again in London. The proofs reached him back in Bockhampton shortly afterwards and *Desperate Remedies: A Novel* was published, anonymously, on 25 March 1871.[45]

The first review, in the *Athenaeum* of 1 April, was remarkably positive: it found the unknown author guilty of 'occasional coarseness' but concluded that if he would 'purge himself' of this fault 'we see no reason why he should not write novels only a little, if at all, inferior to the best of the present generation'. In the context of such encouragement it was galling for Hardy to have to report his occupation in the Census, taken on 2 April, as 'architect's clerk', precisely the way he had been categorized in the 1861 return. For all his efforts in the ten intervening years he had made very little upward progress, and the three volumes of *Desperate Remedies* stood alone as tangible evidence of what he was, against all odds, capable of achieving. The novel was praised again in the *Morning Post* of 13 April, but the 22 April number of the *Spectator* contained a review whose opening paragraphs sounded a very different note:

This is an absolutely anonymous story; no falling back on previous works which might give a clue to the authorship, and no assumption of a *nom de plume* which might, at some future time, disgrace the family name, and still more, the Christian name of a repentant and remorseful novelist,—and very right too. By all means let him bury the secret in the profoundest depths of his own heart, out of reach, if possible, of his own consciousness. The law is hardly just which prevents Tinsley Brothers from concealing their participation also.

The remainder of the review, as Hardy came eventually to recognize, spoke positively of his handling of the rustic characters and his power to arouse in his readers his own 'sensitiveness to scenic and atmospheric effects', but those early sentences seemed so savage and contemptuous that he scarcely had the emotional resilience to withstand their impact. Although he did not himself include in *Life and Work* the account of his reading the review while sitting on a stile at the edge of the Kingston Maurward ewe-leaze and wishing himself dead, it was certainly an anecdote he had often told—and one that showed at this early moment, when his identity was as yet unknown, the extreme vulnerability to hostile criticism that was to recur again and again throughout his life, even in the days of his greatest success and fame.[46]

By the end of March 1871, shortly after the publication of *Desperate Remedies*, Hardy had resumed work for Crickmay in Weymouth and returned to his former lodgings at 3 Wooperton Street. He was still spending most weekends at Bockhampton, however, and a glimpse of the toughly judgemental attitude to human complexity and frailty that prevailed in the Hardy household can be caught in his note of his mother's comment, one Sunday in May, about a man and a woman involved in an incident she had witnessed: 'They were mother & son I supposed, or perhaps man & wife, for they marry in such queer ways nowadays that there's no telling which. Anyhow, there was a partnership of some kind between them.'[47] A long entry in Hardy's architectural notebook taken from a published account of the new St Thomas's Hospital in London probably related to work Crickmay was doing on two Weymouth hospitals at this time, and Hardy seems also to have been involved in such other projects as the restoration of Stoke Wake Church, extensions to schools in and near Weymouth, and alterations to Slape House, Netherbury.[48] The advantages of architecture, as Hardy now engaged in it, were that it allowed ample opportunity for outdoor observation and exercise and could be taken up or left off almost at will. On a Monday morning in April, for instance, he was in Upwey, just north of Weymouth, probably on a professional errand for Crickmay—although he did have relatives in the village, his aunts Martha and Jane Groves and their families. He had, as always, a pocketbook with him and used it first to record a visual phenomenon ('A range of hills endways—the near end brilliant in a green dress softening away to blue at the other') and then to jot down the outline of a story about a village girl who became a school-mistress.[49]

But while this was a sufficiently pleasant mode of existence, it was neither the complete literary life he had long envisaged nor an adequate economic resource for a man contemplating marriage to a young lady with a horse of her own and—as the daughter of a solicitor, the sister-in-law of a rector, and the niece of a canon—considerable pretensions to gentility. He saw Emma Gifford again when he went down to Cornwall in late May, just before his thirty-first birthday, and it was while on his return journey at the beginning of June that he found, on Exeter station, copies of *Desperate Remedies* being remaindered for the derisory price of 2*s*. 6*d*. for the three volumes. As he would later have discovered, Mudie's had the book on offer for just sixpence more. Horace Moule, whom Hardy had apparently not told in advance of the publication of the novel, attempted to salvage the situation with a laudatory notice in the *Saturday Review*. But Moule's review did not appear until 30 September, and although Tinsley agreed to Hardy's suggestion that an extract from it be used in future advertisements, he feared that it had come too late to affect the sales: 'when once a book has been offered cheap it is almost impossible to get the Librarians to buy it in again.'[50]

During the late spring and early summer of 1871, spent partly at Weymouth, subsequently at Bockhampton, Hardy brought to completion a manuscript on which he had done a certain amount of work even before the writing of *Desperate Remedies*.[51] The new novel, *Under the Greenwood Tree*, seems to have derived partly from those early rustic episodes of *The Poor Man and the Lady* that John Morley had admired, and partly from the tale 'entirely of rural scenes & humble life' he had mentioned to Macmillan in September 1868.[52] Many years later, in response to an interviewer's questions as to how he had 'drifted into literature', Hardy replied:

I suppose the impressions which all unconsciously I had been gathering of rural life during my youth in Dorsetshire recurred to me, and the theme—in fiction—seemed to have absolute freshness. So in my leisure—which was considerable—I began to write 'Under the Greenwood Tree' but after writing it about half, laid it aside to write 'Desperate Remedies.' This novel was a success soon after its publication, but under my contract with the publisher I made nothing out of it. However, it encouraged me to go on with 'Under the Greenwood Tree.' I finished it as I began it, which I now regret, because much more could have been made of the story.[53]

In speaking of 'the story' Hardy can scarcely have been referring only to the minimal plot line of *Under the Greenwood Tree*. The unusual beauty of the novel depends very largely upon its lack of 'story', and its subtitle, 'A Rural Painting of the Dutch School', not only reflects a conscious attempt to apply to literature something of what Hardy had learned in his artistic studies but points to a 'composed' quality in the book as a whole. Carefully confined and framed in terms of both time and space, it emerges as a kind of woodland pastoral in which the momentary flurries of the foreground are at once diminished (in their individuality) and magnified (in their representativeness) by being set against the immemorial customs of the community and the inevitable onward movement of the seasons. The characters, though sufficiently established for the purposes of narrative, are players of time-honoured roles, as in a ballad or mumming play, inheritors for their brief moment of joys and sorrows common to all humankind. What Hardy later learned, as a novelist, to 'regret' was the extent to which his parents', and especially his mother's, longevity had effectively prevented him from returning, with a matured technique and a sharpened and more sombre vision, to that intimate childhood world of Higher Bockhampton from which the fictional Mellstock of *Under the Greenwood Tree* had drawn so much of its surface detail. Eight years after his mother's death, when he had long abandoned fiction, he spoke of the basic 'realities' of *Under the Greenwood Tree* as potential material for a book of quite a different kind: 'But circum-stances', he went on, 'would have rendered any aim at a deeper, more essential, more transcendent handling unadvisable at the date of writing.'[54] Like many another beginning novelist, Hardy in his earliest fiction—*The Poor Man and the Lady* and the episodes in other novels adapted from it—drew heavily upon immediately autobiographical resources. But he treated them humorously for the most part, as a kind of protective device, and if he sometimes seems condescending towards the characters of *Under the Greenwood Tree*, that is in part the consequence of self-conscious distancing, although it seems natural enough, given the date and circumstances of the novel's composition, that confusion about his own class situation should surface as tonal uncertainty in a novel dealing so closely with his own back-ground.

The activities, in and out of church, of what Hardy called the Mellstock Quire must have been largely reconstructed from what survived of the old music books and from recollections of the actual Stinsford choir gathered from his parents and neighbours including James Dart who had been one of the players in Hardy's grandfather's time. But the early descriptions of the cottage and of Grandfather James in his mason's clothes come directly from Hardy's own memory, while Mrs Dewy's way of grilling rashers of bacon before an open fire was one he associated with his mother to the very end of his life—on his deathbed he asked for a rasher to be cooked for him before his bedroom fire for just that reason.[55] The topography of the novel conforms almost exactly to that of Stinsford parish, and Hardy's insistence that the book contained no family portraits cannot expunge the impression that some of his parents' tricks of phrase and quirks of personality are directly reflected in the placidly antagonistic domestic dialogues between Tranter Dewy and his wife:

'You've no cause to complain, Reuben, of such a close-coming flock,' said Mrs. Dewy; 'for ours was a straggling lot enough, God knows!'

'I'd know it, I'd know it,' said the tranter. 'You be a well enough woman, Ann.'

Mrs. Dewy put her mouth in the form of a smile and put it back again without smiling.[56]

Offering *Under the Greenwood Tree* to Macmillan on 7 August 1871, Hardy explained that the reviewers' praise of the 'rustic characters & scenery' of *Desperate Remedies* had prompted him to attempt a story entirely of rural life in which the characters would be drawn 'humorously, without caricature'. But the basic debt to *The Poor Man and the Lady* is made explicit by his reference in the same letter to a scene of which the 'accessories' might be recognized 'as appearing originally in a tale submitted a long time ago (which never saw the light)'. Ten days later, in response to an enquiry from Macmillan, Hardy supplied copies of the reviews of *Desperate Remedies*, claiming that, though so contradictory, they seemed to indicate not only that he should not 'dabble in plot again at present' but that 'upon the whole a pastoral story would be the *safest* venture'—a conclusion which perhaps accorded less with the evidence than with the circumstance of his happening to have a pastoral story at hand.[57] Malcolm Macmillan, in mid-September, hinted at a probable acceptance but regretted that the firm was not yet ready to make a final decision. Meanwhile he forwarded a copy of John Morley's report, which was full of praise for the novel's 'extremely careful, natural and delicate' workmanship, but advised the author to study George Sand's rural tales, to restrain his tendencies towards excessive realism, and to 'shut his ears to the fooleries of critics, as his letter to you proves he does not do'. Although Hardy was never to be entirely capable of adopting that last piece of sensible advice, he did obtain, and read, translations of three George Sand novels two or three years later.[58]

No further word came from Macmillan over the next several weeks, and on 14 October 1871—when he was again in Cornwall—Hardy wrote to draw attention to the *Saturday Review* notice of *Desperate Remedies* and request news of *Under the Greenwood Tree*. A reply then came from Alexander Macmillan, on whom publishing decisions finally depended, to the effect that the tale, though charming, was rather slight and too short to be printed in the standard three-volume form. He concluded: 'We could not venture on it now, as our hands are full of Christmas books; besides it is hardly a good time for "Under the Greenwood Tree". But if you should not arrange otherwise before the spring I should like to have the opportunity of deciding as to whether we could do it for an early summer or spring book. I return the MS.'[59] If not ambiguous this was certainly temporizing, and

Hardy and Emma, still together at St Juliot, perhaps took the return of the manuscript as constituting a final rejection: in any case, they could have had little expectation of Hardy's making much money out of such pastoral idylls. Determined to take full stock of his situation, Hardy wrote at once to Tinsley to ask about the sales of *Desperate Remedies* and, more obliquely, to sound out his interest in either *Under the Greenwood Tree*, represented as 'a little rural story' not quite completed, or *A Pair of Blue Eyes*, not given any title but spoken of as a work, still in its early stages, 'the essence of which is plot, *without crime*—but on the plan of D.R.' Tinsley's reply avoided direct reference to either alternative, confining itself to a warning that Hardy was unlikely to retrieve the whole of his investment in *Desperate Remedies* and to a few words of general encouragement: 'I think the "Saturday Review" notice of *Desperate Remedies* should induce you to write another three volume novel. At all events if you do I quite think I shall be glad to take it of you without any risk to you.'[60]

This was as unsatisfactory in its own way as Alexander Macmillan's letter had been, and Hardy was deeply puzzled as to how best to proceed. The manuscript of *Under the Greenwood Tree* must evidently be put aside, with or without the hope of a more positive response from Macmillan in the spring. As for the projected three-volume novel, there was doubt as to the solidity of Tinsley's interest, and even about his own capacity to satisfy the requirements of the critics and the reading public. Attentive as he had been to the often bewildering advice of readers and reviewers, no publisher had yet proved willing to accept his work without a subsidy, and although architecture remained useful as a standby, it demanded time and energy that might otherwise be devoted to writing. He did not respond to Tinsley's gesture, perhaps because the new book was as yet hardly begun, perhaps because of a more fundamental lack of confidence and direction. Staying with middle-class Holders and Giffords in the comfort of the rectory had, if anything, exacerbated the sense of social underprivilege that had provided so much of the impetus for *The Poor Man and the Lady*. As recently as August 1871 he had underlined in his Bible the words 'having men's persons in admiration because of advantage', found in the sixteenth verse of the General Epistle of Jude and silently invoked, a quarter of a century later, in the title of *Jude the Obscure* itself.[61] His mood was not lightened by the necessity of leaving Cornwall once more at the very end of October—apparently the occasion, reflected in the poem 'Love the Monopolist', when on his departure from Launceston station he was hurt by Emma's turning 'round quite | To greet friends gaily' before the train had carried him out of sight.[62]

7

Far from the Madding Crowd

Emma Gifford's 'romantic ideas', so admired by her friend Margaret Hawes, were primarily responsible for her now encouraging Hardy to continue with his writing. She had literary aspirations of her own, an imagination of herself as the wife of a successful author, and doubtless a secret hope that the romance of a literary career would compensate in some degree for Hardy's lack of a commandingly handsome exterior. Hardy himself, though susceptible to such encouragement, was as a prospective husband obliged to consider economic realities, and he could see no immediate alternative to the architectural work in which he was—in one sense fortunately, in another ironically—becoming steadily more experienced, proficient, and sought after. The beginning of 1872 found him in lodgings at 1 West Parade, Weymouth, still working for Crickmay, but just before Easter he went once more to London, to the Bedford Street offices of T. Roger Smith, one of the judges for the Architectural Association prize Hardy had won in 1863 and now busy with submissions to a London School Board competition for the design of new schools.[1] Hardy took lodgings with the family of a tailor at 4 Celbridge Place, a terraced block (now part of Porchester Road) a hundred yards or so from 16 Westbourne Park Villas, and was still enough of a churchgoer to attend service at St George's, Notting Hill, on Good Friday, at St Paul's Cathedral on Easter Day, and at St George's, Hanover Square, the following Sunday, 7 April.[2]

Busy as he was with his work, uncertain as he felt about his literary prospects, Hardy remained keenly interested in the fate of *Desperate Remedies*. Writing to Tinsley on 3 January 1872 he asked for an accounting of the novel's publication and declared, with more bravado than truth, that he had 'rather delayed the completion' of his new manuscript 'till the result of the other is clear'. Tinsley had to be reminded again before eventually sending the account for the novel and then, in March, a cheque for £59 12s 7d.—representing a somewhat smaller loss on the original £75 than Hardy had come to anticipate.[3] Knowing that Hardy was again in London, Tinsley invited him to call at his Catherine Street office, 'as I should like to know what you are going to do about your next book. I hardly think you should be disheartened because the first book has not done well, but this you know best about.' The novelist George Moore once described Tinsley as a 'worthy man' who 'conducted his business as he dressed himself, sloppily; a dear kind soul, quite witless and quite *h*-less,' and Hardy, in *Life and Work*, imitates the broad cockney accent in which Tinsley, meeting him in the Strand one day, demanded that he deliver up his *Under the Greenwood Tree* manuscript.[4] That manuscript, however, he had rather resignedly left at Bockhampton, and it had to be retrieved from there before being sent on to Tinsley on 8 April. By 15 April Tinsley had read it; and on 22 April he made an offer of £30 for the copyright.[5]

That same day, probably as he sat in Tinsley's office, Hardy signed away the copyright for the sum Tinsley had offered.[6] It was an act which caused him much annoyance and inconvenience in later years, but at that moment, lacking both experience and self-confidence, he was glad to get anything at all for a story he had despaired of seeing in print—except, perhaps, at his own expense. The transaction, meagre as it was, gave a renewed sense of reality to his literary ambitions and provided some reassurance at a time when, in addition to all his other personal and professional doubts, he was sufficiently worried about his eyesight to get from Horace Moule the name and address of William Bowman, one of the leading ophthalmic surgeons of the day.[7] The problem proved not to be serious, however, and there is no indication of any further eye trouble at that time or for many years thereafter. By early May 1872 he was correcting the proofs of *Under the Greenwood Tree*, and in early June the two-volume first edition was published, to be greeted shortly afterwards by enthusiastic reviews in the *Athenaeum* and the *Pall Mall Gazette*. Horace Moule's anonymous notice in the *Saturday Review* was long and appreciative, but it was again much delayed and Hardy may have felt some annoyance—in view of Moule's background and of his own—at being taken to task, as he had been in the earlier reviews, for allowing the country characters 'to express themselves in the language of the author's manner of thought, rather than in their own'.[8]

By the time Moule's review made its belated appearance, on 28 September, Hardy's career had already taken some crucial turns. In early July—shortly after Hardy had seen a disturbing prefiguration of his own possible future in the figure of the 'city-clerk' who saw 'no escape to the very verge of his days | From the rut of Oxford Street into open ways'— Tinsley wrote to say that he needed a serial to begin in the September number of *Tinsleys' Magazine* and would be glad to consider 'any portion' of Hardy's new story that he might have ready.[9] Hardy protested that his manuscript needed 'a great deal of re-consideration'—which probably meant that it was as yet unwritten—but was unable to resist either the opportunity of serialization or the £200 which went with it. Somewhat wiser now than he had been in the previous April, he did not dispose of the copyright of *A Pair of Blue Eyes* but only of the right to the serialization and the three-volume first edition.[10] At the end of July, when the school competition entries were submitted, Hardy made his departure from Smith's office. By 7 August 1872 he had supplied copy for the first instalment of his serial—due to appear on 15 August!—and departed by ship for Cornwall.[11]

Before he left London Hardy directed that the proofs of that first instalment should be forwarded, not to St Juliot, but to Kirland House, near Bodmin, the home of Emma's parents and their dependent eldest son, Richard Ireland Gifford junior.[12] On the strength of Tinsley's commission and the promised £200 he evidently felt in a position to make a formal request for Emma's hand. But John Attersoll Gifford greeted his prospective son-in-law with open contempt. He is said to have referred to him in a later letter as a 'low-born churl who has presumed to marry into *my* family', and Hardy once glossed as 'Slander, or something of that sort' a reference he had made in one of his poems to the 'evil' done at Rou'tor Town, identifiable as Bodmin, not far from Rough Tor.[13] Not surprisingly, Hardy did not stay long at Kirland House. By late August he was addressing letters from St Juliot rectory again, and he seems also to have spent some time at St Benet's Abbey, near Lanivet, the home of Captain Charles Sergeant and his wife, friends of Emma's. To this period belongs the foreboding moment, recorded in the poem 'Near Lanivet, 1872', when, pausing to rest one evening on the St Austell to Bodmin road, Emma stretched out her arms against the arms of a signpost and 'Her white-clothed form at this dim-lit cease of day | Made her look as one crucified'.[14]

    In the opening instalment of *A Pair of Blue Eyes*, written hastily in London, Hardy had already drawn upon his Cornish adventure for the first meeting of Elfride Swancourt and the young architect Stephen Smith and for Elfride's distractingly provocative behaviour as Stephen tries to concentrate on drawing and measuring the church he has come to restore: 'Has the reader ever seen a winsome girl in a pulpit?' asks the narrator, with ponderous indirection. 'Perhaps not. The writer knows somebody who has, and who can never forget that sight.'[15] In the ensuing months the unfamiliar pressures of writing against a deadline forced Hardy to rely heavily on recent experiences—even the voyage he had just made from London to Plymouth—and on Emma's cooperation in suggesting usable incidents and details. Emma's references to 'the reserved man', for example, appear almost word for word in one of the later chapters, although it is not clear whether in such instances Hardy was drawing directly upon her letters (as he had upon Eliza's in *Desperate Remedies*) or simply using passages already transcribed into his notebooks. The second instalment of the serial (chapters 6 to 8), written in Cornwall in Emma's company, introduces the lost earring, the game of chess, and other courtship episodes derived from the shared experiences—or joint imaginative resources—of the two lovers. Elfride's astonishment at Stephen's inability to ride a horse similarly originated in Emma's making the same discovery about Hardy, registering it among other accumulating evidence of his being not quite a 'gentleman'. It is nevertheless in this same instalment of the serial that Stephen is assigned a family background even humbler than Hardy's own—a 'journeyman mason' for a father, a 'dairymaid' for a mother. In Hardy's later revisions, extorted by family loyalty rather than by the requirements of the novel itself, Stephen's father became 'a working master-mason' while his mother remained a 'dairy-woman' but one whose 'people had been well-to-do yeomen for centuries'.[16] The autobiographical element is obvious in both instances; not so readily determined is whether those initial downgradings represented a deliberate, even defiant, act of class identification on Hardy's part in the wake of his reception by Emma's father, or simply his adaptation of existing material from the pervasively class-conscious *Poor Man*. Remarkably enough, the relevant portion of the *Pair of Blue Eyes* manuscript is in Emma's hand, and her loyal copying out of the details of Stephen's parentage constituted a symbolic declaration not only that she intended to marry her architect but that she would have done so even if their class differential had been even greater than it actually was.

Despite the high incidence of details drawn from his courtship of Emma, Hardy later insisted that the plot of the novel had been 'thought of and written down' long before he had ever visited Cornwall, and since much of the novel evidently derives from *The Poor Man and the Lady*, it is likely enough that the story was first conceived of as having a Dorset setting and a different heroine but a similar plot line involving a romantic attraction across a well-defined class divide—such as that subsequently incorporated into 'An Indiscretion in the Life of an Heiress', Hardy's *Poor Man*-derived novella of 1878. The manuscript of *A Pair of Blue Eyes* is incomplete, but surviving sections show that Hardy was at one time working with the same 1864–7 calendar and time-scheme he had employed in *Desperate Remedies* and, earlier still, in *The Poor Man and the Lady*. Dorset and Somerset place names—Benvill Lane and Binegar Fair—survive into the early editions, and it was not until 1912 that Hardy altered the reference to 'poor deaf Grammar Cates' that had until then identified the world of Stephen Smith's parents with the worlds not only of *Under the Greenwood Tree*, in which Grammar Caytes (so spelled) also appears, but of Hardy's Bockhampton childhood, where the elderly Rachel Keates (recorded as 'deaf' in the 1851 Census) was an immediate neighbour.[17]

The sections focused on Stephen's parents and on his own situation midway between two distinct social groups living side by side and even interdependently—as the Hardys and the Martins had lived on the Kingston Maurward estate—must have depended heavily on the *Poor Man* manuscript. A chapter such as 'The pennie's the jewel that beautifies a'' points irresistibly towards the underlying continuity among the family relationships, the social patterns, and even the basic dramatic premisses of *Desperate Remedies*, *Under the Greenwood Tree*, *A Pair of Blue Eyes*, and 'Indiscretion', all derived in one way or another from *The Poor Man and the Lady*. Though Hardy adapted the materials from his quarry with considerable skill, it seems necessary to conclude that the parents of Dick Dewy, Edward Springrove, and Stephen Smith had common antecedents in the parents of Will Strong, and that they in turn were composite portraits for which Hardy's own parents served as the principal models. So that it is the vigour of Jemima Hardy that fuels the response of Stephen's mother when detected in a logical inconsistency, even as the irresponsiveness of Stephen and his father reflects the defensive tactics typically adopted by Hardy and Thomas Hardy senior:

'Yes, there, there! That's you; that's my own flesh and blood. I'll warrant that you'll pick holes in everything your mother says if you can, Stephen. You are just like your father for that; take anybody's part but mine. Whilst I am speaking and talking and trying and slaving away for your good, you are waiting to catch me out in that way. So you are in [Elfride's] class, but 'tis what *her* people would *call* marrying out of her class. Don't be so quarrelsome, Stephen.'

Stephen preserved a discreet silence, in which he was imitated by his father, and for several minutes nothing was heard but the ticking of the green-faced case-clock against the wall.[18]

The directness of Hardy's borrowing from his home background is no less remarkable—and no less naked—than his use of episodes from his courtship of Emma. It is as if he were deliberately juxtaposing within the world of the novel the sharply separated halves of his own life. He seems, meanwhile, to have made little effort to bring together those two halves, to introduce Emma to his family, and this passivity and lack of urgency is said to have aroused Emma to the extraordinary—and predictably disastrous—expedient of making an unheralded visit to Bockhampton to plead, or proclaim, her case for recognition and acceptance.[19] Jemima, like Stephen Smith's mother, felt threatened by Emma's social pretensions and what they might imply for her own future relations with her son, and nothing in Emma's appearance or manner was conducive, then or ever, to dispelling the Bockhampton prejudice against her as an interloper who had neither youth, wealth, domestic virtues, nor even a Dorset background, to recommend her. Emma, for her part, could well have been shocked to discover just how 'countrified' the Hardys really were, and if the visit was indeed made it was not repeated before her marriage, or even for some time afterwards.

In mid-August 1872, while Hardy was still in Cornwall, Roger Smith wrote to say that since one of the school designs had been successful in the competition he would be glad to take Hardy on again for a time. Smith's letter prompted debate at St Juliot about the entire direction of Hardy's future career—especially since the design in question seems to have been largely his own work—and evidently precipitated that crucial moment when he 'stood at the parting of the ways' and asked himself whether he would 'rather lose money & opportunities by writing than gain them by not writing'. After putting that same 'test' question to someone else years later, Hardy went on: 'If you can honestly say yes, I think you are called by nature to do it.'[20] His own answer in 1872 was strongly affirmative, but he could well have returned just such a reply at any point during the past several years and the crucial step might even now have been missed or delayed if Emma had not been physically present at the necessary moment and if the immediate decision had not been in itself of a simple undramatic kind—a mere matter of saying no to Smith's offer. Given the understanding which already existed between Emma and himself, the definitive resolution to abandon architecture as a profession could not in any case have been made without her support, grounded though that support necessarily was in simple loyalty and naive romanticism rather than in any serious engagement with economic realities.

The days passed pleasantly away meanwhile, with excursions to Beeny and Tintagel and as far away as Brent Tor, near Tavistock, and Hardy allowed himself to get behindhand with the second instalment of *A Pair of*

Blue Eyes.[21] On 8 September, the final Sunday of his visit, he went with Emma to afternoon service in the now renovated and reopened church at St Juliot, read both of the lessons, from Jeremiah 36 and Romans 9, and recorded the date in his Bible and prayerbook. It was for him a significant occasion, given that the reading of lessons was in effect a class prerogative and that his being invited to read constituted an acknowledgement of his status, not simply as Emma's betrothed, but as a professional man.[22]

Hardy was briefly at Celbridge Place in mid-September and back in Bockhampton by the end of the month, preoccupied with the ongoing serialization of *A Pair of Blue Eyes* and encouraged by a letter of early October in which Tinsley expressed his satisfaction with the novel's early progress: he was, he said, longing to read the third instalment, 'for I *shall lose my reputation* as a judge of good fiction if you don't do great things'.[23] That same autumn George Smith, the publisher of the *Cornhill Magazine*, and Leslie Stephen, its editor, came to much the same conclusion after Frederick Greenwood, editor of the *Pall Mall Gazette*, had drawn their attention to *Under the Greenwood Tree*. Having discovered the name of the author and obtained an address from Horace Moule, Stephen wrote to Hardy on 30 November 1872 to offer congratulations on *Under the Greenwood Tree* ('It is long since I have received more pleasure from a new writer') and seek, for the *Cornhill*, the offer of any new novel he might now have in progress: 'if any agreement could be made between us I have no doubt it would be satisfactory in a pecuniary point of view.'[24] Since the *Cornhill*, first edited by Thackeray, stood in the very forefront of contemporary magazines in respect of both circulation and prestige, this was for a hitherto unknown writer an altogether extraordinary moment. Delighted at so positive an approach from so distinguished a quarter, Hardy replied that he was busy with *A Pair of Blue Eyes*—of which Stephen apparently knew nothing—but would subsequently be turning his attention to a pastoral tale he had in mind, to be called *Far from the Madding Crowd*. Stephen wrote back to say that he regretted the delay but would be patient: 'I like your proposed title,' he added.[25]

Before hearing from Stephen, Hardy had arranged another visit to St Juliot. In a letter of 29 November Caddell Holder had thanked him for the plan he had drawn of a new railway line projected to pass through St Juliot and said that they were '*all*' hoping to see him on 18 December for as long as he cared to stay. 'The young lady,' he added, somewhat coyly, 'Miss Gifford, whom you mention is still here & sends her regards &c &c &c &c.' It is not clear that Hardy did in fact spend Christmas in Cornwall—*Life and*

Work speaks of his staying at Bockhampton until the end of the year—but he was certainly there on 7 January 1873 when he drew up, for Holder's signature, a final statement of the donations and expenses connected with the restoration of St Juliot Church.[26] He was back in Bockhampton by mid-January 1873, however, and remained there for the next several months. On 12 March he sent off the final chapters of *A Pair of Blue Eyes*—not scheduled to appear in *Tinsleys' Magazine* until the July number (published in mid-June) but submitted at this early date in accordance with the standard practice of bringing out the book version of a serialized novel before the serial itself had yielded up its final revelations.[27]

Hardy, with the future *Far from the Madding Crowd* already in mind, had in the meantime attended the annual hiring fair held in Dorchester on 14 February (Old Candlemas Day), watched some of the enacted dramas of hiring and rejection, and heard Joseph Arch, the leader of the National Agricultural Labourers' Union, denounce from a wagon on Fordington Green the inadequacy of agricultural wages and the iniquity of the hiring system itself. As Hardy later testified, he was much impressed by Arch's humour and moderation, his speaking as a 'social evolutionist' rather than as an 'anarchic irreconcilable', and by his capacity to seize and hold the attention of his audience. He was especially touched and amused by the moment when an old labourer in the crowd, moved by the speaker's advocacy, 'held up a coin between his finger and thumb exclaiming "Here's sixpence towards that, please God!" "Towards what?" said a bystander. "Faith, I don't know that I can spak the name o't, but I know 'tis a good thing," he replied.'[28]

Early in April 1873 Leslie Stephen renewed his enquiry about a story for the *Cornhill* and looked forward to an early meeting in London. But for the time being Hardy still lingered at Bockhampton, awaiting the book proofs of *A Pair of Blue Eyes* and enduring the scoldings of his mother, who feared that her son's new social standing would be endangered by his embarking upon so dubious a career as novel-writing. She seems also to have objected to the specificity of the local and family material he had invoked in *Under the Greenwood Tree* and to have been assured that the books would circulate only in London and not penetrate into Dorset itself—a promise impossible to keep in any technical sense but reflected over Hardy's entire lifetime in his determined and remarkably successful efforts to preserve the personal privacy of his parents and siblings.[29] One of the Moule brothers, Charles Walter Moule, also worried over Hardy's change of direction and wrote him a letter of heavy-handed advice upon the desirability of regular employment for men engaged in literary pursuits. Moule evidently felt, as his brother Horace had done, that Hardy lacked the talent or, perhaps, the energy—the physical and psychical resilience—to earn a living by writing alone. He may also have found it hard to reconcile the idea of Hardy as author with what he knew of his background, and the postscript to his letter certainly indicates an awareness of the difficult class transition in which Hardy seemed to be caught: 'I trust I address you rightly on the envelope. I conjectured that you wd prefer the absence of the "Esqre" at Upper Bockhampton.'[30]

Hardy's own sense of the complexity of that transition emerges poignantly from a letter written a year or so later to Geneviève Smith, the accomplished and much-travelled wife of the rector of West Stafford. He alludes admiringly to Mrs Smith's 'varied knowledge & experiences, which are of that precise kind that has a peculiar charm for all engaged in such pursuits as mine', and speaks of his 'having been denied by circumstances until very lately the society of educated womankind, which teaches men what cannot be acquired from books, and is indeed the only antidote to that bearishness which one gets into who lives much alone'.[31] Something of the strength of Emma's initial appeal can be detected in these remarks, but the curious edginess of the letter as a whole was presumably related to his having been waited upon at the Smiths' table the previous evening by James Pole, the butler at Stafford House, whom the Smiths were accustomed to 'borrow' on formal occasions. Pole—later described by one of the Smith daughters as 'an intensely old-fashioned butler'—had all the class-consciousness of his calling, and no doubt objected to being asked to wait upon the son of a local artisan. But the principal source of embarrassment at the Smiths' dinner table had been Pole's angry belief that Hardy had recently 'jilted' his daughter Catherine (Cassie) Pole, a lady's maid at Kingston Maurward House.[32]

The precise nature and duration of Hardy's involvement with the pretty if somewhat insipid Cassie Pole remain obscure, but he seems to have courted her some time in the late 1860s and early 1870s, when she was in her early twenties, and it is even possible that she (rather than Eliza or Jane Nicholls) was the local girl for whom he is said to have originally intended the ring he eventually gave to Emma Gifford. Since Cassie accompanied her mistress Emily Fellowes when she went to London to be married in April 1872, the likelihood is that Hardy broke rather abruptly with her after meeting Emma—or, at any rate, after engaging himself to marry Emma. Cassie died in London in 1894, the wife of a prosperous publican in Shepherd's Market, and it has been persuasively argued that her death was the occasion of Hardy's poem 'At Mayfair Lodgings'.[33] Hardy's relationship with her may earlier have contributed something to the original Dorset-based conception of *A Pair of Blue Eyes*, and the painful evening at West Stafford rectory was undoubtedly one of the sources—perhaps the principal source—for the basic situation of *The Hand of Ethelberta*, in which a butler finds himself waiting upon his own daughter.

The three-volume first edition of *A Pair of Blue Eyes* was published by Tinsley Brothers in late May of 1873. Hardy had made a number of revisions between the serial and the book, most substantially the removal from the opening pages of several paragraphs in which Elfride was introduced as reading a three-volume novel and sighing over the death of its hero.[34] Such concern for the detail of his text stemmed at least in part from Hardy's awareness that the new novel, unlike its anonymous predecessors, was being published over his own name. Fortunately the reviews were generally favourable. Even John Hutton, who had identified himself as author of the offensive *Spectator* review of *Desperate Remedies*, now proved to be a warm admirer of *A Pair of Blue Eyes*, praising it, again for the *Spectator*, as a 'really powerful' story. He did, however, criticize the novel's title as sentimental and its conclusion as unnecessarily bleak, and while Hardy's letters to Hutton have not survived, it is possible to infer from the other side of the correspondence the terms in which he defended himself: 'I agree with you', wrote Hutton on 3 July 1873, 'as to the *truth* of [Elfride's] death: but there are two views of a novel—as a work of art & as what that work is produced for—the advantage and recreation of the public.'[35] That Hardy remained unconvinced may be inferred from the extent to which refusals of comfortable and conventional resolutions became a characteristic feature of his later fiction.

Another early reader of the novel was Horace Moule, who again showed himself to be capable of mingling warm enthusiasm with cold condescension. 'You understand the *woman* infinitely better than the *lady*—' he wrote in May 1873, '& how gloriously you have idealized here & there, as far as I have got. Yr slips of taste, every now and then, I ought to say pointblank at once, are *Tinsleyan*.' Moule signed himself 'Yrs ever & most affectionately', and exclaimed: 'By & bye—only let me be indefinite as to time—I long to meet you again & must & will meet. Besides, I have properties of yours.'[36] That Hardy and Moule had not seen each other for some time seems clear enough, but few details are available of how and where Moule had been living during the four years and several months that had elapsed since his sudden departure from Marlborough. He seems for the most part to have inhabited the fringes of the London literary world, supporting himself somewhat tenuously by examination coaching, journalism, and miscellaneous writing: one undated letter to Hardy (who later ascribed it to 1870) speaks of his having two articles in that evening's London *Echo*, and signed articles by him certainly appeared in *Fraser's* magazine in 1869 and 1871 and in *Macmillan's* magazine in the latter half of 1871.[37] It is striking that Moule, so helpful to Hardy in the mid–1860s, seems not to have introduced him into any of the literary or journalistic circles he himself was presumably frequenting in the early 1870s. Since he seems never to have rated Hardy's abilities especially high, he perhaps feared that he would neither adorn nor feel at home in such circles. Or he may have begun to envy and even resent his protégé's incursions into areas upon which he had long assumed himself to have the superior claim. By July 1872 Moule's financial difficulties obliged him to accept a position under the Local Government Board—where his father was well known for his work in the cause of better sanitation—as an assistant Poor Law inspector for the East Anglian district.

Hardy met Moule again in early June of 1873 during the course of a short visit to London in company with his brother Henry, now 22 years old. He dined with Moule on 15 June, spent the next few days showing Henry around London, and then travelled to Cambridge on the 20th to stay with his friend at Queens', Moule having taken rooms at his old college in order to be closer to his work.[38] They again dined together and in the following 'never-to-be-forgotten' morning they climbed to the roof of King's College Chapel and saw Ely Cathedral 'gleaming in the distant sunlight'. They then parted—'cheerfully'—and it was only in retrospect that Hardy read a sinister significance into his memory of Moule's standing by the mantelpiece the previous evening and, as he talked, pointing unconsciously at a candle whose wax was 'shaping to a shroud'.[39]

That same day Hardy travelled back to London and on to Bath, where he took lodgings in Great Stanhope Street. Emma was staying with her friend Miss Anne d'Arville, an elderly lady whom Hardy had previously met at St Juliot—and remembered, absurdly enough, for her possession of a canary which fell fainting to the bottom of its cage at the sight of a cat or even a picture of one. Hardy and Emma spent the next ten days exploring Bath, Bristol, and the neighbouring countryside, even as far afield as Tintern Abbey.[40] The appearance of John Hutton's review of *A Pair of Blue Eyes* on 28 June—though somewhat offset by the supercilious tone of the notice in the *Athenaeum* on the same day—was for both of them an encouraging indication of the progress Hardy was making in the world of letters. There had also been some recent correspondence with the New York publisher Henry Holt, who was producing editions of *Under the Greenwood*

Tree and *A Pair of Blue Eyes*, and, above all, the active interest shown by Leslie Stephen in the projected *Far from the Madding Crowd*.[41]

When writing to Stephen late in 1872 Hardy had specified of *Far from the Madding Crowd* no more than that it would have as its chief characters 'a young woman-farmer, a shepherd, and a sergeant of cavalry', and he may already have had in mind the specific locations and people—including his aunt and uncle Sharpe—on whom he could most effectively draw in creating such characters and their appropriate settings.[42] But while he again depended heavily upon the 'real' for the substance and detail of his narrative, his essential conception of the book as 'pastoral' was profoundly literary, hallowed by long usage, and bolstered by the allusive possibilities inherent both in the formal traditions of pastoral verse and in the narrative patterns, both romantic and moralistic, of the traditional ballad. On the other hand, the broad melodramatic sweep of the novel, its density of incident, and its dependence upon well-established character types—the Diana Vernon-ish heroine,[43] the dashing soldier villain, the modest but stalwart hero, ultimately successful both in love and in upward social mobility—were more immediately reflective of the Victorian theatre and popular novel, and it can fairly be said of *Far from the Madding Crowd* that much of its success derived from the assimilation of nineteenth-century concerns and situations within a recognizably 'pastoral' framework. Gabriel Oak is thus a traditional shepherd, playing a flute with 'Arcadian sweetness', and at the same time an exceptionally competent Victorian workman, shown in action in a series of closely observed agricultural scenes—one of which, involving a technical description of the causes and effects of sheep rot, was left out of the text as published, perhaps because it threatened to strain the limits of the popularly assimilable.[44]

A Pair of Blue Eyes had been remarkable for its sensitive exploration of such complex figures as the nervously feminine Elfride, a forerunner of Sue Bridehead, and the coldly intellectual and sexually ambiguous Henry Knight. But it had suffered from its too hasty conception and composition, from Hardy's lack of familiarity with the writing of serials, and from his attempt to resolve some of his difficulties by carrying one stage further the cannibalization of the *Poor Man* manuscript. That *Far from the Madding Crowd* marked such an advance in Hardy's achievement and self-confidence was not just because he rose to the opportunity and challenge with which Leslie Stephen had presented him but also because he for the first time put the text of *The Poor Man and the Lady* firmly behind him. That did not of course prevent class and economic differences from playing an important role in the completed novel, as they continued to do in almost all of Hardy's future fiction, nor can it be denied that Gabriel Oak, whose surname constitutes yet another approximation to Hardy, was in the manuscript first called Strong.

It was to the writing of the new story that Hardy turned his full attention when, on 2 July 1873, he returned from Bath to Bockhampton—where 'nightingales sang in the garden' and he still had 'the stimulus and sympathy of his mother's companionship'. He also had the not inconsiderable benefit of his mother's care and cooking, and could indulge in the luxury of working at his manuscript until she called him to a meal—at which summons he would run up to the top of the little hill behind the cottage before coming in to the table. Hardy especially treasured the association between Bockhampton and *Far from the Madding Crowd*, and on the day in 1918 when the manuscript of the novel was sold at auction on behalf of the Red Cross, he went to sit in the garden there and look up 'at the window of the little room in which it was written'.[45] From the first he made no secret of having drawn upon his native countryside and its inhabitants for many of his scenes and characters. Writing to Stephen in 1874 of his desire to stay in Bockhampton until the novel was finished, he explained that his home was 'within a walk of the district in which the incidents are supposed to occur'— the village of Puddletown is clearly intended—and that he found it 'a great advantage to be actually among the people described at the time of describing them'.[46] It is not surprising, therefore, that Joseph Poorgrass's song in the novel, 'I sow'd the seeds of love', should have been associated in Hardy's mind with the Whitings, once the keepers of the beacon on Rainbarrow, or that on Sunday, 21 September 1873, he walked over the heath to Woodbury Hill Fair, on which his fictional Greenhill Fair would be based.[47]

In the evening of that same day—though the news did not reach Bockhampton until two or three days later—Horace Moule cut his own throat in his Cambridge rooms. The reasons for his suicide were explored shortly afterwards in a coroner's inquest, at which evidence was given by Charles Moule, who had been caring for his brother at the time of his death, and by Horace's doctor. The picture that emerged was of a recurrent cycle of depression, recourse to 'stimulants', and resultant incapacity for work— followed by fear of losing employment and hence a return of depression.[48] Moule had never succeeded in conquering the alcoholism his pupil Albert Bankes had observed thirteen years earlier. In the more recent past he had every so often slipped off into the East Anglian countryside and stayed drunk for days at a time, until his brother Frederick, then vicar of Yaxley, near Peterborough, would find him and bring him back to the vicarage to recover. On at least one such occasion he had spoken of suicide and secreted a razor beneath his pillow, and since Charles Moule also declared himself to be familiar with such threats there is perhaps little point in speculating about the immediate 'causes' of Horace's death.[49] He had been for many years an alcoholic, perhaps an opium addict, evidently a potential suicide. He had recently taken on a job which was both demanding and deeply depressing, involving as it did constant visits to workhouses, among whose unhappy occupants he must often have seen examples of what he himself dreaded to become. Coincidentally or otherwise, he had returned from a tour of workhouses just two days before his death.

The ultimate sources of Horace Moule's tragedy lie deeper than those purely academic difficulties specified in a final paragraph that was added—presumably at the instigation of the Moule family—to the report of the inquest published in a London newspaper: 'He was reputed one of the best classics of his time in the university, and was expected to head the classical tripos, but he failed in his mathematical examination, and according to the usage of the university at that period was prevented from competing in classics, and this preyed upon his mind ever afterwards.'[50] Hardy's second wife believed, on the basis of what her husband had told her, that Horace Moule had once had an affair with a 'Mixen Lane' girl of doubtful reputation who became pregnant and was shipped off to Australia, where her son—of whom Moule might or might not have been the father—was later hanged.[51] True or false—and it must be at least partly true despite the suspiciously Hardyan conclusion—this lurid tale belongs to the late 1850s or early 1860s when Moule was living at Fordington, the 1873 date assigned to the apparently relevant poem 'She at his Funeral' leaving open the possibility that the girl, in her 'gown of garish dye', could have been present as a distant observer of the burial of her 'sweetheart'. Another story connected to Moule's suicide is that of his engagement to a governess, 'highly cultivated' and of 'sterling character', whom his sister-in-law, Frederick Moule's wife, thought a 'splendid person', probably capable of solving Horace's difficulties. In another version of the same story the fiancée is referred to as a 'lady of title', but since in both versions the engagement is broken off because of Horace's drinking it seems possible that the woman in question was a governess employed by a titled family—perhaps that of Sir Henry Taylor, the dramatist, for whom Moule once worked as a tutor to one of his sons.[52]

Hardy was deeply shocked by the death of one who had, in many respects, been closer to him than anyone would ever be again. No other man, certainly, would ever subscribe a letter to him, 'Yrs ever and most

affectionately'. The easy assurance of Moule's letters to Hardy reflected the
position of patronage that he had automatically assumed on the basis of
superior age, education, and class, and that in 1873 (so *A Pair of Blue Eyes*
would suggest) Hardy was just beginning to resent. On Hardy's side there
was nevertheless both profound admiration and deep affection. In the copy
of *The Golden Treasury* given him by Moule he wrote the date 'Sept 25. 73'
alongside Shakespeare's sonnet 32, which concludes with the poet's exhortation to the friend who will survive him:

> O then vouchsafe me but this loving thought—
> 'Had my friend's muse grown with this growing age,
> A dearer birth than this his love had brought,
> To march in ranks of better equipage:
> But since he died, and poets better prove,
> Theirs for their style I'll read, his for his love.'

Almost fifty years later Hardy was to declare of Moule that he 'had early
showed every promise of becoming a distinguished English poet. But the
fates said otherwise.' In 1880, when revisiting Queens' College for the first
time, he wrote '(Cambridge H.M.M.)' against the famous stanza of *In
Memoriam*, 'Another name was on the door', and there are similar markings
associating Moule with the lines 'And on the depths of death there
swims | The reflex of a human face' and against the stanza:

> O last regret, Regret can die!
>   No—mixt with all this mystic frame
>   Her deep relations are the same,
> But with long use her tears are dry.[53]

Such a lifelong devotion to Moule's memory seems explicable only in terms
of a complete surrender to his personal charm. In most readings of Hardy's
enigmatic poem 'Standing by the Mantelpiece', subtitled 'H.M.M., 1873',
Moule is imagined as addressing a woman who has broken off their engagement, and the lines can indeed be so construed. But more meaning accrues
to the poem and especially to the candle-wax image when read in homosexual terms, with Moule speaking directly to Hardy himself. Their relationship must, in any case, have had an erotic component, however
unrealized on Hardy's part. For him it had no doubt seemed, and been, the
kind of verbally expressive male friendship characteristic of the period, a
more intense version of the one he had shared with Bastow. Hardy, lacking
Moule's educational advantages, probably knew little or nothing of homo-
sexuality, and if Moule, in June 1873, did make a direct approach it is little

wonder that Hardy bore himself angrily and (as the poem puts it) 'as if surprised', that he subsequently responded so powerfully to Moule's death, or that he should have withheld 'Standing by the Mantelpiece' from publication until his last and, as it proved, posthumous volume.[54]

Moule was buried in Fordington churchyard on 26 September 1873—a religious burial having been made narrowly possible by the inquest verdict of 'Temporary Insanity'—and it was perhaps fortunate for Hardy's state of mind that he was under pressure from Leslie Stephen to submit by the end of the month as much of *Far from the Madding Crowd* as he had so far completed. The required pages of manuscript—'between two and three monthly parts', according to *Life and Work*, 'some of it only in rough outline'—were sent off precisely on 30 September. A week later Stephen wrote to express his satisfaction with such of the novel as he had seen and to raise the possibility that serialization might begin as early as January or February.[55] As the autumn and the manuscript progressed, more letters passed between Hardy and Stephen, then between Hardy and Smith, Elder—publishers of the *Cornhill* and, when the time came, of *Far from the Madding Crowd* in volume form—and by the end of November it had been agreed that the first part of the twelve-part serial would appear in the January 1874 number of the *Cornhill* and that Hardy would receive a total payment of £400.[56]

Hardy had remained at Bockhampton during the autumn, assisting his father for the last time with the annual rituals of cider-pressing—'a work whose sweet smell and oozings in the crisp autumn air can never be forgotten by those who have had a hand in it'.[57] He was to recall such scenes, and his father's unassertive personality, when he came to write *The Woodlanders* and create the character of Giles Winterborne. As he continued to work on *Far from the Madding Crowd* he jotted down ideas for possible stories, notes on conversations with local people—among them James Dart, once a member of the old Stinsford choir—and observations of natural phenomena, including a storm in early November which no doubt provided some of the details of the storm in which Gabriel Oak saves Bathsheba's ricks.[58]

On 8 December Hardy went to London for a few days, staying once again at Celbridge Place, and took the opportunity of calling for the first time upon Leslie Stephen at his South Kensington home:

He welcomed me with one hand, holding back the barking 'Troy' with the other. The dog's name I, of course, had never heard till then, and I said, 'That is the name of my wicked soldier-hero.' He answered caustically: 'I don't think my Troy will feel hurt at the coincidence, if yours doesn't.' I rejoined, 'There is also another coincidence. Another Leslie Stephen lives near here, I find.' 'Yes,' he said, 'he's the spurious one.'[59]

The success of that first meeting led to an invitation to lunch for the following day, when Mrs Stephen and her sister Annie Thackeray wore shawls against the cold and the conversation around the fire was largely of their father, William Makepeace Thackeray. Hardy's own account of the occasion splendidly preserves Stephen's characteristic blend of geniality and moroseness:

We also talked of Carlyle, whom Stephen had visited on the previous day; and he illustrated by enactment the remarkable way in which the philosopher lit his pipe. Somehow we launched upon the subject of David and Saul. . . . I spoke to the effect that the Bible account would take a deal of beating, and that I wondered why the clergy did not argue the necessity of plenary inspiration from the marvellous artistic cunning with which so many Bible personages, like those of Saul and David, were developed, though in a comparatively unliterary age. Stephen, who had been silent, then said, 'Yes. But they never do the obvious thing'; presently adding in a dry grim tone, 'If you wish to get an idea of Saul and David you should study them as presented by Voltaire in his drama.' Those who know that work will appreciate Stephen's mood.[60]

Hardy again travelled westward for what was to prove his last Cornish Christmas, Emma's uneasy relationship with her sister finally resulting in her leaving St Juliot for temporary accommodation elsewhere—probably in her home-town of Plymouth, where, just before the end of the year, Hardy saw for the first time a copy of the *Cornhill* with his own novel given pride of place.[61] Although there is nothing to suggest that the time spent with Emma was other than happy, Hardy grew increasingly uncertain as to the wisdom of his forthcoming marriage even as it became more feasible in economic terms. He became—or remained—susceptible to the attractions of other women, and felt (in his own Dorset phrase) 'quite romantical' about two women in particular. One of these—though he later claimed the feeling to have been 'more on her side than his'—was Annie Thackeray, once described by Leslie Stephen as 'the most affectionate and sympathetic woman' he had ever known.[62] Although she was four years older than Hardy and distinctly plain—'as delightful as she is homely', according to one account, 'and that is saying a good deal'—he was impressed by her parentage and her own authorship of several popular novels, and charmed, as were so many others, by the gaiety, vivacity, and warmth which characterized her tumultuous flood of often inconsequential conversation. Edmund Gosse, who also first encountered her about this time, observed that 'when her mind and her tongue had parted company she was capable of uttering strange oracles'.[63]

Much as Hardy enjoyed Miss Thackeray's company, she did not represent a serious threat to his engagement with Emma. But his feelings for Helen Paterson, the illustrator of *Far from the Madding Crowd*, were of a different order, even though he can have seen her on only a very few occasions. When they first met in the spring of 1874 Miss Paterson was a handsome young woman of 25, a professional artist who had already been on the staff of the *Graphic* for three years. Immediately attracted, Hardy exploited their *Cornhill* association as a basis for further meetings and correspondence. He supplied sketches of Dorset farm implements that she might make her illustrations more authentic, and it was no doubt at his instigation that Miss Thackeray wrote from Southwell Gardens to invite Miss Paterson to dine with Hardy and herself at the Pall Mall Café: they could meet at the restaurant itself, she suggested, or 'if you liked better to come *here* & go with us we wd take gt care of you'.[64] Miss Paterson, however, married the 50-year-old William Allingham, the poet and editor, that same summer, and Hardy was left with his memories—imaginatively inflated as they doubtless were—of the 'charming young lady' whom he described to Gosse in 1906 as 'the best illustrator' he had ever had and the woman he should have married 'but for a stupid blunder of God Almighty'. In the poem, 'The Opportunity (For H.P.)', however, the error is seen as quintessentially human:

> Had we mused a little space
>   At that critical date in the Maytime,
> One life had been ours, one place,
>   Perhaps, till our long cold claytime.
>
> —This is a bitter thing
>   For thee, O man: what ails it?
> The tide of chance may bring
>   Its offer; but nought avails it![65]

By the time Hardy and Helen Paterson met, the writing of *Far from the Madding Crowd* was already well advanced. The serialization had begun sooner than anticipated, and earlier in 1874, fearing that he would run behind the printer, Hardy had remained at Bockhampton, working steadily at his manuscript, from the beginning of January until some time in April.[66] He was sustained in his labours by the good reception that the first instalment had generally received—the *Spectator* declaring that if the story was not by George Eliot, 'then there is a new light among novelists'—and by the warm encouragement and detailed advice he was receiving from Leslie Stephen. Because Stephen, as editor, was in the power position, his recommendations were virtual directives, and not always related to purely literary matters. Like many other magazine editors of the Victorian period, Stephen was fearful of giving offence to his subscribers on sexual and religious grounds, and in a letter to Hardy of 12 March 1874 he confessed to having deleted 'a line or two in the last batch of proofs from an excessive prudery of wh. I am ashamed; but one is forced to be absurdly particular'. Concerned at this point to ensure that the revelation of Troy's seduction of Fanny Robin would be 'treated in a gingerly fashion', he found himself further dismayed, a month later, by the explicitness with which the causes of Fanny Robin's death had been specified. Was there really any need, he wondered, for Bathsheba to find the dead baby in the coffin. Acknowledging that the omission 'certainly rather injures the story' and 'might be restored on republication', he nevertheless continued: 'But I am rather necessarily anxious to be on the safe side; and should somehow be glad to omit the baby.'[67] As Hardy recognized, Stephen's delicate expression of anxiety amounted in fact to a thinly disguised editorial fiat, and the baby was indeed omitted from the *Cornhill* serialization.

It has been strongly argued that Stephen's editorial interventions were so invasive, and so doctrinaire, that they amounted to a kind of censorship, suppressing important aspects of Hardy's early creativity and doing damage to the novel itself. But while it is impossible not to regret some of the changes and omissions made at Stephen's behest, it is no less necessary to recognize the editorial skill with which he guided Hardy, gently but firmly, to the removal of a substantial segment of the sheep-shearing supper and the tightening up of other episodes that had become unduly prolix and unfocused. And since there were sufficient aesthetic grounds for omitting the baby—whose 'cheeks and the plump backs of its little fists' had, in the manuscript, reminded Bathsheba of 'the soft convexity of mushrooms on a dewy morning'—it is possible in at least this one instance to read Stephen's invocation of the *Cornhill*'s super-sensitive readers as a considerate means of enforcing a critical judgement of his own.[68]

Hardy, eager to please, determined to perform well, had assured Stephen in advance of his readiness to compromise: 'The truth is that I am willing, and indeed anxious, to give up any points which may be desirable in a story when read as a whole, for the sake of others which shall please those who read it in numbers. Perhaps I may have higher aims some day, and be a great stickler for the proper artistic balance of the completed work, but for the present circumstances lead me to wish merely to be considered a good hand at a serial.'[69] Hardy had not of course lost sight of those exalted literary aspirations which had first led him to the writing of poetry, nor had there been any lack of 'proper artistic balance' in *Under the Greenwood Tree*, but if writing was to be his livelihood he needed to learn and to accept the limitations within which, as a novelist beginning his career in the 1870s, he must necessarily work. At a moment when he was still struggling for professional recognition, it was crucial to establish himself as someone who could be depended upon to meet his deadlines, sustain his story, and submit instalments containing the requisite number of words and the appropriate density of sufficiently dramatic episodes.

The success of *Far from the Madding Crowd* took him, in the event, well beyond that level of recognition, and impelled him forward into the front ranks of contemporary novelists. Once his identity as the book's author had been revealed in the *Spectator* of 7 February 1874, he soon began to receive approaches from editors and publishers. He cheerfully contracted with the *New York Times* for a short story, but a misunderstanding over the American book publication of *Far from the Madding Crowd* brought him abruptly face to face with some of the more tiresome aspects of professional authorship: 'The sharp practice in literature which apparently exists in America perfectly astonishes me,' he exclaimed in a letter to Smith, Elder.[70] In London again in late April and early May of 1874 Hardy saw Leslie Stephen and Annie Thackeray on a number of occasions, and was introduced to George Smith, founder of the *Cornhill* and head of the Smith, Elder publishing house, and to Mrs Procter, the widow of the poet who had written under the pseudonym of 'Barry Cornwall'. Hardy was now beginning to move in literary circles of some elevation—Mrs Procter, in particular, knew and had known an enormous range of writers, artists, and public figures—and while Emma Gifford was presumably unaware of Hardy's interest, actually or potentially romantic, in Annie Thackeray and Helen Paterson, she was not insensitive to his increasing absorption in his career: 'My work', she wrote in July, 'unlike your work of writing, does not occupy my true mind much.' She added: 'Your novel seems sometimes like a child all your own & none of me.'[71] What she may not have appreciated was the extent to which Hardy's greatly improved literary and hence economic prospects were eroding the last reasons—perhaps, the last excuses—for his further postponing marriage, and in late May he took the anticipatory step of obtaining a passport for himself and his wife, 'travelling on the Continent'.[72]

It was in the middle of July 1874 that the writing of *Far from the Madding Crowd* was finally completed and Hardy's last extended stay at his birthplace came to an end. Some notes of March 1874 about a mail-coach guard who used to live at Higher Bockhampton are almost all that now survive from these final months at home, but it is likely that many more were collected into Hardy's pocketbooks in a deliberate attempt to amass specifically local material for future literary use.[73] It was in the manuscript of *Far from the Madding Crowd*, after all, that he first gave the name Wessex to his fictional region, and there are other indications within the early pages of that manuscript of his becoming progressively aware of the implications and possibilities inherent in the systematic use of a regional or pastoral strategy: in the title of the fifth chapter, for example, the words 'a farming episode' are overwritten and replaced with 'A Pastoral Tragedy'.[74] Although Hardy was always to keep in close touch with his family, his exchange of Bockhampton and the world of his rural subject matter for London and the world of his publishers, critics, and essentially urban audience necessarily constituted a sharp break with both the place and the circumstances of his upbringing. Marriage to Emma Gifford would soon widen and deepen that break, and the composition of *Far from the Madding Crowd* can be seen in the longer view as marking the end of the earliest, happiest, and in certain respects most generously creative period of his career.

8

Marriage

HARDY now returned once more to 4 Celbridge Place. In late July 1874 he went to theatres, made some final revisions to the manuscript of *Far from the Madding Crowd*, and saw a good deal of Leslie Stephen. In August Miss Paterson became Mrs Allingham, and Hardy corrected proofs for the autumn numbers of the *Cornhill*: 'I will speak about the November proof tomorrow,' wrote Stephen on 25 August. 'I saw nothing to alter, unless that it seemed to me in one or two cases that your rustics—specially Oak—speak rather too good English towards the end.'[1] By late summer Emma had come to London to stay 'as country cousin' with her brother Walter, then living in Maida Vale, and at the beginning of September—in the midst of finishing off 'Destiny and a Blue Cloak', the story he had promised to the *New York Times*—Hardy arranged for the wedding to be conducted by Emma's uncle, Dr Edwin Hamilton Gifford, a distinguished theologian who later became Archdeacon of London.[2]

'The day we were married', Emma later recalled, 'was a perfect September day—the 17th, 1874—not brilliant sunshine, but wearing a soft, sunny luminousness; just as it should be.' This was to make the best of otherwise unpropitious circumstances. St Peter's, the parish church for nearby Chippenham Road, where Emma had been staying, was barely four years old, and its lack of history and associations or even of any particular architectural distinction made it a bleak setting for the marriage between a romantic not-so-young lady from St Juliot and the author of *Far from the Madding Crowd*. Family hostility on both sides evidently ruled out St Juliot and Stinsford as possible locations for the wedding and reduced the attendance at the St Peter's ceremony to Hardy and Emma, Dr Gifford, and the two obligatory witnesses, Walter Gifford, Emma's brother, and Sarah Williams, the daughter of Hardy's Celbridge Place landlady.[3] In the register Hardy's profession is firmly entered as 'Author', that of his father as 'Builder', but those differences of class which had already proved to be such a source of friction were writ sufficiently large in the announcement, prepared by Hardy himself, which appeared in the 'Marriages' column of the *Dorset County Chronicle* of 24 September:

HARDY–GIFFORD. Sept. 17, at St. Peter's Church, Paddington, by the Rev. E.H. Gifford, D.D., hon. canon of Worcester, uncle of the bride, Thomas Hardy, of Celbridge-place, Westbourne Park, London, son of Mr. T. Hardy, of Bock-hampton, to Emma Lavinia, younger daughter of J. A. Gifford, Esq., of Kirland, Cornwall.

The entry, interesting for Hardy's identification of himself as a Londoner, is eloquent in terms not only of the prominence given to the name and dignities of the bride's uncle but also of the acknowledged distinction between *Mr* T. Hardy and J. A. Gifford, *Esq.*

Hardy and Emma spent the first night of their marriage in Brighton, at D. Morton's Family and Commercial Hotel, not far from the railway terminus. The next day (Friday, 18 September 1874) Hardy wrote to his brother Henry to 'tell you all at home that the wedding took place yesterday, & that we are got as far as this on our way to Normandy & Paris'. He added a note of thanks for Henry's good wishes and explained that he was 'going to Paris for materials for my next story', almost as if the honeymoon were unimportant in itself and merely the by-product of a necessary piece of literary business. The Brighton weather that weekend was far from kind, but Emma was fascinated by the aquarium —'Seals eyes flash extraordinarily as they flownder over in the water,' she wrote in her little pocket diary—and the pier and the Pavilion offered concerts and other amusements. On the Sunday they went twice to church; on Monday Hardy went for a swim, though the sea was rough. It was still rough when they took the boat to France that evening. After an uncomfortable crossing to Dieppe they went straight on to Rouen and to the Hôtel d'Albion, Emma recording how they went up to their bedroom after the table d'hôte dinner—itself delightedly itemized, like so many subsequent meals—and found that the bed had been turned back and their 'night dresses' laid out upon it.[4]

Armed with an English-language guidebook, they spent the next day visiting the cathedral and some other local sights that were later to figure, if only briefly, in the pages of *The Hand of Ethelberta*.[5] To that extent the trip did furnish materials for the next story—even if subsequent abridgement of the plot complications made it unnecessary for the heroine to go on to Paris, the principal destination of the Hardys. They arrived there in the evening of Thursday, 24 September—'Place de la Concorde, first seen by moonlight,' Emma recorded—and put up at the Hôtel Saint-Pétersbourg, not far from the Opéra. Hardy had prepared for his first foreign expedition, and especially for this portion of it, by purchasing a copy of Murray's *Handbook for Visitors to Paris* and inserting newspaper cuttings about hotels and notes of the correct tips to offer waiters, cab men, and door-openers in theatres. He now took it with him each day as a guide to the Paris sights, enhancing its usefulness by indicating—as any architect might—the direction of north on the plans of the Louvre and adding an occasional comment of his own. A note of 26 September on the Escalier de Marbre at Versailles—that it was 'of every colour marble walls & all'—was later echoed in the description of Lord Mountclere's mansion in *The Hand of Ethelberta*. They visited the Petit Trianon that same day and stopped at a café on their walk back to the railway station to drink *vin ordinaire*, 'like French people', as Emma put it. Among the other sights duly visited were Notre-Dame, the Invalides, the Morgue—Emma finding the three bodies on view to be 'Not offensive but repulsive'—and the Père Lachaise cemetery, where they paid their romantic respects at the tomb of Héloïse and Abelard and picked an ivy leaf from the grave of Balzac.[6]

Emma was fascinated by France, jotting down details not only of food, dress, and furnishings—including those of their bedroom at the hotel—but also of customs ('Les Latrines Publique most strange for English eyes & notions') and what struck her as distinctive characteristics ('Very small babies in Paris'). At the same time she was deeply suspicious of priests—whose age, she decided, could be told by 'their harshness & closeness of expression, like concealed concentrated wickedness'—and uneasy at her own reception in a country where people showed their curiosity more directly and frankly than in England:

Wherever I go, whoever I pass—at whatever time day-time or by night—the people gaze at me as much or more than I at them & their beautiful city—so full of strange things, places—shops—people dress—ways—

Query—Am I a strange-looking person—or merely picturesque in this hat—

Women sometimes laugh a short laugh as they pass Men stare, some stand, some look back or turn, look over their shoulders—look curiously inquisitively—some tenderly [Emma first wrote 'admiringly'] without my being mistaken—they do in a French manner

As it is remarkable I note it—

Children gape too—[7]

Emma, with her long bright hair and her tendency to overdress, was indeed a striking figure, and some of the interested men no doubt believed her to be actively inviting their attention. Though her diary reveals a sensibility sharply perceptive of special qualities of light, colour, and movement, and capable at times of defining them in a vivid phrase, it is no less eloquent of the childlike inconsequentiality she was to display throughout her life. Entirely characteristic was the little farewell to Paris which she jotted down—from a sense of touristic obligation, perhaps, or a desire to compete or communicate with her literary, note-taking husband—while waiting at the Gare Saint-Lazare on 30 September for the train back to Rouen:

> Adieu to Paris.
> Charmante ville [Emma first wrote 'citie']
> Adieu to the Boulevards.
> To the gay shops—
> To the '*gens*' sitting in the streets
> To the vivants enfants
> To the white caps of the femmes
> To the river & its boats
> To the clear atmosphere & brilliant colouring[8]

Given Emma's slowness to respond physically to her husband, and the diminished enthusiasm for the marriage he had himself demonstrated over the past several months, it is difficult even to guess at the kind of personal and sexual relationship the couple managed to establish during their honeymoon. Her undiminished girlishness (she was now nearing 34) scarcely seems propitious, and his suffering from a cold can have done nothing to ease or eroticize the immediate situation. Hardy, who cannot have been insensitive to the Parisian response to Emma's appearance, left no comment whatever on the honeymoon, or none that has survived: the poem 'Honeymoon Time at an Inn' embraced his own marriage only in terms of the bleak future foretold for marriages in general and seems not to have had any specific relation to his own experience. Emma's diary, on the other hand, is lively and voluble but treats almost exclusively of impersonal matters. It is the more remarkable that she should have taken the trouble to return to her diary after being back in England for a few days in order to record an admiring description of a woman observed in the ladies' cabin of the boat bringing them back across the Channel:

The lady on the highest berth in the Steamboat on our return voyage—opposite me—had form flesh & complexion which *can* only belong to *high-fed* & comfortably living people—the combination grand—in her chemise she was a perfect Juno. Flesh, *tinted*—neither dark nor yellow white—perfect flesh & form—

On the next page, among a series of deleted titles for possible sketches or stories, appear the words '"Juno on Earth"—Venus embodied', and the two entries, though evidently written without sexual self-consciousness on

Emma's part, provide a curious and perhaps ominous epilogue to her honeymoon diary.[9]

The Hardys seem not to have made any advance arrangements for their return. Arrived back in London on 1 October, they were obliged to begin house-hunting immediately, first in Wimbledon, where they stayed in a hotel for a few days, then in Denmark Hill, and finally in Surbiton, perhaps drawn there by Hardy's friendship with a Dorset contemporary, Francis Tycho Honeywell, formerly of Weymouth, who had set up as a teacher of music at Surbiton Park Terrace.[10] On 6 October, so Emma's diary records, they arrived at St David's Villa on Hook Road, Surbiton, to find 'Annie & the Retriever playing in the garden with Papa'—an entry that has provoked much biographical speculation as to how John Attersoll Gifford, opposed to the marriage and absent from the wedding, could somehow have become reconciled. Thanks to some remarkable research by local historians, it is now known that 'Papa' was not Emma's father but William David Hughes, the occupant of St David's Villa, the father of 'Annie', and the owner of the retriever. The house itself, renamed Holmbury as early as 1876 and pulled down in 1960, was detached and substantial, described in a sale announcement of 1908 as containing 'Five Bed Rooms, Drawing and Dining Rooms, Library, Kitchen, Scullery, Two W.C.'s and Offices'. Some importance attaches to these details in that the Hardys appear to have shared the house with the Hugheses and not to have occupied a separate apartment.[11]

Hook Road was in the 1870s still an area chiefly of farms and fields, with a small group of houses—including St David's Villa itself—clustered just south of the junction with Ditton Road. But the location, however pleasant in itself, was a little too far from Surbiton station to be ideally convenient, and sharing space with another family seems likely to have had its drawbacks and embarrassments for the newly married couple and especially for Emma, who can have had little if any previous experience of housekeeping without servants. The Hardys clearly knew from early on that they would not be able to stay long in their first home, and almost the only glimpse of the five and a half months spent at St David's Villa is provided by the poem 'A Light Snow-Fall after Frost', whose location Hardy specifically identified as 'Near Surbiton'. The companion poem in *Human Shows*, the better-known 'Snow in the Suburbs', probably belongs to the same period, and it was certainly during the course of a walk from Surbiton that Hardy, on 19 December 1874, saw snow on some graves at Long Ditton and entered in his notebook the characteristic comment: 'A superfluous piece of cynicism in Nature.'[12]

Yet it was while he was living at Surbiton that Hardy first became famous. *Far from the Madding Crowd* was published in two volumes on 23 November 1874, but *Life and Work* insists that the Hardys remained for some time quite unaware of the stir which the novel was making, except that when they went up to Waterloo on the train they often noticed 'ladies carrying about copies of it with Mudie's label on the covers'. Its reception was, in fact, exceptionally warm. In early September, while the serial parts were still appearing, Mrs Procter had written: 'I can hardly make you understand, how one wants the next Number. It is perhaps a taste of Purgatory to wait for the drop of cold water.'[13] To a letter on the subject of Bathsheba, sent by the novelist Katharine S. Macquoid, Hardy wrote a reply that sounded, gently as yet, a note that was to become very familiar over the years: 'I myself, I must confess, have no great liking for the perfect woman of fiction, but this may be for purely artistic reasons.' The imperfections of his own heroines, he explained, were not intended as a 'satire on the sex' but were 'merely portrayed in the regular course of an art which depends rather on picturesqueness than perfect symmetry for its effects'.[14]

The reviews then began to appear—in numbers much greater than for any of Hardy's previous works. His combination of descriptive specificity with melodramatic extravagance worried some of the critics, and there were complaints about abrupt variations in style and treatment and the implausibility of some of the wise and witty speeches assigned to agricultural labourers. But most of the reviews were positive in tone, and all of them took the book seriously—even Henry James's supercilious notice of the American edition ('the only things we believe in are the sheep and the dogs'). To Richard H. Hutton, in the *Spectator*, *Far from the Madding Crowd* possessed a special appeal as a regional novel grounded in intimate knowledge of a functioning community: 'The details of the farming and the sheep-keeping, of the labouring, the feasting, and the mourning, are painted with all the vividness of a powerful imagination, painting from the stores of a sharply-outlined memory. . . . A book like this is, in relation to many of the scenes it describes, the nearest equivalent to actual experience which a great many of us are ever likely to boast of.' Hutton was one of those made uneasy by the philosophical rustics, but John Hutton wrote to assure Hardy that his brother knew too little of the rural poor 'to estimate correctly their intimacy with & constant use of Bible language nor their quaint good humoured cynicism'.[15]

Hardy also received personal recognition from some of his professional colleagues. At some point late in 1874 he was the special guest at one of the regular Fleet Street dinners of the Whitefriars Club, a convivial association of writers and, more especially, journalists. The recollections, a quarter of a century later, of one of the other diners present, suggest that Hardy made little attempt—perhaps did not know how to attempt—to ingratiate himself: 'The rule of no toasts was departed from, and Hardy's health was drunk. He made no pretence to be an after-dinner speaker, and his response was brief and formal.'[16] In mid-January of 1875 George Smith offered Hardy the opportunity—of which he actively availed himself—to make corrections for incorporation in a second printing of *Far from the Madding Crowd*, the first having been almost completely sold out.[17] Hardy could now think of Smith, Elder as 'his' publishers, and he entertained the hope that his previous work might reappear over his own name and with the more distinguished imprint. But Smith advised against any immediate reprinting of *Desperate Remedies*, and when Tinsley was asked to name a price for the copyright of *Under the Greenwood Tree* he demanded £300, precisely ten times what he had paid for it. Although remaining sheets of the novel and the stereotype plates were to be thrown in, the amount was still, as George Smith exclaimed, 'preposterous'. Hardy declined to pay, and never, in fact, regained control of this one copyright, which subsequently passed from Tinsley to Chatto & Windus.[18]

Leslie Stephen had meanwhile shown his own satisfaction with Hardy's work by asking if he could have a new story ready for the *Cornhill* for the following April. Hardy begged for a little more time, and a July starting date was eventually agreed upon. *Life and Work* curiously asserts that serialization began in May 1875 rather than in July, and is again incorrect in giving March rather than mid-January 1875 as the date of Hardy's first submitting to Stephen and to Smith, Elder 'a rough draft of the first part' of *The Hand of Ethelberta*, as his new novel was to be called.[19] On 27 February, impatient for a decision and emboldened by success, he wrote to Smith, Elder, hinted that he was receiving invitations from elsewhere, and continued:

I also find a difficulty in applying myself thoroughly to the story whilst there is any uncertainty about it, which leads me to believe that it would be greatly to the advantage of the tale if we could get this cause of distraction cleared out of the way; and I have thought that you would probably take the same view of the matter on my mentioning it to you.

Although George Smith was nervous at having seen so little of the story, he had sufficient faith in it, or in Hardy, to offer, on 9 March, £700 for English serial and volume publication. In the same month Hardy settled with the *New York Times* for serialization in the United States at the rate of £50 for each *Cornhill* instalment, to be supplied in the form of advance proof sheets—thus assuring himself of another £550, making a total for the novel of £1,250 even before arrangements had been made for such things as American and continental editions.[20]

As if in confirmation of his new standing in the literary world Hardy received that same year invitations to write for a number of other journals, including the *Glasgow News*, *Good Words*, and the *Examiner*. A striking compliment also came from Coventry Patmore, whom he had not then met:

I trust that you will not think I am taking too great a liberty in writing to tell you with what extraordinary pleasure and admiration I have read your novels, especially that called 'A Pair of Blue Eyes.' I regretted at almost every page that such almost [un]equalled beauty and power should not have assured themselves the immortality which would have been impressed upon them by the form of verse.

Although the letter gave Hardy pleasure he was disturbed by the implication that he might, as a writer, be on the wrong track. He was already worried about his lack of interest in manners—as a novelist such as Jane Austen or Henry James would understand the term—and hence about his capacity to sustain satisfactory levels not only of productivity but of popularity. The self-doubting was characteristic, even constitutional, and matters were not helped by Annie Thackeray's breezy assertion that 'a novelist must necessarily like society!'[21]

Although Hardy was not—and could not afford to be—deflected from the career in prose fiction on which he had now so successfully embarked, he was still thinking about poetry, writing it occasionally, making notes for future poems and volumes, even proposing to an unreceptive Leslie Stephen the publication of a series of 'tragic poems'—evidently to be identified with the Napoleonic ballads, 'forming altogether an Iliad of Europe from 1789 to 1815', mentioned in a note of May 1875.[22] And while some of the tentative volume titles in the following list, of 3 April 1873, may have been added when Hardy copied it out at a later date, it remains a remarkable testimony to the early development and subsequent persistence of his poetic interests and objectives:

Titles—	The Look of Life/Lives	Poems imaginative & incidental
	Mindsights & other verses	Poems in Sundry shapes
	Souls of men	Souls shewn in verse
	. . . .	
	Minutes of years	Poems probably final
	Winter flowers & other verses	Winter words said in Verse.

Seemings said in verse   Wintry Things thought in
                                        Verse with other poems.

A Wintry Voice/in
Various Metres
Speaks in Verse[23]

Hardy also sought to bring his experience as a poet to bear upon his current work in prose. Reflecting early in 1875 upon the desirability of cultivating an appearance of slight stylistic casualness, he invoked Herrick's 'sweet disorder in the dress' and concluded that it was simply a matter of 'carrying into prose the knowledge I have acquired in poetry—that inexact rhymes and rhythms now and then are far more pleasing than correct ones'. Ezra Pound's famous remark about Hardy's verse as the 'harvest' of the novels could evidently have been inverted, and Leslie Stephen, looking back from an end-of-the-century perspective upon the first appearance of *Far from the Madding Crowd* recalled his admiration, even at that time, of 'the poetry that was diffused through the prose'.[24]

The Hardys could now afford to live closer to the centre of things, and on 22 March 1875 they moved from Surbiton to 18 Newton Road, Westbourne Grove, within a few streets of Hardy's former lodgings at Westbourne Park Villas and Celbridge Place. Since most of their possessions were left in storage in Surbiton, the Newton Road rooms were presumably being let furnished.[25] The day after their arrival at the new address Hardy received a summons from Leslie Stephen, found him in his library that same evening, a 'tall thin figure wrapt in a heath-coloured dressing-gown', and readily complied with the request that he witness Stephen's signature to a deed of renunciation of holy orders under the provisions of the Clerical Disabilities Act of 1870. Hardy later recalled Stephen's saying, 'grimly', that 'he thought it as well to cut himself adrift of a calling for which, to say the least, he had always been utterly unfit', but of their subsequent conversation he recorded no more—and no less—than that they had subsequently talked of 'theologies decayed and defunct, the origin of things, the constitution of matter, the unreality of time and kindred subjects'.[26] It is an index of Stephen's respect for Hardy's integrity and intelligence that he should have chosen him as sole witness to a document at once so personal and so symbolic. The episode also demonstrates the extent to which Stephen's influence on Hardy—acknowledged by the latter as stronger than that of any other contemporary—was exerted as much through his personality and conversation as through his writings.

Hardy would later tell Virginia Woolf that her father had had a 'peculiar attractiveness for me, & I used to suffer gladly his grim & severe criticisms of my contributions & his long silences, for the sake of sitting with him'.[27] It was in fact remarkably fortunate for Hardy that Stephen not only admired his work but liked him personally and found him good intellectual company. For Stephen was, as philosopher, polemicist, and editor, near the centre of the great contemporary controversies of thought and belief, and it was largely through association with Stephen that Hardy learned to feel more at ease with precisely such topics as 'theologies decayed and defunct, the origin of things, the constitution of matter, the unreality of time'. Hardy's sonnet 'The Schreckhorn', subtitled 'With thoughts of Leslie Stephen', is finely evocative—as Virginia Woolf herself acknowledged—of Stephen's 'spare and desolate figure' and of the 'quaint glooms, keen lights, and rugged trim' of his personality, and it is pleasant to learn that Stephen, on the day of his death in 1904, asked to be given a new poem of Hardy's to read, probably 'A Trampwoman's Tragedy'.[28]

Although Hardy could now think of himself as an established novelist, his background and early experience had given him little conception of what it meant to be a professional writer, and he greeted the success which so suddenly overtook him with a very fearful joy, a tentative grasp, as if unsure of its reality or permanence. He was, in purely practical and economic terms, right to do so. He had indeed raised himself by his own exertions and talents out of the class into which he was born, and he had recently confirmed his new status by marrying a daughter of the middle class. But his married condition exposed him more nakedly than ever to those cruel trickeries of fate that he seems to have accepted as the norm of all human experience. He had forgotten nothing of what he had learned about the reversibility of class transitions and was sharply aware that his abandonment of his architectural career had left him wholly dependent upon an infinite continuation of his literary exertions—above all, upon his capacity to attract invitations from the editors of magazines.

At the time when he was still struggling for recognition Hardy had shown himself to be almost pathetically open to advice from those more experienced than himself, asking Alexander Macmillan to suggest 'the sort of story you think I could do best', writing *Desperate Remedies* in obedience to what he took to be George Meredith's prescription, and telling Leslie Stephen that he wanted chiefly to prove himself a 'good hand at a serial'. He now remained, at the moment of success, extraordinarily sensitive to the strictures of reviewers, as if they represented some body of independent authority vaguely to be identified with the world of literature. But *Life and Work* exaggerates the extent and immediacy of Hardy's response to the negative comments that occasionally qualified the otherwise general praise of *Far from the Madding Crowd*. He was clearly anxious to assert his independence of other writers and to resist categorization as an exclusively rural or regional author—the restrictive fate that had befallen William Barnes—and he thought it best to pursue both those goals by demonstrating an ability to perform effectively in a variety of modes and settings. Those perceptions and decisions, however, dated from at least as early as the summer of 1874, when the serialization of *Far from the Madding Crowd* was still in progress and he was planning for his wedding journey a route and destination that would facilitate visits to French locations already envisaged for inclusion in his next novel. It must therefore have been prior to discussing that novel with Leslie Stephen that Hardy set aside an existing scenario for what eventually became *The Woodlanders* and made the decision not to build upon *Far from the Madding Crowd*'s rich exploitation of the 'given' material of his early background but to set off instead, with an almost perverse determination, in an entirely different direction.[29]

The Hand of Ethelberta certainly begins in Wessex—the region is invoked by name in its opening sentence—and several of its scenes occur there. But it is essentially a social comedy of London life, turning satirically upon inversions of normal master–servant relationships and deriving much of its point from the basic 'idea' of viewing fashionable life from the vantage point of the domestics, upstairs from downstairs. Ethelberta, the daughter of a butler, has aspirations as a poet and makes a successful career for herself as a professional teller of tales, performing at fashionable parties and even on the public stage. She is motivated primarily by a desire to provide her own family—her parents and her nine brothers and sisters—with financial security, and eventually achieves that ambition by becoming the wife of a wealthy viscount. The marriage, however, is loveless and childless, Lord Montclere himself thoroughly disreputable, and Ethelberta in the end somewhat ambiguously presented, as neither wholly happy nor wholly admirable in her success, or even in her self-sacrifice. Hardy's handling of upper-class characters and episodes is more successful than might have been anticipated, but the comic aspects of the novel seem in general much too contrived and the narrative never quite frees itself from a sense of strain—an impression of its having been elaborately 'got up'. It lacks the dense texture of personal experience that toughens all of Hardy's major fiction and seems, indeed, to have been written without any profound creative engagement

It is, of course, possible to argue that many aspects of Hardy's own situation are reflected in Ethelberta's—that some of his closest relatives, including Martha Sparks and Jemima herself, had been servants, and that in presenting a character who used 'storytelling' as a way of advancing socially and economically from such a background he must in some sense have been writing an allegory of his own career. But Hardy had already shown himself in *A Pair of Blue Eyes* to be capable of extraordinary innocence in dealing with autobiographical material, and he seems to have been less interested in the new novel as an exposition of his personal situation than as a generalized fable of both the journeying and arrival costs of upward mobility. It has been argued by more than one critic, and with considerable subtlety and force, that *The Hand of Ethelberta* was constructed by its author as a deliberately subversive work in which Ethelberta's manipulation of a cynical marital market place provided an implicit commentary on the essential dishonesty of a literary market place dominated by the commercial imperatives and bankrupt moral values of the magazine serial—as exemplified by Leslie Stephen and the *Cornhill*.[30] That Hardy always remained a radical thinker on social issues there can be no doubt. But if in *The Hand of Ethelberta* he was indeed returning, as it were surreptitiously, to the material of *The Poor Man and the Lady*, and even to something of its satirical manner, he stopped well short of reviving its 'socialistic' fervour. And if he did incorporate into Ethelberta's career any reflection or prefiguration of his own, it can only have been in ironic terms. The figure closest to Hardy in the novel, after all, is the one who bears the Christian name he would himself have preferred, the pallid Christopher Julian, who makes in his career as a musician just the kind of modest progress Hardy had made as an architect and settles happily at the end of the novel for a quiet marriage and a steady income. It is almost as if Hardy, in the aftermath of his first triumph, were already pondering, as he was to do at the very end of his life, whether he would not after all have been happier as an architect in a small country town. He may also have begun to ask himself about the wisdom of his marriage as set off against that 'family affection between close blood-relations' that seems so reminiscent of Jemima's pairing-off recipe for happy families—and that Christopher at one point in the novel describes as being the 'only feeling which has any dignity or permanence or worth'.[31]

Stephen responded favourably to the successive sections of *Ethelberta* as Hardy forwarded them, but did not repeat—perhaps because the novel interested him less—the intensity of textual engagement he had devoted to *Far from the Madding Crowd*. He worried in May about the propriety of Ethelberta's referring to herself and her verse as 'amorous', and in August took mild fright at 'the suggestion of the very close embrace in the London churchyard'.[32] His most substantial intervention, however, seems to have been a recommendation, prompted by the arrival of the proofs of the first instalment, that Hardy's subtitle, 'A Comedy in Chapters', be omitted from the serial version—on the grounds that it led readers to expect 'something of the farce description', the funniness of the 'professional joker'. Hardy had presumably intended to emphasize the story's artificiality, its availability to abstract and fabular readings, but he promptly agreed to Stephen's suggestion:

My meaning was simply, as you know, that the story would concern the follies of life rather than the passions, & be told in something of a comedy form, all the people having weaknesses at which the superior lookers-on smile, instead of being ideal characters. I should certainly deplore being thought to have set up in the large joke line—the genteelest of genteel comedy being as far as ever I should think it safe to go at any time.[33]

Before he finished the novel Hardy was in fact to risk something very close to farce in the presentation of the various would-be foilers of the marriage between Ethelberta and Lord Mountclere and the subsequent mock-Gothic hide-and-seek at Enkworth Court. Stephen's own dissatisfaction with these developments would be reflected in his coolness towards the possibility of publishing anything else of Hardy's in the *Cornhill*'s pages.

In March 1875 Hardy, as a professional writer, decided to join the recently established Copyright Association, and on 10 May he waited upon the Prime Minister, Disraeli, as one of a deputation of authors seeking an improvement in domestic and international copyright laws.[34] The following day he had engaged himself to travel to Oxford, watch the college boat races, and respond, with Austin Dobson, to the toast of 'Literature' at the Second Annual Shotover Dinner. There is a hint here of a student prank, given that the invitation had come from Francis Griffin Stokes, an undergraduate of Merton College, and that the contents of *The Shotover Papers, or, Echoes of Oxford*, published in thirteen numbers between February 1874 and February 1875, were largely of a satirical cast. But a programme of the dinner has survived, the *Oxford Undergraduate's Journal* of 13 May refers to the 'Shotover Staff' as having entertained 'several distinguished Metropolitan and Oxford Literati' at the Mitre, and it seems necessary to assume that Hardy's visit to Oxford did indeed take place—and to suspect that he may have encountered, in such company, a certain amount of social condescension.[35]

By the time the first instalment of *The Hand of Ethelberta*, somewhat stiffly illustrated by George Du Maurier, appeared in the July 1875 *Cornhill*, the

Hardys had decided to move on again from Newton Road, perhaps because they found city living unduly expensive, probably because London was not proving conducive to intensive literary labour. Having decided to look for somewhere in Dorset, they answered advertisements or made enquiries about houses in Child-Okeford, Shaftesbury, Blandford, Wimborne, and Bournemouth.[36] Strikingly, none of these was within easy reach of Dorchester or Bockhampton. Strong as the pull of Dorset always was, Hardy was not yet ready to confront Dorchester in his new guise as a member of the professional middle class or to place himself and his wife squarely within his mother's orbit. Jemima herself was entirely aware of the situation, if not perhaps of all that lay behind it. When Emma wrote to her in mid-July of 1875 to suggest that she might meet Hardy and herself at Bournemouth, Jemima got Kate to send on her behalf a message that was not overtly hostile but certainly reflected—in its fidelity to her characteristic half-humorous, half-hectoring manner—her strong disapproval of their deliberate avoidance of 'home':

My dear Emma,
    Mother is much obliged to you for your kind invitation but she is so very busy just now that she cannot possibly come. She would like to have come as she says she wants to see you again.
    Mother says you are not to get into the sea or go boating at Bth [i.e. Bournemouth] because she is afraid you will both be drowned or come to some untimely end. You would be much safer she says on Rainbarrows or Cowstairs—
                                                                                Yrs affectly
                                                                                K Hardy[37]

The angry quarrel between Hardy and Emma that erupted shortly after their arrival in Bournemouth may well have originated in their different responses to Kate's letter, but it was no doubt exacerbated by the bad weather and by Hardy's dislike of Bournemouth itself, later the 'Sandbourne' of *Tess of the d'Urbervilles*. On St Swithun's Day, 15 July—if the evidence of the poem 'We Sat at the Window', dated 'Bournemouth, 1875', is to be accepted—they sat and stared at the rain in a mood of mutual hostility:

> We were irked by the scene, by our own selves; yes,
> For I did not know, nor did she infer
> How much there was to read and guess
> By her in me, and to see and crown
>   By me in her.

> Wasted were two souls in their prime,
> And great was the waste, that July time
> When the rain came down.

The essence of the situation emerges more explicitly from the manuscript of the poem, where the first line of this second and final stanza reads: 'We were irked by the scene, by each other; yes.'[38]

Later that same day they left Bournemouth and went by steamer to nearby Swanage, a small port and seaside resort on the 'Isle' of Purbeck. There they found rooms at West End Cottage, a two-storeyed semi-detached house still standing on the hillside above the town, looking out over the bay towards the sea and the cliffs of the Foreland—a setting and outlook ascribed in *The Hand of Ethelberta* to the lodgings taken by Ethelberta upon her first arrival at 'Knollsea', 'a seaside village lying snug within two headlands as between a finger and thumb'. The Hardys' landlord, Captain Joseph Masters, master mariner and lodging-house keeper, also makes an appearance in the novel as Captain Flower, who spoke in a 'rich voice, developed by shouting in high winds during twenty years' experience in the coasting trade', and yet 'slipped about the house as lightly as a girl' while assisting his wife in the preparation of dinner.[39]

The completion of *The Hand of Ethelberta* was Hardy's chief occupation in Swanage during the closing months of 1875. The need to send advance proofs to the *New York Times* obliged him to keep further ahead of the printer than he had done with *A Pair of Blue Eyes* or even *Far from the Madding Crowd*, but he seems to have maintained his schedule without particular difficulty, even though Stephen was still suggesting minor improvements and issuing such admonitions as 'Remember the country parson's daughters. I have always to remember them!'[40] The manuscript was finished in January 1876, well ahead of the conclusion of serialization, and the proofs of the final chapters were sent off to New York by the middle of March. There were, however, only eleven instalments instead of the twelve originally planned. To attempt a twelfth number, Hardy told Smith, Elder in January, 'would be to run the risk of making the latter part dull by undue extension'—and portions even of this shortened text seem diffuse, eked out, and heavily dependent upon immediately accessible or recently 'researched' topographical details from Swanage, Corfe Castle, and Rouen.[41]

Life went on quietly enough at West End Cottage while the novel was in progress. Captain Masters was a constant source of nautical and smuggling anecdotes, the harbour offered regattas and boat trips, the town's ancient stone trade had not yet entirely disappeared, and there were plenty of local sights to visit and sketch. In what was evidently a major reconciliatory gesture, Hardy's sisters Mary and Kate came to Swanage for a fortnight's visit in early September, and several sketches by Mary of scenes in and near Swanage were made during joint expeditions with her brother and his wife, one of them involving a trip around the Isle of Wight in the steamer *Heather Bell*. The visit of the sisters ended on the 13th, when all four set off early by an overloaded carrier's cart, picnicked at Corfe Castle, and then separated, Mary and Kate going on to Wareham (thence to Dorchester), Hardy and Emma returning to Swanage.[42] Included in Emma's diary are a few brief notes related to the composition of her story 'The Maid on the Shore', and that Emma was engaged in some kind of writing at this time, or thought of herself as very actively assisting her husband, is indicated by a remark in Miss d'Arville's letter to her of 26 December 1875: 'You are I dare say both very busy with your new work, which I hope to read when published.' If Emma's participation was at all substantial in any novel of Hardy's other than *A Pair of Blue Eyes* and *A Laodicean* it must have been *The Hand of Ethelberta*. Unfortunately, the manuscript has not survived, Hardy having destroyed even the fragment of it that unexpectedly turned up in 1918.[43]

It was while he was living at Swanage that Hardy first had one of his poems published. In September 1875 Richard Gowing, editor of the *Gentleman's Magazine*, wrote to ask for 'a short sketch, or brief story, or an article on some literary, art or social subject for my next January number— a mere chip from your workshop'. Hardy offered a poem, 'The Fire at Tranter Sweatley's', apparently written while he was with Blomfield in the 1860s. Gowing accepted the poem, and it appeared that November in a text which had suffered mild bowdlerization at the hands of either a cautious editor or an apprehensive author.[44] Henry Holt—with whom, despite the misunderstandings over the American publication of *Far from the Madding Crowd*, Hardy remained on cordial terms—had arranged for simultaneous publication of the ballad in America, and a copy was sent to amuse R. D. Blackmore, whom Hardy had met earlier in the year and addressed in terms of mingled admiration and fellowship. It seemed 'almost absurd', he said, that he had not read *Lorna Doone* before writing *Far from the Madding Crowd*: 'Little phases of nature which I thought nobody had noticed but myself were continually turning up in your book—for instance, the mark- ing of a heap of sand into little pits by the droppings from trees was a fact I should unhesitatingly have declared unknown to any other novelist till now. A kindred sentiment between us in so many things is, I suppose, partly because we both spring from the West of England.'[45] Blackmore's response was very much in kind, and spoke of Hardy's generosity in praising 'one who works in your own field, at any rate to some extent'. But since

Blackmore had found *Far from the Madding Crowd* to be '*in parts* revolting', he was doubtless offended by even the bowdlerized version of 'The Fire at Tranter Sweatley's', and the relationship, though propitiously begun, seems not to have developed further.[46]

9

Sturminster Newton

IN May 1876, just as the *Cornhill* serialization of *The Hand of Ethelberta* had reached its conclusion, Leslie Stephen sought to steer Hardy back to the course he had seemed to be charting with *Far from the Madding Crowd*. Urging him not to allow his own 'perfectly fresh & original vein' to be cramped by an excessive respect for critical canons, Stephen recommended instead the reading of 'the great writers, Shakespeare, Goethe, Scott &c &c, who give ideas & don't prescribe rules'. Especially important, he thought, was George Sand, 'whose country stories seem to me perfect & have a certain affinity to yours'.[1] Hardy did not of course know that he was never again to have a novel serialized in the *Cornhill* or to have the benefits—and occasional drawbacks—of Stephen's editorial guidance. But writing and publishing *Ethelberta* had not been a satisfactory experience, other than in purely economic terms, and it seemed an appropriate moment for reconsidering and ultimately refining his literary options. The previous March he had told George Smith: 'I do not wish to attempt any more original writing of any length for a few months, until I can learn the best line to take for the future.'[2]

In the meantime he was exploring other possible sources of income, at first with mixed success. In writing to Smith he had gone on to suggest that Smith, Elder should bring out cheap one-volume editions of *A Pair of Blue Eyes* and *Far from the Madding Crowd*. He repeated the suggestion in July, but it would be another year before such editions were forthcoming. More immediately gratifying were some negotiations with Freiherr (later Baron) von Tauchnitz, who paid £40 for the rights to publish *The Hand of Ethelberta* in English on the continent of Europe and subsequently added most of Hardy's other novels to his series.[3] Hardy was himself approached by a prospective German translator but had already discovered that translations were more difficult to control or to profit from. In November 1875 he had taken the initiative in writing to Léon Boucher, the author of 'Le Roman pastoral en Angleterre', a long and warmly appreciative article on his work that had appeared in the *Revue des deux mondes*, but while Boucher—writing in English, as Hardy himself had presumably done—thanked Hardy for a kind and flattering letter he was pessimistic about the prospects for any French translation of *Far from the Madding Crowd*, the translation of *The Mill on the Floss* having sold so poorly.[4]

The irritating association of Hardy's work with George Eliot's was kept alive in the summer of 1876 by the appearance of *Daniel Deronda* and the comment in the *Westminster Review* that it was fortunate that *The Hand of Ethelberta* had been published first, 'or else ill-natured critics would have declared that his principal character was only a copy'. To such a criticism, had it in fact been made, Hardy might justifiably have pointed out that George Eliot had, in that same novel, borrowed from *Far from the Madding Crowd* the designation 'Wessex' for certain south-western portions of contemporary England.[5] He could also have cited, in support of his own prior claim to that regional concept, a remarkable article entitled 'The Wessex Labourer' that had appeared in the 15 July 1876 number of the *Examiner*. Charles Kegan Paul, the anonymous author, was warm in his praise of Hardy's intimate knowledge and exact representation of the Dorset countryside, the Dorset peasantry, and the special quality of the region's still isolated way of life: 'Time in Dorset has stood still; advancing civilisation has given the labourer only lucifer-matches and the penny post, and the clowns in *Hamlet* are no anachronism if placed in a west country village of our own day.' The article, which made frequent and familiar use of 'Wessex' as of a term already in general circulation, played its part in determining Hardy's return to the Dorset countryside for the material of his next novel. Not surprisingly, he kept a copy by him and drew upon it, twenty years later, in writing a preface to a new edition of *Far from the Madding Crowd*.[6]

The Hardys had resumed their wanderings meanwhile, still keeping on the far side of an invisible arc centred upon Higher Bockhampton. In early March of 1876 they left Swanage for Yeovil, in Somerset, taking lodgings at 7 St Peter Street, part of a terrace of small houses that no longer exists. Here Hardy corrected the final proofs of the first edition of *The Hand of Ethelberta*, published in two volumes by Smith, Elder on 3 April. It was generally well received by the reviewers, the *Spectator*, for instance, excusing the implausibility of much of its action on the grounds that it could be viewed 'as a humorous fable illustrating the vices and weakness of the upper ten thousand, rather than as a picture of the most characteristic figures in the intellectual society of modern London'.[7] In mid-May of 1876 Hardy and Emma spent a fortnight in London, staying in lodgings at 61 Margaret Street, near Oxford Circus, and viewing the pictures at the French Gallery in company with William Black, the Scottish novelist, a close contemporary whom Hardy had come to know quite well. They then left, on 29 May, for Harwich, the night crossing to Rotterdam, and their second continental holiday.[8]

In Rotterdam they spent two nights at the New Bath Hotel—Emma copying into her diary the menu of the table d'hôte dinner—before setting off on 2 June, Hardy's thirty-sixth birthday, for a tour of the Rhine valley. At the Hôtel de Hollande, on the river bank at Cologne, Emma recorded that her husband was angry 'about the brandy flask'. It is impossible to know whether the flask had been lost, or left behind, or allowed to leak, or whether Hardy, always a near-abstainer, had disapproved of Emma's having brought with her what he perhaps saw as a symbol either of hypochondria or of that weakness for strong liquors which had already wrought such havoc in both their families. But the reference, brief and enigmatic as it is, provides the first specific indication of tension within the marriage. From Cologne they moved south by steamer to Koblenz—Emma trying to define the precise colour of the river as 'a soft whitish green—not blue but brown-white-green'—and thence, on 6 June, to Mainz and another Hôtel de Hollande, described by Emma as a 'very high class, rich hotel'.[9]

The weather was hot, and by the time they reached Heidelberg Emma was becoming exhausted. The evening of their arrival they climbed the tower of the Königsstuhl. Because of the mist, Hardy noted, the landscape was invisible, but the Rhine itself 'glared like a riband of blood, as if it serpentined through the atmosphere above the earth's surface'. Emma was in less poetic mood: '*wished I had not*', she wrote of the climb to the tower. 'Intensely hot, immensely tired, a mist spread everywhere Saw nothing— great fatigue next day.'[10] They moved on, despite her weariness, to Baden Baden, and then to Strasbourg, where, on 10 June, she felt weak and ill, with an ulcerated throat and a sensation 'as if I was either recovering from or going to have a fever'. In *Life and Work* Emma's distress in Strasbourg is attributed to 'excessive walking', and she was perhaps experiencing a recurrence of the 'occasional lameness, suffered from early childhood', that is mentioned in *Some Recollections*. On this occasion she had brandy and drank it, without registering any comment or objection on Hardy's part, and on the following day she had the relief, though also the tedium, of a more than eight-hour train journey from Strasbourg to Metz and then on to Brussels.[11]

The first day in Brussels was entirely given over to a visit to the field of Waterloo, and on the morrow Emma recorded that she was still greatly fatigued and that her husband was 'cross about it'. Two days later things were little better: 'Tom is gone to see the picture gallery which was closed yesterday—so I have missed it altogether. Quite worn out with the day at Waterloo—'.[12] Hardy was the fitter of the two, and by far the more accustomed walker; he also knew precisely what he wanted and needed to see in places to which he might never return; and he had no wish to disturb arrangements—including reservations at good hotels—that had been carefully made in advance. Too much should not be made of marital disagreements generated by the inevitable surprises and stresses of foreign travel, but there is again a hint here that, within two years of their marriage, Hardy was finding Emma something less than the ideal companion, intellectually free and physically active, he had originally believed her to be—and that he was responding to the discovery with irritation rather than with sympathy.

For Hardy the visit to the Waterloo battlefield had always been the major objective of the entire holiday. He had been fascinated since childhood with the period of the Napoleonic Wars—then well within living memory—not only as a conflict on a vast and world-shaking scale but also as a time when George III's summer visits to Weymouth and the scare of a French invasion had brought Dorset temporarily to the forefront of the national consciousness. He was also very much aware that Admiral Thomas Masterman Hardy, a Dorset-born namesake and just possibly a distant relative, had become famous through his association with Nelson, especially at the battle of Trafalgar. The previous summer, on the sixtieth anniversary of Waterloo, Hardy had gone with Emma to Chelsea Hospital to seek out the few pensioners who were still living to tell their tales of that day. Now, on the endpapers of his Baedeker for Holland and Belgium, he drew a 'Plan of Hougoumont—Sketched on the spot by TH.', and in Brussels itself he attempted to identify the house at which the Duchess of Richmond's ball had been held the night before the battle—a historical puzzle which continued to tease him in later years. Since the Hardys' itinerary had been so planned as to bring them back to England, by way of Antwerp, on the eve of another Waterloo Day—no doubt another reason for Hardy's reluctance to change his plans—he was able to go once again to Chelsea and talk with some of the survivors 'in the private parlour of "The Turk's Head" over glasses of grog'.[13] He was, in short, already firmly in the grip of that grand Napoleonic obsession which was to culminate some thirty years later in the publication of *The Dynasts*.

. . .

As one of the last entries in her diary of their continental trip, Emma had written: 'Going back to England where we have no home & no chosen county.' In less than two years they had moved from Surbiton to Westbourne Grove to Swanage to Yeovil, quite apart from house-hunting expeditions and foreign travels, and Emma was weary of such gipsying. The 'search for a little dwelling' begun in Yeovil was now resumed in greater earnest, and on 3 July they moved from Yeovil to Sturminster Newton, a small town in north Dorset situated, once again, just outside the fifteen-mile radius of the *cordon sanitaire* they seem to have placed around Higher Bockhampton.[14] Here they rented Riverside (or Rivercliff) Villa, one of a semi-detached pair on the town's outskirts. It was for many years erroneously assumed that the Hardys had occupied the house immediately adjacent to what is now the recreation ground, but the memorial plaque has since been correctly affixed to the more northerly of the two.[15] Like almost all the houses the Hardys occupied during their married life, Riverside was very much the Victorian 'villa' its name claimed it to be, solid, 'comfortable', and of quite recent construction. The Hardys seem, indeed, to have been the first occupants of the building, and it was Hardy himself who planted in the undivided garden in front of the two houses a pair of 'monkey-puzzle' trees (Chile pines)—perhaps in memory, or emulation, of those growing in the rectory garden at St Juliot. Though unremarkable in itself, the house had, and has still, a splendid situation on a bluff that stands above the river Stour and its water-meadows. The scene is captured in the poem 'Overlooking the River Stour' and in one of Hardy's notebook entries, made shortly after their arrival: 'Rowed on the Stour in the evening, the sun setting up the river. Just afterwards a faint exhalation visible on surface of water as we stirred it with the oars. A fishy smell from the numerous eels and other fish beneath. Mowers salute us. Rowed among the water-lilies to gather them. Their long ropy stems.'[16]

Hardy later spoke of Sturminster Newton as having been the 'happiest time' in his marriage to Emma, and while 'A Two-Years' Idyll', one of his poems about the Sturminster period, certainly acknowledges the capacity of nostalgia to romanticize what at the time of its happening had seemed ordinary enough, it also insists that the 'idyll' was real:

> Yes, such it was;
> Just those two seasons unsought,
> Sweeping like summertide wind on our ways;
> Moving, as straws,
> Hearts quick as ours in those days;

> Going like wind, too, and rated as nought
> Save as the prelude to plays
> Soon to come—larger, life-fraught:
> Yes, such it was.[17]

It was a quickness of heart that enlivened not only their own relationship
but also their attitude towards the people amongst whom they were now
living. Sturminster, a market town of some 1,500 inhabitants, was a focal
point for the eastern part of the Vale of Blackmore, the 'Valley of the Little
Dairies' of *Tess of the d'Urbervilles*. William Barnes had been born nearby at
the very beginning of the century and had written much of his poetry about
the Vale and its way of life, but Hardy himself had previously known at all
well only Blackmore's southern fringes around Melbury Osmond and
High Stoy. Now, however, both he and Emma entered into the life of
Sturminster as though they intended to make it their permanent home.
They were soon friendly with various members and generations of the
Young family, the owners of Riverside Villa, and especially with Robert
Young—'Rabin Hill', the Dorset dialect poet—who was an infinite source
of local anecdotes and traditions, and by the autumn of 1876 they were on
calling and dining terms with several of the leading Sturminster families.
Emma, in particular, was to maintain for many years her friendship with
Mrs Dashwood, the wife of Henry Charles Dashwood, a local solicitor.[18]

The notebook entries Hardy preserved from this period further testify to
an active and outgoing appetite for whatever was lively, local, and curious
—from the 'beheading' of a woman in a twopenny sideshow at Shroton
Fair to the springtime singing of thrushes and blackbirds, 'with such modu-
lation that you seem to see their little tongues curl inside their bills in their
emphasis'. At Blandford Forum, another market town not far distant:
'Night on the bridge at the bottom of the town. Light shines from a window
across the stream; the surface of the stream seen moving on, the little ripples
showing. Occasionally an insect of night touched the water just in the spot
of light, & was, unknown to himself, as visible as in day.' Another note
records a charming remark of Emma's, made in late autumn: 'A gentle day,
when something seems gone from the garden, & you cannot tell what.'[19]

During the closing months of 1876 a further attempt was made to bring
the Hardy and Gifford families closer together. Two of Emma's brothers
came to Sturminster in late October for a brief visit, and in December
Hardy took Emma to spend Christmas with his parents.[20] Surviving studio
portraits of Jemima and of Thomas Hardy senior show them just as they
were at this period, still vigorous in middle age. Jemima's hair seems not to
have turned grey; Thomas, broader and handsomer than his elder son,

looks the solid, moderately prosperous tradesman he had by this time become. Hardy's father that Christmas was evidently very much his kindly self, telling stories of his childhood, when the hobby-horse had not yet died out. But Jemima's mood can scarcely have been so genial. She and Emma never liked or trusted each other, and in later years a mutual antagonism flourished on the basis of real or imagined slights—Jemima, for example, is said to have created a permanent grievance out of Emma's having once served her tea in a cracked cup.[21] Too much, however, has been made, in this and other contexts, of Emma's snobbery. The refusal of trust and liking seems originally to have been Jemima's—believing, no doubt, that her son had married a foolish woman unlikely either to help his career, bear his children, or honour his parents—and Emma's pride of family essentially a retaliatory resource.

In returning to Sturminster at the end of the Bockhampton visit Hardy was also returning to work on his new novel, set not in the Vale of Blackmore where he was now living but in the immediate neighbourhood of his parents' cottage, the spot where he had been born and brought up. It seems on the face of it surprising that Hardy should choose to write about Bockhampton and the heath and yet deliberately persist in living elsewhere, but he was now beginning to realize (in contradistinction to what he had felt at the time of writing *Far from the Madding Crowd*) that because distance enforced a more active and absolute dependence upon memory it could actually enhance the imaginative recovery of past scenes and emotions. Less surprising, though certainly striking, is his having forgone while at Sturminster the opportunity of invoking a landscape that had already been poetically colonized, claimed as it were for literature, in the Dorset poems of William Barnes. A note of 1876 shows that Hardy was vividly aware of the local association with Barnes—'At Bagber—(where Barnes lived): pool: appletrees: remains of garden, &c—all is there except the house'—and he certainly valued his friendship with Barnes himself, then still living, a venerable and venerated figure, on the outskirts of Dorchester. He had already in 1876 received a copy of Barnes's *Poems of Rural Life in Common English* inscribed 'With the Author's kind regards and good wishes for his writings'.[22] There could have been good practical reasons for Barnes's choosing that particular volume rather than one of his more numerous collections of poems in the Dorset dialect—Hardy may even have owned all of the latter—but it certainly points towards a keen awareness and perhaps disapproval on Barnes's part of the younger man's avoidance of the dialect in his own work.

Uncertainty as to his own position in the literary world made Hardy anxious to avoid any appearance of being under Barnes's shadow, and his need as a novelist to appeal to a largely urban audience demanded that regional authenticity be restricted to a point well short of the off-putting obscurity of dialectal exactitude. As early as August 1876 he had addressed this difficult issue in response to an enquiry from the English Dialect Society:

The dialect of the peasants in my novels is, as far as it goes, that of this county: but it is necessary to state that I have not, as a rule, reproduced in the dialogues such words as would from their approximation to received English, seem to a London reader to be mere mispronunciations. But though I have scarcely presented peculiarities of accent & trifling irregularities with such care as could have been wished for purposes of critical examination the characteristic words which occur are in every case genuine as heard from the lips of the natives.[23]

Just how far the writing of *The Return of the Native* had progressed by the beginning of 1877 is not quite clear, but on 5 February Hardy told George Smith that he had sent Leslie Stephen the manuscript 'as far as written'. Stephen did not reject the novel outright but made some temporizing reply, and Hardy, in his anxiety to get into print again, felt himself free to seek publication elsewhere. On 13 February he wrote to enquire about a possible opening in *Blackwood's Magazine* for a 'story dealing with remote country life, somewhat of the nature of "Far from the Madding Crowd"'. In view of Hardy's earlier dealings with Stephen and Smith it seems odd that he should tell John Blackwood, in that same letter, that he had 'not yet written enough to be worth sending', but he had evidently not yet had his manuscript back. On 1 March he wrote to Smith, Elder: 'Will you be good enough to return to me the manuscript of the new story, as soon as you conveniently can: I cannot well get on for want of it, as I have no exact copy.'[24]

On 12 April he wrote again to Blackwood to say that he had just forwarded the first fifteen chapters, an estimated one-third of the novel's total length, adding the reassurance that 'should there accidentally occur any word or reflection not in harmony with the general tone of the magazine, you would be quite at liberty to strike it out if you chose. I always mention this to my editors, as it simplifies matters.' Blackwood, however, declined the novel, objecting that the opening chapters were far too static,[25] and in May Hardy sent it back again to Stephen, only to receive a firm rejection about the middle of the following month. Though Stephen liked the opening, Hardy later recalled, 'he feared that the relations between Eustacia, Wildeve, and Thomasin might develop into something "dangerous" for a family magazine, and he refused to have anything to do with it unless he could see the whole. This I never sent him; and the matter fell through.'[26] After another unsuccessful approach, to the editor of *Temple Bar*, Hardy eventually found a home for the serial version in *Belgravia*. This was a far less prestigious journal than the *Cornhill*, and Mrs Procter, for one, was in due course astonished to find a serial by 'the divine Hardy' in its pages: 'I suppose Hardy could not stand Leslie Stephen,' she concluded: 'I could not.'[27]

The payment from *Belgravia* amounted to no more than £20 for each monthly part, making a total of £240 for the entire novel.[28] That sum did not include publication in volume form, but it still compared poorly with the £700 received for the English serial and volume rights of *The Hand of Ethelberta*. Book publication—subsequently arranged with Smith, Elder, despite the break with Stephen and the *Cornhill*—and American serialization brought in additional amounts, but Hardy found himself rather more dependent than he had anticipated upon such supplementary sources of income as the cheaper one-volume editions of *A Pair of Blue Eyes*, *Far from the Madding Crowd*, and *The Hand of Ethelberta* that appeared in 1877. Hardy was, in effect, turning himself into a competent literary agent, a shrewd though never grasping manager of his professional affairs, fully aware of all the possibilities open to a writer of fiction in that particular period. In March 1877, still exercised over that too hasty sale of the copyright to *Under the Greenwood Tree*, he sought Anthony Trollope's advice as to the most profitable way of disposing of the rights to novels, learning as a result that Trollope himself sold everything to his publishers 'out and out' to save tedious bargaining but believed a royalty arrangement to be best—if one could get it and were not too urgently in need of the money.[29] Royalty arrangements would eventually prove indispensable to Hardy's longer-term financial stability, but in 1877 they were not yet common publishing practice, and he had to be grateful for the modest one-time payments obtained from the sale to Tauchnitz of the continental rights to *Far from the Madding Crowd* and the publication of a children's story, 'The Thieves Who Couldn't Help Sneezing', in an annual called *Father Christmas*.

By the end of 1877 *The Return of the Native* was all but complete. Copy for the first two instalments was sent off on 28 August; by early November three more instalments were ready and Hardy was already turning part of his attention to the kind of historical and regional material he was to draw upon in *The Trumpet-Major*. In September 1877 he had written to a local antiquary, the Reverend Charles Bingham of Binghams Melcombe—the 'original' of Parson Tringham in *Tess of the d'Urbervilles*—to ask where he could find files of local newspapers for the early years of the century or, indeed, 'any county records, notes, or memoranda relating to that time'.[30]

He had also begun his exploration of Hutchins's *History and Antiquities of the County of Dorset*, a crucial resource for his gradual evolution of Wessex into a total imaginative world with a solid, complex, and comprehensively realized existence in space and time.

Several notes from Hutchins appear in the early pages of a notebook that Hardy, with Emma's active assistance, began keeping in the spring of 1876. Unlike the working notebooks he had been keeping for many years, this was in the nature of a commonplace book, recording—usually in summary, sometimes at greater length—whatever struck him as new, interesting, or strikingly expressed during the course of his extensive reading of books, newspapers (chiefly *The Times* and the *Daily News*), and such magazines as the *Saturday Review*, *Spectator*, and *Fortnightly*. The notebook was in frequent use at Sturminster Newton and the fact of Emma's participation—it was she who wrote out the original batch of notes and continued to add others from time to time, including a long series of sayings by the Jesuit Balthasar Gracian from the *Fortnightly Review* of March 1877—is suggestive of the extent to which the Hardys, during these early years of their marriage, saw themselves as a 'team', working together in the common project that was Hardy's career.[31] What the notebook itself most remarkably indicates is the extent to which Hardy, in 1876, was seeking quite deliberately to improve his knowledge of recent and ancient history, European and classical literature, and the history of art. Prominent among the sources quoted and cited in the notebook's early pages are Macaulay's essays, Clarendon's *History of the Rebellion*, G. H. Lewes's biography of Goethe, a translation of an Italian biography of Raphael, the short life of Virgil included in the copy of Dryden's translation that Hardy's mother had given him, a history of ancient Greece, and an article on Aeschylus by John Addington Symonds. Some of the self-consciously 'classical' aspects of *The Return of the Native* clearly had their origin in what it is tempting to think of as Hardy's preparatory reading of such works and, especially, of the translations of Greek tragedy—particularly Aeschylus—to which he seems also to have turned at this period.[32]

Sturminster Newton itself supplied Hardy with material for future use. The episode in *Jude the Obscure* in which Father Time arrives by train without warning, his ticket in his hat, the key of his box on a string round his neck, owes a good deal to the interest aroused in Sturminster in January 1877 by the little girl who arrived at the railway station in care of the guard and carrying a parcel addressed to a local resident who denied all knowledge of the child. It later transpired that the girl's mother had worked as a barmaid while living with the child's father, a publican, and that, after being deserted by another man who had bigamously married her, she sent the child, unannounced, to her own parents, apparently so that she herself might make a new unencumbered start.[33] In describing the Club-day walking and dancing at the beginning of *Tess of the d'Urbervilles* Hardy certainly drew upon what he had seen of such events in the Vale of Blackmore. The anniversary festival of the Sturminster branch of the Dorset County Friendly Society on Whit Monday, 21 May 1877, included a procession with a band, a church service, and a dinner; in the evening the festivities moved to a nearby field, 'where dancing and athletic sports were enjoyed'.[34] Hardy's visit to Marnhull, the 'Marlott' of *Tess of the d'Urbervilles*, on 30 May was probably made in order to witness similar celebrations there, and he specifically recorded his presence at the festivities held at Sturminster on 28 June, the fortieth anniversary of Queen Victoria's coronation. There were sports, and dancing on the green, and Hardy observed that 'The pretty girls, just before a dance, stand in inviting positions on the grass. As the couples in each figure pass near where their immediate friends loiter, each girl-partner gives a laughing glance at such friends, and whirls on.'[35]

The proximity of this note to the account of the Hardys' troubles, that same night, with their servant Jane has additional importance for the genesis of *Tess of the d'Urbervilles*. Although Jane had probably not been with them long—she was presumably the successor to Georgiana, whose dismissal the previous November is noted in Emma's diary—it is clear from their concern for her welfare that they did indeed, as Hardy says in his note, like her very much. When she ran off in the early hours of the morning after having been caught in the act of bringing a man into the house at night, Hardy went to inform her parents, finding them 'poorer than I expected (for they are said to be an old county family)'. A few days later Hardy and Emma seem to have looked for the girl at Stalbridge, where she was rumoured to have gone to join her lover, and on 13 August they learned that she was expecting a baby.[36]

The Hardys' Jane can with some confidence be identified with Jane Phillips, whose two-day-old son Tom died on 28 November 1877 as a result of what the death certificate calls 'Debility from Birth' and was buried at Sturminster by the Reverend S. Keddle on 3 December 1877. Tom's father is nowhere identified, but the parish records show that the child had been privately baptized prior to its death, presumably by its mother, as the Hand children had been by their mother—a sequence of events approximately replicated in the brief life and pathetic death of Tess's child, Sorrow, in Hardy's novel. A Jenny Phillips is named in Hardy's copy of John Hullah's

The Song Book as the singer of several of Hardy's favourite songs, including 'When the rosebud of summer' and 'My Man Thomas', and in view of *Life and Work*'s reference to 'an old county family' it is worth noting that Hutchins includes the pedigree of the Phelips family of Corfe Mullen (a village near Wimborne with which Hardy later became familiar) and records the existence of a family vault there and the decline into cottages of the former mansion of the Phelipses.[37]

References to Jane Phillips occasionally appear in poems associated with this period. The speaker in 'Overlooking the River Stour' regrets that in gazing out at the natural world he had failed to notice the more significant human events occurring, behind his back, within the house itself, and although this could well be an allusion to Hardy's own marriage, the first stanza's reference to 'the wet June's last beam' seems to relate it specifically—the Hardys having spent only one June in Sturminster—to the moment of their troubles with their servant at the very end of June 1877. What Hardy recognized in the fate of Jane Phillips—and dramatized in the story of Tess Durbeyfield—was the sheer power of sexuality and the gross injustice of a social system which threw upon the woman the entire burden of sexual responsibility and guilt. But he also came to see her as a tragic instance of the emotional ferment that could lie beneath the apparent placidity of familiar domestic appearances, and as a warning of the precariousness of that modest everyday happiness which remains unrecognized and unappreciated until it has been irrecoverably lost. 'The Musical Box' is a companion poem to 'Overlooking the River Stour', and whoever is imagined as uttering its central message—' "O make the most of what is nigh!" ' —the bearing of that message is primarily upon the subsequent course of the Hardys' marriage, the fast fading of 'the fair colour of the time'.[38] The point is made quite explicitly in the melancholy final stanza of 'A Two-Years' Idyll', a retrospective assessment of the entire Sturminster experience:

> What seems it now?
>   Lost: such beginning was all;
> Nothing came after: romance straight forsook
>   Quickly somehow
>   Life when we sped from our nook,
> Primed for new scenes with designs smart and tall. . . .
>   —A preface without any book,
>   A trumpet uplipped, but no call;
>   That seems it now.

The book that remained unwritten—like the first stanza's 'plays | Soon to come—larger, life-fraught'—surely included children among its dramatis personae. A wealth of sad and perhaps bitter implication lies behind Hardy's comment on the news that their former servant was expecting a child: 'Yet never a sign of one is there for us.'[39] Although they had not long been married, the Hardys were not especially young in years. At 36, nearing 37, Emma was approaching an age at which childbearing might be difficult and dangerous, and as each year of the late 1870s slipped by the likelihood of her ever having children grew steadily more remote.

In late October 1877 Hardy made a brief trip to Bath to meet his father, who had gone there in search of a cure for his rheumatism—itself largely the consequence of his never troubling to take off wet clothes when coming home from work. Hardy found lodgings for his father, took him to the theatre, saw him safely to the baths the next day, and then returned to Sturminster.[40] Christmas that year seems to have passed without a family gathering at Higher Bockhampton: the evening of 22 December, at any rate, Hardy spent with his friend Dr John Comyns Leach, the local coroner, who was conducting an inquest into the death of a boy at a village a few miles from Sturminster. Hardy held a candle to provide light for the autopsy but otherwise recorded only that the body had been opened by just two cuts, one vertical and the other horizontal.[41]

By the beginning of 1878 the Hardys had arranged to leave Riverside Villa and move closer to London. According to *Life and Work*, Hardy had decided that for professional reasons 'he should have his head-quarters in or near London'. Emma was also ready to move, but for different reasons. She had come to believe that the air from the river was unhealthy and to fret at their living—as one of her brothers had scornfully remarked—in a place so isolated that 'a strange bird on the lawn was an event'. She also believed that her husband, as a successful author, would in London cut more of a figure in the literary world, and that she, too, as a successful author's wife, would have a more satisfying role to play. She had already caused Hardy some embarrassment by exaggerating to Sturminster neighbours the extent of her participation in the actual writing of the novels.[42]

The Hardys left Sturminster just as they were becoming locally known and established. At least two Dorset newspapers recorded their presence, on 5 March 1878, at the Sturminster Literary Institute concert at which a Miss Marsh, from the Somerset village of Keinton Mandeville, sang Sir Henry Bishop's 'Should he upbraid' with a skill and charm which prompted Hardy, years later, to celebrate her performance—'drawing out the soul of listeners in a gradual thread of excruciating attenuation like silk from a cocoon'—in his poem 'The Maid of Keinton Mandeville'.[43] Within two weeks of the concert they had packed up their furniture—most of it purchased new at the time of their moving into Riverside Villa twenty months earlier—spent a final night at the Dashwoods', and left for the house in the London suburb of Tooting on which they had taken a three-year lease during an expedition to London the previous month.[44] It was not to prove a fortunate move in personal or even in professional terms.

10

The Return of the Native

O N 22 March 1878 the Hardys moved into 1 Arundel Terrace, Trinity
Road, Tooting, sometimes called The Larches, the end house of a
three-storeyed red-brick Victorian terrace. Wandsworth Common and
Wandsworth Common Station were only a few minutes' walk away, but the
house was not otherwise notable for charm or convenience. Writing rather
apologetically to Kegan Paul on 21 June, Hardy explained that 'for such
utter rustics as ourselves Tooting seemed town enough to begin with'.
Emma meanwhile sent Mrs Dashwood a harrowing account of the problems of furnishing a house considerably bigger than Riverside Villa.[1]

At Tooting, during the first half of 1878, both the scope and the pace of
Hardy's literary work continued to increase. There were the Napoleonic
ballads, the corrections to the Tauchnitz edition of *Far from the Madding
Crowd*, a new short story ('The Impulsive Lady of Croome Castle'), and the
reworking of what remained of the manuscript of *The Poor Man and the Lady*
into the novella-length story called 'An Indiscretion in the Life of an
Heiress', published in its entirety in the *New Quarterly Magazine* for July 1878
and, across the Atlantic, as a five-part serial in *Harper's Weekly*.[2] The serial
proofs of *The Return of the Native*—running in *Belgravia* from January to
December 1878—had to be corrected and a duplicate set sent across the
Atlantic to *Harper's New Monthly Magazine*, and the novel's illustrator, Arthur
Hopkins (younger brother of Gerard Manley Hopkins), needed guidance as
to the way Eustacia should look and what the mummers would have worn
and carried.[3] Because he expected only a relatively small financial reward
from *The Return of the Native*, Hardy was obliged to pursue other forms of
literary remuneration, and the London move, whatever its negative
aspects, did offer the prospect of his securing more business—and perhaps
more friendly reviews—by making the acquaintance of publishers, editors,

and agents, and mixing in a free and clubbable fashion with the literary world in general.

In the spring of 1878 the editor of a Boston journal asked Hardy to supply some notes for a biographical article—itself an encouraging index of his growing reputation—and received in return a manuscript in Emma's hand that nevertheless embodied the professional image that Hardy himself wished to project. It spoke in particular of his 'higher education' as having been taken in hand by 'an able classical scholar & Fellow of Queen's College, Cambridge', mentioned the two architectural prizes, described his undertaking 'special studies' in the interests of 'becoming an art-critic', and continued: '[B]ut his early taste for romantic literature having revived, he sent a short attempt in fiction to one of the London Magazines: it was accepted at once; & fiction thence forward became his hobby. But he did not altogether neglect art & visited several of the great collections of paintings in Continental Capitals from time to time.'[4] Like so many of Hardy's public statements, the article was not so much inaccurate as misleading. Its exaggeration of the formality and extent of his education and his artistic studies is very much of a piece with the laborious autodidacticism of the notebooks and the sometimes ponderous displays of literary and artistic information in the early fiction. More significant, perhaps, is the impression created of a literary gentleman of wide interests, a countryman by birth, a Londoner by adoption, for whom architecture had been a perfectly natural first career and who had arrived effortlessly at novel-writing in the course of rediscovering an 'early taste for romantic literature'.

The dispatch of this document on 9 May 1878 needs to be correlated with Hardy's election that June to membership of the Savile Club, the principal literary club of the day, and with the entire process by which he 'fell into line as a London man again'. From Tooting he was able to visit galleries and theatres, call on publishers such as George Smith of Smith, Elder, and meet and make friends at the Savile, among them Charles Kegan Paul, now active in London as a publisher and editor, and William Minto, editor of the *Examiner*, who in 1875 had sought to serialize one of Hardy's novels and praised his characterization of Ethelberta as 'even more daring and finer than Bathsheba'. Hardy and Emma could also go together to visit the Alexander Macmillans, who lived quite close by, encountering there such distinguished figures as T. H. Huxley and John Morley.[5]

These occasions would from time to time provide him with 'material': when writing *A Laodicean*, for example, he was able to draw upon his memories of a sudden downpour of rain during one of Mrs Macmillan's garden parties. At the same time, his relative inexperience of the London

literary world tended to expose him to some of that world's most characteristic dangers. London valued facility, energy, panache—the dependable
productivity of a Walter Besant, the infinitely adaptable talent of an
Edmund Gosse—and in none of these did Hardy's genius reside. London
tempted him with journalistic opportunities, invited him to be trivial,
exacerbated his vulnerability to contemporary opinion, undermined him
with sheer occupation—an excess of gossip, shop-talk, dining out, and
'keeping-up'. The founding of the Rabelais Club by Besant in 1879 is
treated in *Life and Work* as an event of major importance—though a certain
wryness enters into the account of the inaugural meeting[6]—and Hardy put
some effort, at least in the 1870s and 1880s, into maintaining cordial
relations with a whole series of second- and third-rate metropolitan littéra-
teurs. This was, however, precisely the literary life towards which he had
aspired—so impossibly, as it then seemed—in the 1860s, the contemporary
counterpart of those earlier worlds so beguilingly evoked in the talk of
Horace Moule and the pages of Thackeray's *Pendennis*. And the friendship
of such a man as Besant—founder of the Incorporated Society of Authors
and indefatigable defender of authors' rights—did at least serve to keep him
informed about current publishing practices and the best ways of maintaining a profitable control over his own productions.

By the spring of 1878 the scheme of *The Trumpet-Major* had taken definite
shape, and from late May onwards, taking advantage of his new location,
Hardy was able to work in the Reading Room of the British Museum on the
background of his native region during the Napoleonic period, enter the
results of his researches into what is now known as his '*Trumpet-Major*'
Notebook, and so supplement what he had been told of his own grandparents' experiences during the period of threatened invasion.[7] Although
the serial of *The Return of the Native* had now run two-thirds of its course, there
were still proofs to correct, illustrations to supervise—his disappointment
with Hopkins's first presentation of Eustacia being quite dispelled by her
appearance in the August number—and various business details to settle: it
was only in September that arrangements were made with Smith, Elder for
publication of *The Return of the Native* in volume form, the payment to be
£200 for an edition of 1,000 copies.[8]

Although parallel serialization had been proceeding in *Harper's New
Monthly Magazine*, rights in the American first edition were again secured by
Henry Holt. The first publisher to bring out a Hardy novel (*Under the
Greenwood Tree*) in the United States, Holt had since published all the other
novels in his one-volume Leisure Hour series, paying Hardy a straight
royalty of 10 per cent of the retail price. Harper & Brothers had now nego-

tiated an independent agreement with Hardy for the publication of *The Return of the Native*, but Holt nevertheless persuaded Joseph W. Harper, Jr., that 'trade courtesy required him to turn the book-right over to me, who had introduced Hardy here'—the same argument as he had earlier used to obtain *Far from the Madding Crowd*.[9] Hardy grew increasingly uneasy in his relationship with Holt, suspecting that he could get better terms elsewhere, and in a letter to Harper & Brothers of 24 June 1878 he made it clear that he would like to do more business with them: 'If at any time you should wish to make a proposal for including novels of mine in your series, it will be treated in confidence. I am not sufficiently acquainted with the usage of American publishers to know if an English author is held to be justified there, as in England, in arranging with whomsoever he chooses for the publication of any particular book or books, irrespective of those that have preceded it.' Meanwhile negotiations with Tauchnitz for a continental edition of *The Return of the Native* completed one more stage in that sequence with which Hardy was now becoming thoroughly familiar: English serial, American serial, English first edition, American first edition, continental edition, cheap one-volume edition.[10]

Much of the remembered happiness of the Sturminster Newton period had its source in the generous and confident flow of Hardy's creative energies as he worked on the manuscript of *The Return of the Native*. He had striven more deliberately than ever before to make the book an unmistakable work of art, not just another run-of-the-mill serial, and hence to prove himself not merely a good serial hand but (to use another phrase from that same February 1874 letter to Stephen) 'a great stickler for the proper artistic balance of the completed work'. In particular, he had sought to enhance the novel's claims to be regarded as a serious work of literature by ordering his story of a primitive and isolated Wessex community in such a way as to sustain unity of place and unity of time and parallel the foreground action with classical and biblical allusions and structural echoes of the patterns of Greek and Elizabethan tragedy.[11] But while the critical reception of the work as published in three volumes by Smith, Elder on 4 November 1878 was characterized by general respect for Hardy as an artist, it displayed a disappointment no less general in *The Return of the Native* as a manifestation of that art. Several reviewers found it cold, intellectual, and unnecessarily depressing, others criticized the theatricality of the scene-painting, and there was a widespread feeling that while the dialogue of the rustic characters was often striking and amusing it was rarely like life: 'The language of his peasants may be Elizabethan, but it can hardly be Victorian.'[12]

The *Athenaeum* review, the source of that smart formulation, was one of the most hostile responses the book received, and one of the earliest. Hardy, venturing for the first time to answer one of his critics in print, wrote a letter which ranged so far beyond the specific point made by the reviewer as to suggest that he was seizing the opportunity to issue a long-contemplated manifesto on issues that were fundamental to his entire position as a regional novelist:

An author may be said to fairly convey the spirit of intelligent peasant talk if he retains the idiom, compass, and characteristic expressions, although he may not encumber the page with obsolete pronunciations of the purely English words, and with mispronunciations of those derived from Latin and Greek. In the printing of standard speech hardly any phonetic principle at all is observed; and if a writer attempts to exhibit on paper the precise accents of a rustic speaker he disturbs the proper balance of a true representation by unduly insisting upon the grotesque element; thus directing attention to a point of inferior interest, and diverting it from the speaker's meaning, which is by far the chief concern where the aim is to depict the men and their natures rather than their dialect forms.

A note made two days before the letter was published is highly suggestive of Hardy's anxiety over the novel's reception—and of the way in which a particular distress could rapidly expand in his mind to quite overwhelming proportions: 'Woke before it was light. Felt that I had not enough staying power to hold my own in the world.'[13]

The critics were not deflected by Hardy's intervention. One of the last to pass judgement, on 8 February 1879, was the *Spectator* reviewer (almost certainly Richard Holt Hutton), who repeated and amplified reservations about the speech of the peasants expressed by earlier critics and developed a sustained criticism of the author's 'gloomy fatalism', his having 'found Schopenhauer far superior to all the prophets and all the seers'. Although the burden of these remarks would be taken up by a great many critics in succeeding years and generations, nothing in Hardy's notebooks or among the contents of his library provides any indication of a familiarity with Schopenhauer's writings at this date. Since Hardy's German, unlike his French, seems always to have remained quite minimal, *The World as Will and Idea* would in any case have become directly accessible to him only on the publication of an English translation in 1883. Edmund Gosse in 1909 told an enquiring scholar that Hardy did 'not admit any influence from Schopenhauer on his work'. He continued: 'The ideas which have animated Mr Hardy's books were already present in his mind and conversation, and were the result of temperament and observation, rather than of "influence".'[14]

Gosse might have added that such ideas were also rooted in both general and particular aspects of Hardy's personal background—a background he had implicitly acknowledged in the first edition of *The Return of the Native* by persuading Smith, Elder to emphasize the novel's unity of place by inserting his own sketch map of 'the supposed scene' as a frontispiece.[15] That map as drawn and printed was deliberately disoriented, so that what should be its north–south axis actually appears as east–west, but it clearly revealed to anyone familiar with the countryside around Dorchester that the place whose unity Hardy sought to project was the tract of heathland immediately adjacent to Higher Bockhampton, the position of the fictional Bloom's End roughly approximating to the location of the Hardy cottage. Given a personal connection so direct and obvious, it seems almost inconceivable that Hardy would consciously have allowed the narrative to fall into autobiographical patterns. Yet the story is that of an idealistic and gifted young man who abandons the professional goals set for him by his ambitious and strong-minded mother, becomes distracted from both practical and idealistic ambitions by his infatuation with a free-spirited woman unexpectedly encountered in a wild and lonely place, and subsequently endures—having largely provoked—the social and perhaps sexual frustrations of his disappointed wife and the bitter hostility which springs up between his wife and his mother. Hardy believed Clement, as Clym Yeobright was christened, to be a name traditional in his own family; he based Mrs Yeobright, Clym's mother, on his own mother; he gave Clym's dead father his own father's and grandfather's love of music and church choirs; and something of his sister Mary went into the creation of the patient, unprotesting Thomasin, whose very name echoes Hardy's own and who in the manuscript was once cast as Clym's sister rather than his cousin.[16] If Emma perceived any of these analogies, one wonders what she can have made of her own role as the beautiful but sexually restless and foolishly romantic Eustacia Vye, the direct though unwitting cause of Mrs Yeobright's death and the active seeker (so the text suggests) of her own.[17]

Emma, however, had already survived the merging of substantial elements of her personality and behaviour into the characterization of Elfride Swancourt, and she was by this time familiar with the transformational processes of her husband's imagination—which is not to say that she had any real grasp of those processes themselves, or of the ways in which they might shift from feeding upon his personal past to feeding into his personal future. Numerous aspects of *A Pair of Blue Eyes*, *Under the Greenwood Tree*, and even *Far from the Madding Crowd* are clearly autobiographical, and the later evidence of *The Woodlanders*, *Tess of the d'Urbervilles*, and *Jude* urges the conclusion that Hardy's best work tended to have strong and specific roots in his own background and experience. It might be argued, indeed, that such rootedness was essential to the fullest and freest flow of his creative impulse, its absence a major source of the relative failure of works such as *The Trumpet-Major* and *Two on a Tower* in which the results of deliberate research do duty for a missing core of personal experience.

Hardy's settings, as all Wessex pilgrims know, are notorious for what might be called their flexible fidelity to actuality: scenes and buildings recognizably 'real' are adapted, developed, shifted, arranged in new topographical relationships, in order to meet the overriding demands of the fiction, the work of art itself. So it often seems to be with characterization and even with individual incidents and passages of dialogue. Hardy's plots may be invented or borrowed, but much of his richest narrative material is reworked more or less directly from the life. If he never tells a wholly autobiographical story, the texture of his work is nevertheless thick with remembered experience and observation, with family and local traditions possessed so absolutely by the imagination as to be indistinguishable from memory itself. Though deeply autobiographical, therefore—and in ways which cannot have been wholly unconscious—*The Return of the Native* is hardly a *roman à clef*. The usefulness of the sketch map is not (despite *Life and Work*'s teasing allusion to the map in *Treasure Island*[18]) as a guide to buried biographical treasure but rather as a reminder of Hardy's having not yet developed those habits of defensive secretiveness that have so often been charged against him.

Of all the 'autobiographical' elements in *The Return of the Native*, the most fascinating consists in Hardy's use of his narrative not to recreate his own past experiences but rather to explore in hypothetical terms a road he had not taken—and, in so doing, to see more plainly, and perhaps justify to himself, the course he had in fact chosen to follow. Clym's decision to reject his profession and return to the heath was quite distinct from the direction of Hardy's life since he had finally given up architecture, and while he had perhaps made some of Clym's mistakes (notably in marrying Emma/ Eustacia) he had not taken the false step of trying to go home again. Hardy had consistently resisted the temptation, and the parental pressure, to meld Emma with the world of Bockhampton, recognizing with a clear-sightedness not available to the blinded Clym—nor, indeed, to his own later self—that such an arrangement would never work. The fact that he had taken the Tooting house on only a temporary basis suggests that a solution to his central dilemma had not yet revealed itself, and that he was in some sense using the writing of his novel not as an act of self-analysis but, more simply, as a way of 'laying out' his situation and problems, of projecting what might have followed—what might still follow—as a consequence of his playing in a radically different fashion the cards dealt him by fate. Like *The Hand of Ethelberta* before it, *The Return of the Native* took on for Hardy himself something of the significance of a private fable or cautionary tale.

In early September 1878, shortly before he first mentioned the sketch map to Smith, Elder, Hardy visited Dorset for ten days and made a series of excursions that asserted, in small and undramatic ways, his new position as an acknowledged man of letters and a member of the professional middle class. He called as a literary equal on William Barnes at Came rectory. He visited Kingston Lacy 'to see the pictures'. When he and Charles W. Moule made a similar expedition to Forde Abbey they arrived outside the normal visiting hours but were invited in and shown round by the owner himself.[19] There was not the slightest suggestion, however, of Hardy's drifting out of touch with his own family. He stayed at Bockhampton as usual, and on returning to London wrote to ask his brother to get their mother to make up her mind to come to London for a visit 'while the fine weather lasts'. With a curious but characteristic affinity for the actual, he wrapped within the letter a chip of wood he had himself taken from the wreck of the *Princess Alice*, a steamship that had sunk in the Thames with heavy loss of life just ten days earlier.[20]

The experience of moving in his old world armed with his new status perhaps gave Hardy the confidence to assert, through the sketch map, his own intimate connection with the scenes he had portrayed. Although not eager to publicize his background, he clearly regarded it with neither shame nor embarrassment. In April 1881, when an article by Charles Kegan Paul linked him with William Barnes as 'sprung of a race of labouring men in a county where the real old families are attached to the soil', he did not respond in print but simply pointed out in a letter to Paul that he came of a line of master-masons, employers of journeymen but never journeymen themselves'.[21] Kegan Paul was, however, a privileged friend, possessed of a special understanding and appreciation of Hardy's work as a result of the twelve years he had himself spent as vicar of the Dorsetshire village of Sturminster Marshall and of his sympathy, during those years, with the aspirations of Joseph Arch and the National Agricultural Labourers' Union. Now a London reviewer and publisher, Paul 'took up' the Hardys following their arrival at Tooting, inviting them to parties and considerably expanding their London acquaintance. Jane Panton, one of the daughters of W. P. Frith, the painter of *Derby Day* and other crowded Victorian canvases, recalled her first meeting with Hardy—'a short, frail-looking man'—in the Kegan Pauls' drawing room during the 1870s, and this was perhaps the beginning of Hardy's friendship with Frith himself and with other members of his family.[22]

Hardy, now as always, was much interested in painting, both for its own sake and as a potential source of images and even techniques relevant to his own work. In a note of April 1878 he praised a painting by an Italian artist, Giovanni Boldini, for its unelaborated representation of 'a young woman beside an ugly blank wall on an ugly highway', and linked it to Hobbema's landscapes as 'infusing emotion into the baldest external objects either by the presence of a human figure among them, or by mark of some human connection with them'. A similar comment, accompanied by a rough sketch, was prompted by another contemporary Italian painting seen at a private view the following November, and Hardy himself made clear in his note on the Boldini that he was seizing upon such examples as confirmation of his own accumulating sense that 'the beauty of association is entirely superior to the beauty of aspect, and a beloved relative's old tankard to the finest Greek vase. Paradoxically put, it is to see the beauty in ugliness.'[23] The shift from the homely and, surely, personal instance (the tankard 'must' have been his beloved father's) to the abstract formulation is typically Hardyan, and the conception itself—so crisply exemplified by the later image of England as 'scored with prints of vanished hands'—had already informed his 'reading' of the Dorset landscape in *The Return of the Native*, especially of the heath itself in the famous opening chapter.[24]

Hardy's explicit acknowledgement of that interconnection is symptomatic of the new authorial self-consciousness evident in several aspects of the novel. Many of its references to art belong with the somewhat obtrusive apparatus of classical references and analogies, largely derived from his recent readings and rereadings of Greek tragedy, by which Hardy sought to elevate the novel above the common run of contemporary fiction. But his telling the Pre-Raphaelite sculptor Thomas Woolner, just a year or two later, that *The Return of the Native* 'embodied' his views on 'the art of the future' was a reflection of his developing interest in the novel form as an appropriate vehicle for the communication of ideas. In the letter to Woolner he specifically drew attention to the opening sentences of Book III:

In Clym Yeobright's face could be dimly seen the typical countenance of the future. Should there be a classic period to art hereafter, its Pheidias may produce such faces. The view of life as a thing to be put up with, replacing that zest for existence which was so intense in early civilizations, must ultimately enter so thoroughly into the constitution of the advanced races that its facial expression will become accepted as a new artistic departure. People already feel that a man who lives without disturbing a curve of feature, or setting a mark of mental concern anywhere upon himself, is too far removed from modern perceptiveness to be a modern type.[25]

Although he is ostensibly writing about art, Hardy's emphasis is clearly upon what he calls—in dull monosyllables as expressive as those of Pope's famous alexandrine—the 'view of life as a thing to be put up with', and the passage falls into place as an element in the overall presentation of Clym Yeobright as a naively idealistic, anxiously cerebrating, and ultimately defeated intellectual.

Clym has often been described as Arnoldian, but Hardy's somewhat dismissive references to the 'ethical systems' Clym has picked up in Paris seem to point rather to Comte, and hence to a deliberate undercutting of those broadly Positivist values—service to others, compromise, and 'loving-kindness'—that had been specifically celebrated in *Far from the Madding Crowd*.[26] Although it was written at Sturminster Newton, during a period subsequently remembered as one of particular happiness, the intellectual content of *The Return of the Native* is significantly denser, more purposeful, and more pessimistic than that of any of his previously published works. It is a difference attributable less to the novel's aspirations to classically tragic status than to the trajectory of Hardy's own reading and thinking during the preceding decade.

A mild melancholia pervades the few notes to have survived from the closing months of 1878. The winter of 1878–9 was a period of increasing tension within the Hardys' marriage—because of its continuing childlessness, perhaps, or because of disagreements over the wisdom of the move to London, or for some unknown reason at which it is impossible even to guess. According to *Life and Work*, 'they seemed to begin to feel that "there had past away a glory from the earth"'. Their relationship is not directly the subject of the specifically dated poem 'A January Night (1879)', but its central lines, 'There is some hid dread afoot | That we cannot trace', chime both with this feeling of loss and with the statement, also in *Life and Work*, that it was at Tooting, a little later on, 'that their troubles began'.[27] That the marriage nevertheless remained strong is indicated by a note of 19 January 1879—headed 'Shines' and entered into the 'Poetical Matter' notebook as potential material for a poem—that preserves with extraordinary and affectionate precision a peaceful moment from the Hardys' domestic life at Tooting:

In the study firelight a red glow is on the polished sides & arch of the grate: firebrick back red hot: the polish of fire irons shines; underside of mantel reddened: also a shine on the leg of the table, & the ashes under the grate, lit from above like a torrid clime. Faint daylight of a lilac colour almost powerless in the room. Candle behind a screen is reflected in the glass of the window, falling whitely on book, & on E's face & hand, a large shade of her head being on wall & ceiling. Light shines through the loose hair about her temples, & reaches the skin as sunlight through a brake.[28]

Little correspondence between Tooting and Higher Bockhampton has survived, but Hardy kept in touch with family events, including in December 1878 the end of his sister Katharine's course at the Salisbury training college and the death of John Antell, his angry shoemaker uncle. In the new year came the more immediately disturbing news that his mother was ill, and at the beginning of February 1879 he left Emma at Tooting and took the train to Dorchester, where he was met by his brother Henry and driven out to Bockhampton in a wagonette pulled by Bob, the horse kept for the family business. Although the weather was unusually cold, Hardy took advantage of the opportunity to visit Weymouth, Portland, and Sutton Poyntz, places directly relevant to *The Trumpet-Major* on which he was now actively engaged, and he learned with wry amusement the fate of some church fittings torn out by John Wellspring, the builder who had done restoration work at Coombe Keynes and elsewhere during his own time with Hicks: 'chickens roost under the gilt-lettered Lord's Prayer and Creed, and the cock crows and flaps his wings against the Ten Commandments'. Because his mother was ill, he spent more time than usual alone with his father, who talked much about earlier times, telling tales about the former west gallery choirs at Stinsford and Puddletown churches and a story about a parson's son who became a miller that probably contributed something, several years later, to the presentation of Angel Clare in *Tess of the d'Urbervilles*.[29]

As soon as he returned to London on 15 February Hardy wrote to Leslie Stephen to sound out the prospects for a *Cornhill* serialization of *The Trumpet-Major*. Stephen replied that he would be interested in seeing the story when it was further advanced, adding that his own preference was for novels like *Vanity Fair* in which the historical characters were kept in the background and a figure such as George III, though felt to be 'just round the corner', was not seen 'in full front'.[30] Although Thomas Masterman Hardy does appear briefly in *The Trumpet-Major* and George III himself— perhaps to tease Leslie Stephen—is once seen 'in full front', this was essentially the method Hardy followed. But precisely because his characters were unknown to history and of relatively humble rank, it was necessary that their lives be seen as meshed within a context of large and intricate historical events, and it was for the sake of such sustaining details that Hardy returned on several occasions to the British Museum, notebook in hand, to continue his researches into histories, memoirs, and especially newspapers of the Napoleonic period.

The Trumpet-Major proved, like its immediate predecessor, somewhat difficult to place. In the wake of Leslie Stephen's temporizing response Hardy seems in May 1879 to have sent a portion of the manuscript to Macmillan, presumably in the hope of serialization in *Macmillan's Magazine*, and in early June he offered John Blackwood 'a cheerful story, without views or opinions' that was 'intended to wind up happily'. Neither approach was successful, but by the end of that same month negotiations with *Good Words*, a popular monthly magazine with a broadly religious readership, were sufficiently well advanced for the editor, the Reverend Dr Donald Macleod, to define for Hardy the kind of material he was seeking: 'We are anxious that all our stories should be in harmony with the spirit of the Magazine—free at once from *Goody-goodyism*—and from anything—direct or indirect—which a healthy *Parson* like myself would not care to read to his bairns at the fireside.'[31] Given the 'cheerful' nature of his story, Hardy could accept these otherwise ominous terms with a reasonable degree of complacency. Accommodating Dr Macleod's ministerial susceptibilities did compel a number of minor changes—mostly matters of moderating swearwords and shifting an event with sexual implications from a Sunday to a Monday—but, as Hardy recalled many years later, it was easy enough to restore the original readings when the novel appeared in book form.[32]

By the summer of 1879 work on the manuscript was well advanced—stimulated by a glimpse of Napoleon's nephew, Prince Napoleon, whose profile struck Hardy as 'altogether extraordinarily remindful of Boney'—and in August he found time to go down to Dorset again to see his convalescent mother. Both his sisters were now school-teaching, and both were at home for their summer holidays. Hardy walked over to Puddletown on at least one occasion and talked with his cousin James Sparks about their common great-great-great-grandfather, said to have lived in Puddletown in the seventeenth century and built there the cottage that had remained in the family ever since. He would also have visited his widowed aunt Mary Antell and seen the little deathbed sketch of her husband drawn by their son, also John Antell, who would later seek Hardy's advice about the headstone he was designing for his father's grave. *The Trumpet-Major* was not forgotten, however. When Emma came down to Dorset a week or so after her husband they soon moved to Weymouth, as the obvious centre for visits to places associated with the novel. It also became the centre for another attempt at family reconciliation as Jemima made the grand gesture of coming over from Bockhampton, despite the wet and exceptionally windy weather, to join her son and daughter-in-law in several of their excursions.[33]

Hardy seems to have begun writing *The Trumpet-Major*, as he had *Far from the Madding Crowd*, with a relatively simple plot line, a broad sense of how the story might go, and then allowed the situations initially established to develop their own momentum. As the writing proceeded he pointed up the class differences between the characters, especially between the potential marriage partners, saw further comic possibilities in Festus Derriman and his uncle, and added new twists to the central plot. By early September 1879 the first fourteen chapters were already in proof and Hardy was putting the finishing touches to the manuscript of the next seven. A few weeks later he sent sketches of early nineteenth-century military and domestic details to the illustrator, John Collier, who used one of them as the basis for the illustration of the miller's kitchen in the February 1881 instalment. Hardy did some last-minute research in the British Museum on 25 November and had probably completed the entire manuscript by the time serialization began that December in the January 1880 number of *Good Words*.[34]

The Trumpet-Major did not absorb all of Hardy's literary energies at this period. His friendship with Charles Kegan Paul had developed into a kind of working partnership useful and profitable to both, and it was during Paul's editorship that the *New Quarterly Magazine* published two of Hardy's earliest and finest short stories: in April 1879, 'The Distracted Young Preacher'—based largely on the smuggling stories he had heard from George Nicholls and Captain Masters and from people still living in the Lulworth district in which the story was set—and in April 1880, 'Fellow-Townsmen', set in the Bridport area. At Paul's request Hardy also wrote for the *New Quarterly* an anonymous review of William Barnes's *Poems of Rural Life in the Dorset Dialect*, entirely positive in its emphases yet recognizing Barnes's avoidance of 'the strong passions which move mankind, great and small', and stressing that his scenes and characters derived not from Dorset generally but specifically from the Vale of Blackmore, 'a limited district . . . having marked characteristics of its own'.[35]

Since Kegan Paul's firm had published the Barnes volume, Hardy's first and only experience as a reviewer involved an element of log-rolling—implicitly acknowledged by Paul's including in the same issue of the *New*

Quarterly a long and generally admiring essay by Mrs Sutherland Orr on 'Mr. Hardy's Novels', the first extended survey of its kind. Paul's own high estimate of Hardy's work appeared in the *British Quarterly Review* of April 1881—to be supplemented in May 1883 by his article on 'The Rustic of George Eliot and Thomas Hardy' in the first number of *Merry England*—and there can be little doubt that he was, after Leslie Stephen, the literary figure who did most to advance Hardy's reputation at this still early period when his work had not yet (as Paul himself put it) 'taken hold on the great popular mind, sometimes slow to discover when a new genius has arisen in the intellectual sky'.[36]

Hardy's popular reputation had, in fact, reached an early peak with *Far from the Madding Crowd* and then fallen back somewhat. But he had remained steadily productive and established himself more firmly amongst his fellow professionals: Walter Besant, in inviting Hardy to join the Rabelais Club, had praised *The Return of the Native* as 'the most original the most virile and most humorous of all modern novels'.[37] Wider recognition resulted in a considerable expansion of Hardy's London acquaintance throughout 1879 and the first half of 1880, and it was while he was living at Tooting that he seems first to have met George Greenhill, teacher of mathematics at the Royal Artillery College, Woolwich, on whom he was to rely, directly or indirectly, for much of the scientific and technical information invoked in his next two novels, *A Laodicean* and *Two on a Tower*. In June 1879 he saw something of the proceedings of an International Literary Congress being held in London and spent a weekend with his friend R. Bosworth Smith (son of the Reverend Reginald Smith of West Stafford and his wife), who was a housemaster at Harrow school.[38] On 10 March 1880 he went with Mrs Procter to lunch with the Poet Laureate and his family and was charmed by Tennyson's geniality and by his praise of *A Pair of Blue Eyes*. He seems especially to have enjoyed Tennyson's asking him to name the first person mentioned in the Bible, to which the correct answer was 'Chap. I'.[39] Browning was often at Mrs Procter's when the Hardys called there during the late winter and spring of 1880, and Hardy persuaded their hostess to make a list of all the celebrities she had known, going back almost to the beginning of the century. High among her current favourites was Henry James, and Hardy—who rather disliked James as a man, much as he always admired him as an artist—recorded with mingled amusement, scepticism, and distaste her assertion that he had made her an offer of marriage.[40]

Hardy was reading James's *Roderick Hudson* at about this time, as well as some of his critical works, including the essay on Balzac in *French Poets and Novelists* and the English Men of Letters volume on Hawthorne. Doubtful perhaps about his own expedition into the past in *The Trumpet-Major*, Hardy extracted from James's Hawthorne study the famous sentence from 'The Custom-House' in which Hawthorne expresses regret at having chosen a historical theme instead of attempting to diffuse thought and imagination 'through the opaque substance of to-day', thus making it 'a bright transparency'.[41] Stimulated by meeting Matthew Arnold at a London dinner in February 1880, Hardy read several of his essays during this same period and entered into one of his notebooks, partly quoted and partly summarized, a passage from 'Pagan and Mediaeval Religious Sentiment' on the relationship between 'the modern spirit' and 'the imaginative reason' that would be central to his next novel, *A Laodicean*, subtitled *A Story of To-day*.[42]

Hardy had proposed *A Laodicean* to Harper & Brothers in response to their handsome offer of £100 for each of the thirteen instalments of a serial that would inaugurate the new European edition of *Harper's New Monthly Magazine*. Asked to find a first-class illustrator for the story, Hardy wrote at once to Helen Allingham, romantically remembered (as Helen Paterson) from the days of the *Far from the Madding Crowd* serial, only to receive by return of post the disappointing information that she had entirely given up book illustration. He then approached three or four other artists more or less simultaneously before finally coming to terms with George Du Maurier, with whom he had already worked during the serialization of *The Hand of Ethelberta*.[43] J. Henry Harper, one of the partners in Harper & Brothers, came over from New York in July 1879, followed later that same month by R. R. Bowker, charged with overseeing the launch of the *Monthly*'s European edition. Within a few days Bowker had called at Tooting and been

received in a pretty parlor by Mrs. Thomas Hardy, with her Kensington-stitch work, and her pet cat; she is an agreeable youngish English lady, immensely interested in her husband's work, and we were at once good friends. Hardy presently came down, a quiet-mannered, pleasant, modest, little man, with sandyish short beard, entirely unaffected and direct. . . . Told me he had the greatest difficulty in remembering the people and incidents of his own stories so that Mrs. Hardy had to keep on the look-out for him. . . . I came home, having made two pleasant friends, I think.

In view of the difficulties that were to attend the completion of *A Laodicean* it was fortunate that Hardy and Bowker should have got on so well from the first. Bowker learned to respect Hardy's professionalism, even in trying conditions, and to think of him as 'a thoroughly good fellow, quietly companionable', while Hardy, for his part, seems to have found Bowker's American straightforwardness entirely congenial.[44]

The numerous social encounters recorded by *Life and Work* for the early summer of 1880 are indicative of Hardy's rapidly expanding circle of London friendships but also of his not being under particular pressure from publishers and editors. Serialization of *The Trumpet-Major* was still in progress in *Good Words* at the time in July 1880 when Hardy contracted with Smith, Elder for its publication in volumes, but he had corrected all the remaining proofs and felt free, at the end of July, to take Emma on another brief continental excursion. They went on this occasion no further afield than north-western France, first to Amiens, to see the cathedral, and thence, on 1 August, to Étretat, where Hardy's love of swimming induced him to stay too long in the chilly waters of the Channel and hence contributed, or so he believed, to his long illness of the following autumn. At the hotel in Le Havre, their next stopping place, they were overcome by just the kind of nervous terror that Jemima had displayed in the London hotel room during Hardy's childhood and spent much of the night setting up barricades of furniture against a wholly imaginary threat of intrusion. They stayed at Trouville and Honfleur before moving on, finally, to Lisieux and Caen, towns which Hardy had already envisaged as stages in Paula Power's pursuit of Somerset in the closing chapters of *A Laodicean*. It is on the beach of that 'romantic watering-place' Étretat, however, that the pursuit ends—the reversal of the Hardys' own itinerary being no doubt deliberate—and Du Maurier later responded to Hardy's expressed admiration for the illustration of that scene by presenting him with the original drawing.[45]

Back in England by mid-August 1880, Hardy applied himself to *A Laodicean* and was able to send off the first instalment well before the end of the month. During these same busy weeks of late August and early September he also completed the final revisions to the forthcoming first edition of *The Trumpet-Major*. The changes were, for the most part, very minor, involving the deletion of some inaccurate dates and the restoration of most though by no means all of the oaths and other offensive details that had been omitted from the *Good Words* version at Dr Macleod's behest. But he also profoundly changed the mood and experience of the ending by explicitly forecasting the trumpet-major's death: John, who in the serial had simply departed 'to blow his trumpet over the bloody battle-fields of Spain', now, in the first edition, went off 'to blow his trumpet till silenced for ever upon one of the bloody battle-fields of Spain'.[46] It was entirely Hardyan of Hardy to thus twist the knife at the conclusion of a book that had been scarcely less of a pastoral idyll than *Under the Greenwood Tree*. In so doing, he compounded the crime of which he was accused by Leslie Stephen, that of allowing the heroine to marry the wrong man, Hardy's objection—that they mostly did—meeting with Stephen's ultimate editorial retort, 'Not in magazines.'[47] The novel has generally been regarded as slight and—unlike most of the other Hardy novels—as especially appropriate for assignment to schoolchildren. Hardy, however, took seriously both his historical researches and the material that had come to him through the oral tradition. He was also unusually attentive to the appearance of the first edition, sending Smith, Elder a copy of the Chandos Classics edition of Butler's *Hudibras* to indicate the kind of red he wanted for the binding and supplying in his own hand the design for the cover, with its twin vignettes of camp and mill connected by a winding path.[48]

11

Illness

HARDY went down to Bockhampton for a few days in mid-September 1880. The talk at his parents' home dwelt largely upon the past disposition of family property, but much of the visit was given over to exploring with his brother Henry the possibility of finding a plot of land in or near Dorchester on which to build a house. This radical shift of direction on Hardy's part marked a corresponding shift in the balance of power as between his wife and his mother. Hardy had thus far preserved the peace by keeping them almost entirely apart, but that policy had severe practical drawbacks. Throughout their six years of still childless marriage he and Emma had moved constantly from one place to another, driven primarily by economic considerations, including his own perceived needs as a literary professional, but also by Emma's vague and always disappointed ambitions for a richer social life. The first serious disagreements between them had occurred, and Hardy seems to have been no longer willing to fight his wife's corner as staunchly as he had done during their first years together. As he later wrote in a poem specifically called 'The Rift', 'We faced but chancewise after that'.[1]

Hardy had long seen residence in Dorset as meeting many of his requirements as a novelist of rural and, more especially, 'Wessex' life, but what now encouraged him to reverse the inner thrust of *The Return of the Native* was a reawakened sense of family responsibility. The clannishness of the Hardys was intense—as both Hardy's wives discovered to their cost. Hardy's marriage had disrupted Jemima's plans for her children to live permanently together in pairs, and it was partly for that reason that it had been so bitterly opposed, and would have been opposed even if he had chosen a different partner. But he still felt—perhaps felt all the more deeply and guiltily—that it was incumbent upon him as the eldest child, as the most prosperous member of the family, and, quite simply, as a Hardy, to assume a greater responsibility for the welfare of his parents and, especially, of his two unmarried sisters. It was a responsibility that he would discharge consistently, generously, even excessively, for the rest of his life.

More immediately, the death of his uncle James at Higher Bockhampton in March 1880—hard on the heels of John Antell's death in December 1878—had reminded him that his own parents were now in their late sixties, that his mother had only recently recovered from a serious illness, and that his father suffered acutely from rheumatism. Henry was well able to run the family building business, and Mary was now headmistress of the Bell Street National School in Dorchester itself, but Kate's departure for college and then for a teaching post on the far side of the county had left Jemima without regular household assistance. And Hardy himself, now aged 40 and in an unexpectedly favourable financial situation, wanted a more settled existence in a home of his own. So the possibility of building in Dorchester was debated—at a family conclave from which Emma was absent—and the decision in its favour constituted a victory for Jemima, and for Emma a corresponding defeat, one which she never forgave and from which she never fully recovered.

At the time a move to Dorchester was first being mooted, family relationships and interrelationships were superficially smooth, or at least quiescent. The experiment of bringing Emma and Jemima together the previous summer had evidently not been an entire disaster. Kate, always far more outgoing than her elder sister, had arrived at a cheerful friendship with Emma that was grounded in the latter's kindness to her while she was attending the training college at Salisbury. Although never in trouble at college,[2] Kate was desperately unhappy, fretting rebelliously against the stern discipline and obligatory performance of domestic duties, and she came to depend a good deal on the reassuring letters Emma wrote her from Sturminster Newton and Tooting. In a letter of 1881, written from her first school in the little north Dorset village of Sandford Orcas, she told Emma to 'write soon and then I'll answer you again like you used when I was at Salisbury'. In a later letter to Emma she reported a conversation with a girl from the college which had suggested that the students there were now 'having rather better times than we used to have', but she added, with an unconscious glance forward to *Jude the Obscure*: 'I don't mind if Tom publishes how badly we were used.' The letter ends, 'Give him my love and the same to you', and is signed 'Yrs very affectly Katie'.[3] Other letters from Kate to Emma in the late 1870s and early 1880s display the same warmth and openness. There are also letters, less open but not notably less warm, from Mary to Emma, and it was while the Hardys were at Tooting that Emma—in what was perhaps a gesture of *rapprochement*—offered to employ as a servant one of Hardy's first cousins from Melbury Osmond. Mary Hand, the eldest daughter of Jemima's brother William, accepted the job—and was subsequently listed as part of the Hardy household in the 1881 census—but told Emma that she did not need to be reimbursed for her fare from Dorset to London: 'I feel I owe you a great deal for your kind consideration when my poor Father died.' [4]

The dangerous and prolonged illness that Hardy suffered during the autumn and winter of 1880–1 contributed further to the suspension of family differences. In mid-October 1880 Hardy and Emma spent a week in Cambridge. They were entertained by three of Horace Moule's brothers, and Hardy's mind was full of poignant and perhaps painful memories of Horace himself. Even his fascination with the shapes made by the dripping wax of the candles in King's College Chapel referred back to the 'shroud' formed by Moule's candle during their last evening together.[5] Hardy felt unwell soon after his arrival at Cambridge, but it was not until he returned to Tooting on 23 October that he acknowledged that something was seriously wrong. The next day his condition had further deteriorated, and a doctor, hastily summoned from nearby, diagnosed an internal haemorrhage and urged an immediate operation. A terrified Hardy and alarmed Emma then appealed to their nearest friends, the Alexander Macmillans, who sent their own doctor. He confirmed the diagnosis and emphasized its gravity but gave it as his opinion that an operation might be avoided if Hardy could be kept in bed, his feet raised above the level of his head, for an extended period.[6]

Hardy accepted the advice and the regime, but the pain was at first so intense that he felt sure that he was going to die—an experience reflected in the poem 'A Wasted Illness':

> Through vaults of pain,
> Enribbed and wrought with groins of ghastliness,
> I passed, and garish spectres moved my brain
>   To dire distress.
>
> And hammerings,
> And quakes, and shoots, and stifling hotness, blent
> With webby waxing things and waning things
>   As on I went.
>
> 'Where lies the end
> To this foul way?' I asked with weakening breath.
> Thereon ahead I saw a door extend—
>   The door to Death.

Hardy, contemplating the experience in retrospect, found like his mother before him an occasion for regret in the realization that recovery meant only that the same terrible route must some day 'be ranged again | To reach that door'.[7] It was, however, to be almost another fifty years before the door was finally reached, and during that long interim he seems to have suffered no other major illness but only a series of milder recurrences of the 'same bladder inflammation' which had brought him low on this one traumatic occasion. The nature and source of that inflammation are not easy to determine. A bladder or even a kidney stone would seem to provide a possible explanation, and it is true that more than six months later, when Hardy was at last able to get up and go out again, he consulted Sir Henry Thompson, the distinguished surgeon, famous especially for his success in removing stones from the bladder. But Kegan Paul had recommended the consultation with Thompson as precautionary only, in order that Hardy might get 'quite free from the fear you had of some worse mischief',[8] and the extraordinary length of Hardy's illness and convalescence tends rather to indicate that the 'bladder inflammation' was complicated by other factors—possibly typhoid fever, contracted during the trip to France. One friend who visited Hardy during his illness remembered him as suffering from jaundice, and it seems in any case entirely likely that total inactivity in an inclined position accompanied by a very restricted diet would prove debilitating in itself and likely to delay recovery.[9]

At the onset of his illness Hardy had already sent off to the printer the first thirteen chapters of *A Laodicean*, equivalent to the first three instalments and a little over, and was probably well advanced with the manuscript for the next few chapters, roughly corresponding to the fourth instalment. But there were still nine instalments left of the thirteen for which he had contracted and Hardy, ill though he was, felt that he had no alternative, professionally speaking, but to deliver each instalment on schedule for as long as humanly possible. His only recourse was to dictate the text to Emma, and in the event it was only her devoted assistance in the multiple roles of nurse, housekeeper, and amanuensis that enabled him to keep up with the printer and so meet his obligations. The expectation of Harper & Brothers that the entire manuscript would be in their hands by December or January had of course become immediately unrealizable, but Hardy staved off any early crisis by putting the finishing touches to the fourth instalment and dispatching it to Bowker more or less on schedule. That was done, heroically, in early November, although he was still in great pain and unable to receive visitors, not only then but throughout the remainder of the month. It was, as he later said of the entire experience, 'an awful job'.[10]

   Hardy's determination not to compromise his carefully cultivated reputation for professional efficiency meant that his outgoing correspondence
must give no hint of the real seriousness of his illness. At a time, therefore,
when Hardy himself was fearing that the illness might prove his last, friends
and colleagues were being told that he was suffering from the consequences
of a severe cold. Bowker, in particular, was assured that the indisposition
'does not affect my writing—indeed it gives me more leisure for the same'.
When such close friends as Charles Kegan Paul and George Smith began
writing to Emma to find out how Hardy really was, a fuller explanation was
required. On 19 November she told Smith that Hardy's illness had 'not
been altogether so severe as has been supposed', although 'a temporary
weakness resulting from the very low diet ordered' had prevented him from
writing himself. The illness, she added, 'has been a sudden local inflamma-
tion that seems to have resulted from a cold, & it will keep him from going
out for some time, as he is mostly obliged to preserve a reclining position,
but his work has hitherto been but little hindered, and we are assured that
his rate of recovery is extremely rapid for the nature of the complaint.' The
qualifications and half-truths here are very Hardyan, and the letter—
like much of the non-extant manuscript of *A Laodicean*—was doubtless
dictated.[11] In so far as the members of Hardy's own family were similarly
put off with half-truths, that was partly because he wanted to save them
from ineffectual anxieties but also because he dreaded the tensions that
might result from their arrival at his bedside. By early 1881, however, when
the worst was safely over, the true situation could be more fully revealed. A
letter from Mary, dated 28 January 1881, gives some sense of the relations
then existing between Emma and her in-laws as well as of the separate and
very different lives that Hardy's parents and siblings were currently living:

My dear Emma,
   I was very glad to hear from you but the iron has again entered into my Soul
respecting Toms illness. I am glad you told me just how he was & I hope he is again
recovering. Perhaps the headache was simply due to keeping the head lower than
usual. If I have a lower pillow than usual my head aches the next morning. I am
glad to find from your letter that our enemies 'winter and rough weather' only
affect you in a modified degree. Poor Katie was reduced, a few days ago, to a few
onions jam and potatoes—a little coal and no candle. She wishes, poor little Soul to
hear from one of you. It is I know as dull and comfortless as the grave at Sandford
[Orcas]. All the schools have been closed but we hope to begin again on Monday.
I don't think there has been such a winter since Granny went to Church walking on
the hedges. . . . I have heard nothing of them from home during the sharp weather
except the Dorchester news which has been that the Bockhampton folk had to live

wholly on potatoes. No bakers could get there I know: but don't be alarmed. Henry is young and strong and they killed a pig quite recently, but I suppose they don't wish to risk Bob's legs if they can avoid it. . . . I should very much like to come and see you again. All this dull weather Katie has been quite lonely & so have I. I wish we could have been with you—if you would have liked us.

Yrs affectly

M. Hardy.[12]

Hardy was able, during that distressing winter, to take mild satisfaction from the generally positive reception of *The Trumpet-Major*, published in three volumes just two or three days after he had taken to his bed. Some reviewers thought the final volume showed signs of hasty writing and found a certain lack of 'finish' throughout, but there was in general a clear and appreciative awareness of what Hardy was setting out to do and of how nearly he was succeeding. The *Pall Mall Gazette*, in particular, put matters squarely:

Mr. Hardy's tales are genuine pastorals, having indeed the form of prose to suit an age which is pre-eminently the age of the novel, but full of a poetry of their own. When we say genuine pastorals, we are thinking not of the exquisitely wrought unrealities of Virgil and of Pope, but of Theocritus, who, dweller in a city though he was, had always the true feeling of country life, and of whom, both when he is serious and in his humoristic touches, Mr. Hardy often reminds us.[13]

A Laodicean, however, the novel with which Hardy was now struggling, was of quite a different character—not especially urban, perhaps, but quite self-consciously modern in setting as well as in spirit, and not in the least pastoral. He did not, therefore, have the option, once the going became difficult, of falling back upon his inherited 'given', the kinds of local and traditional materials that he had so successfully invoked not only in *The Trumpet-Major* but in such earlier novels as *Under the Greenwood Tree*, *Far from the Madding Crowd*, and even *The Return of the Native*. On the other hand, the chapters already in type before the onset of his illness had created an archi-tect hero, George Somerset, and placed him in situations reminiscent of episodes in Hardy's own past: the debate over paedobaptism, for instance, derived directly from those arguments of twenty years earlier with Bastow and the Perkinses. And it was largely by spinning out the architectural 'busi-ness', introducing a series of more or less melodramatic plot developments, and exploiting the notes he had taken during his French and German travels, that Hardy was able to stay the course and fulfil his contract to the satisfaction of Harper & Brothers—if not, perhaps, to their unqualified delight. Hardy had somehow managed to correct the proofs in his own hand throughout his illness, and as time went on he became less and less dependent on dictation, writing the final sections of the manuscript in his own hand—the last page of all on 1 May 1881.[14]

At that date—more than six months after the beginning of his illness—Hardy had still not been out of doors alone. He was confined to his bedroom until well into March—'rather a dreary place to invite friends to', he told Bowker in mid-February—and as late as 6 April 1881 he told George Greenhill:

I am getting on pretty fairly, but don't go out yet—passing my days over the fire, with my feet on the mantelpiece, & a pen in my hand, which does not write as often as it should. . . . I am doing the 12th number of my story, & the nearness of the end prevents my attaining to it quickly—the consciousness that it can be done at any time causing dilatoriness. I should probably have gone out by this time if it had not been for the East wind. But patience is necessary.[15]

Greenhill was one of several London friends whom Hardy learned to appreciate more thoroughly during his illness. Others included his loyal Tooting neighbours, the Alexander Macmillans, Edmund Gosse, then energetically establishing his own semi-scholarly, semi-journalistic career, and Charles Kegan Paul, who had provided information about doctors and tracked down items of information that Hardy needed, or thought he might need, for his novel: on 7 February, for example, he reported a colleague as saying 'that the Telegraphic Instrument with the letters arranged in a circle is known as "Wheatstone's A.B.C. Machine"'.[16]

During these weary months Hardy found himself with all too much time and occasion to reflect upon his work and career, and upon life and art in general. Some of his more aphoristically formulated conclusions found their way, like so much else, into the pages of the novel itself. Other observations, later transferred into *Life and Work*, are so densely argued, and so similar to views expressed throughout the rest of his life, as to suggest that Hardy used this period of personal danger and enforced inactivity as an opportunity to arrive, once and for all, at a personal position on some of the central questions he saw as confronting him as a man and as an artist. A note on Positivism, prompted by the death of George Eliot in December 1880, indicates his continuing to inhabit the optimistic intellectual world of *Far from the Madding Crowd*: 'If Comte had introduced Christ among the worthies in his calendar it would have made Positivism tolerable to thousands who, from position, family connection, or early education, now decry what in their heart of hearts they hold to contain the germs of a true system.' And in April 1881 he and Emma would be invited to the Positivist headquarters at Newton Hall in order to witness the 'presentation' of a daughter of his Dorchester friend Benjamin Fossett Lock.[17]

A few months later, however, there is a distinct shift towards the view of the universe as radically defective, especially in its inability to accommodate the human emotions, that would permeate his later thought, provide the groundnote of the late novels, and gain him that label of 'pessimist' which he so much resented but was never able to shake off:

May 9. After infinite trying to reconcile a scientific view of life with the emotional and spiritual, so that they may not be interdestructive, I come to the following:—

General Principles. Law has produced in man a child who cannot but constantly reproach its parent for doing much and yet not all, and constantly say to such parent that it would have been better never to have begun doing than to have *over-done* so indecisively; that is, than to have created so far beyond all apparent first intention (on the emotional side), without mending matters by a second intention and execution, to eliminate the evils of the blunder of overdoing. The emotions have no place in a world of defect, and it is a cruel injustice that they should have developed in it.

If Law itself had consciousness, how the aspect of its creatures would terrify it, fill it with remorse![18]

The lack of congruence between the views expressed on these two occasions seems not to have disturbed Hardy himself. George Somerset, the hero of *A Laodicean*, adopts a deliberate eclecticism in matters pertaining to archi-tecture, and Hardy seems to have been constantly drawn towards a 'Laodiceanism' of his own—a reluctance to adopt absolute or even firm positions, a willingness to see virtue in all sides of a question, an insistence upon the provisionality of his opinions, and a need to register them rather as a series of tentative impressions than as the systematic formulations of a philosopher. Since the emotions were for Hardy at least as powerful and persuasive as the intellect—hence, perhaps, his attraction to Arnold's concept of 'the imaginative reason'—it becomes necessary to take such disclaimers seriously, and to respond sympathetically, without bemusement or outrage, to those juxtapositions of apparently antithetical statements that occur with some frequency both within Hardy's published works and in the sequences of his surviving notes and reflections.[19]

Hardy's illness had seemed to provide a harsh confirmation of earlier indi-cations, dating back to the 1860s, that he could not for any extended period live in London and remain healthy. It also persuaded him, despite his enjoy-ment of so much that London offered, that it was not an environment in which he could do his best work—that, as *Life and Work* puts it, 'residence in or near a city tended to force mechanical and ordinary productions from his pen, concerning ordinary society-life and habits'. As soon as he was fit to travel, therefore, he and Emma went house-hunting in Dorset once again—the plan for a permanent move to Dorchester having been tempo-rarily set aside, presumably for want of a suitable site—and on 25 June 1881 they moved into a house called Lanherne in The Avenue, Wimborne, now renamed Avenue Road.[20]

Writing to his cousin John Antell, son of the shoemaker, a few days later, Hardy explained that they had come to Wimborne 'for the air, which is considered necessary to my complete restoration', and the town is indeed described in Victorian guidebooks as being both clean and airy. Though small, it was considerably bigger and busier than Sturminster Newton. It was a focal point for the economy of the area, and its ancient minster made it an ecclesiastical and musical centre as well. Little was left, even at that time, of the medieval town, but there were handsome eighteenth-century streets leading off from The Square and some substantial houses on the higher ground to the north. The Avenue itself was in a lower-lying area towards the river and the railway line; its houses were newly built and, as Hardy later recalled, the lime trees to which it owed its name had as yet made little growth:

> They are great trees, no doubt, by now,
>   That were so thin in bough—
>   That row of limes
> When we housed there; I'm loth to reckon when;
>   The world has turned so many times,
>   So many, since then![21]

Sadly, the limes, grown to great trees that overarched the road, were subse-quently cut down to ease the passage of vehicles.[22] Lanherne itself, however, happily survives. Like almost all the houses chosen by the Hardys, it was a typical Victorian villa: detached, solidly built, internally comfortable, and made especially attractive by its possession of a conservatory and a large garden full of fruit trees and bushes and old-fashioned flowers. It was also handy for the railway station, closed in 1964 and now pulled down, but then on a direct line to Waterloo. Since Hardy had no use for the stables and carriage house at the bottom of the garden he made them available to a young Scotsman who was studying farming in the area and lodging near by, the younger brother of Sir George Douglas, a Scottish landowner and gentleman of letters who had already published an admiring sonnet, addressed 'To the Author of "Far from the Madding Crowd"', that began:

'Yours is the empire of an Arcady | More precious than the dreamland of the Greek'. A first meeting with the elder Douglas that autumn, when he came to visit his brother, subsequently developed into one of Hardy's most enduring friendships.[23]

The Hardys spent two years in Wimborne, taking a modest part in its social life but making little attempt to establish themselves as they had done at Sturminster, even though their presence at the ball given by Lord and Lady Wimborne in late December 1881 might well have won them general admission to such society as was constituted by the local gentry and professional middle class.[24] The local Shakespeare Reading Society, which met in private houses, each member taking a part assigned beforehand, attracted Hardy for a time, but he was by now too much the sophisticated Londoner to find anything other than amusement in these amateur occasions: 'The General reads with gingerly caution, telling me privately that he blurted out one of Shakespeare's improprieties last time before he was aware, and is in fear and trembling lest he may do it again.' Hardy himself soon dropped out, leaving behind a reputation as a poor performer who put no expression into his reading. Henry Tindal Atkinson, however, the closest of his Wimborne friends, was much admired for his Shakespearian renditions, winning particular praise for his performance as Shylock in a public reading of the trial scene from *The Merchant of Venice* in May 1883. Although Atkinson was a county court judge on the Dorset, Hampshire, South Somerset, and Salisbury circuit, Hardy liked to refer to him by his former title of Serjeant-at-Law, an ancient legal rank which had become obsolete shortly after his appointment to it in 1864. He was urbane, witty, outgoing, a great reciter of poems—from Macaulay's 'Henry of Navarre' to Hood's 'Faithless Nellie Gray'—and, for the Hardys, a 'genial neighbour' who 'took care they should not mope if dinners and his and his daughter's music could prevent it'.[25]

Clearly, the Hardys did mope, not least because they had from the first assumed that they would move on to Dorchester as soon as building land became available. This sense of impermanence seems, however, to have increased rather than discouraged Hardy's interest in the town and the surrounding area. Much of southern and central Dorset he had known from childhood, largely as a result of the extensive family network into which he was born, and that knowledge had been greatly expanded during his years of visiting and working on village churches on behalf of Hicks and Crickmay. More recently he had spent several months at Swanage, in the south-eastern corner of the county, and the best part of two years at Sturminster Newton, further to the north. He now seized the opportunity of exploring eastern Dorset. He made excursions into the nearby countryside, alone or in the company of his friend Walter Fletcher, architect, land agent, and county surveyor, walking with him on one occasion to the church at Corfe Mullen, where he would have seen the tombs of the Phelipses, the alleged ancestors of Jane Phillips. In July 1881, soon after their first arrival in Wimborne, he and Emma hired a wagonette from a local inn and spent a day visiting Badbury Rings, a large Iron Age fort a few miles to the north-west—although the several pages of notes Hardy made that day dealt not with the fort itself but with the reminiscences of their driver, who had been a postilion in the old coaching days and was full of gossip about the past and present inhabitants of Kingston Lacy and Charborough Park, the two great houses glimpsed along the way.[26]

Also of the Badbury Rings party was Hardy's younger sister Kate, still lonely at her school at Sandford Orcas and delighted to be given a day off for the outing. 'I shall eat such a lot', she warned in advance of her arrival, 'and talk a great deal so I shall be rather troublesome. Come to meet me mind and make a fuss about my coming. I hope you've got some cake.' A letter written after her return begins 'My dearest dears' and describes how fearful she had been of missing her connection during the cross-country train journey—along lines and through stations long since vanished—from Wimborne back to Sherborne. In another warm and affectionate letter to Emma that September she sends thanks for a cape, presumably a birthday present, and announces that she is 'going home tomorrow night as Mary thinks I had better go and see father', Thomas Hardy senior having apparently suffered a fit of nerves in advance of his participation, as singer and violinist, in a village concert got up by the Misses Evangeline and Blanche Smith, daughters of the rector of West Stafford. Kate adds, with characteristic exaggeration, 'I don't know when I have felt so anxious about any thing—never I know. The examinations are nothing compared to it.'[27]

Another visitor to Lanherne that first autumn was Henry Joseph Moule, the eldest of Horace's brothers. Moule, fifteen years Hardy's senior, had known him as a youth and taken a kindly interest in his early exercises in watercolour, but they had lost touch during the intervening years, most of which Moule had spent working as a land agent in Scotland. On the occasion of Moule's first visit they talked 'till the small hours' and discussed ways in which Hardy's literary talents might be combined with the artistic skills that Moule had diligently cultivated over the years. In a subsequent letter to Hardy Moule took up the suggestion, first made by Emma, of 'a book on Dorset written by you with landscape and architectural illustrations by me'. When Hardy turned down the idea, it was ostensibly on the

grounds that it would not pay, but he must also have been reluctant to compromise the autonomy of that fictional world of Wessex with which his
name was becoming so closely associated. The two men nevertheless
remained on the best of terms, despite the difference in their ages, and from
1883 onwards, after Hardy had moved to Dorchester and Moule had
become curator of the Dorset County Museum, their mutual affection and
shared historical interests provided the basis for a friendship that was at
once exceptionally warm and exceptionally relaxed.[28]

Sir George Douglas, writing after Hardy's death, recalled him as possessing
during the Wimborne period 'a robuster figure than any I ever saw again,
robuster and less over-weighted by care. His talk, too, was light and cheerful mainly about literature.'[29] But that is perhaps no more than to say that
Hardy was delighted to entertain a visitor capable of leavening the lump of
Wimborne. He was in fact apprehensively aware of the weaknesses of *A
Laodicean*, shaken still by the physical and emotional debilitation of his illness, and urgently in need of reassurance as to his professional standing as a
writer of imaginative literature—which meant, immediately, fiction,
although notes made during the period of the illness show that poetry was
never far from his thoughts.[30] After a damp and uncomfortable Scottish
tour with Emma in late August and early September of 1881—taking in
Edinburgh, Roslin, Stirling, and the Trossachs and, on the return journey,
Windermere and Chester—Hardy settled down at Lanherne to make the
final corrections to *A Laodicean* in preparation for its publication in three-
volume form. The serial version, meanwhile, was continuing into the
January 1882 number of *Harper's*, and it was not until mid-October 1881
that he could write to Bowker: 'I have examined the revises of Parts 12 & 13,
& find nothing further to correct: so that my task, I believe, is done for the
magazine in that matter.'[31]

Almost simultaneously he received from Thomas Bailey Aldrich, editor
of the *Atlantic Monthly*, a request for a serial for the following year, and
responded promptly with the outline of a new novel. Called *Two on a Tower*,
it would centre on the conflict between a young astronomer's scientific
enthusiasm and his love for an older woman of superior wealth and rank.[32]
Current interest in the Transit of Venus—due to recur in December
1882—had suggested the astronomical theme, although Hardy may also
have recalled the passage in George Eliot's *The Mill on the Floss* in which
Maggie Tulliver concludes that all astronomers must necessarily hate
women 'because, you know, they live up in high towers, and if the women
came there, they might talk and hinder them from looking at the

stars'.[33] The conception of the hero was inspired in part by the youthful seventeenth-century astronomer Jeremiah Horrocks, while the idea of making observations from a tower built for quite other purposes seems to have been suggested by the tower still standing at Charborough Park. The novel's own time-scheme, on the other hand, was entirely contemporary and its specifically scientific emphasis—its attempt 'to set the emotional history of two infinitesimal lives against the stupendous background of the stellar universe'[34]—rendered it, in some respects, even more aggressively 'modern' than *A Laodicean* of so recent and such troubled history. In preparation for the writing of the novel Hardy obtained expert information about lenses and the making of telescopes and contemplated—but seems not to have made—a visit to the Royal Observatory at Greenwich in order to 'ascertain if a hollow memorial pillar, with a staircase inside, can be adapted for the purpose of a small observatory'.[35]

The first edition of *A Laodicean* was published at the beginning of December 1881 to reviews that were for the most part lukewarm but always respectful, never wholly dismissive, and in general considerably more favourable than might have been anticipated. Hardy's attention was, in any case, distracted from them, and from work on *Two on a Tower*, by the distressing controversy that followed the first performance of *The Squire*, by Arthur Wing Pinero, at the St James's Theatre, London, on 29 December 1881. The 'squire' of the title was a woman farmer, and it was immediately apparent that Pinero's conception owed a good deal to *Far from the Madding Crowd*. Still more troubling was the fact that a stage version of that novel, entitled *The Mistress of the Farm: A Pastoral Drama*, had been prepared by Hardy himself in collaboration with J. Comyns Carr, the dramatist and critic, and submitted to John Hare and William Hunter Kendal, the managers of the St James's Theatre, about a year previously. Hare and Kendal provisionally accepted the play and even (so Hardy claimed) put it into rehearsal before finally deciding against it in November 1880. Some time later Kendal's wife, Madge Kendal, the actress, retailed the plot to Pinero, apparently without identifying its source, and *The Squire* was the result.[36]

Hardy knew nothing of Pinero's play until he saw it reviewed in the *Daily News* the morning after the first performance. Puzzled, angry, and more than a little insecure, he rushed to the defence of his professional interests, seeking advice from Tindal Atkinson and composing a letter of protest that duly appeared in *The Times* and the *Daily News* on 2 January 1882, along with a letter from Comyns Carr that cited various corroborative details. The *Daily News* also published a reply from Pinero, admitting that he had read the novel but insisting that his inspiration had come from quite independent sources and that his 'motive, characterisation, and dialogue' were wholly different from Hardy's: 'I merely put my horse's head to the open country and take the same hedges and ditches with him.' Pinero's letter was ill advised, wrote William Black to Hardy that same day: 'We no longer live in an Age of Faith.'[37]

As the arguments rumbled on—the *Theatre* had a 'symposium' on the subject in its February number, *Punch* printed an anti-*Squire* cartoon as late as 8 April—the whole affair became increasingly distasteful to Hardy, as making the entire business of authorship seem as abrasively and sordidly competitive as any other walk of life. A note made on 10 February 1882 spoke poignantly to many features of his past, present, and future career: 'I find that a certain defect in my nature hinders my working abreast with others of the same trade. Architecture was distasteful to me as soon as it became a shoulder to shoulder struggle—literature is likewise—& my only way of keeping up a zest for it is by not mixing with other workers of the same craft.'[38] But if Hardy was hoping that the entire episode would quickly be forgotten, Comyns Carr had seen that there was advantage to be taken of the controversy. He and his wife made a thorough revision of *The Mistress of the Farm*—cutting out the first act, writing a new final act, integrating segments of the printed text with pages of fresh manuscript—got a company together, and opened the play, as *Far from the Madding Crowd*, at the Prince of Wales Theatre, Liverpool, on 27 February 1882.[39] Although Hardy had little part in all this, he was sufficiently encouraged by the enthusiastic reception of the play to travel north in time to catch the final Liverpool performance and his last chance of seeing Marion Terry as Bathsheba. The kind of speech extorted from him at the party following the final curtain would become standard for future occasions when the necessity for speaking at all proved unavoidable: 'I have written many speeches for other people, but when I have to make one myself I'm utterly nonplussed.'[40]

Hardy's lifelong fascination with the theatre—despite distrust of its artifice and contempt for the contemporary fashion for elaborate staging—was much indulged during the 1870s and early 1880s, and it is little wonder that he was impatient with the Shakespearians of Wimborne. He had already met Henry Irving and other leading actors as a consequence of his immersion, while at Tooting, in that London world of clubs and convivial societies—the Savile, the Rabelais, and the rest—in which practitioners of literature, journalism, the theatre, and (in those days) the fine arts were continually being brought together. He wrote to Irving to get seats for *Romeo and Juliet* for Emma and himself on their way home from Liverpool. He invited

Bowker to lunch with the Comyns Carrs and Marion Terry (who failed to turn up).[41] He entered into negotiations for a possible French production of *Far from the Madding Crowd*, and though he had no hand in the disastrous New York adaptation or in the touring performances of the Liverpool production, he did in April attend rehearsals for the London production, which ran for just over ten weeks to general but not universal applause.[42] Mrs Bernard Beere now played Bathsheba while Oak was again played by Ellen Terry's husband, Charles Kelly, of whose occasionally inebriated performances W. S. Gilbert is said to have remarked, 'No one admires Charles Kelly's acting more than I do, but I always feel it more or less indelicate to overhear what he says.' Hardy was present at the successful opening night at the Globe Theatre on 29 April and seems to have responded to the applause by making a brief but presumably silent appearance: 'I should so much like to see Tom on the stage,' wrote Kate to Emma. 'I daresay he looked very nice.'[43]

Hardy had other professional annoyances to put up with in 1882. The *Academy* of 18 February reprinted from American journals two sets of parallel passages purporting to prove that Hardy had plagiarized not only A. B. Longstreet's *Georgia Scenes* in chapter 23 of *The Trumpet-Major* but also a *Quarterly Review* article by 'Nimrod' (Charles Apperley) in chapter 5 of *A Laodicean*. Hardy does indeed seem to have been guilty in these two instances of using notebook material he had earlier copied from published sources, although his source for the passage in *The Trumpet-Major* was in fact the family copy of Gifford's *History of the Wars Occasioned by the French Revolution*, Gifford and Longstreet having themselves drawn upon a common source.[44] That summer he encountered a similar problem from a different angle when a magazine called *London Society* published over his name a poem entitled 'Two Roses'—the work, as it turned out, of another Thomas Hardy, whom Hardy had apparently known during his days with Blomfield. Offended not only by the appropriation of his name but by the badness of the verses to which it had been attached, Hardy wrote to W. Moy Thomas, as secretary of the Copyright Association, to ask what rights he had to the exclusive literary use of his own name when he happened to share it with someone else. As he complained to Thomas, it seemed that he was 'doomed to squabbles this year!'[45] Nor was that to be the last.

Hardy spent the summer of 1882 in Wimborne, working on the manuscript of *Two on a Tower*. The Hardys' cook at Lanherne, a young woman with a broad Dorset accent, later described Hardy as customarily spending much time in the kitchen, smiling at the servants and encouraging them to talk their Dorset talk, and then disappearing into his study (the room behind the conservatory) and writing for the rest of the day, ignoring even meal-times.[46] He seems, even so, not to have given *Two on a Tower* his full creative attention. He allowed his work to be interrupted by short expeditions to Dorchester, where he was still seeking a plot of building land, and to places in the vicinity of Wimborne itself, by a tour in September to Salisbury, Axminster, and various towns in west Dorset, the part of the county he now knew least well—and by a trip of several weeks to Paris during October and early November. This time he and Emma did not stay in a hotel but took a small apartment in the rue des Beaux Arts, did much of their own house-keeping, and spent their days in what seems to have been a pleasantly desultory and essentially amicable fashion, shopping, dining out, seeing sights, buying books, visiting galleries and theatres—though as usual they caught bad colds, attributed to 'the uncertain weather'.[47] As Hardy later confessed to Gosse, the planning of *Two on a Tower* had been careful enough, but 'the actual writing was lamentably hurried having been produced month by month, & the MS dispatched to America, where it was printed without my seeing the proofs. It would have been rewritten for the book form if I had not played truant & gone off to Paris.'[48]

Publication in book form was by Sampson Low, who brought out the novel in three volumes in late October 1882. Some of the reviewers were prepared to be impressed and even moved by the 'astronomical' aspects of the book, and especially by the conversations between Swithin St Cleeve and Viviette Constantine on the tower, but few felt that these elements had been sufficiently integrated into the central story. Almost all expressed some degree of distress at the narrative twists by which Viviette, finding herself pregnant by the absent Swithin, entraps into marriage—and hence into vicarious parenthood—the somewhat pompous Bishop of Melchester. Kegan Paul, himself a former Anglican clergyman, told Hardy it was 'a marvellously comic touch' that the victim should be a bishop, but public comment was generally in line with the *Saturday Review*'s condemnation of the episode as 'extremely repulsive'.[49] The advertisement Hardy himself drew up for insertion in various journals at the beginning of December unwisely emphasized just those aspects of the book that had given offence: 'Being the story of the unforeseen relations into which a lady and a youth many years her junior were drawn by studying the stars together; of her desperate situation through generosity to him; and of the reckless *coup d'audace* by which she effected her deliverance.'[50]

In mid-January 1883 the reviewer in the *St James's Gazette* argued that the bishop's fate not only shocked the reader, as it was evidently intended to do, but insulted the Church. Hardy's defence, printed in the *Gazette* on 19 January, once again seems less than persuasive:

Purely artistic conditions necessitated an episcopal position for the character alluded to, as will be apparent to those readers who are at all experienced in the story-telling trade. Indeed, that no *arrière-pensée* of the sort suggested had existence should be sufficiently clear to everybody from the circumstance that one of the most honourable characters in the book, and the hero's friend, is a clergyman, and that the heroine's most tender qualities are woven in with her religious feelings.[51]

It is impossible not to side with Hardy in the various Grundyan difficulties he encountered during his career, but not always easy to sympathize with the tactics by which he sought to exculpate himself. His response in this particular instance does not begin to meet the real objections of his critics, although its evasiveness pales by comparison with his assertion that there was 'hardly a single caress in the book outside legal matrimony, or what was intended so to be'.[52] There *is*, after all, a difference—on which, indeed, much of the action of the novel turns—between the fact of matrimony and the intention, and what distressed the moralists about that one acknowledged caress was precisely its coinciding with the moment when the marriage between the hero and heroine was known to be invalid—and its being sufficiently prolonged to result in the child subsequently fathered upon the unsuspecting bishop. Hardy appears at his least attractive at such moments, and while his comments are always organized around a kernel of literal truth, he cannot be acquitted of disingenuousness. From time to time he also created difficulties for himself by making misleading or insufficiently transparent declarations of intention, and the editor of the *Atlantic Monthly* was not the last to have grounds for complaining—as Aldrich is said to have done—that Hardy had promised him a family story but supplied instead a story in the family way.[53]

Sending his friend Edmund Gosse a copy of *Two on a Tower* on 4 December 1882, Hardy expressed confidence that he at least would 'perceive, if nobody else does, what I have aimed at—to make science, not the mere padding of a romance, but the actual vehicle of romance'. Gosse first wrote merely to acknowledge the gift and to say how much the American novelist, William Dean Howells, on a recent visit to London, had regretted not being able to meet Hardy, 'the man in all England whom he most wanted to see'. But once he had actually read the novel, Gosse expressed great admiration for it and even greater admiration for Hardy's achievement as a whole:

Your books are very important to me. I look upon you as without approach the best English novelist living. . . . Nothing in your style or manner offends me, although I admit that you are a little Alexandrian sometimes. . . . But you still preserve the great manner, the originality and audacity, the real breath of imaginative inspiration. I watch you as if you were the Dodo. When English fiction loses you, it will lose everything.[54]

Gosse's deliberate cultivation of his famous, his aristocratic, and even his potentially useful contemporaries was an essential ingredient in his career and one of the bases of his eventual influence and success. But if Gosse was eager to please he was also able to please. He had charm, humour, a ready tongue, and a facile and indefatigable pen. That he became the recipient of some of the best letters of Henry James, Robert Louis Stevenson, and many others was chiefly because he was himself so lively and entertaining a correspondent. The devotion with which Gosse pursued his game often became indistinguishable from friendship itself and, in the end, not notably more self-serving than many of the relationships dignified by that name. Although Hardy in later years would come to distrust Gosse, to suspect him, rightly or wrongly, of troublemaking, deliberate indiscretion, and a gossip's inability to resist the pleasures of malice, there can be no doubt that for much of his career it was Gosse who provided him with his nearest approach to an intimate literary friendship.[55]

Hardy would have registered the extravagance in Gosse's letter about *Two on a Tower*, but its warmth and directness provided just the kind of reassurance he needed at that particular moment. His illness and its professional consequences still weighed upon him, as did the 'warm epithets' that had been employed during the attacks on *Two on a Tower*. News had also arrived in late November of the death of Emma's brother-in-law, the Reverend Caddell Holder, remembered in *Life and Work* as a man of 'genuine and genial humour', and life at Wimborne was proving increasingly irksome.[56] 'We propose to leave Wimborne for good about March,' Hardy reported to Gosse in December 1882: 'the house we are in lies rather too near the Stour level for health.'[57] As in 1876, when their departure from Sturminster Newton had been blamed on the air from the higher reaches of the river Stour, so again the environmental explanation did duty for a multitude of others not so readily expressible to outsiders. Hardy was as ready as Emma to be hypochondriacal about dampness and bad air—one of his most frequent recommendations of Dorchester houses in later years was that they were built 'on the chalk'—but she was primarily dissatisfied, as at Sturminster, with the smallness and dullness of the town and its failure to answer to the extravagant expectations of social and literary eminence she continued to project both on her husband's behalf and, evidently, on her own. Mrs Dashwood, writing to Emma from Sturminster at about this time, asked about Hardy's work but continued, with perhaps a touch of irony: 'I hope your stories will emerge one after the other and pleasantly astonish the literary world, they have been concocting in your brain long enough and should now see the light.'[58]

12

Return to Dorchester

Although the Hardys did not get away from Wimborne in April 1883, they were able to do so at midsummer, when the second year of their lease expired. 'We leave this place in the latter part of the month—much to my exhilaration,' Hardy told Gosse on 12 June. 'A man has been here to look at our furniture, which he "carries in his eye" (so he says) till he has made an estimate for removing it.'[1] But if Hardy was glad to turn his back on Wimborne, the time spent there had been by no means unproductive. It had provided him with a comfortable and undemanding context in which to recover from his illness. It had given him the opportunity to get the 'feel' of Dorset again without having to confront the kinds of social pressure that the return to Dorchester would bring. And it had allowed and even compelled him to undertake that reconsideration of his whole career—past, present, and future—which would eventually bear fruit in *The Mayor of Casterbridge* and the other major achievements of the next several years.

Implicit in some notes from the summer of 1882 is the realization, even before the completion of *Two on a Tower*, that he had somehow lost his way in his last two novels and needed to return to the material he best knew and understood and to the narrative modes that had won him his earlier successes and established for his readers a distinctive sense of his individuality. A comment in May 1882 about the 'slow meditative lives of people who live in habitual solitude' finds an echo that August in a more specifically literary formulation: 'An ample theme: the intense interests, passions, and strategy that throb through the commonest lives.' A note made on 3 June, the day after his forty-second birthday, elaborates a theoretical justification for trusting more absolutely to his own deepest instincts as an observer and recorder of the human and natural world: 'As, in looking at a carpet, by following one colour a certain pattern is suggested, by following another colour, another; so in life the seer should watch that pattern among general things which his idiosyncrasy moves him to observe, and describe that alone. This is, quite accurately, a going to Nature; yet the result is no mere photograph, but purely the product of the writer's own mind.'[2]

The Wimborne period also saw the surfacing of some of the social and humanitarian concerns that would be central to Hardy's subsequent life and work. His interest in recording and, whenever possible, preserving oral and physical survivals from the local past found practical expression in his cooperation with the Society for the Protection of Ancient Buildings in its attempts to prevent the destruction of old buildings and oppose the mutilation of churches by the kind of 'restoration' in which he had himself participated while working for Hicks and Crickmay.[3] He offered, in particular, to keep a watchful eye on work being done on Wimborne Minster, and his poem 'Copying Architecture in an Old Minster', though perhaps not written at Wimborne, certainly relates to his experiences at that time— as, in a rather different way, does the broad comedy of jumbled tombstones ('Here's not a modest maiden elf | But dreads the final Trumpet, | Lest half of her should rise herself, | And half some sturdy strumpet!') of 'The Levelled Churchyard'.[4]

By this time, too, the iron had begun to enter into his soul (to use one of his and Mary's favourite phrases) in respect of the sufferings of animals, and there is praise for Emma—to be repeated on many subsequent occasions— for her 'admirable courage' in protesting, on the spot and in defiance of the disapproval of others, against the abuse of horses and other creatures, whether beaten, neglected, or given tasks too great for their strength.[5] Hardy himself was particularly oppressed by the mass slaughter of game birds on local estates: Lord Wimborne's guests, a few weeks before the ball which the Hardys attended in December 1881, had killed in one day 1,418 pheasants, 35 hares, 48 rabbits, and 2 partridges. Early in January 1882, after a conversation with a gamekeeper he had met, Hardy made a note in which his distress visibly rises to the point at which it begins to evolve from the keeper's words the outlines of what was to become one of the most powerful episodes in *Tess of the d'Urbervilles*:

[T]ells me that one day this season they shot—(3 guns) 700 pheasants in one day— a *battue*—driving the birds into one corner of the plantation. When they get there they will not run across the open ground—rise on the wing—then are shot wholesale. They pick up all that have fallen—night comes on—the *wounded* birds that have hidden or risen into some thick tree fall, & lie on the ground in their agony—

next day the keepers come & look for them. (They found 150, on the above occasion, next day)—Can see the night scene—moon—fluttering & gasping birds as the hours go on—the place being now deserted of humankind.[6]

In the novel, of course, Tess suffers along with the birds, their fate in some sense imaging hers.

It was also during the Wimborne period that a deeper, or perhaps a more directly expressed, concern for the rural working class began to appear in Hardy's writings. Although limited space is given to the rural characters in *Two on a Tower*, they are handled sympathetically and allowed to be more specific about their economic hardships than their predecessors in earlier Hardy novels. This was a touchy subject, however, and one that Hardy handled somewhat gingerly in the long essay on 'The Dorsetshire Labourer' that he wrote at the invitation of *Longman's Magazine* during the early months of 1883. Although he personally supported the Liberals in their undertaking to give agricultural workers the vote, he sought, then as always, to avoid in his writings any appearance of espousing a particular political viewpoint: as he told John Morley (to whom and to Gladstone he sent copies of the published essay), 'Though a Liberal, I have endeavoured to describe the state of things without political bias.'[7] Later in 1883 he turned down an invitation to write an article dealing specifically with the political aspects of the agricultural labourers' situation, and even when working to the much broader specifications indicated by *Longman's* he chose to present several separate facets of the subject rather than to argue a case or offer an overall assessment.

Although Hardy has often been discussed as if he were primarily a chronicler of agricultural decline, the evidence of 'The Dorsetshire Labourer' suggests that he viewed the depressed state of agriculture in the early 1880s as less than disastrous. That depression, extending throughout the late nineteenth and early twentieth centuries, is now generally perceived as having been less severe, overall, than used to be believed, and Dorset's emphasis on livestock farming had in any case enabled it to escape the worst consequences of the influx of cheap cereals from North America.[8] Hardy's essay, in fact, does not directly address the general state of agriculture, and while it sharply evokes the exploitation and virtual serfdom to which agricultural labourers had been exposed in the past, it presents their current situation—enhanced by improved wages and a 'pastoral environment'—as reasonably satisfactory. It does, on the other hand, devote a good deal of space to some of the less fortunate effects of that increased mobility which Hardy saw as both the source and the consequence of the labourer's exercise of greater economic power. It laments the loss of the old generations-long intimacies between the land and those who worked it and the disappearance of that 'interesting and better-informed' class of rural trades-men and craftsmen to which Hardy's own forebears had belonged and which he saw as having contributed so much to the self-sufficient village communities of the past. It laments above all, perhaps, the erosion of that oral tradition which had played so important a part in Hardy's own upbringing and been so richly drawn upon in his fiction.[9]

Hardy was too much of a progressive to believe that the social consequences of this historical process were entirely bad, and too much of a realist to imagine that the process could somehow be reversed. But such recognitions only endorsed conclusions already reached about his strengths and needs as a writer and the importance of making an early return to the country of his youth—since reclaimed as the country of his imagination—before the old ways of thinking, speaking, and acting had entirely vanished, and before all the witnesses of the days before his own childhood had finally passed away. The essentially negative impulses which were driving the Hardys away from Wimborne thus served to reinforce the many positive reasons Hardy himself had earlier discovered for a permanent removal to Dorchester, and perhaps did something to reconcile Emma to what she must have seen as a momentous and possibly perilous step.

Hardy's Wimborne writings of late 1882 and early 1883 had included the short stories 'The Romantic Adventures of a Milkmaid' and 'The Three Strangers', and in the summer of 1883 he completed for an American magazine the children's story 'Our Exploits at West Poley', destined to remain unpublished for almost ten years.[10] When 'The Dorsetshire Labourer' and the various revisions of *Two on a Tower* (for the second printing of the first edition, the Tauchnitz edition, and the first one-volume edition) are added, the list testifies to Hardy's revived energy and to that 'versatility of his genius' which was praised, along with much else, by Havelock Ellis in a long and discriminating survey in the *Westminster Review*.[11] But the very range and variety of Hardy's production had its troubling aspects. 'The Romantic Adventures of a Milkmaid'—hastily composed, as Hardy acknowledged, and with occasional sections of the manuscript written out in Emma's hand[12]—was a loosely constructed exercise in fantasy-romance that derived its modest charm from the juxta-position of authentic rural description with the vaguely 'Gothic' elements embodied in the mysterious figure of Baron von Xanten. 'The Three Strangers', on the other hand, was a tightly organized story in which the considerable narrative excitement depended directly upon the integration of the plot with the precisely relevant circumstances of period, setting, and characterization.

If the surrender to non-realism in 'Romantic Adventures' represented the culmination of the phase of Hardy's career most substantially represented by *A Laodicean* and *Two on a Tower*, the future of that career would prove to be in the direction marked out by 'The Three Strangers', later collected as the first in a volume of *Wessex Tales*. In the poem 'He Abjures Love', specifically dated 1883, what seems to be abjured is not love as a personal emotion but rather that 'conception of love as the one business of life' which Havelock Ellis had identified as one of the earliest and most persistent characteristics of Hardy's work. The poem, in this sense, signals a prospective change in both theme and technique, a shift away from love as a dominating motive and from romance as a method:

> No more will now rate I
> The common rare,
> The midnight drizzle dew,
> The gray hour golden,
> The wind a yearning cry,
> The faulty fair,
> Things dreamt, of comelier hue
> Than things beholden! . . .

The implications, however, of such a renunciation, whether personal or professional, are acknowledged in all their bleakness:

> But—after love what comes?
> A scene that lours,
> A few sad vacant hours,
> And then, the Curtain.[13]

The stoicism for which the poem has often been praised is here scarcely distinguishable from disillusion and life-weariness, and it is interesting to set alongside these lines the conservative message—'the sufficiently apparent moral', as Hardy himself phrased it—of 'Our Exploits at West Poley'. If the youthful narrator of that story is occasionally reminiscent of the young Thomas Hardy, there is more than a hint of the mature Hardy in the odd figure of the Man who had Failed, whose wisdom is said to derive from his having 'failed, not from want of sense, but from want of energy' (that lack of which Hardy so often complained), and whose final advice is strongly against meddlesome interference in the established patterns of nature and society: 'Quiet perseverance in clearly defined courses is, as a rule, better

than the erratic exploits that may do much harm.'[14] As he contemplated his
return to Dorchester, Hardy was perhaps already speculating whether it
might not have been better if he had never left—and never embarked upon
at least some of his erratic geographical, professional, and emotional
exploits of the past several years.

Hardy and Emma had anticipated the end of their 'Lanherne' lease by
spending a good deal of time in London during the late spring and early
summer of 1883, 'seeing pictures, plays, and friends'. They lunched with
Browning and Rhoda Broughton at Lord Houghton's and called upon Mrs
Procter, when Browning, who was again present, irritated Hardy by his
habit, during a conversation, of glancing around the room in search of
bigger social game. For Hardy, there was a Rabelais Club dinner in honour
of Henry Irving and a private dinner at which Gosse at last succeeded in
bringing him together with William Dean Howells in the company of such
older acquaintances as Austin Dobson, William Black, George Du
Maurier, and the sculptors Thomas Woolner and Hamo Thornycroft.[15]
Much as he had enjoyed the evening, Howells told Gosse the following
day, 'I felt that after all I had only shaken hands with Hardy across his
threshold.'[16] Though Hardy was not the most clubbable of men, and sometimes entertained doubts as to the wisdom of mixing too much with other
workers in the same craft, he clearly did not envisage an absolute seclusion
from London and its overlapping social and artistic worlds. Nor would
Dorchester be regarded as a place of impregnable retirement: Gosse himself—a quintessential representative of the London literary scene—was, on
21 July 1883, one of the first visitors to the house in the county town to which
the Hardys had moved at the end of June.

Shire-Hall Place, as it was called, formerly the headmaster's house of the
Dorset County School, stood on the west side of Shire-hall Lane (now
Glyde Path Road) immediately adjoining the grounds of Colliton House. A
long, narrow building, it extended along the back of several houses on the
north side of High West Street, and the only access to it from Shire-hall
Lane was through an archway and up a passage. In a letter to Thornycroft,
Gosse referred to it as 'a rambling house. . . of which a townsman said, "He
have but one window and she do look into Gaol Lane." It is indeed a kind
of mole, for the entrance is almost invisible and its burrow extends to the
back of everything.' Writing to his wife he described it as 'a most queer
rambling old house, such as would rejoice your heart, built on ever so many
levels at ever so many periods'.[17]

Hardy had met Gosse at the railway station, walked him to the house, and there introduced him to Emma, whom Gosse somewhat unkindly described in that same letter home as a middle-aged and less handsome version of the notoriously garrulous Mrs William Bell Scott. 'She means', he added, 'to be very kind.' Henry J. Moule joined them at high tea, and in the evening the three men walked together around the town and into the fringes of that countryside by which—like the fictional Casterbridge in the novel Hardy was soon to begin writing—it was so immediately surrounded. Dorchester, Gosse told his wife,

is extremely bright & pretty; there are two barracks just outside it, one cavalry, one infantry, so that the narrow streets are full of colour & animation, & being a country town, the farmers and labourers were crowding in to their Saturday night's shopping, so it looked in the dusk like a bright foreign town. Mr Moule left us presently, but Hardy & I continued to walk in & out of the town, and round the old walls, which now are walks avenued with chestnuts, until 10.30, by the light of the moon.[18]

The next day, a Sunday, Hardy took Gosse to visit William Barnes at his church and rectory of Winterborne Came, just south of Dorchester. Gosse had already corresponded with Barnes and reviewed one of his volumes in favourable terms, but Hardy, setting up the arrangement in advance, knew the old poet well enough to insinuate a touch of supplementary flattery: Gosse, he said, was not only one of Barnes's 'sincerest admirers' but had declared himself ready to 'come to Dorset any day or hour for the pleasure of seeing you'. Barnes, for his part, responded with a characteristic touch of theatricality, performing his pastoral duties with an obtrusive punctiliousness and delivering a standard sermon that was in no way dressed up for the benefit of his literary visitors. After the service Barnes stayed on at the church to hear a choir practice before walking back to the rectory with his guests, talking all the time about antiquarian and philological matters rather than about his poetry, the topic on which Gosse had hoped to draw him out.[19]

Within just a week or two of this visit Hardy found himself attending the deathbed of Barnes's most brilliant pupil, Thomas William Hooper Tolbort, at the house of John Pouncy, the Dorchester photographer. Tolbort, now 41 years old, had risen after his spectacular examination successes to the rank of Deputy Commissioner in the Bengal Civil Service and published transliterations into 'the Roman character', as one of the title pages puts it, of a Persian translation of *Robinson Crusoe* and an Urdu translation of the *Arabian Nights*. He had, however, contracted consumption in the early 1880s and been forced to leave India, spending part of the summer of 1882 in Dorchester and the succeeding winter in Algiers. Hardy's obituary of him in the *Dorset County Chronicle* for 16 August 1883 brings the story to its sad conclusion:

To Dorchester he again returned about three weeks ago, shattered in health, but still full of plans for the future. A sudden accession of his dreadful cough broke down his fragile frame completely, and in five days after his arrival he was dead. Even on the last day that sanguine mood which so often prevails in those who are the victims of this malady permitted him to entertain only a slight suspicion that his death-warrant had come; and there is on this account intense pathos in the words which now lie before me—the last he ever wrote—directions jotted down in pencil (for he could not speak) in a hand remarkably firm and flowing for one in his dying condition. The words are: 'I daresay I shall get over this all right, but in case anything should happen to me before my book is printed I would ask you to get it published for me. . . . The papers are all on the table in the next room—a big heap of them. . . .'[20]

That manuscript, entitled 'The Portuguese in India', proved unpublishable, Tolbort's 'sanguine mood' having no doubt encouraged him to overstate its nearness to completion. So cruelly premature a termination of so hopeful a career moved Hardy deeply and became merged in his mind with memories of Horace Moule, who had helped and encouraged Tolbort and whose own bright promise had ended in a similarly unanticipated disaster. Moule is specifically mentioned in Hardy's obituary of Tolbort, and the two doomed careers may well have contributed something to Hardy's conception of the rise and fall of Michael Henchard, the central figure of *The Mayor of Casterbridge*.

The juxtaposition of the names of William Barnes, Horace Moule, and Hooper Tolbort is indicative of the degree to which Hardy, in these early months of his return to Dorchester, found himself driven, willingly and unwillingly, back upon his past and especially upon his memories of the times, twenty and thirty years back, when he was a schoolboy in Dorchester and then an apprentice architect, criticized from a church pulpit as an overambitious upstart. In the present moment he and Emma were chiefly and for the most part quietly concerned to establish themselves in the town in a manner appropriate to their new middle-class status. Local knowledge of Hardy's humbler background made for a difficult transition. Dorchester was full of people who remembered him from his schooldays or from his years in Hicks's South Street office. His family were still living at Higher Bockhampton, his father and brother still actively in business as jobbing builders, and when, a year or two later, Hardy was elected to the council of the Dorset County Museum he was identified in the council's minutes as 'Mr Thomas Hardy junr', a formula directly indicative of his socio-economic as well as of his biological origins.[21]

It helped a little that his sister Mary was now headmistress of the little infants' school in Bell Lane, and his own new-found reputation as a writer certainly counted for something. If it did not exactly bring him honour in his own country, it at least meant that people knew who he was, and if local gossip responded—as local gossip will—with outward denigration and inner envy, there were others who appreciated and admired his work and valued his friendship. Emma would always feel ignored by the 'county' set, but Evangeline and Alice Smith, accompanied by their father and their brother, Bosworth Smith, soon came to call 'on Mr. Hardy the Author in the nice house', and Mary Sheridan, wife of the grandson of Richard Brinsley Sheridan and daughter of the American historian John Lothrop Motley, was another early visitor.[22] Augusta Everett, wife of the rector of St Peter's Church, invited them to meet Oscar Wilde following his talk on 'The House Beautiful' under the auspices of the Dorchester Lecture Society on 27 September 1883, and a few weeks later Hardy himself was asking Bret Harte to come down from London to give a lecture for the Society and throwing in, all hospitably, the offer of a bed, 'if plain accommodation will suffice'.[23] The Hardys were also on friendly terms with their solicitor, Arthur Henry Lock, whose son later recalled going to a party given at Shire-Hall Place for Emma's young nephew and niece, Gordon and Lilian Gifford, who were staying with them at the time.[24]

There were more formal recognitions of Hardy's return to Dorchester and accession to middle-class status. In April 1884, less than a year after his arrival, he was appointed a justice of the peace for the Borough of Dorchester, swearing the necessary oaths in August, and taking his seat upon the bench early in September. Although his attendance was always erratic, he took his sometimes painful duties with all due seriousness, bought himself a copy of Samuel Stone's *The Justices' Manual*, and—no less characteristically—introduced into *The Mayor of Casterbridge* the scene in which the old furmity-woman turns the tables upon Henchard as he presides over the Borough Petty Sessions.[25] The promptness of Hardy's appointment as a JP suggests that an element of political patronage was involved. Hardy had not hesitated to identify himself as a Liberal; he was on friendly terms with Robert Pearce Edgcumbe, an influential local Liberal and frequent Liberal candidate; and on 3 November 1885, eighteen months after becoming a JP, he sat on the platform together with Pearce Edgcumbe and other prominent citizens at a Liberal Party pre-election meeting held in the Dorchester Corn Exchange.[26]

Election fever was high, the speakers included a government minister, and the audience, made up of Conservatives as well as of Liberals, was estimated by the local newspaper to have numbered somewhere between six and seven hundred. Hardy evidently took no active part in the proceedings, but he must subsequently have questioned—especially when the Liberals lost the ensuing election—the wisdom of alienating large numbers of his fellow citizens not just by publicly identifying himself with a particular party but by arrogating to himself the right to appear before them from the altitude of a raised platform. Hardy never again made so openly political a gesture, and while he remained a Liberal he sought as a writer to distance himself from politics entirely. Declining in 1892 an invitation to nominate Pearce Edgcumbe as a parliamentary candidate, he said that it would have given him pleasure to do so had he not been 'compelled to forego all participation in active politics, by reason of the neutrality of my own pursuits, which would be stultified to a great extent if I could not approach all classes of thinkers from an absolutely unpledged point'. In 1894, however, when he was elevated from a borough to a county magistrate, with the right to serve as a grand juror at the quarterly Assizes, he knew that he again had Pearce Edgcumbe chiefly to thank.[27]

It was while he was living at Shire-Hall Place that Hardy was first 'taken up' by members of the aristocracy. An introduction to Lady Portsmouth in June 1884 was followed in March 1885 by an invitation to visit her and her husband, the fifth Earl, at Eggesford House, their country seat in Devon. Since Emma was forced by illness to remain in Dorchester, Hardy went alone and was more than a little overwhelmed by the welcome he received not only from Lady Portsmouth herself but from her family of young daughters—who were, as he reported to Emma, 'very attentive, & interested in what I tell them'. Hardy was supposed to be continuing with his writing during the visit, and the library was put at his exclusive disposal, but the company and the local countryside proved too attractive and he spent most of his time driving, walking, and talking with Lord Portsmouth ('a farmer-like man with a broad Devon accent') and more especially with his womenfolk.[28]

The pattern of Hardy's subsequent relationship to the world of rich, titled, and handsome women can already be perceived in this first visit to the Portsmouths—if, indeed, it was not already perceptible in his responsiveness, years before, to Julia Augusta Martin and Geneviève Smith. He was well aware of the extravagance of that world, the artificiality of the elegance which made its inhabitants so alluring: 'But these women!' he exclaimed after a London social gathering early in 1890. 'If put into rough wrappers in a turnip-field, where would their beauty be?'[29] Neither that awareness, however, nor his profound sympathy with the victimized women of the lower classes—with those, like Tess, who actually worked in turnip fields—prevented him from enjoying the social and intellectual companionship of upper-class women, nor from responding to their personal attractions. Hardy remained emotionally susceptible to physical and social graces that had been quite unknown to his early experience, and it is possible to perceive in the circumstances of the Eggesford visit—in Emma's absence, in Hardy's delight at finding himself the centre of interest for an 'extraordinarily sympathetic group of women', and in his somewhat insensitive expression of that delight in his letter home—further signs of those difficulties within his own marriage that were to cause such grief only a few years later. Emma's first reaction, however, was to celebrate the social elevation the Portsmouths' invitation seemed to imply. She wrote off to her most distinguished relative, Edwin Hamilton Gifford, recently appointed Archdeacon of London, to tell him the good news, receiving in reply the polite hope that her husband would find his friendship with Lady Portsmouth 'of permanent advantage to him'.[30]

Of particular importance to Hardy in his new Dorchester life was the opportunity to participate in interests and organizations of a specifically local character. He had been for some time a member of the Dorset Natural History and Antiquarian Field Club, and when in January 1884 the Dorset County Museum opened in its new (that is to say, its present) premises under the curatorship of his friend Henry J. Moule, he immediately became a frequent visitor. Even before the reopening of the museum, however, Hardy had found himself at cross-purposes with a prominent local antiquary named Edward Cunnington, who had made a number of significant archaeological 'finds' near Dorchester in the early 1880s—including, according to a recent authority, 'an amber cup, allegedly complete till Cunnington trod on it'.[31] Neither Hardy nor Moule liked or fully trusted Cunnington. Moule, writing on the last day of 1883, reported that he had told Mr Cunnington about some arrow points Hardy had found on the heath, 'carefully concealing name of person & *places*', and Cunnington's excavation of a Romano-Celtic temple at the eastern end of the great Iron Age hill fort known as Maiden Castle was made—almost libellously, one would think—the subject of Hardy's story 'A Tryst at an Ancient Earthwork', published across the Atlantic in the *Detroit Post* in March 1885 but not printed in England until December 1893. Hardy had already made a half-ironical reference to Cunnington as the 'local Schliemann' in a paper that he read at a Dorchester meeting of the Field Club on 13 May 1884, and while that paper was slight and amateur it was presumably Cunnington's animosity towards its author that determined its omission from the club's published *Proceedings* for a full six years thereafter.[32]

Described in Hardy's paper were the skeletons, urns, and other Romano-British relics that had been discovered during the digging of the foundations of the house that Hardy had designed and was having built for himself on the outskirts of the town. His search for a plot of building land, begun before his removal from Tooting to Wimborne,[33] had involved a protracted correspondence with the Duchy of Cornwall, far and away the largest landowner in the area, and ended with the lease and subsequent purchase of a one-and-a-half-acre piece of open ground, a little to the south-east of Dorchester, that had been in the possession of the Duchy since the fourteenth century. The Duchy, however, had recently decided to make some of its extensive Dorchester lands available for building, and by the time formal correspondence about a specific site began in late 1882 both Hardy and the Duchy officials seem to have been quite clear as to its exact location and dimensions. Hardy once privately acknowledged that his application to the Duchy had been specifically approved by the Prince of Wales, who, as heir to the throne, held the title of Duke of Cornwall and depended upon the Duchy for his income—though it remains unclear whether that approval was given on the basis of the Prince's familiarity with Hardy's work or as the result of a recommendation from a mutual acquaintance.[34] Hardy was able, at all events, to include a rough plan of the site in his initial letter of application and be equally straightforward about what he intended to build: 'a villa Residence and Offices, Stabling &c. on plans to be approved of & to cost £1000 at least'. The lease that Hardy was obliged to enter into in the first instance was signed—and witnessed by Henry Tindal Atkinson—in mid-June of 1883, just two weeks before the Hardys' departure from Wimborne, and Kate was able to send them off with a letter that ended '*Success to the building scheme!!!*'[35] A surviving estimate for the installation of a lifting pump for the well is dated 31 August 1883; work on the preparation of the site began on 26 November; and New Year's Eve found Hardy planting some of the hundreds of trees, mostly beech and Austrian pine, that were needed to shelter the house in its high and exposed position but would eventually shut it in to an almost claustrophobic degree.[36]

Hardy was himself the architect of the new house, and its construction was assigned to the Hardy family firm, now largely under the direction of

Hardy's brother. The building grew at a slow pace, but Hardy kept a watchful eye on the work during all its stages. He and Emma remained meanwhile in their rented house in the centre of town, close to the Dorchester shops and markets and within three minutes' walk of the new museum and its handsome reading room, well stocked with works on the history, natural history, geology, and archaeology of the locality, and regularly supplied with the latest issues of the leading newspapers and magazines. Some journals, such as the major quarterlies, were kept and bound, but those auctioned off to members on a yearly basis were likely to include *Punch*, *Graphic*, *Illustrated London News*, *Spectator*, *Saturday Review*, *Chambers's Journal*, *Harper's Monthly*, *English Illustrated Magazine*, *Fortnightly Review*, *Nineteenth Century*, and *Musical Times*.[37] Remote as Dorchester might seem from the perspective of a Londoner, Hardy was never cut off from regular access to the main organs of intellectual communication. The London papers, morning and afternoon, would of course reach Dorchester on the day of publication and it is clear from his literary notebooks and the markings in surviving books from his library that he read his way, during the late 1870s and early 1880s, through numerous works by Arnold, Carlyle, Comte, Macaulay, Mill, Stephen, and Spencer—to mention only the names which most frequently recur—and through books and articles on a wide range of historical, philosophical, and literary topics.

Matthew Arnold's influence was especially strong, and his latest writings were seized upon as they appeared—the 'Wordsworth' essay in 1879, for example, and 'Numbers; or the Majority and the Remnant', one of the American discourses, shortly before a second encounter with Arnold in person at a dinner in June 1884. Although he found Arnold's idealism somewhat remote and rarefied and his specifically religious arguments tiresomely 'hairsplitting', Hardy was deeply sympathetic to his ethical approach and found in his analyses of such phenomena as the 'modern spirit' formulations which gave eloquent expression to some of his own deepest and most instinctive feelings about the great social and intellectual currents in which he was himself so ineluctably caught up. Arnoldian ideas are clearly apparent—which is by no means to say unambiguously endorsed—in novels as diverse as *The Return of the Native*, *A Laodicean*, and *Jude the Obscure*, and there is a real sense in which Hardy's later career, from *Tess* and *Jude* to *The Dynasts* and the reflective poems, constitutes a conscientious exercise in 'the noble and profound application of ideas to life'.[38]

The darker, more sceptical strain in Hardy's thinking continued to be fed meanwhile by some of his reading in general works on philosophy—including Caro's *Le Pessimisme au XIXe siècle* and G. H. Lewes's *The History of*

Philosophy—and in periodical articles focused on such figures as Schopenhauer and von Hartmann, neither of whom he had as yet confronted
directly.[39] But Hardy consistently resisted such labels as pessimist and deter-
minist. At this time in the mid–1880s he was still much influenced by
Positivism, his friendship with Frederic Harrison, the leader of the English
Positivists, dating from this period, and in 1885, writing to John Morley,
now a prominent Member of Parliament, on the issue of Church dis-
establishment, he expressed what proved to be an excessively optimistic
hope for ethical regeneration through gradual modification of the existing
structure and organization of the Church of England:

I have sometimes had a dream that the church, instead of being disendowed, could
be made to modulate by degrees (say as the present incumbents die out) into an
undogmatic, non-theological establishment for the promotion of that virtuous
living on which all honest men are agreed—leaving to voluntary bodies the
organization of whatever societies they may think best for teaching their various
forms of doctrinal religion.[40]

Unbeliever though he was, Hardy retained to the end of his life both a personal attachment to the Anglican traditions of ritual, language, and music
with which he had grown up and a strong sense of the social—what might
now be called the socializing—value of such traditions and of the com-
munal observances in which they were outwardly embodied.

Hardy's journey from London by way of Wimborne was not a frantic flight
from the city: as he told Mrs Sutherland Orr in December 1881, 'I seem to
see more of London now than when we lived in the suburbs. I very frequently run up, & enjoy those very commonplaces of town life which used
to be a weariness.'[41] The move to Dorchester was rather an orderly falling
back upon his oldest, deepest, and surest creative resources. Bockhampton
was now within daily reach, less than an hour's walk away along those same
roads and paths he had travelled daily as a boy and youth, and surviving
notes from late 1883 and early 1884 are full of memories gathered from
elderly people in the neighbourhood. From December there is a personal
reminiscence of the group of trees at Bockhampton known in his childhood
as 'The Birds' Bedroom', and a description of a 'Still life scene' observed
nearby: 'Pond by T. Lock's. Pond wrinkled, a cow having just come out: the
slow waves *bend* the inverted reflections of the other cows without breaking
them. The rich reds & duns are as full coloured in the reflection as in the
reality.'[42] The meticulousness of the perception is familiar—Hardy's verbal
equivalent of Constable's cloud studies—but arguably enhanced by a

pervasive sense of context, as if the status of these particular cows as local and typical, hence regionally immemorial, made them peculiarly available to the Hardyan imagination. While living in Shire-hall Lane Hardy attended and described an unusual number of local events—including a street performance by female itinerant musicians, a production of *Othello* by a group of strolling players, a couple of circuses, the proceedings at the quarterly Assizes, the New Year's Eve bell-ringing in St Peter's Church— very much as if he were deliberately taking opportunities to re-enter the life of the town in all its aspects.[43]

Hardy's reinvigorated interest in regional materials—not just for their own familiar sakes but as offering distinctive particularizations of general themes and universal phenomena—reveals itself most strikingly in the pages of a surviving notebook begun in late 1882. Headed 'Facts, from Newspapers, Histories, Biographies, & other Chronicles—(mainly Local)', it was chiefly used to record materials from printed sources that might prove usable in the writing of future stories or poems: an entry on the first page, on the fallen fortunes of ancient families, is directly anticipatory of *Tess of the d'Urbervilles*. It was with this notebook at hand, and with his next book, *The Mayor of Casterbridge*, specifically in mind, that Hardy sat down, early in 1884, to read his way systematically through the files of the local newspaper, the *Dorset County Chronicle*, for the period beginning January 1826. As he read, he jotted down items that attracted his attention either by their oddity, their incorporation of some ironic narrative twist, or their illumination of the social life of the period—particularly, though by no means necessarily, the life of Dorset itself.[44] Several such items—among them the report of a wife-selling in Somerset—were soon to be drawn upon for narrative and descriptive elements in the new novel, and the entire exercise speaks to a preconceived intention on Hardy's part to establish the fictional Caster- bridge as a densely and concretely realized representation of a busy market town, and to base that representation on whatever research and local memory could recover of the historical Dorchester of the second quarter of the nineteenth century—an approximate terminal point being provided by the allusion, in chapter 37 of *The Mayor of Casterbridge*, to Prince Albert's passage through Dorchester in July 1849.[45]

After the marvellous and in a sense almost accidental successes of *Under the Greenwood Tree* and *Far from the Madding Crowd*—novels which he had writ- ten quite unselfconsciously out of direct experience, delicately reworking the remembered and the traditional—Hardy had listened too attentively to the complaints of the reviewers about the exaggerated presentation of his rustic characters and his excessive indebtedness to George Eliot. Anxious to assert both his competence and his independence, he had quite deliberately set out to do something different in each succeeding novel. Even *The Return of the Native*, though drawing upon deeply personal material, was shaped, perhaps distorted, by Hardy's ambitions for it as both a work of art and a statement about art. It was only with *The Mayor of Casterbridge* that he regained, through what was now an entirely conscious choice of story, setting, and treatment, those levels of achievement at which he had more spontaneously arrived in the finest of his early works.   .

The structural and imaginative grasp of the new novel depended largely upon two central elements which, while not solely determined by Hardy's enhanced professional acumen, were certainly conditioned by it. One of these was the emphasis upon the presentation of a confined and closely knit community seen, as in *Far from the Madding Crowd*, in all phases of its economic and social life. The other was the placement of that community at the centre of a fully developed regional concept. Hardy had learned that his popularity depended largely upon his comic rustics, and he had managed to squeeze a few of them into almost every book. But he also knew that they 'worked' best when presented within contexts to which they naturally belonged. As for the larger world of Wessex, Hardy had become increasingly alert to the benefits that might flow from the exploitation of regional settings (as in the Scottish novels of Sir Walter Scott and, nearer home, in R. D. Blackmore's *Lorna Doone*) and from the linking of novels one with another within some kind of narrative or geographical framework (as in Balzac's *Comédie humaine* or Trollope's Barchester series). The imaginative leap to a comprehensively articulated Wessex may seem in retrospect to have been inevitable, but professional shrewdness probably played as large a part as sheer creative vision in bringing Hardy to the point at which he could clearly see what could and should be done with the world he had thus far only half made. It was therefore with genuine concern that Hardy later wrote to one of his publishers: 'Could you, whenever advertising my books, use the words "Wessex Novels" at the head of the list? . . . I find that the name *Wessex*, wh. I was the first to use in fiction, is getting to be taken up everywhere: & it would be a pity for us to lose the right to it for want of asserting it.'[46]

The broader assertion of Wessex in the pages of *The Mayor of Casterbridge* was to provide the foundation for the greater assurance and more consistent strength of Hardy's final novels. In later years he would make large claims for the historical authenticity of his fictional writings: 'At the dates represented in the various narrations things were like that in Wessex: the inhabitants lived in certain ways, engaged in certain occupations, kept alive certain customs, just as they are shown doing in these pages.' Had he not taken the trouble to discover and verify such details, he went on, 'nobody would have discovered such errors to the end of Time. Yet I have instituted inquiries to correct tricks of memory, and striven against temptations to exaggerate, in order to preserve for my own satisfaction a fairly true record of a vanishing life.'[47] As Hardy acknowledged, a less scrupulous application of surface detail would doubtless have evoked for the mass of urban readers a sufficiently specific image of the rural world in which he wished the lives of his characters to be set. But the concern for accuracy derived both from a deeply personal need to preserve the local past, to keep it alive in memory if not in fact, and from that fundamental puritanism which obliged him in his best and most characteristic work to tell the truth about his characters and follow them unflinchingly to whatever fates their personalities and circumstances ultimately compelled them.

Both impulses—to recreate the local past and project the truths of human experience—are powerfully present in *The Mayor of Casterbridge*. In terms of topography, of history, of social and economic realities, it is easy to recognize everywhere in the presentation of the fictional town the lineaments of the actual town in which it was being written, and the composition of the novel and the construction of the new house in fact proceeded side by side as the twin, obviously interrelated, preoccupations of the Shire-Hall Place period. In terms of characterization and story, it is immediately clear that the mild-mannered and evasively fantastic romances of the years since *The Return of the Native* have been firmly superseded. The subtitle of the first edition, *The Life and Death of a Man of Character*, sounds more strongly than ever before the note of overt moral fable and directly reflects the 'wheel of fate' pattern of Michael Henchard's rise and fall. In almost Bunyanesque fashion, Hardy establishes Henchard in all his particularity of time, place, and class, and then surrounds him with sequences of classical, biblical, and Shakespearian imagery that require him to be viewed as a heroic figure within complexly tragic terms of reference, susceptible to analogies with Oedipus, Samuel, and Lear—even, perhaps, with Heathcliff and Captain Ahab.

As such he is one of Hardy's most remarkable exercises in characterization, the richly and sympathetically imagined embodiment of those qualities of ambition, authority, vigour, violence, and sexual aggressiveness which Hardy knew to be most lacking in himself—though he had a 'source' for at least some of them in his maternal grandfather George Hand. It was perhaps psychically necessary for Hardy that so virile a figure should suffer so catastrophic a fall, yet admiration for Henchard remains the novel's

HARDY'S OWN MAP OF HIS FICTIONAL WESSEX

It is to be understood that this is an imaginative Wessex only, & that the places described under the names here given are not portraits of any real places, but visionary places which may approximate to the real places more or less.

dominant note. For all his faults and self-destructive follies he is clearly a far greater man than those (such as Farfrae) who surround and follow him, and he appears at his strongest at the time of his worst and final defeat. Since Casterbridge was so deliberately modelled upon early Victorian Dorchester, and the novel's social and economic structures were so specifically those of the world Hardy had known as a child, Henchard emerges as representative of those traditional rural beliefs, attitudes, and values which Hardy saw crumbling all around him—doomed, like Henchard, because incapable of withstanding the onset of new ways of thinking and doing, yet leaving behind them a sense of tragic loss at the disappearance of an ancient, deep-rooted, peculiarly English quality of life that could never be replaced or revived.

As the embodiment of those irrecoverable values, Henchard had necessarily to remain without descendants. At the same time, the agony of Henchard's realization that he does not have a daughter, followed though it is by his discovery of a capacity to love Elizabeth-Jane for her own sake, had implications for Hardy's own childlessness—which must by now have been accepted as permanent. But it seems no less significant that it should be not Henchard himself but the modest and womanly Elizabeth-Jane who represents the novel's nearest approach to the distinctively Hardyan voice and point of view. Not only is she endowed with the inconspicuous ubiquity characteristic of Hardy's authorial narrators, but she alone steadily learns and grows in the course of the narrative, achieving through quiet suffering a kind of disillusioned yet compassionate understanding that the reader comes to recognize and accept as wisdom. The note she sounds is close at times to that of Cytherea in *Desperate Remedies*, and if Elizabeth-Jane was in some sense based, like Cytherea, upon Eliza Nicholls, it seems ungracious of Hardy to have linked her name with that of her treacherous sister. He may, on the other hand, have thought of Elizabeth-Jane as incorporating the best qualities of each.

At the very end of the novel Hardy was able to permit himself the full and passionate negativity of Henchard's last testament ('that no man remember me') and then contain and qualify it in terms of Elizabeth-Jane's cautiously positive appraisal of life's possibilities, her belief in the feasibility of 'making limited opportunities endurable' by means of 'the cunning enlargement, by a species of microscopic treatment, of those minute forms of satisfaction that offer themselves to everybody not in positive pain'.[48] It was a proposition that offered cold comfort to contemporary readers at the end of a novel that had in any case offended against conventional expectations by focusing upon a central figure already middle-aged and upon a heroine who neither expects nor receives much from her life. It may, however, have contained a private domestic message, either for Emma or for Hardy himself.

According to *Life and Work*, work on the manuscript of *The Mayor of Casterbridge* began early in 1884, continued 'off and on' during the following summer, and was completed, despite frequent interruptions, in mid-April of 1885.[49] The interruptions included the visit to the Portsmouths at Eggesford House, a trip with brother Henry to the Channel Islands in late August of 1884, at least two busy London visits, and the ongoing need to supervise the building of the new house by his father and brother and their workmen. Typically, he began to doubt the wisdom of the building scheme before it had been finally accomplished. When Lady Portsmouth urged him to abandon 'benighted Dorset' and move to Devon he noted somewhat wryly that 'Em would go willingly, as it is her native county; but alas, my house at Dorchester is nearly finished'.[50]

13

Max Gate

On 29 June 1885 Hardy and Emma made the shortest but most important—and certainly most permanent—of all their removals, from antiquated Shire-Hall Place, in the centre of Dorchester, to the town's south-east outskirts and the brand-new house they were already calling Max Gate. In Hardy's early drawings for the house the name appears as 'Mack's Gate', in obvious reference to Henry Mack, the last keeper of the tollgate that had stood nearby on the Wareham Road,[1] but the jokey Latinization and subtle aggrandizement soon followed. Just once, in a letter to Gosse, Hardy permitted himself the humorous indulgence of calling it 'Porta Maxima'. The site itself was an open field, its situation fairly isolated—though close to the road and within sound of the railway and the whistle of the Eddison steam-plough works—and its elevation sufficient to expose it to the full rigour of the winds from almost every direction.[2] To the south and south-west, however, it commanded magnificent views across Fordington Field to Came Wood, the monument to Admiral Hardy, and the downs that, from their reverse slopes, overlooked Weymouth and the sea. From the upper windows of the new house it was possible (as in the poem 'Looking Across') to look northward over the Frome valley to Stinsford Church and churchyard, Kingston Maurward House, and the heath and woodlands surrounding the Higher Bockhampton cottage itself.[3]

That Max Gate had taken the best part of two years to complete was in part the consequence of its being solidly constructed at a time when building processes (such as the drying time of mortar) were much slower than they have since become, but Hardy brought some of the delays upon himself by giving the job—naturally enough—to his father and brother. The number of men working on the house at one time was never very large—it seems significant that Hardy was one of only two people present when the Romano-British skeletons were dug up—and a reference to Hardy's 'constantly overlooking operations'[4] covers a multitude of family consultations, debates, and arguments. Hardy was no doubt insistent upon a meticulous adherence to the drawings he had himself made for the house he was himself to inhabit, and his father is said to have declared, when it was all over, that he would not build such a house again for a thousand pounds—though whether he was protesting the labour required or the payment received is by no means clear.[5] The main burden of the work and responsibility must in any case have fallen upon Henry Hardy, Thomas Hardy senior being now in his mid-seventies and largely incapacitated by rheumatism.

An early sketch plan shows the house on a north-west/south-east axis, with the main entrance facing north-east, but it was in fact built west/east, with the entrance porch facing almost due south. As originally designed and constructed, Max Gate was indeed a 'villa', as Hardy himself had described it, and by no means on a large scale. On the ground floor there was a modest central hall with a dining room to the left and a somewhat larger drawing room to the right. The kitchen and scullery areas were at the back, together with the hand pump by which all the water for the household had to be drawn up daily. The main staircase, straight ahead, was perhaps a little wider than might have been expected in a house of this size, suggesting that Hardy had already written the poem 'Heiress and Architect' and remembered the architect's final piece of dismal advice: 'Give space (since life ends unawares) | To hale a coffined corpse adown the stairs; | For you will die.'[6] At the top of the staircase was a first floor consisting of three bedrooms, a dressing room, and a water-closet, although one of the bedrooms was used by Hardy as a study. At first, at the time of *The Woodlanders*, the study was at the front of the house, the room over the drawing room; later, at the time of *Tess*, Hardy moved to the smaller room at the north-west corner of the house; the third and final study, with its large eastward-facing window, was built during one of several subsequent extensions to the original structure. Servants, sometimes as many as four, never less than two, were accommodated in the attics. Architecturally the house had one or two unusual features, including a square turret at the west end of the front—balanced only much later by one at the east end—and a glass partition high in the wall of the servants' staircase that let outside light through into the main staircase and the hall below. It also had some particularly attractive details, including the Portland stone window sills and oak window frames and the unusually large south-facing windows on the ground floor whose solid wooden shutters could be closed for warmth, those in the living room folding laterally, those in the dining room sliding upwards.

In a yard at the west side of the house stood a small carriage house and stabling for two horses, although the Hardys never used it for that purpose themselves, always hiring horses and vehicles from the local livery stables as needed. The extensive garden was very deliberately laid out and planted, although it would be a good many years before the former field lost the last of its rawness and took on a thoroughly domesticated appearance. Even in 1895 a visitor could speak of it as 'still only growing into comeliness'.[7] The area immediately to the east and south-east of the house was mostly occupied by a lawn, later divided into two separate lawns. At the far edge of the lawn closest to the house, the preferred spot for taking tea outside in the summer, stood (and stands) the so-called 'Druid Stone', a monolithic slab that was turned up during the digging of the foundations and has recently been identified as a sarsen stone that once formed part of the perimeter of an ancient causewayed enclosure. The ground to the north and north-east became a kitchen garden, an orchard, and a place to hang the laundry; beyond it lay the field that the second Mrs Hardy purchased in the 1920s as a run for her chickens. The remaining area to the south was taken up by the oval driveway running between the front gate on the Wareham Road and the front door of the house itself, and by the thick shrubbery that was encouraged to grow both in the centre of the oval and in the extreme south-west corner of the garden, where the pathetic little stones of the pets' cemetery can still be seen.

A brick wall almost six feet high was built around the southern and eastern sides of the property, where it abutted on public thoroughfares, and within the wall were two thickly planted rows of trees, just far enough apart to allow for a pathway in between. Hardy's preliminary planting of beeches and especially Austrian pines around the perimeter of his property had been designed to provide climatic protection and, secondarily, privacy, but he also wanted to grow within his one and a half acres a wide variety of characteristic English trees and shrubs. He began with a list of possibilities—written out long before and perhaps for quite a different purpose by his uncle, John Antell[8]—that included yew, double-blossom elder, and apple on quince stock, and the garden still contains examples not only of the familiar trees of the Dorset countryside but also of walnut, holly, and spindle. There was also a wych elm until it succumbed to Dutch elm disease. The surviving fruit trees are similarly various, and one or two of them may even be of Bockhampton ancestry.

It is customary to condemn Max Gate as being ugly and uncomfortable, deficient alike in aesthetic qualities and domestic arrangements. In 1912 Arthur Christopher Benson found it 'a structure at once mean & pretentious, with no grace of design or detail, & with two hideous low flanking turrets with pointed roofs of blue slate'. George Gissing, however, called it 'a very nice house' after staying there for a weekend in 1895,[9] and it is clear that the impressions formed by visitors depended very largely upon their particular architectural and social preconceptions. Many of those who made slighting comments were actually sneering at Hardy himself as an *arriviste*. Others were simply accustomed to living in a far more elegant style in far older and grander houses—or, like Benson, within the gracious precincts of Cambridge and Oxford colleges. It is, indeed, hard to defend on any architectural principles the turrets of Max Gate or some of its odder decorative features, except in so far as they can be said to embody distant and even playful allusions to such architectural styles as the Gothic, the neo-classical, and even (in those offending turrets) the Saxon. One generous-minded visitor called it 'a pretty Queen Anne erection'.[10]

Hardy seems almost to have designed the house from the inside out-wards, first deciding upon the number, purpose, and size of the rooms he and Emma required and then contriving to fit those requirements within a reasonably coherent overall structure, at whatever cost in terms of external symmetry. The failure of the various elements of the front elevation to balance one with another is a consequence of Hardy's concern to give each window precisely the size, shape, and location demanded by the function of the room to which it belonged and by the arc of the sun at different periods of the year. The south-facing window of the living room is low, so that those inside can look out; the corresponding window of the dining room is high, to deter those outside from looking in; both are large, in order to catch as much of the sunshine as possible. Although Max Gate became a dark house as a consequence of the unchecked growth of the surrounding trees, Hardy originally designed it to be—what it has now again become—a house full of light.[11]

Much attention has also been paid to the complaints made by Hardy's second wife about the outdated lighting, heating, cooking, and plumbing arrangements at Max Gate: 'We fear no frosts,' she told an American correspondent in 1919, 'as there are no water pipes, practically, in the house. All our water has to be pumped up directly from a well, & heated in kettles & saucepans over the kitchen fire. We have no boilers, no gas, we use oil-lamps & candles for lighting, & have no bathroom even. I expect this is the only house of this size in Dorchester without.'[12] But such comments—understandable in context—have tended to obscure the fact that in the early 1880s the house represented a high standard of middle-class comfort and convenience. One of the reasons it took so long to build was that it had to be provided with its own entirely independent systems for water, drainage, and sewage; its high and isolated position put it for many years beyond the reach of municipal services, and it is not connected to a main drainage system even now. There had to be a well and a pump and a cess pit, candles and oil lamps, and stoves and fires capable of burning either coal or peat—the latter a local product, from the nearby heaths. The Max Gate servants resented the time and labour expended in pumping up water into the roof tank every morning, but the well and the pump were both inside the house, and the tank not only provided running cold water in the kitchen but made it possible to operate the first-floor w.c. The house did not, indeed, possess a bathroom—as distinct from that flushing toilet—until after Hardy had responded to his second wife's complaints, and the servants were obliged to carry jugs of hot water up to the bedrooms for morning ablutions and for the hip baths that Hardy and Emma presumably took— like most English people of their time—at weekly intervals, and in front of a fire. Few English houses had bathrooms in the days before gas geysers and running hot water, and while Florence Hardy's complaints were justifiable in contemporary terms, they reflected her elderly husband's irresponsiveness to improved technology and changed social expectations and had little relevance to the comfortable if somewhat chilly house that he built for himself in his middle forties.

The very red-brick solidity of Hardy's house was disturbing to visitors who came down from London in the expectation of finding him snugly ensconced in an old manor house or thatched cottage. His metropolitan friends in particular were less at ease with the raw modernity and puzzling class pretensions of Max Gate than they would have been with the conventionally picturesque simplicities of Higher Bockhampton. But Emma remained sensitive to the requirements of what she thought of as her station, and Hardy himself was in the 1880s sufficiently a product of his period to want to take advantage of the modern conveniences his income made accessible. Max Gate, even so, was a modest house as first built, containing neither more nor less than the accommodation needed to provide a main bedroom, a separate study, and a spare bedroom for occasional guests. Hardy did not set himself up as a landowning 'gentleman' but as precisely what he now was, a man of the professional middle class, the social equal of the doctor, the solicitor, or, for that matter, the architect in private practice. An early journalistic visitor to Max Gate commented on the lack of ostentation inside the house, observing of the entrance hall that '[t]he appointments here, as elsewhere, are distinguished by a simplicity truly in keeping with the character of the novelist', and of Hardy's study that it was 'solidly furnished, without a single article in it that is not required for use, our author's indifference to *things*, as such, showing strongly here'.[13]

The same anonymous visitor put on record the earliest verbal portrait of Hardy himself, describing him as he rose from his 'writing-table' as

a somewhat fair-complexioned man, a trifle below the middle height, of slight build, with a pleasant thoughtful face, exceptionally broad at the temples, and fringed by a beard trimmed after the Elizabethan manner; a man readily sociable and genial, but one whose mien conveys the impression that the world in his eyes has rather more of the tragedy than the comedy about it, and that he is disposed to rate life, and what it can give, at no very extravagant value.

Apart from the beard, this is already the image of Hardy made familiar by his later fame. Florence Hardy, inserting this quotation into *Life and Work* after her husband's death, supplemented the reference to his height with the words 'he was actually 5 ft 6½ ins.', although Hardy himself, in 1905, laid claim only to '5 ft 6¼, in shoes'.[14] In photographs, standing alongside such a friend as Edmund Gosse, he seems to be distinctly 'below the middle height', and his reputed dislike of being touched[15] sounds very much like resentment of those arm-around-the-shoulder gestures of familiarity and implicit condescension to which short people are peculiarly exposed.

If the Hardy of later years is already clearly recognizable in the designer and first owner of Max Gate, it is no less true that the basic patterns of life and work he adopted at this time remained little changed thereafter. The study was always for him the heart of the house. Though its location shifted, it was always upstairs, as far as possible removed from household activities and callers at the front door, and always impregnable, except by rare invitation to especially favoured visitors. It was there that Hardy, to the very end of his life, spent the greater part of almost every day. 'When he has a story in hand', that early interviewer reported, 'he begins writing immediately after breakfast, and remains indoors until he has finished for the day, even a very little time spent in the open air before beginning proving fatal to any work till after nightfall.'[16] Answering other questions about his working habits put to him by an American medical journalist in July 1884, Hardy intriguingly revealed that it was his habit to 'remove boots or slippers as a preliminary to work'. He also declared that he preferred working at night but found 'day-time advisable as a rule', followed 'no plan as to outline', 'only occasionally' worked against his will, and 'used no stimulant other than tea'.[17] Hardy's personal habits remained as abstemious as they had always been—as, in childhood, they had had to be. He told an enquirer in 1882 that he had never smoked, and as a member of the Dorset County Museum he con-sistently voted to exclude smokers from the reading room for a certain part of each day. He also reported in 1882 that he very rarely drank, having 'never found alcohol helpful to novel-writing in any degree', its effect being 'to blind the writer to the quality of what he produces rather than to raise its quality'.[18] The restorative effects of German beers are nonetheless praised, a fondness for cider is suggested by the poem 'Great Things', and Hardy developed a convenient belief in champagne and St Raphael's wine as tonics. Wine would in any case have been served when there were guests to dinner, and seems to have been more regularly on the table in Hardy's last years.[19]

Although the Hardys had a series of cooks at Max Gate, the standard of cooking seems rarely to have risen above the mediocre. Hardy was perhaps indifferent to what he ate, but his mother was evidently a good cook and his own tastes seem, in fact, to have been definite but simple, tending always towards such basics as kettle-broth and grilled bacon that were associated with, and capable of reviving, the memories of childhood. If mealtime distress was sometimes experienced by sophisticated visitors to Max Gate it must often have derived from unfamiliarity with a somewhat countrified cuisine or from a snobbish readiness to condemn a style of living that was, like the house itself, less gracious than their own. Servants were notoriously a 'problem' for houses on the modest scale of Max Gate, and Emma may not have been an especially skilful manager. At least one visitor was distressed by the way she 'scolded her servants noisily for being late with lunch',[20] and the parlourmaids were for ever getting married, the cooks leaving for other, doubtless more appreciative, situations. The garden which surrounded the house on three sides was also Emma's province for the most part, although it was Hardy who supervised its maintenance, paid the gardener, and refused to allow the trees to be cut back for fear of 'wounding' them.

Hardy's habits of daily exercise took him beyond the garden and into the local lanes and paths, accompanied for the first few years by a black retriever bitch called Moss. But he was not an ambitious walker, and seems in general to have spent a good deal less time outdoors than either his birth, his vocation, or his choice of domicile might have suggested. People meeting him for the first time often remarked upon the paleness of his complexion and his failure to look like a countryman, and it was not until he was released from the sheer hard labour of novel-writing and took, almost simultaneously, to cycling that he can be said to have led an especially active life. Higher Bockhampton is less than an hour's walk from Max Gate, however, and Hardy early formed and long continued the habit of spending some hours there every Sunday. Although relationships between his family

23. Locket miniature of Emma Lavinia Gifford, *c.*1870

24. Thomas Hardy, *c.*1870

25. St Juliot Rectory, *c.*1870; the Revd Caddell Holder, Helen Holder (seated), and Emma Gifford

33. Emma Hardy (*facing camera*), Nellie Gosse, and Hardy on Weymouth Pier, photographed with a pin-hole camera by Edmund Gosse, 1890

34. Hardy and his dog, Moss, in the garden of Max Gate, photographed by Edmund Gosse, 1890

35. Florence Henniker, photographed by Chancellor of Dublin. From the frontispiece to her book, *Outlines* (1894)

36 (*above left*). Rosamund
Tomson, later Rosamund
Marriott Watson. From the
frontispiece to her *Collected
Poems*

37 (*above right*). Agnes Grove.
From the frontispiece to her
book, *The Social Fetich* (1907)

38 (*right*). Hamo and Agatha
Thornycroft

and his wife worsened as time passed, his parents did for some years make occasional visits to Max Gate, and during the severe winter of 1890–1 Jemima, aged 77, once walked alone from Bockhampton along icy roads. Asked why she had set out in such conditions, she retorted, 'To enjoy the beauties of Nature of course: why shouldn't I?'[21]

Hardy's own life at Max Gate was intensely private, centred primarily upon his work and secondarily upon the maintenance of family ties and the observance of family pieties—often at the expense of those marital obligations he had contracted in the face of family opposition. It was a life characterized by daily habits of hard work and plain living, disciplines early learned from his mother and subsequently admired in such men as the Reverend Frederick Perkins. Warned by the example of Sir Walter Scott's Abbotsford, Hardy was determined not to ruin himself by house-building and remained generally faithful to his own dictum that the only way for a writer to cope with success was not to allow it to change his mode of living.[22] Max Gate might be considerably larger and more pretentious than the Bockhampton cottage, but for Hardy himself, shut up in his study and emerging only for meals and exercise, the routines and rewards of each day cannot have seemed remarkably different.

Built into the pattern of life at Max Gate, however, was the annual visit to London during those months of spring and early summer when the 'season' was in full swing. By the time he began to build Max Gate, Hardy saw clearly what he had only dimly and intermittently perceived during the 1870s—that his career as a writer was founded upon his capacity to mediate between essentially rural material and a predominantly urban audience, rather as his childhood and youth had involved a daily experience of seeing 'rustic and borough doings in a juxtaposition peculiarly close'. In his essay on 'The Profitable Reading of Fiction', first published in 1888, he acknowledged that an unfamiliar setting was one of the simplest and most basic sources of reading pleasure—that the 'town man', more specifically, found what he sought 'in novels of the country'.[23] While such a recognition ratified, as it had largely motivated, his decision to settle in his native countryside, it simultaneously confirmed his early and continuing assumption that it was necessary to his career that he maintain his London connections, keep in touch with that 'town man' who represented his chief audience, and move with some regularity in those literary circles on the fringes of 'Society' where professionals and amateurs (including titled amateurs such as Lord Houghton and Lord Lytton) met on friendly terms, and where publishers, editors, and reviewers—past, present, and potential—were also to be encountered. This was an arrangement of which

Emma thoroughly approved, and from the early 1880s until her death in 1912 there were very few years in which the Hardys did not rent a house, a flat, or 'rooms' in London for all or part of the April–July period.

Hardy's apparent weakness for London 'Society' has often been criticized as sheer snobbery and social climbing, and it is certainly true that his engagements in London during the 1880s and 1890s occupy a disproportionate amount of space in the autobiographical *Life and Work*. But he and Emma both enjoyed and took advantage of what London offered in terms of theatres, concerts, museums, and exhibitions, and his membership of the Savile Club was a source of both genial conversation and professional advantage. As his reputation grew Hardy received and accepted invitations to ever more exclusive circles, finding himself as often as not in worlds that were by no means anti-intellectual or closed to talent. The respectful welcomes he received on such occasions gave him a sense not so much of 'arrival'—since he never thought of himself as anything other than an occasional visitor—as of recognition. That he was there at all was an acknowledgement of his status as a successful author, and the active interest of men and women of rank, importance, intelligence, and beauty provided a flattering reassurance to set off against the cheerful incomprehension of most of his own family, the envious disbelief of many of his neighbours, and the multiplying disappointments of his marriage. Emma, meanwhile, had marital disappointments of her own, among them the frequency with which she was excluded from this London world of her husband's and denied opportunities to play that role of successful author's wife for which she had so long yearned and laboured.

Aside from one or two elaborately polite letters to such figures as Frederick Locker and Lord Lytton,[24] there is little indication that Hardy was sycophantic in his relationships with his elegant acquaintances. There was, however, a price to be paid for mixing with the rich and prominent, and when Hardy moved in circles socially superior to his own he found it convenient—like most people in similar situations—to adopt a certain degree of protective coloration. He learned to dress smartly when occasion demanded; he bought books on genealogy, social etiquette, and even billiards, a favourite country-house diversion of the period. He also discovered that in the worlds of fashion and of politics one was by no means immune to the risks of tedium and disillusionment. His friendship with Lady Portsmouth led in the spring of 1885 to invitations from her sister-in-law, Lady Carnarvon, and hence to encounters with Lord Carnarvon's leading colleagues in the Conservative Party, among them Lord Salisbury himself, shortly to become Prime Minister for the first time. The poor opinion that Hardy formed of such figures cannot have been unrelated to his own Liberal sympathies, but it certainly prompted some trenchant generalizations about the relationship between individuals and historical events:

History is rather a stream than a tree. There is nothing organic in its shape, nothing systematic in its development. It flows on like a thunderstorm-rill by a road side; now a straw turns it this way, now a tiny barrier of sand that. The offhand decision of some commonplace mind high in office at a critical moment influences the course of events for a hundred years. Consider the evenings at Lord C[arnarvon]'s, and the intensely average conversation on politics held there by average men who two or three weeks later were members of the Cabinet. A row of shopkeepers in Oxford Street taken just as they came would conduct the affairs of the nation as ably as these.[25]

These are scarcely radical comments, but they serve to indicate the healthy survival, just below the surface, of the strong note of social criticism that had been faintly audible in *The Hand of Ethelberta* but otherwise almost un-sounded in the years since *The Poor Man and the Lady*. They also reflect the steady development—fostered by his reading in philosophy and Greek tragedy—of that larger scepticism about the pattern and purpose of human events that would find its fullest expression in the final novels and in *The Dynasts*.

Although the annual alternation between London and Dorchester con-stituted the basic rhythm of Hardy's life for many years, he did not maintain a rigid separation between those two worlds. His deprecating references to Max Gate as merely the rural retreat in which he did his writing were in part intended to discourage unwanted visitors who would, precisely, interrupt that writing, but particular friends were entertained there from time to time and other people invited down for special reasons. When the American painter John Alexander requested a sitting in September 1886, Hardy replied: 'I could run up to Town for a day, if you are unable to leave; but what I suggest is that you come here & do it. This place is only a cottage in the country which I use for writing in, but we could make you comfortable for a couple of nights.'[26] In general, however, he preferred to see people in London, and his annual visits there were built into the total economy of his life as periods specifically given over to social engagements and obligations, the maintenance of friendships and professional contacts, and the pacifica-tion of Emma. In seeking to discourage any extensive overlapping of the two worlds, he can scarcely have been motivated by mere snobbishness or social vanity. He did indeed tell Kegan Paul in 1881 that he thought 'the less people know of a writer's antecedents (till he is dead) the better',[27] but the acute English ear and eye for nuances of speech and behaviour must have given his London acquaintances a sufficiently shrewd idea of his background and upbringing, if not of just how humble and isolated his childhood had been. What he most deeply cared about was the privacy of his family, increasingly under threat as Wessex became ever more established in the popular imagination as a visitable place.

On 31 December 1885 Hardy recorded a sadness greater than he had felt on most previous New Year's Eves: 'Whether building this house at Max Gate was a wise expenditure of energy is one doubt, which, if resolved in the negative, is depressing enough. And there are others.'[28] Although those additional other doubts were not identified, he was certainly anxious about the reception of *The Mayor of Casterbridge*. It is not entirely clear at what point he finished correcting the proofs of the weekly serial parts for the *Graphic*, but his regret at the sanitization (as to plot) and bowdlerization (as to language) imposed by the *Graphic*'s editor is evident from a note of 2 January 1886, the day the first instalment appeared: 'I fear it will not be so good as I meant, but after all it is not improbabilities of incident but improbabilities of character that matter.'[29] The attempt to shelter *Graphic* readers from the knowledge that Lucetta had been Henchard's mistress had, however, rendered some incidents in the serial version quite strikingly improbable, and Hardy undertook an extensive revision ahead of the novel's appearance in book form. Though he had ample time for the task he seems rather to have rushed it at the last minute. Less than two months before the scheduled publication date he was still 'reading through the proofs', and Smith, Elder, who had agreed to continue as his publishers, were still undecided as to whether the novel should be brought out in the usual three volumes or only in two.[30] Later in the year he confessed to William Dean Howells that he had failed to realize on paper the story 'as it existed in my mind', adding: 'I ought to have improved it much—for the greater part was finished in 1884—a year & half nearly before publication. But I could not get thoroughly into it after the interval.'[31]

Modern critics have generally felt that Hardy, in revising the *Mayor*, made it into one of the most shapely of all his novels, tightly organized and structurally eloquent. Contemporary reviewers, however, were less enthusiastic. They certainly praised the portrait of Henchard as 'almost magnificent in its fullness of expression', but found Elizabeth-Jane 'rather more than a trifle dull' and deplored a pervasive pessimism that seemed unjustified by the situation as presented: '[W]e might', observed the *Pall Mall Gazette*, 'have been spared the concluding Enoch-Ardenism.'[32] While the serial was still in progress, however, the *Church of England Temperance Chronicle*, impressed by Henchard's vow of abstinence, unexpectedly awarded the *Graphic* 'a vote of thanks for giving our movement this friendly lift'.[33] Conclusion of serialization of the *Mayor* on 15 May 1886 and publication of the two-volume first edition by Smith, Elder on 10 May coincided rather too closely with the appearance of the first instalment of *The Woodlanders* in the May 1886 issue of *Macmillan's Magazine*. Hardy had been working on both books at different times during the preceding six or seven months, and in mid-November 1885, when he was still calling the newer novel *Fitzpiers at Hintock*, he recorded that he had gone back to his 'original plot'—evidently to be identified with the 'woodland story' he had 'put aside' in favour of *The Hand of Ethelberta*—and was working from 10.30 in the morning until 12 at night 'to get my mind made up on the details'.[34]

Emma's hand appears quite frequently in the manuscript of *The Woodlanders*, but while it is plain that she was still copying out many of her husband's most heavily corrected pages and assisting him in other practical ways, there is no evidence in this or any other of the surviving manuscripts of her having made any significant contribution to the actual processes of literary composition.[35] She was in any case out of sympathy with the directions Hardy's mind was now taking, and their domestic differences had been intensified rather than reduced by the move to their new home. Much of the trouble originated in Emma's extravagant sense of class superiority— similarly the cause of Grace Melbury's failure to recognize the true worth of Giles Winterborne—but it was at the same time extraordinarily difficult for her to cope with her tough-minded and harsh-tongued mother-in-law, whose grip on her son had never significantly relaxed, and with the stubborn family solidarity displayed by all the Hardys, not least by Hardy himself. Emma's belonging to the 'poor gentry', a class the Hardys affected to despise, was one of the sources of the deep-seated prejudice against her which always prevailed at the Bockhampton cottage. Kate, in her cheerful way, bridged the gap for a time, but the others never quite lost their initial resentment of the marriage, nor was Max Gate ever left in doubt as to how Bockhampton felt. Such tensions had proved sufficiently manageable while the two households were many miles apart, and especially during those early married years when Emma was making a brave effort to 'belong'. But the move to Dorchester boxed everyone in and made possible, and perhaps inevitable, a complexly unhappy situation for which, as the second Mrs Hardy once observed, no one was entirely to blame but everyone a little to blame.[36]

The difficulties already present in the Hardys' marriage even at the time of the move to Max Gate were sharply perceived—more sharply and unkindly, perhaps, than the circumstances then justified—by Fanny Stevenson, who with her husband Robert Louis Stevenson called at the new house in late August 1885. Describing the visit in a letter to Sidney Colvin, Fanny wrote: 'Also we saw [Hardy's] wife—but here one naturally drops a veil. What very strange marriages literary men seem to make.'[37] To a woman friend she was more forthcoming:

[Hardy] is small, *very* pale, and scholarly looking, and at first sight most painfully shy. He has a very strange face, quite triangular, with a nose that bends down very suddenly at the point. His wife, he is lately married, is *very* plain, quite underbred, and most tedious. . . . There was something so modest, gentle, and appealing about the creature that one remembers him as a quite pathetic figure. They had just built a new house, which he recoiled from, preferring the freedom of rooms in an attic, and a 'loose foot', as the hoosiers say.[38]

In June 1886 Stevenson himself wrote to praise *The Mayor of Casterbridge* and ask if he might dramatize it, and a few days later the two men dined together with Sidney Colvin in the latter's apartment at the British Museum, where he was Keeper of Prints and Drawings. Stevenson and Hardy seem never to have met again, but Gosse was to report to Hardy a year later that Stevenson, about to leave for the United States, had included a copy of *The Woodlanders* in his luggage.[39]

It had been a simple matter for Hardy to accept Colvin's dinner invitation, since he and Emma were spending the weeks between early May and late July 1886 in a series of Bloomsbury lodgings, chosen specifically for their proximity to the British Museum Reading Room:

Reading in the British Museum [he wrote in May 1886]. Have been thinking over the dictum of Hegel—that the real is the rational and the rational the real—that real pain is compatible with a formal pleasure—that the idea is all, etc. But it doesn't help much. These venerable philosophers seem to start wrong; they cannot get away from a prepossession that the world must somehow have been made to be a comfortable place for man. If I remember it was Comte who said that metaphysics was a mere sorry attempt to reconcile theology and physics.[40]

Hardy was himself being made uncomfortable by the intense political activity provoked by Gladstone's introduction of the first Irish Home Rule Bill. He was in the House of Commons on 13 May, and probably on other days as well, his long-standing Liberalism shaken by his perception of Home Rule as posing an irreconcilable conflict between what was humanly desirable and what was politically feasible. He also felt that in such circumstances it was specious of either party to claim that it had right as well as reason on its side.[41] The general direction of his thought, indeed, was becoming increasingly pessimistic and disenchanted, to the point of sharing some of the fears that Matthew Arnold and others had recently expressed about the dangers of democracy. A year or so later he would insist that he belonged neither to the right nor to the left but might best be called 'an Intrinsicalist': 'I am against privilege derived from accident of any kind, and am therefore equally opposed to aristocratic privilege and democratic privilege. . . . Opportunity should be equal for all, but those who will not avail themselves of it should be cared for merely—not be a burden to, nor the rulers over, those who do avail themselves thereof.'[42]

Although Hardy never changed his basic political allegiance (apart from a possible Labour vote or two in the 1920s), his opposition to Gladstone's Irish initiatives made it easier for him to accept the fact that most of his London acquaintances were strongly Conservative. One of the newest, and certainly the closest, of his Conservative friends in the spring of 1886 was Mary Jeune, the wife of Francis Henry Jeune, a prominent lawyer and divorce court judge who would be knighted in 1891 and created Baron St Helier just before his death in 1905. Mrs Jeune, whose first husband had been one of the Stanleys of Alderley, took an active interest in politics and social causes, becoming an alderman of the London County Council after her second husband's death, and in the 1880s she was rapidly establishing herself as one of the leading hostesses of the day. Her friendship was to be of great importance to Hardy, not just because he met so many people under her aegis, but because he reached such terms of happy intimacy with the members of her family, and particularly with Dorothy and Madeleine Stanley, her children by her first husband. They called him 'Uncle Tom', confided in him, went with him to the theatre, and displayed an unself-conscious warmth and openness that he found entirely captivating—and that was sustained, especially by Dorothy Allhusen (as she became), to the time of his death. The fact that Francis Jeune happened to be a brother-in-law of Emma's uncle, the Archdeacon, seems to have had little or no bearing upon either the making or the keeping of Hardy's friendships with the various members of the Jeune and Stanley families. Sadly, none of them could 'stand' Emma. 'We all hated her,' Dorothy Allhusen once declared, and the Archdeacon himself seems to have shared their dislike, even if he never quite said, as reported, that she was 'the most horrible woman in the world'.[43]

Hardy also renewed and expanded his circle of literary acquaintances. Henry James was again encountered at a Rabelais Club dinner on 6 June

1886, but neither at this period nor later did the two men develop a relationship of any warmth. The same Rabelais dinner was the occasion of Hardy's meeting Meredith again, apparently for the first time since they had discussed *The Poor Man and the Lady* in 1869. During the course of the summer he also met Walter Pater, 'whose manner is that of one carrying weighty ideas without spilling them', Oliver Wendell Holmes, 'a very bright, pleasant, juvenile old man', indefatigably enjoying his English celebrity,[44] and George Gissing, who seems to have approached Hardy as a relative neophyte addressing an acknowledged master—and with expectations of sympathetic rapport which the event was not entirely to justify.[45]

In late July of 1886 Hardy returned with Emma to Dorchester in order to be able to work more continuously and effectively on *The Woodlanders*. Three weeks later, however, he sent an invitation to Gosse, whose house he had visited several times during the course of the spring and early summer and who was by now the most nearly intimate of his London friends. 'Can you come now?' Hardy wrote: 'Our life here is lonely & cottage-like, as you know, but I think you would be interested in going to one or two curious places in the neighbourhood recently opened up by the railway.' Making it clear that the invitation was to Gosse alone, he explained: 'Next year we hope to have a regulation spare-bedroom for married couples: at present we have only a bachelor's room—my wife particularly wishes you to mention this to Mrs Gosse—to whom she sends her love.' Gosse arrived at the end of August, and the Misses Eva and Alice Smith from West Stafford, calling at Max Gate on the 31st, were able to enjoy 'an old-fashioned cold supper tea with Mr Henry Moule who told ghost-stories and Mr Gosse, a poet and critic'.[46]

One of the places Hardy wanted Gosse to see was Bridport, along the coast west from Dorchester, an area the building of some new railway lines had rendered theoretically easier of access. In practice, however, their visit there was fraught with disaster. Hardy referred apologetically in a subsequent letter to 'that terrible kettle at the Bridport pot-house', and ten years later, in dedicating to Hardy his volume of essays entitled *Critical Kit-Kats*, Gosse amusingly recalled how they had missed the train back from Bridport after being elaborately misdirected by a local inhabitant. As they waited between trains at Maiden Newton on their outward journey, Gosse had taken the opportunity to write home a description of the visit to William Barnes he and Hardy had made the previous day:

Mr Barnes . . . is dying no less picturesquely than he has lived. He has a bed made up in his study, with the books on all the walls, except the one at his back which is hung with a dark green tapestry. He lies in his white bed, for he is now bedridden, in a scarlet dressing-gown, with a dark red soft biretta on his head, his long grey beard falling on his breast, & his white hair scattered on the pillow. He looks like a dying Pope. He was very cordial in welcoming us, & wld not let us go. But he is greatly altered, his memory fails him, & he says the same thing over and over.[47]

When the old poet died on 7 October 1886, Hardy described him in an *Athenaeum* obituary as 'probably the most interesting link between present and past forms of rural life that England possessed'—a man from remote 'pastoral recesses' whose 'great retentiveness and powers of observation' had made him 'a complete repertory of forgotten manners, words, and sentiments'. But while Hardy could write with great sympathy of this aspect of Barnes's career—he might almost have been writing his own obituary of more than forty years later—he felt obliged to enter some reservations about his friend's achievement as a poet. He saw Barnes as a gifted lyricist and a deliberate craftsman, but found something evasive in his use of the dialect and especially in the restrictiveness of his subject matter: 'he entirely leaves alone ambition, pride, despair, defiance, and other of the grander passions which move mankind great and small. His rustics are, as a rule, happy people, and very seldom feel the sting of the rest of modern mankind—the disproportion between the desire for serenity and the power of obtaining it.'[48]

Hardy served on the committee responsible for commissioning the statue of Barnes by Roscoe Mullins that stands outside St Peter's Church in the centre of Dorchester and subsequently edited a selection of Barnes's verse that was published by the Clarendon Press in 1907. More deeply personal was the poem 'The Last Signal', with its evocation of the moment when, as he walked across the fields to Barnes's funeral, Hardy caught a flash of sunlight reflected from the coffin:

> Thus a farewell to me he signalled on his grave-way,
>   As with a wave of his hand.[49]

The imagined gesture and responsive poem represented for Hardy an exchange not just of farewells but of salutes, an acknowledgement of his own succession to the headship of Wessex letters. It may in retrospect seem extravagant to think of Hardy's genius as capable of being rebuked by Barnes's, yet Hardy was always conscious of Barnes as having first revived the name Wessex for the region they shared and as possessing a special claim to be regarded as that region's authentic voice.

In seeking to make the life and values of Wessex understandable to an urban audience Hardy, like any interpreter, always ran the risk of falsifying the original in the interests of comprehensibility, and while he knew that Barnes's distortions went far beyond the mere exclusion of their region's darker aspects, he also recognized the uncompromising 'purity' of Barnes's use of the local dialect and his celebration of that dialect in his specifically philological writings. By returning to Dorchester and building Max Gate, Hardy had sought to re-establish himself in a countryside and a context to which Barnes had been more consistently and continuously loyal. In witnessing Barnes's burial he was simultaneously honouring his friend's life and achievement and claiming the succession to literary proprietorship over their common region and a new freedom to impose upon it an over-lapping fictional world of his own creation.

Relocation in Wessex had not, for Hardy, meant reabsorption into the contemporary regional consciousness. Because the dialect was so powerful a deterrent for readers outside and even inside Wessex, he had determined not to be hemmed in by it. The red brick of Max Gate—in such contrast to the mellow thatched charm of Barnes's rectory of Came, just a little further along the Wareham Road—was precisely indicative of the refusal of the returning native to revert to the assumptions of his own past. Simple as his tastes and even his personal habits remained, devoted as he was to the past of the region and profoundly sympathetic to the fundamental truths (in a Wordsworthian sense) of his earliest experience, Hardy had learned through years of deliberate self-education and of London living that there were other, more sophisticated, and on the whole better ways of thinking and acting—more humane ways, for example, of treating animals, and broader views of the nature of the universe. He was able as an artist to articulate the thoughts and feelings of country people precisely because he could look back upon his own early self from the vantage point provided by a much altered set of attitudes and beliefs.

Hardy never felt totally accepted by his Dorchester neighbours, least of all by those who were of his own class or above it. Florence Hardy once said that in the poem 'To Shakespeare' it was her husband's own situation that had informed his imagination of what Shakespeare's snobbish neighbours might have said upon hearing of his death:

> —'Ah, one of the tradesmen's sons, I now recall. . .
> Witty, I've heard. . . . .
> We did not know him. . . . Well, good-day. Death comes to all.'[50]

The 'ordinary' people of Dorchester, having little understanding of what Hardy did and a lurking resentment of his evident success, also found him somewhat difficult to accept. In certain respects, of course, they were right to be suspicious of what went on behind the trees and boundary walls of Max Gate. Though neither house nor owner could properly be described as suburban, both were in important respects semi-urban. Where Barnes at Came had been a prophet almost exclusively within and to his own country, Hardy was an interpreter of that rural world to an urban world that had grown from it—by historical processes comparable to those later charted in D. H. Lawrence's *The Rainbow*—and lost touch with its original self in so doing. Max Gate was a real house in a real place to whose social, political, and economic realities Hardy was fully responsive. But it was at the same time an outpost of the dominant metropolitan culture from which he sent back to his fellow members eloquent reminders of those ancestral values which they might compromise at need but lose sight of only at their peril.

14

The Woodlanders

RESPONDING to Gissing on 1 July 1886, Hardy expressed the fear that the other's 'keen eye for good work' would be disappointed by *The Woodlanders*, then a quarter of the way through its serialization in *Macmillan's Magazine*: 'It would have made a beautiful story if I could have carried out my idea of it: but somehow I come so far short of my intention that I fear it will be quite otherwise—unless I pick up towards the end.' Both the note of self-deprecation and the particular terms in which it is sounded are familiar enough in Hardy's comments on his work, but he does seem to have experienced real difficulty in writing *The Woodlanders*, and especially in completing it to schedule. He started work on the novel late and then broke off to make the final revisions to *The Mayor of Casterbridge*; he was always under the pressure of completing each instalment in time for advance proofs to be sent across the Atlantic for simultaneous publication in *Harper's Bazar*; and, by no means least, he had not finally learned the impracticability of his attempting serious work in London: 'I have some writing to do whilst in town', he told Stevenson on 7 June, '& *can't* touch it: it is becoming quite a nightmare.'[1]

He also found himself increasingly at odds with Mowbray Morris, the editor of *Macmillan's*. Frederick Macmillan, complimenting Hardy in late March 1886 on the first instalment of *The Woodlanders*, had remarked upon 'one or two little things' Morris had marked in the proofs but insisted that they were 'merely suggestions': '[W]e have no desire to "Edit" your work in any impertinent way.' In September, however, when the serial was well advanced, Morris himself wrote to warn Hardy against overstepping the bounds of propriety in handling the affair between Suke Damson and Fitzpiers. The readers of the magazine, he explained, were 'pious Scottish souls who take offence wondrous easily', and it would therefore be well if the 'human frailty' could be 'construed mild' and Suke not brought to 'too open shame'.[2] Hardy had already accepted, or even initiated, the deletion of the crucial last sentence of chapter 20 ('It was daybreak before Fitzpiers and Suke Damson re-entered Little Hintock'), and he now observed due discretion in treating Fitzpiers's relationships with Suke and, later, Mrs Charmond. He subsequently told two potential dramatizers of the novel that 'the conventions of the libraries &c.' had prevented him from more strongly emphasizing its merely 'hinted' conclusion, 'that the heroine is doomed to an unhappy life with an inconstant husband'.[3]

Like other novelists of his period, Hardy had been obliged to learn—and Leslie Stephen had been well equipped to teach—the practical aspects of being 'a good hand' at a Victorian serial, and he became accustomed to revising and rewriting his work in response to the arbitrary and often unpredictable prohibitions imposed by contemporary magazines and circulating libraries. But he was deeply and increasingly troubled as an artist, and while he was a supporter rather than a public leader in the late nineteenth-century fight for freer literary expression he did publish in 1890 a significant essay, entitled 'Candour in English Fiction', that included a telling description of the circumstances in which the author of a serialized novel could find himself forced to betray both his literary conscience and his 'best imaginative instincts' in order to contrive 'a *dénouement* which he knows to be indescribably unreal and meretricious, but dear to the Grundyist and subscriber'.[4]

Although *The Woodlanders* drew heavily on Hardy's own family background, and especially on what his mother had told him of her Melbury Osmond childhood, he made no attempt to visit that area of north-west Dorset while the novel was in progress. As in the intensely personal *The Return of the Native*, he wrote at a deliberate distance from the locations being recreated in fictional terms, as if hoping to preserve the freshness and vitality of the emotionally charged impressions already stamped upon his imagination. He was accustomed to speak of Wessex as a 'partly real, partly dream-country',[5] and though his immediate reference was to matters of topography the formulation had genetic implications as well. For descriptions of buildings, dress, and decor, for impressions of weather and landscape—the physical and natural aspects of his fiction—he could turn to his notebooks, take down books from his shelves, or undertake research into old newspapers and local records. His characters and their actions and motivations, on the other hand, were the products of a more purely imaginative endeavour for which memory, and especially childhood memory, was a basic creative resource. Hardy seems at this point in his career to have believed that disciplines of personal isolation and physical distance could give access to that resource and thus enable the creation of characters capable, in R. R. Bowker's eloquent phrase, of 'walk[ing] out from the chambers of memory through the gates of the imagination'.[6] Hardy, more prosaically, once told his second wife that as soon as the characters began to take hold of a story and carry it forward he knew that all would be well.[7]

Hardy did not of course feel precluded from revisiting the scenes of *The Woodlanders* once the manuscript had been completed, and it was during such a visit to Melbury Osmond that he made a drawing of Townsend, the house in which his grandmother Betty Swetman had lived with her parents and that he evidently associated with Grace Melbury and her father in the novel.[8] Such associations fed into Hardy's subsequently expressed preference for *The Woodlanders*, 'as a story', over all of his other novels.[9] His imagination was seized by the beauty of the landscape in the vicinity of High Stoy, by the seclusion and restrictedness of the woodland setting, and by his personal memories of his Higher Bockhampton childhood and of the trees at the edge of Thorncombe Wood among which that childhood was so largely spent. The novel also gave him the opportunity to celebrate in the figure of Giles Winterborne the qualities he had learned to admire in his own father, the latter's characteristic dilatoriness and unassertiveness becoming an important part of the overall portrait, and there are hints throughout the book of nostalgic yearnings towards the simpler days and ways that were always identified with Bockhampton in his imagination. The evocation in *Life and Work* of Hardy's assisting in his father's cider-making for the last time in the autumn preceding his marriage is, for example, complemented by the description of Giles Winterborne at the cider press, surrounded by 'that atmosphere of cider which . . . has such an indescribable fascination for those who have been born and bred among the orchards'.[10]

Hardy was never far ahead of the printer during the serialization of *The Woodlanders*, and ten of the twelve instalments in *Macmillan's Magazine* had already appeared by the time he was able to record, at precisely 8.20 p.m. in the evening of 4 February 1887, that the manuscript of *The Woodlanders* was at last complete: 'Thought I should feel glad', Hardy wrote, 'but I do not particularly,—though relieved.' Two days later he paid what had already become his regular Sunday visit to Higher Bockhampton, where his father talked of walking into Dorchester one day in 1830 or thereabouts and happening upon a public flogging of three men at the town-pump on Cornhill. Another group of notes, dating from a little later in the month, is suggestive of the more abstract issues on which he was brooding throughout this period: 'I was thinking a night or two ago that people are somnambu-lists—that the material is not the real—only the visible, the real being invisible optically.'[11] Having once completed his revisions of the serial version of *The Woodlanders* in preparation for his first experience of being published by the house of Macmillan, Hardy made a brief visit to London in early March to be present at a conference on copyright organized by the Incorporated Society of Authors, and then—on 15 March, publication day for *The Woodlanders*—set off with Emma on a long-contemplated visit to Italy.[12]

The early stages of their journey were unpropitious. It snowed in London before they left and there were heavy snowfalls during their overnight train journey across France. When they stopped at Dijon for a meal, so Emma reported in her quite detailed diary of the trip, 'Tom was very vexed, dyspeptic, before & worse now'. On the train from Aix to Turin the con-ductor carried off their tickets for some mysterious reason, and when he was slow to reappear, 'We recriminated,' wrote Emma, '& grew more & more uneasy about them.' They spent a night in Turin and two nights in Genoa, where a visit to the Palazzo Doria helped to counteract the rather depress-ing first impression of the city ('not as the Beauty but the Dowd') which Hardy later invoked in the poem 'Genoa and the Mediterranean'. That afternoon Hardy went out exploring by himself while Emma made friends with a Japanese child and some kittens, although she later complained that Italian cats were all short-haired, unlike the long-haired beauties of France.[13]

The next day they travelled southward to Florence, seeing the landscape of the poem 'Shelley's Skylark' only from the train window but breaking their journey at Pisa long enough to visit the Cathedral and the Baptistery and climb up the Leaning Tower. At Florence they were met by William Barnes's daughter Lucy Baxter and her husband and taken by carriage to the Villa Trollope, at the northernmost corner of the Piazza dell'Indipendenza. At this time a pension run by a Scottish couple, the house had previously belonged to the Trollope family, and Anthony Trollope himself had written *Doctor Thorne* there just thirty years before. There followed several days of regulation sightseeing, sometimes in the company of Mrs Baxter and her sister, usually by themselves: necessarily included were the Medici tombs, the Uffizi, and the Pitti Palace—where Hardy jotted down in his Baedeker brief notes on a bust of Napoleon by Canova ('the morose exprn preserved') and a Canova Venus ('pressing robe to bosom') and sceptically observed of Titian's Magdalene that the artist had been interested only in painting a handsome woman.[14] By the Wednesday evening, Emma recorded, 'Tom is quite wearied out & in his bed'; the next morning, though they both felt exhausted, they went to the Duomo. As they drove back to the pension, Emma, with her usual sensitivity to such matters, noticed that the horse was very weak, but she was disconcerted by the driver's responding to her rebuke not with the 'offensive reply' of a London cabman but with expressions of gratitude for her interest in the animal's well-being.[15]

At the end of the week they took the train to Rome. After two miserable nights at their first hotel ('hard bed, noisy square, & b-gs, noise of fountain as well as traffic, the latter as great as Londons—no sleep') they moved to pleasanter quarters at the Hotel Allemagne in the Via dei Condotti, just below the Spanish Steps. Because Hardy's interest in classical rather than in Christian Rome conveniently coincided with Emma's distrust of Catholicism (the churches seemed to her to be '*full of trash*') they were drawn back repeatedly to the area of the Forum, where Emma on one occasion broke her umbrella while repelling the attentions of a persistent little shoe-black and, on another, courageously intervened to drive off the three thieves who had attacked her husband and stolen a picture he had just purchased.[16] One day they drove out to the Protestant Cemetery on a pilgrimage to the graves of Shelley and Keats, both pre-eminent in Hardy's poetic pantheon. Sending Gosse two violets from Keats's grave later that same day, Hardy reported that he was so overpowered by the prevailing sense of decay in the ancient parts of the city that he felt it 'like a nightmare in my sleep'. There was furious building activity in contemporary Rome, he added, 'but how any community can go on building in the face of the "Vanitas vanitatum" reiterated by the ruins is quite marvellous'.

He made entries in his notebook to this same effect—perhaps with some recollection of the portrayal of Rome in Hawthorne's *The Marble Faun*, read some years previously—and drew upon them when writing 'Rome: Building a New Street in the Ancient Quarter', one of the four poems about the city which he worked up at a later date.[17] On Friday, 1 April, Hardy and Emma made their second visit to the Vatican, but only, as Emma noted, 'after much worrying whether we should go again or not'. They then went on to the Catacombs, where Hardy registered the 'cynical humour' of the monks who acted as guides, and to the Appian Way, which he described to his mother that evening (on a postcard written in a large, round, almost painfully clear hand) in exclusively Christian terms: 'We went to-day along the Appian Way towards the Three Taverns, the road by which St Paul came to Rome, as described in the last Chapter of Acts.'[18]

On 3 April, after staying in Rome a day longer than they had intended, the Hardys returned to Florence and the Villa Trollope. Emma had a cold and felt 'very feverish' in the train but was well enough the next day to call on Mrs Baxter and visit the monastery of San Marco, where she thought the cells 'quite fair-sized chambers seeming very possible to live comfortably in' and decided that Savonarola looked like George Eliot. Fra Angelico, however, seems not to have impressed her, and she confided to her diary the following day that 'old frescoes are horrid entre-nous (Note book & I)'. Hardy got up at 5 o'clock one morning and went to Siena by himself, but the remainder of the week was spent in Florence and filled with sightseeing and social expeditions, including a visit to Elizabeth Barrett Browning's tomb, a call on Violet Paget ('Vernon Lee') and her disabled half-brother Eugene Lee-Hamilton, and a trip to Fiesole with Mrs Baxter that nearly ended in disaster when the horse of their omnibus suddenly bolted. By the final day the Hardys not surprisingly felt 'utterly prostrate', confining their activities to shopping and a farewell call upon the Baxters.[19]

Arriving in Venice on Wednesday, 13 April, Hardy was seriously displeased at finding that their room at the Hotel Angleterre (on the Riva degli Schiavoni) did not face onto the Grand Canal. They had recently met some congenial Americans and did much of their early sightseeing in their company, although the cold, wet weather discouraged lengthy expeditions. On the Sunday Emma had to stay resting in her room ('my knee being jointless') while Hardy, armed with letters of introduction, called on two leaders of the Anglo-American community in the city, Mrs Bronson and Mrs Curtis, known to literary history for their friendships with, respectively, Browning and Henry James. Emma put a brave face on the situation: 'Very disappointing for me', she wrote in her diary, adding, with emphasis, '(*For the best always*)'—although it is not clear whether this was her standard response to disappointments or, more distressingly, a specific recognition that Hardy on his own would probably be more warmly received than if she had gone with him. She was in any case welcomed a little later by both Mrs Bronson and Mrs Curtis, their attentive hospitality combining with some warmer weather to enliven the Hardys' last few Venetian days. Hardy himself, having had Shelley and Browning much in mind throughout his Italian travels, was now especially concerned to identify places associated with Byron, and he would later indulge the rather romantic regret that he had made no attempt to track down local inhabitants who might have remembered Byron's presence in the city some seventy years earlier.[20]

On Friday, 22 April, they left Venice for Milan, where Hardy's imagination was chiefly seized by the city's Napoleonic associations. On the

Saturday he visited the Bridge of Lodi, site of a famous Napoleonic victory, in the company of a young Scotsman, on his way home from India, whom they had met in the train. Emma meanwhile went out to buy presents to take home, including a tie for her brother-in-law, Henry Hardy. The next day they took the train to Lucerne, and spent the night there before going on to Paris the following morning. As they boarded the Paris train in Lucerne, there was what Emma in her diary called an 'altercation' over seats between Hardy and a man with three restless and ill-behaved children whom they had previously encountered on the train from Milan. That Emma was largely responsible for Hardy's defeat in the exchange becomes clear from her own account of subsequent events: 'Changed at Basle—gentleman apologised for not getting out for me—& seemed really sorry—no doubt out of gratitude for my taking his part, & pitying his trying situation with the children.'[21] When they arrived in Paris early Tuesday morning Emma was ill with diarrhoea and unrested: there had been another man in the carriage and she had felt too embarrassed to stretch herself out on the seats as she liked to do when she and Hardy were alone. She was well enough, however, to drive and walk about Paris that day, and to travel back to London the following morning, Wednesday, 27 April.[22]

When Hardy got back to England he found that *The Woodlanders* had already attracted a number of enthusiastic reviews. Its overall reception, indeed, was to prove altogether more favourable, and more thoughtful, than that of its predecessor. *The Times* compared Hardy to Millet and praised his capacity to harmonize the poetry and the penury of rural life. Gosse, writing in the *Saturday Review*, spoke warmly of the book's 'richness and humanity', but made a number of criticisms—one of them, to the effect that Giles was 'a little too consciously treated as the incarnation of a phase of village civilization', rather ungraciously derived from a private remark that Hardy himself had made. Some reviewers found the moral tone distasteful; one blamed Hardy for surrendering to the influence of 'the French novel'; and even Coventry Patmore, incited by Gosse to review the book for the *St James's Gazette*, began with lavish praise of Hardy's previous work but followed up with severe reservations about the repulsiveness of Fitzpiers and Mrs Charmond and the implausibility of an ending which depended—as he, like many readers then and since, assumed—upon the permanent reformation of the deplorable Fitzpiers.[23] Obviously Mowbray Morris was not unique in his sensitivity, but nor was Hardy wrong to fear that he had compromised his novel's conclusion and final effect.

All of the reviews were respectful, however, none entirely negative, and before the end of May it was clear that *The Woodlanders* was Hardy's greatest critical success since *Far from the Madding Crowd*—with which, indeed, it was rather astutely compared by a reviewer in the *Dublin Evening Mail*.[24] Much encouraged, Hardy ventured to send presentation copies of the first edition to Mrs Sutherland Orr's brother Sir Frederick Leighton, the president of the Royal Academy, to Lord Lytton, who responded with a letter of extravagant praise, and to his old hero Swinburne, whom he had never yet met.[25] He was also able to respond with full confidence, as well as considerable economic satisfaction, to an offer of one thousand guineas from Tillotson & Son's Newspaper Fiction Bureau, a syndicated fiction business, for exclusive serial rights to his next full-length novel, although it was well for his peace of mind when he signed the contract on 29 June 1887[26] that he could not foresee the vicissitudes through which the book would pass before it was finally published, as *Tess of the d'Urbervilles*, four and a half years later.

Hardy's gesture in sending his book to Sir Frederick Leighton is indicative of his continuing interest in painting and sculpture at this period. His musings on the nature of reality at the time when he was completing *The Woodlanders* had evidently been touched off by the landscape painting, reputed to be by Bonington, that hung in the Max Gate drawing room: 'I don't want to see landscapes, *i.e.* scenic paintings of them,' he wrote in January 1887, 'because I don't want to see the original realities—as optical effects, that is. I want to see the deeper reality underlying the scenic, the expression of what are sometimes called abstract imaginings.' He continued:

The 'simply natural' is interesting no longer. The much decried, mad, late-Turner rendering is now necessary to create my interest. The exact truth as to material fact ceases to be of importance in art—it is a student's style—the style of a period when the mind is serene and unawakened to the tragical mysteries of life; when it does not bring anything to the object that coalesces with and translates the qualities that are already there,—half hidden, it may be—and the two united are depicted as the All.[27]

It was characteristic of Hardy's visualizing imagination that he should so often use analogies from painting to help define the essentially literary problems he was trying to confront. When, two years later, he saw some Turner watercolours at the Royal Academy, he tried to draw a generalized lesson from what he regarded as Turner's attempt to concoct a 'pictorial drug' capable of producing in the eye of the viewer an effect approximating to that of the unreproducible actuality: 'Hence, one may say, Art is the secret of how to produce by a false thing the effect of a true.'[28]

The profusion of artistic references and visual effects in Hardy's novels and poems is at one level attributable to the intricate interaction between narrative literature and narrative painting prevalent throughout the Victorian period. It seems impossible to determine, for example, the precise degrees of reminiscence and coincidence involved in the relationships between *Under the Greenwood Tree* and Thomas Webster's painting called *The Village Choir*, between Angel's transportation of the milkmaids through the flooded lane and Mulready's *Crossing the Ford*, or between 'Too Late, Beloved!', the abandoned title for *Tess of the d'Urbervilles*, and William Lindsay Windus's *Too Late*—itself a visualization of Tennyson's poem 'Come not, when I am dead'.[29] If the headings given to the successive 'phases' of *Tess* are readily imaginable as the titles of Victorian paintings (e.g., 'Maiden No More', 'The Consequence', 'The Woman Pays'), that is perhaps only to say that Hardy was also working deliberately in terms of moral fable, incorporating within the individual work a moral or social statement which, if not always explicit, would nonetheless be perfectly legible.

But Hardy's artistic interests went far beyond the nineteenth century and the function of paintings as didactic tableaux. He was extraordinarily sensitive to colours—he records covering up a letter lying on a red velvet tablecloth so that it would not 'hit my eyes so hard'—and deeply absorbed in fundamental questions of artistic technique: 'My art', he declared in 1886, 'is to intensify the expression of things, as is done by Crivelli, Bellini, etc., so that the heart and inner meaning is made vividly visible.'[30] He kept up an active acquaintance with a number of prominent sculptors, painters, and illustrators, and used his frequent visits to London to maintain such connections and visit galleries, exhibitions, and museums. He became particularly friendly with Gosse's friend, the sculptor Hamo Thornycroft, and with Gosse's brother-in-law, Lawrence Alma-Tadema, and was on terms of some intimacy with Alfred Parsons, who stayed at Max Gate while preparing the illustrations for Hardy's story 'The First Countess of Wessex', and with the family of William Powell Frith. It was in 1887, following the publication of *The Woodlanders*, that Frith made his own gesture of friendship, referring publicly to Hardy as unsurpassed among living English writers for 'absolute truth to nature and a far sight into the depths of the human heart, . . . He is now his own rival, whom I sincerely hope he will live to throw into shade.'[31]

The Hardys had returned from Italy in time for Hardy to attend his first Royal Academy dinner on 30 April 1887. They subsequently found lodgings in Kensington, at 5 Campden Hill Road, and stayed on in London until late July and the end of a 'season' made especially colourful by the celebrations associated with Queen Victoria's Golden Jubilee. The time passed 'gaily enough'. Mrs Procter was still going strong, with Browning still in regular attendance, though on one occasion so 'sleepy' that he would break off in the middle of the story he was telling, 'forgetting what he was going to say'. At a Savile Club dinner Hardy found himself in distinguished political company—including the then Chancellor of the Exchequer, George Goschen, and a future Prime Minister, A. J. Balfour—and at a Royal Academy soirée he found himself once more in the company of Matthew Arnold.[32] Mrs Jeune was also present on that occasion, and Hardy's friendship with her continued to flourish. His most frequent hostess, however, seems still to have been Lady Carnarvon, and while he had mixed feelings about the entertainment she offered—he noted of one occasion that it was the 'dullest and stupidest of all her parties this season'—he evidently took pleasure in sustaining his friendship with her, with the Portsmouths, and especially with the Portsmouth daughters, who were almost always present. Even that dullest of parties was redeemed by his first meeting with Lady Catherine Milnes-Gaskell, 'the prettiest of all Lady Portsmouth's daughters. Round luminous enquiring eyes.'[33]

Some of the notes Hardy made at this period were later drawn upon for the 'Society' chapters of his late novel *The Well-Beloved*, and it is conceivable that he sometimes attended such functions in the spirit of professional obligation, of 'resignation' to novel-writing 'as a trade', to which *Life and Work* ascribes his occasional appearances at the law courts.[34] Such references, however, seem less reflective of his views at the time than of his concern, in old age, to assert the superior importance of his verse. Though he doubtless found his note-taking onerous, and sometimes engaged in it 'mechanically', the practice had become indispensable to his creative method as a novelist, while the sheer accumulation of so many images, scenes, incidents, and narrative ideas was to prove, in later years, a primary source of his extraordinarily prolonged fecundity as a poet. Note-taking was, of course, a common Victorian activity, partly as an offshoot of the new respect for the methodology of science, but Hardy's persistence in the habit seems also to reflect some continuing insecurity about his educational background and his capacity to hold his own in the exclusive circles in which he now found himself—his 'right', in short, to be where he was. There is more than a hint of self-doubt, inextricably combined with amazed self-congratulation, in the note dated 2 June 1887: 'The forty-seventh birthday of Thomas the Unworthy.'[35]

When, however, Hardy returned to Max Gate at the very end of July he was in unusually high spirits. Responding to a letter from Gosse in late August he dismissed in jocular fashion the almost suicidally depressive states that had once overwhelmed him:

This blackest state of mind was however several years ago—& seldom recurs now. One day I was saying to myself 'Why art thou so heavy, O my soul, & why art thou so disquieted within me?' I could not help answering 'Because you eat that pastry after a long walk, & would not profit by experience'. The stomach is no doubt a main cause, if there is no mental reason: but I totally disagree with those who insist upon blaming the stomach always. In my worst times years ago my digestion was as sound as a labourer's.

At the very end of December he concluded that the year 1887 had been on the whole friendly to him, bringing new experiences and new acquaintances and enabling him, with the successful publication of *The Woodlanders*, 'to hold my own in fiction, whatever that may be worth'.[36]

During the autumn and winter of 1887–8 Hardy was chiefly engaged in the writing of short stories. Though he had produced and sold stories since the very beginning of his career, and been grateful for their supplementation of his income, he had written them only occasionally, and usually in response to specific opportunities. Leslie Stephen, however, had once suggested that he might write a linked series of 'prose-idyls of country life— short sketches of Hodge & his ways',[37] and Hardy now realized that he had already published several stories of good quality—including 'The Distracted Young Preacher', 'Fellow-Townsmen', 'The Three Strangers', and 'Interlopers at the Knap'—that had at least their Wessex settings in common. Once, therefore, he had disposed of 'Alicia's Diary', a cumbersome story dependent in many of its details upon his recent Italian travels, he settled down to write, with far greater care and imaginative investment, what emerged as 'The Withered Arm'. One of the most powerful—and most gruesome—of his shorter narratives, the story drew material not only from familiar Wessex settings, including Casterbridge itself, but also from the half-legendary tales he had heard from the lips of his mother and grandmother—both of whom are invoked in notes surviving from September 1887.[38] When the story was completed he submitted it first to *Longman's Magazine*, which had printed 'The Three Strangers' a few years earlier, only to be told that it was much too grim and unrelieved for a magazine read mostly by girls. Hardy promptly sent it off again, this time to *Blackwood's*, with the comment that the main incidents were essentially true and that he had himself known the two women concerned. *Blackwood's* accepted the story, and it appeared in the January 1888 number—Stephen promptly writing to Hardy to point out, with gentle insistence, that the withering itself was neither scientifically explained nor specifically called hallucinatory.[39]

Having received £24 from *Blackwood's* for his new story, Hardy put it together with the four previous stories he thought particularly well of, offered the collection, as *Wessex Tales*, to Frederick Macmillan, and accepted Macmillan's offer of publication in two volumes at the same royalty of one-sixth the retail price as had earlier been agreed for the one-volume edition of *The Woodlanders*.[40] It was only since the Macmillans had become his publishers that Hardy had begun receiving royalties instead of cash payments for book publication of his works. The new arrangements reflected ongoing changes in the relationship between authors and publishers, but they also indicated—as had Macmillan's eagerness to sign him up for colonial editions of *The Mayor of Casterbridge* and *The Woodlanders*—the growing strength of Hardy's own negotiating position. Within a few years he would have a falling out with Macmillan over the interpretation and application of the agreements between them, but the shift to a royalty system, by giving him a continuing financial interest in his literary properties, not only improved his immediate economic situation but significantly enhanced its stability over the longer term. The sense that things were, in general, going well for him was reflected not only in that genial retrospective assessment of the year 1887 but also in a note made early in 1888: 'Be rather curious than anxious about your own career; for whatever result may accrue to its intellectual and social value, it will make little difference to your personal well-being. A naturalist's interest in the hatching of a queer egg or germ is the utmost introspective consideration you should allow yourself.'[41]

Hardy spent the winter writing at Max Gate, in accordance with what had become and would remain his standard practice. By early March 1888 he was back in London, staying—as, again, he almost always did—at a temperance hotel, although he moved into lodgings when Emma joined him in late April. In London he frequented the Savile Club and the Reading Room of the British Museum ('Souls are gliding about here in a sort of dream—screened somewhat by their bodies, but imaginable behind them'), visited Mary Jeune, Lady Catherine Milnes-Gaskell, and Edmund Gosse, and attended a musical afternoon given by the Alma-Tademas.[42] On 4 May *Wessex Tales* was published, and on the 28th the Hardys left for another holiday in Paris, remaining there for almost four weeks and amusing themselves in a variety of unstrenuous ways. They visited picture galleries and the royal tombs at Saint-Denis, went shopping and to theatres together, and attended the annual running of the Grand Prix at the Longchamp race course. Combining simple curiosity with a vague sense of professional obligation, Hardy visited the Archives Nationales in the Hôtel de Soubise ('much more interesting than I had expected'), inspected an exhibition of manuscripts and drawings by Victor Hugo, and even sat through a few cases of a minor nature in one of the law courts.[43]

Back in London in late June of 1888 they took lodgings at 5 Upper Phillimore Place, one of a series of late eighteenth-century terraces which then stood on the north side of Kensington High Street, just east of Holland House. It was Walter Pater, living nearby, who recalled for them that George III had called the terraces the 'dish-clouts' because of the carved swags of drapery with which they were ornamented. Because the Hardys' bedroom faced onto Kensington High Street they were often disturbed in the early hours of the morning by the noise of the market wagons making their way in from the country to Covent Garden, each with 'its weighty pyramid of vegetables'—an experience irritating at the time but later to be drawn upon in the story 'The Son's Veto'. Though Hardy suffered his usual heavy cold (*Life and Work* calls it 'a rheumatic attack') as a consequence of his holiday, he was soon tasting the standard pleasures of the 'season', visiting the theatre—notably Ada Rehan's performance as Katherina in Augustin Daly's production of *The Taming of the Shrew*—and enjoying the company of such friends as Mrs Ritchie, whom he had not met since she was Miss Thackeray, and Lady Portsmouth, with whom he and Emma had tea. Hardy admired Lady Portsmouth for looking on that occasion exactly 'like a model countess' and, more especially, for being herself: 'She is one of the few, very few, women of her own rank for whom I would make a sacrifice: a woman too of talent, part of whose talent consists in concealing that she has any.'[44]

In mid-July of 1888, shortly after sounding out Lord Carnarvon as to the possibility of his being elected to the Athenaeum Club, Hardy made an unexpectedly early return from London to Dorchester, where part of the drawing-room ceiling at Max Gate had fallen down. Once back in his 'writing-box', he began work on the two stories, 'A Tragedy of Two Ambitions' and 'The First Countess of Wessex', that he had promised to magazines.[45] He had also made longer-term commitments with respect to the novel that would eventually become *Tess of the d'Urbervilles*, the original agreement with Tillotson's specifying delivery of the first four instalments of the serial by 30 June 1889—later put back to September 1889—and 'the remainder by Weekly Instalments, until completed'.[46] In a letter to the novelist Eliza Lynn Linton written on Christmas Eve of 1888, Hardy described himself as 'just in the worrying stage of coming to a decision upon my leading idea of a long story planned sometime ago; & between my own conviction of what is truest to life, & what editors and critics will tolerate as being true to their conventional principles, bless them!'[47]

15

The Writing of *Tess*

IF not much of the new novel had been written by the end of 1888, it had certainly been very much at the front of Hardy's mind. An expedition into central Dorset on 30 September 1888—exactly a year before the first serial instalments would become due—was directly related to the process of thinking himself into the social as well as the emotional texture of his new story, of invoking that sense of historical time and visitable place on which he depended for the essential underpinning of his most ambitious imaginative enterprises. He took a train to Evershot station—actually located in the hamlet of Holywell, a mile or so east of Evershot itself—and walked the short distance northward to visit what remained of Woolcombe, an estate (so he had learned from John Hutchins's *History and Antiquities of the County of Dorset*) formerly in the possession of one of those branches of 'the Dorset Hardys' to which he liked to think himself related. In his notes for the day he invoked for the first time 'The Valley of the Little Dairies' and 'The Valley of the Great Dairies', the fictional names he had given to the vales of Blackmore and Frome, recalled a childhood encounter with an impoverished remnant of the once-proud Woolcombe Hardys walking 'beside a horse and common spring trap', found ample evidence of 'the decline and fall of the Hardys', and concluded with the satisfactorily melancholy reflection: 'So we go down, down, down.'[1] It was a mood appropriately fed by the discovery, at Evershot station, of some mistletoe that had been there 'ever since last Christmas (given by a lass?), of a yellow saffron parchment colour'— evidently the 'source' of the mistletoe which Tess finds hanging meaninglessly over the marital bed after she has made her disastrous confession to Angel Clare. Hardy was now close to the country of *The Woodlanders* and of 'The First Countess of Wessex'—the story he had recently based upon an episode in the past history of the Ilchester family of Melbury House—and before returning to Dorchester that day he walked to the top of Bubb-Down Hill and gazed out over the Vale of Blackmore, associated in his mind with William Barnes, Riverside Villa, and Jane Phillips—and now with Tess Durbeyfield, the as yet unnamed heroine of his as yet unwritten novel.[2]

Thirty and more years later Hardy was to recognize in a young local actress named Gertrude Bugler a striking physical resemblance to Tess Durbeyfield as she had so long existed in his mind, and he once confessed that the association was made more poignant by the fact that it was Mrs Bugler's mother, Augusta Way, seen working as a milkmaid on the Kingston Maurward estate, who had first suggested the figure of Tess to his imagination.[3] The Way family lived in part of the old Kingston Maurward manor house, close by the barn in which Hardy as a child had attended the harvest supper and heard the old ballads so memorably sung, and Augusta, who was 18 in 1888, shared with her sisters in the milking and other chores of the dairy run by their father Thomas Way, very much as Dairyman Crick runs his dairy in *Tess of the d'Urbervilles*. Such associations helped to establish the idea of Tess the milkmaid in Hardy's mind. But once it was so established other images and associations began to accrete to it, including those relating to Jane Phillips of Sturminster Newton. Not only does Jane Phillips's situation conform more closely to the narrative details of the novel than that of any other feasible 'original', but Hardy's memories of her singing make her by far the likeliest possessor of that voice described in the novel as unforgettable by those who had once heard it.

What other elements went into the novel it is impossible to be sure. The early experiences of Mary Head no doubt made their contribution, though her grandson seems to have associated her more specifically with *Jude the Obscure*, and the scene of the midnight baptism certainly owed a good deal to Jemima's memories of her mother's private performance of the baptisms her father had forbidden: Hardy more than once told enquirers that the episode was factual and that he could take them to the bedroom where it had occurred.[4] The suggestion that Kate Hardy 'was' Tess has no plausible basis, the story that she once had an illegitimate child having evidently originated in her own rambling deathbed references to a daughter whom 'they' took away from her. And when Hardy remarked that he would have called the novel *Tess of the Hardys* if it had not seemed 'too personal'[5] he seems chiefly to have had in mind his own family's experience of having come down in the world—becoming in the process Hardys instead of Hardyes or le Hardys, much as the fictional d'Urbervilles had declined to

Durbeyfields, the historical Turbervilles to Troublefields, or the Phelipses
to Phillipses.

Hardy, who gave much attention to the naming of his characters, was
particularly happy in the combination of d'Urberville and Durbeyfield, the
one a Norman-sounding name that nevertheless hints at the urban origins
of the *nouveau riche* family by whom it has been appropriated, the other an
uncompromisingly rural and plebeian name that nevertheless sounds like
an authentic 'corruption'. The naming of Angel Clare was a particularly
bold gesture on Hardy's part—who else, a modern critic once asked, 'would
have dared to give him the name Angel, and a harp too?'—and it may also
have been a very personal one. It has sometimes been assumed that Hardy
took Charles W. Moule as his model for Angel, but he told an interviewer in
1892 that Angel was a 'subtle, poetical man' of 'fastidious temperament'
whose 'great subtilty of mind' alone prevented him from following his
brothers into the Church.[6] Such comments, taken together with Angel's
musical gifts and his uneasy relationship with his parents, seem more
suggestive of Horace Moule than of the amenable and orthodox (though
unordained) Charles, while the episode involving the books of which
Angel's father disapproved was directly based upon the sequence of events
by which the two volumes of Mantell's *Wonders of Geology* came into Hardy's
possession. An identification of Angel with Horace Moule fits well with the
perceptible links between Angel and the morally and sexually fastidious
Henry Knight of *A Pair of Blue Eyes*, and opens up the further possibility that
in Angel and Alec Hardy was dramatizing the two sides of Moule's fatally
divided personality, its combination of extreme refinement with a capacity
for sensual self-abandonment.

The heroine of Hardy's new novel was for a long time called Sue, and in
July 1889 he was suggesting that the novel be called 'The Body and Soul of
Sue', only to change his mind within a week or two in favour of 'Too Late,
Beloved!', a phrase familiar to him from Shelley's 'Epipsychidion'. But
within a late Victorian context it sounded much too melodramatic, and
Hardy was clearly right to opt instead for a title—itself a revision from 'A
Daughter of the d'Urbervilles'[7]—that firmly established Tess's dignity and
individuality and stressed from the first that she was, though born
Durbeyfield, of ancient d'Urberville descent, the inheritor (for good or ill) of
distinctive family traits. *Tess of the d'Urbervilles* is nevertheless a remarkably
cool title for so passionate a book, and it is possible that those earlier titles
were rejected precisely because of the undisguised directness with which
they spoke to Hardy's central concerns. He was obsessed throughout his life
by the struggle between soul and body—*Jude the Obscure* might very appro-

priately have been called *The Body and Soul of Sue*—and once dismissively declared of W. E. Henley's poem 'Invictus': 'No man is master of his soul: the flesh is master of it!'[8]

He was no less haunted by the sheer irrevocability of moments of decision and choice: the opportunity lost, the word unuttered, the road not taken, the beloved recognized or reclaimed too late. It is upon such moments, evoked in all their irony and despair, that so many of his novels and stories turn, as well as some of the most poignant of his poems. Almost always it is a woman who 'pays', who finds herself bereft or betrayed by some such trick of fate or failure of character: what destroys Tess Durbeyfield is not so much her sexual exploitation by Alec as her far more radical betrayal by the man in whom she has voluntarily invested all her trust and love. Whatever its specific sources, *Tess of the d'Urbervilles* was driven into being by the surging movement of human compassion detectable throughout the work in the narrator's scarcely disguised advocacy of the heroine's case—an advocacy confirmed by that polemical subtitle which, at the very last moment, Hardy could not resist inserting: 'A Pure Woman, Faithfully Presented'.[9]

Although Hardy was now well known in Dorchester and quite active in local affairs, he often felt isolated at Max Gate. Writing in mid-April 1889 to John Addington Symonds, confined by illness to the Alpine elevation of Davos Platz, he spoke of himself as being also 'in a sense exiled. I was obliged to leave Town after a severe illness some years ago—& the spot on which I live here is very lonely. However I think that, though one does get a little rusty by living in remote places, one gains, on the other hand, freedom from those temporary currents of opinion by which town people are caught up & distracted out of their true courses.'[10] The end of April, however, found him once again risking those currents and taking Emma up to London for a visit that lasted until the end of July. Although they were in a hotel at first—the West Central temperance hotel, just off Russell Square— they later took 'two furnished floors' at 20 Monmouth Road, Bayswater, a street quite close to the Newton Road house in which they lived for some months in 1875.[11] The summer followed a now familiar course of concerts, theatres, exhibitions, hours in the British Museum Reading Room, and visits and entertainment received and returned. There was talk of Mary and Kate coming up for their Whitsun holiday in early June, but they wrote to Emma to say (apparently without intending a snub of any kind) that they had already arranged to spend the time at Bockhampton.[12]

Hardy, now nearing 50, was becoming sensible of increasing age as well as of growing reputation, and London provided many occasions for him to register the attractions of young women glimpsed in trains and buses or while walking about the city. On 29 May, three days before his forty-ninth birthday, he remarks of a girl seen in an omnibus that she had 'one of those faces of marvellous beauty which are seen casually in the streets but never among one's friends. . . . Where do these women come from? Who marries them? Who knows them?' At the end of June he comments on the beauty of Lady Coleridge, wife of the Lord Chief Justice, encountered at dinner at Mrs Jeune's. On another occasion in July he found himself in the company of Amélie Rives, the American novelist, 'a fair, pink, golden-haired creature, but not quite ethereal enough, suggesting a flesh-surface too palpably. A girlish, almost childish laugh, showing beautiful young teeth.'[13]

Some time in late May or early June 1889 he met Arthur Graham Tomson, a landscape painter of some reputation, and his wife Rosamund, who at the age of 29 was already well-known within the contemporary 'aesthetic' movement and had just published her first volume of verse, *The Bird-Bride*, under the pseudonym of Graham R. Tomson. She was intelligent, gifted, strikingly handsome—an article of 1890 described her as a 'tall, slight, brown-haired woman, with large grey eyes, that at times seemed to be a deep hazel, and a striking individuality pervading her carriage, manner, and dress, the artistic largely dominating the latter'—and no less strikingly independent: she had already divorced her first husband and within a few years she would leave Arthur Tomson for the Australian-born writer H. B. Marriott Watson.[14] Just how much Hardy knew of Rosamund Tomson's personal history it is impossible to tell, but he was at first highly susceptible to her rare combination of literary accomplishment, sexual appeal, and openness of manner and saw in her his ideal of an emancipated woman—self-confident, even assertive, yet evidently less threatening than the 'Faustine' he had met at Walter Pater's the previous summer and categorized as being 'of the class of interesting women one would be afraid to marry'.[15] The copy of *The Bird-Bride* Rosamund Tomson sent to Hardy is dated 7 June 1889 and inscribed 'with the sincere admiration of G.R.T.' His earliest surviving letters to her, in the autumn of 1889, show unusual warmth—they are signed 'Ever sincerely yours' and 'Always yours sincerely'—but also the kind of coy indirection which was to characterize his communications with his closest women friends over the next few years. In one he insists that wild horses would not drag out of him 'that estimate of a poetess's works which came to my ears—till I see her'. In another, he remarks that it is raining but that 'the lovers walk two-&-two just the same, under umbrellas—or rather under one umbrella (which makes all the difference)'.[16]

Hardy eventually broke off the relationship, perhaps after learning of the forthcoming action for divorce, and subsequently claimed that Rosamund Tomson had wanted merely to show him off as one of a long train of admirers.[17] Mrs Tomson, however, possessed ability as well as beauty, and Hardy's deprecating comment betrays an element of deflated vanity. For her the entire episode may indeed have been little more than an almost incidental flirtation with a distinguished older man who could perhaps be helpful to her always difficult career. But for Hardy its impact was considerable. The seriousness of his attraction to her is obvious from the much later poem 'An Old Likeness (Recalling R.T.)', in which she is associated with 'a far season | Of love and unreason',[18] and the experience, whatever it may actually have amounted to, seems to have marked a turning point in his relationship with Emma. Like many men, Hardy perhaps enjoyed the public appearance of sexual privilege almost as much as its actual exercise, and although there is no evidence, and little likelihood, that his adventures went to the point, or even within the range, of adultery, he kept only the slackest of reins on his fantasy life at this time—as *The Well-Beloved* would indicate—and made the most of his many opportunities to be in the company of handsome women and become the recipient of their attention and admiration. He was himself responsible for the seating arrangement at the dinner of the Incorporated Society of Authors on 3 July 1889 which gave him Mrs Tomson on his left hand, Mrs Mona Caird on his right, and Miss Mabel Robinson immediately opposite.[19]

At dinner at the Gosses' on 2 July 1889 Hardy sat next to Agatha, the wife of Gosse's sculptor friend Hamo Thornycroft, who was himself in France. Writing to her husband the following day, she reported that Hardy was 'most attentive & nice, not shy, as he sometimes is, & quite talkative. He wanted to persuade me to go with the Gosses to the dinner of the Society of Authors to-night at the Criterion at which there are to be about 200 people, and at which Edmund [Gosse] makes a speech. He considered it was right I shd be gay while you were away; fearful morals with which to corrupt an inexperienced & innocent person!' The young face that Hardy was seeking to add to the surrounding galaxy that he had already organized for the Authors' dinner belonged on this occasion to the woman (as he told Gosse some years later) whom he thought the most beautiful in England and who had provided him, all unconsciously, with the physical model for Tess Durbeyfield.[20] The extent of Hardy's indebtedness, appreciable from surviving photographs and portraits of Agatha Thornycroft, is implicitly acknowledged in the pages of *Life and Work*, where her mouth is admired in terms precisely similar to those used of Tess's mouth in the novel.[21]

Hardy had apparently done some work on his novel, still called 'Too Late, Beloved!', during his months in London, but he returned as usual to Max Gate for the final weeks leading up to his September deadline. Shortly before his departure he responded to the request of Jack T. Grein and Charles W. Jarvis (soon to be associated in the Independent Theatre) for permission to dramatize *The Woodlanders*. Although the novel had been published only two years previously, Hardy now felt it socially possible—or personally necessary—to face up to the full implications of the fictional situation that he had created but left incompletely explored. He therefore recommended that what had only been hinted at in the final sentences of the novel—Grace's future unhappiness as the wife of a persistently unfaithful Fitzpiers—should in the play be more explicitly brought out. The adapters' first version of the ending was sent to Hardy that September:

FITZPIERS You will come back to me?
GRACE What else can I do? My father says so, he tells me, everybody tells me—to be unhappy.[22]

The dramatization was never produced, but Hardy did at least have the satisfaction of reading a version of *The Woodlanders* that concluded in a manner directly expressive of his intentions.

Hardy's stronger insistence on an 'honest' ending to *The Woodlanders* is highly suggestive of his mood as he settled down at Max Gate in late July or early August to resume work on the *Tess* manuscript at a high pitch of creative and moral excitement, determined to say his say without literary or social compromise. By early September he was well advanced with the new novel, to the point of being able on the 9th to send off to Tillotson & Son a parcel of manuscript representing about a half of the whole.[23] It was at this point that Mabel Robinson spent a 'delightful week' with the Hardys, both of whom were as always '*very* kind':

Max Gate was then raw new & I never thought it shewed talent in the designer, but it was pleasant[.] Hardy shewed me his beautiful manuscripts & after dinner Emma lit a bright fire in the drawingroom and he read aloud bits from the novel he was engaged on. He read very badly & was suddenly overwhelmed with a sense of the inadequacy of his words 'No: No. Its not at all what I thought!' much turning of pages 'Lets try here this is—' etc etc, but neither was *that* what he expected, & he dipped elsewhere in the vain hope of touching his own heart.[24]

At Tillotson's meanwhile the early sections of the manuscript had been passed, unread, to the printer and set up in type to a point just prior to Tess's arrival at Talbothays, ready for serialization to begin. Hardy had not been asked to supply details of his story in advance—it was Tillotson's assumption that every author would naturally give of his best[25]—and it was only when the first proofs reached the firm's head reader that embarrassment set in. Although William Frederic Tillotson himself, the founder of the firm, had died the previous February, his strong Nonconformist beliefs and attitudes were still respected by his successors, and there was general consternation among them at both the narrative content and the moral emphasis of Hardy's story. When he declined to make the changes urged upon him Tillotson's refused outright to publish it, although they remained ready to make the payments to which they had engaged themselves in the original agreement. To this scrupulous gesture Hardy responded with the equally honourable suggestion that the contract simply be cancelled. Tillotson's agreed, and on 25 September 1889 they returned the manuscript along with such proofs as had been pulled—and demonstrated their undiminished goodwill by soliciting a short story for early syndication.[26]

Hardy next made an approach to Edward Arnold, the editor of *Murray's Magazine*. Despite obvious differences between them—Arnold arguing that young women should be protected from knowledge of the world's evil, Hardy insisting that his intention was to prevent those miseries which were the product of ignorance—Hardy persisted in the submission to *Murray's* of his still half-finished manuscript, taking advantage of the ensuing interval to complete the story, 'The Melancholy Hussar', requested by Tillotson's and attend to some damp stains that were showing up inside Max Gate. On 15 November Arnold replied. He had, he said, consulted Mr Murray, his publisher, in the matter, 'and we are agreed that the story, powerful though it be, is not, in our opinion, well adapted for publication in this Magazine.'[27] Hardy sent the manuscript straight off again to Mowbray Morris, the editor of *Macmillan's Magazine*, only to receive little more than a week later a rejection as firm as Arnold's and on essentially the same ground of the story's moral unsuitability for the magazine's presumed readership:

You use the word *succulent* more than once to describe the general appearance & condition of the Frome Valley. Perhaps I might say that the general impression left on me by reading your story—so far as it has gone—is one of rather too much succulence. All this, I know, makes the story 'entirely modern', & will therefore, I have no doubt, bring it plenty of praise. I must confess, however, to being rather too old-fashioned—as I suppose I must call it—to quite relish the entirely modern style of fiction.[28]

According to *Life and Work*, Hardy at this point undertook an extensive revision of the novel, involving the removal and separate publication of its most obviously offensive sections, before offering it to Arthur Locker, the editor of the *Graphic*. The actual sequence of events was somewhat more complicated. Locker had asked for another novel-length serial as early as the autumn of 1887, less than eighteen months after the conclusion of the *Graphic* serialization of *The Mayor of Casterbridge*, but Hardy had repeatedly put him off, perhaps because he preferred to publish in monthly rather than weekly instalments, perhaps because he thought the *Graphic* would not pay enough. He may also have anticipated the possibility or, indeed, the likelihood of bowdlerization. On 13 November 1889, however, while he was in the midst of his dealings with Arnold and Morris, Hardy not only promised Locker a contribution to the Christmas 1890 Number of the *Graphic* but indicated that he was now in a position to contemplate a full-length serial, to begin in January 1891 or at the magazine's convenience. On 18 November, when he had heard from Arnold but not yet from Morris, Hardy accepted Locker's suggestion of July 1891 as a starting date for the new serial. Eleven days later, after Morris's letter had arrived, he told Locker that he now realized it might be difficult for him to submit copy by September 1890, as had been agreed, and sought—and subsequently received—Locker's approval for submission of just half of the manuscript by the end of September and the rest in instalments thereafter.[29]

These negotiations with Locker, though certainly shrewd, do not seem to have been improper. *Life and Work* makes reference to Hardy's having received 'three requests, if not more' for his next serial, and had either *Murray's* or *Macmillan's* accepted 'Too Late, Beloved!' Hardy would still have been able to send the *Graphic* an entirely different work—such as *The Pursuit of the Well-Beloved*, a short novel that he had already 'sketched' some years before and that was in fact serialized in 1892 by the *Graphic's* chief rival, the *Illustrated London News*. Locker had not asked for details of the story Hardy had in mind, and Hardy for his part was anxious to avoid the reputation of unpublishability that might result from yet further rejections from still other journals. And because, like other novelists at this date, his remuneration for the magazine serialization of his work was significantly higher than for its publication in book form, the possibility of publishing the new novel without prior serialization, if attractive in principle, was in economic terms simply impracticable.[30]

During the final weeks of 1889 Hardy occupied himself—quite deliberately, perhaps—with matters other than 'Too Late, Beloved!' He was at Bockhampton as usual on Sunday, 1 December, hearing from his father about old Stinsford burial customs. In the middle of the month he shared with the secretary of the Society for the Protection of Ancient Buildings his anxiety about the threatened destruction of Stratton Church, just to the north-west of Dorchester.[31] Later still Rosamund Tomson sent some photographs of herself, apparently in the wake of a call she had made at Max Gate, and Hardy responded with a decorous note of thanks on Emma's behalf as well as his own. That the photographs—or, rather, a second set received some five weeks later—were of some personal significance to him is suggested by some notes scribbled on the back of a letter the following July:

> Life in Little | Heartache
> Tale of Mrs Tomson's photo.

Although this sounds like an idea for a story, it could equally have been projected as the germ of a poem—conceivably the one called 'The Photograph' that he published almost forty years later.[32] He had told Sir George Douglas at the end of 1888 that he sometimes thought it 'better to fail in poetry than to succeed in prose', and there are several signs of his continuing to write verse from time to time. 'After Schiller', for example, and at least the central idea of 'Heredity' evidently date from 1889, a note of September 1889 shows him returning once more to the evolution of what was at this date called 'A Drama of Kings' and eventually became *The Dynasts*, while 'At Middle-Field Gate in February', about the 'bevy now underground', the village beauties of his childhood, belongs to the winter of 1889–90.[33] In a note ascribed in *Life and Work* to 5 March 1890—but self-evidently written at a later date—Hardy recorded his writing, in the London train, the first few lines of the poem now known as 'Thoughts of Phena', quite ignorant of the fact that his romantically remembered cousin Tryphena Sparks was even then close to death at her home in Topsham, near Exeter, where she had been for several years the wife of a publican named Charles Gale.[34] Hardy and his brother are said to have cycled to Topsham in July 1890 in order to visit Tryphena's grave, but while Hardy did make such a journey it was probably at a later date, and if indeed he cycled he could not have done so earlier than 1896, the year in which he first learned to ride.[35]

The early months of 1890 were spent at Max Gate, completing the six tales, lightly interconnected as 'A Group of Noble Dames', that had been promised to the *Graphic* for its Christmas Number of 1890.[36] Though interrupted by minor illnesses and two brief trips to London, the writing went smoothly enough—perhaps because his creative energies were by no means fully engaged—and when Sir George Douglas came down for the Easter weekend he had two of the tales read aloud to him. Douglas was taken to see William Barnes's grave and to the Isle of Portland, the prospective setting of *The Pursuit of the Well-Beloved*, and after dinner one evening Emma read out from a magazine a short story by Kipling, whose reputation was just becoming established. It must have been an exceptionally weak story, Douglas later recalled, 'for not one of us could find anything to commend in it. "What is he driving at?" was our unanimous verdict.'[37]

Hardy soon learned to take Kipling more seriously. A few weeks later he was summarizing in one of his notebooks what he considered to be the best stories in *Plain Tales from the Hills* and copying down extracts from *Departmental Ditties*—especially from 'The Ballad of Fisher's Boarding House', which he described as 'excellent'. He met Kipling himself in London shortly afterwards,[38] and at a time when there was much controversy over the respective merits of 'realism' and 'romance', and when American critics such as Howells were bearing down hard upon the narrative and stylistic extravagances of Dickens and Thackeray, Hardy no doubt found in Kipling's manner and material a reassuring sign that there were writers—and readers—who still shared his own view that storytellers were essentially Ancient Mariners, justified in delaying the hurrying public only when possessed of 'something more unusual to relate than the ordinary experience of every average man and woman'. Critics such as Howells, he insisted, forgot 'that a story *must* be striking enough to be worth telling. Therein lies the problem—to reconcile the average with that uncommonness which alone makes it natural that a tale or experience would dwell in the memory and induce repetition.'[39]

'A Group of Noble Dames' was dispatched to the *Graphic* on 9 May 1890, two months ahead of the agreed delivery date, and with that task seemingly behind him Hardy set off once again with Emma for London and the pleasures and obligations of the 'season'. In early July Emma was called away to her father's deathbed, but Hardy stayed on in London until the end of the month.[40] In response to a last-minute request by Mary Jeune, among the closest of his London friends, he dashed off a verse epilogue for a special performance of *The Taming of the Shrew* given in support of her Holiday Fund for poor city children. He was not present on 23 July to hear Ada Rehan, who had played Katherina, actually read what he had simply called 'Lines', but the occasion constituted his first appearance as a poet—apart from unattributed fragments in one or two of the novels—since the publication of 'The Fire at Tranter Sweatley's' in 1875, and he was the more exasperated when the verses were promptly dismissed by the *Globe*, a popular London newspaper, as 'poor stuff, poetically—Johnsonian in heaviness of thought, and sesquipedalian in verbal expression'. He retaliated by stirring up the editor of another newspaper to insert in his own pages a mild rebuke to the *Globe* for criticizing so severely what had been written for a charitable purpose and at short notice.[41]

Hardy perhaps felt that he was now old enough—and well enough established—not to have to suffer indignities in passive silence. Still more distressing, however, were his ongoing exchanges with the *Graphic*. The directors of the paper had been offended by 'A Group of Noble Dames' when it came to their attention some time in June, and in the absence of Arthur Locker, the editor, his son William Algernon Locker had written in his capacity as assistant editor a letter all too reminiscent of the communications Hardy had received from Edward Arnold and Mowbray Morris the previous autumn:

Many fathers are accustomed to read or have read to their family-circles the stories in the *Graphic*; and I cannot think that they would approve for this purpose a series of tales almost every one of which turns upon questions of childbirth, and those relations between the sexes over which conventionality is accustomed (wisely or unwisely) to draw a veil. . . .

Now, what do you propose to do? Will you write us an entirely fresh story, or will you take the 'Noble Dames' and alter them to suit our taste; which means slightly chastening 1, 2, 3 &: 4; and substituting others for 5 &: 6?[42]

The four stories Locker wanted revised were (to give them their final titles) 'Barbara of the House of Grebe', 'The Marchioness of Stonehenge', 'Anna, Lady Baxby', and 'The Lady Icenway'; 'Squire Petrick's Lady' and 'Lady Mottisfont' he had rejected altogether as 'hopeless'. Arguments and compromises followed, Hardy made some fairly extensive revisions, and agreement upon the publication of all six stories was eventually reached with the returned Arthur Locker on 30 July.[43]

Although Hardy had not, in the event, been obliged to yield all of the ground so peremptorily demanded of him, he had undergone an experience sufficiently humiliating for a man of his years and standing. The difficulties over *Tess* and 'A Group of Noble Dames', coming hard upon the heels of the milder disagreements over the moral tone of *The Woodlanders*, constituted a rude reminder of his dependence not just upon the judgement of critics and the response of the reading public but also upon the anticipatory censorship of editors and publishers. It nevertheless seems extraordinary that Hardy's awareness of the contemporary cultural climate should not have made him more attentive to the consequences of allowing his stories to drift into waters well known to be dangerous—that he should not have anticipated, for example, the likelihood of an editor's asking, as William Locker did: 'Frankly, do you think it advisable to put into the hands of the Young Person stories, one of which turns upon the hysterical confession by a wife of an imaginary adultery, and the other upon the manner in which a husband foists upon his wife the offspring of a former illicit connection?'[44] It is possible to argue that Hardy was subversively probing what he saw as repressive cultural assumptions, but difficult to understand, if so, why the onset of trouble seems so consistently to have taken him by surprise. Difficult also to determine just how far he can have believed his own assurances to editors that whatever new work he was offering would maintain an impeccable moral tone and give offence to no one. When proved wrong, as he so often was, he responded with superficial cooperativeness, accepting cuts and revisions to serial texts, but with fundamental resentment of the implicit challenge not just to his literary judgement but to his achieved status as an artist and professional. His anger at being dressed down by young Locker found expression only in the scornful references to 'the tyranny of Mrs. Grundy' that he inscribed on the manuscript of the stories,[45] but the episode augured ill for the *Graphic*'s response to the new serial.

By the beginning of August 1890 Hardy was back in Dorset still with work to do on that serial, by this time probably called *Tess of the d'Urbervilles*, although the precise date at which Hardy opted for his final title is not known. In the middle of August, however, Alfred Parsons, the painter and illustrator, was again at Max Gate, and later that same month Hardy took his brother to Paris. The short holiday was tailored primarily to Henry's tastes and expectations, though these did not necessarily run contrary to Hardy's own. The brothers gave their days to fairly strenuous sightseeing and took in a good many places with Revolutionary and Napoleonic associations. They were at the Place de la Bastille on 22 August and at the Arc de Triomphe on the 23rd; three days later, at the Invalides, Hardy wrote 'very fine' in his Baedeker for *Paris and Environs* against the description of the 'twelve colossal Victories' on the walls of Napoleon's tomb. He also pencilled in the back of the Baedeker an index to its descriptions of circuses, cafés chantants, and dance halls (including the Jardin Mabille, said to be 'frequented by the more fashionable "cocottes"'), and during a visit to the Moulin Rouge he was struck—it is tempting to say, inevitably—by the juxtaposition of the cancan performers with the cemetery of Montmartre visible through windows above their heads.[46]

About a fortnight after Hardy's return from France Edmund Gosse and his wife arrived at Max Gate for a five-day visit, during which Gosse took with his 'Kodak' the circular snapshots that constitute the earliest—and very nearly the only—informal photographs of Hardy and Emma to have survived. They show a Max Gate open to the winds, a Hardy still bearded, an Emma distorted by the camera to a disproportionate height. The camera 'gave in', as Gosse put it, before he had 'secured for posterity' the form and features of the Hardys' cat, Kiddleywinkempoops (Trot for short), but he did get a snap or two of their dog, Moss.[47] Much to Hardy's and Emma's distress, Moss died just a few days later, after a savage beating by a prowling tramp, and was buried in the garden. This was the beginning of the pets' cemetery at Max Gate, although it is singular that all the other interments until the death of 'the famous dog Wessex' in 1927 seem to have been of cats—perhaps because, to this childless couple who increasingly and almost pathologically made children of their pets, the experience of losing Moss was too painful to bear repetition.[48]

That autumn of 1890 saw the completion of *Tess of the d'Urbervilles*. Hardy missed by just over a week his deadline for submitting the first half of his manuscript to the *Graphic*: promised for the end of September, it did not go off until 8 October. On the other hand, he was able to supply the remainder before the end of the same month, somewhat earlier than expected. Much was deleted or toned down in the process, and as finally published—with a mock marriage substituted for the seduction or rape of the heroine and the subsequent birth and death of her child omitted—the *Graphic* text achieved decorousness only at a considerable cost in terms of narrative coherence and verisimilitude.[49] The two major excisions from the serial were separately published, 'The Midnight Baptism' in Frank Harris's *Fortnightly Review* and 'Saturday Night in Arcady', roughly corresponding to chapters 10 and 11 of the novel, in W. E. Henley's *National Observer*.[50] Emma wrote out a considerable portion of the manuscript that went to Henley, and in January 1892, when most (though not all) of the 'Saturday Night in Arcady' material had been reincorporated into the text of the first edition, it was Emma who wrote to the editor of the *Spectator* to explain that the word 'whorage', as used by Tess in reference to Car Darch and her companions, had 'ceased in Somerset, Dorset, &c., to carry with it the coarse idea of its root-meaning, being spoken by the most modest to imply simply a company of slatternly, bickering, and generally unpleasant women'.[51]

Hardy had had three different London publishers since 1880: Smith, Elder for *The Trumpet-Major* in 1880 and again for *The Mayor of Casterbridge* in 1886, Sampson Low for *A Laodicean* and *Two on a Tower* in 1881 and 1882, and Macmillan for *The Woodlanders* and *Wessex Tales* in 1887 and 1888. Still, at the age of 50, unsettled in his publishing arrangements, he now took *A Group of Noble Dames* and *Tess of the d'Urbervilles* to the new firm of Osgood, McIlvaine & Co., established in April 1890 as a semi-autonomous London subsidiary of the New York house of Harper & Brothers. In part this was a gesture of friendship towards James Ripley Osgood, who had formerly acted as London agent for Harper. But Hardy also had reason to be satisfied with Harper & Brothers as the publishers, in their various magazines, of the American serial versions of several of his works. They had, in particular, accepted the six 'Group of Noble Dames' tales without the bowdlerizations insisted upon by the *Graphic*.[52] When, therefore, Rudyard Kipling wrote to the *Athenaeum* in November 1890 to accuse Harper & Brothers of sharp practice, Hardy—prompted by Osgood—felt obliged to join with Walter Besant and William Black in sending to the *Athenaeum* a letter testifying to their personal experience of unfailing fairness and liberality on Harper's part. The letter was not intended as an attack upon Kipling himself, nor did Kipling regard it as such, but his poem 'The Rhyme of the Three Captains', first published in the *Athenaeum* on 6 December, nevertheless made lively fun of Hardy ('Lord of the Wessex coast and all the lands thereby') and his co-signatories for demonstrating

> 'How a man may be robbed in Christian port while Three
>   Great Captains there
> Shall dip their flag to a pirate's rag—to show that his
>   trade is fair![53]

At the time when Kipling's ballad appeared, Hardy was in London by himself, Emma having experienced a recurrence of the lameness caused by her 'jointless' knee. He called on Osgood soon after his arrival to learn more details of the unexpected passage of a Copyright Bill by the United States House of Representatives, and was assured that the Bill would also pass the Senate and become law in July 1891, the date at which the serialization of *Tess* was scheduled to commence. As Hardy wrote to Emma that afternoon, the long-term advantages to English authors could not as yet be measured, but the immediate implication would seem to be that the many delays in the publication of *Tess* were to have the effect of bringing it within the scope of the new law: 'If all goes well how fortunate,' he exclaimed.[54]

16

The Publication of *Tess*

HARDY returned to Dorset from London in mid-December of 1890. Encouraged by the financial prospects opened up by the American copyright law, he lay awake before dawn on Christmas Day, 'thinking of resuming "the viewless wings of poesy" ' and finding, as he did so, that 'new horizons seemed to open, and worrying pettinesses to disappear'.[1] In the meantime the proofs of the *Tess* serial had begun to arrive, 'miserably small-typed' and without as yet any indication of where each of the weekly instalments would end and the next begin. Hardy made some suggestions, but was growing impatient with the complexities and compromises of serialization: 'It is immaterial about dividing the parts at ends of Chapters,' he told the *Graphic*'s printing-office manager: 'Any change of scene will do, the next part beginning "Chapter so & so *continued*." '[2] During the early months of 1891 he attended to the *Tess* proofs as they arrived, completed the short stories 'The Son's Veto' and 'On the Western Circuit', and prepared for Osgood, McIlvaine the first book edition of *A Group of Noble Dames*, adding four previously published stories to the six that had appeared in the *Graphic*. His stints of work were diversified by a number of visits to London—by himself in January, with Emma in March—and an increasingly busy programme of social engagements in and near Dorchester itself.[3]

Hardy was again in London without Emma in mid-April. It was dull, he reported; he felt lethargic, and work on the 'Midnight Baptism' sketch for the *Fortnightly* was going slowly. The current burlesque at the Gaiety Theatre had proved disappointing ('"The bogie man" which I went to hear, is not much'), and he could not work up enthusiasm for other forms of amusement. These letters to Emma of April 1891 are quite long and detailed, and as warmly phrased ('My dearest Em', 'Your ever affecte husbd') as might reasonably be expected from a husband writing home to his wife of sixteen years with whom he expected to be reunited within a week or so.[4] Hardy, however, remained sexually suggestive—the moment when a Piccadilly prostitute held a 'long-stemmed narcissus' to his nose would evolve over time into the elaborate fantasy of 'The Woman I Met'[5]—and was still on friendly terms with Rosamund Tomson, and the very length and specificity of the letters, and their stress upon the dullness of London, could conceivably have served as a smokescreen for other activities it was best that Emma should not know about. Sir George Douglas, who had by this date seen the Hardys together in Dorset, in his own home, and in London, believed them to be 'to the full as well assorted as most of the happily married couples that one comes across in life. Each had sacrificed something to the other, but their attachment was strong enough for each to be resigned to that sacrifice.' He especially remarked Hardy's 'unremitted deference and chivalrous consideration' where Emma was concerned, but felt that she herself had little sense of the true quality of her husband's work and was too eager 'to know the people whose names are well known'. Emma, he added, 'belonged essentially to the class of women, gifted with spirit and the power of deciding for herself, which had attracted Hardy in his early manhood. She had the makings of a Bathsheba, with restricted opportunities.'[6]

Though enigmatically phrased, the comment is certainly suggestive of Emma's capacity for independence and impetuosity—the sources equally of her 'admirable courage' in challenging the mistreaters of animals and of what Hardy must have seen as her demeaning support of the man with three children in the dispute over seats on the Paris-bound train. The Hardys' doctor, Dr Frederic Bazley Fisher, recalling his visits to Max Gate in order to treat Hardy for a potentially serious illness in the late 1880s, said much later that he 'realized a good many of the difficulties [Hardy] had had to contend with in his house' and suspected Emma of having been 'the cause of much of the great man's pessimism & depression'.[7] Mabel Robinson, writing of roughly the same period, recalled that Emma's 'thoughts hopped off like a bird on a bough, but never then nor at any other time did the idea cross my mind that her mind (such as it was) was unhinged. It may have been, but as I saw her she was a perfectly normal woman without much brain power but who wanted to be a poet or novelist—I forget which—and found it hard that no-one took her literary accomplishment seriously.' Certainly, she added, Emma 'had not the intellectual value nor the tact it would have needed to hold the heart of her husband against all the world, but she had loved him dearly and was a nice loveable inconsequent little lady of whom one grew very fond.'[8] Emma's discontinuities were part of her charm, the counterpart of those teasing changes of mood that had so contributed to Hardy's enslavement at St Juliot. But they could be exasperating in the practical world of every day. It was not secretiveness or meanness but simple necessity that induced Hardy to keep all financial matters, both business and domestic, in his own hands, and when, in these years, he asked Emma to copy manuscripts and other documents it was often because she yearned for employment rather than because he urgently needed the job done.[9] Hardy's rigorous working habits were by this date firmly established, and Emma, who had once cast herself in the role of his indispensable helpmate, and played that part with some success at Sturminster and Tooting, must have found it a dreary and frustrating experience to be excluded from the Max Gate study for many hours of every day. Employment in literary tasks represented for Emma an opportunity for companionship, a temporary reversion to an earlier time when they had stood together against a complexly hostile world.

They nevertheless lived, visited, and entertained together. They shared in the practical, day-to-day business of maintaining a household and a social life. They remained into the early 1890s—whatever the nature of their sexual relationship, at this or indeed at any period of their marriage— on terms at least of cordiality. But it was one thing for Hardy to remain publicly and even domestically loyal to the woman he had married, quite another for him to admit her to any genuine intimacy of an intellectual or even an emotional kind. Loyalty to Emma stopped short of any diminution of devotion to Jemima, and tensions were sustained and renewed by those long-standing divisions between Max Gate and Bockhampton that Hardy could undoubtedly have tried harder to bridge. He may (like Ethelberta) have seen advantages in maintaining a separation between the two sides of his life—where he had come from and where he had arrived—despite, or precisely because of, their geographical contiguity. The consequences, however, were serious: on his own part, an early developed habit of keeping major segments of his life very much to himself; on Emma's part, a bitter and constantly renewed experience of finding herself isolated in essentially hostile territory. The Hardys were against her, she could never learn to think of Dorset as home, and in marrying Hardy she had in any case expected to live in London and not in semi-rural isolation.[10]

The annual visits to London were thus an essential element in the marriage, and Hardy's growing reputation brought Emma into contact with a gratifying number of 'the people whose names are well known'. It was precisely in London, however, that Emma's eccentricities and impetuosities were most glaringly obvious. Those pretensions to gentility which had so offended her husband's family were in London regarded as inept affectations. She had neither the poise nor the wit—not even the gift of silence—which might have made her acceptable in those circles in which Hardy moved by right of his literary distinction. Worse still was her lack of beauty or a sense of style. Mabel Robinson recalled that Emma's 'masses of silken golden hair' had already 'faded drab' by the time she first met her during the Tooting years. The American novelist Gertrude Atherton, sitting with T. P. O'Connor at a social gathering in the 1890s, saw Hardy walk by in the company of 'an excessively plain, dowdy, high-stomached woman with her hair drawn back in a tight little knot, and a severe cast of countenance. "Mrs. Hardy," said T. P. "Now you may understand the pessimistic nature of the poor devil's work." '[11]

It is not clear how Hardy himself responded to Emma's appearance: in December 1890 he described her as attending a Dorset social occasion looking 'rather well-dressed'.[12] Whatever his own feelings, however, he could not have been unaware of her failure to adapt herself to the circles into which he introduced her. He knew that she was perceived as plain, foolish, and overdressed, and that he himself was often scorned or pitied on her account. He also discovered that there were in London numerous women, handsome, intelligent, and well dressed, who were ready and even eager to claim his attention and be seen in his company. His natural, if not especially admirable, response was to leave Emma behind, at Max Gate or in their London lodgings, whenever he decorously could. For a time Emma accepted this situation, as she had long accepted her husband's occasional outbursts of anger, dutifully enough. It was only later—and particularly after Hardy had seemed in *Jude the Obscure* to be attacking not only the institution of marriage but, by implication, his own marriage—that she was roused to active, bitter, and permanent protest.

Towards the end of April 1891 Emma left Max Gate in charge of Mary Antell and her daughter Mary (known as Polly) and went up to London to share with her husband in the annual ordeal of finding somewhere to spend the months of late spring and early summer that comprised the London 'season'. *Life and Work*, after noting 'their inability to afford a London house or flat all the year round', specifies some of the horrors of this most recent search: 'The dirty house-fronts, leaning gate-piers, rusty gates, broken bells, Doré monstrosities of womankind who showed us the rooms, left Em nearly fainting, and at one place she could not stay for the drawing-room floor to be exhibited.' By the end of the month they had nevertheless rented 'a little flat' at 12 Mandeville Place, just south-east of Manchester Square.[13]

Meanwhile, during the Hardys' absence, a parliamentary by-election was held in the South Dorset constituency and Hardy's friend Robert Pearce Edgcumbe stood as a Gladstonian Liberal.

Hardy, who had sat on the platform with Edgcumbe and other dignitaries at a Liberal Party election meeting in Dorchester in 1885, readily declared his personal support for Edgcumbe. At the same time, he declined to take any further part in the current campaign, basing his refusal chiefly on professional grounds ('the pursuit of what people are pleased to call Art so as to win unbiassed attention to it as such, absolutely forbids political action') but also on his disapproval of the positions taken by both the major parties on the crucial issue of Home Rule for Ireland. Edgcumbe lost narrowly after a bitter campaign.[14] Kate, reporting the outcome in a letter of 15 May, went on to talk of the inspection that she and Mary had just undergone at their school, the death of the Bockhampton cat ('Mother wont hear of having another'), the satisfactory condition of things at Max Gate ('Aunt Mary and Polly are quite happy out at Max. Henry goes in and visits them occasionally, & I have been out a few times'), and possible arrangements for a visit to Mandeville Place which Mary might—and in fact did—make later that month. Kate ended, in her usual cheerful fashion, by sending love to Emma and affectionate wishes to Hardy himself.[15]

In late April 1891 Hardy was notified of his election to the Athenaeum as a person of 'distinguished merit' in the field of literature—the culmination of a process which Lord Carnarvon, at Hardy's own instigation, had set in motion nearly three years previously—and he often used the club thereafter as an impeccably respectable address for his correspondence when in London. He remained for several years, however, a member of the more relaxed Savile, to which such friends as Gosse and Greenhill belonged, and during this particular summer he met Kipling there on a number of occasions. He went, as usual, to galleries, among them the Royal Academy and the English Art Club, and to the theatre, including the first performance of Gosse's translation of *Hedda Gabler*.[16] He was deeply moved by visiting a large private lunatic asylum in the company of T. Clifford Allbutt, a doctor and Commissioner in Lunacy, whom he had recently met at Gosse's, and much touched by what he saw at two London training colleges for women teachers, including the one which his cousin Tryphena had attended more than twenty years previously. He found pathos in the spectacle presented by such communities of young women: 'Their belief in circumstances, in convention, in the rightness of things, which you know to be not only wrong but damnably wrong, makes the heart ache, even when they are waspish and hard.' How much nobler their aspirations were, he added, than those of the people he had recently been encountering at fashionable parties.[17]

Early in June 1891 Hardy went by train to Aldeburgh on the Suffolk coast to spend the weekend with a new friend, Edward Clodd, a banker whose leisure was given to writing works of popular science and anthropology and to publicizing the cause of rationalism. Clodd was accustomed to inviting small groups of congenial companions to spend weekends together at his house on the Aldeburgh sea front, and on this particular occasion, the first of several at which Hardy would be present over the years, the other guests were Walter Besant and J. M. Barrie. Besant, active at this period in the creation of the Society of Authors, was already a good friend, Barrie was fast becoming one, and the weekend provided, as Clodd recorded in his pocket diary, 'plenty of good talk "de omnibus rebus"'.[18] It was perhaps because of Clodd, always eager in the pursuit of new ideas, that Hardy was currently working his way through Schopenhauer's *Studies in Pessimism,* John Addington Symonds's *Essays Speculative and Suggestive,* and at least the first of the two volumes of Frazer's *The Golden Bough.* He was quick to notice correspondences between Dorset folklore and some of the exotic customs and beliefs recorded by Frazer, and one of his notes on Schopenhauer pointed in the direction of *Jude the Obscure*: 'Tragedy. "Only when intellect rises to the point where the vanity of all effort is manifest, & the will proceeds to an act of self-annulment, is the drama tragic in the true sense."'[19]

A Group of Noble Dames had appeared in a handsome one-volume edition at the end of May 1891, to be received with a general lack of enthusiasm and some outright hostility. When a reviewer in the *Pall Mall Gazette* on 8 July especially deplored the horrific aspects of 'Barbara of the House of Grebe', Hardy retorted in a letter published two days later that the tale-within-a-tale structure of the book had been deliberately designed to protect the reader's sensitivities by throwing back the action 'into a second plane or middle distance, being described by a character to characters, and not point-blank by author to reader'. Besides, he added: 'A good horror has its place in art. Shall we, for instance, condemn "Alonzo the Brave"? For my part I would not give up a single worm of his skull.'[20] The trouble with this line of argument, as the reviewer's reply effectively pointed out, was that the technical nicety did little to modify the impact of the narrative itself, and that what was acceptable in fantasy or in the literature of the remote past might prove altogether less palatable within the context of a realistic fiction. Not for the first time, nor for the last, Hardy's vigorous and somewhat blustering reaction to adverse criticism derived not so much from deliberate disingenuousness as from an incapacity to see his work as it might be

seen by others, to appreciate its potential impact upon minds and imagina-
tions not precisely attuned to his own. Later that same year he was to
provide Tillotson's with a prospectus of *The Pursuit of the Well-Beloved* which
concluded with the assurance—no doubt firmly grounded in his own conception of the story as a kind of fantasy-parable—that it contained 'not a
word or scene' that could 'offend the most fastidious taste'.[21] Hardy always
insisted, in response to invitations to write reviews, introductions, and so
forth, that his critical faculties were poorly developed, and some sections of
his paper on 'Candour in English Fiction', published as part of a symposium
in the *New Review* for January 1890, could be said to show a sense less of proportion than of persecution. On the other hand, 'The Science of Fiction',
his contribution to another *New Review* symposium of April 1891, contains a
remarkably concise and coherent statement of the fundamental issues in the
current debate over realism and naturalism.[22]

Although he tended to refer to *A Group of Noble Dames* in somewhat deprecating terms, Hardy ventured to send copies to several of his friends, including Gosse, Clodd, and Lord Lytton. Hutchins's *History and Antiquities of the
County of Dorset* had been his chief source for the quasi-historical narratives
of which the book was composed, but in writing to Lytton he spoke also of
drawing upon 'some legendary notes I had taken down from the lips of aged
people in a remote part of the country, where traditions of the local families
linger on, & are remembered by the yeomen & peasantry long after they are
forgotten by the families concerned'.[23] What he did not say was that one of
the 'aged people' was his own mother, almost certainly a source for the
tradition of the Ilchester family of Melbury House that was eventually
worked up into 'The First Countess of Wessex'. Not altogether surprisingly,
the Earl of Ilchester of the day was distinctly annoyed by the public allusion
to his family past, and his displeasure may have been shared by some of the
other families concerned, but there seems little basis for the story that
publication of *A Group of Noble Dames* led to a general ostracism of the Hardys
by all levels of local society.[24]

Before returning to Dorset from London at the end of July 1891 the Hardys
spent a few days in Suffolk with one of Lady Portsmouth's daughters, Lady
Camilla Gurdon, and her husband.[25] Back at Max Gate Hardy resumed the
task—begun but by no means completed while he was in London—of
preparing *Tess of the d'Urbervilles* for its long-delayed appearance in volume
form. Although this was largely a matter of restoring omitted sections to
their original places, by no means all of the changes made in adapting
the manuscript for serialization were in fact reversed: one fragment, the

description of the dance at Chaseborough which had formed a portion of 'Saturday Night in Arcady', was not reabsorbed into the text until the Wessex Edition of 1912. While he was thus engaged Hardy received a visit from W. Robertson Nicoll, who was anxious to include an article on 'Wessex', together with a map of the fictional places, in the first number of a magazine called the *Bookman* that was about to appear under his editorship. This would be the first publication of a Wessex map—the forerunner of infinitely more than Hardy could well have imagined—and although Hardy declined to contribute a map himself, he supplied Nicoll with enough information to ensure that the one actually printed would be reasonably accurate and comprehensive. 'I have seen a good deal of Hardy lately,' Nicoll wrote to a friend later that same month, 'and am much taken by him. He is certainly the most winning literary man I have ever met—shy and silent in company, but in private remarkably communicative and interesting.'[26]

In September 1891 Hardy and Emma were in Scotland, staying with Sir George Douglas at Springwood Park, his since dismantled house near Kelso, and visiting places associated with Scott. Hardy—who always valued Scott's verse above his fiction and was accustomed to speak of *Marmion* as 'the most Homeric poem in the English language'—was particularly anxious to see and climb Smailholme Tower, the setting of 'The Eve of St John', and Douglas later recalled as peculiarly poignant the sight of Hardy bending silently above Scott's death mask at Abbotsford.[27] The Hardys, said Douglas, were very accommodating guests, who

threw themselves at once into the interests of our family life. A portrait of Mrs Opie by her husband hung in my drawing-room, suggesting to Hardy that I might read them one of her *Simple Tales* after dinner, which of course I was only too pleased to do. Then, next morning after breakfast, Mrs Hardy said at once, 'Let's go and visit the horses,' whereupon she and my sister provided themselves with lumps of sugar, and we trooped off to the stables, which thenceforth became a part of our routine.

Douglas's added comment that Emma, although a horsewoman in her girl-hood, seemed not to possess 'any special knowledge of horses' must have been made in ignorance of the fact that in Dorset she continued to ride, presumably on horses hired from a local livery stable and generally for the purpose of making distant social calls, at least until the autumn of 1893—more than two years later than the terminal date given in *Life and Work*.[28] When Emma attempted one day to make a sketch of Springwood Park there ensued what Douglas recalled as a 'delightful wrangle', though it would seem susceptible of other interpretations: ' "Now you'd better let me touch in the perspective," said the quondam architect; or again, grasping the sketch-book, "Let me put in the trees, and the gable and balustrades will come in almost of themselves." But though Hardy was by much the better draughtsman, and in fact wanted to do the whole picture himself, his good lady had confidence in her own handiwork.'[29]

Hardy and Emma returned by stages down the eastern side of England, visiting the cathedral towns of Durham, York, and Peterborough, and were back at Max Gate by 20 September 1891.[30] On 8 November, when he wrote to thank Douglas for some trees he had sent for the garden at Max Gate, Hardy was correcting proofs for the first edition of *Tess of the d'Urbervilles*. It was at this eleventh-hour moment that he sent Osgood, McIlvaine a new title page for the novel, one that insisted in its subtitle upon Tess's status as 'a pure woman' and declared a personal commitment to her cause in terms of the added epigraph from *The Two Gentlemen of Verona*: 'Poor wounded name! My bosom as a bed | Shall lodge thee.' The subtitle, Hardy later declared, was inserted after his final reading of the proofs 'as being the estimate left in a candid mind of the heroine's character—an estimate that nobody would be likely to dispute'.[31] It was also a deliberate challenge, thrown out in mingled exasperation and assurance. The three volumes themselves appeared just over three weeks later, and Hardy sent off presentation copies to Douglas, to Lady Jeune (as she had become that year as a consequence of her husband's knighthood), and to William Morris, whom Hardy had not met, but who showed in his reply some familiarity with Hardy's earlier novels.[32] Sending a copy also to Alfred Austin, Hardy added by way of delicate compliment a line and a half of verse from the volume Austin had sent him two years earlier, 'Wrestlers born, | Who challenge iron Circumstance—and fail'. What is not quite clear is whether Hardy was applying the quotation to his characters or to himself, as one of the 'poets of contention' to whom, in context, the words refer.[33]

By the end of 1891 Hardy had received a number of encouraging letters about *Tess*. Frederic Harrison claimed the novel as 'a Positivist allegory or sermon'; Charles Kegan Paul called it a 'really great novel', although he was only the first of several people to point out that no parson would have dared to insist that Tess's baby be buried in unsanctified ground.[34] The first reviews were also enthusiastic—the *Speaker* on 26 December finding the novel painful but fine, the *Pall Mall Gazette* on 31 December speaking of it as the strongest English novel for many years—and Hardy was especially pleased by the sympathetic view of Tess's situation taken by the *Daily Chronicle* on 28 December: in a letter to the reviewer, H. W. Massingham, he congratulated him and his paper 'for frankly recognizing that the development of a more virile type of novel is not incompatible with sound morality'.[35] The note of almost unqualified praise was sustained early in the new year by the reviews in the *St James's Gazette*, the *Athenaeum*, and *The Times*. In the *Saturday Review* of 16 January, however, the reviewer—Hardy later decided that it was George Saintsbury—declared that there was 'not one single touch of nature' in any of the characters, that Tess's sexual attractions were too much insisted upon, and—as if echoing Henry James's commendation of the sheep and dogs in *Far from the Madding Crowd*—that the 'terrible dreariness' of the whole tale was relieved only by 'the few hours spent with cows'.[36]

The notice, Hardy told Walter Besant the next day, was an 'absolute mis-representation' but also a personal embarrassment: how could he, after such an attack, re-enter a Savile Club that was full of people who wrote for the *Saturday*? Particularly annoying, as he complained in letters to Gosse and Clodd, was the reviewer's having at one point interpreted a simple typographical error as authorial bad grammar.[37] Hardy's friends tried to dissuade him from taking the unfriendly reviews so much to heart. The *Saturday Review* notice of *Tess* was scandalous, Besant agreed, but there was nothing to be done about it—except to go to the Savile as usual and show that his withers were unwrung. The manifest bad faith of the review, said Gosse, undercut all of its force: in any case, the book was being so praised on all sides—by Besant, by Mrs Humphry Ward, by Henry James—that Hardy should not be concerned with what 'the "Saturday's" ape-leading and shrivelled spinster said or thought'.[38] In the event, as Hardy acknowledged to Gosse on 20 January 1892, orders for the book had actually increased since the review's appearance. Osgood, McIlvaine, in short, had a success on their hands and Hardy, invited to make corrections for a second impression of the first edition, had to write to Tillotson's to beg a little more time for the completion of *The Pursuit of the Well-Beloved*.[39]

The reviews, however, continued to appear. The morality of *Tess* was attacked by R. H. Hutton in the *Spectator* for 23 January, and its theology, specifically the final invocation of 'the President of the Immortals', by Andrew Lang in the February number of the *New Review*: 'If there be a God', Lang expostulated, 'who can seriously think of Him as a malicious fiend?'[40] But the weight of critical opinion continued to be heavily in *Tess*'s favour, and it was only with the publication of a review entitled 'Culture and Anarchy' in the April 1892 number of the *Quarterly Review* that Hardy was again moved beyond irritation to indignation. In addition to repeating some now familiar complaints—that there was an unnecessary emphasis upon the heroine's 'sensual qualifications' for her role, that Hardy displayed an uncertain grasp both of style and of grammar and had quite deliberately told 'a coarse and disagreeable story in a coarse and disagreeable manner'—the reviewer made scornful reference to the 'queer' and 'hole-and-corner' arrangement by which sections of the novel had been separately published in periodicals 'whose editors presumably take a more liberal view of their duties towards their neighbours, or whose readers are more habitually adult'. Hardy himself observed, with perhaps a touch of paranoia, that the *Quarterly* emanated from the same publishing house as *Murray's Magazine*, which had refused *Tess* and subsequently ceased publication. He does not seem to have discovered that the review itself was the work of Mowbray Morris, who had so officiously declined to accept the novel for *Macmillan's* and thus set Hardy upon the path to its dismemberment.[41] Even in the absence of such validation of his senses of irony and persecution, Hardy's condemnation of the review's 'mendacity' was passionate and unforgiving. 'How strange', he wrote after reading it for the first time, 'that one may write a book without knowing what one puts into it—or rather, the reader reads into it! Well, if this sort of thing continues no more novel-writing for me. A man must be a fool to deliberately stand up to be shot at.'[42]

Hardy, buoyed by the novel's popularity, remained in combative mood. When the first one-volume edition of *Tess* appeared later in 1892 he took the unusual step of commenting, in a new preface, upon the critical reception of the novel thus far. Injudiciously, perhaps, he included a scarcely disguised allusion to Andrew Lang as a 'great critic' who had 'turned Christian for half-an-hour the better to express his grief that a disrespectful phrase about the Immortals should have been used'. Not surprisingly, Lang felt himself licensed by such comments to repeat and elaborate his earlier strictures. Whether or not it was he who (as Hardy suspected) originated the term 'Tessimism', his 'At the Sign of the Ship' causerie in the November number of *Longman's* took Hardy sternly to task not only for pessimism but for dubious morality and defects of style and taste. Although Hardy kept public silence thereafter, his hostility towards Lang and Saintsbury never abated. After Hardy's death Saintsbury told his widow that he thought her husband had forgiven him for criticizing *Tess*: 'How little he knew!' she later exclaimed.[43]

Hardy's personal appearance at about the time of the publication of *Tess* was quite strikingly evoked by Rosamund Tomson, in an article published three years later:

As to the outer man, Thomas Hardy presents a curious combination of force and fragility; he is slightly below the middle height, but strongly built, with rugged, aquiline features, pallid complexion, a crisp, closely trimmed brown beard, and mustache short enough to disclose an infrequent smile of remarkable sweetness; hair, neither light nor dark, thickly streaked with gray, and somewhat worn away from the temples; and, most noticeable feature, bright, deep-set eyes, keen as a hawk's, but, for all their watchfulness, full of a quiet *bonhomie*. Indeed, there is something not un-hawk-like about his whole physiognomy, with the predatory expression left out; in no other human face have I seen such a still intensity of observation.

It was a pity, she added, that the nervous strain of sitting for fashionable photographers brought to his usually mobile face 'an expression of almost harsh austerity which those who have the privilege of his intimate acquaintance feel to be a complete misrepresentation of the real man'.[44]

The 'crisp, closely trimmed brown beard' of this description also appears in the most recent of the set of photographs Hardy had himself supplied to the *Strand Magazine* for publication in its November 1891 issue, but it has disappeared, leaving only the moustache behind, from the portrait by a Weymouth photographer that Hardy sent off on 17 March 1892 for publication in an American magazine.[45] The removal of the beard was clearly a symbolic move, prompted—according to the second Mrs Hardy—by the critical and commercial success of *Tess* and the many changes that followed, or were imagined as following, in the wake of that success.[46] The short- and long-term expectation of substantial royalties from both sides of the Atlantic gave Hardy for the first time the sense and reality of financial security, the possibility of accumulating and retaining funds over and above his day-to-day needs. His old dream of a literary life now began to seem realizable in terms quite other than those he had originally projected. Instead of faintly hoping for a country parsonage in which he might write poems for his own satisfaction he now had the prospect of becoming a retired novelist living on the proceeds of his past work and writing poems that had a good chance of reaching an audience.

The sense of financial accumulation—and, implicitly, of an impending culmination of his novelistic career—emerges strongly throughout 1892. In January he asked Clodd, as a banker, about the merits of a particular stock he was thinking of buying, and it was typical of his family-centredness and concern for the future of his still unmarried sisters that some of the shares mentioned to Clodd should have been bought in Kate's name.[47] In September he bought, at auction, a house in the centre of Dorchester (51 High West Street). Intended as an investment and let out over the next few years, the house proved persistently troublesome in terms of both tenant complaints and costly repairs, and Hardy, finding the role of landlord uncongenial and the returns on his investment unimpressive, eventually resold it. Earlier in the year he had spoken of enlarging Max Gate, even while reaffirming his initial intention not to ruin himself by building a great house, as other literary men had done, and the combination of Emma's social ambitions with his own notions of what was due to his new situation led to a gradual elaboration of the style of life kept up at Max Gate, especially when visitors were present.[48]

Hardy, after all, was now a public figure in a way and to a degree that he had not previously experienced, the frequent subject of items of personal or literary gossip in places like the *Athenaeum* and the *Bookman* and even, from time to time, the London newspapers. Literary pilgrims began to descend upon Dorchester in search of an actual Casterbridge and a tangible Wessex and in the hope of catching a glimpse of its creator, the 'Author of *Tess*', as he was now so often called. John Lane was seeking information for a bibliography of Hardy's work, explanatory notes were requested for a Russian translation of *Tess*, and magazines on both sides of the Atlantic wrote to ask for photographs and biographical material.[49] Interviewers of varying degrees of competence and honesty found their way to Max Gate, some by prearrangement, others on a purely speculative basis, and over the succeeding years many so-called interviews would be concocted out of previously published material by people who knew nothing of Max Gate or its master at first hand.

Raymond Blathwayt, one of the most prolific of contemporary interviewers, duly solicited and arranged his visit in advance, and was presumably responsible for arranging the excellent drawing of Hardy in his then study (at the north-west corner of the first floor of an as yet unenlarged Max Gate) that accompanied the interview's original publication. He was also one of the few interviewers to make reference to Emma, describing her with deliberate and indeed elaborate irony—as 'so particularly bright, so thoroughly *au courant du jour*, so evidently a citizen of the wide world, that the, at first, unmistakable reminiscence that there is in her of Anglican ecclesiasticism is curiously puzzling and inexplicable to the stranger, until the information is vouchsafed that she is intimately and closely connected with what the late Lord Shaftesbury would term "the higher order of the clergy".' Blathwayt had evidently been exposed, as were so many other visitors to Max Gate, to Emma's insistence upon her relationship to Archdeacon Gifford. But he had also registered that almost febrile quality, at once attractive in its vitality and disturbing in its excess, that increasingly struck observers as a mark of eccentricity. Hardy, meanwhile, was still making some effort to keep her in touch with his work and his rising literary fortunes: he told Blathwayt, for example, that the scene in which Tess wore the jewels was Emma's idea.[50] Another interviewer that same year noticed that Emma kept in a 'little book' a list of Hardy's Wessex place names and of the actual locations to which they more or less corresponded.[51]

But Emma's listing of Wessex names was a form of bookkeeping that went back at least as far as their Tooting days, and probably earlier. More symptomatic of the current state of their relationship were the secret diaries (begun in or about 1891 but undiscovered until after her death) to which she was now confiding her multifarious complaints against her husband's conduct, attitudes, and beliefs.[52] She was in poor health during the early months of 1892, having never quite recovered from a severe attack of influenza the previous autumn, and the letters Hardy wrote home from London, where he stayed at Lady Jeune's on at least three separate occasions, show no obvious change in tone or content: they still begin 'My dearest Em' and are signed 'Yours affectly'.[53] Even so, his having gone to London alone may itself be significant, and the shaving off of his beard perhaps signalled a determination to appear under his true colours in personal as well as in literary terms.

He certainly took advantage of Emma's absence from London, and of his own enhanced reputation, to expand his range of friendships with hand-some and intelligent women. In March he called for the first time on Charles Kingsley's daughter, Mrs Mary St Leger Harrison, who wrote novels under the pseudonym of 'Lucas Malet', and found her to be a 'strik-ing woman: full, slightly voluptuous mouth, red lips, black hair and eyes; and most likeable'. He wrote her shortly afterwards a warm letter of thanks for the gift of her novel *The Wages of Sin*, and expressed sympathy with the difficulty faced by women writers when handling matters of which they were conventionally supposed to be ignorant. They met again in April, but the relationship seems not to have been long-lived, perhaps because Mrs Harrison did not appreciate Hardy's frankness in telling her that he found the wages of her novel's title—'that the young man falls over a cliff, & the young woman dies of consumption'—to be 'not very consequent'.[54] The names of other women crop up during these months, including those of a 'Miss Norris (ballet dancer)' and Lady Hilda Brodrick ('charming in her girlish naiveté'), who claimed during a 'long and pleasant tête-à-tête' to have wept bitterly over *Tess*.[55]

. . .

On 22 May 1892 Hardy again went up to London by himself to attend the funeral of his friend and publisher James Ripley Osgood. He stayed on at Lady Jeune's after the funeral and began searching, in somewhat desultory fashion, for lodgings in which he and Emma could spend the balance of the London season. Emma came up to join him at the end of the month—they were both guests of the Gosses on 29 May—but before they could get properly settled they were summoned back to Dorchester by the news that Hardy's father had been taken seriously ill.[56] Thomas Hardy senior had lived in seclusion as a semi-invalid for several years—'seen of nobody but ourselves', as his son told Sir George Douglas—and since he was in his eighty-first year a fatal outcome to the illness (identified in the death certificate as atrophy of the liver and exhaustion) seems to have been anticipated from the first.[57] He sank slowly, however, dying at last, without great suffering, on 20 July. Hardy, who had not been present at the moment his father slipped away, took charge of the arrangements for the funeral on 25 July, sent a death notice to the local newspaper, and wrote 'T.H. 23 July 97' in his prayerbook alongside verse 10 of the 90th Psalm: 'and though men be so strong that they come to fourscore years: yet is their strength then but labour and sorrow; so soon passeth it away, and we are gone'.[58] Four verses of the Tate and Brady metrical version of the same psalm, headed 'The grave-side hymn of this parish down to about 1840', appeared on the leaflet that Hardy designed and had printed for the memorial service to his father held at Stinsford Church on 31 July, the Sunday following the funeral. Also on the leaflet was his tribute in Latin to his father's long service as a violinist with the old Stinsford choir: '*In Memoriam Thomae Hardy olim in hac ecclesia viginti annos musici. Ob: Jul: Die XX. A.D. MDCCCXCII, Æ. suae LXXXI.*' The memorial leaflet, deeply felt as an act of filial piety, was significant also as a salutation to those vanished ways and days that the father, in the son's eyes, had so ideally embodied. It was very important to Hardy that his father had died, as the death notice put it, 'in the house of his birth', and that he had asked at the last for a drink of fresh well water to assure himself that he was indeed 'at home'. In his 1855 copy of Horace's *Odes* Hardy wrote 'TH. (sen.)' alongside the beginning of Carminum XXII ('Integer vitae scelerisque purus') and he also applied to his father Hamlet's praise of Horatio as 'A man that fortune's buffets and rewards | Hast ta'en with equal thanks'.[59]

The will of Thomas Hardy, senior, signed in January 1888 in the presence of Mary Antell and her son John, was more ample than might have been expected. Almost everything was left to the financial use of his widow during her lifetime, but after her death his numerous properties were to pass to Henry Hardy. There was doubtless an element of 'rounding up' in Hardy's subsequent description of such properties as comprising '30 acres & about 20 houses', but they certainly included several cottages and the Hardy builder's yard in the village of West Knighton and the 'freehold land called and known as "Talbots" situate in the parish of Stafford'. The bequests to the daughters took effect immediately, Kate Hardy receiving the considerable sum of £500, her better established elder sister £250, while Hardy himself, named co-executor with his brother, was left 'the sum of five pounds and any article of furniture he may choose'.[60] For Hardy and Emma, however, the death of Hardy's father had the more significant consequence of removing an essential element of good-humoured kindliness that had served to temper latent hostilities and keep the Bockhampton and Max Gate households linked, however tenuously, together. There was now no effective buffer between an always implacable Jemima and an Emma who was, with increasing age, revealing her own capacity for obstinacy.

Precisely what drove Emma and the Hardys so far and so permanently apart is not known, but if (as the second Mrs Hardy asserted) Mary and Kate were banned from Max Gate during the twenty years preceding Emma's death,[61] the crucial breach must have occurred in or about 1892. Hardy's own loyalties remained, as always, divided. He did not assert himself to overcome his wife's prohibition, but neither did he break off his own relations with his brother and sisters or interrupt his weekly visits to his mother at Bockhampton. Immediately after his father's death, indeed, he walked in that direction even more frequently than usual, and the breakdown in family relationships could well have been precipitated by Emma's jealous resentment of the demands Jemima was making upon her eldest child in the first lonely days of her widowhood. It was at Bockhampton on a Wednesday at the end of August that Jemima told him that she felt alienated from the furniture around her: 'All those belonging to it, and the place, are gone, and it is left in her hands, a stranger.' But Jemima, as Hardy noted, had lived in the cottage for fifty-three years, and if she could think of herself as a 'stranger' among the Hardys it is little wonder that Emma should have felt so excluded from the clan.[62]

17

Florence Henniker

IN the summer of 1892 Rebekah Owen, an energetic, unmarried American woman of 34, came on a purposeful pilgrimage to Dorchester, dragging her elder sister in her train.[1] She was armed with an introduction from one of the directors of Sampson Low, Marston & Co., Hardy's reprint publishers, talked her way into Max Gate, and was soon on friendly terms with both Hardy and Emma. The more romantic aspects of her relationship with Hardy himself seem to have existed only in her own imagination, but he was certainly flattered and gratified, early on, by her wide and enthusiastic knowledge of his work. The Owen sisters made several expeditions under his or Emma's guidance to Wool Manor, Bindon Abbey, Weymouth, and other places drawn upon in the novels, and on 7 September they all four went to Swanage, where Hardy attended a meeting of the Field Club while Emma showed the Owen sisters around the town. At West End Cottage the now widowed Mrs Masters remembered the Hardys from sixteen years earlier, but Emma declined to go inside, evidently associating the house with a period of relative poverty and with the writing of *The Hand of Ethelberta*, a book she claimed to dislike because it had 'too much about servants in it'.[2] Rebekah Owen has her tiny niche in literary history as the chief of those 'good judges across the Atlantic' who persuaded Hardy to restore to the text of *The Mayor of Casterbridge* the episode of the starved goldfinch which had been included in American editions but omitted from English,[3] but the wearisome persistence of her visits and letters eventually exhausted Hardy's patience and it was left to Emma and, later, Florence Hardy to keep up the Max Gate end of a connection that Miss Owen would not let go and the Hardys did not quite know how to break.

Driving home from Dorchester one afternoon in September 1892, Hardy saw that Stinsford House was on fire, left Emma to continue home in the carriage, and ran across the intervening water-meadows in time to help carry out some of the books and furniture. The near-destruction of the house, following so closely upon the death of his father, brought a further 'bruising of tender memories'. Lady Susan Fox-Strangways had lived there after her romantic elopement with the actor William O'Brien, and his own grandfather had built beneath Stinsford Church the vault that the bereaved and grieving Lady Susan had specified should be just big enough for her husband and herself. His father had sung in the house for Lady Susan in her old age and practised the violin there later on under the watchful eyes and ears of the Reverend Edward Murray. It was there, too, that his mother had worked, and there or in the adjacent church that she had first seen her future husband.[4] Mary Hardy—with almost symbolic appropriateness— was laying flowers on her father's grave when the fire broke out, and Hardy met her in the churchyard. He did not, on the other hand, encounter Emma, although she too made her way to the scene in the company of Bosworth Smith, with whose parents they were engaged to dine at West Stafford that evening.[5]

At the end of that month Hardy was in London, reviewing with Clarence McIlvaine the arrangements for the rights to his novels to be transferred to Osgood, McIlvaine & Co. Most of those rights had been held for some years by Sampson Low, Marston & Co., but Hardy had become dissatisfied with the poor appearance of their much-reprinted editions and was enthusiastically cooperating in the plans, originally projected by James Osgood, for a handsomely produced collective edition.[6] He went on from London to Oxford and thence to Fawley, in the Berkshire countryside south of Wantage, where his grandmother Mary Head had been born 120 years before: 'Though I am alive with the living', he wrote, 'I can only see the dead here, and am scarcely conscious of the happy children at play.'[7] Hardy would draw heavily on these scenes and associations in the novel, eventually entitled *Jude the Obscure*, that he was now taking seriously in hand. He seems already to have foreseen that it would be his last major work of fiction, and the depth of this imaginative engagement with his ancestral past reveals the deliberateness with which he was working towards a personal statement.

The broad directions of such a statement were already being foreshadowed in the weekly parts of *The Pursuit of the Well-Beloved*, which ran as a serial in the *Illustrated London News* from 1 October to 17 December 1892 but appeared in volume form, as *The Well-Beloved*, only in 1897. The novel had two main settings, the curiously isolated world of the Isle of Portland, known to Hardy from childhood, and the crowded drawing rooms of London society. It is not clear to what extent he may have drawn upon personal memories in presenting the Portland episodes, but he seems to have felt free to make use of London occasions and personalities that must have been recognizable at least to those most immediately concerned. Lady Portsmouth, her daughter Lady Gwendolen Wallop, and her niece Lady Winifred Burghclere (née Herbert) were clearly the 'originals' of Lady Channelcliffe and two of the ladies present at her fictional 'assembly'. A dinner at Lady Jeune's in January 1891 at which Ellen Terry was present provided the basis for the novel's description of a dinner at Lady Iris Speedwell's. Hardy's friend, the painter Alfred Parsons, who had chosen to live in London and let others do his thinking for him, is similar in several respects to Alfred Somers, the painter in the novel. Rosamund Tomson supplied certain ingredients in the presentation of Mrs Nichola Pine-Avon, the handsome woman with intellectual aspirations whom the novel's hero rejects but Somers marries. Such dependence may indicate a severe shortage of what Hardy was accustomed to call 'novel padding'.[8] It could, on the other hand, constitute a deliberate if indirect acknowledgement of an autobiographical element within the novel as a whole.

The story, Hardy said on various occasions, was 'a bygone, wildly romantic fancy', sketched long before the appearance of the serial, at a time when he was still 'comparatively a young man'. He jotted down early in 1889 the idea of 'a face which goes through three generations or more' and later insisted that the 'plot' had been suggested by a sculptor's account of how he 'had often pursued a beautiful ear, nose, chin, &c, about London in omnibuses and on foot'.[9] He was also fascinated by Shelley's 'one shape of many names'—the phrase from *The Revolt of Islam* subsequently used as the epigraph to the first edition of the novel—and seems to have been deliberately harking back to *The Woodlanders*, in which Fitzpiers not only quotes Shelley at impressive length but invokes, in cynical justification of his own infidelities, the notion of an ideal beloved capable of manifesting herself in a series of human avatars. In *The Pursuit of the Well-Beloved*—which echoes Fitzpiers's name in that of Jocelyn Pearston (later Pierston), its central figure, and gives the latter's London address as Hintock Road—this aspect of *The Woodlanders* is effectively inverted. Pearston's unresting pursuit of the well-beloved, which renders him as susceptible to feminine beauty at the age of 60 as he had been at 40 or even 20, is described as being 'of the nature of tragedy', however much it might bear 'the aspect of comedy'.[10]

If Hardy had learned since the middle 1880s to perceive the elusiveness of the well-beloved in terms of actual or potential tragedy, that was perhaps because he had been forced to acknowledge to himself the implications of his own attitudes towards Rosamund Tomson and other women known socially or just casually glimpsed—Agatha Thornycroft, Amélie Rives, the prostitute with the narcissus, the 'Cleopatra' in a French railway carriage in the summer of 1890 who seemed 'a good-natured amative creature by her voice, and her heavy moist lips'.[11] Hardy's responsiveness to such encounters was both intense and long-lived: 'The Woman I Met' and 'Thoughts of Phena' are only two among several laments for opportunities left ungrasped at the one ripe moment and swept immediately into that realm of the unattainable where his imagination was always most at home: 'O could it but be', cries the speaker in 'Faintheart in a Railway Train', 'That I had alighted there!' Hardy, 'a young man till he was nearly fifty',[12] had now, in his fifties, been obliged to recognize a growing discrepancy between his increasing age and his undiminished—or perhaps reawakened—sexuality. But what in his as in Pearston's youth had been pleasant fancies or, at worst, transitory adolescent infatuations, had become in his as in Pearston's middle age a source of recurrent anguish, a persistently re-enacted tragi-comedy. For Hardy the situation was exacerbated, its ironies deepened, by the existence of a permanent, increasingly burdensome, yet unignorable domestic tie.

In the serial version of the novel Hardy permitted himself to treat this theme with almost brutal directness. Pearston and Marcia Bencomb marry in haste and become gradually disillusioned with each other over a period of years. She from the first believes that she has married somewhat beneath her; he feels that, as a sculptor 'rising to fame by fairly rapid strides', he had in fact been no bad match 'for a woman who, beyond being the probable successor to a stone-merchant's considerable fortune, had no exceptional opportunities'. He nevertheless recognizes that family enmity would have driven even Romeo and Juliet apart after a month or two, Juliet going to live 'with her people, he with his'. As the narrator observes of the pair: 'In their ill-matched junction on the strength of a two or three days' passion they felt the full irksomeness of a formal tie which, as so many have discovered, did not become necessary till it was a cruelty to them.'[13] Much later in the serial, in one of the numerous plot complications that the book version would significantly modify, Pearston woos and weds a woman much younger than himself who is in fact the granddaughter—and virtual reincarnation—of the woman whom he had abandoned for Marcia's sake forty years earlier. He soon realizes, however, much as Phillotson was to do in *Jude the Obscure*, that she loves someone else, and that humanity if not legality would best be served by letting her go: 'to me', he declares, 'healthy natural instinct is true law, and not an Act of Parliament.'[14]

Emma's distress at these direct attacks on marriage can only have been intensified by the serial's closing episode, in which Pearston, the successful sculptor cursed by the combination of an ageing body with a perpetually restless heart, is seized with hysterical laughter at finding himself finally and permanently yoked to a re-encountered Marcia, now grown shrivelled and old: '"Oh—no, no! I—I—it is too, too droll—this ending to my would-be romantic history."' The entire serial then closes with the exclamation 'Ho—ho—ho!'—outside quotation marks, hence presumably authorial. Hardy's last story, wrote one of Rebekah Owen's friends on the last day of 1892, 'ends pitifully. It reads to me like a disappointed home life, very thinly veiled, in the author's experience.'[15] If *The Pursuit of the Well-Beloved* was being discussed in such terms by mere acquaintances, it could scarcely fail to give offence to Emma herself. And if she perceived the story as reflecting her husband's dissatisfaction with his own marriage, its publication can only have contributed to the further deterioration of that marriage. In so far as it may have constituted for Hardy a conscious act of exorcism, a thera-peutic course of self-flagellation, the exercise was to prove singularly ineffective.

Almost immediately after his return from Oxford and Fawley in early October 1892 Hardy made a special trip to London to be present at Tennyson's funeral. The occasion could not but take on something of the character of a literary concourse—he spoke briefly with Meredith, James, and others, and after the service was taken off by Gosse to lunch with Austin Dobson, Theodore Watts-Dunton, and William Watson—but it was in other respects very much in tune with the depressive mood in which he had remained, perhaps with a touch of self-indulgence, since his father's death. He had a very good place in the Abbey, he told Emma, and 'looked into the grave with the rest as we passed it on our way out'.[16] His former employer Arthur Blomfield (now Sir Arthur) was addressed in a letter of mid-October as one of the few people 'the ravages of time' had left for him to call 'very old friends'. A further melancholy comment, the point of departure for a famous poem, sounded the note of mortality in terms at once deeply per-sonal and immediately apposite to the serial then in progress: 'Hurt my tooth at breakfast-time. I look in the glass. Am conscious of the humiliating sorriness of my earthly tabernacle, and of the sad fact that the best of parents could do no better for me. . . . Why should a man's mind have been thrown into such close, sad, sensational, inexplicable relations with such a precarious object as his own body!'[17] There is a strong suggestion here of a

recent rebuff from a younger woman—possibly Rosamund Tomson—
and it was an odd coincidence, if nothing more, that the illustrator of *The
Pursuit of the Well-Beloved* should have drawn a Pearston who bore a quite
striking physical resemblance to the author himself—as conveniently
represented in the full-page portrait facing the first page of the opening
instalment.[18]

In late 1892 and early 1893 Hardy was occupied with the composition of one
of his finest short stories, 'The Fiddler of the Reels', sent off on 13 January
1893 for publication in a special Chicago World's Fair number of *Scribner's
Magazine*.[19] The negotiations with *Scribner's* had been conducted by A. P.
Watt, a pioneer in the new profession of literary agent, and during the early
1890s Hardy had some dealings with another such agent, William Morris
Colles, whose Authors' Syndicate was closely associated with the Incorporated Society of Authors. Although Hardy usually found himself returning
negative replies to Colles's requests for novels and stories, he did sell some
properties through the Syndicate—notably 'An Imaginative Woman',
published in the newly founded *Pall Mall Magazine*—and during the
summer of 1893 he sought the advice both of the Syndicate and of the
Society of Authors when he ran into difficulties with the house of
Macmillan, as earlier with Sampson Low, over the transfer of rights to
Osgood, McIlvaine.[20] Hardy always held agents at a distance, however,
keeping control over his work very much in his own hands.

In the spring of 1893 he asked the Authors' Syndicate, through Colles, to
prepare typed copies of a one-act play, *The Three Wayfarers*, which he had
just adapted from his short story 'The Three Strangers'.[21] The controversy
over *Far from the Madding Crowd* and *The Squire* had soured Hardy's previous
theatrical experience, and in the years immediately preceding 1893 he had
more than once expressed, publicly as well as privately, a strong distaste for
the contemporary stage and its excessive emphasis upon elaborate scenery
and costumes. In a letter published in the *Weekly Comedy* in November 1889
he went so far as to advocate a form of arena stage: 'The spectators would
then, sitting to a great extent round the actors, see the *play* as it was seen in
old times, but as they do not see it now for its accessories.' The failure of
Grein and Jarvis to get *The Woodlanders* produced, despite approaches to
George Alexander, Henry Irving, and others, only served to increase
Hardy's scepticism about the actor-manager system and its conservative
adherence not only to theatrical spectacle but to the moral assumptions of
the time. It was in realistic anticipation of that conservativism that in 1893
he abandoned his scenario for *Birthwort*, a 'tragic' two-act play that would

have dealt—like the related poem 'A Sunday Morning Tragedy'—with an attempted abortion.[22]

Hardy, even so, remained susceptible to the glamour of the stage. From his earliest days in London he had been a frequent and enthusiastic theatre-goer. He still attended performances of every description—Lottie Collins's 'Ta-ra-ra-boom de-ay' number at the Gaiety, he told Douglas, was 'really a very unusual performance, & not altogether so silly as people say'[23]—and was early and enthusiastically aware of Ibsen's arrival on the English stage. Thanks largely to Lady Jeune, he was on friendly terms with Irving, Ellen Terry, George Alexander, Ada Rehan, and other leading actors of the day. Nor was he insensible of the financial rewards the theatre potentially offered. The notion of adapting already-written material for the stage seemed attractively practicable and in April 1893 Hardy acceded promptly to James Barrie's suggestion that he should make a play out of 'The Three Strangers' for inclusion in a programme of one-act plays to be performed by Janet Achurch and her husband Charles Charrington. The idea had already occurred to him, Hardy replied, and he had even begun to take it in hand: 'I do not know what became of my sketch. However the work wd not be difficult—& I am willing to attempt it again.'[24] He was as good as his word, not only completing the play in good time, but supplying a sketch of the shepherd's cottage, inserting some old dance tunes and figures, and offering to give full details of the dances if required. The morning after the first performance on 3 June 1893 Lady Jeune wrote to scold him for 'running away as you did & leaving us, because everybody was most anxious to see you & they all called for you', but the production as a whole was coolly received and ran only until the end of the week.[25]

It was in the spring of 1893 that the Hardys for the first time took an entire house for the London season, bringing up their own servants from Max Gate. The house, 70 Hamilton Terrace, was in Maida Vale, not far from the church in Elgin Avenue where they had been married nearly nineteen years before. The success of *Tess* was apparent not only in this ampler style of London living but in the expansion of their social activities. There were numerous encounters with the famous, the wealthy, and the well born, and Hardy—famous himself now—moved in these elevated circles with an ever greater assurance. At dinner one evening he sat opposite Princess May of Teck, the prospective bride of the Duke of York (later King George V), and recorded in his notebook, with perhaps deliberate ungraciousness, that she was 'not a bad-looking girl, and a man might marry a worse'.[26] In the less elevated context of an Authors' Club meeting he was sought out by Israel Zangwill, who had recently made a name for himself with his novel *Children of the Ghetto*, and found to be 'oldish' but warm and congenial, 'a nice simple old man'. A few days later Zangwill attended one of the Hardys' 'at homes' at 70 Hamilton Terrace. Emma, 'pleasant, pretty and un peu invalide', chattered away with utter inconsequentiality, while Hardy himself spoke angrily of the delays and restrictions imposed by the conventions of serialization. He also expressed resentment of comments on his work that Henry James was reported to have made in private conversation and some retaliatory distaste for James's recently published story 'The Real Thing': it was 'so futile', he said, and one simply did not believe in the two aristocrats.[27]

On 18 May 1893 Hardy and Emma set off for Ireland, stopping overnight at Llandudno, the setting of that foreboding poem 'Alike and Unlike'.[28] The next day they crossed over to Dublin, where they were to be the guests of the Lord-Lieutenant of Ireland, Lord Houghton, later the Marquess of Crewe. Hardy had been on friendly terms with the writer and reformer Richard Monckton Milnes, the first Lord Houghton, during the years immediately preceding the latter's death in 1885, and had known his son, the current Lord Houghton, for some time. He seems not, however, to have met his host's sister, Florence Henniker, until she welcomed Emma and himself at the Viceregal Lodge. Mrs Henniker was then in her late thirties, the author of three moderately successful novels, and the wife, since 1882, of Arthur Henry Henniker-Major, professional soldier and younger son of the fourth Lord Henniker. Her father's literary and political reputation, her brother's political career, and her husband's military life had brought her an unusually wide range of acquaintances and experiences, and she moved of right in those upper-class circles to which Hardy was admitted only on the basis of his hard-won fame. She was, indeed, a poised, intelligent, educated woman, well qualified, according to Justin McCarthy, to become famous as 'the presiding genius of a salon'.[29] That she never quite attained such a position may be ascribed partly to her uncertain health and partly to the sharpness of her tongue, but more largely to her devotion to her soldier husband and to the somewhat peripatetic life she consequently led. Though not exactly a beauty, she was handsome, assured, and elegantly dressed— in sharp contrast to Emma, who is said to have appeared in Dublin in an outfit of muslin and blue ribbons ludicrously inappropriate to her fifty-one years.[30]

Hardy's attraction to Mrs Henniker was immediate and powerful. 'A charming, *intuitive* woman apparently,' reads the note he made after that first meeting,[31] and while that '*intuitive*' hints at qualities in Mrs Henniker which were soon to be drawn upon for certain aspects of Sue Bridehead's personality, it also reveals a strong element of wishfulness in Hardy's early attitudes towards her, an assumption of a sexual as well as intellectual responsiveness and mutuality that seems simply not to have existed. He had for some time been looking for someone to fall in love with and, in effect, 'chose' Mrs Henniker with little if any encouragement on her part and little initial realization of what was going on. As a woman of intellectual ambitions and accomplishments, mixing freely and easily in many walks of society, as the childless wife, mature yet still attractive, of an often-absent soldier of philistine views, as (by no means least) the daughter of the actively reformist Monckton Milnes—in all these respects Mrs Henniker must have looked like the emancipated woman whom Hardy had long been seeking, an ideal receptacle for his personal vision of the well-beloved.

While the Hardys were still in Ireland during the last two weeks of May they visited the sights of Dublin and shared in the activities and formalities of the Viceregal Lodge and its 'little Court', as Hardy rather sardonically called it. These included a military display on the occasion of the Queen's birthday on 24 May, when he and Emma rode in one of the carriages in the procession through the city, a visit to the scene of the Phoenix Park murders, conversations with his old acquaintance John Morley, then Chief Secretary for Ireland, and various social occasions, including a dinner at which Mrs Henniker played the zither. An apparently trivial notebook entry about the ale or dirty water splashed onto the ladies' clothes during a visit to the Guinness brewery on their final morning in Dublin perhaps served to memorialize for Hardy himself some unexpressed and inexpressible moment of real or imagined intimacy with Mrs Henniker.[32] Later that same day, 25 May, the Hardys set off on a brief tour of the Killarney lakes, returning through Dublin to Kingstown (Dun Laoghaire) on 28 May, and thence to London on the 29th. On the boat to Holyhead they were joined by Mrs Henniker and by General Milman, Keeper of the Tower of London, and his daughter Lena, a young woman of some linguistic and literary accomplishments whom Hardy was to engage in mildly flirtatious, if somewhat desultory, correspondence over the next several months.[33]

Back at Hamilton Terrace the Hardys resumed their active social lives. Hardy met Pearl Craigie, the able and beautiful woman who wrote under the pseudonym of 'John Oliver Hobbes', and Gosse's friend the Dutch novelist 'Maarten Maartens', whose real name was J. van der Poorten Schwartz. He visited the Tower of London under General Milman's guidance and accompanied Emma, Lena Milman, Maarten Maartens, and James Barrie to a performance of the latter's successful play, *Walker, London*. Mrs Henniker was briefly in London that same week, and Hardy went with her, and with her brother-in-law and sister, Sir Gerald and Lady Fitzgerald, to see Ibsen's *The Master Builder*—having already seen *Hedda Gabler* and *Rosmersholm* a few days previously. At the theatre Hardy found an opportunity for some private conversation with Mrs Henniker and even for a declaration of affection, evidently received with distinct coolness: he was trying, he wrote on 17 June, to 'redress by any possible means the one-sidedness I spoke of, of which I am still keenly conscious', adding, with awkward formality, 'I sincerely hope to number you all my life among the most valued of my friends.'[34]

Hardy's early letters to Mrs Henniker are nakedly exploitative of whatever links—as substantial as literature or as tenuous as architectural history—might be established between them. He sent her a handbook on the history of architecture, recommending that she familiarize herself with certain sections, and arranged to give her a conducted tour of Westminster Abbey and other buildings nearby: 'Oral instruction in actual buildings', he rather transparently observed, 'is, of course, a much more rapid and effectual method than from books, and you must not think it will be any trouble to me.' He suggested a rendezvous at Sloane Square underground station, not far from Cadogan Gardens, where Mrs Henniker was staying with her sister, and they seem to have met there once or twice again in early July, during another of Mrs Henniker's short trips up to town from the house in Southsea that she and her husband had taken for the duration of his current Portsmouth posting.[35] Mrs Henniker's letters for this period have not survived, but it is clear from those of Hardy's that are still extant—some having been destroyed by Mrs Henniker, others perhaps by Hardy himself after her death—that she was keeping him very much at arm's length, declining to be drawn into exchanges of a romantic or potentially physical nature: 'Well—perhaps you are right [he wrote on 20 June] about the story of the two people spiritually united—as far as the man is concerned.' Hardy's grudging tone suggests that he was seeking something more concrete than spiritual affinity, and while later letters speak of his trying 'desperately' to dispel the intensity of his emotions by distractions and occupations of various kinds, the frequency and explicitness of such allusions, together with the confessions of 'poor results', reveal a lingering hope that his persistence will in the end be rewarded, that his correspondent will soften and relent—at least to the extent of engaging in a sympathetic dialogue.[36]

Nor did Mrs Henniker remain entirely immune to such implicit appeals. Whatever her motives in giving Hardy, on 30 June, some of her verse translations from the French and Spanish, he could scarcely have been blamed for interpreting as coquettish, or cruelly teasing, the receipt of such lines as these:

> We were together,—her eyes were wet,
> But her pride was strong, & no tears would fall;
> And *I* would not tell her I loved her yet,
> And yearned to forgive her all!
>
> So, now that our lives are for ever apart,
> *She* thinks—'Oh! had I but wept that day!'
> And *I* ask in vain of my lonely heart—
> 'Ah! why did I turn away?'[37]

When, a little later, Hardy jokingly threatened to give lessons in architecture to other attractive women of their acquaintance, she evidently responded with a gratifying (if mock-serious) display of jealousy: 'I will religiously obey orders about the architectural lessons,' Hardy wrote on 16 July. 'You shall hold the copyright in them. Is not that promise very handsome of me?' The remainder of that same letter, however, is more sternly written, showing clearly that Hardy had already realized that Mrs Henniker's views upon morality in general and marriage in particular were likely to prove too rigidly conventional to allow of any relationship that went beyond the strictly 'platonic'. Referring to their having both been reading Shelley's 'Epipsychidion', he wrote:

I had a regret in reading it at thinking that one who is pre-eminently the child of the Shelleyean tradition—whom one would have expected to be an ardent disciple of his school and views—should have allowed herself to be enfeebled to a belief in ritualistic ecclesiasticism. My impression is that you do not know your own views. You feel the need of emotional expression of some sort, and being surrounded by the conventional society form of such expression you have mechanically adopted it. Is this the daughter of the man who went from Cambridge to Oxford on the now historic errand! Depend upon it there are other valves for feeling than the ordinances of Mother Church—my Mother Church no less than yours.

Hardy's allusion to her father's early advocacy of Shelley suggests the extent to which his investment in Mrs Henniker had been of a theoretical rather than an entirely instinctual nature. So, equally, does a veiled reference, in the same letter, to his earlier disappointment in Rosamund Tomson and his conclusion that he must, in future, 'trust to imagination only for an enfranchised woman'.[38]

The Hardys left London for Dorchester in the first half of July, but on the 19th Hardy went back alone to stay once more with the Jeunes, taking a roundabout route in order to spend a few hours with Mrs Henniker in

Southsea.[39] On 5 August he entered into a notebook some lines from Dante Gabriel Rossetti's 'Spheral Change', taken from the copy of his *Poetical Works* just given him by Mrs Henniker:

> O dearest, while we lived and died
>   A living death in every day,
> Some hours we still were side by side
>   When where I was you too might stay
>   And rest and need not go away.
> O nearest, furthest! can there be
>   At length some hard-earned heart-won home
> Where—exile changed to sanctuary—
>   Our lot may fill indeed its sum,
>   And you may wait, and I may come?[40]

The sentiment is in some respects strikingly similar to that of Hardy's own poem 'At an Inn', based on the visit he and Mrs Henniker made to Winchester together on 8 August. They met at Eastleigh, a railway junction just north of Southampton, and Mrs Henniker seems immediately to have made it clear, once and for all, that things could not be as Hardy wished. As the poem 'The Month's Calendar' puts it: 'You let me see | There was good cause | Why you could not be | Aught ever to me!'[41] Arrived in Winchester, they lunched at the George Inn, attended Evensong in the cathedral, and walked a little way out of the town to the spot from which, at the end of *Tess*, Angel and Liza-Lu watch the black flag rise above the prison in confirmation of Tess's execution.[42] It was a pilgrimage sadly appropriate to Hardy's mood. As the poem 'At an Inn' so painfully suggests, a meeting which had all the external appearance of a lovers' tryst—to the point that at the George Inn he and Mrs Henniker were taken for a married couple and shown into a bedroom together—proved in fact to be something very different:

> And we were left alone
>   As Love's own pair;
> Yet never the love-light shone
>   Between us there!
> But that which chilled the breath
>   Of afternoon,
> And palsied unto death
>   The pane-fly's tune.[43]

In the final stanza the breath-chilling presence is identified as the 'laws of men', and a letter of 17 August, alluding to an indiscreet (and now vanished) letter he had sent her two weeks earlier, makes it clear that Hardy had something close to contempt for the conventionality of Mrs Henniker's thinking: 'If I shd never write to you again as in that letter you must remember that it was written *before* you expressed your views—"morbid" indeed! *petty* rather—in the railway carriage when we met at Eastleigh.'[44]

Mrs Henniker's views did not, even so, drive Hardy away. Though 'In Death Divided' is in every sense a funereal poem, it sounds a faint note of acceptance or at least resignation in its affirmation of 'The eternal tie which binds us twain in one'. The sexual element in the relationship perhaps had declined in importance, and even for Hardy it may not have been dominant from the first. As 'A Thunderstorm in Town' suggests, and as Florence Hardy once confirmed, Hardy and Mrs Henniker never exchanged a single kiss, although Hardy, confiding in Clodd three years after the event, did speak of their having clasped hands beside the high altar in Winchester Cathedral.[45] Since it is not at all clear what conclusions Hardy had projected for his courtship, Mrs Henniker's unresponsiveness may have been a source of unacknowledged relief. But the experience, in all its delusive excitement and ultimate disappointment, was certainly productive of personal pain as well as of renewed hostility to those imprisoning aspects of marriage already cruelly portrayed in the pages of *The Pursuit of the Well-Beloved*. For Hardy as poet there was also a usable residue in the form of intensely emotional memories, similar in mood to his voiced regrets for Louisa, Tryphena, and all the other lost prizes of earlier days, and only to be exceeded by the grieving and guilty response to the death of Emma that produced the 'Poems of 1912–13'.

Most moving, perhaps, of all the poems associated with Mrs Henniker, and certainly eloquent of Hardy's longer view of the relationship, is the second stanza of 'A Broken Appointment':

> You love not me,
> And love alone can lend you loyalty;
> —I know and knew it. But, unto the store
> Of human deeds divine in all but name,
> Was it not worth a little hour or more
> To add yet this: Once you, a woman, came
> To soothe a time-torn man; even though it be
> You love not me?

The poem is remarkable in itself as an example of Hardy's capacity to evolve verse of almost classical elegance out of such essentially humdrum material—as an instance, too, of marvellously enriching revision, in that substitution of 'time-torn' for the earlier 'soulsad'.[46] But it implicitly brings against Mrs Henniker a charge of hardness and selfishness, of a lack of what the first stanza calls 'lovingkindness' (always one of the most fundamental of Hardyan positives), and she does indeed seem—for all her charm and passionate advocacy of humanitarian causes—to have been a little lacking in personal warmth: Florence Hardy, who was very fond of her, once said of Sir George Douglas that he appreciated Mrs Henniker, 'as few did'. As Hardy did not hesitate to inform her, she certainly showed insensitivity in reading out portions of his letters to her family and friends. And in praising Hardy to a friend in 1915 the adjective she chose was the patronizing 'unspoiled'.[47] Yet she could scarcely have known, and probably never did know, the depth and complexity of Hardy's feelings for her, the extent to which he had so unreasonably focused upon her the accumulated dreams and desires of so many disappointed years.

In late August 1893 Hardy and Emma travelled to Shropshire to spend a few days with Catherine Milnes-Gaskell and her husband at Wenlock Abbey, where Hardy enjoyed Lady Catherine's attractive company, talked sexual politics on the basis of her confession that she had once engaged in a 'wanton' flirtation, and indulged his melancholia by discussing with her 'suicide, pessimism, whether life was worth living, and kindred dismal subjects'. Such topics were extremely germane to the new novel on which he would shortly begin working. He had already visited Oxford in June to get the flavour of the Commemoration festivities,[48] but prior commitments required that the first weeks after the return to Max Gate at the end of August should be devoted to work on short stories.

On 14 September he sent off to Colles the manuscript of 'An Imaginative Woman', the story of a romance-that-never-was between a publishing poet and an 'impressionable, palpitating' young married woman with literary ambitions of her own. The poet, Robert Trewe—called in the manuscript Crewe, the maiden name of Mrs Henniker's mother—is physically different from Hardy himself but distinctly similar in his extreme sensitivity to unfair criticism ('"lies that he's powerless to refute and stop from spreading"') and in being 'a pessimist in so far as that character applies to a man who looks at the worst contingencies as well as the best in the human condition'.[49] Trewe is also the author of a 'mournful ballad on "Severed Lives"' that sounds very much like a counterpart to 'In Death Divided' or to 'The Division', another poem in the same group. Ella Marchmill does not especially resemble Mrs Henniker—except in having eyes whose 'marvellously bright and liquid sparkle' is said to be characteristic of persons of an imaginative 'cast of soul'—but a connection is unmistakably established by the militariness of her surname, by her husband's occupation of 'gunmaker', and by the use of Solentsea (i.e. Southsea) as a setting.[50] That the story was in certain limited respects an ironic reworking of Hardy's recent emotional adventure seems clear enough; on the other hand, its affinities with *The Well-Beloved* suggest that *Life and Work* is perhaps correct in indicating that its essential features had been sketched at an earlier date.[51]

In October, after a few pleasant days spent with the Jeunes at their country house near Newbury, Hardy gathered together nine previously published short stories under the title of *Life's Little Ironies*—the collection into which the as yet unpublished 'An Imaginative Woman' would eventually be inserted.[52] By 22 October 1893 he was able to tell Mrs Henniker that the stories were ready to go off to the publisher, and to declare himself free to 'turn to the "Desire"', the story—eventually published as 'The Spectre of the Real'—on which they were already jointly engaged.[53] The idea of a literary collaboration, first mooted at least as early as July, had gained impetus following Hardy's acceptance of the limitations Mrs Henniker had placed upon their relationship. Mrs Henniker's more consistent emphasis upon their shared literary interests had been largely motivated by her eagerness to deflect Hardy from his pursuit of other forms of attachment, but she was by no means unaware of his potential usefulness to her own career. The silver inkstand she gave him in September 1893 was practical enough in itself—'Oddly enough I am badly off in inkstands,' Hardy gallantly declared[54]—but it also hinted at the direction she felt his interest and activity might best take.

The survival of two typescripts of the story and a set of corrected proofs for its initial magazine publication provides copious evidence of its complicated composition, and detailed analysis of those materials has recently revealed that Mrs Henniker's role in the collaboration was significantly larger than had previously been supposed.[55] That the plot was essentially Hardy's is obvious from its incorporation of a central 'poor man' and 'lady' pairing, the inconveniently timed return of a husband believed dead and other features from *The Pursuit of the Well-Beloved*, and one of those familiar Hardyan deaths by drowning that can plausibly be traced back to his exposure in childhood to tales of his namesake's fatal tumble into the Frome. He had, however, discussed the plot with Mrs Henniker, offered her a choice between alternatives,[56] and accepted with only minor changes the scenario she prepared after making that choice. It was then she, not Hardy, who filled out that scenario and wrote the story in its entirety. Hardy not only read her manuscript but revised it throughout, entirely rewriting the conclusion, before sending it off to a Miss Tigan—one of the professional typists who were becoming an increasingly familiar feature of the publishing scene—with instructions to return the manuscript to himself but send the completed typescript directly to Mrs Henniker. The letter he wrote to her the same day, 28 October, shows him sharply and almost guiltily aware of having altered the ending of the story without her consent:

Will you please read it from the beginning (*without* glancing first at the end!) so as to get the intended effect, & judge of its strength or weakness. It is, as you wished, very tragic; a modified form of Ending II—which I think better than any we have thought of before. If anything in it is what you don't like please tell me quite freely,—& it shall be modified. As I said last time, all the wickedness (if it has any) will be laid on my unfortunate head, while all the tender & proper parts will be attributed to you. Without wishing to make you promise, I suggest that we keep it a secret to our two selves which is my work & which yours. We may be amusingly bothered by friends & others to confess.

Mrs Henniker was also asked to pencil in any changes or additions she thought necessary, especially with respect to the heroine's wedding morning, where she might be able to supply details 'that would only be known to a woman'.[57] Although the typescript survives, the faintness or subsequent erasure of many of the pencil markings makes it difficult to determine just which of the ink revisions inscribed by Hardy had in fact been suggested by his collaborator. She certainly insisted upon the restoration of several passages descriptive of butterflies and bird-tracks and other natural phenomena that Hardy had omitted during his revision of the manuscript—not 'because they weren't good', he had taken care to explain, 'but because the scale of the story was too small to admit them without injury to the proportion of the whole'.[58]

The changes were sufficiently extensive to make a fresh typescript desirable, and it was the carbon copy of this second typescript, still further revised, which was sent off to Jerome K. Jerome's magazine *To-Day*, accompanied by a firm instruction in Hardy's own hand: '*To the printer.* Insert all *accents* & hyphens, & punctuation precisely as in copy. TH.'[59] Hardy had conducted the negotiations for the sale of 'The Spectre of the Real' through the agent A. P. Watt, chiefly to encourage him to be active in future in Mrs Henniker's behalf. But Watt, as Hardy acknowledged to his collaborator on 1 December, got them a 'very fair' price for so short a tale[60]—and, he might have added, for so sour an exploration of social and sexual mismatching. Hardy's obsession with the evils of marriage obtruded itself throughout in ways that Emma, once again, can only have found deeply offensive, and that Mrs Henniker herself toned down two years later when collecting the story in her volume *In Scarlet and Grey*.

18

The Making of *Jude*

Busy as he was in the autumn of 1893, Hardy found time to lend some architectural assistance to his builder brother. He had always made his expertise available to Henry as need arose. Just a year or two earlier he had provided the design and working drawings for Talbothays, the substantial house built by the family firm some two miles east of Max Gate on the piece of land that their father had called Talbots. It is possible that Henry expected to be married and to move into the new house with his bride. Or the family may have planned more comfortable accommodation for their newly widowed mother, now entering her eighties. In the event, and for whatever reason—the collapse of Henry's marriage plans, perhaps, or Jemima's refusal to leave Higher Bockhampton—Talbothays was let out until 1911, when Henry finally took occupation in company with his sisters Mary and Kate.[1] The task Hardy shared with his brother in 1893-4 was the extensive renovation of the little Frome valley church of St Peter's, located in West Knighton, conveniently close to the Hardy building yard. At West Knighton Henry was the contractor, Thomas the architect and supervisor, and together they reroofed the chancel, rebuilt the gallery, uncovered and restored an old arch, and made alterations to some of the windows. The restoration overall was discreetly and inoffensively done, although Hardy's essentially imitative designs for the new windows could scarcely be said to have conformed to the doctrines of the Society for the Protection of Ancient Buildings, of which he was in principle such a strong supporter.[2]

Accidentally or otherwise, Hardy's involvement in the West Knighton project overlapped with the composition of *Jude the Obscure*, a novel with a stonemason hero and deep roots in his own life and background. His poem 'The Young Glass-Stainer', written in November 1893 on the basis of the

West Knighton experience, is lightly suggestive of some of the resulting linkages:

> 'These Gothic windows, how they wear me out
> With cusp and foil, and nothing straight or square,
> Crude colours, leaden borders roundabout,
> And fitting in Peter here, and Matthew there!
>
> 'What a vocation! Here do I draw now
> The abnormal, loving the Hellenic norm;
> Martha I paint, and dream of Hera's brow.
> Mary, and think of Aphrodite's form.'[3]

The West Knighton experience fitted in with the more deliberate journeys that Hardy was making to Oxford and his grandmother's village of Great Fawley in order to get the 'feel' of the unfamiliar actualities he was about to transpose into fiction, to expose perception and memory to whatever numinous presences might still linger in places associated with past events and vanished people. By taking up pencil and measure again, refamiliarizing himself with the sights and sounds of tradesmen at work, the smell and texture of the materials used, the ring of hammer on stone, he could the more readily think himself back into the period and contexts in which the new novel was set.

Although so much of the emotional impetus of *Jude the Obscure* sprang from Hardy's own experience, its narrative materials were drawn from many different sources, among them his grandmother's early years in Berkshire, the lives and personalities of John Antell and Horace Moule, and the joys and agonies of his recent relationship with Mrs Henniker. It was in London in April 1888, at the time of a House of Commons debate on secondary education and 'the ladder from the primary schools to the university', that Hardy seems first to have thought of writing a short story about a young man's inability to go to Oxford and his subsequent struggles, failure, and suicide. According to the preface to the first edition of *Jude*, the scheme of the novel was 'jotted down in 1890, from notes made in 1887 and onwards, some of the circumstances being suggested by the death of a woman in the former year'.[4] Because Hardy's cousin Tryphena Sparks died in 1890 it has generally been taken for granted that she was the woman intended. But Hardy often used 'former' to mean 'earlier',[5] and the passage makes likelier sense if so read.

Tryphena's personality and life—apart from her college and teaching experiences, for which Hardy had other available precedents—had little similarity to Sue Bridehead's, and if the death that Hardy found so disturbing did in fact occur in 1890 it seems quite possibly to have been the execution, on 23 December 1890, of 24-year-old Mary Wheeler, also known as Mrs Pearcey, found guilty three weeks earlier of the murder of the wife and child of Frank Hogg, a man whom she had known for several years. The murder, carried out with considerable brutality, had attracted much public interest, and Hardy, happening to arrive in London on the day of the verdict, mentioned in a letter to Emma that people everywhere were reading about it in the newspapers. A remarkable feature of the case, specifically commented upon by a leader-writer in *The Times*, was that Mary Wheeler's feelings for Frank Hogg seemed not to have been of a specifically sexual nature, the emphasis—as in Sue's relationships with the Christminster undergraduate and, later, with Jude himself—being on 'friendship', on the maintenance of a kind of intimate comradeship.[6] Given the purely circumstantial nature of the evidence against Mary Wheeler, her youth and obvious intelligence, and the violence of her own death, her story could have so affected Hardy as to become an integral part of the imaginative and emotional context of *Jude* and an underlying presence in the narrative itself.

Although the death of Hardy's aunt Mary, his mother's sister, the widow of John Antell the shoemaker, has also been ascribed to 1890, it did not in fact occur until November 1891 and can scarcely have occasioned the reference in the *Jude* preface.[7] But her death and funeral, which he seems to have attended, would certainly have brought back memories of his visits to Puddletown in the late 1860s, attracted there by the presence of both his charming young cousin Tryphena and the darkly fascinating John Antell, his uncle by marriage. An undated notebook entry—'Poem. "The man who had no friend"—Auto. by John A-tell sen. Cf. "The Two Leaders." Swin.'[8]—hints enigmatically at Hardy's continuing fascination with John Antell's personality and fate, his sense of his gifted uncle as having been driven to drinking and violence, to isolation and self-disgust, and ultimately to an early grave, as a consequence of his having been denied the educational and societal opportunities that could have fostered his remarkable talents. Hardy must also have registered the anger that had prompted Antell, dying of a wasting disease (presumably cancer, or 'Lumbar abscess', as his death certificate called it), to pose for the remarkable photograph in which he stands, bent and emaciated, alongside a placard bearing the accusatory words 'SIC PLACET', evidently addressed to God, Fate, or even the President of the Immortals. Though not, apparently, based on the Antell photograph, the illustration of 'Jude at the Milestone' drawn by William Hatherell for the final serial instalment of *Jude* is strikingly reminiscent of it. Hardy, congratulating Hatherell on the illustration, called it 'a tragedy in itself'.[9]

That first preface to *Jude the Obscure* spoke of the final version of the novel as having been written 'from August 1893 onwards into the next year', but the crowding events of the latter half of 1893 had in fact prevented Hardy from making much initial progress: 'What name shall I give to the heroine of my coming long story when I get at it?' he asked Mrs Henniker on 22 October. 'I don't quite know when that will be, though it must be this winter.'[10] In mid-November, when he was tentatively negotiating with the *Graphic*, through Colles, and with the *Illustrated London News*, through Clement Shorter, he told the latter that the story was still in too chaotic a state for him to be able to estimate its eventual length. Writing to Mrs Henniker again on 1 December he confessed himself reluctant to get down to serious work on his manuscript, but added: 'However, as it is one I planned a couple of years ago I shall, I think, go on with it, & probably shall warm up.'[11] It was also in December that he came to terms with Harper & Brothers over the sale of all the serial rights, an arrangement that avoided the necessity of supplying duplicate copy for a separate American printing and enabled him to work through his English publishers, Osgood, McIlvaine, the English agents for Harper's and for the European edition of *Harper's New Monthly Magazine*.[12]

Intensive work on the manuscript now began—'I am burying myself alive here in hope of doing a little writing,' he wrote Lena Milman from Max Gate on 23 December—and by mid-January 1894 he could report to Mrs Henniker that he was 'creeping on a little with the long story' and becoming more interested in his as yet 'nebulous' heroine as she took on 'shape & reality'.[13] Such progress, though encouraging, was not without its attendant problems. Hardy had, as usual, assured his publishers that the forthcoming novel would not offend 'the most fastidious maiden', but by early April he felt obliged to inform them that the story was carrying him into such 'unexpected fields' that he dared not predict 'its future trend'. He offered—'promptly and magnanimously', as J. Henry Harper later acknowledged—either to cancel his agreement with Harper & Brothers or allow them to make whatever changes in the serial they felt to be necessary. Harper, having 'pledged' to print 'nothing which could not be read aloud in any family circle', chose the latter alternative; Hardy agreed to do some rewriting; and the serial version actually published between December 1894 and November 1895 was in consequence severely and, in some respects, ludicrously watered down. Episodes such as the pig-killing and Arabella's seduction of Jude were modified or omitted altogether; Jude and

Sue were obliged to live not together but 'near'; and the one child (instead of two) murdered by Father Time was Sue's by adoption only.[14] Hardy had long learned the virtues of compromise in such situations. As recently as January 1894 he had assured the editor of the *Pall Mall Magazine* of his willingness to delete an offending passage from the text of 'An Imaginative Woman', adding: 'I always give editors *carte blanche* in these matters: as I invariably reprint from the original copy for the book-form of my novels.'[15] Textually, the serial of *Jude* is of importance only in so far as Hardy allowed some of its bowdlerizations to survive into the first edition. But it was a painful episode in his professional and, indeed, personal history, and one that contributed its share of bitterness to his long-standing and still-accumulating dissatisfaction with the novel-writer's trade.

When the first instalment of the serial appeared it was called 'The Simpletons', but someone pointed out that a novel called *A Simpleton* had already been published in *Harper's* in the early 1870s. Hardy then reverted to his earlier, discarded title 'Hearts Insurgent', and it was under that regrettably lurid heading that the remainder of the serial appeared, Hardy's third thought, 'The Recalcitrants', having reached New York only after the second instalment had gone to press.[16] The evidence of the surviving manuscript has been variously and indeed conflictingly read, but it is clear that the central themes of the novel, education and marriage, were present from the first, and that Hardy always conceived of his central characters as challenging conventional attitudes towards both.[17] His problem as he tried to get the novel under way was to establish interconnections that would be functional in both narrative and thematic terms. Jude clearly had to go to Christminster; it was also necessary that he fall in love with his cousin; the puzzle—only temporarily troublesome—was to justify Sue's presence in Christminster and allow a meeting to take place. If, as appears, Phillotson had originally no part in the opening pages of the manuscript, that was perhaps because there were other ways of setting Jude on the road to Christminster and because it was only at a later stage that Hardy realized Phillotson's potential *both* as a partner in the sexual quadrille and as the motivator of Jude's educational ambitions.

Jude seems, in the manuscript, to have been first called Jack, with a possible glance towards John Antell. The status of Jude as the patron saint of lost causes was doubtless in Hardy's mind when making the change, and since he had on his shelves a copy of Charlotte M. Yonge's then standard *History of Christian Names*[18] he evidently chose his hero's name in full consciousness of its ill-omened similarity to Judas Iscariot. Indeed he drew deliberately upon that association in establishing from the first the sense of his hero as doomed to perpetual homelessness and pariah-hood. Jude's surname was at one time Head, after Hardy's grandmother, at another Hopeson, a heavily allegorized version of his great-grandmother's maiden name of Hopson (or Hobson), and went through other variations before becoming fixed as Fawley, the name of the Berkshire village that Hardy had recently visited for the sake of its associations with Mary Head and her forebears. The ancestral allusion thus removed from the name of the hero reappeared in the names of the heroine, Sue Bridehead, and of the village, Marygreen, from which Jude sets out on his journey in search of knowledge and self-knowledge. Consciously or otherwise, Jude became for Hardy the embodiment of an entire series of personal, familial, and social grievances that included the hardships encountered by his sisters as students and teachers, the poverty and violence suffered by his mother and both his grandmothers, and John Antell's anger against the world and its creator, as well as his own struggles for education, advancement, and sexual happiness. Horace Moule's tragic alternations between intellectuality and sensuality seem also to have been drawn upon, and Moule's alleged son in Australia was perhaps merged with the unaccompanied child at Sturminster station to constitute the 'original' of Jude's son Father Time.

Jude thus possesses obvious links with Hardy's biography, and even with such shadowy antecedents within Hardy's work as the schoolmaster of 'An Indiscretion in the Life of an Heiress' or, still further back, the hero of *The Poor Man and the Lady*. Sue's origins, on the other hand, remain less clear. Although Hardy's heroines had often been exasperating creatures, given to flirtation and various forms of deliberate and innocent sexual teasing, they had rarely exhibited any fundamental uncertainty as to their suitability for, or willing acceptance of, the traditional female roles. Writing to Gosse in November of 1895, Hardy described Sue as 'a type of woman which has always had an attraction for me—but the difficulty of drawing the type has kept me from attempting it till now'. The self-repressive austerity and sexual 'Laodiceanism' of Paula Power, in *A Laodicean*, strongly suggest that Hardy had in fact attempted an early version of the 'type' as early as 1881. What sharply distinguishes Paula from Sue, however, is the depth of her emotional commitment to Charlotte De Stancy, her 'more than sister'.[19] For all her fastidiousness in her relations with men, Sue displays no such compensatory preference for members of her own sex.

Hardy, in fact, pointedly eschews an obvious opportunity for the exploration of Sue's relationships with women of her own age. Melchester Training College, which Sue attends, was directly based on the Salisbury training college Hardy's two sisters had attended, many years apart, and where Kate, in particular, had been bitterly unhappy: 'I don't mind if Tom publishes how badly we were used,' she had once declared. Mary's resentment seems to have been softened by memories of her college friendship with Annie Lanham, later the wife of her cousin, Nathaniel Sparks,[20] and Hardy himself, visiting two London training colleges for women in 1891, had been moved by the thought of such friendships. None appear in *Jude* as published, however, and the college might not have been introduced at all had it not been for its association with Mary and the extent to which Hardy's presentation of the intimacy between Jude and Sue depended upon his sense of Mary as his own 'earliest playmate—a kind little sister, sharing with him, gladly, all she had, proud of him beyond words'.[21] Jemima rather than Mary was perhaps the 'relation' whose thoughts would so 'jump' with his own that 'after a long silence, both of us, in the same breath, would speak of some person or thing apparently quite absent from the thoughts of either five minutes before', but the central importance of his emotional and intellectual intimacy with Mary is reflected in the poem 'Conjecture', where she is mentioned in the same breath as Hardy's actual wives: 'If there were in my kalendar | No Emma, Florence, Mary, | What would be my existence now—.'[22] In childhood, he said, 'she was almost my only companion', and because of the isolation, both geographical and temperamental, in which they grew up, their early playing and sharing developed into a kind of defensive alliance against a largely uncomprehending world that can be imagined as approaching the marriage of true minds achieved by Jude and Sue at the time of the Great Wessex Agricultural Show, when they seem 'almost the two parts of a single whole'.[23]

Phillotson also speaks of Jude and Sue as resembling 'one person split in two', attributing the phenomenon partly to their cousinship. But cousinship in the novel was perhaps an available device for confronting a still closer degree of consanguinity. To think of Jude's early identification with Sue as deriving much of its validity and force from Hardy's feelings for Mary does at least provide a context for the deletion from the manuscript of a passage in which Jude looked at the sleeping Sue and saw in her 'the rough material called himself done into another sex—idealized, softened, & purified'. It also lends point to Phillotson's comparison of Jude and Sue to Laon and Cythna, in Shelley's *The Revolt of Islam*.[24] Shelley, after all, had first conceived of Laon and Cythna as brother and sister, and Hardy's habitual idealization of the relation between the sexes in Shelleyan terms was heavily dependent upon his own memories—themselves no doubt idealized—of the perfect understanding that had existed between Mary and himself in early childhood.

In deliberately insisting, within the novel itself, upon Sue's full name, Susanna Florence Mary Bridehead, Hardy was indirectly acknowledging his principal 'sources' for her representation. The Apocrypha's story of innocent Susanna and the lascivious Elders was perhaps sufficient justification for the first of those names, but Tess Durbeyfield was once to have been called Sue, and the name seems to have had for Hardy a special significance that perhaps stemmed from the romantic history of Lady Susan O'Brien. That Lady Jeune's first names were Susan Mary Elizabeth may or not be significant, though she was an especially dependable friend of Hardy's at this period. Sue Bridehead's Mary certainly points to Mary Hardy, and her Florence scarcely less directly to Florence Henniker. As Hardy once acknowledged in conversation with Edmund Clodd, Mrs Henniker was his most immediate 'model' for Sue Bridehead, especially in her elusive and teasing phases, and it was Mrs Henniker he had chiefly in mind when, in a remarkable letter, he told Gosse that there was

nothing perverted or depraved in Sue's nature. The abnormalism consists in disproportion: not in inversion, her sexual instinct being healthy so far as it goes, but unusually weak & fastidious; her sensibilities remain painfully alert notwithstanding, (as they do in nature with such women).[25]

To think of Mrs Henniker as essentially epicene doubtless provided Hardy with a personal explanation and excuse for the rebuff he had received. Within the novel itself, however, he was obliged to confront Jude's own challenge of engaging with a woman of complex sexual instincts and attitudes whose considerable intellectual gifts made her entirely capable of analysing her situation at any given moment, articulating her views, and acting decisively upon her conclusions.[26] It was a challenge that helped to shape the novel, Hardy having been taken into those 'unexpected fields' by his realization of how an initial Mary-based conception, functioning largely as a contrast to the destructive sexuality of Arabella, could be expanded and intensified by his recent experiences with the fascinating but unresponsive Mrs Henniker and become a crucial element in Jude's final tragedy.

The novel's second title, 'The Simpletons', emphasized the idealistic folly of a young couple who attempt to share a private and independent life, isolated from the values and prejudices of the society that surrounds them. Consciously or otherwise, the title also reflected wryly upon Hardy's own attempts to create an oasis of satisfaction to which he could escape from the desert his own marriage had increasingly become. 'Let us off and search, and find a place | Where yours and mine can be natural lives': so begins the poem, 'The Recalcitrants', which preserves another of the abandoned titles for *Jude*.[27] This is the grand motive of the life which Jude and Sue try to make together. That the attempt is doomed was implicit in its fictional premisses, but also in Hardy's recognition, painfully soon after meeting Mrs Henniker, that he would have to 'trust to imagination only for an enfranchised woman'.[28] If the book's implied judgement of Sue's character and conduct remains to the end uncertain or inconsistent, much is attributable to the ambiguities of Hardy's inspiration—what can be admired in a sister is likely to be deplored in a mistress—and to the unstable mix of devotion and resentment that characterized his entire relationship to Mrs Henniker.

Emma always hated *Jude*, having inevitably registered—with a sense of the deepest betrayal—not only its central attack on marriage and marriages but, worse still, its incorporation of elements of her own personal history in the presentation both of Arabella and of Sue. If 'The Place on the Map' is indeed to be associated with Hardy's and Emma's courtship, then its implied narrative is echoed, even travestied, in Arabella's false pregnancy. If Emma, as Hardy once declared, was indeed an agnostic at the time of their first meeting, then the subsequent shifts in her attitudes and beliefs could be seen to be reflected in Sue Bridehead's melancholy decline from brilliant independence to bleak religiosity.[29] Though perhaps not privy in detail to the composition of *Jude*, she certainly knew of her husband's friendship with Mrs Henniker—of which, in fact, he seems to have made little or no secret, mentioning the Winchester visit to the gossip-loving Rebekah Owen within a few weeks of its taking place.[30] Some degree of publicity, after all, was needed to give validity to their status as literary collaborators, and Mrs Henniker, who had neither desire nor motive for secrecy, put Hardy's name on the dedication page of her short-story volume, *Outlines*, published at the end of 1893.

However much, or little, Emma knew or guessed about the deeper levels of Hardy's attachment to Mrs Henniker, she became resentful of the slur which Hardy's collaboration with another woman seemed to cast upon her own literary pretensions. She had attempted to write before this time— 'The Maid on the Shore', begun in the 1870s, seems to have been completed in the late 1880s—and early in 1894 she sought to place some of her work through the literary agent A. P. Watt, the very man whom Hardy had entrusted with the cultivation of Mrs Henniker's career.[31] Emma would publish a few poems and articles later on, and although nothing seems to have come of the 1894 initiative it was significant of a growing tendency on Emma's part to assert her independence, to try to live a life separate from her husband's, and even in opposition to it.

The withdrawal into the Max Gate attic was still some way in the future—the attic itself had not yet been built—and she remained devoted to her Evangelicalism, to the prevention of cruelty of animals, and to the prosecution of a variety of religious, humanitarian, and feminist causes. In taking up such causes she found not only outlets for her considerable energies but also convenient platforms for the harassment of her husband: 'His interest in the Suffrage Cause is nil, in spite of "Tess",' she wrote to a woman friend, probably in November 1894, '& his opinions on the woman question not in her favour. He understands only the women he *invents*—the others not at all—& he only writes for *Art*, though ethics show up.'[32] She also became increasingly vocal in expressing her long-standing grievance against the socially demeaning aspects of her marriage: 'A man who has humble relations', she told Clodd in 1895, 'shouldn't live in the place where he was brought up.' A few years later, talking to Desmond MacCarthy about her husband's family, she would declare that the less one had to do with 'the peasant class' the better,[33] and it is clear that Emma's growing estrangement from her husband was as nothing compared to her outright hostility towards those whom she regarded as the real enemy, Hardy's implacable mother and obsessively devoted elder sister. Early in 1896, recuperating in the seaside resort of Worthing from a distressing attack of what was probably shingles, and with time and motivation to revisit and refresh her accumulated grievances, Emma addressed and sent to Mary Hardy a letter so extraordinary, and so eloquent of both her predicament and her personality, that it deserves to be quoted in full:

Miss Hardy

I dare you, or any one to spread evil reports of me—such as that I have been unkind to your brother, (which you actually said to my face,) or that I have 'errors' in my mind (which you have also said to me,) and I hear that you repeat to others.

Your brother has been outrageously unkind to me—which is *entirely your* fault: ever since I have been his wife you have done all you can to make division between us; also, you have set your family against me, though neither you nor they can truly say that I have ever been anything but, just, considerate, & kind towards you all, notwithstanding frequent low insults.

As you are in the habit of saying of people whom you dislike that they are 'mad' you should, & may well, fear, least the same be said of you; what you mete out to others shall be meted to you again; & I have heard you say it myself, of people. I defy you ever to say such a thing of me or for you, or any one, to say that I have ever done anything that can be called unreasonable, or wrong, or mad, or *even unkind*! And it is a wicked, spiteful & most malicious habit of yours.

Now—what right have you to assert that I have been no 'help' to my husband? That statement, false & injurious, as it is, you have constantly repeated without warrant or knowledge of the matter.

How would you like to have your life made difficult for you by anyone saying, for instance, that you are a very unsuitable person to have the instruction of young people?

You have ever been my causeless enemy—causeless, except that I stand in the way of your evil ambition to be on the same level as your brother by trampling upon me. If you did not know, & pander to his many weaknesses, & have secured him on your side by your crafty ways, you could not have done me the irreparable mischief you have. And doubtless you are elated that you have spoiled my life as you love power of any kind, but you have spoilt your brother's & your own punishment must inevitably follow—for God's promises are true for ever.

You are a witch-like creature & quite equal to any amount of evil-wishing & speaking—I can imagine you, & your mother & sister on your native heath raising a storm on a Walpurgis night.

You have done irreparable harm but now your power is at an end.

E.

If you will acknowledge your evil pride & spite & change your ways I am capable of forgiving you though I cannot forget or trust your nature but I can understand your desire to be considered cleverer than I which you may be I allow.

Doubtless you will send this on to your brother but it will not affect me if you do as he will know from me that I have written thus to you—which I consider a duty to myself.[34]

Mary Hardy presumably did share this letter with her brother as well as with her mother and sister. But she then put it into the hands of the family solicitor, primarily as evidence against Emma should an intra-family lawsuit ever come about, but perhaps also as a precaution against Emma's challenging her position as headmistress of the Bell Street junior girls' school. The letter shows Emma at her paranoid worst, but it also generates sympathy for the difficulties of her situation—outnumbered by the Hardy family, excluded from its conclaves, and powerless in the face of its solidarity—and for the energy and independence with which she nevertheless sought to make her voice heard: 'T.H. has always so much to say by voice, & pen,' she protested to Rebekah Owen a few years later, 'that letter-writing is my only resource for having all the say to myself, & not hearing his eloquence dumbly.'[35] The accusation brought against Mary and her accomplices is essentially—and plausibly—that of 'evil-wishing & speaking'. Disappointingly unspecified, on the other hand, are the reasons for Emma's calling her husband 'outrageously unkind'.

During the early years of their friendship Hardy and Mrs Henniker often exchanged books which interested them both, each making annotations for the other's attention in the single copy being passed between them. A pocket edition of Browning, first given to Hardy by Mrs Henniker in July 1894, was one such volume, and it was presumably Hardy who drew the marginal line against the conclusion of 'Confessions': 'We loved, sir—used to meet: | How sad and bad and mad it was— | But then, how it was sweet!'[36] Another, earlier that same year, was *Keynotes*, a collection of short stories written by 'George Egerton', the pseudonym of Mrs Chavelita Clairmonte, who later married R. Golding Bright, Hardy's dramatic agent in the 1920s. The stories in *Keynotes* had created something of a sensation by the directness with which they treated of the relations between the sexes, and while Hardy's marginal annotations have to be read as contributions to the half-humorous debate being carried on with Mrs Henniker, they do tend to echo the standard male attitudes of his time. Alongside a reference to 'the eternal wildness, the untamed primitive savage temperament that lurks in the mildest, best woman', Hardy writes: 'This if fairly stated, is decidedly the *ugly* side of woman's nature.' A teasing note on the word 'woman' in the same passage reads: 'Hence her inferiority to man??' And an observation on the unreality of men's imaginary conception of women provokes the response: '*ergo*: *real* woman is abhorrent to man? hence the failure of matrimony??'[37] Just a little earlier, in his contribution to a June 1894 *New Review* symposium on the desirability of providing young women with pre-marital information as to the facts of life, Hardy raised 'the general question whether marriage, as we at present understand it, is such a desirable goal for all women as it is assumed to be; or whether civilisation can escape the humiliating indictment that, while it has been able to cover itself with glory in the arts, in literatures, in religions, and in the sciences, it has never succeeded in creating that homely thing, a satisfactory scheme for the conjunction of the sexes'.[38]

　　Despite the now intractable differences between his family and his wife, the established patterns of Hardy's domestic life continued much as before. Throughout January and February 1894 he was at Max Gate, working on the *Jude* manuscript and playing his usual part in family and local affairs. His regular Sunday visits to Higher Bockhampton continued and in February, with Henry's assistance, he set up in Stinsford churchyard the tombstone he had designed for their father's grave. In April, as the result of another initiative taken by Robert Pearce Edgcumbe, he was elevated from his existing position as a local magistrate to membership of the county bench and took his seat there for the first time.[39] He stayed at Lady Jeune's for a few March days—during which Emma, alone at Max Gate, was found by one friend to be in 'her *most* affable frame of mind'—and met there and at Lady Londonderry's several of the leading politicians of the day, together with a sprinkling of journalists and soldiers.[40] He took most pleasure, however, in a visit to the theatre with his hostess's daughters, Dorothy and Madeleine Stanley, by whom, as he told Emma, he was more amused than by the play itself: ' "I do hope it will be something very *risqué*" [said] Dorothy. "So as to make our hair curl!"—the point of it being that they wd turn round & ask me *if it was risqué*—not knowing of their own judgment.'[41] That he was still writing to Emma in such cheerful terms suggests that he at least was trying to keep their domestic life on an even keel and that her animosities were being for the most part directed outward.

Life's Little Ironies, Hardy's third collection of short stories, was published by Osgood, McIlvaine in late February, to favourable reviews. Shortly afterwards he successfully negotiated for the first edition of *Jude the Obscure* a royalty of 20 per cent on all copies sold instead of the 15 per cent he was currently receiving for *Life's Little Ironies*. There must also have been discussion of plans for the first collected edition of his novels, scheduled to appear following the expiration of the Sampson Low agreements that summer. He had already, after some initial difficulties, arrived at an amicable accommodation with the house of Macmillan by which they surrendered whatever rights they might have in *The Woodlanders* and *Wessex Tales* in return for the inclusion of all of Hardy's fiction (apart from the irrecoverable *Under the Greenwood Tree*) in their Colonial Edition. An agreement to this effect was signed by Hardy on 21 May 1894, after he had pointed out that the draft prepared by the publisher omitted *Desperate Remedies*—a book, he characteristically added, which always sold well.[42]

In mid-April 1894 Hardy and Emma moved into 16 Pelham Crescent, South Kensington, bringing with them their own servants from Max Gate. *Life and Work* lists some of the many people of rank and fame Hardy encountered during the course of the season and specifically mentions the frequency with which it was somehow deemed appropriate that he should, as the notorious author of *Tess*, be introduced to the reigning beauties of the day. He did not challenge that assumption, and Lady Jeune, well aware of his prejudice in favour of good-looking women, was careful when introducing him to the portrait-painter Winifred Thomson to insist that she was 'a *very* nice girl clever pleasant your sort but *not* pretty'.[43] Hardy did indeed find Miss Thomson congenial; he praised the portrait of himself she painted the following spring and wrote to her over a number of years in that slightly arch, mildly flirtatious style he reserved for women whom he liked but did not deeply care for.[44] In late May, and no doubt at other times, he was able to see something of Mrs Henniker, and on 25 April he reminded Clement Shorter, as editor, that her *Outlines* had not yet been reviewed in the *Sketch*— a piece of frank 'log-rolling' to which Shorter responded not only with the extorted review but also with a full-page portrait of Mrs Henniker herself. Another portrait, in the *Illustrated London News*, was accompanied by Hardy's own unsigned account of Mrs Henniker's career, praising in her work qualities closely akin to that 'intuitiveness' he had first registered in her personality—'emotional imaginativeness, lightened by a quick sense of the odd, and by touches of observation lying midway between wit and humour'.[45]

That Hardy himself—in part because of Mrs Henniker—was currently in a distinctly darker and even brooding frame of mind is suggested by the appearance of the Pelham Crescent address or the date, sometimes both, against several passages in his Bible. By this stage of his life he customarily used markings in his Bible and prayerbook only to register his attendance at a specific service. These from the spring and early summer of 1894, however, are from a variety of sources in both testaments, rather as if he were searching both for passages with which he was already familiar—the first chapter of Ecclesiastes ('Vanity of vanities, saith the Preacher') is dated 'May 7 1894'—and, more randomly, for any that might speak to his current anxieties. He wrote 'June 26 1894', for example, at the head of chapter 3 of the General Epistle of James, with its tirade against ill-speaking: 'But the tongue can no man tame; it is an unruly evil, full of deadly poison.' Whether he had Emma in mind, or some upsurge of London or Dorchester gossip, or William Archer's recent accusation that he had introduced 'a note of sensuality' into English fiction—or something altogether different—it is impossible to tell.[46]

Hardy made a number of short expeditions out of London during that spring of 1894. On 30 April he went with Clodd to dine with Meredith at Box Hill. In mid-May he joined Grant Allen the novelist and Edward Whymper the Alpinist in another weekend visit to Clodd's house at Aldeburgh, telling Clodd during a confidential talk of the 'restrictions on his travelling about with a lady', presumably Mrs Henniker, and expressing his view that a woman should have the freedom to choose the father of her child and males be collectively required to contribute to the support of all children.[47] In mid-June he went down to Dorchester for a few days to make arrangements for the extensions to Max Gate—a new kitchen and scullery, with a new study for himself above, and two small attics above that—which were to be carried out during the autumn. Emma, who had again been unwell, took the opportunity to go off by herself to Hastings, to enjoy the sea air and put into practice her new programme of independence. Hardy, too, was beginning at 54 to feel some of the effects of increasing age. At dinner at Lady Jeune's one evening in May he talked until his throat was tired, a recurring problem and a major cause of that quietness of speech noted by many people who met him, and when moving out of 16 Pelham Crescent at the end of July he hurt his back while dragging a heavy portmanteau downstairs.[48]

Work on 'The Simpletons', as it was still called, had continued intermittently in London during the spring and summer, much of it a matter of bowdlerizing copy already submitted. No more than a third of the novel had been written by the time he returned to Dorchester at the beginning of August; with serialization due to begin in December, completion of the remaining two-thirds began to take on a certain urgency—and to exact a certain personal cost. 'I am going to have a tremendous holiday some time or other,' he told Gosse at the beginning of September, and added: '[A] night or two ago, when I was standing on the Quay at Weymouth just before the departure of the Channel boat, I felt inclined to walk aboard & go across under the starlight.'[49] The mid-September 1894 date on Hardy's sketch of Old Grove's Place, Shaftesbury, the house to which he imagined Phillotson as taking Sue after their marriage, provides a possible clue to the stage of the narrative he was then approaching, but the final pages, according to the date on the manuscript itself, were not written until March 1895.[50]

The delays were chiefly caused by Hardy's ostensibly reclusive existence at Max Gate being subject in fact to a whole series of personal and professional distractions. He spent more than a week in London in October, sat on the bench at the County Petty Sessions on three occasions during the course of the autumn, and kept up his regular Sunday visits to Bockhampton, where his mother, now in her early eighties, was still capable of producing for her son's benefit an anecdote she had not previously told, or of singing 'Come ashore, Jolly Tar, with your trousers on' and other popular songs and ballads that she had heard in her youth and young womanhood.[51] A constant source of disturbance was the building in progress at Max Gate itself. On 13 November Emma complained that her husband's writing obliged them to stay in the house while work went forward. Twelve days later Hardy explained to H. Macbeth-Raeburn, the artist, that because of the alterations they were 'huddled into fewer rooms than usual' and thus unable to offer him a bed when he came down to discuss the frontispieces he had been commissioned to prepare for the forthcoming Osgood, McIlvaine collected edition.[52]

At the beginning of 1895, with *Jude* still unfinished, Hardy was obliged to turn at least part of his attention to the prefaces needed for each of the new collective edition's sixteen volumes: the preface to the first volume, *Tess of the d'Urbervilles*, is dated January 1895, three months ahead of the publication date. The textual work on the successive volumes of that edition had been complicated, and to a degree duplicated, by Hardy's promise to incorporate the same corrections and revisions into the corresponding volumes of Macmillan's Colonial series, but he was now, as always, a consummate professional, and all his commitments appear to have been completed on time.[53] The prefaces, eventually written over a period of roughly a year and a half, reflected Hardy's genial contemplation of the fictional world he had created over the previous quarter-century and was now about to leave permanently behind him. The textual revisions themselves were primarily directed towards the reinforcement of that world by making the topographical references in the different works more consistent one with another and thus enhancing the coherence asserted in the title, 'Wessex Novels', that he had chosen for the Osgood, McIlvaine edition as a whole.

Hardy seems from the first to have conceived of Wessex as possessing a more than purely regional integrity, as becoming in course of time and composition a distinct, internally coherent fictional entity, an imaginative construct grounded in geographical actuality. As he recalled in February 1895 when writing the preface to the Osgood, McIlvaine edition of *Far from the Madding Crowd*: 'The series of novels I projected being mainly of the kind called local, they seemed to require a territorial definition of some sort to lend unity to their scene. Finding that the area of a single county did not afford a canvas large enough for this purpose, and that there were objections to an invented name, I disinterred the old one.'[54] Strictly speaking, Hardy was anticipated by William Barnes in his use of Wessex in a contemporary sense, but he must certainly be credited with the name's acceptance 'as a practical provincial definition' and with the transformation of a 'dream-country' into an actual, visitable place—'a utilitarian region which people can go to, take a house in, and write to the papers from'. By the mid–1890s maps of Hardy's Wessex were already beginning to appear, and one of the distinctions of the Osgood, McIlvaine volumes was their inclusion of the first such map specifically endorsed by the author—the earliest volumes displaying in their maps such *Jude*-related locations as Marygreen and Alfredston well ahead of the novel's publication, as the edition's eighth volume, in November 1895.[55]

Commercial shrewdness had of course entered into Hardy's initial perception of the possible advantages of creating a separate regional world: he was well aware of the precedents set by Scott, Balzac, R. D. Blackmore, and especially Trollope. But the invention and progressive elaboration of Wessex also answered magnificently to his ambitions as a regional historian, his desire to record as faithfully as possible the details of a vanishing way of life and thus justify the claim, articulated in the general preface to the Wessex edition of 1912–13: 'At the dates represented in the various narrations things were like that in Wessex: the inhabitants lived in certain ways, engaged in certain occupations, kept alive certain customs, just as they are shown doing in these pages.'[56]

That Hardy's novels, stories, poems, and autobiographical writings constitute a remarkable and invaluable portrait of rural life in the southern counties of nineteenth-century England there can be no doubt. To a large extent, however, it was a portrait based less on direct observation than on the resources—rich, irreplaceable, but not inevitably reliable—of the oral tradition. When, in 1894, Edward Clodd raised a question about the folk beliefs incorporated into 'The Superstitious Man's Story' from *Life's Little Ironies*, Hardy assured him that 'every superstition, custom, &c., described in my novels may be depended on as true records of the same (whatever merit in folklorists' eyes they may have as such)—& not inventions of mine'. What that in fact meant was that he had depended for those as for so many other details upon that 'old woman' his mother's memories of Melbury Osmond.[57] Jemima, again, was presumably the 'aged friend' invoked in the 1896 preface to *Wessex Tales*, who had known the original of Rhoda Brook of 'The Withered Arm' and told the author that he had weakened the story by describing Rhoda as throwing off the incubus at night instead of in broad daylight, as had actually occurred. Hardy agreed that 'the occurrence of such a vision in the daytime is more impressive than if it had happened in a midnight dream', and went on to acknowledge the deceptive role his own memory had played: 'Readers are therefore asked to correct the misrelation, which affords an instance of how our imperfect memories insensibly formalize the fresh originality of living fact—from whose shape they slowly depart, as machine-made castings depart by degrees from the sharp hand-work of the mould.'[58] For Hardy 'living fact' had an integrity to which fiction could offer, at best, a poor approximation, an authenticity that the novelist ignored at his peril. Hence those pocketbooks and notebooks, and the anxiety that impelled the correction of topographical details in works already published. But there are of course historical risks involved whenever 'living fact' translates into 'living memory', even when that memory is first-hand—rather than second- or third-hand, let alone 'traditional'—and has not acquired too many 'advantages' through frequent retellings.[59]

Despite his insistence that the backgrounds of the Wessex novels had been 'done from the real', Hardy did not specifically accept, even though he did not deny, the identification of Dorchester with Casterbridge, of Sturminster Newton with Stourcastle, Weymouth with Budmouth, and so on. In maps and texts alike Hardy used the real names of natural features— Stour, Frome, High Stoy, Vale of Blackmore, etc.—to establish the geography of his fictional Wessex and render it recognizable and even accessible, but places of human construction and habitation were given the names— Mellstock, Shaston, Melchester, etc.—that he had himself invented. He also reserved the freedom to adapt the details of topography in response to the needs of the text: as he said of the historical settings of *The Dynasts*, it was 'sometimes necessary to see round corners, down crooked streets, & to shift buildings nearer each other than in reality (as Turner did in his landscapes)'.[60] So in *The Mayor of Casterbridge* the house imagined as Lucetta's was moved some distance from its actual Dorchester location next to the Hardys' then address in Shire-hall Lane; so the mill in *The Trumpet-Major* selected features from different mills at Sutton Poyntz, Lewell, and Upwey; so the barn in *Far from the Madding Crowd* drew upon actual barns at Abbotsbury and Cerne Abbas.

Hardy visited some of the scenes of his novels in March 1895 in company with Macbeth-Raeburn, who went also to Boscastle and Oxford to sketch the frontispieces for *A Pair of Blue Eyes* and *Jude*. An Easter visit with Emma to the Jeunes' country house just north of Newbury provided an opportunity to return once more to some of the villages associated with Mary Head—and now with Jude Fawley.[61] The manuscript of *Jude the Obscure* itself was finally finished, although its title remained in doubt. When talking to Macbeth-Raeburn in March, Hardy referred to it as 'The Simpletons'. In a Memorandum of Agreement dated 4 April 1895 he granted to Osgood, McIlvaine & Co., for a period of seven years, the exclusive British publication rights to a work called 'Hearts Insurgent' or 'such other title' as he, the author, might select.[62]

In the early spring of 1895 Hardy was still working on the successive volumes of the Osgood, McIlvaine edition but finding time to contribute a concluding episode to Mrs Henniker's story 'A Page from a Vicar's History' and then negotiate with Clement Shorter its publication in the *English Illustrated Magazine*.[63] He also took in hand a dramatization of *Tess of the d'Urbervilles*. The popular success of *Tess*, and its obvious dramatic and melodramatic qualities, had provoked much talk of its possible adaptation to the stage, and Hardy was besieged by a series of well-known actresses—from Mrs Patrick Campbell and Elizabeth Robins to Bernhardt and Duse—who urged upon him by letter, in person, or through intermediaries their claims to create the part of Tess. As on other such occasions, Hardy found it difficult to reject such applications out of hand and caused himself much embarrassment by allowing a number of imperious women to believe that he had them exclusively in mind for the part.

Hardy was at first enthusiastic about the play. Discussions with Johnston Forbes-Robertson and Mrs Campbell began in April 1895, and in early May, writing to Emma about the service flat he had taken for the season, Hardy listed among its advantages its proximity not only to Victoria Station, the Army & Navy Stores, and Westminster Abbey but also to Mrs Campbell: she lived, he reported, 'in an adjoining block—& if the play goes on that may be convenient for the work'. By July Mrs Campbell was pressing him for a commitment as to her future representation of 'the dear woman Tess', and Hardy was assuring her that she *'must* be the Tess now we have got so far'.[64] But the anticipated production agreement with Forbes-Robertson ran into endless delays and complications. No resolution had been reached by the time Hardy returned to Max Gate in late July 1895, when the matter was put aside while he recovered from an attack of what he called 'English cholera'.[65]

His distress at the beginning of that visitation was doubtless exacerbated by awareness of the divorce action being brought by Arthur Tomson against his wife Rosamund. She, writing as Graham R. Tomson, had recently caused Hardy some embarrassment by reporting in an American journal that his first approach to the Duchy of Cornwall about the purchase of land for the building of Max Gate had met with a dusty reception from the official involved, and that the land had become available only as a result of the personal intervention of the Prince of Wales, the hereditary holder of the Duchy.[66] Responding to a worried letter from the Duchy official concerned, Hardy agreed that his initial reception had in fact been entirely courteous and correct, and then added: 'A woman is at the bottom of it, of course! I have reason to know that the writer of the account is a London lady, pretty, & well known in society (The signature is not I believe her real name). Why she should have written it I cannot say—except that it was not to please me; for such gossip annoys me greatly even when true.' Neither in that letter, however, nor in a brief denial published in the *Dorset County Chronicle*, did he acknowledge what he had indiscreetly confided to Rosamund Tomson and later confessed to his friend Edward Clodd—that the Prince had indeed played some role in approving the final decision. Hardy perhaps feared that this public linkage of his name with Mrs Tomson's could lead to his being mentioned in the course of the divorce action, but it was in fact undefended.[67] Mrs Tomson continued her career as Rosamund Marriott Watson until her death in 1912, and Hardy owned a copy of her posthumously published collected poems. That she continued to haunt his memory is suggested not only by the poem 'An Old Likeness (Recalling R.T.)' but also by an undated note for another possible poem: 'A letter comes in the handwriting & postmark of a lady long since dead (e.g. the one I received like Graham Tomson's). He fears to open it, (delayed in P.O. say).'[68]

In early September 1895, just before the *Jude* proofs began to flow in, Hardy and Emma spent a few days at Rushmore on the Dorset–Wiltshire border, the estate of General Augustus Lane Fox Pitt-Rivers, the archaeologist, whose wife Alice was a sister of Mary Jeune's first husband Constantine Stanley. Rushmore was remarkable not only for the archaeological 'digs' which Pitt-Rivers had carried out on the property but also for the Larmer Tree Gardens, a combination of *ferme ornée*, amusement park, menagerie, and theatre that he had built up over the years and opened, without charge, to the general public. The Hardys' visit on 4 September had been timed to coincide with the annual sports day for the area, followed, after nightfall, by dancing on the lawns in a moonlight supplemented by thousands of lamps strung amongst the trees. It was a romantic scene and moment, quickened still further for Hardy by his leading off the country dancing in partnership with his host's youngest daughter Agnes, the wife of Walter (later Sir Walter) Grove.[69]

Agnes Grove was in her early thirties at this date, beautiful, elegant, and intelligent, with ideas of her own on such matters as women's suffrage, and with literary ambitions which she had as yet scarcely ventured to pursue. Hardy found her attractive and sympathetic; she was no doubt flattered by the attentions of the 'author of *Tess*'. That first encounter was extremely brief—Mrs Grove left for the Continent with her husband the following morning—but she and Hardy were to meet and correspond with some frequency over the next few years. She in effect took over Florence Henniker's vacated place as Hardy's literary 'pupil', accepting the role with rather more complaisance than her predecessor had generally displayed.[70] The dance at Rushmore, according to *Life and Work*, was the last occasion on which Hardy, 'passionately fond of dancing . . . from earliest childhood', ever 'trod a measure. . . on the greensward'. In the poem 'Concerning Agnes', written after Lady Grove's death in 1926, his retrospective vision becomes absorbed by the memory of that night 'when the wide-faced moon looked through | The boughs at the faery lamps of the Larmer Avenue'. Because of her death, he lamented,

> I could not, though I should wish, have over again
>   That old romance,
> And sit apart in the shade as we sat then
>   After the dance
> The while I held her hand, and, to the booms
> Of contrabassos, feet still pulsed from the distant rooms.

Hardy was immediately aware of the parallels between his meeting with Agnes Grove and his meeting with Florence Henniker two years previously. Writing to the latter on 11 September 1895, shortly after his return to Max Gate, he did not mention Mrs Grove herself but described the Rushmore experience as a whole as 'the most romantic time I have had since I visited you at Dublin'.[71]

The weekend of 14–16 September 1895 the Hardys entertained two visitors at Max Gate, Clarence McIlvaine, Hardy's publisher, and the novelist George Gissing, a friend of long but still somewhat uncertain standing. Always warily appreciative of each other's work, Hardy and Gissing were distinctly uncomfortable in each other's company, and the correspondence begun in the middle 1880s had soon been allowed to lapse. But in mid-July 1895, after an interval of nine years, they met again at the Burford Bridge Hotel, south of London, where a dinner for George Meredith was being given by the Omar Khayyám Club, under the presidency of Edward Clodd. Hardy and Gissing both made brief speeches at the dinner in praise of the guest of honour—Hardy recalling Meredith's encouraging reception of the 'very strange and wild' manuscript of *The Poor Man and the Lady*—and as the gathering broke up Hardy suggested that Gissing might write to him if he felt inclined to do so. In September Gissing took up that suggestion, and Hardy responded with the invitation to Max Gate.[72]

The weekend was marred for Gissing, as he told his brother, by the obtrusive presence of Emma—'an extremely silly & discontented woman, to whom, no doubt, is attributable a strange restlessness & want of calm in Hardy himself'. It was to the influence of this 'paltry woman', as he called her in another letter, that he was also inclined to attribute Hardy's disturbing tendency to talk of 'fashionable society', of 'lords & dignitaries', and it is indeed sufficiently clear that Hardy was anxious to keep the conversation, so far as possible, on topics to which Emma might conceivably have something pertinent to contribute. When Gissing complained that Hardy, 'good, gentle, and poetically minded' though he was, read little and did not even know the names of flowers, he was judging his host in terms of the 'high culture' of a Meredith and the technical knowledge of such a natural-history enthusiast as Grant Allen, not of that deeper and more instinctive relationship to local history, culture, and countryside upon which Hardy's distinctive strengths as a writer depended. Hardy, Gissing sadly concluded, 'is a very difficult man to understand, & I suspect that his own home is *not* the best place for getting to know him'.[73]

Painful as Hardy's current differences with Emma sometimes became, they were not such as to render the entertainment of visitors problematic, and later that same month Edward Clodd and William Archer—dramatist, critic, and source of the comment on Hardy's 'sensuality'—came to Max Gate for a few days and were taken for a 'romantic walk' on the heath after dark. Hamo and Agatha Thornycroft arrived without notice one afternoon and found Hardy and Emma together at tea, in which the visitors, tired from cycling over the hills near Maiden Castle, were happy to share. The Thornycrofts' advocacy of the virtues of bicycling seems to have been instrumental in arousing the Hardys' active interest in that new and increasingly fashionable form of amusement, exercise, and locomotion. They were now of course in their middle fifties, but Emma, with the confidence of a horsewoman, took quickly to the saddle, and by the following January Hardy had also taken it up in order 'to keep her company'.[74]

He had been attending meanwhile to the final stages of the publication of the book version of *Jude the Obscure*. In August he had completed the preparation of printer's copy—a process he described to Florence Henniker as one of 'restoring' the manuscript to its 'original state'—and written a deliberately challenging preface: 'For a novel addressed by a man to men and women of full age; which attempts to deal unaffectedly with the fret and fever, derision and disaster, that may press in the wake of the strongest passion known to humanity, and to point, without a mincing of words, the tragedy of unfulfilled aims, I am not aware that there is anything in the handling to which exception can be taken.'[75] In September the proofs arrived, and his further corrections, though mostly minor, were numerous and occasionally significant. The paragraph about Gibbon was introduced into the scene in which Jude hears the voices of Christminster's past; Biblioll replaced Sepulchre as the name of the college whose Master sends Jude a dusty answer; the sexual references tended to become more explicit; and there was less stress on the cousinship of Jude and Sue and more on their comradeship. The closeness of Hardy's scrutiny of *Jude* may not have been exceptional—he was always a meticulous proof-reader—but it sorts happily with the comment, in his 12 August letter to Mrs Henniker, that he was 'more interested in this Sue story than in any I have written'.[76]

19

The Publication of *Jude*

ON 1 November 1895 *Jude the Obscure* was published by Osgood, McIlvaine as a single volume, the familiar Victorian three-volume format for novels having virtually disappeared following recent industry-wide changes in publishing and distribution practices. That same day Sir George Douglas arrived at Max Gate for a short visit and was alone with Hardy in his study when the first copy of the novel was delivered: 'The auspices, I remember, were not flattering, the weather being gloomy, whilst Mrs Hardy was suffering from an accident sustained in learning to cycle.' Douglas believed, moreover, that the author was not 'lifted up by a sense of work well done' and 'as little expected conspicuous success for his new work as he did the resounding obloquy which was to be its portion'.[1] Hardy perhaps had higher hopes for *Jude* than Douglas appreciated, but his past encounters with negative criticism had still left him ill prepared for the depth, directness, and extent of the hostility he now encountered. Even those critics who praised *Jude* as a masterpiece were liable to express dismay at its unrelieved darkness, discomfort at its blunt treatment of controversial issues, and irritation at its insistent purposefulness. Those who saw it as a disaster—not least in its startling departure from the manner and matter of its author's previous work—felt free to express themselves with open vituperation.

The *Guardian* (the Church of England newspaper) called it on 13 November 'a shameful nightmare, which one only wishes to forget as quickly and as completely as possible'. The *Pall Mall Gazette* review of 12 November, headed 'Jude the Obscene', indulged in a blank trivialization of Hardy's passionate narrative:

And so in due course an unblessed family appears; and soon early and later infants are attracting momentary attention by hanging each other with box-cord on little pegs all round the room. After this come inquests, and remorse, and a new consciousness of sin, ending up in the re-marriage of all the divorcees, making, to the best of our reckoning, a total of six marriages and two obscenities to the count of two couples and a half—a record performance, we should think. And they all lived unhappily ever after, except Jude, who spat blood and died; while Arabella curled her hair with an umbrella stay and looked archly at her old acquaintance the itinerant quack.[2]

The London *World*, under the title 'Hardy the Degenerate', retracted its earlier protest against the bowdlerization of the serial version of the novel,[3] poked clumsy fun at such scenes as the pig-killing: 'Perhaps, as the novel was primarily destined for an American audience, all this talk of chitterlings and "innerds" was meant as a delicate compliment to the inhabitants of Porkopolis, Ohio'. It then proceeded, in tones of high moral earnestness, to accuse Hardy of offering, in Sue, an unfortunate model for 'not a few neurotic would-be heroines of real life' and of modelling himself upon 'the methods of Zola and Tolstoi—Zola of *La Terre*, and Tolstoi the decadent sociologist. . . . Humanity, as envisaged by Mr. Hardy, is largely compounded of hoggishness and hysteria.'[4] Hardy's anguished response to such attacks emerges from the many letters he wrote that November. To such friends as Mrs Henniker, Lady Jeune, Douglas, Clodd, and Gosse he insisted again and again—often in almost identical words—that *Jude* was not at all intended as a purpose novel, least of all as a 'manifesto on the marriage question', that the pig-killing scene was at once a deliberately humanitarian gesture and a dramatization of Arabella's essentially animalistic nature, and that his only fear had been that the book would be perceived not as hostile to morality but quite the reverse—as too strongly endorsing the Christian exhortation to mercy and as downright 'High-Churchy' in its emphasis upon Sue's final return to orthodoxy.[5] Exaggerated as some of these protestations undoubtedly were, they scarcely matched the grotesque distortions of some of the reviewers.

Especially revealing of Hardy's bewilderment and distress, and his resentment at the unreliability of even the warmest of his literary friends, was his acknowledgement on 10 November of Gosse's review in the *St James's Gazette* two days previously. The review was in many respects intelligent and sympathetic, but Gosse, like many another reader then and since, had found the bleakness of the story excessive and more than a little gratuitous, and hinted as much in his opening sentences:

It is a very gloomy, it is even a grimy, story that Mr. Hardy has at last presented to his admirers. . . . The genius of this writer is too widely acknowledged to permit us to question his right to take us into what scenes he pleases; but, of course, we are at liberty to say whether we enjoy them or no. Plainly, we do not enjoy them. We think the fortunes, even of the poorest, are more variegated with pleasures, or at least with alleviations, than Mr. Hardy chooses to admit. Whether that be so or no, we have been accustomed to find him more sensible to beauty than he shows himself in 'Jude the Obscure'. . . . We rise from the perusal of it stunned with a sense of the hollowness of existence.[6]

Hardy's letter acknowledged the perceptivity of some comments Gosse had made on the geometrical structure of the novel, and closed 'with sincere thanks for your review'. But failing, finally, to contain his irritation at the tone and phrasing of the review's first paragraph he added a postscript that was eloquent both of his dissatisfaction with his friend's lukewarmness and of his own profound commitment to the novel and its hero:

One thing I did not answer. The 'grimy' features of the story go to show the contrast between the ideal life a man wished to lead, & the squalid real life he was fated to lead. The throwing of the pizzle, at the supreme moment of his young dream, is to sharply initiate this contrast. But I must have lamentably failed, as I feel I have, if this requires explanation & is not self evident. The idea was meant to run all through the novel. It is, in fact to be discovered in *every* body's life—though it lies less on the surface perhaps than it does in my poor puppet's.[7]

When Gosse accepted, shortly afterwards, an invitation to write a further review of the novel for *Cosmopolis*, a new international magazine, Hardy sought to guide him towards a better informed and more consistently sympathetic reading. At the urging of his worried publishers, he seems also to have inspired the article 'On Some Critics of *Jude the Obscure*' contributed by Sir George Douglas to the January 1896 number of the *Bookman*.[8]

The later reviews—including those by William Dean Howells, H. G. Wells, and Havelock Ellis—were distinctly more favourable to the novel than the early ones had been.[9] But Hardy had still to endure the opprobrium of Jeannette Gilder in the New York *World*,[10] of Mrs Oliphant ('The Anti-Marriage League') in *Blackwood's*, of A. J. Butler ('Mr. Hardy as a Decadent') in the *National Review*, and of a good many others.[11] It is possible to argue that there were, on balance, as many positive reviews as negative ones, and that Hardy ought, in any case, to have been thicker-skinned and certainly less surprised: 'My word, we should cultivate a little stoicism,' Andrew Lang had observed to Clodd on learning of Hardy's response to his criticism of *Tess*.[12] But the thinness of Hardy's skin was inseparable from those personal qualities, and those aspects of his personal history, that made him a great novelist, and while the spectacle of Hardy angrily at bay is by no means attractive, it ought not to be particularly surprising.

Hardy in this unhappy episode again showed himself capable, like Jude Fawley, of being both 'Simpleton' and 'Recalcitrant'. His apparent astonishment at the responses to his work made first by editors and then by reviewers is of a piece with his apparent failure to realize the extent to which the directness of his treatment of the relationships between men and women, reinforced by his disinclination to accept marriage as the necessary goal and conclusion of fictional action, was bound to meet with criticism and resistance: Mrs Oliphant, after all, was perfectly justified in discussing *Jude* within an 'anti-marriage' context. When Hardy was challenged on such issues ahead of serial publication, he had always been prepared to execute a tactical withdrawal. Because the publishing system of the day demanded publication of a novel in book form ahead of the appearance of its final serial instalment, Hardy had really no choice other than to write from the start what he intended ultimately to publish. The serial, however important financially, was textually ephemeral and indeed disposable, available therefore, if needs must, to infinite adaptation and even mutilation. The full, the original, the always intended text could be restored ahead of book publication, and occasional revisions perhaps introduced on the basis of the reception of the serial and the rereading involved in the act of restoration itself—the reconsideration of omissions or alterations made under pressure sometimes revealing them to have been, after all, improvements. Once, however, a restored text had appeared in volume form, Hardy was much less willing to give ground, even on points of a purely technical nature. When a reader objected that Angel Clare would in real life have been sentenced and jailed as an accessory to the murder of Alec, Hardy did not simply dismiss the objection as a foolish irrelevancy. Instead, he disputed his correspondent's interpretation of the law and insisted that even if Angel had been sent to prison the shortness of his sentence would have allowed him to be present as a free man on the day of Tess's execution—and thus on the novel's final pages.[13]

Unfairly attacked, Hardy did not consider long or deeply the justice or appropriateness of his own first self-defensive lunges. Nor, in his unwillingness or inability to separate attacks on the work from attacks on the author, did he readily forget or forgive those who had wounded him. Hardy's personal application of public references emerges with unusual vividness from the burning of *Jude* announced in a letter to the *Yorkshire Post* by William Walsham How, Bishop of Wakefield—a churchman and hymn-writer of some distinction whom Hardy nevertheless dismissed as a 'miserable second-class prelate'.[14] In some respects this was a comic episode, and *Life and Work* does observe that burning a good thick book is by no means easy and that since the Bishop chose the height of summer for his gesture he presumably had to stoke up a fire especially for the purpose.[15] But Hardy was deeply disturbed by so symbolic an act on the part of a representative of 'that terrible, dogmatic ecclesiasticism—Christianity so called (but really Paulinism *plus* idolatry)' which he saw as persistently hostile to morality, to progress, and even—since it had so little in common with 'the real teaching of Christ'—to religion itself. He was also angered to discover, after How's death, that he had instigated the withdrawal of the novel from W. H. Smith's huge circulating library: 'Of this precious conspiracy Hardy knew nothing, or it might have moved a mind which the burning could not stir to say a word on literary garrotting.'[16]

The protest against literary garrotting, a term neatly combining censorship with economic strangulation, rests solidly enough on objections of both a principled and a practical nature, but it is followed in *Life and Work* by a comment of quite another kind: 'The only sad feature in the matter to Hardy was that if the bishop could have known him as he was, he would have found a man whose personal conduct, views of morality, and of the vital facts of religion, hardly differed from his own.'[17] What is remarkable about this passage is not so much that Hardy should have imagined that he and the Bishop—meeting, say, in the Athenaeum Club—might have profited from knowing each other, but that he should have felt the necessity, in such a context and on such an issue, not merely of defending his work but of protesting his personal virtue and sense of morality. It is of course likely that, by the time Hardy wrote *Life and Work*, he had learned rather more about Bishop How and his by no means contemptible achievements.

If Hardy was capable of being hurt by attacks from people he had never met, it is not surprising that attacks from people he knew should have stunned him with a sense of betrayal. His distress at the possibility that fellow members of the Savile Club had written hostile reviews of *Tess* reflected his sense, ingrained from childhood, that friendship was inseparable from loyalty. He may also have rather bitterly realized that his years of investment in metropolitan clubbability and *bonhomie* were not, after all, standing him in good professional stead. Of Mrs Oliphant, who not only criticized *Jude* in *Blackwood's* but wrote to commend Bishop How for consigning it to the flames, *Life and Work* rather plaintively complains that Hardy had gone out of his way to visit her in Windsor during an illness.[18] When he learned, years after the event, that Henry James and Robert Louis Stevenson had exchanged views on what they considered the abominable style and factitious sexuality of *Tess of the d'Urbervilles*, Hardy called them the Polonius and Osric of novelists and exclaimed: 'How indecent of those two virtuous females to expose their mental nakedness in such a manner.' Nor was his old friend Edmund Gosse ever quite forgiven for telling Hardy to his face that *Jude* was the most indecent novel ever written.[19]

One might say, with Andrew Lang, that Hardy should have been capable of keeping his personal life distinct from his literary life. Yet many writers more self-confident than Hardy would have found difficulty in overlooking so hurtful a remark from so close a friend, and for Hardy the conventional distinction between the professional and the personal, the world of the imagination and the world of everyday, seems scarcely to have existed. Far more than financial success or social reputation was ultimately at stake in the reception of criticism by a man whose working and personal lives were so indistinguishably intertwined, virtually one and the same— who drew so persistently upon known and experienced actualities and lived most intensely in, and almost exclusively for, those hours spent in his study every day he was at home at Max Gate. At the most immediate level Hardy regarded hostile reviews as direct and deliberate reflections upon his professionalism, as asserting that he was *not*, as a matter of practical competence, a good hand at a serial, a novel, a short story, a poem, and as thereby damaging his reputation and endangering his sales. Such criticism also tended, by extension, to cast a shadow over the position he had achieved as a result of his literary success, to expose him to personal ridicule, and to bring more sharply into view those aspects of his life, often admirable in themselves, that the class conventions of the day had taught him to regard as sources of embarrassment—the humble background, the lack of a university education, the gulf between his Higher Bockhampton beginnings and those literary and social circles he now presumed to inhabit.

To remark upon the rawness of his sensitivity to negative or querulous commentary is, in effect, to recognize that indivisibility, to register the tense, suspicious, hard-won, and hard-clenched integrity with which Hardy strove to realize himself as an artist within the context not of the ideal life he would have wished to lead but of 'the squalid real life'[20] imposed upon him by the quirks of his own personal fate and the exigencies of that system of commercial publishing through which alone he could win his way to a fuller self-expression. Hardy had cherished from the first an elevated conception of the artist's role. He had a great admiration for Shelley, a type of the artist as hero, and could praise Henry James, whom he disliked personally, for being a dedicated artist, 'a real man of letters'.[21] He was ruthless in the demands he made, as an artist, upon himself and upon an imperfectly comprehending Emma. And when in defending his own work he twisted and turned, argued extravagantly or evasively, it was because he felt, with something close to panic, a threat not just to his fortunes as a tradesman of letters but to the integrity of his artist self.

By the mid–1890s Hardy's income from royalties looked sufficiently large and sufficiently stable to enable him, in those non-inflationary times, to think of abandoning prose fiction in favour of that return to poetry he had contemplated for so long. He seems therefore to have determined from the first that in *Jude*, his final novel, he would say his say without hesitation or compromise, denounce, once and for all, those denials of educational and sexual justice, of simple humanity, that he saw as widely present and every-where implicit in the British class system, and give expression at last to feel-ings which had been simmering in his memory and his imagination since before *The Poor Man and the Lady*. The success of the already controversial *Tess of the d'Urbervilles* had provided a springboard from which to launch the final comprehensive challenge of *Jude*, and *Life and Work* contains several invocations of authorial bravado under fire, among them the slogan, attributed to Benjamin Jowett, 'Never retract. Never explain. Get it done and let them howl.'[22] In practice, however, he proved to have been ill prepared for the psychological stresses consequent upon so extensive and painful a public exposure, or for the impact of such stresses upon matri-monial crises, disappointments in relationships outside of marriage, depres-sion over advancing age and the likelihood of declining health, and disillusionment with what passed for literary comradeship.

The darkness of the final weeks of 1895 was not entirely unrelieved. Hardy especially valued the letter in which Swinburne, acknowledging the gift of a copy of *Jude*, praised the novel for its beauty, terror, and truth, and there were other congratulatory messages from Mrs Craigie, Ellen Terry (who nonetheless found the novel's language unnecessarily coarse at times), and 'George Egerton', the author of *Keynotes*, who praised the characteriza-tion of Sue as a psychologically penetrating treatment of 'a temperament less rare than the ordinary male observer supposes'.[23] In London together for a short visit at the beginning of December, Hardy and Emma saw Forbes-Robertson and Mrs Patrick Campbell in *Romeo and Juliet* and dined with them afterwards. He also saw Mrs Henniker and other friends and by the time of his return to Dorchester was able to assure Sir George Douglas that *Jude* was 'going very well' and that London society was 'not at all represented by the shocked critics'.[24]

Early in 1896 Mrs Campbell stayed in Dorchester, at the King's Arms, for several days and spent a good deal of time at Max Gate: on 12 January she reported to a friend that she had been dancing improvised steps to old tunes played by Hardy on his fiddle.[25] The possibility of a London production of the *Tess* play was again being actively canvassed. Hardy called on Mrs Campbell to discuss the matter when he was in London in early February; there were more negotiations with Forbes-Robertson and his partner Frederick Harrison; and in mid-March Hardy sought the advice of Henry Arthur Jones as to the kind of terms that were being discussed.[26] He did arrange, through Harper & Brothers, for a New York production with Minnie Maddern Fiske in the title role and, as he later learned, a text extensively revised by one Lorimer Stoddard. That version had its first performance on 2 March 1897, and was taken after its New York run on a North American tour, but the anticipated London production failed to materialize. *Life and Work* attributes the breakdown in those negotiations to the furore over *Jude*, but the letter Hardy wrote in August 1896 to a distressed Mrs Patrick Campbell alluded vaguely to other complicating factors, and there could well have been problems with the dramatization itself.[27] He was nevertheless obliged to go through the formality of a London copyright 'performance' to coincide with the American first night and, in 1900, to make a public disavowal of any participation in a 'pirated' version that played for a while in London until an injunction was successfully brought against it on behalf of Mrs Fiske.[28]

In February 1896 Emma suffered for the first time a severe attack of a kind that was to dog her for the rest of her life. She and Hardy called it eczema but it was perhaps, as Lady Jeune suggested, shingles. While Emma was resting at home and, later, recuperating on the Sussex coast—her ferocious letter to Mary Hardy was dated simply from Worthing—Hardy himself went twice to London, where he accompanied Lady Jeune and her daughter Madeleine to a masked ball at Mrs Crackanthorpe's ('the most amusing experience I have lately had'), sat to Winifred Thomson while she completed the portrait begun the previous year, and called on Florence Henniker and her husband—whom he described when writing to Emma as 'really a very good fellow'.[29] Although he was still taking a hand in Mrs Henniker's literary career from time to time, Hardy was much more actively engaged in encouraging and advising Agnes Grove, whose ambitions were polemical rather than purely literary in nature. He suggested possible topics of current interest, read and revised her drafts, and gave assistance, often of a very direct kind, in placing the finished work in magazines. He was deeply involved, for example, in the composition and publication of the essay 'Our Children. What Children Should Be Told', published in the July 1896 issue of the *Free Review*, even the proofs passing through his hands on their way to the author herself.[30]

At the beginning of April, Emma's health having somewhat improved, they took up London residence in the usual way and in the same house at 16 Pelham Crescent as they had occupied in 1894. It was now Hardy's turn for illness and depression. A letter to Lady Jeune mentioned a chill, rheumatism (his father's particular scourge), and other unspecified discomforts, and after being house-bound for two or three weeks he took the advice of a doctor Lady Jeune had recommended and went off with Emma to try for himself the virtues of Brighton air.[31] The Sussex climate not proving especially efficacious, they returned after a week or so to Pelham Crescent. Agnes Grove was among those who took tea there shortly afterwards, and Hardy encountered her on other occasions during the course of the season. They were both guests at a party given by Herbert and Margot Asquith and at the wedding of Hardy's young favourite Dorothy Stanley to Henry Allhusen, and during one of the band concerts at the Imperial Institute that Hardy loved to attend he was in a sufficiently exuberant and sentimental mood to lead Mrs Grove through a few turns of the 'Blue Danube' waltz.[32]

By the time he and Emma returned to Max Gate on 23 July 1896 Hardy had completely thrown off all traces of illness, and in early August he completed his work for the Osgood, McIlvaine 'Wessex Novels' edition by writing the preface to *Under the Greenwood Tree*. This out-of-sequence placement of *Under the Greenwood Tree* was a consequence of Hardy's having sold the copyright a quarter of a century earlier, but it provided a happy opportunity for the edition to be rounded out with an affirmation of loyalty to the customs and values of his Bockhampton childhood as symbolized by the old handwritten and hand-bound music books of his father's and grandfather's that had now passed into his own keeping: 'Some of these compositions which now lie before me, with their repetitions of lines, half-lines, and half-words, their fugues and their intermediate symphonies, are good singing still, though they would hardly be admitted into such hymn-books as are popular in the churches of fashionable society at the present time.'[33] The continuing importance of music as an element in the lives of the Hardys emerges from a letter to Kate at the end of June in which Hardy offered to send or bring from London any music she might want. Other family continuities were less secure. When he went to see his mother at Bockhampton immediately upon his return from London he found her perceptibly shrivelled ('her face looked smaller') and realized that this most precious link with the past must in due course be broken.[34]

In mid-August 1896 Hardy and Emma set off together on an eight-week holiday, spent partly in England and partly in Belgium. They went first to Malvern, Worcester, Warwick, and Kenilworth, stayed a week at Stratford-upon-Avon, and then travelled, somewhat circuitously, through Coventry and Reading—the Aldbrickham of *Jude* and a town, as *Life and Work* observes, where Mary Head had lived for a time—on their way to Dover and the Continent.[35] At Dover, however, Emma suffered an accident while riding the bicycle (painted green and nicknamed 'The Grasshopper') that she had chosen to take with her, and they were forced to remain on the English side of the Channel for almost two weeks while she recovered. During that period Hardy—with characteristic punctiliousness—reread *King Lear* and wrote the date, together with his own and Emma's initials, against 'Dover Beach' in the copy of Matthew Arnold's *Poetical Works* he had brought with him. Given the context of the extended holiday, it is tempting to interpret that marking of 'Dover Beach' as reflecting a perhaps shared attempt to halt and reverse the erosion of the marriage. That it might, on the other hand, be no more than a travel note, as in Hardy's marking of his Baedekers, is suggested by its juxtaposition to the title of the poem rather than to the famous exhortation, 'Ah, love, let us be true | To one another!'[36]

The Grasshopper accompanied the Hardys to Belgium in mid-September, underwent many adventures, became a burdensome nuisance, and arrived back safely with them at Max Gate in mid-October. The Belgian portion of their itinerary included Ostend, Bruges ('a bygone, melancholy interesting town'), Spa, and Dinant, where Hardy became much concerned for the fortunes and fate of the first really compulsive gambler he had ever encountered. At Brussels they stayed 'for association's sake' at the Hôtel de la Poste, their lodging during their previous visit. Unfortunately, the hotel 'had altered for the worse' since the 'bright days' of twenty years earlier, and the main impact of the revisitation of old scenes was a sombre realization of time's passage and life's decay: 'It is 20 years since I was last in this part of Europe', wrote Hardy to Mrs Henniker from Liège, '& the reflection is rather saddening. I ask myself, why am I here again, & not underground!' He had nonetheless taken pleasure in visiting the galleries in Bruges and Brussels and in the renewed opportunity to walk (as he did, alone, on 2 October) over the field of Waterloo. It will never be known what, if anything, Emma said about the trip in her 'secret' diary, and if she kept one of her customary travel diaries, that too has disappeared. But the simple fact of the Hardys having contemplated, undertaken, and survived a complicated eight-week holiday would seem in itself to argue the maintenance of reasonable levels of mutual civility and accommodation, perhaps even of active goodwill. On the whole, Hardy told Mrs Henniker, in a letter written from Max Gate on 12 October, it had been 'an agreeable

& instructive time—the English half of it perhaps more so than the foreign one'.[37]

Florence Henniker's inclusion of 'The Spectre of the Real' in her short-story collection *In Scarlet and Grey*, published in the autumn of 1896, provided the occasion for a brief renewal of the kind of attack recently directed against *Jude the Obscure*, Mrs Henniker being solemnly advised by the *Spectator* that 'Mr. Thomas Hardy, in his later phases, is hardly a judicious literary counsellor'.[38] Hardy assured Agnes Grove in mid-November that he was himself 'basking in fields of innocence at present', with nothing forthcoming other than 'A Committee-Man of "The Terror"' in the Christmas Number of the *Illustrated London News*. He had, however, sold the *Saturday Review* another story, 'The Duke's Reappearance', based on a Swetman family tradition from the late seventeenth century, and was about to undertake a revision of *The Pursuit of the Well-Beloved*, as serialized four years previously, in order to make it publishable in volume form as *The Well-Beloved*: 'I fear I shall not be in London much, if at all, before Christmas,' he told Mrs Grove three weeks later, 'having rashly promised my publisher to have some copy ready by that date.'[39]

The Owen sisters reappeared in Dorchester in November 1896 and called as usual at Max Gate. Emma regretted, in a subsequent letter, that they had found the household in some disorder as a result of her long absence in the early autumn. She added, good-humouredly enough, that she was still experiencing domestic difficulties, Hardy having moved his study once again, going 'bit by bit, & book by book, leaving a room unfit for use till the workmen have been!' And there were, as always, problems with the servants: 'Our new maid has the footfall of an earthquake! and daily crashes the china—*placidly*! but she is sweet-tempered and sweet to look at. The "boy" who says he has been a page, gapes at the visitors, & hardly gets them in, or out, of the house.' Similarly staccato comments in this same letter are directed towards her reading. She has just finished Richard Le Gallienne's novel *The Quest of the Golden Girl*: 'exquisitely poetical at the beginning—crisply amusing in the middle, though somewhat licentious—& very pathetic at the end—which is quite unexpected'. *John Gabriel Borkman*, just published for the first time in an English translation, has also been read: 'Ibsen has excelled himself in it—pathetic, powerful & true to the characters in their positions.'[40]

Emma's habitual vehemence could be engaging and even amusing, and it made her a lively if, at times, an alarmingly discontinuous letter-writer. It also made her a fervent and forceful if not especially coherent advocate of the social and religious movements to which she was becoming increasingly—and often publicly—committed. One of the many sources of her detestation of *Jude* had been its cheerless presentation of the human condition, and by the mid–1890s she was moving away from Hardy intellectually no less decisively than he was moving away from her emotionally. His increasingly outspoken criticism of established institutions and values ran directly counter to her own deepening religiosity, centred in an old-fashioned Evangelicalism and characterized by hostility to Roman Catholicism and enthusiasm for a limited group of humanitarian causes. Writing to Rebekah Owen in February 1897, she lamented that her correspondent was 'a Jude-*ite*' and went on to voice her abhorrence of the 'blank materialism' of authors and their 'pride of intellect' and to declare her own devotion, deepening with increasing age, to 'ameliorations & schemes for banishing the thickening clouds of evil advancing'.[41]

Emma's nephew Gordon Gifford, who was attending school in Dorchester at this period and spending much of his time at Max Gate, always insisted that while husband and wife were certainly 'at odds' over *Jude*, the marriage itself could not be called unhappy. But the 'strange restlessness & want of calm' Gissing had observed in Hardy in 1895 was clearly related to a fundamental condition of unrest within the household as a whole. Ford Madox Ford's story of Emma's imploring Richard Garnett to stop the publication of *Jude* was almost certainly apocryphal, but it sounded sufficiently authentic—or perhaps just sufficiently mischievous—to gain wide circulation.[42] Alfred Sutro, the dramatist, recalled that when he praised *Jude* during a visit to Max Gate shortly after its publication, Emma sharply responded that it was the first novel Hardy had published 'without first letting her read the manuscript; had she read it, she added firmly, it would *not* have been published, or at least, not without considerable emendation. The book had made a difference to them, she added, in the County. . . . Hardy said nothing, and did not lift his eyes from the plate.'[43] As time went on Hardy was to resort increasingly to such silences as the best available means of covering his own embarrassment and avoiding scenes of an even more distressing character. He had become accustomed over the years to living with Emma's inconsequentialities, but he could muster only silent resignation in response to her public scoldings and open unheralded displays of antagonism and independence.

Henry Joseph Moule and his daughter, calling at Max Gate shortly before Christmas 1896, found Emma in an affectionate frame of mind and Hardy himself similarly in good spirits.[44] Moule was of course an old friend, and the cheerful Max Gate atmosphere may not have survived his departure, but Hardy, while extraordinarily consistent at the deepest levels of personality and of purpose, was at a more superficial level liable to quite rapid shifts in thinking, feeling, and mood. His darkest depressions could not only coexist with outward geniality but alternate with periods of actual cheerfulness, and he seems at times to have been perfectly capable, if not of deliberately generating depression, at least of surrendering to it willingly enough. Those darker moods, after all, were often fortunately productive— from the 'melancholy pleasure' found in designing a tombstone for a favourite cat whose loss had plunged him into despair[45] to the creative pinnacle attained following Emma's death in the 'Poems of 1912–13'.

There was, however, nothing in the least factitious about the bleakness that pervaded the finest verse of 1895–6. If *Jude the Obscure* is the story of a man who has touched bottom, then Hardy himself seems to have plunged dangerously close to despair in such poems as 'Wessex Heights' and the three parts of 'In Tenebris'. Florence Hardy once said that it wrung her heart to reread 'Wessex Heights' because she knew it was written in the aftermath of the reception of *Jude*, when Hardy was 'so cruelly treated'. It was no less significantly written in the aftermath of his deeply painful rejection by Mrs Henniker:

> As for one rare fair woman, I am now but a thought of hers,
> I enter her mind and another thought succeeds me that she prefers;
> Yet my love for her in its fulness she herself even did not know;
> Well, time cures hearts of tenderness, and now I can let her go.[46]

Both 'Wessex Heights' and 'In Tenebris', however, speak primarily to the more generalized despair of 'One who, past doubtings all, | Waits in unhope'—to an almost suicidal sense of isolation not only from human affection and trust ('friends can not turn cold . . . For him with none') but from the entirety of a grotesquely brash and optimistic age, a world in which 'nobody thinks as I'. If there is self-pity here it is, as always, balanced and corrected by a relentless honesty. The acknowledgement in 'Wessex Heights' of a certain falseness to 'my simple self that was'[47] reflects Hardy's acceptance of a degree of personal responsibility for what was happening to his life, a readiness both for a life of greater retirement and more even tenor, perhaps even for the kind of reconciliatory gesture implicit in the long holiday with Emma. Seized with such quietist ambitions, Hardy could think of the return to poetry as offering not only greater possibilities of artistic fulfilment but also, more mundanely, a technique for polemical indirection, a means of obtaining a hearing for ideas which, directly expressed, might well be howled down:

Perhaps [he told himself in October 1896] I can express more fully in verse ideas and emotions which run counter to the inert crystallized opinion—hard as a rock— which the vast body of men have vested interests in supporting. To cry out in a passionate poem that (for instance) the Supreme Mover or Movers, the Prime Force or Forces, must be either limited in power, unknowing, or cruel—which is obvious enough, and has been for centuries—will cause them merely a shake of the head; but to put it in argumentative prose will make them sneer, or foam, and set all the literary contortionists jumping upon me, a harmless agnostic, as if I were a clamorous atheist, which in their crass illiteracy they seem to think is the same thing. . . . If Galileo had said in verse that the world moved, the Inquisition might have let him alone.[48]

Hardy himself was not to be left altogether in peace by the reviewers of *The Well-Beloved*, the extensively revised book version of *The Pursuit of the Well-Beloved*. When Osgood, McIlvaine first published it on 16 March 1897, in a single-volume format matching that of *Jude* and the remainder of their collected edition, the initial response was extremely favourable, if occasionally a little puzzled. On 24 March, however, the London *World* came out with a review, 'Thomas Hardy, Humorist', that was very much along the lines of its 'Hardy the Degenerate' attack of fifteen months previously. Expressing relief that Hardy had, in the new novel, 'resolutely abandoned all references to the pigstye', the anonymous reviewer condemned with heavy sarcasm the improbabilities and improprieties of the plot and declared: 'Of all forms of sex-mania in fiction we have no hesitation in pronouncing the most unpleasant to be the Wessex-mania of Mr. Thomas Hardy.' Scorning, with obvious reference to the controversy over *Jude*, the 'usual talk' of the author's 'whole-hearted devotion to the truth', the piece concluded with just the kind of *ad hominem* attack which had so distressed Hardy on that earlier occasion:

Mr. Hardy has once more afforded a dismayed and disgusted public the depressing spectacle of genius on the down grade. Matthew Arnold once rudely referred to Burns as 'a beast with splendid gleams,' a description which was irresistibly recalled to the present writer by the perusal of *Jude the Obscure*. For in that book there were undoubtedly some splendid gleams. There are none in *The Well-Beloved*.'[49]

These are—for better or worse—no longer the sort of terms in which literary disagreements are customarily aired, and it is necessary to catch the flavour of such reviews in order to understand the nature of Hardy's response. Refusing to allow himself to be cheered and reassured by the many positive reviews, or by the excellent sales, Hardy expressed repeatedly to friends and acquaintances his dismay at the open malice of the *World* reviewer and his astonishment that so innocent a story could be so perversely read. The 'horrid stab', he told Mrs Henniker, was the more astonishing in that one of his reasons for republishing the novel in book form was that 'it cd not by any possibility offend Mrs or Mr Grundy, or their Young Persons, even though it cd be called unreal & impossible for a man to have such an artistic craze for the Ideal in woman as the hero has'.[50] Hardy wisely declined the invitation of the editor of the *Academy* to reply to the *World* in kind, observing that abuse of so personal a nature best answered itself, but that did not deter him from writing privately to the editor of *The Times* to express the hope that their reviewer would not be influenced by what the *World* had said. Nor did he hesitate to comment: 'What foul cess-pits some men's minds must be, and what a Night-cart would be required to empty them!'[51]

Although the peculiar violence of the review makes comprehensible the violence of Hardy's own language, it remains once again remarkable that he should not have been more fully prepared—even after Ibsen, even after *Jude*—for adverse reactions to a story that so narrowly skirted so many sexual taboos and seemed, as a sympathetic reviewer put it, so comic 'in the abstract'.[52] What exacerbated Hardy's anger and distress was the effort he had made to render the book version of the novel less outspoken and less overtly hostile to marriage than the 1892 serial had been—hence less offensive to Emma and, as a kind of bonus, less exposed to attacks by reviewers. Such neutral pages as those dealing with fashionable London life were left essentially as they stood in *Pursuit*, with some pointing up of the social satire here and there: of the political discussions at Lady Channel-cliffe's, for example, it was now said that 'No principles of wise government had place in any mind, a blunt and jolly personalism as to the Ins and Outs animating all'.[53] Rewritten or replaced, on the other hand, were several sections treating directly of the relationships between Pierston (as his name was now spelled) and the various temporary incarnations of the well-beloved, to the point that the novel in its revised form scarcely dealt with marriage at all, either thematically or as an element in the action, and became much more consistently a fable of the artistic temperament—defensively but not unreasonably described by Hardy himself as 'a fanciful, tragi-comic half allegorical tale of a poor Visionary pursuing a Vision'.[54] Particularly striking was the deletion of the sardonic 'Ho—ho—ho!' that had concluded the serial and its replacement by a quietly ironic portrayal of Pierston as cured of his Shelleyan restlessness at the cost of the evaporation of all his ambitions and capacities as an artist. Looking even older than his years, he enters into a marriage of amicable elderly non-sexual convenience, fosters a scheme for 'the closing of the old natural fountains' on the 'Isle', pulls down, on account of their dampness, some 'old moss-grown, mullioned Elizabethan cottages', and builds 'new ones with hollow walls, and full of ventilators'.[55]

These are, on the face of it, images of emasculation and surrender, pointing—if indeed they have any autobiographical significance—towards a resigned acceptance of age and its familiar accompaniments, declining sexuality and diminished creativity. And Hardy did exclaim to Gosse, just after the novel's publication: 'I, too, am getting old like Pierston!'[56] But the ending of the book version of the novel is the product of a maturer vision than the ending of the serial. Like Ethelberta and Clym before him, Pierston becomes the half-sympathetically, half-ironically presented exemplar of the route not to be taken. Hardy indeed accepted what was implicit in Pierston's story, the interdependence of romantic and creative aspiration, but saw that acceptance in potentially positive terms, as an affirmation of the continued indivisibility of the two, on into the future. To have made poor choices in life—in marriage, for instance—need not mean the death of the spirit, and if the revision of *The Well-Beloved* constituted for Hardy a Prospero-like burning of his books, it was in the rooted anticipation of an early Phoenix-like re-emergence of the poet from the ashes of the novelist. 'Poetry certainly has not had its day,' he had assured Sir George Douglas several years earlier. 'You must remember that the Muses have occasionally to "draw back for a spring"—or, as they themselves would probably express it, *reculer pour mieux sauter*. & they may have been doing so lately.'[57]

20

Keeping Separate

Hᴀʀᴅʏ had apparently determined the contents of *Wessex Poems* in February 1897, nearly two years ahead of its first appearance in December 1898, and he had certainly made by then the remarkable decision to illustrate the volume with his own sketches. In making up such a volume of verse he was able to draw upon richer resources than his contemporaries are likely to have suspected, his abandonment of poetry during the fiction-writing decades having been far from absolute. Poems had been completed but left unpublished, *The Dynasts* had been brooded upon, planned and replanned, and partly drafted,[1] and notebooks had become filled with material potentially usable in possible poems. Apart from items entered into Hardy's 'Studies, Specimens' notebook from the 1860s or retrospectively gathered into his later 'Poetical Matter' notebook, little of that material survived the systematic destruction of Hardy's pocketbooks that was carried out partly by Hardy himself before his death and partly by Sydney Cockerell after it.[2] But while the available evidence for Hardy's continuing poetic activity is thus disappointingly sparse, what the pocketbooks typically contained can readily be inferred from the few surviving fragments: ideas for possible topics or titles; descriptions of weather and other natural phenomena; rough drawings of places, people, and paintings seen; snatches of overheard conversations; vignettes of human predicaments and personalities; notes on possible images; outlines for entire poems and even fragmentary drafts. There can be no doubt of the passion and determination with which Hardy kept his poetic ambitions alive. Relatively few poems, even so, were brought to their final form in the period between *Far from the Madding Crowd* and *Tess of the d'Urbervilles*, and most of the poems in *Wessex Poems* itself were either revised from drafts dating back to the 1860s or conceived and composed during the early to mid-1890s.

In the spring of 1897 the Hardys went up to London as usual, leaving Max Gate in the charge of one of the servants and Hardy's correspondence in the hands of Kate. Both the sisters had recently resigned from their teaching positions at the Bell Street girls' school,[3] Mary on grounds of ill health, Kate because it suited the family for her to do so, because her brother's financial support made it possible, and because she was glad to leave a profession for which she had never felt well suited. Hardy had a few years previously purchased for his sisters a house in Dorchester, close to the school, in which they could live during the working week. Jemima, however, was now in her eighties and needing attention on a daily basis, and once Mary and Kate had retired they were able to spend much more of their time at the Bockhampton cottage, where Henry still remained. Because of the excitement roused in that spring and summer of 1897 by the forthcoming Diamond Jubilee celebrations, Hardy and Emma failed to find anything suitable to rent, and after ten uncomfortable London days they took the somewhat extreme step of retreating to lodgings in Basingstoke, about an hour's train ride from Waterloo. They nevertheless managed, during a series of one-day or overnight visits, to see London friends, pictures, and plays (including two by Ibsen), and attend once again the concerts at the Imperial Institute. In mid-June, about a week ahead of the official Jubilee ceremonies, they returned briefly to Max Gate before setting off for Switzerland and another continental holiday.[4]

Writing from Berne, their first destination, on 20 June 1897, Hardy reported only on the depressing density of the cloud cover: 'up to the present the statement that there are mountains in Switzerland seems a groundless tradition.' Interlaken, reached two days later, provided finer weather and Alpine sightings, and over the next few days they visited Grindelwald, took a steamer trip on Lake Thun, and travelled on to the (now-vanished) Hôtel Gibbon in Lausanne.[5] Pleased to find himself there on the 110th anniversary of Gibbon's completing *The Decline and Fall of the Roman Empire*, Hardy sat out in the hotel garden until midnight 'and imagined the historian closing his last page on the spot, as described in his *Autobiography*'. Hardy's poem on the occasion, 'Lausanne. In Gibbon's Old Garden: 11–12 p.m.', not only embodied something of his personal sense of intellectual embattlement but did so in language suggested by a recent reading of Milton's *The Doctrine and Discipline of Divorce*:

> 'Still rule those minds on earth
> At whom sage Milton's wormwood words were hurled:
> *"Truth like a bastard comes into the world*
> *Never without ill-fame to him who gives her birth"*?'[6]

By the end of the month the weather had turned uncomfortably hot. At Zermatt on the 29th Emma had a frightening ride on a mule to the Riffel-Alp Hotel and its view of the Matterhorn while Hardy laboured up on foot. Learning on his arrival that an Englishman—later identified as James Robert Cooper, father of one of the two authors known collectively as 'Michael Field'—had mysteriously disappeared while following that same route a few days earlier, Hardy retraced his own steps but could find nothing suspicious—and reported as much in a letter to *The Times*. This odd piece of officiousness on so hot a day made Hardy physically exhausted and when they moved on to Geneva he was obliged to rest in the hotel while Emma went exploring on her own and succeeded in locating the tomb of Sir Humphry Davy, the natural philosopher, whom she was able to claim as a distant relative. When they reached Paris a few days later, Emma again set off alone to look for her nephew Gordon Gifford, who had been attending a school there in order to improve his French.[7]

Writing to Mrs Henniker just before his departure from Geneva, Hardy declared that he had given no thought to novels, his own or other people's, since correcting the proofs of *The Well-Beloved*. As soon as he got back to Max Gate, however, he found himself revising a story, 'The Grave by the Handpost', that he had promised for the Christmas Number of the *St James's Budget*, and trying to sort out the confusion which had arisen over two rival French translations of *Tess*.[8] In mid-July he was briefly in London at the invitation of Lady Jeune in order to attend a Jubilee dinner celebrating the progress made by women during the reign of Victoria. It was a large gathering and although Helen Allingham was also present it is quite possible that she and Hardy did not actually meet. Shortly thereafter, while some building work was being done at Max Gate, he and Emma went on another but briefer holiday excursion that took them just beyond the boundaries of Dorset to Wells, Longleat, Frome, and finally Salisbury, where they stayed for several days.[9] Writing from there on 7 August to ask Kate if she would like to 'run up' for a day, Hardy noted that the training college was closed for the holidays and that she would therefore be spared 'unpleasant reminders'.

The same letter speaks to his appreciation, as in the poem 'A Cathedral Façade at Midnight', of the beauty of the cathedral and the peace of the Close at night,[10] and annotations made, as of old, in his Bible, prayerbook, and recently purchased copy of *The Cathedral Psalter* show that he attended Evensong in the cathedral with Emma two or three times during the Salisbury visit. Listening to a reading from the sixth chapter of Jeremiah, he was struck by the applicability to himself, as an agnostic ostensibly engaged in worship, of the twentieth verse—'To what purpose cometh there to me incense from Sheba, and the sweet cane from a far country? your burnt offerings are not acceptable, nor your sacrifices sweet unto me'—and evidently had it in mind when writing and illustrating his poem 'The Impercipient', a moving testimony to the coexistence of a persistent yearning to believe with an unyielding incapacity to do so.[11] Later that same month Hardy was back in Salisbury again for a brief meeting with Romain Rolland's sister, Madeleine Rolland, whose interests he had recently been trying to protect in the squabble over translation rights to *Tess*. He had already been impressed by the excellent English of Mlle Rolland's letters, and this first meeting was to lead to a long friendship maintained almost entirely by correspondence—in which Emma also took an active part, venturing now and then to write in a vividly inaccurate French.[12]

Although they had recently travelled into Somerset and Wiltshire by train, Hardy and Emma were now seeing more and more of their local Dorset countryside by bicycle. Emma, whom neighbours claimed to recall as affecting a green outfit of the kind advocated by Mrs Bloomer, was acknowledged to be the more skilful of the two, and she seems to have gone so far as to participate in a 'Bicycle Paper Chase' organized in Dorchester one Saturday afternoon in April 1897.[13] But her confidence betrayed her into the kind of impetuosity she so often displayed on paper and in conversation, and an accident when out riding with her husband in early September resulted in her being incapacitated for some time by a badly bruised ankle. Hardy, however, continued to ride his cherished Rover 'Cob' throughout the autumn. A few days were spent accompanying Rudyard Kipling in his unsuccessful search for a house in the Weymouth area, and there was a moment of amusement, perhaps touched by chagrin, when the elderly occupant of one of the inspected premises proved never to have heard of either of her celebrated visitors.[14] Other cycling expeditions, alone or with his brother, were made as far afield as Sherborne in north Dorset, or even across the Somerset border to Wells and Glastonbury. The advantage of cycling for literary people, Hardy told Sir George Douglas on another occasion, was that 'you can go out a long distance without coming in contact with another mind,—not even a horse's—& dissipating any little mental energy that has arisen in the course of a morning's application'.[15]

Pleading 'physical reasons that always prevent my making a speech, & almost prevent my dining out', Hardy in November 1897 declined an invitation to respond to the toast of 'Literature' at a forthcoming dinner of the Royal Institute of British Architects. When, in the same letter, he nevertheless reaffirmed his sense of comradeship with the profession he must have had very much in mind his engagement in the restoration of West Knighton Church and the building of Talbothays as well as his recent assistance to the Society for the Protection of Ancient Buildings in the form of technical reports on the dilapidated church at East Lulworth and an old inn at Maiden Newton that was being threatened with destruction.[16] Some of the illustrations he was preparing for *Wessex Poems* were also architectural in character, and he may have taken advantage of his visit to East Lulworth to go further along the coast to Eliza Nicholls's former home at Kimmeridge and make the drawing of Clavel Tower that accompanies 'She, to Him' in the published volume. He clearly enjoyed these expeditions during the winter of 1897–8, whatever memories they brought back, and felt invigorated by the way in which his discovery of the bicycle, his abandonment of fiction, and his return to poetry had come together as if in a single movement of liberation and renewal. 'As to a novel from me', he told William Archer,

I don't incline to one. There is no enlightened literary opinion sufficiently audible to tempt an author, who knows that in the nature of things he must always come short of real excellence. I mean that the little sound & just opinion we get is swamped by the flood of ignorant & venal opinion, & is as if it were not uttered at all. And zest is quenched by the knowledge that by printing a novel which attempts to deal honestly & artistically with the facts of life one stands up to be abused by any scamp who thinks he can advance the sale of his paper by lying about one.[17]

Hardy's sense of release from such pressures emerges almost gaily from a letter to Kate written from 9 Wynnstay Gardens, Kensington, shortly after he and Emma had moved into a flat there for the London season of 1898: 'The young people seem to cycle about the streets here more than ever. I asked an omnibus conductor if the young women (who ride recklessly into the midst of the traffic) did not meet with accidents. He said "Oh, nao; their sex pertects them. We dares not drive over them, wotever they do; & they do jist wot they likes. 'Tis their sex, yer see; & its wot I coll takin' a mean adventure. No man dares to go where they go."' Hardy did some reading at the British Museum in preparation for *The Dynasts* and resumed his faithful patronage—even in inclement weather—of the concerts at the Imperial Institute. Music was of deep importance to him throughout his life, and his visits to London provided him not only with access to theatres, museums, art galleries, but almost his only opportunities to hear good music well played. His tastes were catholic, gratified by performances of military bands as well as by orchestral and chamber concerts, and as he remarked to a friend, 'to be honest I am never tired of music'.[18]

Emma's niece Lilian Gifford was at Max Gate that summer, and Lilian's brother Gordon arrived in September—at the Hardys' instigation, but with the ready acquiescence of the parents. Both visits were prolonged to the end of the year and Gordon in particular spent extended periods at Max Gate over the next few years while attending local schools, first Hardye's grammar school in Dorchester itself, later the Dorset County School at Charminster, preferred by Emma as being 'better class'.[19] Though devoted to Hardy, Gordon Gifford was less attached to his aunt, and the two male members of the household are said to have sat in mutually sympathetic silence during Emma's tirades—much as Hardy and his father seem to have coped with Jemima's outbursts at Higher Bockhampton. Gordon Gifford later denied that the Hardys' marriage had been, in his experience, an unhappy one, but he did acknowledge that his aunt, as 'a very ardent Churchwoman and believer in the virtues and qualities of women in general', had strongly objected to *Jude the Obscure* and to the views of some of its characters.[20]

Hardy, for his part, was fond of all children who were quiet and well behaved—Edmund Gosse's daughter Sylvia spoke of him as understanding small children and as never failing to come upstairs to say good night to her brother and herself when he was visiting the house[21]—and the presence of Gordon and Lilian at Max Gate was one of several factors that helped to maintain a not entirely illusory impression of domestic regularity. For all their many differences, the Hardys were at one in their love of children, animals, and plants. They still dined together, entertained together, went to London together, cycled together, and took holidays together. That their domestic life remained for the most part on a manageable level had much to do with Emma's ability to discharge much of her animosity into her diaries and with Hardy's discovery of silent endurance rather than hopeless contestation as the most effectual response to his wife's tirades. He did not, of course, read Emma's letters, nor did he know of those diaries in which she was corrosively recording her grievances against him.

The situation at Max Gate was considerably eased by Emma's programme of greater separateness and independence. She was now quite prepared to go by herself to London, where she had joined a women's club, the Alexandra, and to take trips to the Sussex seaside when so prompted by her health or her mood. Since the additions to the rear of Max Gate Hardy had moved his study to the new east-facing room on the first floor and Emma had claimed the two attic rooms on the second floor, one of them over the new study, the other over the previous study at what had been (before the extensions) the building's north-west corner. 'I sleep in an *Attic*— *or two!*' she exclaimed to Rebekah Owen. 'My boudoir is my sweet refuge & solace—not a sound scarcely penetrates hither. I see the sun, & stars & moon rise & the birds come to my bird table when a hurricane has not sent it flying.'[22]

In this retreat Emma spent much of her time sewing, reading, and painting: in early 1899 she was attempting a portrait of Gordon Gifford, 'a lovely youth of the chestnut kind at present'. She was also writing both prose and verse and trying to get the results published. 'The Egyptian Pet', a brief and occasionally touching article on cats ('Always give a cat free ingress and egress and attend to his voice, remembering that he has no language but a cry'), appeared in the *Animals' Friend* in 1898 and was later reprinted, so Emma's note on her own copy records, as a leaflet 'for circulation in Dublin etc.' Otherwise she succeeded in publishing little beyond occasional letters to the newspapers, most of them protesting against cruelty to animals: one on 'The Destruction of Larks' appeared in *The Times*, for example, another, on the public whipping of a tiger, in the *Daily Chronicle*.[23] The editor of the *Vegetarian* informed her in March 1898 that a story she had submitted had probably been destroyed, no stamps having been enclosed to cover the cost of its return, and in early July a story called 'The Inspirer' was declined by the editor of *Temple Bar*—a journal to which Hardy had advised Agnes Grove to send a story.[24]

None of this deterred Emma from criticizing the publications of others. Her husband remained her most frequent target, but in March 1897 she attacked Edward Clodd on the score of the rationalist arguments advanced in his recent book *Pioneers of Evolution*: 'The chapters I greatly object to, are those with which you seem to have taken so much pains to say—There is no God—there is no Christ.' Such writings, she insisted, caused despair to those of 'weak faith', though her personal position remained strong and clear: 'In spite of the theory of evolution, for my part I still believe that man was always man.' She went on: 'I do not see why we should have doubts as to immortality, or that we should not be able to rise in *myriads* invisible to such eyes as ours. In the plan of creation there is no permanence of form, size, time, or quantity: all is limitless.'[25]

At the time when *Wessex Poems and Other Verses* was published by Harper & Brothers in mid-December of 1898, Hardy himself had for some time been out of the public eye. Immediately after the volume appeared, he again became a controversial figure. For his first significant appearance as a poet he had drawn on the entire range of the verse he had written to that date, almost as if more concerned to expose the full compass of his work than to display it and himself in the most favourable light. But what made the volume seem so idiosyncratic was Hardy's deployment of thirty-two of his own drawings, some hauntingly effective, others relatively crude in both conception and execution. The opening poem, 'The Temporary the All', was not only headed by an enigmatic drawing but immediately confronted readers with challenges that were to recur throughout the volume and are now recognizable as characteristically Hardyan—the dense stresses, the strict yet unfamiliar stanza form, the inverted syntax, the archaisms and odd coinages, and the profoundly pessimistic mood, unromantically and unfashionably eloquent of non-progression and unfulfilment:

> Mistress, friend, place, aims to be bettered straightway,
> Bettered not has Fate or my hand's achieving;
> Sole the showance those of my onward earth-track—
> Never transcended![26]

The argumentative movement of the poem, from a hopeful past to a melancholy, backward-looking present, anticipates the way in which the volume as a whole follows a roughly (though by no means invariably) chronological sequence from such poems of the 1860s as 'Amabel', 'Hap', and 'Neutral Tones', through some of the rare poems of the 1870s and 1880s, most of them directly or indirectly related to the novels of the period, to those such as 'Friends Beyond', 'Thoughts of Ph—a', 'At an Inn', and 'The Impercipient' that had been written in comparatively recent years. Oddly grouped, as 'Additions', at the very end of the book are the broadly comic 'The Fire at Tranter Sweatley's' (somewhat revised from its previous appearance), the rather plodding 'Lines' spoken by Ada Rehan on behalf of Mary Jeune's charity, the sardonically moralistic 'Heiress and Architect' and 'The Two Men', and, finally, 'I Look Into My Glass', the finest and most obviously personal of these later poems:

> I look into my glass,
> And view my wasting skin,
> And say, 'Would God it came to pass
> My heart had shrunk as thin!'
>
> For then, I, undistrest
> By hearts grown cold to me,
> Could lonely wait my endless rest
> With equanimity.

> But Time, to make me grieve,
> Part steals, lets part abide;
> And shakes this fragile frame at eve
> With throbbings of noontide.[27]

Hardy felt little optimism about the likely response to his first appearance as a poet—and especially, or so he told Gosse, to his elevation of content above form at a time when poetry was generally regarded as 'the art of saying nothing with mellifluous preciosity'. The change of direction, so long contemplated in private, was totally unheralded in public, and several of his friends and admirers were not only surprised but dismayed, Meredith exclaiming: 'What induces Hardy to commit himself to verse!'[28] Some of the reviews were savagely dismissive: the *Saturday Review* spoke of 'this curious and wearisome volume, these many slovenly, slipshod, uncouth verses, stilted in sentiment, poorly conceived and worse wrought. . . . It is impossible to understand why the bulk of this volume was published at all—why he did not himself burn the verse, lest it should fall into the hands of the indiscreet literary executor, and mar his fame when he was dead.'[29] The illustrations, if mentioned at all, were typically invoked as a means of indirectly and sometimes snidely commenting on the verse itself: their impact, declared the *Westminster Gazette*, 'like that of Mr. Hardy's best poems, is curiously in advance of their technical merits'.[30] But for the most part the reviewers were not so much hostile as puzzled and unsure. It was 'difficult to say the proper word', as E. K. Chambers confessed in the *Athenaeum*, and even so sympathetic a critic as Lionel Johnson, author of one of the earliest books on Hardy's fiction, qualified his praise of the 'arresting, strenuous, sometimes admirable' poems with regret at their almost uniform grimness and absence of humour. The entire volume, Johnson complained, might have been entitled 'The Temporary the All', and to call it *Wessex Poems* seemed 'somewhat cruel to Wessex, which is not an wholly Leopardian land'.[31] Hardy had in fact been reading Leopardi—noting, for example, his observations on ancient customs of ceremonially mourning a birth in the family and rejoicing in a death—and readily acknowledged to Johnson that his criticism might have some validity.[32]

Hardy devoted several somewhat querulous pages of *Life and Work* to the reception of *Wessex Poems*, but would seem in the end neither to have had nor to have felt any great cause for dissatisfaction, his real complaint being not so much that the critics had been unkind as that they had been so comprehensively imperceptive in their 'inevitable ascription to ignorance' of poetic form 'what was really choice after full knowledge. That the author loved the art of concealing art was undiscerned.' More significant in any case, and more reassuring, were the letters of congratulation received from such friends as Leslie Stephen, Theodore Watts-Dunton, and Swinburne, and he was sufficiently vain—or perhaps sufficiently insecure as a poet—to send Mrs Henniker a list of the poems that Swinburne had specifically praised.[33]

The most persistently adverse reaction to *Wessex Poems* seems to have come from Emma, who found the one poem addressed directly to her, 'Ditty (E.L.G.)', to be an inadequate compensation for the criticism of herself she discerned in 'The Ivy-Wife' or for the various poems she knew, guessed, or suspected to refer to other women, among them Eliza Nicholls, Tryphena Sparks, and Florence Henniker. She may also have been alert to some of the personal allusions Hardy had incorporated into the drawings. When, however, she confided her unhappiness to Alfred Pretor—a Dorset-born classicist and minor novelist, fellow of St Catharine's College, Cambridge, with whom she had recently struck up a semi-literary friendship—she was told that her darker fears were quite unfounded: 'T. has said again & again to me', Pretor circumspectly wrote, 'little casual things that are absolute proofs that all his reminiscences are little fancies evoked from the days of his youth & absolutely without bearing on the real happiness of his life.' When an unpersuaded Emma persisted in the objection that Hardy's treatment of her, in print as in life, displayed monstrous ingratitude, another letter from Pretor counselled her to be content with her lot as the helpmeet of genius and assured her that people did indeed believe that she copied and even composed passages in her husband's books. After all, he ambiguously added, 'such an ideal union as the Brownings is (I venture to think) unique, at any rate between two such gifted people'.[34]

The Brownings figured largely in what was fast becoming Emma's standard rhetoric of complaint and self-pity. Believing that she was her husband's superior in birth, family connections, and education, and only slightly his inferior in literary gifts, she took great offence at the scant attention being paid to her and her opinions by her husband's friends and, increasingly, by her husband himself. She also objected to Hardy's taking the management of their lives and of the household itself more and more into his own hands, as he had evidently felt it necessary to do. 'He should be the last man to disparage marriage!' she indiscreetly complained to Rebekah Owen in April 1899. 'I have been a devoted wife for at least twenty years or more—but the last four or five alas! Fancy it is our silver wedding this year! The *thorn* is in my side still.'[35] Her jealousy was exacerbated rather than disarmed by Hardy's self-protective conscientiousness in keeping her informed as to his meetings and correspondence with Florence Henniker, Mary Jeune, and Agnes Grove. Resentful of Hardy's encouragement of the literary ambitions of such women and his apparent forgetfulness of those earlier times when he and she had worked together as a team, she continued—as Pretor's comments show—to talk in extravagant terms of the role she had played in the writing of the Wessex novels.

That Emma had given her husband much help in times past there can be no doubt. Incidents and details suggested by her were incorporated in novels as early as *A Pair of Blue Eyes* and as late as *Tess*; she endured the tedium of taking down Hardy's dictation during the composition of *A Laodicean* and perhaps on other occasions; she copied into 'Facts' and 'Literary Notes' and other of Hardy's cumulative notebooks a great many items that Hardy had simply jotted down on whatever scrap of paper happened to be at hand; she kept her own records of Hardy's invention and occasional alteration of 'Wessex' place names; she materially assisted in the completion and submission of some of the novels and stories by recopying manuscript pages that had undergone especially heavy correction; and she from time to time wrote out letters and documents on her husband's behalf. Although her participation in such tasks was greater in the earlier stages of their marriage than in the later, it seems to have continued in some form at least into the early 1890s.[36] But it was never an independently creative participation, nor was it ever as substantial as Emma claimed in the exaggerated accounts she was accustomed to deliver to neighbours, visitors, and journalistic interviewers. Her persistence in indiscriminately advancing such claims on private, social, and even professional occasions was profoundly irritating to Hardy himself, and one of his responses was to destroy the manuscript of *A Laodicean* as well as pages in her hand that he came across in the manuscripts of other novels.[37]

Emma, of course, saw things somewhat differently. To Isa MacCarthy, mother of the ambitious young Desmond MacCarthy, she acknowledged that she was 'prejudiced against authors—living ones!—they too often wear out other's lives with their dyspeptic moanings if unsuccessful—and if they become eminent they throw their aider over their parapets to enemies below, & revenge themselves for any objections to this treatment by stabbings with their pen'.[38] To Winifred Thomson's sister Elspeth, disillusioned by the early stages of a somewhat middle-aged marriage to Kenneth Grahame, the author of *The Wind in the Willows*, she had earlier sent a still more alarming message:

I can scarcely think that love proper, and enduring, is in the nature of men—as a rule—perhaps there is no woman 'whom custom will not stale.' There is ever a desire to give but little in return for our devotion, & affection—their's being akin to children's—a sort of easy affectionate*ness*—& at fifty, a man's feelings too often take a new course altogether. Eastern ideas of matrimony secretly pervade his thoughts, & he wearies of the most perfect, & suitable, wife chosen in his earlier life. Of course he gets over it usually, somehow, or hides it, or is lucky!

Interference from others is greatly to be feared—members of either family too often are the cause of estrangement. A woman does not object to be ruled by her husband, so much as she does by a relative at his back,—a man seldom cares to control such matters when in his power, & lets things glide, or throws his balance on the wrong side which is simply a terrible state of affairs, & may affect unfavourably himself in the end.

Keeping separate a good deal is a wise plan in crises—and being both free—& *expecting little* neither gratitude, nor attentions, love, nor *justice*, nor *anything* you may set your heart on. Love interest—adoration, & all that kind of thing is usually a *failure—complete*—some one comes by & upsets your pail of milk in the end. If he belongs to the public in any way, years of devotion count for nothing. Influence can seldom be retained as years go by, & *hundreds* of wives go through a phase of disillusion,—it is really a pity to have any ideals in the first place.[39]

Emma's case against husbands in general was essentially an elaboration of her case against her own husband, the phrase about 'a relative at his back' obviously alluding to Mary Hardy or, more probably, Jemima, still very much alive at Bockhampton and still regularly visited there by her still devoted son. 'I have suffered much', Emma told Isa MacCarthy a little later on, '& greatly from the ignorant interference of others (of the peasant class).'[40] It is impossible, even so, to uncover at all precisely the biographical and perhaps psychological sources of the bitterness underlying Emma's destructive advice to Elspeth Grahame, or to speculate at all responsibly as to possible assignments of blame. Given such lack of knowledge, given also the extraordinary accident and immediate impact of Thomas Hardy's and Emma Gifford's first meeting at St Juliot, it is tempting to see that encounter and its consequences as ironically encoded in 'The Convergence of the Twin', Hardy's famous poem about the *Titanic* and its predestined iceberg:

> Alien they seemed to be:
> No mortal eye could see
> The intimate welding of their later history,
>
> Or sign that they were bent
> By paths coincident
> On being anon twin halves of one august event,

Till the Spinner of the Years
Said 'Now!' And each one hears,
And consummation comes, and jars two hemispheres.[41]

Bertha Newcombe, an artist friend of the Hardys, visited them at Max Gate in March 1900 and reported in a letter to Nellie Gosse that she had felt much sympathy and pity for the way in which Emma was 'struggling against her woes. She asserts herself as much as possible and is a great bore, but at the same time is so kind and goodhearted, and one cannot help realising what she must have been to her husband. She showed us a photograph of herself as a young girl, and it was very attractive.' Emma also gave Miss Newcombe, as she had given Mabel Robinson, her own version of how she had first met the 'ill-grown, under-sized young architect' in Cornwall, discovered his genius, and encouraged him to write. 'I don't wonder', Miss Newcombe continued, 'that she resents being slighted by everyone, now that her ugly duckling has grown into such a charming swan. It is so silly of her though isn't it not to rejoice in the privilege of being wife to so great a man?'[42] Emma might have termed that very much an outsider's view. If it was her privilege to marry a man of genius it was also her misfortune. Hardy's life—externally so uneventful, internally of such intense creative preoccupation—was conducted with the necessary ruthlessness of an artist with work to do, and he had become over the years increasingly unwilling, or unable, to treat Emma with the patience she required or provide her with the audience she craved. By a relentless process of action and reaction, her personal religious and moralistic obsessions deepened as the irreligion and immorality of her husband's work became, in her eyes, more and more pronounced, with the result that while in the 1890s she was still content to assure people that her husband did not in fact mean what he said on such matters, she came before she died to see him as a living embodiment of precisely those evils to whose eradication she was so devoutly dedicated.

On 2 June 1899, Hardy's fifty-ninth birthday, Emma gave him a Bible. That November, perhaps on the occasion of her own fifty-ninth birthday, she put her name into a copy of Mary Wollstonecraft's *A Vindication of the Rights of Women*.[43] Whatever Hardy may have read domestically into such gestures, his public life with Emma went on much as usual. In May they returned to Wynnstay Gardens (though to a different flat), and at the end of the month Hardy went off to Aldeburgh on the Norfolk coast to spend the Whitsun weekend with Clodd and his other guests, including Walter Besant and

Flinders Petrie, the Egyptologist.[44] He visited Meredith again at Box Hill and spent a day or two with Dorothy Allhusen (the former Dorothy Stanley) at her house adjoining Stoke Poges churchyard. He was much impressed during this visit by the Duchess of Manchester's faultless recitation, at Gray's graveside, of the whole of the 'Elegy in a Country Churchyard', not only because the young and beautiful Duchess reminded him of a dairy-maid who had mindlessly repeated biblical passages when he was conduct-ing Sunday school at Stinsford as a youth, but also because the 'Elegy' had always been of peculiar importance to his sense of himself as the novelist and poet of isolated localities—so much so that on a later occasion he asserted that Stinsford, the Mellstock of *Under the Greenwood Tree*, *was* Stoke Poges.[45]

Back in Dorset in mid-July 1899 the cycle rides were resumed with much enthusiasm and energy, although a tour with Henry through the New Forest to Southampton proved too tiring on account of the heat and was cut short after two days. One Sunday in August Hardy and Emma cycled to the north Dorset village of Turnworth to visit the rector, the Reverend Thomas Perkins, who was congenial to Hardy as a doughty campaigner on behalf of the Society for the Protection of Ancient Buildings and to Emma as a crusading anti-vivisectionist. They stayed on to attend a harvest festival in the church that Hardy had been instrumental in restoring thirty years earlier and then cycled the seventeen or so hilly miles back to Max Gate in the moonlight.[46] Hardy was again in his cycling knickerbockers when James Milne of the *Daily Chronicle* suddenly descended upon him in late August to seek an interview on the subject of Stonehenge, about to be put on the market by the owner of the land on which it stood. Hardy agreed to be quoted on such a subject, although it seemed curious, as he told Mrs Henniker, that he should be approached as an authority on Stonehenge solely on the strength of a single scene in *Tess of the d'Urbervilles* when some-one like Lady Grove's father, General Pitt-Rivers, had 'devotedly crawled among the stones on his hands & knees inspecting rabbit-holes, &c.'[47] In the course of arguing that the monument should be purchased for the nation, Hardy in fact displayed an impressive knowledge of the ruins and of the problems involved both in protecting them from the elements and in preserving them from the threat of transportation to the United States, where he believed they would be rendered meaningless by the loss of all associations. His interest in Stonehenge thus re-aroused, Hardy took advantage of an invitation to a house party at the Jeunes' the following month to arrange for his hosts to meet him at Stonehenge, explore the site with him, and then drive him back to Arlington Manor in their motor car.[48]

This was probably Hardy's first experience of such a vehicle, but if he was struck by its juxtaposition to the antiquity of Stonehenge he was much more disturbed by the implications, both immediate and historical, of the hostilities looming in South Africa that had been the principal topic of conversation among his fellow guests. As the war against the Boers, a crisis of British imperialism, became increasingly a reality, Hardy was torn—as he freely acknowledged—between a principled abhorrence of war and an irresistible responsiveness, now as in childhood, to the excitement generated by military activity. As he wrote to Mrs Henniker on 11 October: 'I constantly deplore the fact that "civilized" nations have not learnt some more excellent & apostolic way of settling disputes than the old & barbarous one, after all these centuries; but when I feel that it must be, few persons are more martial than I, or like better to write of war in prose & rhyme.'[49] Learning that Major Henniker was about to leave for South Africa with a contingent of the Coldstream Guards, Hardy wrote to wish him 'good fortune' and a 'speedy return', and took the letter with him to Southampton, where he stood at the dockside to watch the troops depart. He had hoped to meet Major Henniker there, but the Coldstreams, it transpired, were to leave the next day; the following morning, therefore, he roused up Gordon Gifford at an early hour, made him some fortifying cocoa, and sent him off on his bicycle to observe the scene and deliver the letter to Major Henniker by hand.[50]

Hardy's experiences, supplemented by his nephew's, became the basis of 'The Departure' (later 'Embarcation'), a poem published in the *Daily Chronicle* on 25 October. Much as he had been moved by the spectacle at Southampton, he remained critical of the failure of 'this late age of thought, and pact, and code' to settle disputes other than by 'the selfsame bloody mode' of ancient times. A few days later, indeed, the sight of an artillery battery moving out from the Dorchester barracks, at night and in pouring rain, on its way to South Africa prompted 'The Going of the Battery: Wives' Lament', a poem not overtly hostile to the war as such but unromantically and even pathetically insistent upon the bleakness of the particular scene and the deprivation and anxiety of those left behind.[51] Not surprisingly, Hardy was distressed by the unqualified jingoism of Swinburne's sonnet 'The Transvaal', published in *The Times* in mid-October, and wrote to congratulate George Gissing on having publicly criticized Swinburne's final exhortation, 'Strike, England, and strike home', for its irresponsible pandering to 'the old blood-thirst'. Gissing's demurral, Hardy told him, was 'the right word at the right moment'.[52]

Before the end of the year the first military engagements had been fought in South Africa and the first lists of casualties were beginning to arrive back in England. Hardy again made a quick response in such poems as 'The Dead Drummer', 'At the War Office after a Bloody Battle'—a scene, as he told Mrs Henniker, that he had not witnessed but could readily imagine— and the magnificent 'The Souls of the Slain', whose prescient truth to the experience of subsequent wars was grounded in its author's highly developed sense of history.[53] It was indicative of the profound change in Hardy's habits of thinking and writing that the verses should now come so swiftly and, on the whole, so richly, even while he found some difficulty, that November and December, in finishing the last two prose narratives he was ever to write, 'Enter a Dragoon' for *Harper's New Monthly Magazine* and 'A Changed Man' for Clement Shorter's *Sphere*.[54] Christmas Day 1899 was largely taken up with writing to the editor of the *Daily Chronicle* in defence of his recently published poem 'A Christmas Ghost-Story', criticized in that morning's *Chronicle* on the grounds that its central figure, the 'puzzled' military ghost who asks when Christ's message of peace was 'ruled to be inept, and set aside', was scarcely heroic enough to be identified with 'one of the Dublin Fusiliers who cried amidst the storm of bullets at Tugela, "Let us make a name for ourselves!"'[55] Arguing with point, erudition, and humour ('Hamlet's father, impliedly martial in life, was not particularly brave as a spectre'), and gently insisting that his portrayal had ample warrant both in logic and in literary precedent, Hardy concluded:

Thus I venture to think that the phantom of a slain soldier, neither British nor Boer, but a composite, typical phantom, may consistently be made to regret on or about Christmas Eve (when even the beasts of the field kneel, according to a tradition of my childhood) the battles of his life and war in general, although he may have shouted in the admirable ardor and pride of his fleshtime, as he is said to have done: 'Let us make a name for ourselves!'[56]

On the issue of the war, at least, Max Gate spoke with very nearly a united voice, Emma's sounding somewhat the more trenchant in the private letter she wrote to Rebekah Owen just two days after her husband had sent his public letter to the *Daily Chronicle*: 'But the Boers fight for homes & liberties—we fight for the Transvaal Funds, diamonds, & gold! is it not so? . . . Why should not Africa be free, as is America? Peace at any cost of pride, & aggrandisement, is my idea.'[57]

Hardy followed the war news avidly, visited the Dorchester barracks in early February 1900 after learning that another local unit was about to leave for the war zone, and implicitly consented to the successful prosecution of the war once it had begun. He was, however, fundamentally out of sympathy with the resort to arms as an instrument of policy or with the imperial idea that policy sought to uphold, and profoundly disturbed by doubts as to the validity of the cause itself and by awareness of the sufferings both of men and of horses. Even before the outbreak of the war he had urged that horses not be 'employed in battle, except for transport'; once the fighting had begun he was the more acutely distressed at the plight of 'the mangled animals too, who must have terror superadded to their physical sufferings'.[58] 'How horrible it all is,' he exclaimed in February 1900: 'I take a keen pleasure in war strategy & tactics, following it as if it were a game of chess; but all the while I am obliged to blind myself to the human side of the matter: directly I think of that, the romance looks somewhat tawdry, & worse.' He added that he had recently shocked one of the Moule brothers by suggesting that since nearly 2,000 years of Christianity had failed to teach countries 'the rudimentary virtues of keeping peace,' there seemed no good reason not to abandon it in favour of some other religion, such as Buddhism.[59] As hostilities gradually diminished towards the end of 1900, and the first troops began to return home, Hardy wrote and published the most broadly acceptable, because least polemical, of his Boer War verses, 'Song of the Soldiers' Wives'. It was, he assured Mrs Henniker on Christmas Eve, the last of his 'war effusions, of which I am happy to say that not a single one is Jingo or Imperial—a fatal defect according to the judgment of the British majority at present, I dare say'.[60]

This sense of disconnection between his own views and those of the country at large exacerbated Hardy's sense of being at odds with his potential audience: 'I am puzzled what to do with some poems, written at various dates, a few lately, some long ago,' he wrote in October 1900. 'If I print them I know exactly what will be said about them: "You hold opinions which we don't hold: therefore shut up."' English reviewers, he continued, 'go behind the book & review the man', with 'paralysing' consequences for those who would otherwise have 'developed' the English novel, 'possibly in a wrong direction in many cases, but ultimately towards excellence'.[61] His own literary energies were now entirely devoted to the writing of verse, his novels concerning him only retrospectively, as financially significant 'properties' to be managed and kept in the public eye. He had felt some anxiety about his financial position when his abandonment of fiction was followed early in 1900 by the threatened bankruptcy of Harper & Brothers, whose absorption of Osgood, McIlvaine & Co. had resulted in their becoming his principal publishers on both sides of the Atlantic. After yet another reorganization, however, Harper & Brothers not only emerged from their

39. Max Gate, 1901; Hardy with bicycle; Emma Hardy with Gordon Gifford in foreground; windows of Emma's attic and Hardy's final study visible at far right; photographed by Clive Holland

40. Hardy's final study, 1900

41. Thomas Hardy, *c.*1886, photographed by Barraud

Thomas Hardy.

ELLIOTT & FRY   Copyright   55, BAKER STREET
LONDON. W.

42. Signed photograph of Thomas Hardy, *c.*1900

43 (*left*). Emma Hardy in early middle age

44 (*below*). Jemima Hardy in an invalid carriage shortly before her death

45. 'But Mr Hardy, Mr Hardy, if you only knew all the circumstances': cartoon by Will Dyson
(1880-1938). *From the original drawing*

46. The pets' cemetery, Max Gate

47. Emma Hardy, *c.*1905

48. Portrait of Hardy by Jacques-Émile Blanche, 1906

A Singer Asleep

~~A South-Coast Nocturn~~

By Thomas Hardy.

(A.C.S. 1837 — 1909)

I.

In this ~~high niche beside~~ fair niche above the ~~sleepless~~ unslumbering sea
That sentrys up & down all night, all day,
From cove to promontory, from ~~cape~~ ness to bay,
The Fates have fitly bidden that he should be
          Pillowed eternally.

II.

— It was as though a garland of red roses
Had fallen ~~upon~~ about the hood of some snug nun
irresponsibly When ~~in my primest~~ ~~his years failed~~, dropped as from the sun
In fulth of ~~canzons~~ numbers peaked with musical closes
Upon Victoria's formal middle time
          His leaves of rhythm & rhyme.

III.

O that far morning of a summer day,
When down a terraced street whose pavements lay
Glassing the sunshine into my bent eyes,
I walked & read with a quick glad surprise
          New words, in classic guise;—

IV.

The
~~That~~ passionate ~~notes~~ of his earlier years,
Fraught with hot sighs, sad laughters, kisses, tears?—
Fresh-fluted notes, yet ~~by~~ from a minstrel who
Blew them not naively, but as one who knew
          Full well why thus he blew.

V.

I still can hear the brabble & the roar
At those thy tunes, O still one, now passed through

difficulties but sought to stimulate the sale of Hardy's fiction by publishing, at sixpence each, paper-covered editions of *Tess of the d'Urbervilles* and, a little later, *Far from the Madding Crowd*. Although Hardy's royalty on these was necessarily small, it was reassuring to be told that no less than 100,000 copies of the sixpenny *Tess* had been printed for sale in the United Kingdom alone.[62]

Hardy was still advising Lady Grove from time to time on the progress of her writing, now returned from an unsuccessful excursion into fiction to what was for her the solider ground of lightly satirical essays on contemporary manners. Her two visits to Max Gate in early 1900, followed by her criticism of the contents of some pamphlets her hostess had pressed upon her, were perhaps instrumental in provoking a jealous Emma to literary emulation.[63] Stimulated—or perhaps irritated—by her husband's publication of poems in the pages of the *Westminster Gazette*, she submitted one of her own, only to receive from the editor a suggestion that it might be made 'a little simpler & more uniform in metre'.[64] Clement Shorter, with whom she had recently begun to correspond, proved more responsive, to the point of including one of her poems in the editorial section of the *Sphere* of 14 April 1900:

SPRING SONG

Why does April weep?
   And why does April smile?
And why look we both sad and sweet
   A-wondering all the while?

If the winter's nights have flown,
And its dark days so lone,
And the summer's love's a-warm,
Coming like bees a-swarm

Will not the sun's heart glow
To ours in a steady flow
Of joy and sure delight,
Of new deeds, and thought of might?

But none know what summer's days may bring.
That's why we weep and smile, come Spring.

Writing to Rebekah Owen shortly after the publication of her sonnet, as she called it, Emma remarked that two words—not specified—would have been altered in the last verse had she been sent proofs. Shorter, for his part, had somewhat undercut the gallantry of his gesture by explaining to his

readers that he was publishing Emma's poem 'as one of the most enthusiastic admirers of her husband's books'.[65] When another of Emma's poems,
'The Gardener's Ruse', appeared on the literary gossip page of the *Academy*
a year later, it too was introduced in terms of lightly veiled dismissal: 'Mrs.
Thomas Hardy tells us in the following interesting lines how rose trees are
planted in Wessex.' Of rather more interest, however, is the extent to which
the dependence of the rose upon the onion dug in to feed its roots could
have been intended by Emma as a metaphor for her own unappreciated
role in her husband's success:

> Down far in the earth, hidden its worth,
>   The Onion, coarse and meek,
> Sought the roots of the roses, to give scent to its posies,
>   And brilliance in colour—a Freak![66]

Hardy told Sir George Douglas as early as mid-March of 1900 that he
and Emma felt disinclined to take a house or flat in London for the duration
of the 'season'. The war was not yet over, Emma felt 'pulled down very
much' and insisted that she did not in any case 'care greatly for the season
& the extravagance, & attrition, of society'. They did, however, spend a few
weeks in June at the West Central Hotel, Southampton Row.[67] Hardy, who
went up to London ahead of Emma and left again a week before she did,
saw something of Lilian Gifford and especially of her brother, who had
begun studying architecture in the offices of Sir Arthur Blomfield's old firm,
now run by his two sons. Hardy had for some time been giving Gordon
lessons in architectural theory and practice, taking him on visits to local
churches and other buildings of architectural interest and going to some
pains to encourage and develop his skills as a draughtsman. When some
of Gordon's architectural drawings of the ruins of Cerne Abbey were
published in a professional journal, the *Builder*, it was not only at Hardy's
instigation but with the accompaniment of his anonymously contributed
descriptive text. In January 1900 he arranged with Charles Blomfield for
Gordon to receive more systematic training in London, pointing out that he
had been able to teach his nephew in accordance with the firm's traditions.
In London that spring he checked on Gordon's progress and showed him
how to use the library of art and architectural history at what is now the
Victoria and Albert Museum. He also saw Mrs Henniker and spent
another weekend at Stoke Poges with Dorothy Allhusen.[68]

By the end of June the Hardys had returned to Max Gate, where they
received several groups of visitors over the next few weeks. Gordon Gifford
was invited down for a short visit; Lilian stayed for a longer period extend-

ing into the new year and joined Hardy and Emma, sometimes separately, often together, in cycle rides to Upwey, Cerne Abbas, Bulbarrow, and other places made attractive by their scenery or associations.[69] Hamo and Agatha Thornycroft arrived, bringing their bicycles, in late July; A. E. Housman, Edward Clodd, and Arthur Symons—a somewhat surprising assortment— were there together the first weekend in August. Clodd, who arrived on the Friday, ahead of the others, recorded a few details of his visit. On the Saturday morning he played croquet on the front lawn with Hardy and Lilian Gifford, chatted with Hardy as they strolled around the garden, and then walked with him to Winterborne Came to visit William Barnes's grave. Housman and Symons arrived that afternoon, and on the Sunday, after a rainy morning which Clodd and Lilian devoted largely to chess, Hardy took his three guests to visit Maumbury Rings and Maiden Castle. There was more croquet after tea that day, but in the evening, after dinner, Symons read some Housman, Housman read some Symons, Clodd read some Robert Bridges, and the talk was all of poetry. On the Monday, a Bank Holiday, the four men took the train to Weymouth and walked up onto Portland to see the assembled ships of the Channel Fleet. Clodd left for London early on Monday morning, the entry in his diary—the source of all these details—concluding 'Mrs H. chatted to me as of yore, re Tom'.[70]

In October news came of the serious illness of Helen Holder, the widow of the Reverend Caddell Holder, and Emma left for the Hampshire seaside town of Lee-on-Solent to nurse her sister and try to set her financial affairs in order. As Helen Holder's condition worsened and Emma's absence from home was prolonged, Hardy became somewhat restive. Though Lilian was a pleasant enough companion for a cycle ride she was something of a nuisance to have around the house, especially as she had no real resources of her own and was not prepared to undertake any domestic tasks. In a news-filled letter of 6 November 1900, signed 'Yours affly', Hardy strongly hinted, without specifically insisting, that Emma should come home for a while and attend both to her niece and to household affairs in general. Emma did return briefly in mid-November, and for another day or two at the end of the month, but she otherwise remained at Lee-on-Solent until after Helen Holder's death and funeral in the first weeks of December. When Emma wrote to say that her sister had died, Hardy in his reply showed concern for her own physical well-being, and perhaps for her emotional state: 'I feel rather anxious lest you should have broken down under your exertions. There is now no need for continued effort, as, in settling up bills of a deceased person, Valuation for Probate, &c, the law allows a reasonable time for relatives to act in. So "take it stiddy" as they say here—

the case now being no longer one in which a sick person is dependent on what you do.'[71]

Hardy's anxiety that Emma should return home in early November may have been provoked in part by the return to Dorchester of Rebekah Owen, who remained throughout the next several weeks a sometimes amusing but often troublesome presence, constantly pressing for walks, cycle rides, visits to Max Gate, and inscriptions in her copies of Hardy's books. Miss Owen, who still liked to imagine that her relationship with Hardy had a strong romantic ingredient, thought of Lilian Gifford's presence on these occasions as that of a 'chaperone', and in a letter of 27 November 1900 gave a vivid, if exaggerated, description of her as being 'as fat as butter and the image of a China doll, with bushy frizzy dark hair, round red cheeks between which the tiny nose is scarcely visible'. The same letter cited the latest gossip about the Hardys, including Mrs Sheridan's 'She leads him a Hell of a life'.[72] Emma herself, writing to Rebekah on 31 December 1900, spoke warmly of Lilian ('She is a bright little soul & we do not like to part with her to her parents') but gloomily of her own situation and of the world in general:

Do you read much of the new poetry—so involved, obscure, & so much of it? There is a mystical poem by Yeats—'The Shadowy Land' What does it mean? That no woman's love is worth offering to a man, who is as a god? ... Supposing women had always held the reins of this world would it not have been—by now, getting near the goal of happiness? This is a *man's world*—& in spite of their intellect shown most especially in science! it is in fact a terrible *failure* as to peace & joy—[73]

There is so much of Emma in this passage: her strenuous literary aspirations, generally pathetic in their consequences but by no means contemptible in themselves; her earnest feminism, fed by raw resentment against her own husband but also by flashes of genuine insight; her belief, as urgent as it was confused, in not merely the possibility but the sheer necessity of a world better and happier than the one, full of war and cruelty and injustice, into which she had been born.

It seems an unkind coincidence that Hardy should have published, just two days before Emma's New Year's Eve letter to Rebekah Owen, some verses in which his own violently conflicting impulses had proved magnificently capable, if not of intellectual at least of creative resolution. 'By the Century's Deathbed' was published by the *Graphic* as a reflection upon the moment of transition from the end of the nineteenth century to the beginning of the twentieth. Under its later title, 'The Darkling Thrush', it still eloquently testifies to the role of emotion in all of Hardy's thought—to that 'imaginativeness' of his reasoning which enabled a persistent hoping for the best even within the context of a profound conviction of the worst:

> So little cause for carolings
>   Of such ecstatic sound
> Was written on terrestrial things
>   Afar or nigh around,
> That I could think there trembled through
>   His happy good-night air
> Some blessed Hope, whereof he knew
>   And I was unaware.[74]

21

Pessimistic Meliorist

REVIEWERS of *Wessex Poems*, echoing the reception of Hardy's later novels, repeatedly invoked the term 'pessimism', as if in so doing they were simultaneously defining a distinctive philosophical position and enforcing an adverse critical judgement. Hardy's exasperation at being so crudely categorized was exceeded only by his overwhelming sense of the inconceivability of 'optimism' in a world of such radical imperfection. Picking up a reference to Browning in an article on 'Form in Poetry' for which Gosse had taken *Wessex Poems* as his text, Hardy exclaimed: 'The longer I live the more does B.'s character seem *the* literary puzzle of the 19th century. How could smug Christian optimism worthy of a dissenting grocer find a place inside a man who was so vast a seer & feeler when on neutral ground?' In a much later note, prepared for inclusion in *Life and Work* but not in fact used there, he drew a specific contrast between Browning's outlook and his own: 'Imagine you have to walk [a] chalk line drawn across an open down. Browning walked it, knowing no more. But a yard to the left of the same line the down is cut by a vertical cliff five hundred feet deep. I know it is there, but walk the line just the same.'[1]

Hardy's troubled musings upon the nature of existence and the problem of evil emerge with particular directness from an interview that William Archer conducted at Max Gate in February 1901. Having ventured the proposition that there might be 'a consciousness infinitely far off, at the other end of the chain of phenomena, always striving to express itself, and always baffled and blundering', Hardy accepted Archer's suggestion that this might be considered a new version of 'the good old Manichean heresy, with Matter playing the part of the evil principle—Satan, Ahriman, whatever you choose to call it'. He insisted, however, that he did not necessarily believe that what Archer had called the 'evil principle' would ultimately prevail:

For instance, people call me a pessimist; and if it is pessimism to think, with Sophocles, that 'not to have been born is best,' then I do not reject the designation. . . . But my pessimism, if pessimism it be, does not involve the assumption that the world is going to the dogs, and that Ahriman is winning all along the line. On the contrary, my practical philosophy is distinctly meliorist. What are my books but one plea against 'man's inhumanity to man'—to woman—and to the lower animals? . . . Whatever may be the inherent good or evil of life, it is certain that men make it much worse than it need be. When we have got rid of a thousand remediable ills, it will be time enough to determine whether the ill that is irremediable outweighs the good.

Challenged by Archer to say whether he really believed that mankind was ridding itself of such an evil as war, Hardy confidently declared:

Oh yes, war is doomed. It is doomed by the gradual growth of the introspective faculty in mankind—of their power of putting themselves in another's place, and taking a point of view that is not their own. In another aspect, this may be called the growth of a sense of humour. Not to-day, not to-morrow, but in the fulness of time, war will come to an end, not for moral reasons, but because of its absurdity.[2]

Hardy's vision of the future was to become much darker during and after the First World War, but this unusually open exposition of his ideas at the very beginning of the century makes it possible to reconcile strands in his thought that might otherwise seem inconsistent. Fundamentally pessimistic about the human condition, in the sense that he believed birth and coming to consciousness to be a kind of original doom, Hardy could nevertheless respond with compassion to human (and animal) suffering and bring a reformist zeal to bear upon evils perceived as social and hence as potentially susceptible to amelioration or even eradication. Agnostic though he was, he could also remain perpetually alert to the possibility, however faint, of some 'blessed hope' of which the most diligent search had thus far left him 'unaware'.[3] Abstractly, theoretically, generally he could see only an incomprehensible and probably meaningless universe; concretely, practically, specifically he cared deeply about the human condition, perceived value in individual lives, asserted such traditional and officially Christian values as charity and what he liked to call 'loving-kindness', and thought that things could and indeed did get better.

Where Hardy differed from so many of his contemporaries was in the absoluteness, the literalness, with which he believed that not to be born was best, that consciousness was a curse, and that while death might distress the bereaved the dead were not themselves to be pitied. '*Heu mihi, quia incolatus meus prolongatus est!*, wrote Hardy inside the back cover of his copy of *The Missal for the Use of the Laity*, marking also the passage and its translation ('Woe is me, that my sojourning is prolonged!') at the point at which they occurred within the volume. In February 1896 he insisted in conversation with Clodd that he wished he had never been born and, 'but for the effort of dying, would rather be dead than alive'. On Christmas Day 1890 he made a note for a poem: '*The amusement of the dead*—at our errors, or at our want- ing to live on.'[4] He told the grieving Rider Haggards that a child's death was 'never really to be regretted, when one reflects on what he has escaped', and when writing to Mrs Henniker about the fighting in South Africa, at a time when her husband was still on active service there, allowed himself to remark: 'It is sad, or not, as you look at it, to think that 40,000 will have found their rest there. Could we ask them if they wish to wake up again, would they say Yes, do you think?'[5] Ungracious as such opinions must have seemed to their recipients, they were for Hardy statements of the obvious, inherent in that bleak view of the human lot which gave him the courage— or perhaps the cruelty—to execute Tess and destroy Jude.

Whatever their formal austerity, Hardy's views did not teach him stoic detachment. That extraordinary capacity for imaginative identification which gave such strength to a novel like *Tess* was liable, at the level of every- day living, to take the form of an almost morbid sensitivity to the sufferings of others, and especially to the sufferings of animals. Lack of children no doubt had much to do with the extreme and indulgent fondness both Hardy and Emma displayed towards their pets, but it was at one level a protective tenderness entirely consistent with Hardy's larger vision of the scheme of things. When, in early April 1901, his favourite cat—'*my* cat—the first I have ever had "for my very own"' was run over, like other Max Gate cats before and after it, on the nearby railway line, Hardy exclaimed: 'The violent death of dumb creature[s] always makes me revile the contingencies of a world in which animals are in the best of cases pitiable for their limitations.' He had already expressed his distress at the involuntary and uncompre- hending sufferings of horses and mules on the battlefields of the Boer War, and when, in the summer of 1901, he was invited to share in the rejoicing at the demise of the Royal Buckhounds, he declared that 'the hunting of tame stags' was 'but a detail' to one who believed, as he did, that it was in any circumstances 'immoral and unmanly to cultivate a pleasure in compassing the death of our weaker and simpler fellow-creatures by cunning, instead of learning to regard their destruction, if a necessity, as an odious task, akin to that, say, of the common hangman'.[6]

. . .

Despite the loss of the cat, the prolongation of the war in South Africa, and other sources of particular or general distress, Hardy felt somehow re-invigorated by the initiation of a new century and a new reign. Although he observed Queen Victoria's death in February 1901 with a poem of sober praise—written, so he claimed, during a bad headache, sent off immediately to *The Times*, and not revised before publication—he responded with instinctive cheerfulness to the 'general sense of the unknown lying round us, which in itself is a novelty. . . . [W]hat French editors call "Le God save" has to be sung somewhat differently by me when I feel musical, & my money all looks old-fashioned pending the new coinage.' Writing to Florence Henniker on 2 June, his sixty-first birthday, he spoke of the 'cheerful time' he had spent at Aldeburgh the previous weekend with Clodd and such fellow guests as Anthony Hope Hawkins, author of *The Prisoner of Zenda*, and James Frazer of *The Golden Bough*. Physically, he was still suffering from the effects of an earlier attack of influenza and had spent the day 'lying down, in sheer languor', but his mental condition was such that he could not recollect a year in which he had met his birthday 'with more equanimity'.[7]

The persistence of this lighter mood throughout most of 1901 perhaps reflected the establishment of some workable, if temporary, *modus vivendi* with Emma. She was in poor health and low spirits during the early part of the year and unwilling, for the second year running, to go to the trouble of taking a house or flat for the London season. They did, however, go up to town for a few weeks in May and June, staying in lodgings at 27 Oxford Terrace, on the south side of what is now Sussex Gardens.[8] Hardy made his customary visit to the Private View of the Royal Academy, always a major social event of the season, and went with Emma to concerts by the violinists Ysaÿe and Kubelik and presumably to other performances as well. The music London could offer continued to rank high among his incentives for going there each year, and it was in April 1901 that he alluded to the recent deaths of Sir John Stainer and Sir Arthur Sullivan and confessed to a much deeper interest in the history of the concert hall than in the history of the theatre. A few years later he made much the same comment to Henry W. Nevinson, the essayist and journalist, adding that he thought Tchaikovsky's music 'had exactly the modern note of unrest' but that he liked most of all to 'go to St. Paul's to hear the chanting'.[9]

Returning to Dorchester in the middle of June, the Hardys received shortly thereafter a visitation by the Whitefriars Club, a society of London journalists, some 100 of whom came down to Dorset on 'A Pilgrimage to Wessex' and were entertained to tea in a marquee erected on the Max Gate lawn. The arrangements for the visit had been made chiefly by a journalist named Charles J. Hankinson ('Clive Holland'), whose persistent attentions and proliferating articles over the years irritated Hardy to the point of eventually refusing him admission to Max Gate. The leader of the party, 'Prior' for the day, was Clement Shorter, shown in surviving photographs as sitting next to Hardy in the centre of the group. He, too, was a man whom Hardy learned to distrust and dislike, although his multiple editorships made him useful as an occasional log-roller and publisher of 'inspired' paragraphs. Soon after the Whitefriars visit, indeed, Hardy got Shorter to put into the *Sphere* a brief refutation of an American newspaper report to the effect that the Whitefriars members had found the Wessex countryside intrinsically dull, its interest lying exclusively in 'the novelist's interpretation of it'. As Hardy tartly observed, precious little of Wessex had in fact been visited: 'The pilgrims were not absent from London much more than twelve hours altogether, returning there the same evening; and it is utterly impossible to see the recesses of this county in such a manner, not to mention those adjoining.'[10]

As the Whitefriars party drove into Dorchester along the road from Puddletown, they did not realize that the old lady waving a handkerchief to them from the roadside was Thomas Hardy's mother—Jemima having determined, despite her daughters' objections, to salute the folk from away who had come to pay their respects to her now famous son.[11] Always absolute in her opinions and now in her eighty-eighth year, Jemima had become very much a 'woman of character', as Hardy himself was to call her at her death a few years later: strong-willed, sharp-tongued, set in her ways, and more than a little tyrannical. When in the summer of 1903 the Smith sisters of West Stafford visited the Bockhampton Hardys they found that 'the talk of the daughters who showed us their treasures, and the 90 year old Mrs. Hardy, in its salt and savour, made the ordinary party talk very insipid by contrast'. Writing to a relative a few months later, Mary Hardy passed on a piece of advice that her mother had delivered 'with her old decisiveness': 'I hope', she added, 'her message will not offend but that you will only perceive she is as outspoken as ever.'[12] Though in full possession of her mental faculties, Jemima had become shrivelled in face, bent in body, and progressively confined to her bed. Her health was a constant source of anxiety, her restlessness at her enforced inactivity a frequent cause of domestic friction. Since her daughters were no longer teaching they were ready at need to devote themselves to her care, and although they kept their house in Dorchester they spent more and more of their time at the Bockhampton cottage. Kate in particular, assisted by her cousin Polly Antell (who had been taken into the household following her own mother's death), became almost entirely occupied with nursing and housework. Henry, having let his new house at Talbothays, was still living at the cottage with his mother, while Hardy himself continued as always to be a frequent visitor. It was entirely consistent with the dominance of Jemima's personality, and with that family loyalty she had so persistently preached, that her children should have rallied so staunchly to her support in her declining years.

Among the other relatives who came to Bockhampton during this period were James and Nathaniel Sparks, the sons of Jemima's nephew, Hardy's cousin, Nathaniel Sparks, who had gone to Bristol and become a maker and repairer of violins. In August 1902 the two young men cycled over from Bristol, following a scenic route Hardy had mapped out for them. Before they set off Mary Hardy wrote to tell James that he and his brother should call first at her own house in Dorchester itself, 'as Mother is too old to receive any one at Bockhampton and her house is small, which your Father will explain to you. No 12 Wollaston Rd is my house as you know, where I am supposed to live, but I stay a good deal of my time at Bockhampton especially in the summer.' In a letter dated November 1903 and addressed from 'In Mother's bedroom', Mary described to James's father how things then stood at the cottage:

Henry jogs on, not troubling much about what is going to happen next. Katie and Polly do what they can to make the best of their rather quiet life here for on account of Mother's age and illness they don't go out much. . . . Mother wants to get up but we fear if she attempts to come down stairs we shall have some trouble in getting her back again.[13]

During the Sparkses' visit to Bockhampton, so Nathaniel later recalled, Jemima spoke of Emma, in a broad Dorset accent, as 'A thing of a 'ooman', insisting that 'She were wrong for I'—and, by implication, for her son. Writing to James Sparks after the brothers' return to Bristol, Kate Hardy also made gentle fun of her mother's unrepentant use of the dialect: 'I played the harmonium in Church one Sunday because the organist was gone to Bristol. Mother said: "Well—be 'ee all Bristol crazy?"'[14] Kate's long-standing musical connection with Stinsford Church—to which she would later donate the money for a new organ—was especially important at this period as justifying occasional excursions from the cramped and somewhat difficult situation at the cottage. There was talk at some point of her marrying Charles Meech Hardy from Puddletown, a first cousin twice removed, with whom the Sparks brothers stayed for a time during their 1902 visit. But Hardy, who liked Charles Meech Hardy and sometimes employed him to do building work on the house at 51 High West Street, seems to have been among those who disapproved of him as a husband for Kate—perhaps because he had a reputation as a heavy drinker—and the marriage never took place.[15] Some kind of engagement or 'understanding' between Kate and Charles seems nevertheless to have drifted on in desultory fashion—references to him in Kate's diary are often entered in a (readily decipherable) code—until terminated by Charles's marriage to Elizabeth Veal in 1916, when he was 57 and Kate 60.[16]

Both the Sparks brothers had exceptional artistic gifts, James becoming an art teacher in Exeter, Nathaniel a distinguished engraver who exhibited regularly at the Royal Academy. Hardy recognized these qualities in his two young relatives, helped them from time to time in their careers, and kept in touch with them over the years, even though their one call at Max Gate in 1902 was marred by Emma's refusal to have anything to do with them.[17] When Nathaniel Sparks senior learned from his sons of Hardy's desire for a cello he found and sold him, at a very reasonable price, the one which now stands in the replica of Hardy's study in the Dorset County Museum: 'No doubt', said Hardy in his letter of thanks, 'the old viol has many a score time accompanied such tunes as "Lydia", or "Eaton".' And he added, tapping into their shared memories of the Puddletown of a half-century earlier, 'the latter was the tune with which they used nearly to lift off the roof of Goddard's chapel of a Sunday evening.' What Hardy could not have anticipated was the role the younger Nathaniel would eventually and somewhat controversially play as a collector and interpreter of family letters, memorabilia, and gossip.[18]

The cheerfulness with which Hardy had greeted the new century had much to do with the sense of satisfaction with which he looked forward to the preparation and publication of his second volume of verse. Negotiations with Harper & Brothers went slowly, however, and it was not until late May of 1901 that agreement was reached for the publication of an edition of 1,000 copies (half of them for England, the other half for the United States) of a book tentatively entitled 'Poems of Feeling, Dream, and Deed'. And it was not until early July that the Whitefriars Club had come and gone, and left him free to turn his full attention to the tasks of final selection and revision. Upon its eventual publication, as *Poems of the Past and the Present*, in mid-November 1901, the collection enjoyed a generally favourable critical reception—despite the uncertainty expressed by a few reviewers as to whether Hardy was writing poetry at all—and a second printing of 500 copies was ordered within two or three weeks.[19] The poems on the war which Hardy had published in national newspapers had helped to make him better known as a poet, and it was perhaps for that reason that he placed them at the beginning of the volume, preceded only by the 'reverie' on the death of Queen Victoria.

Poems of the Past and the Present marked a distinct advance over its predecessor in almost every respect. Though still extremely heterogeneous, somewhat quirky in organization, and unequal in quality, it displayed those features less abrasively than *Wessex Poems* had done. More importantly, it contained a number of individual poems of great distinction and a sequence of thematically related texts, placed at the beginning of the section entitled 'Miscellaneous Poems', in which Hardy asserted and enforced—relentlessly, repetitiously, yet incrementally—the central tenets of his world view: 'The Mother Mourns', 'I Said to Love', 'At a Lunar Eclipse', 'The Lacking Sense', 'Doom and She', 'The Subalterns', 'God-Forgotten', 'The Bedridden Peasant', 'By the Earth's Corpse', 'To an Unborn Pauper Child'.[20] In such poems, and in the three parts of 'In Tenebris' (placed separately from the other poems as reflecting a more directly personal grief), Hardy established, once and for all, the characteristic features and dominant mood—brooding, anguished, and discomforting—of his philosophical verse. God is 'unknowing', Nature blind or asleep, controlling Doom indifferent to human suffering, the speaker himself 'One who, past doubtings all, | Waits in unhope'.[21] Sir George Douglas, in his *Bookman* review of January 1902, shrewdly observed that the poems grouped as 'Miscellaneous' were in fact those which had 'the most definite common characteristics' and were most strongly 'cumulative' in their effect. Such beauty as the poems possessed lay, for Douglas, in their very austerity, but while he recognized the courage with which Hardy had given voice to his deeply pessimistic conclusions about the nature of the universe, he declined to accept the proposition that life was essentially and necessarily such a meaningless affair: 'The vast majority in this world are not unhappy.'[22]

Although Hardy had no complaints about the way Harper & Brothers had handled *Poems of the Past and the Present* or, indeed, any of his previous books, he was displeased that their absorption of Osgood, McIlvaine & Co. had resulted in his being published in London by 'a subordinate member of a New York house'. By February 1902, when Clarence McIlvaine wrote on behalf of Harper & Brothers to invite renewal of the agreement originally made with Osgood, McIlvaine & Co. for the 'Wessex Novels' edition, Hardy had already decided to find another English publisher, even while retaining Harper & Brothers as his publishers in the United States. McIlvaine protested that Hardy's defection would damage the firm's reputation, and Hardy, mindful of old loyalties, made a point of obtaining from G. Herbert Thring and Anthony Hope Hawkins, both officers of the Incorporated Society of Authors, an assurance that, since the contract with Osgood, McIlvaine had been signed for a limited term only, he was perfectly within his professional and moral rights in allowing it to lapse. Anxious to soften what McIlvaine so evidently regarded as a severe blow, Hardy allowed an extra six months beyond the end of the original contract during which Harper & Brothers could continue to act as his sole publishers and sell off as much as they could of existing stocks. He also undertook to try to persuade the new publishers, whoever they might be, to enter into negotiations for the purchase of plates and of any stock still on hand.[23]

Hardy did not approach the Macmillans until after his dealings with McIlvaine had been concluded, but it is clear that he had long intended to move in their direction whenever the opportunity offered itself. He had always been grateful for the interest Alexander Macmillan had shown in his early work, and though his subsequent dealings with the firm had not been uniformly happy he was well satisfied with their handling of the colonial editions of his novels and had formed a high estimation of Frederick Macmillan, the current head, on both personal and professional grounds. The latter responded to Hardy's initiative with understandable enthusiasm, guaranteeing that if the move was indeed made Hardy would never have cause to regret it. A comprehensive agreement was drawn up, giving Hardy a royalty of one-fourth of the selling price on books sold at six shillings and upwards, one-fifth on those sold at prices between four and five shillings, and one-sixth on all cheaper volumes; the existing arrangement for a royalty of fourpence a copy on all Colonial Library volumes was reconfirmed. Once Hardy had signed this agreement in April 1902, Macmillan suggested that even though the change of publishers would not formally take place until October, when the extended Harper contract ran out, there was no reason why the printing of titles in the new Macmillan format should not begin. Hardy agreed, stipulating only that he be allowed to make a number of minor revisions, including the incorporation of changes to the preface of *Far from the Madding Crowd* already made for the sixpenny edition recently published by Harper, and a toning down of the much-criticized pig's pizzle scene in *Jude the Obscure*.[24]

Emma, one of the most intransigent objectors to *Jude*, had also disapproved of numerous poems in *Poems of the Past and Present* not specifically identified but sweepingly characterized to Rebekah Owen as 'personal—moans, & fancies etc.' Her troubles with her husband, she insisted, would be less irksome if only 'his later writings were of a more faithful, truthful, & helpful kind', and she doubtless took a grim satisfaction in his receiving, on his sixty-second birthday, a cutting from the *Daily Mail* that, though sent in fun, could have occasioned gossip had the story been picked up by one of the Dorchester newspapers: 'For assaulting his aged mother-in-law with a bust of the late Mr. W. E. Gladstone Thomas Hardy was yesterday fined 10s. and costs at Wood Green.'[25] The birthday happened to coincide with news of the much-delayed conclusion of the Boer War, an event recognized at Max Gate by the flying of a celebratory flag. Less happily, it was also a day on which Emma had another of her accidents, so compounding the low spirits and lack of energy that had earlier deterred the Hardys from planning any extended visit to a London expected to be unusually crowded and expensive in a coronation year. They did not, in fact, go up to London during the entire 1902 'season' but stayed at Max Gate throughout the spring and summer.[26] In October, however, they made a brief holiday trip to Bath. On Sunday, 26 October, Hardy went with Emma to morning service at Bath Abbey and then rode to Bristol on the bicycle he had brought with him, attending Evensong at St Mary Redcliffe before setting off on the return journey. Another expedition from Bath to Bristol— possibly to call on Nathaniel Sparks and his family—was the occasion of his falling off his bicycle, being 'rubbed down by a kindly coal-heaver with one of his sacks', and thus becoming such an object of pity that the woman from whose shop he sought to purchase an old copy of Hobbes's *Leviathan* had not the heart to ask him more than sixpence for it. He was much embarrassed to discover later that it was a first edition: as he confessed to Mrs Henniker, had he known that at the time he would 'hardly have had the conscience to take it'.[27]

Hardy and Emma had spent a week together at Bath during the period of their courtship, twenty-nine years previously, and in 1877 Hardy had gone there with his father—evidently the occasion he recalled when telling Florence Henniker that this October 1902 visit had been 'as pleasant as could be in a place last visited to see those who are now dead'. Bath was also full of other, more famous ghosts: 'I stayed [he told Douglas] close to where Pitt was living when he received the news of Austerlitz that is said to have killed him, & looking out of window in the small hours I could in fancy see his emaciated form.'[28] However strongly the Hardys had been drawn to Bath by its personal associations, the invocation of Pitt shows that Hardy himself also had in mind the needs of the manuscript of *The Dynasts*, on which he was just beginning to work in earnest. Although a grand work on the Napoleonic period had been in contemplation from at least as far back as 1875, the final scheme for *The Dynasts* as published was apparently drawn up some time late in 1897.[29] Hardy had always intended it to be in verse, and had gradually come to conceive of it as a verse drama, not for stage performance but distantly modelled, even so, on Shakespeare's histories, with their differing levels of action and their occasional use of 'chorus' figures. The choice of blank verse for the central historical sequences was, in the circumstances, almost automatic, but there was no ready solution to the basic difficulties involved in treating of such material in verse of any kind, and he was fortunate to be free of the pressures he had known as a writer of fiction, to be able to work at his own pace and take up and lay down the manuscript as mood and occasion prescribed.

Hardy's mind dwelt much upon the past at this period, because of *The Dynasts*, because of the increasing frailty of his mother, and because of a sharper awareness of his own advancing years. During the course of the summer he had written three letters to the *Dorset County Chronicle* about Dorchester's early theatres and associations with Edmund Kean, the actor. A few months earlier, in response to Rider Haggard's request for his observations on the history of the Dorset agricultural labourer, he had welcomed recent economic improvements in the labourers' situation but regretted, as in his essay on 'The Dorsetshire Labourer', that their increased mobility had so disrupted the continuities of the oral tradition: 'I can recall the time when the places of burial, even of the poor and tombless, were all remembered; the history of the squire's family for 150 years back was known; such and such ballads appertained to such and such localities; ghost tales were attached to particular sites; and secret nooks wherein wild herbs grew for the cure of divers maladies were pointed out readily.'[30] He increasingly saw his own published works as a repository of such vanishing information, and in one of his letters to Frederick Macmillan early in 1902 he had touched upon the possibility of an annotated edition, somewhat along the lines of Scott's *magnum opus* edition, that would give 'a really trustworthy account of real places, scenery, &c'.[31]

Wessex as a literary phenomenon he claimed as very much his own property, protesting in that same letter to Macmillan how unfair it was 'that capital shd be made out of my materials to such an extent as promises to be done'. He objected, strongly and publicly, when he was accused of having caused confusion by popularizing an unhistorical identification of Wessex with Dorset—insisting that in his writings and his maps alike he had always included five other counties—and was distressed by the omission of the words 'The Wessex Novels' from the proof of the half-title of *Tess of the d'Urbervilles*, published in October 1902 as the first volume under the new Macmillan imprint. As he told Frederick Macmillan: 'For commercial reasons, not to speak of literary ones, I fancy the words should be retained. Many people have heard of the Wessex novels who do not know their individual titles. This inclusive title is, moreover, copyright, & as several writers have used "Wessex" in their productions since I began it they may annex "Wessex Novels" if we let the name drop.'[32]

Hardy's sense of proprietorship was endorsed by the continuing flood of 'pilgrims' from London and other parts. A visit by 200 members of the Institute of Journalists in September 1905 again required the erection of a large marquee on the Max Gate lawn. A year later Hardy was away from home at the time of a similar visitation by members of the Society of Dorset Men in London but wrote to suggest that he had in a sense already welcomed them to the neighbourhood 'in a rather lengthy speech of some twenty volumes, which I hope you will take as delivered on the occasion'.[33] The early years of the century also saw a proliferation of such topographical guides as Bertram Windle's *The Wessex of Thomas Hardy* (1902), Wilkinson Sherren's *The Wessex of Romance* (1902), Charles G. Harper's *The Hardy Country* (1904), Sir Frederick Treves's *Highways and Byways in Dorset* (1906), and Clive Holland's *Wessex* (1906).[34] At once amused and slightly appalled by the bookmaking he had provoked—he remarked of Harper's *The Hardy Country* that it was 'rather hard upon the landowners of this part of England that their property should be so called by these tourist-writers'—Hardy was shrewd enough to recognize that the circulation of such volumes could only enhance the sale of his own books.[35] Partly for that reason, partly in order to limit the propagation of error, he cooperated with Windle and his illustrator, Edmund New, wrote a brief foreword to a guidebook to Dorchester, and took a lively interest in the paintings by Walter Tyndale that were used to illustrate the Clive Holland volume. He worked most closely, however, with Hermann Lea, an enthusiastic Dorset photographer, who produced a first, slim volume, *A Handbook to the Wessex Country of Thomas Hardy's Novels and Poems*, in 1905 and then, in 1912, what amounted to the authorized version of Hardyan topography, the profusely—if not very vividly—illustrated *Thomas Hardy's Wessex*.[36]

Hardy was of course capable of being annoyed by the tourists and literary pilgrims who bought and used such books. He complained to Lea that he had been unknowingly 'Kodaked' while visiting the Higher Bockhampton cottage, and insisted that neither the topographical details nor the photographs included in *Thomas Hardy's Wessex* should be so specific as actually to invite such intrusions upon his own privacy or that of other members of his family.[37] Passionate believer though he was in the dictum (misquoted from Southey) that he commended to the Wessex Society of Manchester in January 1902—'Whatever strengthens local attachments strengthens both individual & national Character'—Hardy had no intention of infringing upon the privacy of his family or of publicly revealing the precise nature and degree of his attachment to, and dependence upon, his own locality. He was initially reluctant to contribute a foreword to a new edition of the Dorchester town guide for fear that his doing so would discourage the Wessex pilgrims from believing that they were 'penetrating a disguise which (as is quite true) I had no wish for them to penetrate'.[38] Lea, however, had become a trusted friend who could be counted upon to keep a confidence, and Hardy went so far as to supply the actual wording of two passages in the *Handbook* devoted to explaining that the fictional Wessex corresponded not to Dorset alone but to 'the Wessex of history' and that the towns, villages, and houses given fictional names were only '*suggested* by such and such real places', even though they might in practice be quite readily identifiable.[39] It was another step in that adoption of authorial disguises which began with the placing of anonymous paragraphs in newspapers and magazines and ended, many years later, in the ghost-writing of his official biography.

In the first week of 1903 the Hardys went up to London for a day or two in order to attend the wedding of Madeleine Stanley, Lady Jeune's elder daughter, and St John Brodrick (later Viscount Midleton), at that time Secretary of State for War in the Conservative Government led by A. J. Balfour.[40] They otherwise spent the winter at Max Gate, where Hardy continued to work on the first part of *The Dynasts*. In February 1903 he withdrew from the committee overseeing the restoration of the ancient church of Fordington St George, protesting that the changes envisaged went well beyond what he considered practically necessary, aesthetically desirable, or historically appropriate. A few weeks later he inspected a font in the church on behalf of the Society for the Protection of Ancient Buildings, and over the succeeding years he continued to make such protests as he could against the grandiose rebuilding which more than doubled the size of the church in the period between 1906 and 1927.[41]

Hardy was still acting as a local magistrate from time to time, though he had sat only on the county bench since being elevated to it in 1894, and in the early years of the new century he made a number of appearances as a grand juror at the thrice-yearly Dorset Assizes. Since the task of grand juries was not to try cases but to decide whether there existed prima facie grounds for trial, Hardy was not required to pronounce upon the guilt or innocence of the accused, nor was he involved or even necessarily present when sentences were handed down. When called upon, for example, to 'find a true bill against two murderers', he and his fellow jurors were being asked to pass judgement solely upon the technical validity of the indictment itself.[42] Hardy's taste for the theatrical was gratified by the pomp and solemnity of the Assizes, and while he doubtless enjoyed the local distinction his position conferred it would be equally true to say that he conferred distinction upon the proceedings by his presence: one of the Dorchester clergy spoke after Hardy's death of having seen 'more than one of His Majesty's judges look up sharply and curiously to identify the possessor of the quiet voice that answered "Here" to the name "Thomas Hardy" when the roll was called'.[43] Such occasions gave Hardy the satisfaction of performing a responsible social and legal function without having to pronounce upon ultimate issues of life and death, and in April 1903 it was from within this context that he rather evasively responded to an American enquiry as to his views on capital punishment: 'As an acting [i.e. active] Magistrate I think Capital Punishment operates as a deterrent from deliberate crimes against life to an extent that no other form of punishment can rival. But the question of the moral right of a community to inflict that punishment is one I cannot enter into in a necessarily brief communication.'[44]

Emma was again in poor health in the spring of 1903 and hesitant about taking London lodgings for the season. Hardy went up to 'a couple of bachelor's rooms in St John's Wood' while she was regaining her strength and summoning up her courage, and at the very end of May he accepted an invitation from Clodd to spend the Whitsun weekend at Aldeburgh with Shorter, Flinders Petrie, Henry W. Nevinson, Alfred Cort Haddon, the anthropologist, and Hugh Clifford, the colonial administrator, recently returned from service in Borneo. The talk one evening, Clodd recorded in his diary, was largely on the 'race question'; the following evening it was too various to summarize, prompting him to 'sigh for a phonograph to fix it'. In London a week or so later Clodd, Shorter, and Hardy went to Madame Tussaud's waxworks after hours, as the guests of the current proprietor, John Tussaud, who allowed them to handle the Napoleonic relics. Five years later, after reading the third and final volume of *The Dynasts*, Shorter would recall to Clodd 'how, in the incubating period of that book, we three pranced about Tussauds' by night, Hardy wearing the Waterloo cocked hat!'[45]

Emma did eventually come up to London at the beginning of June 1903, leaving Max Gate in the charge of Hardy's old friend Henry Joseph Moule, who was recuperating from a serious illness and enjoying such ready access to the surrounding countryside. Moule's wife Margaret and the Hardys' servant Bessie Churchill kept Emma informed as to the welfare of her cats and the situation at Max Gate generally, although it was to Hardy that Bessie wrote about a problem with 'the soft water pump'. Emma, however, was soon driven home again by the bitter cold and persistent rain, which continued and even worsened immediately following her departure: 'I have known about 30 London Junes', said Hardy in a letter home, 'but never remember such an one as this.'[46] The weather moderated towards the end of the month, and Hardy—though displeased at having been recognized by the other people at his lodgings—stayed on long enough to escort Lilian Gifford to the Royal Academy soirée at the beginning of July: 'It was such a novelty & a delight to her', he told Emma the next day, 'that I was so glad I took the trouble; she never saw anything at all like it before, poor child, & though I felt past it all, I enjoyed it in an indirect way through her eyes.'[47]

Back in Dorchester for the remainder of the summer, he discovered that the inconveniences of fame as experienced in London could become still more acute when brought to his own doorstep: 'The usual rank & file of summer tourists have called here,' he reported to Mrs Henniker, '& I have given mortal offence to some by not seeing them in the morning at any hour. I send down a message that they must come after 4 o'clock, & they seem to go off in dudgeon.' But he turned the edge of the complaint by describing his own experience of being shown over Montacute House in Somerset the previous week: 'The amusing thing was that the residents sat like statues, reading in their library, & without speaking a word, whilst I was inspecting it, as if they, too, were part of the architecture. They are a very ancient family, I admit.'[48] There were, as always, other callers at Max Gate—James Sparks, for example, came in early September to finish a bronze medallion of Hardy he had begun on a previous visit—but Hardy was now working intensively, and even urgently, on the final stages of Part First of *The Dynasts*. He told Clodd several months later that he had originally intended not to publish that part by itself but to wait until the entire work was ready; on his return to Max Gate from London, however, 'I had a sudden feeling that I should never carry the thing any further, so off it went'. Impulsively or not, he dispatched the manuscript to an apparently unprepared Frederick Macmillan on 28 September, pointing out—doubtless to Macmillan's increasing dismay—that while complete in itself it constituted only the first part of an intended trilogy.[49]

The Macmillan house had by this time reissued—sometimes with revisions, sometimes not—all of the volumes it had taken over from Osgood,

McIlvaine, including *Wessex Poems* and *Poems of the Past and Present*. But bringing out the three thick parts of *The Dynasts* was by no means an attractive commercial enterprise. Nevertheless, as Frederick Macmillan wrote to the firm's New York office after Hardy had submitted the manuscript of Part Second, 'It must, of course, be published although the first part was a disastrous failure, but we cannot afford to disoblige an author of Mr. Hardy's standing.'[50] Hardy was presumably unaware of his publisher's lack of enthusiasm for a work in which he had himself invested so much time, labour, and emotion over so many years. *The Dynasts* was for him an infinitely fascinating project, and he involved himself to an unusual degree in the details of its production. He it was who suggested that the spine of the first volume should carry a single star rather than the words 'Part First', since the latter might 'suggest incompleteness too forcibly to the would-be purchaser', and his comments to Frederick Macmillan on the specimen page testify to the eye for typography and book design which he had developed over the years:

The size of the print-page I note, is 5¾ in. by 3⅜ therefore I gather you propose to reset the book when, later on, it is brought into the 3/6 uniform edition, as it could not be cut down to that size without looking ugly. If it should be desirable to avoid resetting I suggest that the type-page be kept as in the old books 5¼ inches by 3 inches—the type being *small pica* old style for the main part, & *brevier* for the stage directions—so as to get the matter into the smaller compass.[51]

The proofs reached him for correction in mid-October 1903, but hold-ups in the printing of the American edition set back publication until the following January. Short as the delay was by comparison with the long years the work had already been in gestation, an anxious Hardy found that it wore upon his nerves. Literary journalists were pressing him for information about the title and subject of the new book, he told Frederick Macmillan in November: 'Is there any harm in letting them know a little?' Writing to Florence Henniker just before Christmas he regretted not having been able to send her 'an early copy of the drama' as he had hoped. It would be out early in January, he added, 'though whether it will interest you at all, or anybody, I am in heathen ignorance, never having attempted the kind of performance before'.[52]

22

The Dynasts

HARDY's uncertainty over his forthcoming public appearance in yet another new guise—as author of a verse drama designed to be read rather than performed—was compounded by his domestic worries. Lilian Gifford had again been staying at Max Gate, and in mid-November 1903 Emma carried her off on a visit to Dover and then, purely on impulse, across the Channel to Calais. Messages exchanged between Emma and Bessie Churchill, the Max Gate parlourmaid, were chiefly concerned with the health and comfort of the four household cats. On learning that one of them had been brought home after an absence at the vet's, Emma counselled: 'Keep Marky away from Pixie—perhaps also from Snow-dove they will try to chase her off.'[1] Hardy, who wrote frequently, also mentioned the cats but his inclusion of local gossip and family news suggests that he was chiefly concerned to keep Emma in touch with home and with reality. While she was at Dover he could accept her absence with some equanimity, but once she and Lilian had gone to France he began to show signs of anxiety and drop ever broader hints as to the desirability of an early return. Fearing further unheralded movements, he warned her not to let herself run short of money, since it would take time to send funds from England, and urged: 'Mention the *town* when you give yr address as I am not sure sometimes. Also leave yr address when you come away, in case a late letter arrives, but the best plan is to stay to the day you say you are going to leave on. Wherever you go (if you go anywhere else) it will be best to keep near the sea, as you may get a cold inland, particularly at Paris.'[2]

Hardy ended this letter of 21 November by wishing Emma a pleasant Channel crossing, but more than a week later, after he had himself been up to London and caught his usual cold, she still showed no signs of returning. He now wrote with greater urgency, but still without peremptoriness, as if fearing to provoke her into a contrary response:

I think your wise course wd be not to stay there *much longer.* as winter weather may bring an illness, & from my experience Friday night & yesterday I know the misery of being unwell at an hotel—much more seriously ill, alone, with a foreign doctor. . . . Perhaps your plans may be influenced by the news Bessie tells me that she is not going to be married after all, but will stay on here with us. This will enable us to go away anywhere after Christmas—not to London, but to some place where influenzas do not abound.[3]

Bessie Churchill wrote to Emma the same day to confirm her willingness to stay on and do the cooking, if Emma would pay her higher wages and employ a parlourmaid to perform the other household duties. Whether or not Emma had originally taken flight in the face of an impending servant crisis, she did now make a last sketch of Calais, dated 30 November, and return to Max Gate in the first week of December. When writing to Florence Henniker Hardy put a bold face on the whole episode: 'Em spent a month partly at Dover, partly at Calais, the air there having an invigorating effect upon her, but I did not go on to her as I had intended.' It nevertheless seems clear that he had been disturbed by his wife's escapade and that the relative calmness of his letters had been hard-won.[4]

Part First of *The Dynasts*, finally published on 13 January 1904, met with a respectful but uncertain reception from its early reviewers. The sources of their difficulty were obvious enough. Although its form was dramatic, it was not intended for stage presentation. Although written in verse, much of that verse was of an obviously and even deliberately prosaic quality. Although divided into acts, there were six such acts in this first volume, instead of the classical and familiar five, and a total of nineteen promised for the work in its three-volume entirety. Although most of the space was devoted to the re-creation of great historical events, Hardy's preface to the first part made it clear that the reader was expected to supply sufficient knowledge and imaginative sympathy to flesh out the presented material with supplementary information and understanding:

A panoramic show like the present is a series of historical 'ordinates' (to use a term in geometry): the subject is familiar to all; and foreknowledge is assumed to fill in the curves required to combine the whole gaunt framework into an artistic unity. The spectator, in thought, becomes a performer whenever called upon, and cheerfully makes himself the utility-man of the gaps.[5]

Hardy probably meant no more than that 'foreknowledge' of the subsequent pattern of historical events (e.g. that Nelson will die in his moment of triumph) could extort from the reader an intensely emotional response to scenes not especially dramatic or moving in themselves. A number of reviewers nevertheless affected disapproval of this apparent shifting of the burden of responsibility from off the author's shoulders and onto the reader's, while others were offended, irritated, or simply puzzled by the curious machinery of the commentating 'phantasmal Intelligences' and the fundamental assumption of the entire work that the force ultimately controlling the universe was that blind, unconscious power invoked in the opening lines:

SHADE OF THE EARTH

What of the Immanent Will and Its designs?

SPIRIT OF THE YEARS

It works unconsciously, as heretofore,
Eternal artistries in Circumstance,
Whose patterns, wrought by rapt aesthetic rote,
Seem in themselves Its single listless aim,
And not their consequence.[6]

Two of the most acute among the early reviewers, Max Beerbohm and A. B. Walkley, agreed in finding that the scale and mode of presentation had the effect of reducing the individual historical figures to the stature of marionettes. Walkley extorted mild humour from his proposal for *The Dynasts* to be presented as a puppet play; Beerbohm, though his final judgement was more favourable than Walkley's, permitted himself some broader touches:

I confess that I, reading here the scene of the death of Nelson, was irresistibly reminded of the same scene as erst beheld by me, at Brighton, through the eyelet of a peep-show, whose proprietor strove to make it more realistic for me by saying in a confidential tone, '''Ardy, 'Ardy, I am wounded, 'Ardy.—Not mortally, I 'ope, my lord?—Mortally, I fear, 'Ardy.' The dialogue here is of a different and much worthier kind; yet the figures seem hardly less tiny and unreal. How could they be life-sized and alive, wedged into so small a compass between so remote and diverse scenes?

Beerbohm also concurred with Walkley in finding the Wessex peasants the only genuinely human figures, marring by their very vitality the work's overall unity of effect.[7] It was Walkley, however, with his considered rejection of 'closet-drama' as a form, who provoked Hardy to write to the *Times Literary Supplement* in defence of *The Dynasts* in particular and of 'unactable play-like poems'—such as Shelley's *Prometheus Unbound* and Byron's *Cain*—in general. He argued not only that the artistic spirit was 'at bottom a spirit of caprice', so that an artist might quite legitimately 'borrow the methods of a neighbour art', but that Walkley was wrong in asserting that a work written in dramatic form did not lend itself to private reading:

It surely ought to have occurred to him that this play-shape is essentially, if not quite literally, at one with the instinctive, primitive, narrative shape. In legends and old ballads, in the telling of 'an owre true tale' by country-folks on winter nights over a dying fire, the place and the time are briefly indicated at the beginning in almost all cases; and then the body of the story follows as what he said and what she said, the action being often suggested by the speeches alone. . . . Of half-a-dozen people I have spoken to about reading plays, four say that they can imagine the enactment in a read play better than in a read novel or epic poem. It is a matter of idio-syncrasy.[8]

By thus insisting upon the narrative character of *The Dynasts* Hardy underlined its essential continuity with the world of his fiction, and, indeed, with the origin of that fiction in the taletelling of his childhood—just as he had expressed the hope, before the first part appeared, that it would prove to be 'as readable as a novel'. A little later on he agreed with Arthur Quiller-Couch's suggestion that he had been impelled to find a new form by a growing sense of the inadequacy of the novel as a means of 'expressing how life strikes us', and he perhaps saw the multiple viewpoints of *The Dynasts*, its omnipresent commentating voices, as providing a solution to that problem of philosophical inconsistency which had troubled him in novels such as *Tess* and *Jude*. The combination of the machinery of the spirits with the conventions of the dramatic soliloquy also offered a possible means of representing those 'true realities of life, hitherto called abstractions' that had at once fascinated and eluded him in *The Woodlanders*.[9] In more recent years the resources of radio have made possible a fuller realization of the text than either private reading or the occasional attempts at public staging could supply in Hardy's own day. It has also become possible to argue that those bird's-eye views of battlefields and panoramic sweeps of entire con-tinents which seemed so extraordinary in the first years of the twentieth century are potentially cinematic, and that Hardy in seeking for a narrative form more expansive and more flexible than the novel as he knew it was groping towards the methods of a 'neighbour art' that had not yet been fully born. A proposal for a film version of *The Dynasts* was in fact brought forward following the Granville Barker stage production of 1914–15, but Hardy had disapproved of that production and perhaps feared that the film would simply reproduce it.[10]

When Walkley, in a subsequent comment, succeeded in demonstrating some of the flaws in the theoretical position Hardy had adopted, the latter retorted, in a second letter to the *Times Literary Supplement*, that the 'real offence' of *The Dynasts* in the eyes of the critics lay not in its form but in its philosophy, its unfashionable world view.[11] The accusation was certainly inaccurate as far as Walkley himself was concerned, and only partly true of the reviewers in general, but it represented a strategy and a rationalization entirely consistent with Hardy's long-established habit of attributing hostile criticism to some specific cause which had little directly to do with the literary quality of the work under discussion—the 'pure woman' issue in *Tess*, for example, or the 'marriage question' in *Jude*. He may genuinely have believed that the reviewers' response to *The Dynasts* was 'in truth, while nominally literary, at the core narrowly Philistine, and even theosophic'. In private correspondence, however, he freely admitted that the work lacked 'finish'. He had been 'appalled', he told Gosse on 31 January, by some of the verbal infelicities he had encountered in the printed text, and the quality of the verse, line by line, paragraph by paragraph, would provide the theme of much of the most serious, and most damaging, criticism of *The Dynasts* both at the time of publication and over the succeeding years.[12]

Writing to his rationalist friend Edward Clodd in March 1904 Hardy was at pains to insist that there was nothing supernatural about his phantom observers and commentators: '[T]hey are not supposed to be more than the best human intelligence of their time in a sort of quintessential form. I speak of the "Years". The "Pities" are, of course, merely Humanity, with all its weaknesses.' Shifting levels, he alluded to an illness of Meredith's and to the death of Leslie Stephen ('They are thinning out ahead of us') and spoke of the recent loss of an old Dorchester friend of forty-seven years, 'a man whose opinions differed almost entirely from my own on most subjects: & yet he was a good & sincere friend—the brother of the present Bp. of Durham, & like him in old fashioned views of the Evangelical school'. This was Henry Joseph Moule, the eldest of the Moule brothers and much the closest to Hardy in the twenty years since he had returned to Dorchester to live. Two days earlier Hardy had described the funeral to Henry Joseph's brother Arthur, then pursuing his missionary labours in China, and added some observations of a deeply personal kind. That very afternoon, he reported, his mother had told him in her now feeble voice of her first sight of the Reverend Henry Moule conducting a drumhead service at the Dorchester barracks as long ago as 1830. She had known Henry Joseph Moule himself for more than sixty years and had sent to his funeral a wreath made at Bockhampton from 'the old fashioned flowers up there (which he had often admired)'.[13]

Just two weeks later, on Easter Sunday (3 April) 1904, Jemima herself was dead. The death certificate cites 'Senile decay' and 'Heart failure', and over the past several years she had been increasingly deaf, bedridden, and 'out of sight of the world'. But it is evident from Hardy's recent letter to Arthur Moule and his responses to the condolences of friends that his mother's mind and memory had remained relatively unaffected. She 'took a keen interest in the fortunes of "The Dynasts," down to 3 or 4 weeks ago', he told a London acquaintance, and to Clodd he wrote that she 'did not seem to me to be old, since she was mentally just as she had been since my earliest recollection'.[14] It is not clear that Hardy was present at the moment when his mother died—it was Henry, as one 'present at the death', who informed the registrar—but the mingled regret and relief at her passing is finely captured in his poem 'After the Last Breath':

> There's no more to be done, or feared, or hoped;
> None now need watch, speak low, and list, and tire;
> No irksome crease outsmoothed, no pillow sloped
>   Does she require.
>
> Blankly we gaze. We are free to go or stay;
> Our morrow's anxious plans have missed their aim;
> Whether we leave to-night or wait till day
>   Counts as the same.
>
> The lettered vessels of medicaments
> Seem asking wherefore we have set them here;
> Each palliative its silly face presents
>   As useless gear.
>
> And yet we feel that something savours well;
> We note a numb relief withheld before;
> Our well-beloved is prisoner in the cell
>   Of Time no more.
>
> We see by littles now the deft achievement
> Whereby she has escaped the Wrongers all,
> In view of which our momentary bereavement
>   Outshapes but small.[15]

The photograph of Jemima shortly after her death was presumably taken by Hermann Lea, who had earlier made the photograph of Mary Hardy's painting of her mother in old age that Hardy now supplied for reproduction in a number of national papers, including the *Graphic* and the *Sphere*. He also sent the *Book Monthly* a copy of a drawing of their mother that Mary had made at an earlier date.[16] Herbert von Herkomer, the illustrator of *Tess*, saw one of the reproductions, Hardy reported to Mary, and expressed regret that he had not been given a chance to paint Jemima himself: ' "Such a profile as that we painters don't get every day. It would have been a fine opportunity!" And he drew her profile in the air with his finger as if he were painting her.'[17] Hardy supplied brief reminiscences of his mother to be published without attribution in several papers, wrote the short obituary published in *The Times* and (slightly abbreviated) in the *Dorset County Chronicle*, and responded through the *Daily Chronicle* to allegations that he had neglected his mother by allowing her to go on living in the relatively humble Bockhampton cottage: 'though she was the owner of several comfortable freehold houses not far off, she preferred to remain in the original inconvenient one.'[18]

Jemima's death, at the age of 90, had long been expected, and her sufferings towards the end made her passing no occasion for rational regret. Yet, as Hardy confessed to Clodd, 'one does regret.'[19] It was not just that Jemima was his mother. She had also been, as he wrote, just a little romantically, in *Life and Work,* 'a woman with an extraordinary store of local memories reaching back to the days when the ancient ballads were everywhere heard at country feasts, in weaving shops, and at spinning-wheels; and her good taste in literature was expressed by the books she selected for her children in circumstances in which opportunities for selection were not numerous.'[20] But even on 10 April, the day she was buried, neither the background nor the foreground could remain entirely free of shadows. The *Dorset County Chronicle* simply reported at the end of Jemima's obituary that the funeral had already been 'conducted quietly at Stinsford church . . . the chief mourners being the deceased's sons and daughters'. An annotation in Hardy's prayerbook similarly indicates that only Mary, Henry, Katharine, and Polly Antell were with him at the service, and it seems clear that Emma—whether out of unquenched resentment, spousal insistence, or genuine tactfulness—had simply stayed at home.[21]

The death of his mother made Hardy acutely aware that the procession of the generations was about to falter and fail. He and Emma had no children; his brother and sisters had not married; Jemima had no grandchildren. Writing to Clodd of the gap, 'wide, & not to be filled', that had been created by her death Hardy observed: 'I suppose if one had a family of children one would be less sensible of it.' Such recognitions seem, at least in the short run, to have made not for increased bitterness between Hardy and Emma but for eased tensions and gestures towards normality. On the other hand, the diary entry Clodd made after dining with the Hardys at the Shorters' in June 1904 recorded Emma as boasting that twelve Cambridge men had 'praised her writings' and as taking 'her usual little digs' at her husband, who seemed for his part to have 'learned the virtues of silence & patience'.[22]

That summer, for the first time in several years, the Hardys took a house in London—at 13 Abercorn Place, Maida Vale, close to the church in which they had been married thirty years before—and remained there for the best part of two months. The address, however, was that of Emma's brother Walter, the father of Gordon and Lilian, and it is not clear what financial or other arrangements had been made between the two families, nor whether the deteriorating health of Walter himself was in any way a factor. Gosse entertained Hardy several times that June and July, and Emma's name made a rare appearance alongside her husband's in 'The Book of Gosse', the record which Gosse kept of his guests.[23] While they were away in London Max Gate became subject to the invasion of unpleasant odours from the new sewage treatment works in the Frome valley, and while Hardy felt it necessary to return Emma stayed on in London until she was assured that all was at least temporarily well.[24] Once she was home again, Hardy lent her his unofficial assistance in the performance of her duties as a judge (with Lady Conan Doyle) of the *Tatler*'s competition to determine, on the basis of photographs, the three prettiest babies in the United Kingdom. In January Hardy had observed in a letter to Alice Rothenstein, William Rothenstein's wife, that they were much interested in babies at Max Gate, perhaps because they had none of their own. In September, when the results of the *Tatler* competition had been decided, Emma was able to report to Shorter, as the *Tatler*'s editor, that at Max Gate they both felt the winner of the third prize was 'not a beauty exactly—he looks somewhat cross—but has fine limbs'.[25] Trivial as the occasion may seem, Hardy's participation seems eloquent both of a lingering regret for the childlessness of his marriage and of a continuing investment of some kind in the marriage itself.

Hardy and Emma certainly remained at one in their devotion to their cats. One visitor at about this period reported that there were boards laid from one piece of furniture to the next, so that the cats could walk around the room without descending—or condescending—to the floor. Another, startled at Hardy's coming to the door in his stockinged feet, was told by Emma: 'I never let him wear his boots in the house until the kittens are three weeks old, in case they get hurt.' A run of feline disasters in October 1904 began when Snowdove, like so many of the Max Gate cats, was cut in two on the railway line. Emma relayed the sad news to friends while Hardy wrote to Hamo Thornycroft, as a sculptor, to ask where he could get a chisel sturdy enough to keep its edge while he carved Snowdove's name on the piece of Portland stone he proposed to place over her grave in the pets' cemetery in the Max Gate garden.[26]

That same month news came from India of the suicide of Violet Nicolson, the author of 'Pale hands I love' and other romantic love lyrics under the pseudonym of 'Laurence Hope'. Hardy seems to have met her only once, and to have harboured reservations about her verse, but he greatly admired her as an 'impassioned & beautiful woman'. When, therefore, he was told that her suicide had been prompted by the death of her husband General Malcolm Nicolson, many years her senior, he was deeply moved by contemplation of the devotion which had resulted in so desperate and romantic a gesture. 'The author,' he wrote in an unsigned obituary for the *Athenaeum*, 'was still in the early noon of her life, vigour, and beauty, and the tragic circumstances of her death seem but the impassioned closing notes of her impassioned effusions.'[27] Much to Hardy's annoyance, the introduction he wrote for a posthumous collection of Laurence Hope's poems was entirely omitted by the publisher, probably because it incorporated so much of what Hardy had already said in the obituary and failed to offer any alternative to 'impassioned' as a means of characterizing either the author or her work.[28]

October 1904 also saw the death of Emma's brother Walter, the father of Gordon and Lilian Gifford. This was an occasion for shared distress, but also for concern as to the situation in which Lilian and her brother now found themselves, Walter Gifford having left almost nothing and his pension from the Post Office (his former employer) ceasing abruptly with his death.[29] Gordon Gifford's architectural training, to which Hardy had contributed, would prove sufficient to ensure him a modest career in local government: by November 1902, in fact, he had already left the Blomfields for the relative security of the position in the Architect's Department of the London County Council in which he remained—quiet, cordial, but uncommunicative—until his retirement forty years later.[30] But as Lilian grew older her always unstable personality combined with her poor education and extravagant social vanity to render her difficult to live with and virtually unemployable. She became a pathetic figure, drifting about from one cheap lodging to another, a constant burden on her brother, a frequent visitor to Max Gate, and a permanent object of Hardy's charity.

Although 1904 had brought more than its share of melancholy events, Hardy was in good spirits during its closing months, largely because he was working on the second part of *The Dynasts*: 'I am doing the battle of Jena just now,' he told Mrs Henniker in late September, '—a massacre rather than a battle—in which the combatants were *close* together; so different from modern war, in which distance & cold precision destroy those features which made the old wars throb with enthusiasm & romance.'[31] Although Part First of *The Dynasts* had sold poorly, it had received a great deal of public notice and been recognized as a work, whatever its faults, of philosophical seriousness, moral earnestness, national celebration, and almost epic scope. It added, at the very least, a new dimension to the public perception of Hardy and had much to do—along with his advancing age and the corresponding recession into the past of the furores over *Tess* and *Jude*—with the honours that began to come his way during the Edwardian years.

The first of these, an honorary Doctorate of Laws from the University of Aberdeen, was especially appreciated by its recipient as a gesture from that world of formal education he had never known as a young man. Although the journey north was a long one—'almost as far as to the Pyrenees'—he determined to receive the degree in person, and in sending Herbert Grierson, Professor of Rhetoric at Aberdeen, the measurements to be used in ordering a doctoral gown, he demonstrated an appropriately pedantic precision, specifying his height as 5 feet 6¼ inches 'in shoes', his shoulder measurement ('over coat') as 45 inches, his chest measurement as 38 inches ('under arms & over coat'), and the distance round his head as 22½ inches.[32] Arriving in Aberdeen in early April 1905, he was immediately charmed by the city and by the cordiality of his welcome at the university. Above all, he delighted in the ceremonials and accoutrements associated with the degree ceremony itself, and although a dozen or so honorary degrees were granted that day the reception accorded to Hardy by the largely undergraduate audience was said by a local newspaper to have been the most enthusiastic of all: 'The cheers that greeted the name of the eminent author were loud and prolonged, and were followed by the hearty singing of "For He's a Jolly Good Fellow".'[33]

For two months during that same spring of 1905 the Hardys took a flat in 1 Hyde Park Mansions—on Marylebone Road near the junction with Edgware Road—and pursued, together or separately, the kind of social round that had been so familiar to them in the 1880s and 1890s: concerts at the Queen's Hall and elsewhere; plays, including Shaw's *John Bull's Other Island* and *Man and Superman*; a conversazione at the Royal Society; a dinner meeting of the Omar Khayyám Club; a farewell dinner given by the Lord Mayor of London for the retiring American ambassador, and so on.[34] In June Hardy called on his old hero, Swinburne, at the house in Putney where he was living with Theodore Watts-Dunton, and found him looking boyish and even impish. They found no difficulty in agreeing that they had been the most abused of modern writers—for *Poems and Ballads* and *Jude the Obscure*—and Swinburne described seeing in a Scottish paper a paragraph expressing disapproval of Hardy's Aberdeen degree: 'Swinburne planteth, Hardy watereth, and Satan giveth the increase.' Swinburne himself had received no honours of any kind, but that same year Hardy lent his support to a proposal to nominate him for the Nobel Prize for Literature—something he had apparently not quite dared to do in January 1902 when the British Nobel Prize Committee, of which he was a member, had decided to support Herbert Spencer.[35] Before returning to Dorchester in early July of 1905 Hardy went down to Box Hill to call on George Meredith, another of the literary figures who had loomed so large for him in his beginning years. Meredith, though pleased to see his visitor, later confessed that he was 'afflicted by his twilight view of life' and had felt obliged to conceal his real opinion of *The Dynasts*—that Hardy could have 'made it more effective in prose—where he is more at home than in verse, though here and there he produces good stuff'. Hardy had 'no imagination', he told Clodd, and his verse could scarcely be called poetry at all.[36]

In mid-September 1905 Hardy went to Aldeburgh at Clodd's invitation to participate in the celebrations marking the 150th anniversary of the birth of George Crabbe. Emma, as usual, did not accompany her husband to Suffolk, explaining on this occasion that she and Hardy could never leave Max Gate at the same time 'until some sweet spirit acts as caretaker'. The French scholar René Huchon was present at Aldeburgh, also Clement Shorter and his wife Dora Sigerson, a much-published Irish poet with strongly nationalistic opinions. Shorter tried to draw Hardy out but, as one of the other guests recalled, Hardy 'remained unobtrusively himself, speaking in his gentle refined voice when he had something to say, but never for politeness' sake or for any other conventional reason'.[37] Though Hardy can scarcely be said to have been 'influenced' by Crabbe's realism, he certainly acknowledged him as a significant predecessor, writing in a note of about this date: 'The beauty in "Ugliness" or "Commonplace"—e.g. a dusty road. This, which has been recognized in prose, (I have exemplified it often), has not been much done in verse. Crabbe had the materials, but did not use them properly—i.e. make them beautiful—In painting the English Art Club attempts it.'[38]

As this note suggests, Hardy the poet had by no means forgotten his past as a novelist. In July he sent F. W. Maitland his reminiscences of Leslie Stephen as he had known him at the time of the writing of *Far from the*

Madding Crowd. Responding in October to a volume of stories and prose sketches by Arthur Symons, he rather ponderously questioned whether it was proper to write inconclusive 'slice-of-life' sketches about fictional characters who existed, after all, solely in the author's own imagination. Though Symons's slight and slightly precious pieces were a far cry from the massive 'documentary' novels of Zola, Hardy's general distrust of 'realism', of the 'slice-of-life' school, was founded precisely on what he perceived as its abandonment of total creative responsibility. Zola in particular, though remarkable as a social reformer, he persisted in finding 'no artist, & too material'.[39]

Hardy himself took a public stand on a number of social and even political issues during the course of the year, adding his name to a telegram protesting against the Russian government's imprisonment of Maxim Gorky and to a letter in *The Times* that called for a better understanding between England and Germany. In November 1905 he wrote to Israel Zangwill, again for publication, a letter strongly supportive of the ultimate establishment of a Jewish state in Palestine. Acknowledging that if he were a Jew he would almost certainly be 'a rabid Zionist', Hardy expressed a profound interest—originating, perhaps, in that *History of the Jews* received from his godfather in childhood—in 'a people of such extraordinary history and character—who brought forth, moreover, a young reformer who, though only in the humblest walk of life, became the most famous personage the world has ever known'.[40] These were matters on which Hardy and Emma thought very much alike, and when her husband's letter appeared, with others, in the *Fortnightly Review* of April 1906, Emma wrote Zangwill a letter of her own, recalling a childhood interest in the Jews and offering such support (to the amount of seven shillings) as she felt able to afford:

For weeks & months past I have had it in my mind to offer a mite, (I am poor *personally* on account of helping relatives) a small sum it is, but if you can imagine from what I have said, the feeling more than a sentiment, a burning desire, with which I offer it, you will accept it in the spirit I wish, yes, a burning desire to be one in so grand a scheme. I have often found too, that I am fortunate for others—and may I be so now! I have not liked to write before but I have decided to do so after reading your article & the letters yesterday but I am an atom beneath the clouds & upper regions you will probably think. Please treat this as *strictly confidential*.

In acting more independently of each other the Hardys had in certain respects arrived at a closer intellectual affinity than they had known for some years—which may be simply to say that by living more apart they had less opportunity to probe and inflame their differences. Direct evidence

as to the state of the marriage is, as always, extremely meagre, but during
the middle years of Edward VII's reign they do seem to have maintained a
reasonably stable relationship. Emma spent much of her time in her attic
'eerie', as she called it, writing, reading three newspapers a day, and keeping an alarmed eye on current political developments in England and in
France, 'the country I love most after our own—& the one I shall want to fly
to perhaps some day or other when fighting comes on here, or our beautiful
free land changes its character'. But she came downstairs to at least the
evening meal, went to London with her husband in the old way, and seems
to have felt less necessity to make slighting references to his work. Hardy
was not being wholly facetious or disingenuous, evidently, when he told
Clement Shorter, at Christmas 1905, that he and Emma were 'having a nice
dull time' at home at Max Gate.[41]

At the end of 1905 Hardy was awaiting publication, early in the new year, of
Part Second of *The Dynasts*, which would deal chiefly with the Peninsular
War and bring the historical material to a point shortly before the beginning of Napoleon's fatal Russian campaign. The manuscript had been
completed at the end of September and sent shortly afterwards to
Macmillan, where it was received with resignation rather than active enthusiasm, English sales of the first part having been distinctly poor. Proofs were
forthcoming in early November but, as with the first part, English publication was delayed by uncertainty as to the American publishing arrangements. Since sales were again expected to be low, it was eventually decided
not to print a separate American edition of Part Second but simply to send
across the Atlantic some 250 unbound copies of the English edition.[42]

For Hardy, who had never anticipated substantial sales of any of his
poetry, the completion of Part Second represented, as he told Mrs
Henniker, the removal of 'a great weight' from his shoulders, since he was
now two-thirds of the way through his task and no longer felt 'such a huge
bulk of work' ahead of him. He went on to refer to that day's celebrations of
the centenary of the battle of Trafalgar, in which Admiral Thomas Hardy
of Portisham had played so prominent a role, and to assert that his brother
and sisters at Bockhampton were 'the only people we can discover in this
part of the county who are still living in the same house they occupied on the
day of the battle 100 years ago (in the direct line of descent)'.[43] Such continuity of occupation was probably less unusual than Hardy claimed, but
the observation is suggestive of the degree to which his contemplation of the
past continued to be inextricably linked with thoughts of his own family and
his own region. Although there were no Wessex scenes in Part Second of

The Dynasts, it had sprung no less surely from that childhood fascination with Napoleon and Napoleonic times which had been stimulated by the talk of his elders, the survival of visible relics in the local countryside, and his sharing the name of Nelson's flag-captain on the *Victory*.

Hardy well knew, however, that the elders from whom he had heard so many tales of the past had not shared his own obsession with that past. He understood their songs, their lore, their anecdotes, whether personal or inherited, to have been simply a part of what they naturally and unreflectingly carried with them down that stream of time he had invoked in the opening chapter of *The Trumpet-Major*. A note dating from the period 1906–8 records some thoughts that had come to him as he walked from Bockhampton across the ewe-leaze he had so often traversed as a child: 'Thinking how at B. we are always looking back at those who have gone before, who did not look back in their time, but found the present all-sufficient.'[44] And in the poem 'Night in the Old Home', the speaker, having represented himself to the ghosts of his ancestors as a 'thinker of crooked thoughts upon Life in the sere', is admonished to cultivate a wiser passivity:

'—O let be the Wherefore! We fevered our years not thus:
Take of Life what it grants, without question!' they answer me seemingly.
'Enjoy, suffer, wait: spread the table here freely like us,
And, satisfied, placid, unfretting, watch Time away beamingly![45]

Few men can have been less capable than Hardy of letting be 'the Wherefore'. For him, as for Arnold in 'The Scholar Gypsy', such 'unfretting' seemed as idyllic as it was unrealizable, and as he himself advanced in years his imagination became ever more centred upon an idealized past peopled by faultless inhabitants. Though such conservatism—even resurrectionism—would become a source of irritation and even grief to those around him, it was for Hardy an essential source of his continuing creativity on into old age. As those of the generations ahead of him died off, so such symbols and totems as the family graves at Stinsford had to take their place, in order that the rituals of memory and celebration might still be sustained. Even the cello purchased from Nathaniel Sparks was destined not for use but for memorialization: it figures prominently in the sketch, entitled 'Silent Christmas Voices. The Study, Max Gate (Fiddle Corner)', that he drew on Christmas Eve 1905 in allusion and tribute to the musicianship of his father and grandfather, to his own childhood memories, and to the lost world-that-never-quite-was of the Mellstock Quire.[46]

23

After the Visit

O N 2 January 1906 Hardy was writing to a young woman to thank her for the 'box of sweet flowers' she had sent him. They were, he said, 'at this moment in water on the table, & look little the worse for their journey'.[1] His correspondent was Florence Emily Dugdale, born on 12 January 1879—six months ahead of his own fortieth birthday. The second of the five daughters of Edward Dugdale, an Enfield schoolmaster, and his wife Emma, a former governess, Florence Dugdale had been brought up in solid lower-middle-class comfort and exposed to a thoroughly conventional set of religious, moral, and domestic values. Quiet, studious, and 'sweet-tempered' as a girl and young woman, though always delicate in health, she first attended the St Andrew's (Church of England) girls' school in Enfield, transferred at the age of 12 to the local Upper Grade School, where she once came top of her class in 'Composition', and then, aged 15, took the almost automatic next step—given her family background and the paucity of career alternatives then available to women—of becoming a pupil-teacher.

In 1897, after spending four years of stressful teaching and frequent ill health at the same St Andrew's girls' school she had herself attended as a child, Florence Dugdale suffered the bitter disappointment of passing the Queen's Scholarship Examination for entrance to training college with a first-class placing, only to be denied admission on medical grounds.[2] This setback forced her to seek professional certification by qualifying for an Acting Teacher's Certificate, a far more exacting and time-consuming process that required additional teaching —at the St Andrew's boys' school of which her father was headmaster—and part-time attendance at Cusack's Day Training College in central London. Although often ill, especially with throat infections, and frequently exhausted by the multiple burdens of teaching, studying, and travelling to and fro between Enfield and the city, Florence enjoyed the classes at Cusack's—as her elder sister later recalled, she 'ever was a better, more willing student than a teacher'—and eventually obtained the certification she sought. But that was not until 1906, when she was already 27, by which time the repeated bouts of laryngitis and pharyngitis had amply confirmed the medical assessment made nine years previously—that her health was not sufficiently robust to withstand the rigours of elementary school teaching.[3]

She was also temperamentally unsuited to such work. Shy and melancholy, even depressive, she preferred withdrawal into the world of literature to confrontation of schoolroom realities. There were always books at home when she was a child—her father had run a small bookshop in Enfield for a time and been the local agent for the Society for the Propagation of Christian Knowledge—and an early love of reading gradually developed into an ambition to be a writer, both for writing's sake and as an alternative to teaching as a means of livelihood. Around the turn of the century she began contributing occasional articles, stories, and theatrical reviews to the local newspaper, the *Enfield Observer*, whose editor was a friend of the family. She also became very friendly with a local writer named Alfred Hyatt, sympathizing deeply with his pathetic struggle against physical and financial handicaps and admiring his capacity, in the face of such difficulties, to sustain himself as a working journalist and anthologist and even keep alive his aspirations as a poet.[4] Although Florence Dugdale was still teaching at the time she first met Hardy in 1905, she had made gestures towards financial independence by placing a few items in such London newspapers as the *Globe* and the *Daily Mail* and beginning her active if never very remunerative career as a writer of children's stories. *Old Time Tales*, *Cousin Christine*, and *Country Life* were all published by Collins between 1906 and 1908, and several others, with titles such as *Jack Deane's Reward*, *Little Lie-A-Bed; and Other Stories*, and *Jennie, Who Did Not Like Christmas*, were brought out by the SPCK. Hardy had found himself in a similarly uncertain situation before he made the final choice between architecture and literature, and it was sympathy for Miss Dugdale's aspirations and difficulties as well as responsiveness to her person and personality that first drew him towards the woman who was to become his second wife.

Florence had a long-standing admiration for Hardy's work—first stimulated by encountering the cliff scene from *A Pair of Blue Eyes* as quoted and illustrated in a volume called *Gleanings from Favourite Authors*—and in August 1905 she wrote to ask if she might call upon him at Max Gate. Hardy's response, addressed to 'Dear Madam' and signed 'Yours truly T. Hardy', was both formal and formulaic: 'As you are not going to print anything about your visit I shall be happy to be at home to you some afternoon during this month, if you will send a post card a day or two before you are coming.'[5] That very first visit—so Florence told Richard Purdy many years later—was made in company with Mrs Henniker, whom she presumably knew from their common membership of one or other of the women's clubs and professional organizations then flourishing in London. As etiquette required, the two visiting ladies had arranged to call upon the lady of the house, but when they arrived at Max Gate a horse and light carriage were waiting at the front door and it became quickly apparent that Emma had forgotten their appointment and was about to depart on some errand of her own. A page in uniform ushered them into the dining room, announced that Mrs Hardy was not at home, and sent away the carriage—leaving Emma trapped somewhere upstairs. A few minutes later Hardy himself appeared, greeted Mrs Henniker warmly, and proceeded to make tea for them himself with his 'capable fingers'. Emma did not materialize and Hardy chatted on with a freedom and ease that—as Florence later learned—was quite unlike the silence he customarily maintained in Emma's voluble presence. He escorted his guests out of the house when the time came for their departure, and as they stood in the drive Florence both impressed and moved him by drawing attention to the scent from the privet, still in flower in the second half of August. This was a phenomenon he had never noticed for himself—and a moment that neither of them ever forgot: 'Until then the faint scent | Of the bordering flowers swam unheeded away', Hardy wrote in 'After the Visit', a poem specifically dedicated to Florence Dugdale that he first published in August 1910.[6]

From the very first Hardy felt attracted to Miss Dugdale by her quiet seriousness, her large solemn eyes, her literary ambitions, and, not least, her open admiration of him as a great author. The acquaintance gradually deepened. She evidently called again at Max Gate before the end of 1905: 'I do not think you stayed at all too long, & hope you will come again some other time,' Hardy assured her in a letter dated 2 January 1906.[7] In September of that year he gave her two signed photographs of himself, and by year's end, armed with a ticket to the Reading Room—sponsored by a well-known Enfield figure named John McEwan—she was visiting the British Museum on Saturdays and holidays in order to look up references and historical details Hardy needed for the completion of the third and final part of *The Dynasts*. She later acknowledged that Hardy probably invented some of these tasks, 'knowing the pleasure I took in "helping" him'.[8]

Part Second of *The Dynasts*, published 9 February 1906, was generally well received, and Hardy had, in any case, assured himself of some positive if private responses by sending out presentation copies to a numerous group of friends and acquaintances, including Gosse, Clodd, Mrs Henniker,

Arthur Symons, Henry Newbolt, and Sidney Lee, Leslie Stephen's successor as editor of the *Dictionary of National Biography*. Gosse in particular was warm and even gushing in his thanks, calling the volume a 'magnificent success', suggesting that Hardy's imagination was now flowing 'with greater freedom' than it had done in Part First, and exhorting his friend: 'Slacken not in winding this glorious poem up to a noble and thrilling conclusion.'[9] When writing to friends Hardy tended to apologize for a certain hurriedness of execution, as he had done when Part First appeared, and sometimes went on to promise extensive revisions when the work was published in its entirety. But when Arthur Symons ventured to argue the basic inappropriateness of using verse for a historical subject, Hardy was firm in his own defence, arguing that 'unemotional writing which has no claim of itself to verse-form may properly be attracted into verse-form by its nearness to emotional verse in the same piece. Leave alone plays, some of our best lyrics are not lyrical every moment throughout, but the neutral lines are warmed by the remainder.'[10]

That spring and early summer of 1906—from mid-April to mid-July— the Hardys occupied the same flat in Hyde Park Mansions that they had rented the year before. Hardy went with Henry Arthur Jones to see H. B. Irving in *Othello*, was induced by Arthur Symons to attend a private performance of Wilde's *Salome*, and slipped in, alone, one afternoon to see a performance of Maxim Gorky's *The Bezsemenoffs*. Henry Nevinson, who happened to encounter him there, noted that he was 'in his usual mood, gentle, sensible, unpretentious', but became 'a little alarmed' after the performance at the prospect of going to a Lyons teashop, 'being used only to an A.B.C.' As they emerged from the teashop, Hardy was brought up short by a newspaper placard announcing 'Family Murdered with a Penknife': 'He couldn't get over that,' Nevinson recalled. 'The vision of the penknife seemed to fascinate him'[11]—perhaps because he associated it with the long-ago but never forgotten death of Horace Moule.

Hardy told Nevinson that he preferred concerts to plays, and he seems at that period to have taken a particular interest in Tchaikovsky and Wagner. He attended a series of Wagner concerts in the spring of 1906 and confessed his own preference, whatever the current taste might dictate, for late Wagner as for late Turner, 'the idiosyncrasies of each master being more strongly shown in these strains'. He added, in terms that perhaps reflected a sense of his own endeavour in *The Dynasts*: 'When a man not contented with the grounds of his success goes on and on, and tries to achieve the impossible, then he gets profoundly interesting to me. Today it was early Wagner for the most part: fine music, but not so particularly his—no spectacle of the inside of a brain at work like the inside of a hive.' To the more specifically 'fashionable' aspects of the season he paid little heed: London, he told Mrs Henniker in June, was 'carrying on its old games of the season as usual; though I have nothing to do with them.'[12]

Although harassed by the heavy cold he seemed to catch in London every spring, Hardy remained generally fit and well. That did not, however, prevent his being portrayed by the French painter Jacques-Émile Blanche as already far gone in decrepitude. It was exceptionally hot in London on the day in June when Hardy sat for his portrait, and Blanche—concerned perhaps to justify the image he had created on the canvas rather than to recall Hardy's actual appearance—later described how, in the excessive heat of the studio, 'La lumière froide du zenith, dans un ciel bleu dépouillé par la chaleur, teintait d'un vert cadavérique le crâne, les joues plates, la moustache tombante de mon nouveau grand ami.' Told that Blanche had made him look ten years older than he was, Hardy remarked: 'time will cure that fault.'[13] That August, at all events, he was fit enough to go with his brother Henry on a cycling tour of Lincoln, Ely, Cambridge, and Canterbury, and one day in September he cycled to Yeovil and back in company with his younger sister, probably to visit some distant cousins who lived there.[14]

Shortly after returning to Max Gate from London in mid-July 1906 Hardy had told Gosse that he was 'trying to enter into' the third part of *The Dynasts*. He worked without particular urgency, permitting himself to break off for occasional cycling expeditions, but by the end of October he was describing himself as 'distractedly trying to give something like a clear picture of that maelstrom of confusion the Battle of Leipzig'.[15] Part Third would emerge as considerably longer than either of its predecessors, but Hardy seems to have moved quite easily through its densely crowded incidents—Borodino, the retreat from Moscow, Vittoria, Leipzig, Napoleon's exile and return—with the prospect of the culminating presentation of Waterloo as a constant incentive to progress. His imagination, as Gosse had suggested after reading Part Second, now seemed to be flowing with greater freedom and confidence, and he felt more assured about his own philosophical position, both as incorporated into the structure and argument of *The Dynasts* and as capable of independent formulation. In May 1906 he had taken the (for him) unusual initiative of writing to the philosopher J. McT. E. McTaggart to express his admiration of McTaggart's *Some Dogmas of Religion*, in which he had found support for the philosophical position he had himself taken in *The Dynasts*. Central to Hardy's developed conception of *The Dynasts*, as he explained in a June 1907 letter to an enquiring critic, was the possibility that 'the Unconscious Will of the Universe' was 'growing aware of Itself' and might ultimately become not merely conscious but sympathetic.[16] It was in this sense that he was able to think of himself as a 'meliorist' and end the third and final part of the drama on a note of modest optimism.

It was not, however, a kind of optimism that made for short-term cheerfulness. As he observed in October to his old Positivist friend, Frederic Harrison:

I, too, call myself a 'meliorist', but then, I find myself unable to be in such good spirits as you are at the prospect. In regard of Sport for instance, will ever the great body of human beings, of whom the commonplace & degenerate breed most, ever see its immorality? Worse than that, supposing they do, when will the still more numerous terrestrial animals—our kin, having the same ancestry—learn to be merciful? The fact is that when you get to the bottom of things you find no bed-rock of righteousness to rest on—nature is *un*moral—& our puny efforts are those of people who try to keep their leaky house dry by wiping off the waterdrops from the ceiling.

For some readers Hardy's especial concern with cruelty to animals has always seemed mildly eccentric, beside the main point. And yet Henry Nevinson, who had another long conversation with Hardy in the autumn of 1906, was surely right to identify Hardy's feeling for animals as a logical as well as an emotional extrapolation from the wincing rawness of his response to all forms of suffering. Recalling Hardy's tales of the slaughter of game birds and of the hangings, whippings, burnings, and other brutal punishments dealt out to human beings in Dorchester's not-so-very-distant past, Nevinson commented: 'These subjects have for him a horrible fascination that comes of extreme sensitiveness to other people's pain. I suppose that if we all had that intensity of imagination we should never do harm to any human being or animal or bird, certainly not in cruelty.'[17]

To this display of what might be called his emotional extremism Hardy added, at the end of November 1906, a rare glimpse of the continuing radicalism of his broader socio-political outlook. Asked by Millicent Garrett Fawcett, a leading figure in the women's suffrage movement at that date, to contribute to a projected pamphlet on the suffrage issue, Hardy replied that he had long 'been in favour of woman-suffrage', but not, perhaps, for the usual reasons:

I am in favour of it because I think the tendency of the women's vote will be to break up the present pernicious conventions in respect of manner, customs, religion, illegitimacy, the stereotyped household (that it must be the unit of society), the father of a woman's child (that it is anybody's business but the woman's own, except in cases of disease or insanity), sport (that so-called educated men should be encouraged to harass & kill for pleasure feeble creatures by mean stratagems), slaughter-houses (that they should be dark dens of cruelty), & other matters which I got into hot water for touching on many years ago.

I do not mean that I think all women, or even the majority, will actively press some or any of the first mentioned of such points, but that their being able to assert themselves will loosen the tongues of men who have not liked to speak out on such subjects while women have been their helpless dependents.

It is scarcely surprising that Mrs Fawcett, thanking Hardy for his letter, regretted her inability to use it as planned: 'John Bull is not ripe for it at present.'[18]

Hardy continued to work on Part Third of *The Dynasts* throughout the winter and into the early months of 1907, finishing the first complete draft on 29 March at 11.30 at night. From mid-April to mid-July he was in London with Emma, again at the Hyde Park Mansions flat, and encountering, among others, George Bernard Shaw and his wife, Lady Grove and her husband, the Blanches, the Maxim Gorkys, H. G. Wells, Joseph Conrad, and J. M. Barrie, one of his closest friends from this period onwards. He went with Emma to the Gosses' on 7 June and lunched three days later at the House of Lords, where Gosse was luxuriating in his privileges as Librarian, a position to which he had been appointed in 1904.[19] When, late in June 1907, the Hardys went to Windsor for a royal garden party they travelled down in the train with Blanche, who later reported Emma ('au long voile vert victorien') as insisting that Hardy, despite the hot sun, should walk up the hill to the Castle instead of taking one of the seats in the waiting carriage. It was not in fact an especially long walk, but Blanche took Emma's imperiousness to be the cause of her husband's notorious pessimism and painted a cruel verbal portrait of her as an ageing woman reft of all her former charm and freshness: 'décharnée, l'âge l'ayant comme rapetissée, elle plastronnait, gardait le sourire stéréotypé d'antan, comme si le photographe le lui avait fixé une fois pour toutes.'[20]

The process of getting Part Third of *The Dynasts* into publishable shape began with Hardy's return from London to Max Gate in mid-July 1907. Early in August he was trying to cut the manuscript down, but when, on 10 October, he sent it off to Frederick Macmillan, he was forced to acknowledge that it was longer than its two predecessors, making *The Dynasts* probably 'the longest English drama in existence'.[21] The proofs arrived in December and by the end of the year Hardy had almost finished correcting them, feeling after his long involvement in Napoleonic events 'like an old

Campaigner—just as if I had been present at the Peninsular battles & Waterloo (as they say Geo. IV imagined of himself)'. Though glad to be almost finished with his massive task, Hardy confessed that he would 'miss the work', and as the end of the year approached it was just such a sense of residual emptiness and anticlimax that he reported both to Mrs Henniker and to Gosse, though insisting to the latter that he was not 'habitually gloomy, as you can testify'.[22] He was also discouraged by the difficulties encountered, even at this moment in time and in his own career, in placing a poem such as 'A Sunday Morning Tragedy'—rejected by the editor of the *Fortnightly* in October on the grounds that his magazine 'circulate[d] among families'—and perhaps by the news that the Nobel Prize for Literature had been awarded to Kipling, whose genius he admired but whose political views he deplored. As he observed to Florence Henniker, 'It is odd to associate him with "peace".'[23]

The Dynasts Part Third was published on 11 February 1908 to almost universal acclaim. Though reviewers sometimes questioned particular aspects of the work—its verse, its historical accuracy, its philosophy—there was widespread agreement that it was a great and unique achievement. Later critics, however, have tended to see the grandeur of the overall design as being seriously undercut by weaknesses of detail, by slack rhythms and inert language. Working either directly from the original texts or by way of an intervening prose draft, Hardy found it all too easy to 'poeticize' his sources into a technically correct and minimally serviceable blank verse,[24] and the absence of the obligation to rhyme removed the most fruitful—the most stimulative of happy invention and variation—of all the disciplining limitations to which he normally subjected himself as a poet. *The Dynasts* did, however, increase Hardy's own confidence in his capacity to write effectively in a wide range of forms, and enhance the public perception of him as not merely a great writer but *the* great writer of his day, demonstrably superior to authors such as James and Conrad who expressed themselves only in prose, and challenged only by the somehow less respectable Kipling, whose Nobel Prize could not quite compensate for his lack of anything equivalent to Hardy's capacity for sheer grandeur of description, narration, and emotion.

Writing to Florence Dugdale on 29 April 1907, shortly after his arrival at Hyde Park Mansions, Hardy had referred to a piece of work she had done for him at the British Museum and suggested that she might join him in 'hunting up something' at the South Kensington Museum the following Saturday afternoon, when she would not be teaching: 'I will look for you in the architectural gallery at 4—say by the Trajan column—But please do not come if it is wet, as you have had such a bad cold this winter.' He was anxious about the strain of school-teaching upon Miss Dugdale's rather light voice and frail physique and distressed by her exploitation as a writer of children's stories, advising her to hold out for a substantially larger sum for her next undertaking than the publisher had offered: 'the *lowest* you should agree to is 21 guineas—a guinea a thousand words. It is poor pay at that.'[25] Though their relationship seems to have remained somewhat formal—a copy of the pocket volume containing both *Wessex Poems* and *Poems of the Past and the Present* is inscribed 'To | Miss Florence Dugdale | with the Author's kind regards. | June 1907'—Hardy began to exert himself on Florence's behalf in various practical ways, not only by giving her occasional employment himself but by recommending her to the editor of the *Daily Mail Books Supplement*, to which she had already contributed a few items, and to his own publisher, Macmillan. Miss Dugdale, he told Maurice Macmillan, was a certificated teacher but would be better employed in doing the kind of literary work, including the editing of children's books and classroom texts, to which her tastes and abilities impelled her: 'I may mention', he added, 'that she is skilled in shorthand & the use of the typewriter.'[26] He also helped her with her own writing, successfully submitting to the *Cornhill* on her behalf a short story, 'The Apotheosis of the Minx', that incorporated in its structure and themes a number of distinctively Hardyan elements.[27]

The developing relationship with Florence Dugdale reawakened—or perhaps simply reinforced—Hardy's old susceptibility to feminine companionship and caused him to fret anew at the restrictions placed upon him by his own marriage. Those restrictions were partly legal but more importantly moral, at least in the sense that he had married Emma in deliberate opposition to the wishes of both their families and that to break openly with her now would constitute not only an act of personal disloyalty but an invalidation of one of the decisive acts of his life. He must also have shrunk, at this time and later, from the hostile publicity that would inevitably accompany such a step. It is at the same time understandable that Hardy, now approaching 70, should have indulged a little the vanity of knowing that other women—younger, handsomer, cleverer than Emma—still valued his friendship and that it was not altogether ridiculous to allow himself to be attracted to them. A letter to Mrs Kenneth Grahame of late August 1907 referred in passing to the young women 'in fluffy blouses' who distracted his attention when he rode on the tops of omnibuses.[28]

Lady Grove, in particular, remained an occasionally distracting presence. She was a frequent visitor at Hyde Park Mansions during the London 'season' of 1907—Blanche refers, no doubt with his usual extravagance, to her presiding over Emma's little 'at homes'—and in the autumn she sent Hardy the proofs of her book *The Social Fetich*, a lightweight and lightly amusing commentary on contemporary manners. He read the proofs with great attentiveness and occasional sternness, correcting her grammar and usage ('If you italicize one French word you must another') and suggesting ways of avoiding verbal repetitions. Alongside a passage devoted to the ascending warmth of the endings of letters—from 'Yours truly' all the way to 'Your very loving' and, finally, 'Your most loving'—he wrote approvingly: 'This is delightful! Would that some charitable person would bestow some of the latter ones upon me!' Earlier, fussing over the precise form of the dedication of *The Social Fetich*, he had permitted himself to become quite 'romantical', as he put it, over his memories of 'that dance on the green at the Larmer Tree by moonlight'. He ended that letter by insisting that he was 'long past all such sentiments', but it seems clear that they were, on the contrary, always liable to overwhelm him—to shake his 'fragile frame at eve | With throbbings of noontide'.[29]

Emma's response to *The Social Fetich* once again underlined for Hardy the painful contrast between what might have been and what actually was. Given Lady Grove's rather obtrusive presence at Hyde Park Mansions that spring, given also the subject of her book, its title, its dedication, and the handsome photograph of its author that formed the frontispiece, it was perhaps inevitable that Emma should have something to say about it. The criticisms she made in a letter to Lady Grove herself were both broad—'the disturbing elements of life generally in this present century are of such immensity & *importance* that the use or abuse of words are after all not matters of like importance'—and specific:

Perhaps you have already discovered an inaccuracy to be corrected in a new edition on page 12. In the use of the word *inculcate* with *into* instead of 'with which' & past participle. There is an infelicity in the sentence following the word 'wit' which has a different sense from unwittingly—By-the-bye 'witting' is a pretty word but seldom used—never perhaps, neither by you. You may think me hypercritical perhaps but I love words, & pounce upon sentences by early habit having to search for errors & misprints. In the daily papers how many occur! My father allowed us no *slang*, no obsolete words no *affectations* at all—'plain English'. He was a fine classical scholar & a courtly man at *home* & abroad! Good-breeding meant simple manners with much stateliness then—a combination never achieved now—all is changed—culture even abhorred by some of the self-educated '"Deportment," what is that?' they say. There is so much elasticity every way—but the old times seem best to those who knew them. However, I must own to liking a 'Cosey' & the *hot tannin* produced under it which benefits me as St Raphael's wine does invalids— *its tannin* though being COLD. Few people, I know do care for the ingredient, therefore *no* tea-cosey for visitors![30]

Though by no means unintelligent, the letter is entirely characteristic of that self-absorbed, unreflecting randomness of Emma's which had long been a source of such embarrassment and even difficulty for her husband.

In September 1907 Hardy took the trouble to comment in some detail on *Our Fatal Shadows*, Mrs Henniker's latest novel, moderating his necessary praise by a sense of what he would himself have done with the same heroine:

Of course *I* should not have kept her respectable, & made a nice, decorous, dull woman of her at the end, but shd have let her go to the d— for the man, my theory being that an exceptional career alone justifies a history (i.e. novel) being written about a person. But gentle F.H. naturally had not the heart to do that. The only thing I don't care much about is her marrying the Duke's son—whom she did not love; an action quite as immoral, from my point of view, & more so even, than running off with a married man whom she did love would have been. But convention rules still in these things of course.[31]

That his interest in fiction, though diminished, remained very much alive was confirmed by his venturing, in the proofs of *The Social Fetich*, to replace Lady Grove's rather bleak account of an encounter with an uncooperative shop assistant with a brief passage of his own that was instinct with imaginative sympathy: 'What could have happened? It was never explained. Probably there had only overflowed on me, by chance, a pent-up, well-justified indignation for heaps of wrong done her by society, wealth, or general circumstances, though I personally had had nothing to do with them.'[32]

Hardy also found himself being drawn back once again into theatrical matters, although at the local and amateur rather than the metropolitan and professional level. A programme of dramatized episodes from *Far from the Madding Crowd*, staged by Harry Pouncy, a Dorchester journalist and lecturer, in the autumn of 1907, was followed early in 1908 by the presentation of a scene from *The Trumpet-Major* as an illustrative accompaniment to a lecture in Dorchester Town Hall on 'Napoleon and the Invasion of England' and by the performance of three Wessex scenes from *The Dynasts* as part of the town's 'Maie Fayre' festivities.[33] As a perhaps inevitable sequel to these experiments, *The Trumpet-Major* was dramatized in its entirety by

A. H. Evans—a Dorchester chemist whose son Maurice was to become famous as a Shakespearian actor—and produced in November 1908 by a group of local amateurs, the Dorchester Debating and Dramatic Society. This, the first of the so-called 'Hardy Plays', attracted a fair amount of attention from the London critics, although, as Hardy observed to Harold Child of *The Times*, the production itself was unsophisticated, its chief interest lying in the fact that so many of the actors would, in effect, be re-enacting the lives of their own great-grandparents.[34]

As it turned out, Hardy had a severe cold at the time of the Dorchester performance of *The Trumpet-Major* and Emma had to go by herself.[35] Earlier in 1908 it was she who had been attacked by severe bronchitis and worried by failing sight, to the extent that she felt unable to go to the trouble of taking a London flat for the season. Hardy nevertheless went up by himself for a series of short visits, sleeping at the West Central Hotel and using the Athenaeum Club as his main base. When Emma spoke of coming up to London in late June or early July, Hardy arranged with the West Central for a double room to be made available. At the same time he raised so many questions about her health, the London heat, the discomforts of the hotel, and so on, as to make it clear that he was not eager for her presence.[36] Hardy was presumably seeing Florence Dugdale during this period—he recommended stories of hers, or perhaps the same story, to two different magazines in July and August 1908—but there is no evidence to suggest that Emma had any sexual peccadilloes of her husband's in mind when she told Rebekah Owen, in May 1908: 'My Eminent partner will have a softening of brain if he goes on as he does & the rest of the world does.'[37]

Emma, however, persisted in coming up to London that June of 1908, primarily because she was eager to participate in a large-scale demonstration in support of the women's suffrage movement scheduled for 21 June. As an active member of the London Society for Women's Suffrage she had taken part in the London demonstration of 9 March 1907; along with Millicent Fawcett, Annie Kenney, and other leading figures, she had contributed to a 'symposium' on the suffrage issue published in the March 1907 issue of the *Woman at Home* magazine; more recently still, on 6 March 1908, the *Nation* magazine had published in its correspondence columns a long and passionate letter of hers in which the general case for women's rights was advanced with a good deal of energy and force.[38] She temporarily resigned from the London Society in September 1909, however, because of her opposition to the acts of violence being committed by some of the more militant 'suffragettes', and never again became fully active in the movement. She did continue to send modest donations, but her attention thenceforward was devoted primarily, and passionately, to 'the Protestant cause', perceived as under increasing threat 'because of the aggressive attempt of the R.C. Hierarchy to interfere with our simple services & subvert free-flourishing England & *aggressive* attitude of the *Roman* C.s *generally*'.[39]

Hardy's hesitation about Emma's attendance at the 1908 rally sprang not from opposition to the cause but from concern as to the risks to her health and safety that her participation might involve. Improvements to Emma's attic rooms were similarly a primary objective of the fairly extensive programme of building work put in hand at Max Gate that autumn. Hardy had now arrived at a plateau of modest affluence that put such a project well within his means. Though the sales of *The Dynasts* and the poetry volumes remained modest, the royalties from the novels and stories continued to flow in, both from existing editions and from Macmillan & Co.'s successful marketing of its new 'pocket' editions.[40] Nor is this impression contradicted by his sale of 51 High Street West, Dorchester. Now that his income was reasonably stable and other forms of investment had become practicable, Hardy was glad to be no longer involved in the tedious and sometimes distasteful business of finding suitable tenants, and negotiating leases with them, while maintaining the property to their satisfaction too often turned out to demand something more than a simple assurance that the house was 'a particularly dry one', standing as it did 'on solid chalk'.[41]

As soon as the building work began at Max Gate Emma suddenly departed, cancelling a garden party she had arranged and forgetting to inform two of the guests, who came all the way from north-west Dorset on the appointed day. Although she seems to have planned to go only to Dover, her first communication to her husband was a postcard sent from Calais on 10 September 1908, announcing that she had just arrived there straight from London, having reached Dover and found the Channel ideally smooth for a crossing. Hardy, remembering Emma's previous excursion to Calais, took the news with what was perhaps deliberate calmness. He again wrote frequently and at some length, sending news of the three cats, Marky, Kitsey, and Comfy, reporting on the progress of building operations, and adding a cautionary note or two: 'You must mind not to be too friendly with strangers, as you don't know who's who in a town through which the worst (& no doubt best) of the earth pass on their way out of our country when it gets too hot for them.'[42] The work at Max Gate went smoothly enough, but the new plaster in Emma's room simply would not dry. Perhaps, suggested Hardy on 19 October, she should stay away until the beginning of November. Just three days later, however, she unexpectedly reappeared, hard on the heels of a warning telegram.[43]

Shortly after her return Emma wrote a lively but disorganized article, 'In Praise of Calais', that was published in the *Dorset County Chronicle* at the very end of December 1908. While admiring the colour and vivacity of the town, and especially the area around the harbour, she was sternly disapproving of some of its social defects:

The drainage still is imperfect, and the running of slop-water from the houses into its gutters is the greatest defect, which may be a hindrance to its favour with English people, who, however, find it healthy. The East wind clears all. The defect is put up with by the natives, who are well accustomed to it; but it causes surprise that the Municipal Council does not see the disadvantage of allowing its continuance, as well as some other obsolete practices, such as allowing the cellar trap doors to be open, the unnecessary whipping of horses, the use of dogs as draft animals, the trams running close to the pavements in one of the principal streets instead of starting them at a further distance—a bell, however, is constantly ringing a warning, and there being no provision for the winding up of the numerous clocks.

The complaints reflected familiar preoccupations of Emma's, as did her curt dismissal of Calais cathedral as 'not important: it holds the usual paraphernalia of a Continental Roman Catholic country'.[44] Her religious prejudices, always strongly Protestant, were now beginning to take on the stature of obsessions, and it was with the deepest distress and disapproval that she learned in June 1908 of Rebekah Owen's conversion to Roman Catholicism. 'I cannot comprehend', she replied, 'how the world of 1900 odd can turn again to Roman Catholicism for Christianity, & accept such a *travesty* of Christ's life, teaching & death! The fact that its secret stretching forth for power over the person & means of the people of our free & enlightened England should have any success is marvellous notwithstanding the inundation of nuns, bishops priests etc.' Though she did not shrink from specifically theological arguments, her main emphasis was upon what she saw as the repressive aspects of Catholicism: 'Consider, would you bear to see a near relative persecuted as a "heretic" with cruelty & say it was your duty to God. The Bible to be taken from you, & traditions & ordinances, & prohibitions of men substituted. Not to read God's truth, not to be permitted to enter a Protestant Church to hear it—not to listen or to read *this*. Ah if you read the Bible with a prayer The Spirit of Truth will reveal it to you & Satan's guile will be gone.'[45]

Emma's sudden return to Dorchester prevented Hardy from attending that evening's vestry meeting at Stinsford Church and contributing his architectural expertise to a discussion of repairs to the church fabric. Hardy's always active involvement with local affairs and local people can easily be overlooked in following the course of his extraordinarily productive literary career and his relationships with notable members of the London literary and social worlds. Friendships maintained through face-to-face meetings were no less important for leaving only a meagre record in terms of correspondence, and the much regretted Henry J. Moule had been only the closest of the several Dorset friends with whom Hardy kept in touch to the time of his death, or of theirs. Hermann Lea was one such, Alfred Pope another, brought closer in later years by a shared interest in local history. Others included Hardy's solicitor Arthur Lock, and his son H. O. Lock; Reginald Thornton, the banker, of Birkin House, near Dorchester, and the Wood Homers of Bardolf Manor.

Hardy's obligations as a JP were at least intermittently fulfilled during these opening years of the century, and he later served several terms as a governor of the Dorchester Grammar School, always mindful of the important role his namesake, the Elizabethan Thomas Hardye, had played in the school's early history.[46] He lent his sympathy and active support to the local dramatizations of his work, especially when the proceeds were to be devoted to charitable purposes, and Stinsford Church was only one of several buildings that he inspected and reported upon in the interests of their preservation. His attempt in such instances was always to reconcile associative and aesthetic values with simple realism: his impression of St Catherine's Chapel, Abbotsbury, he told the Secretary of the Society for the Protection of Ancient Buildings in September 1908, was that 'to prevent its falling, the alternatives are the Scylla & Charybdis of putting in new stones, or cementing over the old ones, exposure having crumbled them a good deal'.[47]

Hardy also took on a literary task in which local sentiment strengthened professional obligation. When, in January 1907, he was first invited to edit a selection of William Barnes's poems for the Clarendon Press, Hardy pleaded his need to complete *The Dynasts*. A year later, however, he agreed to undertake at least the selection of the poems. About a hundred, he thought, would be enough, perhaps more than enough, to cover Barnes's best work, and even some of those, marred by the presence of 'an unfortunate stanza or two of a prosy didactic nature', need not be printed in their entirety. Sections were omitted from several poems on this dubious principle, while difficulties over copyright made the task more tedious than Hardy had anticipated and obliged him to print early versions of poems that he believed to have been greatly improved by Barnes's subsequent revisions.[48] It was only when the proofs of the text had been corrected that he agreed to supply a preface to the volume, using the occasion to emphasize that his participation had been an act of local and personal piety, per-formed almost in the spirit of a translator of a dead language: 'I chance to be (I believe) one of the few living persons having a practical acquaintance with letters who knew familiarly the Dorset dialect when it was spoken as Barnes writes it, or, perhaps, who know it as it is spoken now.' He had there-fore attempted to select judiciously, introduce warmly, gloss whenever necessary, and so make it possible for something of Barnes's quality and charm to convey itself to 'persons to whom the Wessex R and Z are uncouth misfortunes, and the dying words those of an unlamented language that need leave behind it no grammar of its secrets and no key to its tomb'.[49]

Within six months of the publication of the *Select Poems of William Barnes* on 24 November 1908 the deaths occurred of two other writers who, in their very different ways, had influenced Hardy's early literary ambitions and the shape of his subsequent career. The response of the press to the news of Swinburne's death in April 1909 roused Hardy to an anger reminiscent of his indignation at the reception of *Poems and Ballads* more than forty years earlier: 'The kindly cowardice of many papers is overwhelming [Swinburne] with such toleration, such theological judgements, hypocriti-cal sympathy, and misdirected eulogy that, to use his own words again, "it makes one sick in a corner"—or as we say down here in Wessex, "it is enough to make every little dog run to mixen".'[50] The following month, during one of several forays to London that spring—Emma having again declined to take a London lodging for the season—Hardy came suddenly upon a placard announcing the death of George Meredith. Although he thought Swinburne by far the better writer, Meredith's departure from the literary scene was of more directly personal significance to Hardy in that it left him in a position of clear pre-eminence among living English authors. It was almost inevitable that he should be asked, early in June, to succeed Meredith as president of the Incorporated Society of Authors, and although he finally accepted the position he questioned the Society's wisdom in appointing someone whose work had been so controversial: 'No recent English writer has been so roundly abused by the press as I have been in past times, with the single exception of Swinburne, & he is dead.' Nor, he added, could he 'undertake never to kick over the traces again, for on one point I am determined—to exhibit what I feel ought to be exhibited about life to show that what we call immorality, irreligion, &c, are often true morality, true religion, &c, quite freely to the end'.[51]

In early July 1909 Hardy was again in London, attending the rehearsals and then the successful Covent Garden first night of Baron Frederick d'Erlanger's opera *Tess*. The adaptation by d'Erlanger and Illica (co-librettist of *La Bohème* and *Tosca*) was of course in Italian, and since it ended with Tess disappearing—apparently to commit suicide—immediately following her confession to Angel, it is not surprising that Hardy should have been left with little sense of its relationship to his own novel. The newspaper critics gave particular praise to Emmy Destinn's performance in the title role, but while Hardy agreed that her voice was magnificent he had difficulty in associating her portly figure with the Tess of his imagination.[52] He had evidently wanted to take Florence Dugdale to *Tess*, but felt obliged to ask Emma whether she thought it worthwhile to come up from Max Gate for the occasion. The question was put in an uncharacteristically rambling and repetitious letter whose very disconnectedness perhaps suggested to its recipient that it might be advisable for her to put in an appearance. It was at this point that Clodd, at Hardy's prompting, offered to escort Miss Dugdale to the opera, leaving Hardy free to take care of Emma, and although it has been alleged that Florence and her escort left the theatre early in order to avoid detection, Clodd's only concern seems to have been not to miss his last train home.[53]

Hardy found Clodd's sceptical cast of mind extremely congenial, and had gradually become more intimate with him, especially during the hearty Aldeburgh weekends, than with any other of his male companions, with the possible (though unknowable) exception of his brother Henry. Gosse was a much older friend, but Hardy had long been wary of Gosse's propensity for gossip and had not yet recognized Clodd's own capacities for indiscretion. He had been at Aldeburgh over the weekend of 2–5 July, and in the train back to London talked to Clodd more frankly than he had ever done before about his 'strained relations' with Emma and about the 'amanuensis' whom he might one day bring to Aldeburgh with him. After meeting Florence on the night of the opera Clodd made complimentary references to her in a letter to Hardy and suggested that they both come to Aldeburgh soon. Gratefully embracing the invitation, Hardy said that he had known his 'young friend & assistant' for several years, was concerned for her health and general welfare, and wanted to get her away to the seaside lest she should 'break down quite'. If she did come to Aldeburgh, he added, there would be 'such a clicking of the typewriter as never was in your house before (she is not really what is called "a typist", but as she learns anything she has learnt that, though as I told you she writes original things, is a splendid proof-reader, & a fine critic, her taste in poetry being unerring—only doing my typewriting as a fancy)'.[54]

Florence was too unwell to go to Aldeburgh at the beginning of August as originally arranged, but she and Hardy were there for a week in the middle of the month. One day, while sailing on the river Alde in Clodd's boat, they stuck on a mudbank and were left stranded by the falling tide. Clodd flew a flag of distress, Hardy energetically waved his handkerchief, and a punt eventually came to their rescue. But the local paper reported the incident, headlining it 'Eminent Authors on the mud', and Hardy became alarmed at the possibility of the story's being picked up by the national press.[55] But if Emma was as yet unaware of the increasingly important role Florence was playing in her husband's life, the relationship could scarcely have been described as secret. Various friends of Clodd's—including William Archer, the theatre critic, Professor J. B. Bury, the historian, and the Reverend Robert Frew—were also at Aldeburgh during the period of the August visit; Florence wrote to her family from Clodd's; and in October 1909 she and Hardy visited Chichester Cathedral together and then set off in company with Henry Hardy on a trip to York, Durham, and Edinburgh.[56]

Florence's availability for a series of shared expeditions during the summer and autumn of 1909 was a result of her being no longer in continuous employment, having taught her last class at her father's school in Enfield early in 1908 and subsequently supported herself by her writing and by the typing she did for Hardy and Florence Henniker and perhaps for others.[57] Though the details are unclear, she seems also to have acted on various occasions as companion to the mentally ill wife of Sir Thornley Stoker, a distinguished Dublin surgeon, brother of the author of *Dracula*. Florence probably met the Stokers through her friendship with the Irish writer Katharine Tynan Hinkson, who in October 1911 inscribed a copy of her *New Poems* 'To my dear Florence Dugdale from her loving K.T.H. October 1911'. Hinkson lived for many years in Enfield, knew Florence's literary friend Alfred Hyatt, and was friendly with Clement Shorter, the editor of the *Sphere*, and his wife, the Irish poet Dora Sigerson.[58]

Florence began acting as temporary companion to Lady Stoker even before she abandoned teaching: she was certainly at the Stokers' elegant Dublin house over the 1906–7 new year, perhaps while Lady Stoker's regular attendant was on holiday.[59] The arrangement seems always to have been maintained on a friendly, flexible, and informal basis, but it presumably brought Florence not only some interesting encounters with members of the Dublin social and artistic world but also some of that financial remuneration of which she stood so urgently in need. She was in any case devoted to both the Stokers—'my dear lost friends in Dublin', as she called them in later years—and her affection was evidently returned. They bought her a typewriter when she was first trying to break away from teaching, and at Sir Thornley's death in 1912 she inherited the considerable sum of £2,000.[60] At an altogether different level was Florence's performance of journalistic chores for Clement Shorter's *Sphere* magazine. It has been suggested that she acted as the *Sphere's* fashion correspondent for the six months beginning June 1908, but the evidence, though shrewdly assembled, is entirely circumstantial, and it is not clear that she had met Shorter by that date. She did, however, write book reviews for the magazine over a number of years, and during 1909–10 she worked for several months as a newspaper reporter for the London *Standard*, an experience she later alluded to as 'the most degrading work anybody could take up'.[61]

Although the friendship between Hardy and Florence Dugdale was now deep and intimate, it is questionable whether it was, or became, actively sexual. Hardy would scarcely have been so eager to accompany Florence to Clodd's if he had been conducting the sort of liaison for which his solitary visits to London would have provided much readier opportunities. The great attraction of Clodd's was simply that they could be together, as an accepted couple, without seriously risking Florence's reputation. There was of course a sexual element in Hardy's attraction to Florence: when, during these years, she recited to him the last line of his poem 'The Revisitation', 'Love is lame at fifty years', he cried out that it was not true.[62] But it seems doubtful whether she, with her strong ties to a warm and thoroughly conventional home background, was quite the liberated woman he had been searching for in the early 1890s, and it is perhaps significant that she confessed, many years later, to an inability to 'enter into' the lovemaking described in Marie Stopes's novel *Love's Creation*: 'a lack of real feeling on my part I suppose.'[63] Nor would it have been easy for Hardy, at the age of 69, to have overcome the reticences of a lifetime.

But Hardy was not restrained, at this or any time, by any degree of emotional reticence, and the poems written about Florence Dugdale, like those written about Florence Henniker fifteen years earlier, are full of the anguish of impermanence, of meetings in uncomfortably public places, of partings so accelerated that the happiness of the moment had scarcely had time to be realized: 'On the Departure Platform', 'After the Visit', and the poignant 'To Meet, or Otherwise' ('By briefest meeting something sure is won; | It will have been').[64] But though they are as surely love poems as those to Mrs Henniker, addressed to the 'girl of my dreams', 'maiden dear', and 'she who was more than my life to me', their persistent theme is that of 'human tenderness', of the beloved's 'mute ministrations to one and to all | Beyond a man's saying sweet'.[65] What Hardy valued above all in Florence Dugdale was a gentleness, a peacefulness, a quietness even, such as he had scarcely ever known before in his relationships with women. She was admiring, anxious to serve and to please; because she had literary ambitions of her own she could be helped and encouraged, as Mrs Henniker and Lady Grove had been before her; unlike them she had neither the beauty, the personality, nor the consciousness of superior social class to make her resentful of such patronage and assertive of her own independence.

Despite the opportunities he had had of seeing Florence in London, in Aldeburgh—where they spent a weekend with Clodd at the end of October—and elsewhere during the second half of 1909, Hardy was deeply depressed, overwhelmed by a sense of what he had missed in the life he now felt to be slipping away from him: 'I am not in the brightest spirits, to tell the truth,' he told Florence Henniker in November 1909. 'Still, who can expect to be at my age, with no children to be interested in.'[66] Precious as Florence Dugdale had become, it only accentuated his depression to be unable to see any way in which she could become a part of his everyday life. Max Gate, where he must necessarily spend so much of his time, was the one place to which she could not come: 'Did my Heartmate but haunt here at times such as now', he wrote in 'The Difference', 'The song would be joyous and cheerful the moon; | But she will see never this gate, path, or bough, | Nor I find a joy in the scene or the tune.'[67]

Though the preparation and publication of a new collection of poems was normally a period of intense absorption, the forthcoming appearance of *Time's Laughingstocks* did little to engage Hardy's energies or relieve his gloom. He had not published such a volume since 1901 and felt renewed uncertainty as to the likely critical response, especially since he had included not only 'A Trampwoman's Tragedy' and 'A Sunday Morning Tragedy'—both rejected by magazine editors as likely to cause moral offence—but also 'Panthera', which he had been advised to omit on religious grounds. As Hardy told Frederick Macmillan (now Sir Frederick) in September 1909, scholars were thoroughly familiar with the legend he had drawn upon—that of the Roman centurion who believes the figure on the Cross to be the son he had unknowingly fathered some thirty years earlier—and he had even gone so far as to rewrite the poem in such a way as to throw doubt on the truth of the events narrated. Even so, he did not 'want to provoke acrimony amongst well-meaning but narrower minded people for the sake of one poem, good or bad', and would therefore leave Macmillan to decide whether or not it ought to be left out.[68] Macmillan, with that decisiveness upon which Hardy had already learned to depend, took the view that the poem ought certainly to be published, and while 'Panthera' did indeed cause distress to a few reviewers when *Time's Laughingstocks* appeared in early December 1909, the general response to the volume was extremely favourable. Even Hardy acknowledged that it had been received 'wonderfully well', and sales were brisk enough to exhaust the first printing of 2,000 copies and necessitate a second printing early in the new year.[69]

In March 1910 Hardy went with Florence Dugdale to stand beside Swinburne's grave at Bonchurch on the Isle of Wight. Though much offended by the cross which had been placed over the tomb, Hardy made the visit the occasion of his tribute, in 'A Singer Asleep', to the poet whose early work had impinged so disturbingly 'Upon Victoria's formal middle time' and seized his own imagination when he first 'read with a quick glad surprise | New words, in classic guise'.[70] Hardy and Florence were in Aldeburgh shortly afterwards, and that spring they were often together in London, where Hardy introduced her to Lady Gregory as his 'young cousin' and Florence published in the London *Standard*, for which she was perhaps still working, the article she had written, with Hardy's active cooperation, to mark the occasion of his seventieth birthday, 2 June 1910. Clodd's own seventieth birthday was due at the end of that same month and Hardy persuaded him to 'sit' for a similar article, also to be written by 'my secretary Miss Dugdale'.[71]

24

A Funeral

EMMA was also nearing 70, and had been in indifferent health for some years. In May 1906, while gardening at Max Gate, she suffered a seizure of some kind: 'My heart seemed to stop; I fell, and after a while a servant came to me.'[1] Her description of this as her 'first strange fainting-fit' suggests that it was followed by others, but by 1910 her general health had markedly improved. She resumed cycling that summer after having felt well enough in the spring to accompany her husband to London and renew her private assault upon the world of letters. It was, as usual, Hardy who found, at 4 Blomfield Terrace in Maida Vale, what was to prove their last London flat, and Emma followed at the beginning of May, bringing with her one of the Max Gate maids to answer the door and do the shopping.[2] It was at just this moment that the death of Edward VII occurred. Hardy watched the funeral procession from the vantage point of the Athenaeum Club and on his own birthday, two weeks later, he was moved by the reflection that he was, at 70, a year older than the dead king.[3]

Now that he had, as it were, officially reached old age he determined to find a way of drawing Florence Dugdale more directly and permanently into the basic rhythms of his life. Since the relationship did not involve him in technical 'infidelities' to Emma, it was exasperating that it should have to be conducted with such discretion. Since he could make good use of Florence's secretarial skills and she—with feelings intricately compounded of personal affection, literary idealism, and sheer dislike of journalism—was only too eager to place them at his service, it seemed ridiculous that he should not be able to avail himself of such assistance on a more regular basis. Florence and Emma were both members of the Lyceum Club, founded in 1904 as a meeting place for women with literary and other intellectual interests, and it was apparently at this time, and perhaps at Hardy's suggestion, that Florence ingratiated herself with Emma at a Lyceum Club event by coming forward to help her when she got into a muddle with the pages of a speech she was supposed to be delivering. It was certainly in early June 1910 that Florence received an invitation to one of Emma's 'at homes' at Blomfield Terrace, and it was Hardy himself who saw to it that Lady Grove and the novelist May Sinclair were invited on the same day—perhaps on the principle that the presence of women with whom he was already known to be friendly might prevent Emma from divining the true nature of his relationship with Miss Dugdale.[4]

Emma responded with eager impulsiveness to Florence's quiet charm and readiness to be of service. At the next Thursday 'at home' but one Florence was given the honour of pouring out the tea; in early July, when Emma had already left for Max Gate, Florence wrote to assure her that she had visited the Blomfield Terrace flat as requested and found that all was well; and later that same month she went down to Max Gate in person as Emma's guest and assistant.[5] By this time she was on intimate terms with Emma, encouraging her literary ambitions and Protestant prejudices, typing her manuscripts—religious writings in prose and verse, the memories of her childhood later published as *Some Recollections*, even her ageing Cornish romance 'The Maid on the Shore'—and doing her best to get them published. They talked of collaborating in a novel, and Florence, without being at all religious, was sufficiently anti-Catholic to be able to enter sympathetically into Emma's 'campaign' against the infiltration of the Church of England by the forces of Rome.[6] Because Florence's surviving letters to Emma during the latter half of 1910 contain praise of writings which she must have known were of little value, and endorsement of attitudes which she must have thought extreme and even obsessive, it is easy to accuse her of hypocrisy and callous deception. But it is clear that she felt a genuine affection and sympathy for Emma, that she was amused and occasionally charmed by her lively if disconnected chatter, and that she believed it to be the course of kindness to indulge her in schemes and ambitions which, however unrealistic, did no one any harm. Emma, after all, was an elderly lady of 70, forty years Florence's senior; she was also technically the patroness, Florence the protégée; and on neither ground would the latter have felt it appropriate to venture upon criticisms and contradictions.

Florence of course knew that the continuation of her relationship with Hardy made it important for her to remain on good terms with Emma. But she may never have permitted herself to think very deeply about what she was doing or where it might lead her. She can scarcely have indulged in any thoughts of marrying Hardy—there was no reason to think that Emma would die first or soon—and if she was not Hardy's mistress, she had no reason to feel that she was doing anything particularly wrong. It is in any case perfectly clear that as she got to know both Hardy and Emma better, and saw at first hand what conditions at Max Gate were like, her sympathies became for a time quite evenly balanced. By 23 June 1910, when she met Clodd to talk over the article she was writing about him, she had already decided that Hardy was 'a great writer, but not a great man'.[7]

By the autumn of 1910 Florence had become accepted almost as a regular part of the Hardy household. Miss Dugdale, 'my handyman, as I call her', had arrived with her typewriter the previous day, Hardy told Clodd on 15 November, and on that same date he mentioned in a letter to Henry Newbolt that a 'friend' who was staying at Max Gate had read some of Newbolt's poems to Emma and himself the previous evening.[8] Even before that visit, however, Florence confided to Clodd—with an indiscretion that would have deeply shocked Hardy had he known of it—that she had learned to view the 'Max Gate menage' in a somewhat comic and ironical light. Although Hardy had professed to be in despair over the death of Kitsey, his favourite cat, his letters showed that he was nonetheless 'very pleasurably excited' over the forthcoming Dorchester production of a dramatization of *Under the Greenwood Tree*, and that he was taking 'a melancholy pleasure' in devising an inscription for Kitsey's headstone in the Max Gate pets' cemetery.[9] When Florence accused him of ingratitude in daring to write of Kitsey, 'That little white cat was his only friend', Hardy only smiled and protested that he was not writing about himself exactly but about some 'imaginary man in a similar situation'—and the poem did eventually take the shape now known as 'The Roman Gravemounds'. Emma, Florence reported, remained 'good to me, beyond words', and grew more affectionate than ever: 'I am *intensely* sorry for her,' she added, 'sorry indeed for both.'[10]

Hardy managed to tie Florence more tightly to him in a number of ways during the course of her various visits to Max Gate that autumn. He took her to visit his sisters at Higher Bockhampton; he had her sketched by William Strang when he came down in September to make a portrait of Hardy himself; and the date 25 September 1910 and the words 'Maiden Castle' attached to a tiny bunch of dried flowers evidently memorialize an occasion of special emotional significance.[11] None of this made life at Max Gate any easier for Florence. Precisely because of the sympathy she felt for both husband and wife it became increasingly painful for her to be a witness, sometimes the occasion, of an antagonism that always threatened to burst out into violent quarrels. During the November visit Emma not only suggested to Florence that they should go off to Boulogne together, because that would 'have a good effect on TH', but insisted that Hardy looked very like Crippen, a notorious murderer then much in the news. She added that she quite expected to find herself dead in the cellar one morning. When Florence returned a month later to spend Christmas at Max Gate she had to endure, on Christmas Day itself, an appalling quarrel between Hardy, who wanted to take her with him to Bockhampton to visit his sisters, and Emma, who declared that the sisters would poison Florence's mind against her. The upshot was that Hardy went off by himself, Emma 'went up to her attic-study to write her memoirs', and Florence was left alone for several hours, vowing 'that no power on earth would ever induce me to spend another Christmas day at Max Gate'.[12] Thenceforward, she seems to have avoided visiting Max Gate while Hardy and Emma were both present. She nevertheless continued her friendship with Emma, though dodging the threatened visit to Boulogne by suggesting, on her father's authority, that it would be too cold for a winter holiday.[13]

It was during this period of private distress that Hardy received some of his most cherished public honours. In November 1908 he had gently declined the offer of a knighthood from the Prime Minister, H. H. Asquith—who would nevertheless include him among the Liberal sympathizers listed as potential recipients of peerages during the Parliament Bill crisis of 1913. In June 1910, however, the name of Thomas Hardy appeared in the first Birthday Honours List of the new king, George V, as a recipient of the Order of Merit, a greater and more appropriate distinction, and less invidious in social terms. Among the many letters of congratulation he received, that from Evangeline Smith sounded the happiest note: 'How pleased your dear Mother would have been!'[14] Emma, who would dearly have liked to become Lady Hardy, subsequently complained that it was characteristic of her husband's selfishness that he would accept honours for himself only. Hardy was nervous in advance of the investiture on 19 July, and Florence Dugdale was asked, independently, by Hardy's sisters and by Emma herself (who remained at Max Gate), to keep an eye upon him that day and see that he was properly dressed. All went off well enough, although Hardy feared that he had 'failed in the accustomed formalities' and was so flustered when he rejoined Florence that he could not at first find the insignia of the Order, which he had dropped, loose, into one of his pockets.[15]

Four months later, on 16 November 1910, Hardy received the freedom of the Borough of Dorchester. Although the honour was long overdue, and even now had perhaps been extracted from doubtful councilmen only by the recent royal distinction of the Order of Merit, it meant more to him, precisely because it was local, than any national or international recognition could do. His satisfaction was reflected in the unusual length and eloquence of his speech of thanks, which turned both on the need to preserve the visible relics of the local past and on the sadness of the realization that the 'human Dorchester' he had once known could not be so preserved. He had now, he said, to go to the cemetery to find 'the Dorchester that I knew best. There the names on the white stones, one after the other, recall the voices, cheerful and sad, anxious and indifferent, that are missing from the dwellings and pavements.' The speech itself was a deeply felt testimony to his sense of local identification, made all the more poignant by its being immediately followed, that same evening, by *The Mellstock Quire*, the dramatization of *Under the Greenwood Tree* done by A. H. Evans, the Dorchester chemist, and performed by an entirely local cast. The peculiar emotional significance of the occasion was further intensified by its being probably the only time in his life when Hardy was present in the same room not only with his brother and his sisters and with Emma, who sat beside him on the platform in elaborate evening dress, but also with Florence Dugdale.[16]

Although Florence Dugdale no longer visited Max Gate when Hardy was there, she still saw him with some frequency. A visit to Weymouth enabled her to be at Higher Bockhampton for the celebration of his seventy-first birthday on 2 June 1911. Earlier in the year she had accompanied Hardy, his brother, and her own sister Constance on a visit to Lichfield, Worcester, and Hereford cathedrals, and shortly after Hardy's birthday she joined in a similar expedition to Carlisle and the Lake District that Hardy had planned as an alternative to staying in London and experiencing the excitements and discomforts associated with the coronation of King George V—to which he had been officially invited but from which he excused himself on grounds of 'unavoidable circumstances'.[17] Also of the Lakes party was Florence's father, who had long been aware of the friendship between Florence and a man considerably older than himself. In contriving such groupings Hardy was as always concerned to avoid compromising Florence's own situation, but he seems at this period to have had the further goal of bringing about a marriage between Constance Dugdale and his own 60-year-old bachelor brother, partly because he saw such a marriage as beneficial to both the potentially contracting parties, but also because it promised to provide occasion and excuse for Florence to visit Dorset more often.[18]

In late July Florence went with Emma to the seaside resort of Worthing for what she rather surprisingly described to Mary Hardy as 'a delightful fortnight', during which she went swimming once and sometimes twice a day. She seems not to have accompanied Hardy and Kate in a tour of north Somerset and south Devon that was cut short because of the hot weather,[19] but she was certainly in Weymouth for a week or two in early October, and in early December one of Hardy's sisters—presumably Kate, Mary's health having been declining for some time and beginning to give cause for anxiety—acted as chaperone for an expedition to Bath, Gloucester, and Bristol. Shortly afterwards Hardy sent Florence a card bearing, cryptically enough, a text from Galatians: 'Ye have been called unto liberty.' The message sounds significant and may indeed have been so, given that the remainder of the same verse reads: 'only use not liberty for an occasion to the flesh, but by love serve one another.' On the other hand, it may simply have registered Hardy's sense of Florence's relief at being released from the constant companionship of Kate, whose ebullient temperament and country manners she could well have found a little oppressive. Florence on her return home reported to Clodd that Hardy seemed well and even light-hearted, and that she had concluded—since Mrs Henniker during a recent visit to Dorchester had also found him in excellent spirits—that his depressive moods ought not to be taken too seriously.[20]

Florence, whom Hardy was now addressing as 'My dearest F.', was still doing occasional typing for Emma, for Hardy himself, and especially for Mrs Henniker. But she was also writing things of her own, and although she found a ready if poorly paying market for most of her children's stories she continued to depend a good deal on Hardy's assistance in her ventures into adult fiction. He was again active in securing acceptance of her story 'The Scholar's Wife', and of a distinctly feeble little sketch called 'Trafalgar! How Nelson's Death Inspired the Tailor'. And the intimacy of his involvement in the composition and publication of 'Blue Jimmy the Horse-Stealer', published over Florence's name in the February 1911 issue of the *Cornhill*, has recently been revealed by close analysis of its surviving page proofs and traceable sources.[21]

Still more remarkable in some respects was his unproven yet almost certain collaboration in a trio of children's books illustrated by E. J. Detmold, twin brother of C. M. Detmold and a much-admired animal painter in his own right. In each of the three large and matching volumes, *The Book of Baby Beasts* (1911), *The Book of Baby Birds* (1912), and *The Book of Baby Pets* (1915), Florence Dugdale is named as the author of the brief prose 'descriptions' that accompany each of the full-page Detmold illustrations. Each such prose piece, however, is preceded by a short poem, also evocative of the creature in question, and for these poems no authorship is ascribed. It has been, and remains, a reasonable assumption that since the poems were clearly not part of Detmold's contribution to the books, they must have been written by Florence Dugdale. But three of the poems, one from each volume, have long been accepted as the work of Hardy himself,[22] and since they are so similar in kind and competence to the other fifty-four lively, amusing, sometimes poignant, occasionally casual, but generally skilful poems for children that the volumes contain it is no less reasonable to speculate that Hardy was the author of all of them—including, for example, 'The Llama', from *The Book of Baby Beasts*:

THE LLAMA

Mere beast of burden though I be
I am proud of my utility;
And therefore should not feel depressed
But for one fact to be confessed:
It is that, being a simple Llama—
An understudy in Nature's drama
Of him that heads our family,
The Camel—large compared with me,
(I only carry a hundredweight
And he a thousand as his freight)—
I feel myself looked down upon
In pitying comparison,
As if, whatever my application,
I only were an imitation.

However, now, as I have heard
Without much grief, Mules are preferred.[23]

That such poems do not clamour for inclusion in the Hardyan canon can undoubtedly be argued. Most of them, on the other hand, are at least as successful as the three already admitted there, and they all have interest as potential witnesses to his humour, his sympathy with animals (as in 'The Polar Bear', 'The Elephant', and many others), his basic poetic skills, his fondness for writing under cover, and, by no means least, his attachment to Florence Dugdale. There is absolutely no indication that Florence herself ever wrote verse, let alone verse so consistently combining simplicity with dexterity, but ample evidence, on the other hand, of the ease with which Hardy himself could turn off a poem. Specific evidence also exists of his active cooperation in the *Baby* books project. In a note to Florence attached to his pencilled manuscript of 'The Yellow-Hammer', written for *The Book of Baby Birds*, Hardy wondered whether the poem might be ornithologically inaccurate, then added: 'If so, will write a different verse.' Archival research has yet to produce further confirmation of Hardy's authorship of these poems, but their imaginative sympathy and technical deftness certainly tend to endorse the contention of Bernard Jones, their perceptive editor, that 'To read all of them with an awareness of their original [i.e. *'Baby'* book] context is to come irresistibly to the conclusion that they can be no one else's.'[24]

In the aftermath of *The Dynasts*, Hardy's own work was going well, and he was becoming increasingly at ease with himself as a poet. For whatever reasons—his long apprenticeship in both verse and prose, the sheer creative tenacity that drove him to worry at lines until he got them exactly right, the trenchant simplicity of his assumption that poetry was an entirely natural medium of human expression and, as such, entirely appropriate to almost any human situation—Hardy found that verse flowed, not freely perhaps but certainly frequently, from his pen. The editors of periodicals often asked him for poems, he told Sir Frederick Macmillan in September 1910: 'Tragic narrative poems, like the Trampwoman's Tragedy, seem to be liked most, & I can do them with ease.'[25] The years 1910–12 would, in the event, prove more remarkable for love poems such as 'To Meet, or Otherwise', for brooding philosophical excursions such as 'A Plaint to Man' and 'God's Funeral', and for demonstrations such as his *Titanic* verses, 'The Convergence of the Twain', of the extraordinary gift for the occasional poem that would have equipped him to be an outstanding Poet Laureate.[26] His religious and social opinions were not, however, to everyone's taste, and when the position became vacant in 1913 the choice fell on Robert Bridges—who was, as Hardy himself decorously observed, 'on the whole, a very good, & what is more, a safe man'.[27]

There was a garden party at Max Gate in September 1911 and Hardy gave active support that autumn to the forthcoming production by the Dorchester amateurs of a double bill consisting of his own play *The Three Wayfarers*, adapted from the story called 'The Three Strangers', and a dramatization of 'The Distracted Preacher' by A. H. Evans.[28] He also became deeply involved in the preparation of an Anglo-American *édition de luxe* of all his works, verse as well as prose, which had recently been agreed upon, and when in early 1912 the arrangements with the American publisher unexpectedly collapsed, he readily welcomed Sir Frederick Macmillan's alternative proposal for the production by his own firm of a 'definitive' edition with a first printing of 1,000 copies and a price of 7s. 6d. per volume, of which 1s. 6d. would go to the author.[29] Writing to Florence Henniker about the original American proposal, Hardy had described himself as 'not altogether elated' at the prospect of 're-reading old books of mine, written when my spirits were brisker than they are now, & full of artistic errors which cannot be altered'. That he was nevertheless deeply and actively concerned for the accuracy of his own texts emerges strongly from what he was saying to Macmillan at about the same time: 'Lying awake last night,' he wrote on 28 June 1911, 'I was thinking that unless I correct those proofs myself there will be errors in the text—of a minute (the worst) kind—that will endanger the reception of the edition by our reviewers, & by impairing its value in a literary point of view, injure its commercial success. . . . The fact is that the literary insight of America cannot be depended upon.'[30] Though disappointed that he was still not to receive, as Stevenson, James, and Kipling had already done, 'the dignity of an edition-de-luxe',[31] he was well satisfied with the alternative Macmillan proposal and the associated design and production arrangements.

To this Wessex Edition, as Macmillan had suggested it be called, Hardy proceeded to devote weeks and even months of concentrated work, giving all his texts a thorough revision, updating his authorial prefaces, adding a new 'General Preface', and dividing the prose volumes into categories that would have the effect of separating the major from the lesser works and at the same time, as he told Macmillan, give reviewers something to write about.[32] He also supplied Macmillan with his own map of his fictional Wessex, suggesting that it could either be used as it stood or be professionally redrawn with the addition of ships, fishes, trees, and other decorative devices such as the old mapmakers had affected. Macmillan chose the second of these alternatives and the map as published in each of the Wessex volumes was duly provided with whale- and dolphin-crowded seas. It was Hardy, too, who specified both the photographer (Hermann Lea) and the individual photographs to be used as frontispieces to the successive volumes.[33]

The experience of reading through his own work was, on the whole, deeply satisfying. During the process of correcting the proofs of *The Return of the Native*, he told Florence Dugdale on 22 April 1912, 'I got to like the character of Clym before I had done with him. I think he is the nicest of all my heroes, and *not a bit* like me.' Reading *The Woodlanders* for the first time in many years, he found that he liked it '*as a story*, the best of all. Perhaps that is owing to the locality and scenery of the action, a part I am very fond of.'[34] Though this scarcely amounts to the self-congratulatory pleasure that so charmingly exudes from the pages of Henry James's preface to the New York Edition of *The Ambassadors*, it is an indication—among many others— that Hardy's tendency in later years to make deprecating remarks about his fiction was chiefly a strategy for insisting upon the less generally acknowledged excellence of his verse. In a conversation with Gosse in early September 1912 he even canvassed the merits of *Desperate Remedies*: 'A melodrama, of course,' Gosse reported him as saying, 'but better as a story than one would think. Have you read it lately? Don't you think, just as a story, it is rather good? Of course, I put all that in just in obedience to George Meredith. He said there must be a story. I did not care.' Hardy spoke of the novel, Gosse recalled, 'as if it was some book written a long time ago, by someone who was no longer of much importance'.[35]

Hardy had displayed much the same modesty the previous year when he allowed, and even encouraged, Sydney Cockerell, director of the Fitzwilliam Museum in Cambridge, to take away several of his most important manuscripts and present them to institutional libraries on both sides of the Atlantic. The task was entrusted to Cockerell, whom he had only just met, not just because he was impressed by Cockerell himself and by his past role as secretary to William Morris and the Kelmscott Press, but because he genuinely and indeed characteristically felt that it would 'not be becoming for a writer to send his own MSS to a museum on his own judgement'. He therefore specified that negotiations should be carried through without publicity of any kind and that the distribution should be made entirely on Cockerell's responsibility rather than his own. Cockerell did, in the event, obtain Hardy's approval for his dispositions, which saw the manuscripts of *Tess of the d'Urbervilles* and *The Dynasts* go to the British Museum, *The Trumpet-Major* to the Royal Library at Windsor Castle, *A Group of Noble Dames* to the Library of Congress, *Wessex Poems* (complete with its drawings) to the Birmingham City Museum and Art Gallery, and—not altogether surprisingly—both *Jude the Obscure* and *Time's Laughingstocks* to the Fitzwilliam Museum itself.[36]

Modesty did not, however, prevent Hardy from taking pleasure in the further honours which came his way, especially those conferred by his literary colleagues. Indeed, his pleasure seems to have been enhanced by the very unexpectedness of such recognition, as if it had never ceased to amaze him that he had somehow become a great man in the world's eyes without ever ceasing to be rather an insignificant figure in his own. When in 1912 the Royal Society of Literature decided to present him with its gold medal on the occasion of his seventy-second birthday, he asked that the occasion be private, and Henry Newbolt and W. B. Yeats duly went down to Max Gate to make the presentation on the Society's behalf. Already made uncomfortable by the absence of other guests, and by the awkwardness of a lunch at which Hardy talked exclusively with Newbolt about architecture while Emma discoursed to Yeats upon the lives and habits of the two cats who sat on the table beside her plate, the visitors were moved to protest at Hardy's determination to exclude his wife from the ceremony proper. Emma also 'remonstrated' at first, but when Hardy stood firm she quietly left the room and the presentation went forward with all the formality of a public occasion. When the time came for his expression of thanks—which took the form of a warning against the increasing corruption of the English language—Hardy insisted on reading the speech aloud, explaining that he had already supplied copies to the London newspapers, who would report that he had addressed the deputation, and that it would not be proper of him to turn them into liars.[37]

Hardy's behaviour on this occasion lends some colour to Emma's frequent complaint that her husband wanted all the glory for himself and would share none of it with her. Some years earlier she had warned Clement Shorter that he had better not publish a portrait of her in the pages of the *Sphere*: 'I think the photo: must be returned—as I fear that T.H: will not like it added to his affairs he has an *obsession* that I must be kept out of them lest the dimmest ray should alight upon me of his supreme story—"*This to please his family*," chiefly. He is like no other man—or himself as "*was*"'.[38] On the other hand, Hardy perhaps had some justification for feeling that the award was indeed being made to him alone—despite the claims Emma had so often made of having written much of the fiction herself—and for fearing that the occasion might be marred by some embarrassing intervention on her part. By that summer of 1912 her eccentric behaviour, shifting between paranoiac protest, childish playfulness, and aggressive religiosity, had become very marked, showing itself not only in her public and domestic behaviour but also in the writings, both verse and prose, to which she now devoted so much of her time.

At the very beginning of 1911 Emma had completed 'Some Recollections', that charming evocation of her childhood and of her first meeting with her husband, and incorporated into its final paragraph a declaration not only of religious faith but of an essentially optimistic and even cheerful attitude towards life that could scarcely have been more at odds with her husband's world view:

I have some philosophy and mysticism, and an ardent belief in Christianity and the life beyond this present one, all which makes any existence curiously interesting. As one watches *happenings* (and even if should occur *unhappy happenings*) outward circumstances are of less importance if Christ is our highest ideal. A strange unearthly brilliance shines around our path, penetrating and dispersing difficulties with its warmth and glow.[39]

Against this happier aspect of Emma's faith must be set its darker, more obsessive side. Her violent hatred of Catholicism was reflected in her support for a wide range of Protestant organizations: her charitable contributions for the year 1909 included, in addition to a number of societies in aid of animals and children, the National Church League, the Protestant Alliance ('against all encroachments of Popery'), the Evangelical Alliance, the Children for Protestantism, Protestantism in Parliament, the Tower Hamlets Mission, and the Christian Colportage Association for England. Colportage was Emma's special field of evangelical endeavour. She was a great believer in the efficacy of pamphlets and much given, in and out of season, to leaving them in the shops and houses she visited. As she told a young relative in October 1911: 'I have been scattering beautiful little booklets about—which may, I hope, help to make the clear atmosphere of pure Protestantism in the land to revive us again—in the *truth*—as I believe it to be. So I send you some of them. Do read & *pass them on*.'[40]

At the end of 1911 Emma arranged with a Dorchester printer for the private printing of a slim volume entitled *Alleys* which contained fifteen of her poems, ranging from the little nature poem 'Spring Song' to the ponderously patriotic 'God Save Our Emperor-King', structured as an 'antiphon' between India and Great Britain and bearing the very recent date of November 1911. 'Ten Moons', the most interesting of a small group of what might perhaps be called visionary poems, was rendered unduly mysterious by printing errors—especially one which rendered the 'world' of line 2 as 'whirled'—that have here been corrected:

> In misery whirled
>   Is this One-Moon world,
>   But there's no sorrow or darkness there
>   In that mighty Planet where
> There is no night.
>   Ten moons ever revolving
> All matter its long years resolving
>   To sweetness and light.[41]

A fuller exposition of her religious beliefs appears in the similarly printed prose volume *Spaces*, subtitled 'An exposition of Great Truths by a new treatment', and dated from Max Gate in April 1912. Its contents consist of a rhapsody on 'The High Delights of Heaven', a homily on the need to be an 'acceptor' rather than a 'non-acceptor' of God's salvation, a vision of the Day of Judgement, and a brief dramatic dialogue depicting Satan's ejection from Heaven. That third part, headed 'The New Element of Fire', contains a very specific timetable for the Day of Judgement itself:

The Last Day must not be considered as literally a day of twenty-four hours more or less, but as any prolongation, neither must the sound of the Trumpet—that awful call—be supposed to be one sudden shout, for the Divine order is usually slow, lengthy, culminating from an almost unnoticeable beginning. So will the end of all here on earth follow that order—an earthly day is, as it were, a hundred years or more by heavenly reckoning. . . . And then will occur the general darkening of the sun, moon, and stars by blackest clouds, as at the Crucifixion, and the power of that awful Trumpet accelerated till the final blast, when suddenly a spot of light will appear in the East at 4 o'clock a.m. according to western time—and dark night of Eastern time or about that hour, varying at distances, the hot sunshine there gone completely, leaving however the weariness and dreariness of the afternoon heat of hot latitudes.[42]

The unquestioning sincerity of Emma's faith was a major source of the impervious serenity that enabled her to pursue her own preoccupations quite unaffected by, because oblivious to, the effect she was having on other people. What *Spaces* chiefly projected, however, was an impression of a mind at once obsessed, muddled, and naive. Even the benign Charles Moule, now President of Corpus Christi College, Cambridge, had advised Emma against its publication,[43] and Hardy's own embarrassment can readily be imagined.

Emma's elderly religiosity was from Hardy's point of view the culmination of three decades of marital difficulty and discomfort, serving as such to confirm him in the long-held opinions he summarized for Mrs Henniker in October 1911 in answer to her criticism of H. G. Wells's *The New Machiavelli*: '[Y]ou know what I have thought for many years: that marriage should not thwart nature, & that when it does thwart nature it is no real marriage, & the legal contract should therefore be as speedily cancelled as possible. Half the misery of human life would I think disappear if this were made easy.' He allowed that there could be difficulties in putting such a policy into effect, especially when children were involved, but nevertheless restated his position shortly afterwards when contributing to a magazine symposium on 'How Shall We Solve the Divorce Problem?', published early in 1912.[44]

Because Hardy saw no hope of ameliorating his situation in the world as it was, he had long ago determined to bear his lot with whatever stoicism he could muster, to avoid public exposure of his domestic difficulties so far as that proved feasible, and to maintain his wife, in social and economic terms, in the manner she had a right to expect. There is, in all the circumstances, something admirable about the resolution and dignity with which he maintained such a position. At the same time—as he himself later saw—it was a position based on principle rather than on sympathy, on obligation rather than loyalty or affection. Precisely because of his long-standing intellectual adherence to a particular view of marriage, Hardy was perhaps too apt to find confirmation for that view in his own experience, too rigid in his judgements of Emma, too quick to abandon hope (always an enticing option for one of his temperament) and settle comfortably into a self-justifying satisfaction at being so cruelly frustrated by fate and circumstance—by the treachery of the flesh, the elusiveness of the well-beloved, and the injustice of the prevailing social order. He had also learned all too well those techniques of passive resistance so long practised by his father in his dealings with Jemima. What Hardy was most to regret, most to blame himself for, in later years, was precisely the inflexibility of his behaviour towards Emma, his failure to see her as a fellow sufferer, and his betrayal of that moral and emotional touchstone of 'loving-kindness' he had so movingly embodied in his own finest work.

It is not necessary, however, to judge him more harshly than he did himself. He had work to do, after all, a creative need and obligation to whose imperatives he had necessarily—and properly—to respond. Criticism of Hardy's conduct during these years seems sometimes to ignore the fact that he was an artist. It is as if he could have been forgiven for grandly sinning, in traditional artist fashion, like a Byron or an Augustus John, but did not deserve sympathy for the lack of enthusiasm with which he tried to live with his own great mistake. Nor is it appropriate, in sympathizing with Emma, to underestimate either the extent of her deterioration or the gravity of its public and private consequences. Emma's vanity, gaucherie, unpredictability, and exasperating foolishness emerge with painful vividness from the entry which A. C. Benson made in his diary immediately following a visit to Max Gate in company with Edmund Gosse in early September 1912.

Benson's impression of Emma, whom he had not previously met, was of 'a small, pretty, rather mincing elderly lady with hair curiously puffed & padded rather fantastically dressed' whom Gosse took by both hands and addressed in 'a stream of exaggerated gallantry which was deeply appreciated'. Gosse, for his part, recorded of that same visit that Emma greeted them effusively, 'absurdly dressed, as a country lady without friends might dress herself on a vague recollection of some nymph in a picture by Botticelli'. After lunch—rather coarse fare, according to the fastidious Benson, in the 'rather slatternly' dining room, with streaks and stains showing on the purple distemper—Gosse mischievously insisted that Emma should smoke one of the cigarettes he had produced. Hardy did not, of course, smoke; Emma declared that she had never done so either, but nevertheless 'lit a cigarette & coughed cruelly at intervals, every now & then laying it down & saying "There that will be enough" but always resuming it, till I [Benson] feared disaster. Hardy looked at her so fiercely & scornfully that I made haste to say that I had persuaded my mother to smoke.' In conversation with Gosse that same afternoon Emma voiced her usual complaint that Hardy, full of self-conceit, was becoming ever more difficult to live with, accepting only honours he could keep to himself, and refusing to let her have a motor car. She later showed Benson around the dining room, 'talking in a low hurried voice, as if she was thinking aloud & not regarding me at all', and then the garden, where she became so absorbed in pinching the pods of the *Noli me tangere* to make them eject their seeds that she went on doing it 'with little jumps & elfin shrieks of pleasure'.[45]

Benson, accustomed to the manicured elegance of Cambridge colleges, had some rather acid comments to make on Max Gate itself as a house at once mean and pretentious, uncomfortable and shabby, sunk deep, dark, and airless in the midst of a jungle-like plantation—hopelessly overgrown by trees and shrubs as a consequence of Hardy's reluctance to 'injure' any growing thing even by pruning or cutting back. He found Hardy himself to be of unprepossessing appearance ('One would take him for a retired half-pay officer, from a not very smart regiment') and thought that his manner, while certainly kindly and courteous, was lacking in openness, showing something of the instinctive self-protectiveness of his peasant background. But that lack of 'openness' was primarily an effect of the frozen terror with which Hardy both awaited and greeted his wife's eccentricities of word and deed, and as Benson looked back upon the visit he was above all oppressed by a sense of 'something intolerable' in the thought of 'the old rhapsodist' having 'to live day & night with the absurd, inconsequent, huffy, rambling old lady'. It was true that Hardy did not behave very agreeably towards Emma either, but 'his patience must be incredibly tried. She is so queer, & yet has to be treated as rational, while she is full, I imagine, of suspicions & jealousies & affronts which must be half insane.'[46]

Benson was, of course, a dreadful snob who did not in any case care for women, and his distaste for Emma must be read in that context. But Emma had struck Gosse as odd and difficult ('she means to be very kind', he had told his wife) as long ago as 1883, and almost everyone who encountered her came to similar conclusions. Even those who spoke of her as lovable and childlike often did so in terms suggestive of condescension or pity. Hardy could unquestionably have treated her with greater kindness and consideration; he might also have taken more actively and imaginatively into account the loneliness she endured as a consequence of his confinement to his study for so many hours of almost every day. But it is common enough for irritation, anger, and despair to be provoked with peculiar vehemence by the deterioration, for whatever reason, of the object once beloved. During their early continental holidays Hardy had got angry whenever Emma felt too tired to keep up with him. So, in later years, he got angry when she acted gauchely, dressed inappropriately, talked foolishly—while her natural response to that anger, whether prompted by defiance or by sheer nervousness, was to intensify whatever in her behaviour was giving offence. And while the programme of keeping apart, suggested by Emma and embraced by her husband, certainly made for a reduction in day-to-day tensions, it also entrenched their basic differences to the point at which they finally stopped listening to each other.

Well before 1912 the situation had been pushed beyond any real hope of recovery. Hardy's friend Sir Clifford Allbutt, as a Commissioner in Lunacy, once gave it as his unofficial opinion, conditioned by the standards and practices of the time, that Emma was probably certifiable, and Hardy's poem 'The Interloper'—with its epigraph, 'And I saw the figure and visage of Madness seeking for a home'—suggests that he believed the symptoms of Emma's condition ('that under which best lives corrode') to have been visible, had he been able to recognize them, from the time of their first meeting.[47] Emma would have been happier in her later years if Hardy had been more patient and sympathetic, if he had not become emotionally attached to Florence Dugdale, if he had not possessed such extraordinary dedication and longevity as an artist, even if he had not brought her to live in a place where she had never felt at home. But her personal tragedy might well have overtaken her whatever route her life had taken.

There is no suggestion either in Gosse's account or in Benson's that Emma was suffering from an illness or disability of any kind. What they do emphasize, on the contrary, was her display of a considerable and even excessive physical energy—in Benson's phrase, a 'flighty & peevish activity'.[48] She had certainly been busy in and around Dorchester during the first eight months of 1912. In February, for the first time in many years, she attended a Dorset Field Club meeting with her husband, rather pathetically exhibiting a coloured illustration of an ancient gold collar that she had drawn in Cornwall before her marriage, and on one hot day in mid-July she held a garden party at Max Gate.[49] Later in July she hired a two-horse brake to take the young members of the Fordington St George Needlework Guild to the seaside, supplying the party with a picnic on the beach and more refreshments back at Max Gate and presenting each child with a cup and saucer. Lilian Gifford was again invited to stay for much of the summer—

until she quarrelled with Emma and was banished—and it was presumably the need to entertain their bored and rather lethargic niece that prompted the Hardys to take her to Weymouth in August to see a performance of *Bunty Pulls the Strings*, a popular comedy of the day which Hardy himself had already seen in London two months previously.[50]

Emma's health, however, had evidently been poor—though not dramatically so—for some time. Hardy, in *Life and Work*, speaks of her as having been 'in her customary health and vigour' during the summer months but as 'weaker later on in the autumn, though not ill' and complaining at times of her heart.[51] She now had a maid, 14-year-old Dolly Gale, to sleep in the attic bedroom next to her own, bring up her breakfast and lunch (she still went down to dinner), and perform such personal—and sometimes distasteful—tasks as brushing her hair and scalp to relieve the eczema with which she was afflicted.[52] During those more troublesome autumn months Emma seems to have suffered, sometimes severely, from angina attacks and from the gallstones that were presumably the source of the back pains that Dolly Gale tried to alleviate by patting or rubbing, and although she seems not to have consulted a doctor she did have occasional recourse to a standard painkiller, *Liquor opii sedativus*, prepared largely from opium, sherry, and alcohol. On Sundays she would sometimes get the gardener to pull her to Fordington church in a Bath chair, not because she had become entirely immobile but because the walk was too far for anyone in poor or indifferent health—and because Hardy had persisted in his refusal to set himself up with a car and chauffeur.

One day in mid-November 1912 Emma was taken out in a hired car to visit her friends the Wood Homers, beyond Puddletown. That night she had a violent attack of what Hardy persuaded himself was dyspepsia. During the next few days she had severe back pains and felt too unwell to eat but still declined to see a doctor. On 22 November she was well enough to copy out, in a neat hand, a cheerful little poem called 'Winter!' ('Gaze, gaze at the Mosses! | Winter joys for flower losses') and to write down, more clumsily and pathetically, six lines of verse beginning 'Oh! would I were a dancing child'.[53] On Monday, 25 November (the day after her seventy-second birthday), Emma kept to her room as usual until summoned downstairs to the tea table by the importunities of Rebekah and Catharine Owen, who had come to Dorchester to see the performance of *The Trumpet-Major*, a revised version of the 1908 dramatization, the following Wednesday. She came in very slowly, so Rebekah Owen later recalled, wept a little, and was obviously depressed, but she so resisted the idea of seeing a doctor—pleading her fear of operations—that the Owen sisters 'thought it as likely to be nerves and melancholia as anything'. When Dr Gowring did come the following day, Emma is said to have refused to let him examine her; in any case, according to Hardy, he treated her only for the weakness from which she was suffering, largely as a result of lack of nourishment.[54]

When Dolly Gale looked in upon her mistress at about eight o'clock the next morning, 27 November, she was terrified by the change that had taken place, by Emma's distorted face and moans of pain. Told to summon Hardy, who was already working in his study, just at the foot of the attic stairs, she had (according to her own account) difficulty in persuading him of the seriousness of the situation: 'Your collar is crooked,' he said. When he did follow her back up the stairs—perhaps the first time he had climbed them in many weeks—he found Emma already too far gone to speak. Within a few minutes she was dead, leaving on her desk a pencilled note directing one of the servants to fetch from the chemist's a supply of her usual painkiller: 'Mrs Hardy finds that she must have Liq: Op: Sed:—which she knows to take.' The causes of death were subsequently certified as impacted gallstones and heart failure—or, as Dr Gowring put it to Hardy, heart failure 'from some internal perforation'.[55] The diagnosis, as Hardy recognized, clearly indicated that 'mischief had been working for some while', but there seems no reason to question the truth of his statements, in so many letters written at the time to people who knew Emma well and had seen her recently, that her death was 'absolutely unexpected', by the doctor as well as by himself, and that while she had certainly been in indifferent health for some time he had no suspicion that anything was radically wrong—that she was other than 'robust and sound and likely to live to quite old age'. Her family were certainly shocked at the news of her death, nothing in her recent letters having led them to suspect that she was ill.[56]

Emma was buried at Stinsford the following Saturday, 30 November, in the plot which Hardy had already marked out for her, and for himself, alongside the graves of his parents and grandparents. Although Emma had herself worshipped at churches in Fordington and Dorchester—and might in any case have chosen other company—Hardy can scarcely have considered an alternative location. His whole conduct towards Emma had been founded on the principle that she was his wife, whom he had chosen in the face of all the world, and it would have been unthinkable that she should lie apart from him in death. And after all, to put Emma alongside Jemima was no more of an offence and affront to the memory of the former than to the memory of the latter. Mary Hardy did not attend the funeral, no doubt invoking her own illness as an available and possibly genuine excuse, but the wreaths placed on Emma's coffin did include one inscribed with 'affectionate memories' from her Hardy relatives. There were other ironies. Neither Emma's cousin Charles Gifford (who was suffering from a 'nervous breakdown'), nor her nephew Gordon Gifford, was present at the funeral, while her niece Lilian arrived at the churchyard only after the service was over. Nor was Emma attended to her grave by any of those literary friends and London dignitaries who were to crowd to her husband's funeral fifteen years later. Yet the shape of her posthumous triumph was already fore-shadowed in the wording of Hardy's wreath: 'From her Lonely Husband, with the Old Affection.'[57]

25

A Second Marriage

IMMEDIATELY upon Emma's death Kate Hardy moved into Max Gate to act as her brother's housekeeper. Florence Dugdale was already in Weymouth, having come down, like the Owen sisters, to be present at the performance of *The Trumpet-Major*, and when Hardy summoned her to Max Gate they seem to have behaved with what Emma's loyal young maid, taught by Dorchester gossip to regard Florence as Hardy's 'mistress', regarded as unseemly levity. A death can of course provoke complex responses from the living, and it is likely enough that both Hardy and Florence were at first seized by a sense of the freedom and opportunity that Emma's departure had so unexpectedly created. But the moment for euphoria soon passed. Florence went back to Enfield for a few days, and when she returned to Max Gate in early December she found not only that Kate was still in command but that Lilian Gifford had moved in too. There were in any case business matters to be attended to, letters to be written, malicious tongues to be challenged and, if possible, silenced. Hardy, criticized for allowing the performance of *The Trumpet-Major* to go forward on the day of his wife's death, sent to *The Times* a supplementary obituary of Emma that included a statement to the effect that 'Mr. Hardy' had not interfered with the play simply out of consideration for those who had come a long way to see it.[1]

Very shortly after Emma's death Hardy embarked upon the process of imaginative re-creation that would result in the 'Poems of 1912–13'. By 13 December he was writing to Clodd about the way in which one tended, after a bereavement, to forget all recent differences and go back in memory to 'the early times when each was much to the other—in her case & mine intensely much'. Four days later he told Mrs Henniker that he was reproaching himself for not having paid more attention to Emma's health:

In spite of the differences between us, which it would be affectation to deny, & certain painful delusions she suffered from at times, my life is intensely sad to me now without her. The saddest moments of all are when I go into the garden and to that long straight walk at the top that you know, where she used to walk every evening just before dusk, the cat trotting faithfully behind her; & at times when I almost expect to see her as usual coming in from the flower-beds with a little trowel in her hand.[2]

The note, and even some of the vocabulary, of Hardy's rhetoric of remorse is already audible in that letter, and at the end of 1912 and beginning of 1913, as he later recalled, he wrote more poems than he had ever done in a comparable space of time. All were about Emma, stimulated by a yearning to expiate what he now acknowledged as his neglect of her in recent years, and by a still more poignant sense of the contrast between the magic of their first meeting and the desolation of their final years together. Both sets of emotions were sharpened and intensified by the discovery, when he began going through Emma's papers, not only of 'Some Recollections' but also of the secret diaries she had kept since their marriage and which, as he now discovered, had been largely devoted, during the last twenty years or so of her life, to harsh comments upon her husband's conduct, character, and genius.

Although precise datings are not always possible, the earliest poems seem to have been those of immediate loss and self-reproach—'Your Last Drive', 'Rain on a Grave', 'Lament', 'Without Ceremony' ('It was your way, my dear, | To vanish without a word') and 'The Walk':

> You did not walk with me
> Of late to the hill-top tree
>   By the gated ways,
>   As in earlier days;
>   You were weak and lame,
>   So you never came,
> And I went alone, and I did not mind,
> Not thinking of you as left behind.[3]

The magnificent poems which harped back specifically to the earliest days of their romance were almost all of them products of the melancholy pilgrimage which Hardy made to St Juliot in early March 1913—the forty-third anniversary of that first meeting at the rectory door. Hardy's choice of his brother as his companion on this sentimental expedition is, on the face of it, surprising. But Henry, with his bluff commonsensicality and hearty dislike of Emma, no doubt served as a brisk reminder of past and present realities and as a healthy antidote to the deliberateness with which Hardy was setting out to immerse himself in the scenes and memories of his courtship.

Hardy had already displayed an unusual range of different and some-times conflicting moods. Florence Dugdale, writing to Clodd from Max Gate on 16 January 1913, could speak of his having regained what Kate had described as the happy laugh of his young manhood and, in the next sentence, go on to describe the depressing effect upon him of his nightly reading of what she later called those 'diabolical diaries' of Emma's: 'Nothing could be worse for him,' she understandably, but perhaps mis-takenly, exclaimed. When Hardy went off to Cornwall she felt such luxuri-ating in misery could only do him harm: 'He says that he is going down for the sake of the girl he married, & who died more than twenty years ago. His family say *that* girl never existed, but she did exist to him, no doubt.' She comforted herself with the thought that, as Kate had observed, no great damage would be done ' "so long as he doesn't pick up another Gifford down there" ', and felt justified when Hardy himself confessed, in a letter from Boscastle, that the visit had been a very painful one and that he could not think what had possessed him to make it.[4]

But it is perfectly clear from the verbal and rhythmic control of the poems written about Emma at this time that Hardy remained ultimately in com-mand of his emotions. As on previous occasions, what gave him pain was precisely what provided the fuel for his art, and what more than anything else determined the embodied passion of the finished product, whether in prose or verse, was the intensity of the original creative impulse—the degree to which his imagination had been seized by a sense of compassion-ate identification with suffering guessed at or actually witnessed, some place or person perceived as richly symbolic, or a crucial personal experience revisited and intensified. 'Hereto I come to view a voiceless ghost', he wrote in the opening line of 'After a Journey', and the poem as a whole is nothing less than a deliberate invocation and confrontation of the Emma he had met in 1870 and drifted away from all too shortly thereafter:

> Yes: I have re-entered your olden haunts at last;
> > Through the years, through the dead scenes I have tracked you;
> What have you now found to say of our past—
> > Scanned across the dark space wherein I have lacked you?
> Summer gave us sweets, but autumn wrought division?
> > Things were not lastly as firstly well
> > > With us twain, you tell?
> But all's closed now, despite Time's derision.[5]

Such intensification could, up to a point, be consciously pursued and achieved, induced almost as if by contemplative discipline. Regret for Emma, like regret for Kitsey ('the little white cat was his only friend'), flourished in a condition of deep melancholy that was to some degree willed, consciously cultivated—a kind of enclosed mental garden within which Hardy's creativity could uniquely flourish but that he was nonetheless capable of entering or leaving almost at will. There were, however, times when this trick of the imagination did not quite come off, when the marvellous poetic tact—the held balance between directness of thought, grainy naturalness of language, and elegance of form—was coarsened by a hint of morbidity, of sheer self-flagellation. One such poem, 'The Sound of Her', about hearing Emma's coffin lid being screwed down, Hardy was persuaded not to publish.[6]

Before his return from Cornwall in March 1913 Hardy arranged for a memorial to Emma, designed by himself, to be placed on an interior wall of St Juliot Church, where it was inspected and approved by Gordon Gifford the following August. Before the end of April he had seen to the erection of her tombstone, again to his own design, in the churchyard at Stinsford.[7] For Florence Dugdale, Hardy's obsession with his dead wife was both painful and bewildering. Painful because she knew from first-hand experience what his last years with Emma had been like, and because in sanctifying Emma he seemed to be undervaluing her own devotion. Bewildering because he seemed not to make, in his own mind, any clear correlation between his feelings for Emma and his feelings for Florence. In the same letter in which he dismissed Emma's abuse of him in her secret diaries as 'sheer hallucination in her, poor thing, & not wilfulness', he could go on to tell Florence that once she returned to Max Gate he would keep her there till spring: 'If I once get you here again won't I clutch you tight.' While he was visiting Boscastle, deliberately pursuing his newly found obsession, he could at the same time insist upon his continuing need for Florence's presence: 'Looking back it has seemed such a cruel thing altogether that events which began so auspiciously should have turned out as they did. And now suppose something shd happen to you, physically, as it did to her mentally! I dare not think of it, & I am sure you will not run any risk if you can help it. I have told H[enry] I am charging you strictly to stay indoors, & he ridicules the idea that you will listen to me for a moment.'[8]

In April 1913 Hardy visited Mrs Henniker's house in Suffolk at a time when Florence was there in the role of secretary and companion. He then went on by himself to Aldeburgh, where he talked to Clodd at length about

Emma and the way in which her delusions about being followed and con-spired against were consistent with what he deemed to be 'the mad strain in the family blood'. He spoke also of Emma's belief that she was the author of the Wessex novels and referred to a story of hers, called 'The Inspirer', about a wife who inspired her husband's novels. Whether he knew that this was one of the manuscripts that Florence had typed out for her in the autumn of 1910 is not entirely clear.[9]

Once she arrived back at Max Gate later that spring, Florence seems to have remained there more or less continuously, despite Hardy's (entirely justified) fears of what Dorchester gossip would say if it discovered her presence, even if 'chaperoned' by Kate, Mary, or Lilian Gifford. Hardy was apprehensive, too, of the inquisitiveness of Clement Shorter—unaware that intimate details of his domestic life were being regularly conveyed by Florence to Clodd, who was accustomed to pass on all such tidbits to Shorter. It was perhaps in an attempt to purchase Shorter's discretion by a controlled indulgence of his curiosity that Hardy invited him down to Max Gate with Clodd for a long weekend in mid-July 1913. The two visitors were taken to Bockhampton, to Emma's grave, and to Talbothays, to which Henry Hardy and his sisters had recently moved. Clodd found Henry 'a well-set, sensible man' and the two sisters 'quite as Miss Dugdale told me— ladylike, refined, well-informed', and observed that it was a shame that Hardy had allowed 'his half mad wife' to forbid them and their mother access to Max Gate. It was also a shame, he thought, that Hardy had not let him 'know these good folk earlier. He should be proud of them.'[10] It might have been difficult for Hardy to make Clodd and Shorter understand that it was precisely because he was so proud of his family, and so devoted to them, that he had sought so tenaciously to protect them from the public eye.

This slight shift in Hardy's attitudes towards his family was directly related to the final departure of Mary, Kate, and Henry from that Bockhampton cottage which—as Hardy noted on 1 January 1913 when making out the cheque for the last quarterly rent—the Hardys had occu-pied for 112 years. The old lifehold lease had expired in 1892 upon the death of Hardy's father, but the owners of Kingston Maurward, though unwilling to sell the property, had allowed the Hardys to go on living there at a very modest rent. The move to Talbothays was a sharp and in many respects a sad break with the past, but once Jemima had died her three unmarried children—especially the cheerfully extroverted Kate and Henry—had inevitably succumbed to a desire for modern convenience. As Mary told their cousin Nathaniel Sparks, it was a wrench to leave Bockhampton, but the house there had got out of repair and it seemed a pity not to occupy

Henry's 'comfortable new one'. By June 1913 they were well established at Talbothays and Mary was able to report to her elder brother that Henry's garden was growing well, its successive rows of vegetables already giving it the look of their father's garden 'in the olden time'.[11]

Florence meanwhile was helping Hardy with his voluminous correspondence—typing or writing out letters he had drafted and sometimes sending them over her own initials as 'Secretary'[12]—and beginning to get the disorganized household into good order. Max Gate itself, as Benson had remarked the previous year, was in a sadly run-down condition, and during the autumn of 1913 Hardy had it redecorated throughout and added a small conservatory, leading out of the drawing room, to the east side—projects, as Florence reported to Clodd, that amused him 'tremendously'. He was, indeed, as cheerful and affectionate as she had ever known him, and she, for her part, was endeavouring to accommodate herself, not gladly but perforce, to his poetic obsession with an extravagantly idealized Emma. When, however, he suggested to Florence that she should wear half-mourning in perpetuity as a sign of devotion to Emma's memory, she began to wonder whether there might not be 'something in the air of Max Gate that makes us all a little crazy'.[13]

What she found most difficult to endure was the continuing presence of Lilian Gifford. Lilian had learned long before to regard Max Gate as her second home, and although she had recently quarrelled with Emma she had evidently seen her aunt's death as an opportunity to reintroduce herself into Hardy's domestic life on a more permanent basis, as a substitute for the wife he had lost and the daughter he had never had. When presenting him with a lamp on the first anniversary of Emma's death she called him 'Daddy-Uncle' and declared that she always thought of him in those terms.[14] Florence saw Lilian not so much as a threat to her own position but rather as a constant, irritating reminder of the woman whose lingering presence—more formidable now than ever in life—she was trying to exorcize. She complained to Clodd in December 1913 that while Lilian sought to ingratiate herself with Hardy by talking sentimentally of Emma and of St Juliot, she refused to help in the house, gave herself superior airs, made contemptuous references to Florence's family background—and provoked, on the occasion of a visit by Florence's sister Constance, a scene such as she had previously encountered only when staying at Max Gate in Emma's time.[15] Hardy had known Lilian for a long time and was sympathetic towards her precisely because her childlike speech and behaviour reminded him of Emma, but by the beginning of 1914 Florence had made it clear that if Lilian did not leave she could herself neither remain at Max Gate nor go through with the marriage 'compact' into which she and Hardy had already entered. Florence knew that marriage would give her the position—and the respectability—she needed, but she also realized that it would be meaningless unless she had clear authority over the running of the household. Both Kate and Henry supported her in this view—Henry saying that it was the only way to avoid a life of misery—and Lilian was sent away, having first been provided with a degree of financial security in the form of an annuity and some stocks.[16]

During this period of domestic upheaval, emotional disturbance, and extraordinary creativity Hardy led a public life even quieter than usual. In June 1913, however, he went to Cambridge to receive the honorary degree of Litt.D. He stayed with Sydney Cockerell, who had been largely instrumental in prompting the honour, and lunched with the Vice-Chancellor, S. A. Donaldson, at Magdalene. It was there that A. C. Benson found him, wearing a Doctor of Laws gown by mistake and looking 'very frail & nervous, but undeniably pleased'. Mary wrote to congratulate him, reminding him of his abandonment of his Cambridge ambitions in the 1860s: 'Now you have accomplished it all with greater honour than if you had gone along the road you then saw before you.' Florence's already wifely concern was for his health, and she began what was to prove a long and voluminous correspondence with Cockerell by warning him that Hardy was being much troubled by varicose veins and must rest his leg horizontally to prevent any clot of blood being carried to the heart or brain. That November Hardy was again in Cambridge to be installed as an Honorary Fellow of Magdalene, taking pleasure in the company of Clifford Allbutt, A. E. Housman, and others, and again in the splendour of his (presumably more appropriate) robes.[17]

At the beginning of 1913 Macmillan published the last two of the original twenty volumes of the Wessex Edition, which had begun to appear in April 1912. That same summer Hardy rather doubtfully put together a volume of previously uncollected stories, calling it *A Changed Man* after the story he thought, on the whole, to be the best of a rather poor bunch. Since he protested that he would never have revived the stories at all if they had not been so frequently reprinted in cheaper American editions, he was gratified by the warm reception given the volume upon its appearance in late October. 'This book', wrote Gosse, 'is a cluster of asteroids, which take their proper place in your planetary system, and differ from your novels only in the matter of size. They are uniformly and wonderfully worthy of you, and are wholly precious.'[18] Not surprisingly Sir Frederick Macmillan raised the possibility of reprinting 'An Indiscretion in the Life of an Heiress', the one extensive prose work which remained uncollected. Hardy replied that the story had been omitted from *A Changed Man* as being only a shadow of the larger work from which it had been abstracted, but added, remarkably enough: 'I thought it might be amusing in my old age to endeavour to restore the original from the modification, aided by my memory & a fragment still in existence of "The P. M. & Lady"—merely a few pages.'[19]

This reawakened interest in *The Poor Man and the Lady* was perhaps stimulated by the visit Hardy apparently received, some time in 1913, from Eliza Bright Nicholls, whose relationship with him in the 1860s had been an important element in the novel's emotional context. She had never married, never discarded Hardy's ring or portrait, and seems to have persuaded herself, upon hearing the news of Emma's death, that her long devotion might yet receive its due reward. Whether out of courtesy or curiosity—or out of a sense that she was another woman to whom he had behaved less well than he might have done—Hardy agreed to see her at Max Gate, only to tell her, when she arrived, that he intended to marry Miss Dugdale.[20] Another figure from his early life, Louisa Harding, the subject of 'Louisa in the Lane', had died in September 1913 and been buried in Stinsford churchyard, while a more recent attachment, Rosamund Tomson, had also passed away—as Rosamund Marriott Watson—in December 1911. By a final little Hardyan irony, Florence Henniker had been widowed in February 1912, less than a year before the death of Emma. Hardy wrote a short poem to General Henniker's memory but seems not at any point to have contemplated making Mrs Henniker a proposal of marriage. He no doubt felt that their moment—like that of the lovers in his story 'The Waiting Supper'—had long passed, but he was also conscious that she had never at any point returned his devotion and that he himself had in any case become too deeply and happily committed elsewhere. Florence Dugdale, for her part, had been made the more ready to contemplate marriage to a man thirty-eight years her senior by the recent deaths of Alfred Hyatt and Sir Thornley Stoker, the only other men for whom she seems to have cared at all deeply.

Hardy probably proposed marriage to Florence Dugdale as early as 16 April 1913, the date attached, together with the simple inscription 'To F.E.D.', to another of those bunches of dried flowers that seem to have marked important stages in their relationship. When Clodd visited Max Gate in mid-July Florence was certainly able to tell him in confidence that such a proposal had been made and at least tentatively accepted. The apparently hasty arrangements for the marriage itself, on 10 February

1914—a special licence was obtained as late as 6 February—evidently reflected nothing more than a desire to keep the affair private. No one outside the two families concerned was told of the approaching event, and the ceremony at Enfield Parish Church was held at eight o'clock in the morning—in the presence only of Henry Hardy and of Florence's father and youngest sister. The newly married couple left for Dorchester immediately, just ahead of a crowd of reporters who had somehow got wind of the event and arrived at Mr Dugdale's door an hour or so later.[21] They were also successful in reaching Dorchester station before anyone had had time to organize the formal civic welcome they had especially dreaded.

Although Hardy insisted in a letter to Lady Grove that the occasion had not been without romance, he represented it to most of his friends in severely practical terms. 'We thought it the wisest thing to do,' he told Cockerell, 'seeing what a right hand Florence has become to me.' To Frederic Harrison he remarked that the step had been soberly taken in the hope that 'the union of two rather melancholy temperaments may result in cheerfulness, as the junction of two negatives forms a positive'.[22] To both Cockerell and Harrison he had spoken of the satisfying continuity provided by Florence's former friendship with Emma, and he developed the same point for Florence Henniker's benefit in a letter made ungainly by conflicting memories and emotions:

I am rather surprised that *you* were surprised at the step we have taken—such a course seeming an obvious one to me, being as I was so lonely & helpless. I think I told you in my last letter that I am very glad she knew Emma well, & was liked by her even during her latter years, when her mind was a little unhinged at times, & she showed unreasonable dislikes. I wonder if it will surprise you when I say that according to my own experience the second marriage does not, or need not, obliterate an old affection, though it is generally assumed that the first wife is entirely forgotten in such cases.

To the current rector of St Juliot he declared that the romance of St Juliot would abide nonetheless, even if he lived to be 100.[23]

Had the second Mrs Hardy been aware of the terms in which her husband was speaking of their marriage she might well have felt a degree of foreboding. Her situation was not, in any case, an easy one. She had married not just to escape the alternative prospect of becoming an old maid and eking out a meagre living by various forms of secretarial and literary drudgery, but out of profound admiration for Hardy's genius and a deep appreciation of his kindness towards her. His 'tender protective affection', she confided to a woman friend later that year, was like that of 'a father for a child'. It was, as she acknowledged, 'a feeling quite apart from passion', balanced, on her own part, by a similar non-sexual protectiveness and concern. That she and Hardy could have had a child of their own was mentioned as a possibility in a letter Florence wrote to Marie Stopes as late as September 1923: 'He said he would have welcomed a child when we married first, ten years ago, but now it would kill him with anxiety to have to father one.' But in 1923 Florence was well into her mid-forties and by addressing the issue in terms only of Hardy's age and not of her own she would seem to have been resisting confidences rather than offering them, and neither her exchanges with Marie Stopes nor Hardy's reputed boasts of his sexual capacity in old age can be taken as reliable evidence of their marital relations.[24]

But although at the time of her marriage Florence was capable of seeing the situation in perspective, of recognizing that her role thenceforward was to serve that great man her husband as secretary, companion, housekeeper, and, when necessary, nurse, she was, at 35, still a young woman. She was also, as Hardy had recognized, the possessor of a temperament scarcely less depressive than his own, and over the years she would prove capable of descents deep into melancholy, impulsive confidences to people believed to be sympathetic, and suspicions, jealousies, and resentments, sometimes justified, sometimes not, of those who seemed to threaten her position or her capacity to carry out efficiently the many different tasks that position involved. Her husband's continuing tenderness towards Emma's memory and Emma's relatives was just one such irritant she could well have done without. Much as Emma, in her time, had been exasperated by Hardy's refusal to place her feelings and interests above those of his own family, so Florence responded with ill grace to the brief visits paid to Max Gate by both Gordon and Lilian Gifford within the first year of her marriage, and especially to Gordon's insistence that Emma had promised—on what authority is not clear, unless she had counted on being the survivor of the marriage—that Max Gate and its contents would be left to him.[25]

When Hardy and Florence first returned to Max Gate after the wedding, they were both kept busy for several days responding to the many letters and telegrams of congratulation that had poured in. Later in that same month of February 1914 they spent a brief 'honeymoon' in Teignmouth, Dartmouth, and Torquay, and during the ensuing spring Florence was able to enjoy some of the public rewards of being the wife of so famous a man. They went to Cambridge together at the beginning of May, were entertained in London by Gosse and by Lady St Helier (formerly Lady Jeune), who organized a large dinner party in their honour, with Mr and Mrs

Winston Churchill prominent among the guests, and spent a weekend with Sir Henry and Lady Hoare at Stourhead, their magnificent estate just over the Wiltshire border.[26] Although Hardy was much less interested in having visitors at Max Gate than Florence would have liked, there were enough of them to present an occasional pleasant diversion: Ellen Glasgow, the American novelist, in June; Henry Dickens, Charles Dickens's last surviving son, in early July; and Amy Lowell, American poet and biographer of Keats, at the end of that same month. Hardy meanwhile was working with happy intensity at the final revision of the volume which was to contain 'Poems of 1912–13' and discussing with Sir Frederick Macmillan the plans for a limited *de luxe* edition of his works—which must, he insisted, include the poems, even if they had to be printed in smaller type.[27]

Although he wrote that spring of 1914 what seemed in retrospect the prophetic stanzas of 'Channel Firing', Hardy always declared that he had not had the slightest anticipation of the approaching conflict. All his philosophical assumptions, indeed, as embodied in poems such as 'The Sick Battle-God', had tended in the direction of an eventual improvement in the relationships between men and between nations, especially as the senselessness of modern warfare came to be more generally appreciated.[28] That August's outbreak of war on so vast a scale seemed entirely to undercut all such views, and he was forced to reconsider even the note of limited long-term optimism on which he had concluded *The Dynasts*, his treatment of the previous European conflagration. Her husband seemed to have been aged ten years by the war, Florence told Sydney Cockerell on 15 August: 'I think he feels the horror of it so keenly that he loses all interest in life.' At the end of the month Hardy himself gloomily observed to Cockerell that the enforced recognition of the brutality of the age 'does not inspire one to write hopeful poetry, or even conjectural prose, but simply make one sit still in an apathy, & watch the clock spinning backwards, with a mild wonder if, when it gets back to the Dark Ages, & the sack of Rome, it will ever move forward again to a new Renascence, & a new literature.'[29]

As that autumn of 1914 drew on, Hardy's despondency over the war news was matched by Florence's increasing dismay at the nature and difficulty of the task she had voluntarily assumed. Hardy's reluctance to change his ways, or anything around him, greatly restricted her freedom of action in household matters. Just as he could not bear to wound the Max Gate trees, even by prudential pruning, so he was soft-hearted towards servants whose inefficiency seemed attributable to some handicap or misfortune for which they were not to blame. When their parlourmaid persuaded them to hire her deaf-and-dumb but appealingly pretty sister, who at first made little contribution to the work of the house, it was Hardy who insisted that she be kept on. Florence, relatively unaccustomed to servants, or to household management, found such worries '*soul-destroying*', and in mid-October, when the cook served up a 'simply uneatable' meal on the occasion of a visit by Harley Granville Barker, she was close to despair.[30]

It is understandable, therefore, that her response to the publication of *Satires of Circumstance* on 17 November was one of profound distress, Hardy having brought together in this volume those 'Poems of 1912–13' that constituted the most poignant expression of his regret for the decay of his first marriage and, by general consent, probably the highest point of his achievement in verse:

> Woman much missed, how you call to me, call to me,
> Saying that now you are not as you were
> When you had changed from the one who was all to me,
> But as at first, when our day was fair.
>
> Can it be you that I hear? Let me view you, then,
> Standing as when I drew near to the town
> Where you would wait for me: yes, as I knew you then,
> Even to the original air-blue gown!
>
> Or is it only the breeze, in its listlessness
> Travelling across the wet mead to me here,
> You being ever dissolved to wan wistlessness,
> Heard no more again far or near?
>
> > Thus I; faltering forward,
> > Leaves around me falling,
> > Wind oozing thin through the thorn from norward,
> > And the woman calling.[31]

Florence was not deaf to the eloquence of such poems, but she found herself defenceless in their presence, unable to prevent herself from reading them as a series of directly personal statements of the most negative kind: 'It seems to me', she wrote to Lady Hoare, 'that I am an utter failure if my husband can publish such a *sad sad* book. He tells me that he has written *no* despondent poem for the last eighteen months, & yet I cannot get rid of the feeling that the man who wrote some of those poems is utterly weary of life—& cares for nothing in this world. If I had been a different sort of woman, & better fitted to be his wife—would he, I wonder, have published that volume?' When Lady Hoare very sensibly pointed out that many of the poems were essentially dramatic and that Hardy the man must not be held directly responsible for the utterances of Hardy the poet, Florence thanked her for restoring her sense of perspective.[32] Such reassurance did not, however, entirely remove her sense of grievance at the inclusion of so many poems to Emma, nor alter her more fundamental perception of the kind of life that now stretched before her.

Though she never lost her admiration and affection for her husband, nor her sense of being privileged to serve and cherish his genius, many of the day-to-day realities of her marriage were not of an enlivening kind. It was not simply that Max Gate was made gloomy by its trees, burdensome by its domestic worries, and lonely by its location, nor even that Hardy, for all his simplicity and sympathy, was showing with advancing age a perhaps inevitable tendency towards greater rigidity, obstinacy, and querulousness. It was also that she had, while still a comparatively young woman, to stand aside and watch the decay of what remained of her youth and her original ambitions. Although she continued to write book reviews and stories, it was clear that Hardy would have preferred her not to, especially when they took such shapes as the crudely patriotic tale, ' "Greater Love Hath No Man . . .": The Story of a Village Ne'er-Do-Weel', which she published, as Mrs Thomas Hardy, in the *Sunday Pictorial* for 13 June 1915—and immediately felt 'rather ashamed of'.[33] Although she liked to get away to pay brief visits to London and her family, Hardy so fretted while she was gone that she became increasingly reluctant to leave him, even for a single day. And even if she had accepted that her marriage would bring her no sexual satisfaction, the celebration of Emma in *Satires of Circumstance* now seemed to deprive it of its last shreds of romance. Writing in early December 1914 to sympathize with Rebekah Owen in the recent death of her sister, Florence allowed herself to exclaim, in an apparent reference to Alfred Hyatt, that she had herself lost, some three years before, the friend who had been more to her 'than anything else in the world . . . the only person who ever loved me—for I am not loveable'.[34]

Florence Hardy's deeply personal reading of *Satires of Circumstance* as a wholly pessimistic volume was echoed, in impersonal terms, by most of the reviewers. Even Lytton Strachey, one of the more perceptive among them, spoke of its prevailing mood as one of melancholy—'the melancholy of regretful recollection, of bitter speculation, of immortal longings unsatisfied; it is the melancholy of one who has suffered, in Gibbon's poignant phrase, "the abridgment of hope".'[35] The presence of the 'Satires of Circumstance' themselves, the sequence of bitterly ironic narratives that Hardy had hesitated to include, did much to distort the reception of the volume. Because the title made them seem self-evidently central, critics felt obliged to respond to them, and tended in so doing to repeat what had already become established commonplaces—Hardy's previous collection, after all, had been called *Time's Laughingstocks*. Even those, such as Laurence Binyon in the *Bookman*, who recognized the tenderness and poignancy of the 'Poems of 1912–13' rarely engaged with them at all fully, while those hostile to Hardy found it easy to ask, in the tone formerly adopted by some of the critics of *Jude*, whether one who dwelt so consistently on 'the seamy side of things' had any right to be called a poet at all. It was perhaps as well that Gosse kept to himself the characteristically self-deprecating inscription on the copy of *Satires of Circumstance* he had received from its author: 'To Edmund Gosse: the mixture as before of unstable fancies, conjectures, & contradictions: from Thomas Hardy.'[36]

It was, in truth, a deeply depressing and distressing time. As the scope and violence of the war increased Hardy felt his whole framework of assumptions—both abstract and day-to-day—severely shaken. He was fundamentally hostile to war and even, so the 1913 poem 'His Country' would seem to suggest, to patriotism itself in any narrowly nationalistic sense, and his distrust of Britain's past record of imperialist aggression made him question at first the role his country had played in the events that had brought the war about.[37] He soon became persuaded, however, that Britain was 'innocent for once', that the fundamental source of conflict had been the will to power of the German rulers, and that Britain had had to fight because Germany had left it no alternative. On grounds of simple compassion he soon joined in appeals on behalf of Belgian refugees, a cause to which he later contributed a second poem in response to a request from Henry James, writing on behalf of Edith Wharton.[38]

But he was by no means immune to the prevailing wartime fever. At the very beginning of the war he wrote and promptly published ' "Men Who March Away" ', designed specifically as a marching song and qualified in its patriotism only by the incorporated reference to the poet himself as the 'Friend with the musing eye' who watched the marchers 'With doubt and dolorous sigh'.[39] In early September 1914, in the hope of making some contribution to the national interest, he participated along with Barrie, Galsworthy, Chesterton, Arnold Bennett, H. G. Wells, and many other writers in a meeting summoned by C. F. G. Masterman, Chancellor of the Duchy of Lancaster, to consider what role eminent authors might play in formulating and publicizing British principles and war aims. The minutes of the meeting record Hardy as saying only that 'a list of German misstatements' should be published, 'together with answers to them in succinct language', but he was certainly one of the fifty-two writers who put their names to a statement of British war aims that was published on 10 September 1914 both in *The Times* and in the *New York Times*, where it was accompanied by facsimile signatures.[40]

In early October his letter of protest against the German shelling of Rheims Cathedral appeared in several British newspapers,[41] and by November the national clamour for ever more volunteers had impelled him to write to Lord Kitchener, then Secretary of State for War, and to the Prime Minister, H. H. Asquith, with specific suggestions as to the lessons that might be learned from the recruiting methods adopted during the Napoleonic Wars. 'I think,' he wrote to Kitchener,

if something of the old style of doing it—minus the liquor—could be generally adopted, it might have a productive effect. I refer to the systematic and persistent 'beating up' through the streets of towns, with a band of fifes and side-drums; two lines four deep of old sergeants (past service) with drawn swords, full uniforms, and ribbons and flags flying, followed by a company of recruits who have already joined, also with ribbons in their hats, a halt being made on reaching corners and open spaces and a brief speech delivered by one of the sergeants. One pound notes were spitted on their swords a hundred years ago, but these would not be essential.

In a subsequent letter to Sir Courtenay Ibert, clerk to the House of Commons, he addressed the possibility of conscription on the basis of something similar to 'the militia ballot of the Napoleonic time'. He recalled old people as saying that those on whom the lot fell would often find and pay a substitute if they could afford to do so, and observed that if any such system were to be reintroduced 'a point would be whether substitution should be allowed or not'. His final suggestion was that a 'rush for voluntary enlistment' could probably be stimulated by introducing a 'system of conscription paying only half or two-thirds the bounty that would be paid on voluntary enlistment beforehand'.[42]

It was within this tense and highly emotional context that Hardy, in late September, gave permission for the presentation at London's Kingsway Theatre of Harley Granville Barker's stage version of *The Dynasts*. He had not, of course, intended *The Dynasts* to be performed, and he would object strongly to several features of the actual production, but the circumstances gave him no real choice but to embrace Granville Barker's proposal and offer whatever assistance he could. By early October he was actively involved in the selection and occasional revision of performable episodes and in writing a new prologue designed to anticipate—and if possible dispel—the obvious objection that France was not now the national enemy but the national ally.[43]

Since England, right or wrong, was engaged in another life-and-death struggle, the author of *The Dynasts* could not but wish and work for its survival; nor did he have any sympathy with those who directly opposed the war on political or pacifist grounds. At the same time, the author of 'A Christmas Ghost-Story', 'The Souls of the Slain', 'The Sick Battle-God', and 'Channel Firing' could not entirely surrender to the national war hysteria. His poem 'In Time of "the Breaking of Nations"', derived from notes made at St Juliot in 1870, was completed in 1915, and in the April 1915 number of the *Fortnightly Review* he published 'The Pity of It', with its poignant insistence upon the similarities between the German language and the dialect of Dorset:

> Then seemed a Heart crying: 'Whosoever they be
> At root and bottom of this, who flung this flame
> Between kin folk kin tongued even as are we,
>
> 'Sinister, ugly, lurid, be their fame;
> May their familiars grow to shun their name,
> And their brood perish everlastingly.'

As he put it to Florence Henniker when sending her a proof of the poem: 'I, too, like you, think the Germans happy & contented as a people: but the group of oligarchs & munition-makers whose interest is war, have stirred them up to their purposes—at least so it seems.'[44] That final qualifying note of scepticism, audible in the poem itself, is only a distant echo, even so, of Hardy's Boer War verses. But he was older and less flexible now, and saw that the likelihood of defeat was greater, and its potential consequences far graver, than they had been at the beginning of the century. In the first months of the war he had entertained a lively fear of a German invasion, and he believed, early and late, that Germany was unlikely to be beaten—a characteristic 'full look at the Worst' that enabled him, so Florence told a friend in 1916, to remain relatively calm in the face of the military and other disasters the war entailed.[45]

Nor was the war by any means the only source of anxiety for Hardy at this time. Florence, who had suffered painfully from sciatica at the beginning of the year, had to go up to London in late May 1915 to undergo an operation designed to cure her 'nasal catarrh'. After the operation, performed by a surgeon, later a friend, named Macleod Yearsley, she spent a week in a nursing home in Welbeck Street established by Hardy's distinguished Dorchester contemporary Sir Frederick Treves, and then a day or two with Lady St Helier before returning home. Since Florence was in good hands throughout and receiving visits from her own family—since, too, he had such a dread of doctors and hospitals and was in any case still weak from the severe attack of diarrhoea he had suffered on a recent visit to London—Hardy decided to stay at Max Gate.[46] Concerned at the possibility that she would try to resume her normal activities too quickly, he wrote to urge Florence to stay longer at the nursing home, adding: 'I don't at all mind paying the extra days'—an offer that would seem to qualify, if not necessarily contradict, Florence's indiscreet complaint to Rebekah Owen that she would be paying all the costs of the operation herself.[47]

While Florence was away in London, recovering from her operation, Hardy was told by his sisters that he ought to make his will in favour of someone who had been 'born a Hardy', their preference being for Basil Augustus Hardy, a grandson of Hardy's cousin Augustus, the third son of his father's older brother James. Hardy seems not to have been moved by the suggestion, having neither met the young man in question nor formed a high opinion of his father, the Reverend Henry Hardy, a Church of England clergyman. But the discussion did prompt him to think seriously about a possible inheritor of Max Gate. He finally fixed upon Frank George, the son of a Bere Regis publican and Charles Meech Hardy's sister Angelina, hence technically his own first cousin once removed. After some years of working in banks in Dorchester and Bristol, Frank George was called to the bar at Gray's Inn and—with occasional assistance from Hardy himself—seemed headed for a respectable legal career. At the beginning of the war, however, he had volunteered for the Army and been commissioned as a lieutenant in the Dorset Regiment. A recent visit by Frank George to Max Gate had confirmed Hardy's liking and respect for a young man who had worked his way determinedly upwards and was one of the very few Hardys who had shown any interest in, or aptitude for, education and the life of the mind.[48]

Gordon Gifford, who still cherished hopes of inheriting Max Gate, fell further out of favour in the early summer of 1915 when he contracted a marriage for which Hardy seems to have evinced little enthusiasm. Florence, taking a malicious satisfaction in this turn of events, made the tongue-in-cheek suggestion that the young couple should be presented with 'the Gifford relics', including the portrait of the Archdeacon, but Hardy responded that he had bought them all from the Giffords at a good price and proposed to hang on to them.[49] Talk of heirs reminded Florence of her own childlessness and of the 'sort of compassion' with which the local mothers showed her their babies, and she seems to have found some compensation in cherishing—much as Emma, abetted by Hardy, had spoiled her cats—her wire-haired terrier Wessex, who had first entered the Max

Gate household in December 1913, when he was four months old. Wessex was quarrelsome, snappish, and generally ill behaved, a perpetual cause of trouble and anxiety, but Hardy treated him with a tenderness and indulgence even greater than Florence's.[50]

Although profoundly depressed by the worsening war news, Hardy was in excellent health that summer. He paid Hermann Lea to take Florence and himself out for drives in his car—to the seaside with Kate or Henry, into Devon to call on Eden Phillpotts—and welcomed several callers at Max Gate. Even so, he seemed to Florence to be growing more and more of a recluse. His mind still dwelt upon the past—he was now corresponding with distant relatives of Emma's about the whereabouts of the Gifford family graves—and he refused either to go up to London or to invite people down to stay.[51]

At the end of August 1915 domestic worries and irritations were temporarily overlaid by the news that Frank George had been killed in action at Gallipoli.[52] Hardy was much shocked, and while there may seem a touch of extravagance and even of factitiousness about his grief for someone he did not in fact know especially well, he was certainly moved, both personally and, as it were, dynastically, by the loss of the young man he had thought of as the probable inheritor of Max Gate and who was, as he told Mrs Henniker, 'about the only, if not the only, blood relative of the next generation in whom I have taken any interest'.[53] The ungainly term 'blood relative'—so suggestive of Jemima's obsession with family exclusivity— served in this instance to except from the generalization Emma's nephew and niece Gordon and Lilian Gifford, in whom Hardy had of course taken a great deal of interest,[54] while the reservation 'if not the only' minimally allowed for his genuine if fitful interest in the artistic careers of Nathaniel and James Sparks. It mattered, however, that Frank George had been a Hardy rather than one of the somehow less essential Hands. Hardy called on Frank's mother and sisters, offered them financial assistance, and continued in subsequent years to make himself accessible to any members of the family who came to call at Max Gate.[55] He wrote a short obituary for *The Times*, and by the end of September he had composed the poem 'Before Marching and After (In Memoriam F.W.G.)' and sent it off for publication in the *Fortnightly Review*.[56]

A nearer and more severe bereavement was soon to follow. Since September 1912 Mary and Kate had been gradually settling into Henry's house at Talbothays, emptying first the Bockhampton cottage and finally the house they had formerly occupied together in Wollaston Road,

Dorchester. In June 1915 the last remnants of the Wollaston Road furniture were sold at auction and the sisters settled down, with Henry and with Polly Antell, in an isolation that Mary at least found congenial[57] and that was intruded upon only by close friends and members of the family—including, virtually every Sunday, the elder brother and his young wife, occasionally accompanied by one or other of Florence's sisters. Margaret Soundy, the youngest, recalled of one of her visits to Talbothays that Mary sat on an ottoman throughout, saying nothing but gazing with admiration into Hardy's face. Hardy had referred to Mary as 'almost a hermit' as early as 1906, though still keeping up with her painting, and as she became more of an invalid she went out less and less, the only significant expedition, regularly repeated until she was in her seventies, being the annual day trip to London and back to see the Summer Exhibition at the Royal Academy.[58] At the beginning of November 1915, however, Mary became severely and distressingly ill with emphysema, and on the 24th—three years almost to the day after Emma's death and within a month of her own seventy-fourth birthday—she died. Hardy prompted Clement Shorter to publish in the *Sphere* a photograph of the self-portrait Mary had painted several years previously and contributed largely to the obituary notice that appeared in the local newspaper, laying particular emphasis upon her talents in music and painting: 'Her facility in catching a likeness was remarkable, and hence, in respect of a family record on canvas—that which, whatever its shortcomings, is valued in proportion to its reproduction for us of the faces we wish to remember—she painted to good purpose.' Of Mary's personality he said, briefly but sufficiently: 'Under an often undemonstrative exterior she hid a warm and most affectionate nature.' And in *Life and Work* he spoke of her—perhaps with Emma's old hostility in mind—as having been 'remarkably unassertive, even when she was in the right, and could easily have proved it'.[59]

Mary suffered a great deal during her last illness, but in death her face seemed to Kate more than happy, reminding her of how she used to look when they were living together at Denchworth. There was little enough serenity at Talbothays during the next few days, however. Kate was at first 'utterly bewildered' at her sister's death, Henry quarrelled with his brother because the latter was unwilling to go back to Talbothays after the funeral, and Florence, unused to country ways, had already been appalled by the rituals of death as observed in the Hardy family, and especially by Kate's repeated insistence that she kiss the corpse.[60] No less shocking to her, however, was the haggling and bickering that resulted from Mary's having left no will or other instructions for the disposition of the quite considerable amount of money that—thanks primarily to Hardy's watchful generosity—had been in her possession. Once Kate had been assured that the money would come to her, the strain was removed, but the serious illness of Henry during December, following the slight stroke he had suffered in the spring of 1914, brought once more to the fore the whole question of who should eventually inherit the family money when all those of the present, entirely childless, generation had passed away. The overwhelming concern was that the inheritor should be '*a Hardy born*', and while Florence could to some extent appreciate how peasant instinct and family loyalty could combine with personal memories to generate such feelings, she also gained from Kate's tenacity her first real insight into what Emma had been up against in her dealings with the Hardys.[61] Her own situation, moreover, was by no means entirely different, for where the Hardys had scorned Emma for being 'poor gentry' they were no less suspicious of the lower-middle-class Dugdales and of the designs which Florence's relatives might have, singly and collectively, upon Hardy's prospective estate. 'I shall miss Mary very, very much,' she told Rebekah Owen, 'for she had a much more amiable and placid disposition than the others, and also she rather held them in check.'[62]

Hardy took Mary's death with apparent calm, seeming to be relieved that she had been spared further pain, but his temporary avoidance of Talbothays is suggestive of severe inner distress, and by the middle of the month he had developed a heavy cold and taken to his room. Though the cold was real, its seriousness was exaggerated in order to justify a withdrawal that was primarily emotional. He announced to Florence that he never wanted to go anywhere or see anyone again but to live on quietly at Max Gate, shut up in his study, and Christmas was made miserable by his continuing refusal to see anyone other than Florence in her capacity as nurse—a role, she nevertheless assured Rebekah Owen, in which she felt entirely happy.[63] Kate, grieving over Mary and exhausted by her nursing of Henry, felt desolate and deserted, but Hardy's profound shock at the death of the sister who had been so much to him in childhood and early manhood apparently left him unready to encounter the other sister who so acutely reminded him of Mary yet meant so much less to him. On 10 February 1916, the second anniversary of Hardy's wedding, Kate went up to Max Gate to offer her congratulations, only to find that he seemed not to want to see her.[64] Writing to Nathaniel Sparks senior, she reported that her brother had changed greatly and aged considerably since Mary's death, and even at the beginning of April, when Hardy at last resumed his old habit of Sunday visits to Talbothays, the conversation struck Kate as altogether flatter and duller than it had been when Mary was alive.[65]

26

Life-Writing

Mary's death had made Hardy think more intensively about his own, and in February 1916 he began arranging for Florence and Sydney Cockerell to become his joint literary executors, recompensed out of royalties for their services. He completed the design for Mary's tombstone in Stinsford churchyard, saw to its proper execution, and ensured that it was correctly positioned in relation to the two accompanying tombs, one for Thomas and Jemima, the other for Emma—and eventually, so Hardy intended, for Florence and himself. When Florence's friend Ethel Inglis was taken on a visit to Stinsford in May 1916 Hardy produced a brush for cleaning the family tombs and used a penknife to scrape away the moss on the stone of Robert Reason, the 'original' of Mr Penny in *Under the Greenwood Tree*, saying as he did so that he felt just like Old Mortality.[1]

Nor had his obsession with Emma's memory yet faded. He kept in touch with Gordon and Lilian Gifford and required Florence, rather against her inclinations, to do the same. He also cultivated other Gifford relatives— even those who had never known Emma in her lifetime—and called upon some of them at Launceston while on a brief visit to St Juliot with Florence in September 1916. Melancholy as the purposes of the expedition were, Florence was at least able to regard it as a much-needed disruption of Hardy's increasingly reclusive habits.[2] The actual visit to St Juliot passed off pleasantly enough, with an inspection of the tablet to Emma's memory in the church itself and tea at the rectory with the current incumbent and his sister, but when they visited Tintagel Church in order to see how much it had changed in the years since Emma had sketched it, Hardy was appalled to be told by the vicar, in peremptory tones, to get out of the way of the processional route of the choir. It was almost the only time, Florence later recalled, that she had seen him really angry. Writing to Cockerell from Tintagel, she expressed the hope that her husband had 'found the germ of an Iseult poem'—a hope that seven years later bore fruit in *The Famous Tragedy of the Queen of Cornwall*.[3]

Florence's feelings about Cockerell fluctuated greatly during the course of 1916, and would long continue to do so. On the one hand he was immensely helpful to Hardy, almost like a son; on the other, he was so domineering as to be quite frightening. Florence's own voluminous correspondence with Cockerell vacillated accordingly from extremes of intimacy to extremes of hostility and ultimately to silence, but, like Rebekah Owen, Lady Hoare, Ethel Inglis, and other of Florence's correspondents, he became over the years the recipient of much personal information that Hardy must have intended to be—and imagined to have been—kept strictly within the walls of Max Gate. Privacy was very much on his mind at this particular moment when a sharpened sense of personal mortality was merging with family grief and wartime disasters to close him in upon himself and prompt the raising of drawbridges that had previously allowed ingress, however limited, from the outside world. He was narrowing down his range of trusted friends and becoming more than ever sensitive to gossip, even on quite trivial matters. Clodd, the accommodating host of Aldeburgh days, was now shut out of all confidence following detection of his readiness to share secrets with Shorter, and there was a moment of sheer terror when news arrived that he was about to publish his reminiscences. Florence, at her husband's bidding, sent off a letter of stern warning, but Clodd's *Memories*, when it arrived, proved to be of the discreetest kind, containing nothing—as Florence assured their author—'that the most ultrasensitive person could object to'.[4]

Shorter himself had for some time been beyond the Hardyan pale, even though Florence liked him and remained grateful for his having given her literary work before her marriage and kept her on ever since as a reviewer for the *Sphere*. During the war years he fell still further into disfavour by his doubtless profitable fondness for issuing private printings of Hardy's poems. Finally exasperated in May 1916 by Shorter's request for permission to do a similar limited-edition reprint of 'To Shakespeare after Three Hundred Years', Hardy returned a negative reply and encouraged Florence to publish the poem herself. Cockerell, who had recommended this course of action, oversaw the printing of the pamphlet at the Chiswick Press, where more than a dozen similar pamphlets would be printed over the next few years.[5] Their active cooperation in these projects helped to bring Cockerell and Florence closer together, at least for the time being.

Apart from the brief visit to Cornwall, Hardy stayed at Max Gate throughout the whole of 1916. It was astonishing, he observed to Gosse in December, that he, who had once been half a Londoner, should not have been to London all year. His routine was now one of long hours of work in his study each day, interrupted only by meals and a modicum of exercise. He would descend from his room at teatime, especially if visitors were present, and break off finally for the day when he came down to dinner—after which Florence would read aloud to him until he went to bed at 10.30 or so. When the work was going with especial smoothness he hated to interrupt it at all, believing as he did that when the wheels were going round it was a mistake to stop them, lest they proved impossible to restart. There were days, therefore, when he would have all meals, including dinner, in his study and even give up his daily walk.[6]

Hardy continued to be very productive as a poet and became more than ever insistent upon the superiority of his verse over his prose. He was impatient with books and articles about him which made no reference to the poetry, and in June 1915—in a gesture that seems attributable either to supreme vanity or to the most modest practicality—he asked Cockerell to go to the British Museum to arrange for the addition of 'poet' to 'novelist' after his name in the library's main catalogue.[7] No volume of new poems appeared during the year 1916, but Hardy took much interest in the compilation and publication, on 3 October, of *Selected Poems of Thomas Hardy*, containing a few poems not previously published but chiefly designed to make his verse more immediately accessible to a wider public in terms both of its modest price (*2s. 6d.*) and its exclusion of poems he thought likely to give offence. When Cockerell expressed regret at the omission of 'A Trampwoman's Tragedy', Florence concurred but explained that Hardy had wanted a volume that could be given 'to a school girl, or the most particular person'.[8]

During that autumn Hardy also completed the William Barnes section—consisting of a biographical survey, a critical preface, and a small group of poems—of the fifth and final volume of Thomas Humphry Ward's anthology *The English Poets*. He did little more than extract material from his Clarendon Press edition of 1908, but his willingness to undertake the task reflects the persistence, in this as in so many other matters, of long-standing loyalties. A significant element of local loyalty went, for example, into his *Wessex Scenes from 'The Dynasts'*, performed by the Dorchester amateurs in June 1916. Although these *Wessex Scenes* were based upon those presented in Dorchester in 1908, Hardy undertook a good deal of revision and expansion in preparation for the new production. A little romance thread, for example, involving a young waiting-woman and her soldier husband, was introduced in the opening scene and tied up in the third and last, for no very apparent reason other than to give more substance to the part of the waiting-woman, played by a young local actress named Gertrude Bugler who had made a striking Marty South in A. H. Evans's 1913 adaptation of *The Woodlanders*. Hardy was actively involved in the whole production, devoting to it much of the late spring of 1916, and he was present at most of the rehearsals of the original Weymouth performance, insisting, however, that the interest of the production lay 'not in the artistic effect of the play—which was really rather a patchwork affair, for the occasion—but in the humours of the characters whom we knew in private life as matter-of-fact shopkeepers & clerks'.[9] It was remarkable that a man of his age—he was now 76—should have been willing and able to devote so much energy to such a project, but Florence noticed that what had started out as a source of pleasurable excitement became in the end a cause of constant worry, and she resolved to discourage his participation in any future productions: 'He is too old for the worry and responsibility,' she complained, 'for of course if it is a failure it will reflect on him. It *has* worried him so.'[10]

Because the proceeds of the performances went to the Red Cross, Hardy was able to regard his labours as a contribution to the war effort. The news of the war, however, continued to be mostly bad, and the Dublin rising of Easter 1916 only confirmed Hardy's prejudice against all things Irish. On the other hand, he responded sympathetically to the plight of the German prisoners-of-war housed in a wartime hospital not far from Dorchester: 'T.H's kind heart melted,' Florence told Cockerell, 'at the sight of the wounded & he expressed his sympathy with them by eloquent gestures to which they responded in a most friendly manner . . . & now he is sending them some of his books in German—for their library.' Inevitably, Hardy registered the irony implicit in the location nearby of another hospital in which a great many English wounded lay in an equivalent state of helplessness, 'each scene of suffering caused by the other!'[11] Early in the following year some German prisoners came to Max Gate with their guards to remove trees from the kitchen garden and make room for more potatoes. 'They are amiable young fellows', Hardy reported to Florence Henniker, '& it does fill one with indignation that thousands of such are led to slaughter by the ambitions of Courts & Dynasties. If only there were no monarchies in the world, what a chance for its amelioration!'[12]

In the early stages of the Russian revolution of 1917 Hardy was very much of two minds, for while he felt sympathetic to the revolution in the abstract, there was no doubt that Russia's slackening its effort against Germany was greatly adding to the burden on the Allies. Throughout this whole dark period of the war he tried to sustain a balanced view. In March 1917 he published, at government request and after immense labour, his poetically unimpressive 'A Call to National Service', with its exhortation to all classes of men and women to come forward 'That scareless, scathless, England still may stand', but his belief in the necessity of his own country's survival and in the essential justice of its cause did not prevent him from publicly defending the *Cambridge Magazine*'s policy of publishing translated extracts from German and other foreign newspapers and thus, as he said, enabling England to be seen 'bare and unadorned—her chances in the struggle freed from distortion by the glamour of patriotism'. As he told John Galsworthy, he found it difficult to write patriotic poems, since he saw the other side too clearly.[13] The prevailing bleakness of his outlook was reflected in his anticipatory comment on *Moments of Vision*, being prepared for publication at the end of 1917: 'I do not expect much notice will be taken of these poems: they mortify the human sense of self-importance by showing, or suggesting, that human beings are of no matter or appreciable value in this nonchalant universe.'[14] As he struggled to see the present in an historical perspective, his mind dwelt, as so often before, upon the long and bitter Napoleonic struggle. He noted the anniversaries of Quatre Bras and Waterloo as they occurred, and declined an invitation to the contemporary French battlefields in company with James Barrie and John Buchan with the thought that if he wanted 'to feel military' he would have to content himself with the battles of the past.[15]

Although his reluctance to make such a trip at the age of 77 had been entirely understandable, it seemed part and parcel of that more general immovability which had been steadily coming over him of recent years and which Florence, for his sake and certainly for her own, was anxious to combat. They did, however, stay with Barrie in Adelphi Terrace for two nights at the end of July, when Hardy's old memories of his days with Blomfield merged with the novel experience of watching searchlights sweep the sky over south London in search of German aircraft. Florence had earlier won a small victory when she was allowed not only to go to Enfield to be present at her sister Margaret's wedding to a young airman named Reginald Soundy, but also to invite the couple to spend their honeymoon at Max Gate: 'Bravo F!!!!!' exclaimed Kate Hardy, who had made her own first London visit in many years in order to be present at the wedding.[16] In June Florence went up to London to see Macleod Yearsley again, and consult another specialist who prescribed a course of bacteriological inoculations as treatment for the chronic pharyngitis which had now been diagnosed. To Rebekah Owen she once again complained of having to pay her own medical costs: 'Of course were I Lilian Gifford a cheque would be written joyfully.'[17]

Florence's expression of resentment seems, as on a good many other occasions, to have been somewhat in excess of what the situation really warranted. Hardy shared Kate's and Henry's dislike and distrust of the medical profession: 'If you send for a doctor I shall be ill' was his customary cry whenever Florence became anxious about his health. He evidently had no faith that the inoculations would have any effect, Florence herself having expressed fear that the money would be wasted. At the same time, he felt it improper to prevent his wife from spending her own money as she saw fit. She had a small private income derived from the investment of Sir Thornley Stoker's legacy; she earned something from her journalism; and although no formal settlement was made at the time of her marriage, it seems to have been established early on that she would meet from her own resources such personal outlays as went beyond the allowances her husband made her for clothes, household expenses, and so on.[18] That Hardy might even so have paid his wife's medical bills it is impossible to deny, and his broader reputation for meanness in old age seems traceable very largely to his having achieved affluence too late to be fully at ease with it. Though taught—one might almost say programmed—to be always and unhesitatingly supportive of his parents and siblings, he otherwise fell back upon the careful habits of his own earlier years and upon those policies of prudent restraint in anticipation of potential disaster that he and his sisters had learned from their mother and from generations of past experience, a kind of racial memory. Some allowance must also be made for the desperate wartime situation, the decline in the value of investments, the constant sense of the need for austerity, especially at the height of the German submarine campaign, and Hardy's apocalyptic fears of the state to which his own household might conceivably be reduced: in April 1917 he was wondering whether he and Florence could, if driven to it, feed Wessex and even themselves upon the cow-parsley which grew so profusely at Max Gate.[19]

Florence's persistence in writing complaining letters to Rebekah Owen and Sydney Cockerell involved her in acts of indiscretion that Hardy would never have countenanced, had he become aware of them, and in a kind of disloyalty that was disturbingly similar to her predecessor's. But whereas Emma had obviously intended her complaints to get abroad, Florence at least requested her correspondents to keep her revelations to themselves: 'My dear Betty,' she implored Rebekah Owen, 'if anything should happen to me I *entreat* you to burn every scrap of my writing. I do write so carelessly & injudiciously that I fear there are letters of mine preserved that I should hate to have seen.'[20] Such letters were no doubt an essential element in her psychological economy, as were Emma's protests in hers—an occupation, a release, even a kind of revenge, during the long solitary hours spent waiting for Hardy to emerge from his study, an opportunity for utterance in a world that hung always on his words but never on his wife's, an outlet for a sense of grievance that was fed as much by the exasperations of house-keeping and of dealing with Hardy's relatives as by the behaviour of Hardy himself. Not many months of marriage had been needed to bring her to a sharper appreciation of how difficult it had been for Emma to confront, without friends, allies, or even local roots of her own, the solid phalanx of the Hardy clan. At bottom, however, there remained Florence's own melancholy temperament. As she herself fully recognized, it not only predisposed her to the 'profuse grumbling' that she claimed did not really 'mean very much' but plunged her into moods so profoundly depressive that she could scarcely control—and sometimes did not seek to control—the reckless extravagance of her complaints and accusations.[21] Since the mood of exasperation or despair was often exhausted by the mere act of expressing it in writing, she was sometimes surprised by the response of her correspondents to letters she had dashed off and then promptly forgotten.

A three-day trip to Plymouth and Torquay with Hardy in October 1917 was marred by heavy rain and by Hardy's persistence in visiting the decaying houses and overgrown graves of departed Giffords. A still sterner trial was the publication, on 30 November, of *Moments of Vision*. Hardy had engrossed himself with great enthusiasm in the completion of the volume, and when he was correcting the proofs in early September Florence reported him as being extremely cheerful, as he always was when a piece of work had reached that stage. She felt, however, that the volume, like *Satires of Circumstance*, showed her in a poor light, suggesting by its continual memo-rialization of Emma that 'T.H's second marriage is a most disastrous one & that his sole wish is to find refuge in the grave with her with whom alone he found happiness. Well—all things end somewhen.'[22] Florence had been familiar with the contents of the volume long before its publication—she and Cockerell had joined forces in August to dissuade Hardy from includ-ing 'The Sound of Her'—and she ought, perhaps, to have been mollified by Hardy's inscription in her own copy: 'From Thomas Hardy, this first copy of the first edition, to the first of women Florence Hardy. Nov: 1917'.[23] She might also have recalled the wise advice about the danger of identifying the poet with the man that Lady Hoare had sent her at the time when *Satires of Circumstance* appeared. But she did none of these things, until—up in

London for another round of visits to specialists—she broke down and wept at a matinée of *Dear Brutus*, that poignant play about the 'might-have-beens' of life, and had to be comforted and reassured by an 'old friend of my husband', almost certainly the author of *Dear Brutus* himself, Sir James Barrie.[24]

The new volume, larger than any of its predecessors, did indeed contain a great many poems devoted to Emma in the mood, if not always of the quality, of 'Poems of 1912–13'. The scenes and occasions of these later poems, however, now extended beyond the St Juliot days to other phases of the marriage, and the fading of romance was confronted for the first time in terms of Emma's mental deterioration—notably in 'The Interloper' but also, by implication, in 'Near Lanivet'. Autobiographical themes unrelated to Emma were also sounded in the numerous examples of what, in an abandoned title for the volume, Hardy once called 'Moments from the Years'[25]—poems prompted by vivid recollections of past experiences. Such moments were often quite spontaneously brought to mind by some memory-triggering accident of sight, sound, touch, or smell. They could also emerge from the deliberate stimulation of memories in which Hardy was quite consciously indulging when he looked from Max Gate out across the fields to Kingston Maurward and the woods that hid Higher Bockhampton, when he walked upon Puddletown heath or along the path to Winterborne Came, when he wandered among the graves in Stinsford churchyard, or when he leafed his way through his old pocketbooks and pondered upon things he had seen, thought, sketched, or half-written in years long gone.

It was upon just this kind of exercise that Hardy was engaged in September 1916 when he walked up onto the heath, stood on the old coach road, and 'had visions' of George III and his court, of Admiral Hardy, and of his mother as a child.[26] In October 1917 he cited 'In Time of "the Breaking of Nations"', the poem he had recently written on the basis of notes made at St Juliot in 1870, as an instance of his 'faculty . . . for burying an emotion in my heart or brain for forty years, and exhuming it at the end of that time as fresh as when interred'. Intense autobiographical recovery is indeed central to almost all his best work, in verse and prose alike, and much as Florence hated those melancholy visits to Stinsford churchyard and the rare expeditions to St Juliot, they made a crucial contribution to the extraordinary poetic creativity of Hardy's old age—and to the exceptional happiness with which, as Florence proudly reported to Cockerell, Hardy approached the end of 1917. On New Year's Eve she repeated the good news to Rebekah Owen, characteristically couching it within a disconsolate comment of her own: 'My husband is very well & amazingly cheerful in spite of his gloomy poems. I wish people knew that he was really happy, for strangers must imagine that his only wish is to die & be in the grave with the only woman who ever gave him any happiness.'[27]

The persistence of a retrospective mood throughout 1917 was intimately related to the beginning of work on the biographical narrative that was for the most part written by Hardy himself but eventually published, after his death, as *The Early Life of Thomas Hardy* and *The Later Years of Thomas Hardy*, a two-volume official biography attributed, on the title pages, to Florence Emily Hardy. Just when and how the scheme was first conceived and decided upon is by no means clear. Such circumstances as Mary's death, Henry's serious illness, and Hardy's own advancing age all played their part, as doubtless did Cockerell's gift of the third-person autobiography of the early nineteenth-century radical boot-maker named Thomas Hardy— no relation but in some respects a kindred spirit—who explained in his preface that he had chosen to write in the third rather than the first person in order to 'obviate the necessity of calling the great *I* so repeatedly to my assistance'.[28] If this was intended as a hint, Cockerell soon became more explicit, urging Hardy in a letter of December 1915 'to write down something about yourself—& especially about that youthful figure whose photograph I have got, & of whom you told me that you could think with almost complete detachment'. With Florence's help, Cockerell continued, Hardy could create a rich account of his own childhood, 'even if, as you have intended, only landmarks and special episodes of the later years are recorded'.[29] Cockerell and Florence seem to have been allies in this particular campaign, and it may well have been, as asserted in the prefatory note to *Early Life*, at Florence's 'strong request' that the project was first deliberately embarked upon.[30] It offered her, after all, the opportunity to make herself directly useful to her husband and help in protecting his posthumous reputation and at the same time find purposeful, congenial, and sustained employment for her own under-used literary energies.

Hardy was, as he had always been, an intensely private man who felt (as many another author has done) that the world should be concerned only with his writings, not with the life or personality of the writer himself. But by 1917 he was approaching 80. He had been famous for many years, exposed to the importunities of literary pilgrims, the sensationalism of journalists, and the bookmaking of academics. Particularly alive in his memory was the distressing experience of reading F. A. Hedgcock's *Thomas Hardy: penseur et artiste*, published in Paris in 1911. Hedgcock was a serious scholar and his book primarily a critical study, but it opened with a biographical chapter to which Hardy took violent exception, writing in the margins of his copy such comments as 'All this is too personal, & in bad taste, even supposing it were true, which it is not. , . . It betrays the cloven foot of the "interviewer".' He effectively discouraged the publication of an English translation of Hedgcock's book, and attempted to extort from subsequent interviewers the promise that nothing he said would be quoted in print.[31] Obliged to recognize that such assaults on his privacy would continue for the rest of his life, and on into the years after his death, he eventually became persuaded that, if biographies there must be, they could best be thwarted, countered, or at least given a favourable direction by the prior publication of his own version of his life's significant events. Given the circumstances in which he found himself—given above all the presence of a collaborator who had already written and published books of her own—it was relatively easy to move from the idea of a third-person autobiography to that of an 'official' biography written by the subject but destined for posthumous publication over the name of the collaborator.

Work on the project began in earnest during the calamitous wartime summer of 1917, and much of its subsequent progress can be followed in Florence's numerous and indiscreet letters to Sydney Cockerell. 'I have been taking notes,' she told him on 23 July 1917, 'but find them very difficult to do without constantly referring to T.H. for verification, and he is now almost at the end of his present job—revising his note-books (they are practically diaries)—and we are going to work together. At least that is what we propose doing. Man proposes—.'[32] In September 1917 she wrote to say that Hardy was happily at work on the last batch of proofs for *Moments of Vision* and that as soon as he had finished the job he intended 'to go on giving me facts about his life. I have got as far as the time he started work in London, but a lot can be filled in. He seems quite enthusiastic now about the idea, and of course I love doing it.'[33]

Hardy seems first to have written—or possibly dictated to Florence—an account of his early life that went as far as his first year or so in London. Stimulated by that initial exercise in retrospection, he then went through all the little pocketbooks of observations, plots, and occasional drawings that he had kept at least since the 1860s, cutting or copying out individual items for incorporation into the composite narrative he was building up. He also sorted through and largely destroyed the mass of incoming correspondence that had accumulated over the years. So far as his own outgoing letters were concerned, the need for secrecy made it impossible to seek their return from the friends to whom he had sent them, and his only resort was to search out the drafts or copies he had retained of particularly important letters, although these tended not to be personal communications but letters written for publication in newspapers and magazines. The 'Materials'—the collective Max Gate term for items set aside for potential inclusion—were not in any case regarded as entirely sacrosanct, Hardy being perfectly prepared, if need be, to modify old notes and letters that no longer struck him as happily phrased, or gently refurbish the original diary entries in the light of subsequent events. Such adjustments of the historical record were entirely in accordance with the accepted flexibilities of the Victorian 'Life and Letters' tradition, and became significant only because so many of the original documents were subsequently destroyed.

The actual composition of the 'Life' was conducted with the degree of secrecy deemed to be necessary for Florence's sake, as the ostensible author, as well as for Hardy's own reputation, both immediate and posthumous. Hardy's holograph manuscript was written in his study in the strictest privacy, the sheets slipped under the blotting paper whenever anyone entered, and then handed over page by page to Florence to be typed up in three copies, a ribbon copy and two carbons. Hardy would correct and revise the third of these copies (the second carbon), and then pass it to his wife for her to transfer the changes into copy two (the first carbon) and subsequently, when his final approval had been given to them, into the ribbon copy intended for the printer—which would, in theory, contain no visible trace of his participation. By the end of 1919 the narrative seems to have been completed up to the end of May 1918 and to have been put temporarily aside, a note in Hardy's hand certifying it as 'in approximately printable condition' up to that point.[34] He did come back to it later, however, inserting a little, revising a great deal, and continuing to add to the 'Materials' the diary entries, copies of letters, and miscellaneous notes that Florence would be able to draw upon in writing the final chapters.

Told, so to speak, in cold blood, the circumstances in which the Hardy 'Life' was written and originally published can be, and have been, made to sound eccentric, fantastic, and vaguely discreditable, and neither Hardy nor Florence can be wholly exonerated from the charge of disingenuousness. At the same time, the title page of *The Early Life of Thomas Hardy*, the first of the posthumously published volumes, would come remarkably close to strict accuracy in its statement that the volume had been 'compiled' by Florence 'largely from contemporary notes, letters, diaries, and biographical memoranda, as well as from oral information in conversations extending over many years'. And for Hardy and Florence it was at the time and in the circumstances a perfectly sensible, down-to-earth undertaking, putting

Florence essentially in the position of an authorized biographer blessed with unlimited access to an ideally cooperative subject and enabling Hardy to throw over what he wanted to say the aura of authenticity and impersonality implicit in the use of the third-person point of view. The directly confessional and revelatory impulses were entirely foreign to him, and he had in any case woven his richest autobiographical experiences into the very texture of his novels and poems. His concern as he approached the end of his life was simply to set out what he regarded as the basic record of his career, pay tribute to his forebears, obtain a final hearing for his thoughts on the nature of existence, cruelty to animals, and other favourite topics, and project on into the future the protective cover he had so long and earnestly kept in place over the deepest sources of his inspiration and the innermost recesses of his extraordinarily private self.

Although most reviewers responded positively to *Moments of Vision*, a few confessed themselves puzzled and even repelled by its melancholy and unconventionality. The *Athenaeum*'s reference to the writing as displaying 'something of the gracelessness of a youth learning to skate' was one of the comments that prompted Hardy to jot down harsh comments about the imperceptiveness of reviewers and their incapacity to appreciate that art might be deliberately employed in the concealment of art. To Florence Henniker he complained that although the fifty or so reviews his publishers had sent him were certainly 'friendly enough', all but five or six of them were 'deplorably inept, purblind, & of far less *value* than the opinion of one's grocer or draper . . . I always fancy I could point out the best, & the worst, in a volume of poems, which none of these did. But perhaps that is my self-conceit, for I have had no experience as a reviewer.' He was also provoked by the persistence of the conventional romantic view of what 'true poets' must necessarily be like: 'They must all be impractical in the conduct of their affairs; nay, they must almost, like Shelley or Marlowe, be drowned or done to death, or like Keats, die of consumption.' What was so often forgotten, despite his own poem, 'An Ancient to Ancients', published in *Late Lyrics*, was that some of the greatest writers of the ancient world—Homer, Aeschylus, Sophocles, and Euripides—had done their best work in old age, their 'poetic spark' always latent but its 'outspringing . . . frozen and delayed for half a lifetime'.[35]

Although Hardy's successful career as a novelist had provided him with the springboard from which to launch *Wessex Poems*, it had subsequently proved something of an impediment, allowing and even encouraging reviewers to seize on what they saw as the prosaic qualities of his verse as an occasion for lamenting his abandonment of prose. He himself believed that his being 'unpoetically' old in years and uninterestingly domestic in his habits further discouraged critics from taking him seriously as an artist, and that it was therefore increasingly necessary to insist upon the absoluteness of his dedication to what he had described in the General Preface to the Wessex Edition as 'the more individual part of my literary fruitage'.[36] He dwelt upon this difficulty when, in February 1918, he supplied Edmund Gosse with information for 'Mr. Hardy's Lyrical Poems', the article he was writing for the *Edinburgh Review*: 'For the relief of my necessities, as the Prayer Book puts it, I began writing novels, & made a sort of trade of it; but last night I found that I had spent more years in verse-writing than at prose-writing! (prose 25½ yrs—verse 26 yrs) Yet my verses will always be considered a bye-product, I suppose, owing to this odd accident of the printing press.'[37] Gosse duly pointed up this theme in his own opening paragraph and then proceeded to survey the whole of Hardy's poetic career from 1860 to *Moments of Vision*, stressing his friend's remarkable capacity for discerning and dramatizing the extraordinary and the ordinary, the tragic and the mundane: 'There is absolutely no observation too minute, no flutter of reminiscence too faint, for Mr. Hardy to adopt as the subject of a metaphysical lyric. . . . [H]e seems to make no selection, and his field is modest to humility and yet practically boundless.' Astonishingly, however, Gosse dismissed *Satires of Circumstance*, containing 'Poems of 1912–13', as the most dispensable of Hardy's volumes, a judgement that fully justified Hardy's oblique reference, in thanking Gosse for the article, to his having read it 'as if it were concerning a writer altogether unknown to me'.[38]

The year 1918 was devoted almost entirely to the completion of 'Life and Work' and to the various clearing-out and tidying-up operations associated with it. By 11 June Florence had typed up the narrative as far as 1895. Later that same month, after Hardy had revised the typescript up to 1892, he insisted, much to Florence's distress, upon burning the holograph manuscript for the entire 1840–92 period. In the autumn he spent much of his time going through the piles of reviews that had accumulated over the years, eliminating almost everything of a 'belittling or invidious nature', and pasting the items he wished to preserve into the large scrapbooks which still survive.[39] Since those scrapbooks contain a fair number of somewhat hostile reviews, it would appear that by 'belittling or invidious' Hardy meant not so much critically disparaging as dealing offensively in personalities.

Hardy worked at these tasks with immense energy and eagerness, insisting that they be done right even at the cost of the laborious revision, rewriting, and sometimes retyping of what Florence had thought of as finished work. Though she remonstrated from time to time, she had already learned that Hardy would not go back on a decision once made. Apologizing to Rebekah Owen in February 1918 for Hardy's refusal to autograph his new book for her, she explained that at his age there was naturally a certain 'fixity of purpose'. Yet he wonderfully retained, she told Cockerell, 'that inner radiance of his: a true sun-shine giver', and while the war news was deeply depressing they had neither of them 'ever expected that we should defeat Germany'.[40] Hardy reacted with horror to the suggestion that Florence's sister Margaret might have her baby at Max Gate, but proved perfectly willing to allow Margaret to stay with them during her pregnancy, even though, as Florence confessed, he much preferred the two of them to be alone there together. When the time came he raised no objection to the child's being named Thomas in his honour, and doubtless thought what Florence said—how much a baby would have been welcomed at Max Gate in years gone by. To Mrs Henniker, however, he commented a little sourly on the event, observing that if he were a woman he would 'think twice before entering into matrimony in these days of emancipation, when everything is open to the sex'.[41]

Apart from a brief illness in October and a severe attack in March that was blamed upon eating a tart made of bottled plums, Hardy remained well and physically active throughout most of 1918. When in April he and Florence made a sentimental visit to the Higher Bockhampton cottage (now occupied by Hermann Lea) on the afternoon the recently rediscovered manuscript of *Far from the Madding Crowd* was being auctioned at a Red Cross sale in London, Hardy found the cycle ride something of an effort. But it had been his first outing of the year, and he made many more such trips in the course of the spring and summer, most of them to Talbothays, where he and Florence were frequent visitors, some a little further afield.[42] He also continued his modest participation in local affairs. Although he had rarely served as a JP on the Dorchester bench since becoming a county magistrate in 1894, Hardy returned there on five occasions in the years 1917–19, chiefly in order to adjudicate in a number of food-profiteering cases. He seems to have seen it as another form of war work, but Florence, faced with the day-to-day difficulties of shopping in a time of severe food shortages, was exasperated by his fining their own grocer £15 for selling ground rice at a halfpenny per pound too much.[43] In January 1918 he had taken a lively interest in the local revival of *The Mellstock Quire*, and at one of the last rehearsals of the dances incorporated into the production he picked up a fiddle and played one of the tunes: 'He did not dance', Florence told Cockerell, 'but he was *longing* to I could see, & would have footed it as bravely as any.'[44]

Cockerell made two visits to Max Gate in 1918, and had by this time established himself almost as a member of the household. There were visits, too, from actual members of the family, including Frank George's siblings and a granddaughter of Christopher Hand, whose early reputation as a heavy drinker had yielded in later years to his local fame as one of the regular prizewinners at the Puddletown Cottage Garden and Horticultural Show.[45] Max Gate remained, however, on the fringes rather than at the centre of the Hardy network, its owner's habits and routines tending to discourage unheralded visits. The Higher Bockhampton cottage had always functioned as the clearing-house for family news and local gossip, as well as a focus for the preservation and recital of family memories and local legends, but now that no Hardys lived there its role had passed, with some inevitable diminishment, to Talbothays, and especially to Kate, whose diary for these years makes frequent mention of visits from relatives and family friends. Through his own visits to Talbothays Hardy thus remained in touch, directly and indirectly, with a range of relatives and connections that included the children and grandchildren of several cousins, even as he continued to keep up with Florence's parents and sisters and with several of Emma's relatives.

He bought the house Charles Meech Hardy was living in at Puddletown in order to prevent his being turned out, and when, after his death, his widow left Puddletown, Hardy wrote to assist her admission to an almshouse.[46] When Gordon Gifford made it known, early in 1923, that he was worried about losing his position as an architect with the London County Council, Hardy asked Lady St Helier, as an alderman of the council, to make enquiries of the head of Gordon's department, and was soon able to assure his nephew that his position was quite secure. He was also exercised about the future of Lily Whitby, a granddaughter of William Jenkins Hardy and first cousin of Frank George, although he did not feel comfortable with the suggestion that she should stay at Max Gate when Florence was away. And Florence herself, though dubious as to the wisdom and appropriateness of some of Hardy's financial gestures, did not deny or belittle her husband's kindness and generosity to distant relatives, 'even those he dislikes'.[47] Though sharply conscious of his own childlessness, and that of his brother and sisters—'I am at the fag end of my family,' he wrote to one of Emma's cousins in 1919—Hardy held tenaciously to his belief in the family as a force for cohesion and a focus of loyalty, and told Sir George

Douglas how much he regretted 'the way in which families scatter themselves with a light heart'.[48]

Hardy's omission of most of his uncles, aunts, and cousins from the family tree he drew up at about this time has frequently been regarded as a sign of deliberate obfuscation or snobbishness, or indeed of both. But 'The Hardy Pedigree', never intended for publication, sprang like most such exercises from Hardy's interest in his personal ancestry, in the identity of his own grandparents, great-grandparents, and other forebears, and quite naturally took the form of an inverted pyramid, with his own name at the foot of the page, linked to left and right with the corresponding genealogies of his two wives, headed 'The Gifford Pedigree' and 'The Dugdale Pedigree'. Hardy duly indicated the number of siblings in his parents' families, but any attempt to record each name and the name of each spouse—let alone the names of all the children and all the children's children—would have resulted in a hopelessly confused and crowded page. He had nearly sixty first cousins, after all, and although one of Martha (Sparks) Duffield's grandsons had been brought to England in 1902 to be admired at Max Gate and christened in Puddletown Church[49] it would have been impossible for Hardy, with the best will in the world, to identify all the Australian descendants of Martha Duffield and her sister Emma (Sparks) Cary, trace the tentacular ramifications of his Aunt Martha's family in Canada, or even keep track of the multi-generational host of Hands and Hardys who had scattered to London, Bristol, Windsor, and other parts of the British Isles. Hardy has also been accused of being concerned only with those family members and connections who belonged or attained to the middle class. That does not in fact appear to be a sustainable generalization, but even if it were, that would only be to say that he took an entirely natural interest in those few relatives who had, like himself, departed in some way from the otherwise monotonous family pattern of employment and marriage within the inherited boundaries of occupation and class. If he gave particular attention to such remote relatives as the Childses, that was partly because they displayed some literary interests—otherwise rarely discoverable in his background—but also because he had access to genealogical information volunteered by the family's living members.

27

Tea at Max Gate

Hardy's fame and popularity, reinforced by the lure of Wessex itself, brought an ever-increasing stream of visitors to Max Gate, and it was at teatime that Hardy routinely made himself available to each day's intake. As early as 1918 Florence could write in her diary: 'No-one to tea—blessed relief.' John Cowper Powys, during the following summer, found Hardy ready to talk 'gaily and cheerfully' about 'all manner of little things', from a punctured bicycle tyre to 'the names in the cemetery near Portland Bill'. Recounting the visit to his brother Llewelyn, Powys described Florence as looking like 'a grave ascetic art student or a Chelsea socialist, follower of William Morris', with 'her hair parted Madonna-wise and a very responsible air'.[1] Clement Shorter, though dignified in Florence's eyes by the recent loss of his wife, forfeited her good opinion and confirmed himself in Hardy's low one by arriving uninvited at Max Gate on its owner's seventy-eighth birthday and behaving badly throughout his visit. When the literary journalist Arthur Compton Rickett came to tea, Hardy suspected him of biographical designs and delayed coming downstairs from his study for more than an hour.[2]

Among the newcomers to Max Gate none created deeper impressions than Siegfried Sassoon and Charlotte Mew. Sassoon was Hamo Thornycroft's nephew, and Hardy, 'always longing to come across some great new poet', as Florence told an American correspondent early in 1918, had taken an early and eager interest in his work. They exchanged letters for a time but did not meet until 6 November 1918, when Sassoon immediately became Hardy's '*adored* young friend' and, for Florence, 'one of the most brilliant, & handsome & likeable young men I know'.[3] Miss Mew, first brought to their attention by Cockerell, proved to possess singularly little personal charm ('a plain shabby little thing'), and to be not Hardy's type of woman at all.[4] But her conversation and her poems were alike impressive, and Hardy and Florence both became deeply interested in her work and welfare.

Another welcome visitor was Elliott Felkin, a lieutenant stationed at a nearby prisoner-of-war camp, who quickly established himself as a favourite at Max Gate and became the recipient of many Hardyan observations and reminiscences. One day Hardy took Felkin on the standard tour of Stinsford churchyard and showed him Emma's tomb:

> As he talked about it and her his voice became quavery, and there were tears in his eyes, and all the time we were round the spot he lost the thread of what he was saying. . . . He said if you ever want to put up a tomb that you think won't be much cared for, put one up like that, not a cross, which falls over and has bad lettering. That will last for hundreds of years. I thought of it like that because, you see, I have no descendants. He said he could not make up his mind about the inscription— 'THIS FOR REMEMBRANCE'—which was partly from Shakespeare and partly from the Bible, and where to put it, at the head or the side. I felt at first embarrassed by all these private questions, but he went on talking quite simply about it, so that one could give frank answers.

Hardy had, Felkin noted, an extraordinary capacity for 'treating young people not as if you were pretending to make yourself young out of politeness, nor as if you were instructing or guiding by the wisdom of experience, but as if you really felt that age and youth had something to give each other. . . . I should like to be like that when I am old.'[5] Though certainly growing old and becoming forgetful of recent events, Hardy was in good health and, as Florence told Cockerell, his memory of his early childhood was still 'miraculous'. 'When I first met him', she added, 'he was so wonderful—he was writing "The Dynasts" and his mind was luminous. Not but that he isn't far beyond the average young man even now.'[6]

The Armistice of November 1918 was greeted at Max Gate with relief but not with much optimism. The event is not even mentioned in the pages of *Life and Work*. But at the beginning of May 1919 the return of peace, endorsed by the return of spring, did rouse Hardy to the point of taking Florence on a short visit to London, where they stayed with Barrie at his Adelphi Terrace flat. Hardy went with Barrie to the Royal Academy dinner; with Florence he attended the Royal Academy Private View, called on Maurice Macmillan and on the Gosses, dined at Lady St Helier's, and lunched with Sir Frederick and Lady Macmillan.[7] Although the Royal Academy dinner had been the occasion for the trip, the need to discuss several matters with Sir Frederick Macmillan had perhaps been its principal motivation. A new volume of the Wessex Edition, containing *Satires of Circumstance* and *Moments of Vision*, was shortly to appear (Hardy read proof later that same month); a one-volume *Collected Poems*, incorporating all the volumes thus far published, was also to be brought out that autumn, in a format matching that of the one-volume edition of *The Dynasts*; and Macmillan had recently set in motion arrangements for the publication of the thirty-seven-volume Mellstock Edition, a replacement for the projected *édition de luxe* whose publication had been thwarted by the outbreak of the war.[8]

Although the war's end meant that 1919 was relatively free of deaths and mourning, that August brought one especially troubling and poignant piece of news. Lilian Gifford, whose mother had died in February, had now been diagnosed as a paranoiac and committed, as 'a person of unsound mind', to the London County Council asylum at Claybury in Essex. Florence, distressed by thoughts of her own past hostility to Lilian, went to Claybury to see her. She also saw Gordon Gifford and his wife and, since Lilian's mind seems not to have been at all dangerously disordered, was able to arrange for her to be released from confinement a year or so later on the basis of financial and other guarantees both from Max Gate and from some of Lilian's relatives.[9] Although Lilian had been admitted to Claybury as a 'pauper', Hardy had in fact provided for her more liberally than Florence had imagined: in addition to the small but by no means derisory annuity, which was still intact, he had purchased in her name some gilt-edged securities that Lilian had subsequently traded for more speculative stocks. Because of Lilian's relation to Emma and his own affectionate memories of her as a child and young woman, Hardy at first spoke of having her to live at Max Gate as soon as she was released, but Henry, Kate, and of course Florence were all opposed to the idea, and he himself—despite, as Florence wryly observed to Cockerell, his habit of idealizing people as soon as they were out of reach—recognized that Lilian's unreasoning discontents were all too reminiscent of Emma's afflictions, and that it might be unwise to expose himself to the repetition of an experience which had already caused such anguish.[10]

That October Siegfried Sassoon came to Max Gate for the weekend, bringing with him the 'Poets' Tribute', a handsomely bound volume containing holograph copies of poems by forty-three poets—from Bridges, Kipling, and Yeats to Graves, Sassoon, and D. H. Lawrence. Hardy was touched by the gesture and pleased to be honoured in such a fashion, and set himself the not inconsiderable task of thanking personally, and distinctively, each of the poets involved.[11] He also took more trouble than might have been expected in composing the little speech he made at the opening, on 2 December 1919, of the Bockhampton Reading-Room and Club, erected in Lower Bockhampton as a local war memorial almost on the spot where Robert Reason's shoemaker's shop had once stood. Hardy's immersion in the past was now so habitual and so intense as to threaten almost to overwhelm the present, and it seems to have surprised neither Florence nor himself that he saw a ghost in Stinsford churchyard that Christmas Eve, just after putting a sprig of holly on the grave of the grandfather he had never known. A figure in eighteenth-century costume said, 'A green Christmas'; Hardy replied, 'I like a green Christmas'; but when he followed the strange figure into the church he found no one there.[12]

On 2 June 1920, Hardy's eightieth birthday, Augustine Birrell, Anthony Hope Hawkins, and John Galsworthy arrived at Max Gate to present him with an address of congratulation from the Incorporated Society of Authors. Barrie—with whom Hardy had stayed in April when he attended the wedding of Harold Macmillan and Lady Dorothy Cavendish—was also at Max Gate that summer and was confirmed in his sense of Hardy's having 'something about him more attractive than I find in almost any other man—a simplicity that really merits the adjective *divine*—I could conceive some of the disciples having been thus'.[13] Charles Morgan, as manager of the Oxford University Dramatic Society, saw much of Hardy during the visit he made to Oxford in February 1920 to receive an honorary D.Litt. and attend an OUDS production of scenes from *The Dynasts*. To Morgan's eyes there was something self-protective in Hardy's determination to be 'unspectacular', 'something deliberately "ordinary" in his demeanour which was a concealment of extraordinary fires'. At the same time, by neither pretending that he was young nor presuming upon his years, Hardy achieved without apparent effort or artifice the easy relationship with his juniors that Elliott Felkin had so admired. It was also in 1920 that Sydney Cockerell's friend Katharine Webb remarked how Hardy had changed in thirty years from 'a rather rough-looking man, dressed very unlike his fellows, with a very keen alert face and a decided accent of some kind', to 'a refined, fragile, gentle little old gentleman, with. . . a gentle and smooth voice and polished manners'.[14]

Looking back upon the world and his own career from the vantage point of his eightieth year, Hardy found little cause for rejoicing. The immense material advances in the years since his birth had not been accompanied by any corresponding progress in 'real civilization'—in human kindness, in consideration for other people and for the lower animals. The war was over but the peace concluded at Versailles in June 1919 seemed to him disastrous, a view for which he found support in his reading of John Maynard Keynes's *The Economic Consequences of the Peace*. Nor did he see much hope for a future which depended upon 'the young and feeble League of Nations'. To his old friend Pearce Edgcumbe he speculated about 'our probable retrogression during the next 60 years to the point from which we started (not to say further)—to turnpike-road travelling, high postage, scarce newspapers (for lack of paper to print them on), oppression of one class by another, etc., etc.' Art and poetry, he believed, would be among the first casualties of the impending decline in civilization, and the belief was sustained by the continuing incomprehension (as he somewhat extravagantly saw it) of his own work.[15]

In July 1919 he wrote a stinging letter to Robert Lynd about his failure, when reviewing *Moments of Vision*, to recognize the onomatopoeic element in the poem 'On Sturminster Foot-Bridge'. He was still more dismayed by the February 1920 issue of the *Fortnightly*, in which Frederic Harrison attacked his pessimism on personal as well as on literary and philosophical grounds: 'Byron, Shelley, Keats, were all exiles from home, decried, destined to early death abroad. And yet their pessimism was occasional. But Thomas Hardy has everything that man can wish—long and easy life, perfect domestic happiness, warm friends, the highest honour his Sovereign can give, the pride of a wide countryside.' Clearly, then, Harrison concluded, the 'monotony of gloom' in his verse 'is not human, not social, not true'. Hardy spent two days drafting replies, but was eventually dissuaded by Florence from sending any of them; his long friendship with Harrison, however, he regarded as totally at an end.[16] When Alfred Noyes, a far less intimate acquaintance, made a similar attack on Hardy's 'philosophy' later that same year, Hardy did respond, and at some length, insisting that, like many other thinkers, he saw the power behind the universe not as malign, as Noyes had argued, but simply as without feeling, purpose, or morality of any kind whatsoever—and as, in any case, unknowable:

In my fancies, or poems of the imagination, I have of course called this Power all sorts of names—never supposing they would be taken for more than fancies. I have even in prefaces warned readers to take them only as such—as mere impressions of the moment, exclamations, in fact. But it has always been my misfortune to presuppose a too intelligent reading public, and no doubt people will go on thinking that I really believe the Prime Mover to be a malignant old gentleman, a sort of King of Dahomey,—an idea which, so far from my holding it, is to me irresistibly comic. 'What a fool one must have been to write for such a public!' is the inevitable reflection at the end of one's life.[17]

To many of Hardy's friends his insistence upon the unfairness of contemporary criticism seemed unreasonable and lacking in proportion. But Hardy did not undertake statistical surveys of favourable and unfavourable comments, nor had he lost with age the sensitivities of earlier years. The famous public figure of the 1920s was the same man who, fifty years earlier, had been rendered utterly wretched by a review of the anonymously published *Desperate Remedies*. And while he had become accustomed to the trivialities and crudities of journalistic reviewing, he could still be brought close to despair by displays of incomprehension on the part of 'serious' critics, especially those who had enjoyed his friendship over many years. It was perhaps not surprising that he was deeply impressed by the calmness and repose of the cathedrals of Exeter and Wells when he visited them that spring, and felt that he would have preferred to be a cathedral organist to anything else in the world.[18]

Katharine Webb thought Florence 'the most melancholy person' she had ever encountered, full of complaints about her inability to get away from Max Gate, especially during the grim winter months 'when the dead leaves stick on the window-pane and the wind moans and the sky is grey and you can't even see as far as the high road'. The trees at Max Gate were indeed thicker and higher than ever, making it increasingly difficult to grow flowers successfully, and Florence wondered whether Hardy's having been walled in by trees for so much of his life might not be one reason for the 'sombre hue' of his work.[19] Meanwhile the servant problem had again become acute and the viciousness of Wessex—who not only bit postmen and terrorized servants but had once killed a stoat after a long and bloody battle—was prompting talk (neither for the first nor the last time) of having him put to sleep. Hardy, however, persisted in his indulgence of the dog, giving him an eiderdown to lie on in the study and feeding him goose and plum pudding at Christmas, but making no offer to clear up the mess when he was, predictably, sick. Lady Cynthia Asquith, accompanying Barrie on a visit to Max Gate in 1921, reported with perhaps a touch of extravagance that throughout dinner Wessex—the 'most despotic dog' she had ever encountered—was 'not under, but on, the table, walking about quite unchecked and contesting with me every forkful of food on its way from plate to mouth'.[20]

Hardy's reluctance to take initiatives or spend money was a continuing obstacle from Florence's point of view. He pleaded poverty when she first talked of replacing the old kitchen range at Max Gate with a new and more efficient one; some months later, however, the new range was installed. Florence, indeed, seems mostly to have got her way in the end, at least so far as household matters were concerned. It was for Florence's convenience and pleasure that a telephone (Dorchester 43) was installed at Max Gate, not for Hardy's (who claimed to be 'bad at it'), and her frequent complaints about the primitivism of the house, specifically its lack of a bathroom and of hot water on tap upstairs, were finally answered in May 1920 by the beginning of work on the installation of an upstairs bathroom.[21] Though so set in his ways, so immovable in his likings and dislikings, Hardy was still capable of occasional flexibility and even of a little self-irony: 'We are reading Jane Austen,' reported Florence on 8 July 1920. 'We have read "Persuasion" & "Northanger Abbey", & now are in the midst of "Emma". T.H. is much amused at finding he has *many* characteristics in common with Mr Woodhouse.'[22]

Reading aloud to her husband after dinner, often for an hour or more at a stretch, was for Florence a regular and sometimes a trying task, given the persistent weakness of her throat. She also had other responsibilities. The publicity surrounding Hardy's eightieth birthday had finally confirmed his status as the universally acknowledged grand old man of English letters, and some of the implications of that status soon revealed themselves to the couple at Max Gate. The influx of letters and telegrams at the beginning of June was enormous, and the burden of answering them fell largely upon Florence's shoulders. She also had the unpleasant responsibility of keeping away from Hardy the people he did not wish to see, and of ensuring that those who were admitted to Max Gate did not stay too long. Hardy was well, but increasingly frail and easily tired, especially when attempting to play the genial host. When an army officer with a reputation as a boxer called in 1920, Hardy took off his jacket and engaged in mock fisticuffs, and John Middleton Murry once spoke of the extraordinary act of kinetic memory by which the octogenarian Hardy, sitting with Murry's nine-month-old daughter on his knee, succeeded in accurately recollecting from childhood the way to contort a handkerchief into the shape of a rabbit.[23]

Visitors, encountering the great man in lively and cheerful mood, did not realize that he was exerting himself for their benefit after having already put in a full day's work in his study—described by one privileged visitor in 1921 as 'bare, simple, workmanlike and pleasantly shabby', its 'well-faded walls. . . distempered an unusual shade of coral-pink'.[24] It was there that Hardy sat for much and often most of each and every day, writing, reading proofs, answering letters, and keeping a close watch on the health and prosperity of his many publications. Nothing was allowed to interfere with his morning's labours, and at lunchtime he was always tired and unwilling to engage in conversation. After a rest, however, he was quite fresh again, ready to return to his study for another stint, and re-emerge at 4.30 or so to greet teatime visitors. Florence regretted that this schedule meant, among other things, that they could never accept invitations to lunch, but she realized that it was only by resisting such temptations and distractions that her husband was able to remain actively at work so far into his old age. Hardy himself told a visitor that summer that, whatever his mood, he went to his study every day and wrote something, it scarcely mattered what: 'I never let a day go without using a pen. Just holding it sets me off; in fact I can't think without it. It's important not to wait for the right mood. If you do, it will come less and less.'[25]

One of Hardy's tasks during the spring and early summer of 1920 was the correction of proofs for the Mellstock Edition. He had taken the opportunity to change some of the topographical references in *A Pair of Blue Eyes* so as to connect the novel more directly with the St Juliot area and thus with Emma. The only alterations to the other prose volumes were of minor errors in the earlier Wessex Edition that readers had drawn to his attention or that he had himself spotted from time to time, and in the event he read proof only on the corrected pages of *A Pair of Blue Eyes*. He certainly undertook no systematic reconsideration of the texts, and did not think of the new edition as in any sense challenging what he regarded as the 'definitive' status of the Wessex. He did, on the other hand, read the proofs of the seven poetry volumes (including the three volumes of *The Dynasts*) on the grounds that 'no human printer, or even one sent from Heaven direct, can be trusted with verse'.[26] Although he continued to rate his verse more highly than his fiction and sometimes referred to the latter in disparaging terms, he well knew that his novels remained his principal source of income.

He became for that reason somewhat agitated when, in May 1920, Harper & Brothers announced that because of rising costs they proposed to reduce the author's royalty on one of the editions they had in print in the United States. The elaborate summary of his past dealings with the Harper firm that he then sent to Sir Frederick Macmillan provides a remarkable insight into Hardy's careful record-keeping and the anxious zeal with which he watched over his publishing affairs.[27] In these later years Sir Frederick Macmillan and the other Macmillan partners were always willing to give advice on technical matters and, if so requested, to assist in negotiations with foreign publishers, would-be translators, anthologists seeking reprint rights, and representatives of film companies, who had from an early stage regarded *Far from the Madding Crowd* and *Tess* as attractive 'properties'.[28] Hardy nevertheless continued to the end of his life to perform on his own behalf a great many troublesome tasks that, later in the twentieth century, would routinely have been delegated to agents and accountants.

While Hardy remained financially dependent upon the continuing and even increasing popularity of his novels, made available by Macmillan & Co. in a range of attractive and modestly priced formats, he sometimes spoke of them as if they possessed, as works of literature, a purely anti-quarian interest. When Florence Henniker evinced an interest in *Two on a Tower*, Hardy sent her a copy. 'On looking into it it seems rather clever,' he remarked, with the same unselfconscious simplicity—or profound self-knowledge—that enabled him to say, when Mrs Henniker asked what happened after the end of the novel, that history did not record whether or not Swithin St Cleeve married Tabitha: 'Perhaps when Lady C. was dead he grew passionately attached to her again, as people often do.' Expressing mild dissatisfaction with the rather abrupt conclusion of a novel by his friend Eden Phillpotts, Hardy remarked that if he himself were to write another novel—as he had no intention of doing—he would surprise his readers by going back to the old-fashioned style, practised 'in Fielding's time & onward', of telling the reader what finally happened to all the characters.[29]

In poetry, on the contrary, he remained eager to catch the sound of new and distinctive voices. The arrival of presentation copies of Ezra Pound's *Hugh Selwyn Mauberley* and *Quia Pauper Amavi* was at first greeted with polite discretion: 'I will not try to express my appreciation of their contents, as I am a very slow reader; & as, moreover, your muse asks for considerable deliberation in estimating her.' But Hardy later grappled with the poems and made what Pound called the 'impractical and infinitely invaluable suggestion' that 'Homage to Sextus Propertius' might be made more accessible by being retitled something like 'Sextus Propertius Soliloquizes'. When Robert Graves, introduced by Siegfried Sassoon, spent a weekend at Max Gate with his wife, Nancy Nicholson, in August 1920, Hardy inquired about his working methods. Told that a particular poem was in its sixth draft and would probably need two more before it was finished, Hardy said that he had himself never made more than three, or at most four, drafts of a poem for fear of its 'losing its freshness'. He showed little sympathy for *vers libre* or other radical shifts in the technique of poetry, declaring that 'All we can do is to write on the old themes in the old styles, but try to do a little better than those who went before us'.[30]

At the time of the Graveses' visit Hardy had been happily busying himself with the restoration of the disused Norman font at Stinsford—although he had himself been christened in the eighteenth-century marble font presented to the church by Lora Pitt but subsequently removed.[31] He got out his old architectural notebook and took it with him not only to Stinsford itself but to the church at Martinstown, where he made a drawing of a similar font, and to the three Dorchester churches, in each of which he measured the height of the font above the floor and the height of the officiating step.[32] He got a similar retrospective pleasure from the country dances and the mummers' play of 'St George' as incorporated into the dramatization of *The Return of the Native* with which the Dorchester amateurs were reviving the pre-war 'tradition' of the annual Hardy play. Hardy had little hand in the adaptation of his own novel, but childhood memories made possible an approximate reconstruction of the mummers' play itself. That Christmas of 1920 the Hardy Players, as they now called themselves, appeared at Max Gate in mumming costume and performed the play in the drawing room before an audience consisting of Hardy, Florence, Kate, Henry, and the Max Gate servants. Carol singers outside sang the old Bockhampton carols and the entire occasion, so Florence reported to Cockerell, gave Hardy 'intense joy'. Hardy's brief reference to the *Play of Saint George*, produced 'just as he had seen it performed in his childhood', provided an appropriate conclusion to his direct participation in the composition of *Life and Work*,[33] although his breaking off the manuscript as of the end of 1920 by no means ended either his tinkering with the text as typed or his adding to the collection of 'Materials' for Florence's eventual use.[34]

Gertrude Bugler, playing Eustacia Vye in the Hardy Players production of *The Return of the Native*, had also taken the disguised Eustacia's role in the performance at Max Gate, and Hardy's responsiveness to her charms had been an important ingredient in his enjoyment of the occasion. Florence, putting a brave face on the situation, acknowledged to Cockerell that Gertrude Bugler looked 'prettier than ever in her mumming dress. T.H. has lost his heart to her entirely, but as she is soon getting married I don't let that cast me down *too* much.' But Hardy's feeling for Gertrude was something more complex than an old man's fondness. Although her father, prosaically enough, was a Dorchester confectioner who made his premises available to the Hardy Players for their rehearsals, her mother had been the dairymaid living in the old manor house at Kingston Maurward who became, all unknowingly, one of Hardy's 'sources' for the inspiration of *Tess*. Gertrude's own fresh beauty and slightly open-mouthed eagerness were extraordinarily reminiscent of Agatha Thornycroft and of the image of Tess Durbeyfield that Herkomer had captured in his drawings for the *Graphic*. She had already impersonated some of Hardy's most appealing female characters, and there is no doubt that she was impelled, both by genuine awe of Hardy and by her own natural desire for admiration and attention, to make herself as charming and agreeable to him as possible, not least because the publicity accorded *The Return of the Native* in the London papers had given her theatrical ambitions of a larger though as yet unfocused kind.

Hardy, still susceptible at 80 to feminine beauty, found Miss Bugler quite captivating. To her, he seemed always a fatherly figure, and she was for him, in one respect, the incarnation of the ideal daughter he had never had. But in so far as she 'was' Tess Durbeyfield she also embodied the inextricable mesh of association and emotion that Hardy invested in perhaps the most personal of all his characters. Miss Bugler was indeed married (at Stinsford Church) in September 1921 to a farmer cousin also surnamed Bugler, but her change of status did not remove her from the scene as completely as Florence could have wished. Her new home was at Beaminster in north-west Dorset and she was much preoccupied during the next two or three years with marriage and, eventually, motherhood; but she kept up her association with the Hardy Players, whose 'star' she was, and did not forget that Hardy, after the final performance of *The Return of the Native*, had suggested that she might one day play the part of Tess.[35]

Early in 1921 Florence was experiencing acute depression and some pain—though both seemed to disappear once she was away from Max Gate—and in April she went to London to have six of her teeth taken out, in accordance with the alarming orthodoxy of the time: 'I trust the extraction has been for the best,' Hardy wrote to her at Mrs Henniker's, 'though I don't quite see how the removal of a symptom cures a disease.' She was also worried about the future prospects of her sister Margaret Soundy, who stayed at Max Gate with her son Tom before leaving for Canada at the end of April: 'We are so occupied by the pranks of a two-and-a-half-year-old boy', Florence reported to Cockerell, 'that we haven't time to think of anything else.'[36] Hardy himself remained remarkably fit, still entirely capable of walking to Stinsford and cycling to Talbothays. Though occasionally afflicted by eye trouble he refused to see an oculist and persisted in his loyalty to the pair of cheap spectacles he had himself picked out at the counter of the Civil Service Stores many years before. In late July 1921 he persuaded himself that he had heart trouble, but when the doctor was eventually summoned he reassuringly, if unromantically, diagnosed indigestion. Hardy then stopped talking about his heart but sent Florence back to do some more work on the 'Materials'.[37]

In April 1921 Hardy and Florence attended a special 'Warriors' Day' performance of *Far from the Madding Crowd*, Gertrude Bugler having added Bathsheba to her repertoire of Hardyan heroines, and in June they drove with Cecil Hanbury, the current owner of Kingston Maurward (hence of the cottage at Higher Bockhampton), to see the Hardy Players perform the Bathsheba episodes again in the castle ruins at Sturminster Newton. Hardy had tea with the cast at Riverside Villa, where he had lived with Emma in the 1870s, and insisted that Gertrude Bugler, who had been invited to come back and stay there, should sleep in the room in which he had written *The Return of the Native*. A day or two later Hardy drove over with Florence to visit the Granville Barkers at Netherton Hall, and in July he opened a fête in Dorchester in aid of the county hospital, observing in his brief speech that he 'almost' remembered the original construction of the building and had known personally its architect, Benjamin Ferrey.[38]

These, however, were exceptional excursions. On most days Hardy ventured out only into the immediate vicinity of Max Gate, just far enough to give Wessex and himself some exercise. But there was nothing truly reclusive about such an existence, at least during the warmer months of the year. Increasing use of the motor car contributed greatly to the rising incidence of visitors at Max Gate, making it seem 'almost suburban',[39] and the procession of teatime callers kept up steadily throughout the spring and summer of 1921 and on into the autumn: Barrie, Sassoon, E. M. Forster, G. Lowes Dickinson, Cockerell, Middleton Murry, Galsworthy, and many others, known and unknown, old friends and strangers, neighbours and pilgrims from far distances. The conversations so doggedly recorded by Vere H. Collins took place at this period. Walter de la Mare came for the first time in 1921 and was an immediate favourite. Masefield arrived with the somewhat embarrassing gift of a model full-rigged ship he had made with his own hands: it was just what Hardy had always wanted when he was a boy, Florence confided to Forster, but he wasn't sure what to do with it now. A more obviously appropriate gift was a copy of the first edition of Keats's *Lamia, Isabella, the Eve of St. Agnes and Other Poems*, presented to Hardy by a group of his 'younger comrades in the craft of letters' on the occasion of his eighty-first birthday.[40]

'I am getting to know quite a lot of the Young Georgians,' Hardy remarked to Mrs Henniker in July 1921, '& have quite a paternal feeling, or grandpaternal, towards them.'[41] The reminiscences of such visitors speak uniformly of Hardy's geniality and benignity, a radiating kindliness expressing itself in terms of good manners and flattering attentiveness rather than of articulated wisdom. H. J. Massingham, who visited Max Gate with his father in 1921, could later recollect little of what was actually said but vividly retained the impression Hardy had made upon him:

A man slow, deep-rooted, full of treasure within but hidden from the prying eye. A man who might have been mistaken for a country doctor, old-style, with humour in the mouth and tragedy in the eyes, but neither revealed except by that close scrutiny that awe and manners forbade. A kind host, a gentle manner of speaking, a low voice, an attentive listener with head slightly cocked of one side, like a bird's. No glitter whatever in the talk which (on his side) was reminiscent, as all true country things are.

That same year Hardy received two young men from the University of Birmingham with the utmost graciousness and talked fully and freely with them—which is not to suggest that he said anything he had not said many times before. His conversation in these later years became, indeed, more than a little repetitious, so that Cockerell, as a frequent visitor, once noted in his diary that there had been conversation 'as usual' about Shakespeare, Keats, and Shelley.[42] 'Ah, yes, Hardy,' said E. M. Forster once. 'Such a nice man. He always wanted to know if you'd had enough tea.'[43]

Now that he was in his eighties, and famous, Hardy relaxed to some extent his concern for certain points of principle that had meant much to him in former years. A visitor of 1920 was much puzzled by Hardy's declaring, in response to a remark about his having pulled out 'all the stops' in *Jude*: 'Do you think so? My views on life are so extreme that I do not usually state them.'[44] What he perhaps meant was that he had learnt, since *Jude*, not to change his mind about the state of the world and of the universe, but to save some of the wear and tear consequent upon speaking that mind in public. At his age, and with so much work behind him, it no longer seemed necessary, profitable, or congenial to continue to testify in season and out, and he had for some time taken the position that it was possible to be too vocal in a good cause. His sometimes discomforting facility for seeing all sides of a question had in any case obliged him to acknowledge that those who held radically different views might be perfectly sincere and honourable and, within their own terms of reference, perfectly justified. As early as 1912, after revising *Jude* for the Wessex Edition, Hardy had told Cockerell that when he read the new preface and postscript, 'you will say to yourself (as I did to myself when I passed the proof for press) "How very natural, & even commendable, it is for old-fashioned cautious people to shy at a man who could write that!"' And in 1918, rereading a sermon against *Tess*, he became convinced that the preacher was probably a good man.[45]

Hardy's last years saw fewer direct challenges, public or private, to critics and reviewers, and a less strenuous insistence upon the deliberate non-observance of certain social and religious forms. He went to church from time to time, chiefly because he enjoyed the singing and the long-familiar rituals, but also because the church had once been a centre of village life and might still, in a time of immense social and political upheaval, have a cohesive and 'disciplinary' role to play. 'I believe in going to church,' he told J. H. Morgan. 'It is a moral drill, and people must have something. If there is no church in a country village, there is nothing.' The request of Mrs Hanbury of Kingston Maurward that he stand as godfather to her daughter Caroline was one that Hardy would in the past have refused, but now, in 1921, he not only consented but wrote a little poem for the occasion, inscribed it on parchment, and presented it in a silver box.[46] When, in that same year, Robert Graves and Nancy Nicholson told him that their children had not been baptized, he merely observed that 'his old mother had always said of baptism that at any rate there was no harm in it, and that she would not like her children to blame her in after-life for leaving any duty to them undone.' He added: '"I have usually found that what my old mother said was right."'[47]

Florence found her husband's ancestor worship extremely oppressive at times: she blamed the 'atmosphere of Mellstock Churchyard' for the melancholy tone of one of her letters to Cockerell. But those walks to Stinsford were still making their contribution to an extraordinary poetic flow that showed no sign of drying up. 'Voices from Things Growing in a Churchyard' was written in 1921, stimulated by the experience, of reading through some of the old Stinsford parish registers,[48] and in November 1921 Hardy told Sir Frederick Macmillan that he had enough poems for a new volume. A suggestion made in the same letter—that sales of the one-volume editions of *The Collected Poems* and *The Dynasts* might be enhanced by the publication of thin-paper issues—was characteristic of his unremitting attention to his own literary affairs, even as its prompt acceptance was reflective of Macmillan's eagerness to accommodate, so far as possible, the wishes of the firm's most famous author who happened also to be, if not the best-selling, then certainly one of the most consistently selling.[49]

Royalties from Macmillan for the year 1920 amounted to something over £3,400, Florence reported to Cockerell (surely without Hardy's knowledge), and film and other subsidiary rights brought in £1,000 more. 'And yet I think,' she added, 'that T.H honestly believes that poverty & ruin stare him in the face. Argument does not convince him—merely irritates.' When visitors came to lunch or dinner, Hardy, mindful of the lavish hospitality he had received from wealthy friends in town and country, felt an obligation to entertain in some style, if not always with much grace. Appeals to his sympathy or his sense of family loyalty could often open his purse. But he otherwise lived with the utmost frugality, partly from habit, partly in the long-held belief that an author could only retain a sense of proportion and keep in touch with his essential material if he continued to live after his success in the same manner as he had lived when he first began writing.[50]

The standard generalizations about Hardy's meanness in old age are intrinsically suspect for being based almost exclusively upon the prejudiced comments of Max Gate servants and the evidence of others—including Florence herself—who knew him only in old age, when many people become tight-fisted. Few of the Max Gate servants felt any particular affection or admiration for their employer. He had never been accustomed to servants in his earlier years and had little sense of how to conduct himself towards them. He was inconveniently around the house all day long and sharply resentful of interruptions to his work. He was an object of perpetual suspicion, on the basis of local gossip about his irreligiousness and immorality, and gave offence to staff and tradesmen alike by his failure to appreciate that a tip which might have been adequate in the 1880s was certainly not so in the 1920s.

It is true that Hardy's income in his last years was very substantial and that he could have well afforded to keep Florence better supplied with money for household and other expenses. But his habits had long been formed by that time, and they included a hatred of waste—he was not the only elderly Victorian to remove coals from a fire which had been heaped too high—and an imagination of disaster, fed by childhood memories, by the riskiness of his profession, by the real difficulties and prospective perils of the First World War, and by the social and economic dangers which seemed to threaten England and Europe in the immediate post-war period. Everything in Hardy's experience had taught him to be cautious about money. He had been poor himself, and remained sharply and painfully aware of what it meant to be lacking in social and economic status. He had taken extraordinary financial risks in shifting in his early thirties from his first hard-won career in architecture to one that had promised few chances of success and none of permanent security, and when he abandoned fiction in the 1890s he was gambling that his novels would continue to sell in sufficient quantities to support his indulgence in yet another new career, as a poet, from which he anticipated financial loss rather than financial advantage.

He was, not least, his mother's son, imbibing from her a family history of poverty and a peasant tradition of thrift and prudence. He had also learned from her a keen and almost obsessive sense of family loyalty, the need and obligation to look after one's 'own'. Though he was himself childless, there had always been the two unmarried sisters for whom he felt responsible and a large number of impecunious and often envious relatives from whose importunities he naturally shrank but to whose genuine difficulties he tried to be responsive: 'He does so much for others,' Florence rather grudgingly wrote, '& has quite a little crowd of annuitants.' Florence was the most directly affected—and by far the most vocal—of those who deplored the tight hold that Hardy kept upon his purse, but she freely acknowledged that while he was careful over shillings and pence he was often indifferent to larger sums and certainly not in the least interested in the accumulation of money for its own sake.[51]

In January 1922 Hardy was in bed with a severe chill accompanied by acute diarrhoea. He could eat little but found sustenance in an occasional half-bottle of champagne. Florence thought it was influenza, which she herself came down with shortly afterwards, but he himself described it after the event as 'the old bladder complaint'. There had been a traumatic day or two when their own doctor, seconded by a colleague, had diagnosed cancer and Florence had frantically summoned her sister Eva, a trained and experienced nurse.[52] Although this fear was soon dispelled, Hardy took several weeks to recover his full strength. By early February, however, he was out of bed and writing for his forthcoming volume of poems the preface that he had determined and brooded upon while he was ill. He later told Gosse that the illness had 'caused' the preface. Florence came upon him one day talking to himself about the iniquities of critics, until he suddenly burst out with: 'I wrote my poems for men like Siegfried Sassoon.'[53] Once the preface, now called 'Apology', was completed he was anxious to assure himself that it was not too bitter—too 'cantankerous' as he put it—in its animadversions upon critics and reviewers. Florence thought the whole thing a mistake but hesitated to say so, and the decision was left to Cockerell, who urged publication with only minor revisions. Hardy accepted his advice, along with his offer to help in correcting the proofs of the volume, and the 'Apology' was duly included.[54]

Although devoted in part to restating Hardy's foreboding vision of the contemporary world, the 'Apology' chiefly reflected his long-standing resentment against those who insisted upon the ungainliness of his verse and the bleakness of his philosophy, and while it was in itself, as Florence recognized, a fine piece of argumentative prose, its tone and content naturally drew protests from that class of reviewers and critics against whom it was chiefly directed. Even Gosse claimed to have read it 'with surprise, and even with some pain', and pointed out that Hardy alone seemed to be unaware of the reverence with which he was now regarded. He also picked up on Hardy's having taken the opportunity to express his particular annoyance at Harrison's *Fortnightly* article and at a more recent piece in the *Fortnightly Review* by Joseph M. Hone:

It appears [wrote Gosse in the *Sunday Times*] that 'a Roman Catholic young man' has reproved him for the 'dark gravity of his ideas'. Let that young man be produced and exhibited in a glass case, for he is a rare specimen. What in all the earth does it matter what some young Catholic (or some old Protestant, if it comes to that) has been silly enough to say? There is always somebody willing to court attention by an imbecile paradox. . . . It is part of Mr. Hardy's genius, no doubt, to be sensitive, but I am vexed to find that he feels a pea under the seven matresses of our admiration.

Practically, logically, Gosse's expostulations were unanswerable. But that extreme, delicate, ever-troubling sensitivity of Hardy's could not be argued away, and it constituted a larger element in his 'genius' than Gosse's qualification allowed for. As Hardy himself observed, what counted was not the strength of the blow itself but the nature of the material on which the blow fell.[55]

When *Late Lyrics and Earlier* appeared in May 1922 it was generally well received, and Hardy persuaded himself that the 'Apology' had done much to assure its success. The volume was in any case a remarkable publication for a man in his eighty-second year, roughly half the verses, so the 'Apology' claimed, having been written 'quite lately'. Dates appended to some of the other poems range from the 1860s onwards, and although it is clear that Hardy had gathered in, with or without revision, a number of works deemed insufficiently strong or insufficiently 'finished' to be included in earlier collections, the volume as a whole does not show any significant falling off. It opens with the disarming cheerfulness of 'Weathers', apparently one of the latest written of the poems, and is generally less sombre in mood than either *Satires of Circumstances* or *Moments of Vision*—although Mrs Henniker, even so, ventured to suggest that it was much sadder in tone than Hardy was himself.[56] The several poems about Emma—including 'The West-of-Wessex Girl', 'A Man Was Drawing Near to Me' (suggested by 'Some Recollections'), 'The Marble-Streeted Town', and 'A Duettist to her Pianoforte'—are for the most part gently nostalgic in feeling.[57] They are also offset by poems commemorative of other women—Helen Paterson ('The Opportunity'), Louisa Harding ('The Passer-by'), and the Miss Marsh who sang at the Sturminster Newton concert in 1878 ('The Maid of Keinton Mandeville')[58]—and Florence seems not to have felt, as she had

50 (*left*). Florence Emily Dugdale, aged 19

51 (*below*). Thomas Hardy and Florence Dugdale on the beach at Aldeburgh, August 1909

57. Thomas Hardy in old age, photographed by Wheeler of Weymouth

58. Thomas and Florence Hardy with Gwen Ffrangcon-Davies and Philip Ridgeway at Max Gate;
Hardy holds acting script for *Tess of the d'Urbervilles*

59 (*above*). Florence Hardy, *c.*1930

60 (*left*). Hardy with Edmund Gosse in the porch
of Max Gate, 1927

61. Stinsford churchyard, showing Hardy family tombs in the foreground and a part of Stinsford House to the right of the church, photographed by Leslie Greenhill

done when the two preceding volumes were published, that *Late Lyrics* cast doubt upon the validity and happiness of Hardy's second marriage by retrospectively celebrating his first. Florence and Cockerell had both hoped that the new volume would contain a poem about Wessex, but Hardy declared that he could write one only if the dog were dead—a consummation devoutly desired by a succession of servants and postmen but still some years away. Meanwhile, so Florence assured Cockerell, Wessex was bearing up well and continuing to 'snarl & growl & fly at people with all his accustomed spirit & sweetness'.⁵⁹

Evident in the controlled and economical prose of the 'Apology' was an alertness and suppleness of mind that owed more than a little to the continuing stream of teatime visitors to Max Gate. Like Tennyson at Farringford in the previous century, Hardy was much annoyed by 'pilgrims' who lurked outside the gate to get a glimpse of him as he walked out to the letter-box that had—for his convenience—been let into the garden wall just beyond the front gate or who clung to the parapet of that wall in an attempt to peer over. Visitors who made a polite approach, preferably by letter, were rarely turned away, whether they were famous or unknown, local or foreign. Hardy on these normally teatime occasions would customarily settle into a smooth reminiscential rhythm, sometimes exasperating Florence by his narrative indiscretions in the presence of 'third rate people' whom she suspected of biographical intentions: 'T.H. tells them all sorts of things that are in my book,' she complained to Cockerell, 'and I shiver as I see them greedily drinking in all they hear and obviously making mental notes. It really would be wiser to keep them all away, but it is difficult to do so.' But the 'Life' itself, Cockerell was assured in August 1922, was now 'finished, so far as is possible, & put away', and the appearance at Max Gate of such established friends as Sassoon, Barrie, Cockerell himself, and the Granville Barkers gave pleasure to both Hardy and Florence. Every now and then a newcomer would fill them with delight—Edmund Blunden, for example, who reminded Hardy of Keats, seemed to Florence every inch a poet, and reduced even Wessex to fawning adoration.⁶⁰

Florence Henniker, now in her late sixties, stayed in Dorchester for a week that summer of 1922 and drove with the Hardys into the Vale of Blackmore and other parts of the local countryside. Dorothy Allhusen came down with her daughter in November, and she too had to be asked to stay in the town rather than at Max Gate—an apparent ungraciousness that embarrassed Florence, mindful of the hospitality so readily extended by Mrs Allhusen and her mother in the past, but that Hardy's age made unavoidable. Max Gate was not a large house, its toilet and bathroom facilities were limited, and Hardy lacked the physical and nervous resilience to be exposed to visitors at all hours. As time passed even his teatime performances became something of a strain, causing him to collapse into near-exhaustion after the last guest had left and giving Florence occasions and cues for wry reflections upon the illusory image of health and vigour her husband projected to people who knew nothing of the care and attention he required during the remainder of the day.[61]

28

Plays and Players

In early September 1922 Florence's elder sister Ethel Richardson was asked to stay at Max Gate for a few days while Florence went up to Enfield to see her parents. Mrs Richardson played to Hardy on the piano—everything from cathedral chants to modern dance tunes—and found him, despite the frailty of his appearance, to be in manner, bearing, and conversation 'like a man twenty years younger'. At breakfast one morning she was vouchsafed a glimpse of the puritanical absoluteness of Hardy's dedication as an artist. Responding to the news that Granville Barker and his wife proposed to spend the winter in Italy, he declared that Barker had evidently given up all thought of writing: ' "For it is impossible," he said "to write, & have other interests. In writing, as in all work, there is only one way—*to stick to it.*" '[1]

One day that October of 1922 Hardy walked to Talbothays and back, something Florence had not expected him ever to do again. He went with Florence to vote against Labour in the municipal elections at the beginning of November, though Florence at least 'felt mean in doing so', and took a lively pleasure in a new honour which came his way in the form of an honorary fellowship of Queen's College, Oxford.[2] As the winter drew on, however, he slid into one of the old depressive spirals from which he had for some years been almost entirely free. Emma's birthday on 24 November—consistently forgotten in her lifetime, as Florence wearily remarked—was now a major date on the Max Gate calendar, especially since it precisely coincided with the day on which Mary had died. In 1922 the day's pervasive melancholy was extended and intensified by the arrival, just three days later, of the tenth anniversary of Emma's death. 'E.'s death-day, 10 years ago,' reads Hardy's notebook entry. 'Went with F. & tidied her tomb, & carried flowers for hers & the other two tombs.' In December a mild attack of the flu bereft him of what remained of his energy and spirits: 'He said', Florence told Cockerell on the 17th, 'he had never felt so despondent in his life. And he told me that if anything happened to me he would go out & drown himself, which, considered rightly is a compliment, isn't it.' Hardy, however, had recovered with a rapidity that Florence attributed to his drinking 'two bottles of champagne—not all at one go, but two glasses twice a day. That seems always to do him more good than anything.'[3]

Different as Florence was from Emma in so many respects, there were also some curious similarities between Hardy's two marriages, prominent among them Florence's insistence upon keeping up with her own writing. Hardy had of course been immensely supportive of the writing career of Miss Dugdale, but it is clear from Florence's correspondence with some of her women friends that he felt very differently about publishing wives. Unlike Emma, Florence seems wisely to have avoided verse, but 'War's Awakening: How Duty's Call Came to a Bachelor Girl' and other unabashedly patriotic pieces contributed to the *Sunday Pictorial* during the war years[4] were followed, at least into the early 1920s, by a series of articles for another Sunday tabloid called the *Weekly Dispatch*. Typically billed as 'the wife of our greatest novelist', she appeared in 1922 and 1923 as the author of such items as 'A Woman's Happiest Year', 'No Superfluous Women', and 'The Dress Bills of Wives', even as she continued from time to time to write for the *Sphere* anonymous reviews of such new novels as Clement Shorter chose to send her way.[5] Though no complaint against Florence's writing appears in any of Hardy's known correspondence, he must surely have winced at what she wrote for the *Weekly Dispatch*, and regretted both the general worthlessness of the novels Florence agreed to review and, it must be said, the prevailing vapidity of her criticisms. Florence's persistence in such endeavours, like Emma's before her, can be read, positively enough, as a declaration of partial independence, but Hardy's toleration of them, however grudging it may have been, would seem also to be deserving of some sympathy and respect.

In 'A Woman's Happiest Year', published on 27 August 1922, Florence had described the great rewards women could find 'in willing self-surrender and devotion to others'. Unfortunately, the self-abnegatory role she herself had chosen did not always sit comfortably on her shoulders. Just two months earlier she had begged Siegfried Sassoon to call her 'anything rather than Mrs Hardy. That name seems to belong to someone else, whom I knew for several years, & I am oppressed by the thought that I am living in *her* house, using *her* things–&, worst of all, have even stolen her name.' That November, looking back over the years to the moment of Emma's death, she felt able to identify it as marking 'a clear division' in her own life, 'for on that day I seemed suddenly to leap from youth into dreary middle-age'. She acknowledged that she had not had serious responsibilities to carry before that time, but the despondent remark clearly reflected—as she moved through her early forties, faced sickness and surgery, coped with the increasing difficulties of life with her octogenarian husband, and anticipated with dread the miseries of yet another Max Gate winter—a profound and all too familiar sense of all that, as a woman, she had never had. Nor was she much cheered, as she sat writing to Cockerell in mid-December, by the sound of her husband playing a Christmas hymn 'on that most pathetic old piano' that was itself a remnant and reminder of his former marriage.[6]

In early January 1923, stricken by illness and by the death of her long-time maid and companion, Mrs Henniker telegraphed to ask if Florence could come and keep her company for a while. Florence arranged for two of her sisters to come down to Dorset, Constance to Max Gate, Eva to Talbothays, while she herself went up to Mrs Henniker, who had let her London house and was living in colder and damper conditions at Epsom. Already broken down in both health and spirits at the time of Florence's visit, Mrs Henniker died of heart failure in early April, and there was an emotional moment at Max Gate when Hardy's letters to her, which had been bequeathed to Florence, were unsuspectingly opened by the latter in Hardy's presence. Although Hardy's only surviving note on Mrs Henniker's death is brief enough—'After a friendship of 30 years!'—both he and Florence felt the loss severely, and the empty place she left in the ranks of Hardy's trusted friends and comfortable correspondents would never be filled.[7]

There had been other occasions for mourning, individually less painful but cumulatively distressing, over the last few years. Charles W. Moule, the last of the 'seven brethren', died in 1921, Emma's cousin Charles Edwin Gifford in 1922, and Charles Meech Hardy in 1923. Later in 1923 the death occurred of Sir Frederick Treves, surgeon to the royal family and saviour of the 'Elephant Man', who had gone to the same Dorchester school as Mary Hardy. 'So friends & acquaintances thin out,' Hardy had soberly observed to Mrs Henniker in March 1922, '& we who remain have to "close up".' He had long got beyond the point of regarding death as a calamity, and was so accustomed to contemplating the early prospect of his own departure—and so absorbed in the ritualization of his griefs for Emma and Mary—that these more recent losses fell into place as little more than episodes, pauses for regret and salutation, in his own continuing pilgrimage. On 22

September 1921 he had written the day's date in his Spenser alongside the lines:

> Sleep after toyle, port after stormie seas,
> Ease after warre, death after life, does greatly please.[8]

Far more agitating were his expedition to Queen's College, Oxford, in June 1923, and the Prince of Wales's much-trumpeted call at Max Gate in July. For the two-day visit to Queen's, the first and only time he was there as an Honorary Fellow, he and Florence travelled to Oxford by car, passing through Salisbury and Wantage and making a brief diversion to Fawley in order to search for ancestral graves in its little churchyard. In Oxford itself they were somewhat over-entertained, but Hardy had made up his mind in advance as to the Oxford sights he wanted to see once again—the curve of the High Street, the Martyrs' Memorial, the Shelley Memorial—and made sure they were included in his itinerary. The return journey was made by way of Winchester, another of those cathedral towns to which he was so devoted, and the New Forest, where they picnicked 'in the simple way that Hardy so much preferred'.[9]

There was nothing simple about the preparations for the Prince's visit on 20 July. Additional servants had to be brought in to handle the catering, cigars had to be purchased, and Florence was much flustered because of Max Gate's limited toilet facilities: 'And he will want to wash his hands—etc—here which is terrible. You know what our house is like.' But Hardy himself, she somewhat bemusedly added, 'is *pleased*'. When the anxiously awaited day came, everything went off smoothly enough, Florence behaving with such determined normality that Hardy subsequently scolded her for being too cool. The conversation could not in the nature of things be very lively, however, and it was Sassoon who subsequently spread abroad the Prince's most notable utterance: 'My mother tells me you have written a book called *Tess of the d'Urbervilles*. I must try to read it some time.'[10] Kate, Henry, and Polly Antell had been told that they might, if they wished, secrete themselves in one of the upstairs rooms at Max Gate while the royal visit was taking place, but Kate and Polly contented themselves with watching the Prince drive into town while Henry simply ran the Union Jack up the Talbothays flagpole. Hardy and Florence went to Talbothays the following day, but they were both, to Kate's eye, 'highly strung' and made off at the approach of some friends of Henry's.[11]

During the spring of 1923 Florence had consulted Macleod Yearsley about a swelling in her neck. Hardy also wrote to Yearsley, in a letter eloquent both of his affectionate anxiety for Florence and his unchanging dread of the surgeon's knife, and received the temporarily reassuring news that, since the 'little gland' was not 'appreciably' larger, Florence had no immediate need to contemplate an operation.[12] She was, indeed, especially active that year, and although photographs of her sitting between Hardy and the Prince of Wales on the Max Gate lawn suggest no lightening of her habitual melancholy, it is only fair to add that the Prince seems equally oppressed and Hardy only slightly less so. It was presumably with the Prince's personal blessing that Florence subsequently obtained from the Duchy of Cornwall the field adjoining the original Max Gate property for use as an extra paddock for her poultry—a dutiful and domestic gesture that she light-heartedly counterbalanced by persuading T. E. Lawrence to give her a ride in the sidecar of his motorcycle.[13]

Lawrence, then secretly serving as 'Private Shaw' at the army camp near Wool, had sought out Hardy by writing to Robert Graves, who had in turn written to Florence, and when he made his first appearance at the Hardys' tea table in April 1923 the liking and admiration on both sides was immediate and strong. Lawrence subsequently returned to Max Gate whenever his duties would allow him to do so—trying, not always successfully, to avoid encounters with other visitors who might know and recognize him. Hardy, he reported to Graves, was 'so pale, so quiet, so refined into an essence', and so totally absorbed in the Dorset of the Napoleonic era, that to return to the camp after a visit to Max Gate was like waking up from a restful sleep: 'There is an unbelievable dignity and ripeness about Hardy: he is waiting so tranquilly for death, without a desire or ambition left in his spirit, as far as I can feel it: and yet he entertains so many illusions, and hopes for the world, things which I, in my disillusioned middle-age, feel to be illusory. They used to call this man a pessimist. While really he is full of fancy expectations.'[14]

There were many other visitors to Max Gate that year. Bernard Shaw and his wife joined Lawrence at lunch one day. John Drinkwater arrived with his future wife, the violinist Daisy Kennedy, who played for them on Hardy's own fiddle. Lady St Helier came for what was to prove the last time. Marie Stopes motored over from her lighthouse on Portland.[15] The reactions of these and other callers naturally varied. H. G. Wells and Rebecca West found Max Gate and its inhabitants infinitely dismal and depressing, but Romain Rolland, calling there with his sister, the translator of *Tess*, was struck by both Hardy's physical agility and his mental alertness ('sa mémoire est précise, son esprit ferme, clair, sans trace de vague ou de sentimentalisme') and described him as having 'l'air d'un vieux petit docteur suisse'. The American scholar Roger L. Loomis was there in June and recalled many years later that 'No one could have been more friendly to me a perfect stranger, more cheerful, more communicative.' As another visitor, one of the daughters of the Bankes family, drove off, Hardy appreciatively observed that she was a fine figure of a woman.[16]

Loomis had been able to talk authoritatively about the Tristram legend, whose Cornish aspects were at that period very much in Hardy's mind. He had recently astonished Sir Frederick Macmillan, and almost everyone else, by producing the completed manuscript of *The Famous Tragedy of the Queen of Cornwall*, a poetic drama whose theme and setting derived from the emotional and geographical circumstances of his long-ago meeting with Emma Gifford in Cornwall in 1870 and his return to those scenes in the company of his second wife in 1916. Immediately after publication of the play on 15 November 1923 he spoke of it as '53 years in contemplation, 800 lines in result, alas!'[17]

The lack of any rich metaphorical or prosodic vitality in the verse of *The Queen of Cornwall* needs to be judged and understood in terms of Hardy's description of it, on the title page, as having been 'Arranged as a Play for Mummers'—as if it had pre-existed in a more poetic and literary form and was now to be presented somewhat in the mode evoked in the preface to Part First of *The Dynasts*:

a monotonic delivery of speeches, with dreamy conventional gestures, something in the manner traditionally maintained by the old Christmas mummers, the curiously hypnotizing impressiveness of whose automatic style—that of persons who spoke by no will of their own—may be remembered by all who ever experienced it.[18]

Such an invocation of mumming conventions and insistence upon absolute simplicity of staging was evidently designed to emphasize the play's elemental ingredients of love, jealousy, and death, and to disarm critics whose expectations might be pitched unrealistically high. The Tintagel setting and Hardy's earlier references to Emma as 'an Iseult of my own' are indicative of a heavy personal investment dating back to 1870, and if the play does not readily lend itself to either an autobiographical or an allegorical reading that is perhaps because Hardy disinterred and revised it specifically for performance by the Hardy Players with Gertrude Bugler in the role of Iseult—although she was, in the event, prevented by pregnancy from taking any part in the production.[19]

Scarcely less remarkable than Hardy's composition of the play was the care and effort he put into its production. In July 1923, before making the text available to the local group, he sent a copy to Harley Granville Barker, who responded with a long letter of appreciation and advice. In October, after attending one of the early rehearsals, Barker sent a series of specific suggestions to be passed on to Alderman T. H. Tilley, director of the Dorchester production. Of the actors Barker observed: 'I think they're all on the right lines. They only need more courage and precision and *not* to do one or two things.'[20] Hardy concerned himself with the musical setting, heard the actors read through their parts, and sent Harold Child, who was to review the play for *The Times*, a long explanation of certain technical aspects, notably the preservation of the unities, the use of the English term 'Chanters' instead of the Greek 'Chorus', and the attempt to make the characters as timeless as possible. Although the critics were generous in their comments on the play, few of them picked up on what Hardy himself had regarded as its most remarkable structural feature: 'compactness and continuity without a moment's break in the action'.[21]

Hardy's involvement with *The Queen of Cornwall* continued well into 1924. Rutland Boughton, the composer, was in correspondence with him in January about a musical version of the play and asked if more songs could be introduced as a way of relieving the tragic tone of the text as published. Hardy readily agreed, saying that he had 'always meant to revise it a little, to bring it roughly to the average length of Greek plays'. He supplied some of the enlargements himself, approved Boughton's proposals for the incorporation of appropriate lyrics from his existing volumes of verse, and became even more enthusiastic about the production after meeting Boughton in person and finding that he liked him very much despite his outspoken communist sympathies.[22] Hardy determined to attend one of the performances of *The Queen of Cornwall* at that summer's Glastonbury Festival, only to be thrown into great anxiety at the last minute by the prospect of making so long a journey by car. Florence, accustomed by now to her husband's panics and indecisions, told Cockerell that the only remedy was to remain quiet and allow him to calm down. Before she had finished her letter, indeed, she was able to report that Hardy had already forgotten about Glastonbury and was busily writing a poem: 'He asked me which was the better phrase "tender-eyed" or "meek-eyed". I pointed out that "tender-eyed" is used in the Bible (in reference to Leah) as meaning "sore-eyed"—which was why Jacob didn't want her. So a little biblical knowledge is handy at times: "tender-eyed" was promptly abandoned.'[23]

As this little episode suggests, Hardy's moods of anger or anxiety tended to subside almost as suddenly as they erupted. But the moods themselves could be intense. In the spring of 1924 Hardy was 'nearly driven frantic' by

Rutland Boughton's alarmed report of an unauthorized production of *The Queen of Cornwall* with musical settings that seemed to threaten both his position and his work. When, however, Florence suggested to her husband that he should hand over all such business matters to Cockerell, to one of the Macmillans, or even to a more recent friend, John Middleton Murry, he gradually became less agitated, only to be thrown back into despair a day or two later by a revival of the public controversy begun earlier that year by the savage attack on his style and reputation in George Moore's *Conversations in Ebury Street*. Moore's literary antagonism towards Hardy dated back at least as far as the publication of *Esther Waters*, just a year or two after that of *Tess*; his more specifically personal enmity seems to have originated, more recently, in Gosse's telling him of Hardy's wish not to encounter him again at Gosse's house.[24] After *Conversations in Ebury Street* appeared, Murry won Hardy's approval by stoutly supporting him in the pages of the *Adelphi*; other friends, as Hardy bitterly observed, could have come to his defence but stayed safely silent instead: 'As for that ludicrous blackguard G.M.', Hardy told Murry in April 1924, 'my concern has been for the unfortunate gentlemen his disciples. What a disgrace for them. They must be a timid lot, not to protest, & remind me of performing dogs in a show, obeying their master with fear & trembling lest they shd get the hot iron behind the scenes.' For Hardy, passionate in his opposition to cruelty to animals, these were powerful images to invoke. But his anger had already thrown him back upon still stronger and cruder resources of language. In March 1924 he told Murry that he knew little of Moore's work, having mentally classed him among those writers who were negligible and therefore need not be read, and could not understand why the English press took him so seriously: 'Somebody once called him a putrid literary hermaphrodite, which I thought funny, but it may have been an exaggeration.'[25]

In 1923 Hardy sat for his portrait—a little restlessly at times—to both R. G. Eves and Augustus John. Upon seeing a photograph of the John painting, he is said to have remarked: 'Well, if I look like that the sooner I am under ground the better.' There was talk of a Sargent portrait later in the year, but while Hardy was attracted by the idea he would not consider going to London to sit. As Florence told Cockerell, his patience was not inexhaustible, and in 1924 the presence of the Russian sculptor Serge Youriévitch over a period of several days so put him out that he would not speak at lunchtime while Youriévitch was there but sat with his face permanently hidden behind *The Times*. 'And it seems rather late', Florence sadly observed, 'to have all these paintings & busts done.'[26]

Augustus John figured ambiguously in a dream that Hardy described in the autumn of 1923 in response to a request from Helen Granville Barker, who had accompanied her husband on his recent Dorchester visit:

In the morning of Oct 21: 1923 I dreamt that I stood on a long ladder which was leaning against the edge of a loft. I was holding on by my right hand, & in my left I clutched an infant in blue & white, bound up in a bundle. My endeavour was to lift it over the edge of the loft to a place of safety. On the loft sat George Meredith, in his shirt sleeves, smoking; though his manner was rather that of Augustus John. The child was his, but he seemed indifferent to its fate, whether I should drop it or not. I said 'It has got heavier since I lifted it last.' He assented. By great exertion I got it above the edge, & deposited it on the floor of the loft: whereupon I awoke.

Although the dream has been persuasively interpreted in sexual terms, it is at least possible, given the fact that Meredith and John were fellow artists, that the baby somehow 'represented' the perceived burden of creative responsibility. On 15 December 1919 Hardy told Cockerell: 'My dreams are not so coherent as yours. They are more like cubist paintings & generally end by my falling down the turret stairs of an old church owing to steps being missing.'[27] Violet Hunt once recorded what she represented as Hardy's account of 'his one perennial dream': 'I am pursued, and I am rising like an angel up into heaven, out of the hands of my earthly pursuers. . . . I am agitated and hampered, as I suppose an angel would not be, by— a paucity of underlinen.' But if Hardy did indeed tell such a tale, it was doubtless in a tone of sceptical amusement. As he told Florence in April 1923, he once thought he heard his mother calling him, but since nothing happened afterwards he concluded that dreams need not be heeded.[28]

On his eighty-fourth birthday, 2 June 1924, Hardy received more letters and telegrams than ever, and the task of responding to them fell, as always, largely upon Florence's shoulders. In marrying Hardy ten years earlier she had not only assumed the standard and, at that time, inevitable responsibilities associated with the running of Max Gate but also accepted, whether explicitly or implicitly, the role of full-time or at least permanently available secretary to Hardy himself. She was still typing up Hardy's manuscripts— poems, prefaces, reworkings of segments of 'Life and Work'—but was chiefly involved, on a daily basis, in helping him to keep up with the mass of correspondence that flooded in upon him as the most famous writer of his time. Autograph seekers were a particular irritant, especially when they sent autograph albums or copies of Hardy's own books in the hope of getting them inscribed, and it seems to have been Max Gate policy to keep such volumes until a request was received for their return, at which point they would be sought out, parcelled up, and put back—still unsigned—into the mail. 'Alas,' wrote Florence to Rebekah Owen, shortly after Hardy's eightieth birthday, 'I am afraid the autograph hunters will be unsatisfied. Every now and then one writes for his, or her, album to be returned (or book) which is done. To see to all this properly requires a permanent paid secretary.'[29]

For some time, however, a young typist (and poet) named May O'Rourke had been employed at Max Gate on a part-time basis, primarily in order to assist Florence when the load of correspondence became especially heavy. Hardy still wrote most of his personal letters in his own hand, but for those considered less important a different procedure was usually followed. On the back or at the foot of the incoming letter Hardy would draft or briefly sketch a reply, just a few words often proving sufficient, and then pass the document on to be typed by Florence or May O'Rourke and, in most cases, to be signed or initialled by them as well. The original incoming document, now amplified by Hardy's draft, would then be kept for purposes of record. There were variations on this basic system, but its essential purpose was always to conceal his authorship, foil both the systematic and the casual hunter of autographs, and achieve some saving in time and trouble without any significant loss of control or need for genuine delegation. May O'Rourke put on record, years later, her memories of a Max Gate full of activity, kindness, and good humour, a Hardy always pensive and sometimes stern but never morose, a Florence capable of youthful gaiety, and a Wessex moved to aberrant behaviour only by the nervous strain of an 'obvious determination to be as nearly human as possible'. Hardy liked her but doubted her discretion, and Florence, after Hardy's death, would have occasion to protest at the published article in which Miss O'Rourke, a devout Catholic, had sought to explain and to some extent excuse the irreligious aspects of Hardy's writing—what she called his 'frenzied outbursts of unbelief'—as being the implicitly pitiable 'ravings of a man in pain'.[30]

Although Miss O'Rourke lightened the shared secretarial load, Florence remained responsible for the bulk of the correspondence as well as for all typing that was of a more confidential nature—thoroughly earning the day trip she made to London to meet Cockerell and go with him to *St Joan*.[31] At the beginning of July Hardy took pleasure in a visit from the Balliol Players, a group of Oxford undergraduates who performed an English version of the *Oresteia*, entitled *The Curse of the House of Atreus*, on the Max Gate lawn to an audience consisting of Hardy, Florence, and Harley and Helen Granville Barker. T. E. Lawrence had wanted to be present but could not get free from his military duties that afternoon. He had, however, entertained the Hardys and E. M. Forster to a sumptuous tea at his Cloud's Hill cottage ten days earlier, and continued to be a frequent and much valued visitor at Max Gate, admired by Florence, in particular, as 'one of the few entirely satisfactory people in the world'.[32]

The early autumn of 1924, however, was for Florence, hence for Hardy, a period of anxiety and even crisis. What had previously been diagnosed as a swollen gland on Florence's neck was now declared to be a potentially cancerous tumour, and she went once again to London to undergo, on 30 September, an operation for the removal of the tumour at the hands of James Sherren, the surgeon, who was the son of a Weymouth bookseller. Sherren reported to Hardy the next morning that the whole of the tumour had been successfully removed and that Florence's condition was quite satisfactory. Cockerell, in London, wrote twice to Hardy that same day and exerted himself both to keep Hardy reassured and to provide cheerful company for Florence at the Fitzroy Square nursing home. May O'Rourke, arriving at Max Gate the morning of the operation, was shocked by Hardy's physical appearance, and even after news of the operation's success had arrived he remained as if 'dazed'. He felt additional distress, and some guilt, at not being on hand in London himself, but Florence could only have been disturbed by his frail and fretful presence and Wessex, Hardy insisted, would have 'broken his heart (literally) if we had both gone away'.[33]

By 9 October Florence felt well enough to return home and Henry Hardy, with a local chauffeur to do most of the driving, went up to London to fetch her in the car that he had purchased that summer—and that had made him, according to Florence, ten years younger. Elaborate plans were laid for the journey to and from town, Hardy supplied route maps for the driver and rugs for the patient, and Henry embraced the whole project with great enthusiasm: 'He is simply delighted over it I am sure,' wrote Kate to her elder brother, '& gets the hour of starting earlier & earlier, like father used to do in quite a merciless way. Do you remember?' All was safely accomplished, but it was after dark before the party reached Max Gate and Hardy (as he touchingly recorded in the poem 'Nobody Comes') spent an anxious hour or two standing at the house gate while car after car rushed by without stopping, having 'nothing to do with me'.[34]

Florence remained deeply worried about her future health—May O'Rourke, indeed, believed that the persistent dread of cancer was largely responsible for her subsequent periods of 'inexplicable depression'—and it was while she was still weak from the operation itself that she had to endure the excitement, anxiety, and occasional embarrassment of Hardy's involvement in the local production of his own dramatization of *Tess of the d'Urbervilles*, first written in the 1890s but not in fact performed either at that time or since. Hardy's version of the production's history was that in 1924 the Hardy Players, led by Alderman T. H. Tilley, extracted the play from him against his better judgement. Other evidence suggests that he had long wanted to produce it, with Gertrude Bugler as Tess, but had been deterred by the doubts expressed by Tilley and others as to the play's propriety and hence its suitability for the conservative Dorchester audience. Now that the production was finally determined upon, Hardy put even more of his heart into it than he had done into *The Queen of Cornwall* the year before. Tilley called at Max Gate while Florence was away—the only visitor Hardy would see during that period—and brought with him miniature models of the staging. In October there were discussions and rehearsals at Max Gate, and even a rehearsal in Wool Manor itself (the imagined scene of Tess and Angel's disastrous honeymoon) at which Gertrude Bugler as Tess, Dr E. W. Smerdon as a balding Angel, and Norman Atkins as a dark and villainous Alec went over the confession scene between Tess and Angel and Tess's subsequent re-encounter with Alec.[35]

Hardy's interest in Gertrude Bugler had always stayed very much alive. In 1922, when she was recovering from the miscarriage that had prevented her from appearing in that year's production of *Desperate Remedies*, Hardy had sent her a silver vase full of carnations, using one of the other Hardy Players as an intermediary in order to avoid publicity.[36] Since her casting as Tess, however, his attentiveness had become increasingly noticeable and increasingly noticed. By the time of the play's first performance in Dorchester on 26 November it had given rise to a good deal of local gossip, largely generated by the jealousy of other members of the cast at the attention being paid to Mrs Bugler by visitors and journalists as well as by Hardy himself. She sat next to him at the tea given for the players between the matinée and evening performances, and Florence interpreted as intimate whispering what Mrs Bugler later blamed upon Hardy's saying quietly to her something about Augustus John that John, sitting on Hardy's other side, was not to hear. At the Weymouth performance on 11 December Hardy, behind the scenes, pointed out that Mrs Bugler was wearing her wedding ring and offered to hold it for her; later, just before the scenes in which Tess was supposed to be married, Hardy gave her back the ring by putting it on her finger as in the marriage ceremony.[37]

Florence had borne with her grievances and jealousies, real or imagined, on the assumption that the performances would soon come to an end and

Mrs Bugler return permanently home to Beaminster with her baby and her husband. But as Tess Mrs Bugler had been deeply moving in her beauty, her calm passivity, and her vulnerable innocence, and the enthusiastic response of some of the visiting critics from London had led to talk of the play's being produced in London with Mrs Bugler in the title role. Hardy told her that he did not quite like the idea of her going away to London: 'We are so proud of you down here that we wish to keep you for ourselves, so that you may be known as the Wessex actress who does not care to go away, & who makes Londoners come to her.' He recognized, however, that she had become seized with ambitions for a London acting career, felt that he had no right to stand in her way, and indeed did whatever he could to arrange for a series of matinée performances of the play to be put on at the Haymarket Theatre the following spring. At the same time he made it clear to Frederick Harrison, the Haymarket manager, that he had also discussed with Lewis Casson the longer-term possibility of a London production with Sybil Thorndike as Tess.[38]

On 10 January 1925, when Cockerell arrived at Max Gate, he found a heavy cloud over the house as a consequence of Hardy's continuing infatuation. Cockerell told Florence the next day that, given Hardy's age, she ought to view the situation in a comic light, to which she replied that she had attempted to do so but that Hardy had spoken to her 'roughly' and shown that she was in the way. The next day was still worse. Florence told Cockerell that she had worried during the night until she thought she would go mad, and she complained bitterly that Hardy showed no consciousness that the date was 12 January, her birthday, but was entirely taken up with discussions with Frederick Harrison and Mrs Bugler about the proposed Haymarket matinées, now regarded as a settled thing.[39]

Rehearsals at the Haymarket were scheduled to begin in April 1925, but at the beginning of February Florence suddenly appeared at Mrs Bugler's Beaminster home, saying that she was there without her husband's knowledge and begging Mrs Bugler, for his sake, to withdraw from the entire scheme. She argued that, despite his age and health, Hardy would insist on going to London to see the performances, that he would go to Mrs Bugler's dressing room, and that the resultant publicity would be bad for both his nerves and his reputation. In order to convey to the astonished Mrs Bugler some sense of the reality and depth of Hardy's infatuation, Florence told her that he had written poems to her, including one in which the two of them were imagined as going off together: 'But I destroyed it,' she added.[40] Shocked by such an assault, already aware that her husband and child would rather she did not go to London, Mrs Bugler wrote to Harrison to withdraw from the agreement she had entered into. Harrison, in his reply, regretted her decision but acknowledged that it was probably a wise one. She also wrote to Hardy, explaining that she could not bear to be parted from her daughter, that her husband was unenthusiastic about her going, and that she had no right to sacrifice their happiness. While he, too, accepted her decision—evidently in the belief that it had been freely taken—he also permitted himself a note of genuine regret: 'Although you fancy otherwise, I do not believe that any London actress will represent Tess so nearly as I imagined her as you did.'[41]

Gertrude Bugler never forgave Florence for denying her the chance of appearing in the West End in 1925. When, with Florence's active encouragement, she did at last play Tess in London after Hardy's death, she felt that she was already too old to embark upon a professional career as a romantic actress. Florence certainly emerges unhappily from this entire episode, the one occasion when her emotions ran beyond her control and drove her to interfere injudiciously and even cruelly in someone else's life and career. Clearly, Hardy had been behaving in ways Florence did not know how to cope with or contest, and the gossip already rife in Dorset could well have become a national scandal once it found its way into the London press. She may also have genuinely believed that there was more of natural charm than of developed skill in Mrs Bugler's acting and that the course she wished to follow was likely to end in disappointment. Essentially, however, Florence had surrendered to the melancholia induced by her operation, by her anxiety about her marriage, especially as it might be perceived by outsiders, and by the strain—earlier signalled by the onset of headaches and severe nervous disorders—of looking after Hardy when he was himself overwrought. She was also momentarily overwhelmed by a sense not just of her own advancing age but of her lack of precisely those things in which Gertrude Bugler, young, beautiful, and already a mother, appeared so rich. Her own life, she had tried to explain to Mrs Bugler in December 1924, was bound up entirely and exclusively in her marriage: 'Unlike you I have no child to promise future happiness, no career before me—everything seems to lie behind.'[42]

Once Mrs Bugler had withdrawn from the Haymarket scheme, Hardy was free to come to terms with Lewis Casson and Sybil Thorndike. But they wanted changes in the script and structure that he felt unable to accept, and the project was finally taken in hand by a little-known manager, Philip Ridgeway, at the out-of-the-way Barnes Theatre. Hardy was grateful to Ridgeway for energetically attacking obstacles at which so many had faltered in the past, and was therefore prepared to deal generously with him in the matter of royalties and performing rights. He was ill prepared, however, to cope with persistent requests for the American and colonial rights to the play well in advance of the opening night of the Barnes production, and became engaged both directly and through Florence in a bewildering correspondence as to just what Ridgeway might and might not be allowed to have and do. When Ridgeway was searching for a suitable Tess, Hardy had recommended that he consider Gertrude Bugler if no London actress seemed right for the part. Barrie seems also to have mentioned Mrs Bugler, and even after the choice had finally fallen upon Gwen Ffrangcon-Davies, Florence's reawakened fears prompted her to take steps to ensure that there would at least be no more Hardy plays in Dorchester itself.[43]

Though Gwen Ffrangcon-Davies was not, as Gertrude Bugler had been, the physical approximation to Hardy's ideal image of Tess, she was a highly intelligent actress, deeply interested in the structure of the play as well as in its production, and capable of making sensible suggestions for its improvement. She came down to Max Gate in August with Ridgeway and A. E. Filmer, the producer, to go over details of the play, and Filmer, who had been alarmed at the 'theatrical impossibility' of the script as it had been delivered to him, was much relieved when Hardy gave him a free hand to make whatever practical alterations he saw fit—later described by Filmer himself as not involving significant cuts or changes to the text itself but chiefly 'a matter of rebuilding (mainly to give each scene an effective curtain) and readjustment of speaking cues'.[44] In December 1925, after the play had been successfully launched, the whole cast came down to Dorchester to put on a performance in the Max Gate drawing room, Hardy having followed both his doctor's orders and his own inclinations in refusing to go to London to see it, either at Barnes or after it had transferred to the Garrick Theatre in the West End. Florence, on the other hand, had gone to an early performance at Barnes and been photographed, in an enormous two-tiered hat, presenting a bouquet to Gwen Ffrangcon-Davies.[45] The Max Gate performance itself garnered a good deal of unexpected attention in the London press, Ridgeway having apparently infiltrated a gossip-writer or two into the visiting cast under the guise of 'extras'. 'That Ridgeway', as Florence now referred to him, subsequently persuaded Hardy to accept reduced royalties for a week in order to cover the cost of the Dorchester trip, even though, as she said, it had been undertaken to publicize the play rather than to give Hardy pleasure. Nevertheless, the occasion did please and interest him and even move him to attempt a little speech just as his visitors were preparing to leave.[46]

29

Last Things

HARDY'S creative energies found their chief outlet at this period in the compilation, revision, and publication of yet another volume of verse, at first unpromisingly called 'Poems Imaginative & Incidental: with Songs and Trifles', later renamed *Human Shows Far Phantasies Songs and Trifles*—a less commonplace title, as Hardy remarked to Sir Frederick Macmillan, and easier to remember, since it would in practice simply be called *Human Shows*. The manuscript was sent to Macmillan at the end of July 1925, and once the proofs arrived Cockerell's assistance in reading and correcting them was again volunteered and gratefully accepted.[1] Although most of the poems in the volume were evidently of recent composition, a substantial number had originated in old notes or drafts that Hardy had come upon while sorting out his papers a few years earlier, the volume as a whole giving much the same impression of, so to speak, homogeneous miscellaneity as *Late Lyrics* and indeed all of the previous collections. There are several poems about Emma and St Juliot, others, such as 'The Absolute Explains', are of a philosophical cast, and there is even one about the death of Horace Moule ('Before my Friend Arrived')'.[2] Familiar Hardyan themes are everywhere rehearsed: the dangerous power of sexual attraction in 'At Wynyard's Gap' and 'The Turnip-Hoer', the cruelties of sexual mismatching in 'A Hurried Meeting' ('"Love is a terrible thing: sweet for a space, | And then all mourning, mourning!"'), while even 'To C.F.H.', the little christening poem for Caroline Hanbury, ventures to ask 'what | You think of earth as a dwelling-spot, | And if you'd rather have come, or not?'[3]

Sensitive to what had become the standard complaint about his sombreness of tone, and anticipating that the new volume would be similarly greeted, Hardy went through the list of contents as set out in the page proofs, marking each title with a 'T' (for tragedy), a 'C' (for comedy), an 'L' (for love song), or an 'O' (presumably for 'other'), and jotted down the results of his calculation on the flyleaf:

Total:	152 poems.
	—of these there are, roughly
60—	poems of tragedy, sorrow or grimness
	⌠ 65 of a reflective dispassionate kind
92	⎨ 11 of the nature of comedy
	⌡ 16 love-songs & pieces, mostly for music
that is	
	Tragedy or sadness 2/5 of the whole
	Reflection, love, or comedy 3/5- - - -[4]

The most remarkable feature of *Human Shows* was perhaps its very existence as the newly produced work of a man in his eighty-sixth year. In 'Why Do I', the volume's closing poem, the speaker asks 'Why do I go on doing these things? | Why not cease?'[5] But Hardy himself continued to do the things he had already done so long and so well. He would provide the poems for yet another volume before he died, and the persistence and intensity of his thinking, working, and writing during this ninth decade resulted in its emerging as one of the most productive periods of his entire career. What made such old-age creativity possible was Hardy's physical and mental resilience in combination with the extraordinary quantity, range, and depth of literary work that he had already accomplished—the 'harvest', to use Ezra Pound's term, of more than the novels—and the constant revisitation and reinforcement of memory such work had simultaneously demanded and achieved. Important as his notebooks and pocketbooks continued to be, there was also a sense in which the experiences of his childhood, so crucial to his prose and verse alike, had become fully available to his creative imagination only as they were gradually released by the passage of time, by accidents of later experience, or by specific actions taken, whether deliberately or incidentally, by Hardy himself.

An element of imaginative self-projection had entered from the first into his otherwise professional researches into local history and local newspapers. Each newly created Wessex location had to be supplied with an invented or appropriated history, and his revisions of successive collective editions returned him repeatedly to the rich resources of his personal past. The writing of such poems as 'Wessex Heights' and those gathered into 'Poems of 1912–13' had taught him that personal memories, like personal ghosts, were capable of being summoned by the conscious or unconscious practice of specific contemplative techniques—as when he stood on the old coach road on the heath and conjured up visions of figures both famous and familiar who had formerly passed that way.

That study at Max Gate in which Hardy spent so much of every day was itself a kind of memory-box, a repository of objects rich in associations: books dating back to his earliest years and even to his parents' and grandparents' times; family photographs and portraits of admired writers such as Shelley and George Eliot; illustrations to *Tess* and *Jude* and other novels; a painting that had once belonged to William Barnes; the portable writing desk he had bought as a boy from the father of Sir Frederick Treves. Florence Hardy, showing the study to Richard Purdy some eighteen months after her husband's death, spoke of his devotion to old and familiar objects and pointed out the presence on his desk of an old pair of scissors, a paperknife that had belonged to Emma, another paperknife that she had herself unsuperstitiously bought him the day before their marriage, the inkwell given him by Florence Henniker, and the perpetual calendar set permanently at Monday, 7 March, the day and date of his first arrival at St Juliot.[6] A cello stood in one corner of the room together with the violin that he had himself played as a child, and among the many books visible on the study shelves were the four massive volumes of John Hutchins's *History and Antiquities of the County of Dorset*—much annotated by Hardy, as Purdy soon discovered, and with an inserted newspaper cutting dating from as late as August 1927. Stored away in the cupboards, along with so much else, were Hardy's own early sketches and the tattered music books once used by his father and grandfather as members of the old Stinsford choir.[7]

By walking across the water-meadows of the Stour that lay to the north of Max Gate, Hardy could arrive within an hour at the cottage of his birth or, within half an hour or less, at Stinsford Church and churchyard, his increasingly hallowed place of communion with the beloved dead. Sympathetic visitors such as Elliott Felkin had been taken there from time to time, but it was in a letter written in 1924 to an older friend, A. C. Benson, that Hardy went so far as to use Shelley's phrase in *Adonais* for Keats's grave in Rome to evoke the emotional significance of Stinsford as the nearby 'slope of green access' that he deliberately frequented for the sake of reviving his memories of childhood, 'finding no pain in so doing.'[8] He seems not to have recognized that the authenticity of the original memories would inevitably be compromised by his repeated acts of revisitation, nor would such knowledge necessarily have troubled him. What he did know was that memories, true or false, were for him a primary source of emotions, hence of poems, and that he could most effectively invoke them by entering into the presence of memorials, whether natural or man-made, of the local, personal, or dynastic past.

In 1925 the publication in the United States of an unauthorized and occasionally offensive biography of himself was sufficient to turn Hardy's attention back to his own complex act of self-memorialization. He rejected Maurice Macmillan's proposal of April 1926 that the first part of the 'Life' typescript be set up in type in anticipation of his death, fearing that knowledge of its existence and its contents would be leaked by the printers, but he nevertheless took that typescript once more in hand in order to give it yet another careful revision. 'This may be wise, or the reverse,' Florence wrote to Macmillan. 'However he is greatly interested.'[9] T. E. Lawrence, now stationed at Cranwell, had meanwhile read one of the copies when Florence sent it to him in early 1926, and Sassoon had to be admitted at least partly into the secret when Harper & Brothers approached him with the suggestion that he write 'the authorized biography'. Florence remained unsure even now as to Hardy's intentions regarding the 'Life', and recommended that one of the Macmillans should come to Max Gate to receive his instructions at first hand. When Daniel Macmillan duly arrived, Hardy made it clear that he was 'not disinclined' to eventual publication of the biography. That July, however, he was still so busy tinkering with the typescript, putting in new notes and then taking most of them out again, that Florence could see no early prospect of completion.[10]

Hardy was in these years keeping a diary-style 'Memoranda' notebook for Florence to use in writing the final chapters of the 'Life', and in his entry for 31 December 1925 he recorded that they sat up late: 'Heard on the wireless various features of N.Y. Eve in London—dancing at Albert Hall, Big Ben striking twelve, singing Auld Lang Syne, G.S. the King, the Marseillaise, hurrahing.' A year later, on 31 December 1926, his notebook read simply: 'New Year's Eve. Did not sit Up.'[11] While Hardy had certainly not made an invariable practice of seeing in new years, the difference between the beginning and end of 1926 seems significant of a more general if not immediately obvious decline. In January 1926 he resigned from the board of governors of the Dorchester Grammar School, the last public body in which he had continued to be at all active, and finally assumed his favourite role, as *Later Years* would put it, of the 'man with the watching eye'—apparently Florence's imperfect memory of the line 'Friend with the musing eye' from the poem ' "Men Who March Away" '.[12]

Hardy was now beginning to show his eighty-six years, but husbanding his energies to the point that he rarely became tired. When a hernia was diagnosed he refused to wear the light truss recommended by his doctor, and Florence told Cockerell that scarcely anyone now had any influence over her husband, the only exceptions being Sir Frederick Macmillan and Dr Henry Head, the neurologist, a friend of some years who was now living near by.[13] Although Hardy had never pursued a programme of deliberate austerity, it is clear from the recollections of Ellen ('Nellie') Titterington, a housemaid at Max Gate from 1921 to 1928, that he continued to live the relatively simple life that he had always believed in, practised, and advocated—especially for authors. Max Gate had at this period a complement of servants that was fairly standard for its size and class and the amount of entertaining done: a cook, a housemaid, and a parlourmaid who 'lived in' and a full-time gardener who 'lived out'. Its daily routine, as described by Miss Titterington, began with tea and hot water (for washing) delivered to the separate but interconnecting bedrooms at 7.45 a.m., and continued with a cooked breakfast in the dining room at 9 a.m., a substantial lunch around 1 p.m. (at which Hardy always ate a baked custard pudding for dessert), a somewhat minimal tea, often with visitors present, at 4 p.m., and at 7.30 p.m. a relatively light dinner of which Burgundy, Stilton cheese, and Dorset knob biscuits seem to have been regular features. Florence then read aloud to Hardy until around 10 p.m., at which point she would prepare him a nightcap of some kind with the hot water the servants would have left at the dining-room door before retiring to their beds in the Max Gate attics.[14]

For Hardy himself, until the last two or three weeks of his life, the unattributed hours in this daily schedule were spent working alone in his study, Florence being left downstairs with Wessex but otherwise alone with her household and secretarial responsibilities and more than enough time in which to type, as she continued to do, her long, sometimes querulous, and often indiscreet letters to Cockerell and to such other Hardy-watchers as Sassoon, Forster, Gosse, Marie Stopes, T. E. Lawrence, and (a portent of the future) Howard Bliss, an early collector of Hardy books and manuscripts.[15] Inside his study Hardy was still busily writing verse, and if much of it was, as Florence said, promptly burned, he was still fully capable of turning off within two or three days a little poem like 'The Aged Newspaper Soliloquizes', in celebration of the 135th birthday of the *Observer*, of making the revisions that contributed so distinctively to the final versions of 'He Never Expected Much' and other poems in the posthumously published *Winter Words*, and of keeping an ever-watchful eye on the publication and reprinting of his works.[16]

He took a particular interest in the fortunes of the touring version of *Tess*, with Christine Silver in the title role, and again found himself entangled, with Florence, in a bewildering correspondence with Ridgeway, Macmillan, Golding Bright (who was acting as Hardy's dramatic agent), and others about Ridgeway's grandiosely conceived and importunately advanced proposals for stage versions of all of Hardy's novels. Florence in her letters, while not disguising her dislike of Gertrude Bugler, made a point of praising aspects of her performance as Tess and suggesting that she ought to be considered for other parts. In September 1926, at Hardy's suggestion, she went with Mrs Bugler to the Barnes Theatre to see John Drinkwater's dramatization of *The Mayor of Casterbridge*, a production that Hardy himself was able to see shortly afterwards at a 'flying' matinée put on at Weymouth largely for his benefit. The applause for him personally, both inside and outside the theatre, was loud and enthusiastic, giving him, perhaps for the first time, some tangible sense of how enormous his popular reputation had become—everywhere, that is to say, except in Dorchester itself, which had known him and his family too long to allow itself to be unduly impressed or to have its suspicions of his irreligiousness and immorality entirely dispelled.[17]

The Balliol Players came again to Max Gate in June 1926, performing on this occasion a translation of the *Hippolytus* of Euripides. In July Virginia Woolf called with her husband Leonard, subsequently entering in her diary perhaps the most vivid of all the many impressions of Hardy as he was in old age: 'a little puffy cheeked cheerful old man, with an atmosphere cheerful & businesslike in addressing us, rather like an old doctors or solicitors, saying "Well now—" or words like that as he shook hands.' Where so many friends and visitors had registered a fundamental simplicity in Hardy, Mrs Woolf saw 'no trace . . . of the simple peasant' but rather a complete assurance, a confident sense of a mind made up on all questions and of a life's work satisfactorily and in any case finally and irreversibly accomplished. The word 'simplicity', perhaps as roughly synonymous with 'straightforwardness', did however figure in the final summing-up of her impressions of the visit:

There was not a trace anywhere of deference for editors, or respect for rank, an extreme simplicity: What impressed me was his freedom, ease & vitality. He seemed very 'Great Victorian' doing the whole thing with a sweep of his hand (they are ordinary smallish, curled up hands) & setting no great stock by literature; but immensely interested in facts; incidents; & somehow, one could imagine, naturally swept off into imagining & creating without a thought of its being difficult or remarkable; becoming obsessed; & living in imagination.[18]

Virginia Woolf's characterization of Florence, though perhaps ungenerous in its invocation of childlessness, was no doubt accurate enough in substance: 'She has the large sad lack lustre eyes of a childless woman; great docility & readiness, as if she had learnt her part; not great alacrity, but resignation, in welcoming visitors; wears a sprigged voile dress, black shoes,

& a necklace.'[19] Florence had been depressed by Wessex's obvious decline and increasingly worried about some pains of her own she had mentioned to Cockerell earlier in the year. She was also worn down by the sheer burden of looking after a man who was at once frail and energetic, instinctively and inconveniently reclusive yet capable of being cheerfully gregarious for an hour or two each day, and ultimately answerable—in his own judgement and indeed in her own—only to the imperatives of his genius. Thoroughly imbued with Hardy's own views of existence—they both, she had told a correspondent in March, felt that consciousness must be a disease which ought not to exist—she lacked his facility for sublimating those views into poetry and consequently brooded upon them, and upon her own life, in ways that at once fostered and fed upon the intensity of her natural melancholy.[20]

In June 1926 Hardy sent up to Macmillan some corrections to both the one-volume edition and the Wessex edition of *The Dynasts* with the intention of making them 'exactly alike, never to be touched again'. His eighty-sixth birthday, earlier that same month, was made the occasion of 'He Never Expected Much', a dispassionate retrospect upon a life he saw as having been undramatically composed of those 'neutral-tinted haps and such' his childhood had taught him to expect. In November he made what was to prove his last visit to the Higher Bockhampton cottage to arrange for tidying up the garden and further 'secluding' the building itself from public view.[21] That Christmas both he and Florence were plunged into grief by the death of Wessex, who was finally put to sleep on 27 December after having been ill for some time with a tumour. Wessex was Florence's dog. He had arrived at Max Gate just a few months before her marriage, and while it was Hardy who had spoiled him the most, it was always Florence who had taken responsibility for his misdeeds and protected him against the vengeance of those whom he had insulted or injured. 'Of course he was merely a dog,' she wrote to Cockerell, '& not a good dog always, but *thousands* (actually thousands) of afternoons & evenings I would have been alone but for him, & had always him to speak to. But I mustn't write about him, & I hope no one will ask me about him or mention his name.'[22]

Siegfried Sassoon, visiting Dorchester and Max Gate in January 1927, sent Gosse from the King's Arms—' "the room which Mrs Henniker always used to have" (so T.H. says)'—a description of Hardy in 'what is, to me, his most characteristic attitude. Perched on the least *easy* chair, supporting his head with one hand, & gazing downward with a gentle & rather wistful expression. I noticed this evening,—when the half-lit room was dealing gently with his face—the great beauty of his expression.' There were some indications of an increasing weariness—'I think I've had enough of Napoleon!' he confessed to Sassoon on that same occasion—but no obvious slackening either of creative activity or of literary care-taking. In a letter to Sir Frederick Macmillan later that month Hardy spoke humorously of himself as a 'long-seller' rather than a 'best-seller', agreed to the republication of some poems in the pages of a popular magazine on the grounds that it would constitute 'a sort of advertisement', and hinted at the desirability of reprinting *Wessex Poems* complete with its illustrations.[23]

Three weeks later he wrote to propose the publication of a new edition of *Selected Poems* which would incorporate some of the verses published since its first appearance in 1916. By 18 September he had completed the pleasant if slightly worrying task of choosing the additional poems and was able to send off to Sir Frederick Macmillan the printer's copy for the enlarged selection. Although most of the new poems were from the most recent volumes— *Moments of Vision, Late Lyrics, Human Shows*, and *The Queen of Cornwall*—he had also included some songs from *The Dynasts* and gone back to *Wessex Poems* and *Time's Laughingstocks* to pick up 'Hap', 'The Fiddler', and, most strikingly, 'A Trampwoman's Tragedy', which in 1916 had still been judged unsuitable for a volume that might be used in schools. Concerned that Macmillan might think the revised text ran to too many pages, Hardy pointed out that the corresponding volume of Wordsworth contained an even greater number of poems, and that while there were fewer in the Byron volume some of them were 'rather long'. He was not at all anxious about the book's publication, he assured Macmillan, 'but felt it best to make sure you had the corrections in case anything should happen'.[24]

In March 1927 Hardy issued a brief public statement in support of the activities of the League for the Prohibition of Cruel Sports, and drew upon childhood memories in contributing to a pamphlet issued as an appeal for financial contributions to a Fund for the Preservation of Ancient Cottages. In July he made his last major public appearance on the occasion of the laying of the foundation stone of a new building for the Dorchester Grammar School, which was moving from the centre of the town to its outskirts. The site, not far from Max Gate, was open and windy, just as Max Gate itself had been when it was first built more than forty years before, and the weather on the actual day of the stone-laying proved to be blustery and unseasonably cold. But Hardy led the procession of dignitaries across the muddy field and delivered, in a firm and clearly audible voice, a speech chiefly—and characteristically—devoted to speculative ruminations about his Elizabethan namesake who had been the school's leading benefactor:

'He was without doubt of the family of the Hardys who landed in this county from Jersey in the fifteenth century, acquired small estates along the river upwards towards its source, and whose descendants have mostly remained hereabouts ever since, the Christian name of Thomas having been especially affected by them.' No less characteristic was his endorsement of the choice of the site itself as being 'not so far from the centre of the borough as to be beyond the walking powers of the smallest boy', and as promising to be incomparably healthy, 'with its open surroundings, elevated and bracing situation, and dry subsoil, while it is near enough to the sea to get very distinct whiffs of marine air'.[25] Detectable here are those still-painful memories of his childhood trudges between Bockhampton and Dorchester, as well as the slightly suspect geological and climatic reasons by which he had so long justified, to himself and to visitors, the otherwise somewhat inconvenient location of Max Gate.

Although Hardy was tired by the Grammar School stone-laying, Florence was able to report, just three days later, that he was working 'tremendously hard', and that she had therefore had an opportunity to slip away and take her ailing mother, in Weymouth for a few days, for one or two drives into the Dorset countryside. Outings by chauffeur-driven hired cars now provided both Hardy and Florence with their principal source of recreation. In May they had been driven over to lunch with the Ilchesters at Melbury House and been offered a tiny Sealyham puppy named Suzanne as a replacement for Wessex—a gift they decided they could not accept, Hardy having already been presented with a blue Persian cat named Cobweb. On his eighty-seventh birthday they drove into Devon to spend the day with the Granville Barkers at Netherton Hall—and thereby dodge the threatened attentions of an American journalist.[26] In June Hardy received what proved to be a last visit from Sir Edmund Gosse (as he had been since 1925), a friend for more than fifty years. In July Sassoon came, and the Masefields, and the Balliol Players performed again on the Max Gate lawn.[27] On 6 August Hardy accepted the dedication of Gustav Holst's new tone poem, *Egdon Heath*, inspired by the opening chapter of *The Return of the Native*, and a few days later he accompanied the composer himself on a drive across the heath to Puddletown Church and the wooden choir gallery in which Hardy's grandfather had sometimes performed. Later in the month Hardy and Florence motored to Bath and back in the one day, Hardy seeming quite fresh when they got back, so Florence told Cockerell: it was *she* who felt tired.[28] September brought a visit from John Galsworthy and his wife, an extended outing to Ilminster and Yeovil, and the acceptance of lunch invitations to Charborough Park and Lulworth Castle. At the end of the month Florence was able to speak of her husband as being 'very well indeed', although occasionally 'rather troubled by strange sensations about his heart'. She hoped these were merely the effects of indigestion, but Hardy—like Emma, she might have interjected—disliked being medically examined.[29]

That autumn Hardy continued active. On 25 October he attended at the Dorset County Museum a meeting directed to the preservation of a Roman mosaic pavement recently discovered in Fordington.[30] In November he corrected proofs of the enlarged edition of *Selected Poems*, made a few minor revisions to the text, and suggested that since some people foolishly confused 'Selected' with 'Collected' it might be sensible to change the title to *Chosen Poems of Thomas Hardy*. At the end of November he expressed particular delight at the arrival of copies of the handsome large-paper edition of *The Dynasts*: 'There was great excitement here when they came', he told Sir Frederick Macmillan, '& they are all that I expected. Leslie Stephen used to say that all modern books & newspapers would have perished in 100 years, but I fancy these volumes will hold out. I notice that you have embodied all the latest corrections, & I hope the booksellers will do well with their stock.' Hardy, indeed, retained to the last his old concern for the physical appearance, the textual correctness, and the financial viability of the volumes that bore his name. During the late summer he had been rereading, and reconsidering, some of his short stories in preparation for a one-volume collected edition proposed by Macmillan, and a note indicating that he would have preferred a less conventionally comfortable ending to 'The Romantic Adventures of a Milkmaid' is dated as late as September 1927.[31]

Hardy had by now stopped making even the most minor additions to the 'Materials' upon which Florence was to draw for the final chapters of the 'Life', and she herself began to keep an intermittent diary, taking particular note of those childhood reminiscences that at this period flowed so freely and clearly into Hardy's mind. On 4 November she recorded what proved to be his final visits to the churchyard at Stinsford and to his brother and sister at Talbothays, and her long entry for Armistice Day, 11 November, described his coming down from his study to listen to a broadcast service from Canterbury Cathedral and stand thinking of Frank George during the two minutes' silence. Later that same day, they took what Florence described as their customary 'melancholy little walk' alongside the railway line at the back of Max Gate and watched, as they had done so often before, the passing of a trainload of Portland stone.[32] When they reached home Hardy—moved, perhaps, by some obscure impulse associated with the emotions of the morning—became concerned for the welfare of Florence's chickens and asked the gardener to build a shelter to give them better protection against the cold. Later that same day, his thoughts still running on the blocks of building stone they had seen, he told Florence that 'if he had his life over again he would prefer to be a small architect in a country town, like Mr. Hicks at Dorchester, to whom he was articled'. A day or two later he had Henry Bastow, his fellow pupil at Hicks's, much upon his mind.[33]

A few days later still, his thoughts returning to the question of ambitions and their realization, he declared that 'he had done all that he meant to do, but he did not know whether it had been worth doing', adding that his one literary ambition had been to 'have some poem or poems in a good anthology like the Golden Treasury'. His mood, clearly, was that of 'He Resolves to Say No More', the poem which was to stand at the end of his posthumous final volume:

> Why load men's minds with more to bear
> That bear already ails to spare?
>   From now alway
>   Till my last day
> What I discern I will not say.

Yet Florence Hardy, after her husband's death, denied that the poem should be regarded as his final statement and insisted that he had in fact experienced a great outburst of creativity late in 1927 and felt that he could have gone on writing almost indefinitely.[34]

The usual period of combined mourning for Mary and Emma at the end of November was marked—pathetically, as it seemed to Florence—by Hardy's wearing 'a very shabby little black felt hat' and carrying a black walking stick.[35] But he kept up his work on the selection and revision of the poems that he wished to include in the new volume he was planning to publish on his ninetieth birthday. When *Winter Words* in fact emerged nine months after Hardy's death it proved to be somewhat shorter than most of its predecessors but in every way comparable to them in its range of theme, subject matter, and technique. Whether or not Hardy had deliberately withheld until this moment such intensely personal poems as 'Standing by the Mantelpiece', specifically associated with Horace Moule, it is impossible to say, but it is certainly remarkable that so many phases of his life were reflected in this final volume:[36] Higher Bockhampton ('Childhood among the Ferns', 'Yuletide in a Younger World'), Louisa Harding ('To Louisa in the Lane'), Eliza Bright Nicholls ('The Musing Maiden'), his early London years ('In the Marquee'), the winter he and Emma spent at Swanage ('The Lodging-House Fuchsias'), and an unidentified woman, perhaps Jane Nicholls, to whom he had once been attracted ('A Countenance').[37] His friendship with Lady Grove, who had died in 1926, was movingly commemorated in 'Concerning Agnes'; Wessex, already memorialized in stone in the pets' cemetery ('The Famous Dog Wessex Aug. 1913–27 Dec. 1926. Faithful, Unflinching.'), received an overdue poetic tribute in 'Dead "Wessex" the Dog to the Household'; and there were other poems, evidently related to Hardy's own history or that of his family ('A Mound', 'Family Portraits'), whose precise bearing now seems irrecoverable.[38] Though the poems thus gathered together had originated in almost every stage of Hardy's poetic career from the 1860s onward, several were of very recent date: it was at teatime on 27 November 1927, the anniversary of Emma's death, that Hardy first showed Florence the manuscript of 'An Unkindly May', a poem typically worked up from an earlier draft or note and gently expressive of that intense compassion for all living things that had caused him such anguish throughout his life and prompted his concern for the Max Gate chickens just two weeks before.[39]

On 1 December Florence told Cockerell that she expected to be approached with the suggestion that H. M. Tomlinson be permitted to write a biography of her husband: 'Of course there is only one reply.' Hardy himself, she reported in the same letter, was 'very well, . . . exceedingly cheerful & busy. Not a cloud in the sky.' Five days later she reported that Hardy had felt tired and kept indoors all day, which was 'rather unusual with him'. He nevertheless seemed well and alert, had delighted in a visit from Dorothy Allhusen two days previously ('She & T.H. were talking of old times, of the pranks she used to play when she was a child, & he stayed with her mother'), and was looking forward to a visit from Sassoon the following day. On 8 December Hardy was again not feeling quite himself, but he was alert enough to comment that Stephen Tennant, who had accompanied Sassoon, was the only person he had ever known with a walk like Swinburne's, and Florence felt justified in assuring Cockerell that there was nothing seriously amiss.[40]

When Hardy went to his study the morning of 11 December, however, he found himself, for the first time in his life, quite unable to work. He took to his bed thereafter, spending just a few hours downstairs each day, and by the middle of the month Florence was obliged to tell Gosse that Hardy had tired himself on 10 December by talking too much—to a representative of Harper & Brothers, as she later explained. His heart had been affected in consequence, although the doctor expected that a day or two's rest would set all to rights.[41] Four days later Hardy was still in bed and seemed very weak; he was said to have a chill, but his entire system was beginning to wear out and a few days later Florence found that he could no longer follow her when she read aloud, although she did subsequently read him some poems he asked to hear, among them de la Mare's 'The Listeners' and Browning's 'Rabbi Ben Ezra'.[42] There had been a great rush to dispatch the text of Hardy's own poem 'Christmas in the Elgin Room' in time for its publication in *The Times* on 24 December 1927, and when Gosse sent an immediate note of praise and appreciation Hardy roused himself sufficiently on Christmas Day itself to scribble a pencilled note of thanks and even to summon up a flash of the humour that had so consistently marked their correspondence over the years: 'I am in bed on my back, living on butter-broth & beef tea, the servants being much concerned at my not being able to eat any Christmas pudding, though I am rather relieved.'[43]

On 30 December Florence reported to Cockerell that Hardy was about the same. The doctor remained worried about his heart, but his having lunched that day on pheasant and champagne seemed an encouraging sign. She was doing all the nursing herself at present, she added, and it was perhaps a good thing that Henry and Kate had not offered to come. In the early days of 1928 Hardy's condition steadily worsened, and his exhaustion, both physical and mental, became so pronounced that the local practitioner, Dr E. W. Mann, summoned in Dr E. How White, a specialist from Bournemouth, for an urgent consultation. Dr White's opinion that Hardy's organs were all sound and his arteries those of a much younger man gave rise to temporary optimism, but the patient's strength did not return, the long period in a recumbent position produced fluid at the base of the lungs and the fear of hypostatic pneumonia, and by 8 January his condition had become critical.[44] On 9 January Florence, who had already enlisted her sister Eva's nursing expertise, summoned Cockerell by telegram to Max Gate, although neither he nor anyone other than Florence, Eva, Henry, and Kate was allowed into the sickroom itself. Cockerell arranged for a professional nurse to relieve Florence and Eva of some of their burden, but Hardy refused to have her in the room and Florence—remembering her husband's old fear of doctors and operations—said that it would kill him at once.[45]

On 9 January Sir James Barrie arrived, staying at a hotel in the town. The following day Hardy showed some signs of rallying, to the point of signing, in a hand of scarcely impaired firmness, a cheque for his annual subscription to the Pension Fund of the Incorporated Society of Authors, of which he was still president. On the 11th he took delight in the arrival of a huge bunch of grapes, a present from Newman Flower of Cassells, and asked for a rasher of bacon to be grilled for him in front of the open fire in his bedroom, as bacon had been cooked in his mother's time.[46] A touch of his mother also asserted itself that afternoon in the tough unforgivingness which impelled him to dictate brief bitter epitaphs on two men, G. K. Chesterton and George Moore, whose personal remarks about him had given lasting offence. 'Heap dustbins on him,' he wrote of Moore: 'They'll not meet | The apex of his self conceit.' He seems also, in quite another mood, to have asked Florence to read him a stanza from Fitzgerald's version of the *Rubáiyát of Omar Khayyám*.[47]

When Kate called at Max Gate that day she found the prevailing mood of optimism difficult to share: 'I saw Tom,' she wrote in her diary, 'but I am afraid he is not going to be here long. He looks like father & altogether I cannot blind myself to what is coming.' At 8.15 that evening she telephoned to see how things stood, and was again given an encouraging report. At about that same time Dr Mann was concluding one of his regular calls. While he was there Hardy chatted cheerfully about ways of celebrating his recovery and mentioned that he had been reading J. B. S. Haldane's recently published *Possible Worlds*, but found it too deep.[48] But at about 8.30, Hardy suffered a severe heart attack, and Dr Mann, summoned by telephone, apparently got back to Max Gate in time to be present, with Florence and her sister, at the moment of death.[49]

Of the details of that death and its immediate aftermath it is impossible to speak with confidence. Eva Dugdale, at Hardy's side during his final confused minutes, later recalled his speaking the word 'blood', muttering some remarks about herself—'She is such a little person yet she has seen such big operations'—and then, as she was taking his pulse, crying out 'Eva, what is this?' She held his hand to reassure and support him, but his grip weakened and death came.[50] Florence, who once told Dorothy Allhusen that when Hardy knew he was dying a look of horror passed over his face, included in her draft description of Hardy's death, but not in the 'official' account in *Later Years,* a passage to the effect that just before his final loss of consciousness 'a few broken sentences, one of them heartrending in its poignancy, showed that his mind had reverted to a sorrow of the past'. She must also have been the authority for her solicitor's saying that Hardy had passed away with 'broken words' about Emma on his lips.[51] An incompletely preserved letter Florence wrote to Clodd within a week of her husband's death does indicate that some such utterance may indeed have been made, but not, apparently, on that final day, and Nellie Titterington, sitting within earshot in the dressing room adjoining Hardy's bedroom, certainly concurred with Eva Dugdale in recalling his last words as being 'Eva, what is this?'[52] What is not in any doubt is that the death of Thomas Hardy, poet and novelist, occurred on 11 January 1928 at 9.05 p.m.—just in time for Cockerell to telephone the BBC and have an announcement made at the end of the nine o'clock news.

30

Afterwards

ONCE Hardy was dead, little remained for Dr Mann to do beyond certifying the cause of death as 'cardiac syncope', with old age itself as a contributory factor. A telephone call to Talbothays that evening received no reply, Kate and Henry, reassured by what they had been told at a quarter past eight, having seen no reason to depart from their usual custom of not answering calls after they had gone to bed. Eva Dugdale washed the body and prepared it for burial without the aid of an undertaker. She had also to remove a light growth of beard, Hardy not having been shaved since he had stopped shaving himself just a few days earlier.[1] The following morning, Cockerell, who had slept in his clothes in the Max Gate dining room, was at last admitted to the bedroom, where he assisted Eva in fitting Hardy's scarlet doctoral robe over his white nightshirt. 'Hardy's expression', he wrote in his diary that evening, 'is noble, majestic and serene—that of the Happy Warrior.'[2] When Nellie Titterington cycled to Talbothays with the news just before eight o'clock, Henry and Kate went straight to Max Gate and found their brother wearing 'the same triumphant look on his face that all the others bore—but without the smile'. Also admitted to the death chamber was an Irish Catholic priest, Father James O'Rourke, who had visited Max Gate a few months earlier and now urged his request to see Hardy's body with such earnestness and gentleness that Florence felt unable to deny it.[3]

Cockerell and Barrie now began to assert their male authority over what Cockerell, in a letter to his wife, had already referred to as 'the housefull of women' and to advance what they represented—and doubtless believed—to be the claims of the world of letters and of the nation as a whole. Though Florence was consulted, she was too tired and distressed to be able to resist their arguments. Cockerell, named as a literary executor, acted as if he were a fully empowered executor and opened up Hardy's will on the Max Gate kitchen table within an hour or two of the death. He soon persuaded himself that while the will specified interment at Stinsford—where Hardy's parents and grandparents were buried and his first wife was already lying beneath the tombstone he had designed to accommodate his own name as well—the wording was sufficiently conditional to allow for the consideration of other possibilities.[4]

Cockerell and Barrie had already agreed that Poets' Corner, in Westminster Abbey, was Hardy's only appropriate resting place, and by the time Henry and Kate arrived to view their brother's body that morning of the 12th—Florence's birthday, though nobody noticed it—the decision to request interment in Westminster Abbey had already been made. Barrie, who had returned to London on 10 January, rapidly marshalled the support of Stanley Baldwin, the Prime Minister, and Geoffrey Dawson, the editor of *The Times*, in order to secure for Hardy a privilege that no novelist had been granted since Dickens, no poet since Tennyson, and that had been consistently denied to a long series of distinguished agnostics. Following Meredith's exclusion from the Abbey in 1909, Hardy himself, in a letter to Gosse, had only half-jokingly proposed the creation of 'a heathen annexe . . . strictly accursed by the Dean and clergy on its opening day, to hold people like Meredith, Swinburne, Spencer, &c. The Abbey itself is, as [T. H.] Huxley said, a Christian temple after all.' Such, however, was Hardy's fame and national standing that by the late afternoon of the 12th the Dean of Westminster had already given the necessary permission.[5]

Henry and Kate, with their strong sense of local and family pieties, were entirely stunned by these developments, and especially by the news that their brother's body would have to be cremated and only his ashes given Abbey burial. To them, as to many of their conservative Dorset neighbours—as probably, indeed, to Hardy himself—cremation was an alien and even abhorrent practice, and the mere mention of the word served only to intensify the already clamorous local objections to Hardy's being separated in death from the part of England with which he had been so deeply and so famously identified. Kate seems to have felt that her brother would not have 'refused' burial at Westminster, but Cockerell recorded Henry as being 'very emotional and strongly against the Abbey', and their cousin Theresa, James Hardy's daughter, still living at Higher Bockhampton, was prominently reported as declaring that 'Tom' should be 'buried among his own people, where he so much wanted to be buried'.[6]

Another shock awaited Kate and Henry when they learned that Florence, grieving, exhausted, and confronted by conflicting demands, had accepted as a compromise solution the well-meaning if ill-advised suggestion made by the vicar of Stinsford that Hardy's heart be removed before cremation and given a separate burial in Stinsford churchyard. It was only

by chance, wrote Kate in her diary, that she and Henry had called at Max
Gate on the 13th and so seen Hardy's body for the second and last time.[7]
That evening of the 13th Dr Mann returned to Max Gate in company with
his partner, Dr Nash-Wortham, in order to remove Hardy's heart in preparation for the body's transfer to Woking for cremation early the following
morning. The procedure itself was performed in Hardy's bedroom by
Nash-Wortham, who was a surgeon, not by Mann himself, and the heart,
once removed, was wrapped in a small towel and placed in a biscuit tin
obtained, with some urgency, from the Max Gate kitchen. The tin was then
carefully sealed and taken away by Dr Mann, to be brought back to Max
Gate the following day (the 14th) and placed in the burial casket, which was
itself immediately sealed.[8] Meanwhile, by an irony that Hardy would himself have appreciated, there had arrived by post at Max Gate an article on
medieval heart burials, off-printed from the current volume of the Dorset
Field Club's published *Proceedings*.[9] But the existence of ancient precedents
for these somewhat macabre proceedings did not, of course, silence
popular disapproval or the outrage of some of Hardy's friends. Clodd, for
example, found the compromise 'very repellent', Gosse called it 'medieval
butchery'.[10]

At eight o'clock in the morning of Saturday the 14th Hardy's coffined
body was taken from Max Gate, placed in a hearse, and driven to the
crematorium at Brookwood, near Woking. Barrie accompanied the coffin,
oversaw the cremation, and subsequently delivered the urn containing the
ashes to the Westminster Abbey authorities. Despite the early hour and
inclement weather, numerous reporters and photographers were on hand
at Max Gate to record the occasion and make their contribution to the
development of the week's major news story. Hardy's death had been
greeted everywhere with editorials, obituaries, photographs, and feature
articles, and the note sounded in the two-column obituary published in *The
Times* of 12 January—that English literature had been deprived of 'its most
eminent figure'—was echoed and enlarged upon not only in the British
press but in newspapers around the world.[11] The Westminster Abbey
service itself, held on Monday, 16 January, was a national event. Although
no member of the royal family was present—both the King and the Prince
of Wales having sent aides to represent them—the names of the pall-
bearers were sufficiently eloquent of Hardy's standing. The Prime Minister
and the leader of the opposition (Ramsay MacDonald) were supported by
the heads of the two colleges (Magdalene, Cambridge, and Queen's,
Oxford) of which Hardy was an Honorary Fellow and six of the leading
literary figures of the day: Sir James Barrie, John Galsworthy, Sir Edmund

Gosse, A. E. Housman, Rudyard Kipling, and George Bernard Shaw. Many of the reserved seats in the Abbey were occupied by people with famous names, among them Arnold Bennett, John Masefield, Sir Arthur Pinero, John Burns, Jane Harrison, Gwen Ffrangcon-Davies, Walter de la Mare, Leonard and Virginia Woolf, and by members of the Macmillan firm which, as Hardy's publisher, had been responsible for organizing the occasion. The seats available to the public were all filled long before the service began and large crowds waited outside in the pouring rain for the opportunity to file past the open grave in Poets' Corner.[12]

Florence and Kate, escorted by Cockerell, were the chief mourners at the Abbey service. Henry, who had been in poor health, represented the family at the heart burial being held simultaneously at Stinsford, where the crowd was smaller, the formalities fewer, and the weather kinder. Kate, who felt numbed by the dismal trip to London and back and by the Abbey service itself, noted in her diary that at Stinsford, by contrast, 'the good sun shone & the birds sang & everything was done simply, affectionately & well'. Even the Stinsford service, however, was not without its ironies. Gertrude Bugler, who was there, was distressed by the presence of a woman friend of Hardy's who had come straight from riding to hounds without having had, or taken, the time to change out of her hunting dress.[13] A third event taking place at that same time was the memorial service in St Peter's Church, Dorchester, at which Dorchester paid its formal respects to the man who had made it famous—and someone had the imagination to include the time-honoured Tate and Brady 'graveyard' hymn that had been played and sung at the funeral of Hardy's father. In accordance with a mayoral request, the local shops were closed for the one-hour duration of the three simultaneous services.[14]

'I regret Hardy's funeral service,' wrote T. E. Lawrence from Karachi. 'So little of it suited the old man's nature. He would have smiled, tolerantly, at it all: but I grow indignant for him, knowing that these sleek Deans and Canons were acting a lie behind his name. Hardy was too great to be suffered as an enemy of their faith: so he must be redeemed.'[15] What continued to haunt Florence, however, were not so much the elaborate religious formalities accompanying the burial of her agnostic husband as the controversial decisions that had determined the disposal of his bodily remains. There were, of course, those who understood her dilemmas and the difficulties she had faced. A man like Hardy, Bernard Shaw told her, did not belong entirely to himself, nor would he have begrudged the people the performance at the Abbey any more than he had resented receiving American pilgrims at Max Gate.[16] That was what Kate Hardy also believed, and there is some evidence that Hardy had himself allowed for a possible assignment to the Abbey. The clause in his will that requested burial at Stinsford included, as if incidentally, a reference to supplementary 'considerations detailed in my directions to my Executors on a separate paper', and although that paper is not known to have survived it was perhaps the 'notice', consenting to an Abbey burial 'if the nation desires it', that Kate and Henry were told of, though not shown, the morning after Hardy's death. What does survive is Hardy's full-scale design for the memorial tablet to himself that would eventually join the memorial to Emma already installed in St Juliot church. Though the place of burial was given as 'STINSFORD, DORSET', those words differed from the rest of the meticulously completed drawing in being only lightly pencilled in, and it may not have been entirely coincidental that the space thus tentatively occupied proved an almost exact fit for the 'WESTMINSTER ABBEY' that appeared on the tablet as actually completed.[17]

Even the much-criticized double or, rather, divided funeral had its defenders, who argued that it had very satisfactorily enabled Hardy's heart to find its proper resting place in Wessex even while his ashes had been, as it were, claimed by the nation. Florence herself wrote to Sir Owen Seaman, the editor of *Punch*, to express her appreciation of the brief stanza of his own which he had put into the issue of 18 January 1928:

> The Nation's Temple claims her noblest Dead,
> So to its care his ashes we confide,
> But where his heart would choose a lowlier bed
> There lay it, in his own loved countryside.[18]

She was nonetheless deeply and painfully aware that in yielding to the pressures exerted by Barrie and Cockerell she had given countenance to a situation whose proliferating grotesqueries resembled one of Hardy's own most melancholic exercises in prose and verse—a satire of circumstance indeed, one of time's laughingstocks, an outrageous instance of life's little ironies. As time passed, she came to feel more and more strongly that the decision had been a terrible mistake, but told herself that she had been under such stress as to be scarcely responsible for her own actions.[19]

In the immediate aftermath of her husband's death Florence devoted herself, with an expiatory fervour reminiscent of Hardy's grieving over Emma, to carrying out both the provisions of his will and the tasks to which she was more privately committed. Before the end of 1928 she had seen through the press, with exemplary if suspicious promptitude, *The Early Life of Thomas Hardy*, the first part of the official biography that had always been intended to appear over her name. Hardy had specifically given her the responsibility of making, after his death, whatever additions or deletions she thought proper, and while it is sometimes difficult to distinguish alterations Florence made on her own initiative from those made while Hardy was still alive, she certainly removed or abbreviated, at Sir James Barrie's urging, a good many of her husband's unlovely diatribes against critics and reviewers and several of his listings of people encountered in London drawing rooms.

But such passages did have a function to perform in Hardy's original narrative. The lists of metropolitan notables and miscellaneous aristocrats helped to fill out the record of years whose truly significant events—the onset of middle age, the desolation of his first marriage, the abortive affairs of the heart with other women—were too private and painful for public revelation. They further served, however indirectly, to reflect his enjoyment of a world that offered at the very least a colour and glamour, a quality of conversation and perhaps of cooking, certainly an appreciation of his distinction as an author, that contrasted sharply and on the whole favourably with daily life at Max Gate. They also made a small but useful contribution to the implicit 'life and times' aspect of the book, and Hardy, being Hardy, may genuinely have felt that readers might be interested in his having met Lord Salisbury or even 'Mr Stephen (a director of the North-western Railway)' rather than in Lord Salisbury's and Mr Stephen's having met Thomas Hardy.[20] Vain though Hardy undoubtedly was of his achievements as a poet and even as a novelist, he seems obscurely to have felt that, considered apart from his writings, he was essentially an uninteresting person who had lived an unexciting life and therefore needed all the external support and social consequence he could muster in order to cut a sufficient figure in his own biography. He often claimed to take 'no interest in himself as a personage',[21] and *Life and Work* reads at times precisely as if it were being directed towards the creation of a self who might provide a conceivable subject for just such an enterprise.

Undertaken by Hardy chiefly as a means of deflecting the unwelcome attentions of would-be biographers, the official 'Life' became for Florence yet another worrisome responsibility. Publication of *Early Life* was in itself an important task for her to have completed, and in so doing she had not only added two important early letters from Hardy to his sister Mary that might otherwise have been destroyed but also inserted, at Barrie's instigation, a number of anecdotes that Hardy had been accustomed to tell about his childhood and youth, including the important detail of his disliking to be touched.[22] The second volume, called *The Later Years of Thomas Hardy*, required much more work than the first, the last two chapters, covering the period since 1920, having to be written almost from scratch on the basis of the documents that Hardy had accumulated to just such an end. Publication of the two volumes gave her a somewhat spurious literary reputation of her own, but she always insisted upon the enormous assistance she had received from her husband, even though loyalty to his memory and to his passionate desire for secrecy made it impossible for her to reveal the exact circumstances in which the work was written.

Under the terms of Hardy's will, which gave her possession of Max Gate and the income from all her husband's publications, Florence became a wealthy woman, and she was able to enjoy a number of luxuries that had previously been denied her, either by her husband or by simple circumstance. She bought herself a car and hired a chauffeur, and in the hope of making a more stimulating life for herself—and avoiding what she saw as the desolation of Max Gate winters—she rented an elegant London apartment in Adelphi Terrace, where her husband had worked for Blomfield in the 1860s and where Sir James Barrie now lived.[23] But she had little experience of personal happiness. She soon quarrelled with the overbearing Cockerell, with whom she had become yoked in the literary executorship under one of the more disastrous terms of Hardy's will, and became embroiled in painful controversies over such difficult issues as the disposition of Hardy's books and papers and the form to be taken by a proposed national monument to his memory.[24] She felt deep if sometimes unreasonable disappointment and bitterness at what she perceived to be her abandonment by many of Hardy's admirers who had cultivated her friendship during his lifetime. She had, above all, counted on Barrie's affection and support, even to the point of expecting a proposal of marriage, and when he too proved elusive her depression was correspondingly deepened.

As time went on she largely abandoned her London campaign, spent more of her time in Dorchester, and became increasingly active as a magistrate, a leading member of the Dorchester Hospital Management Committee, and the chairman of the Mill Street Housing Society, a small-scale but effective provider of cheap but well-built housing in the poorer parts of the town. She looked out for the needs of her own family, especially her youngest sister Margaret Soundy and her two children, renewed contact with old friends such as Sassoon, Lawrence, and Max Beerbohm, and formed important new friendships with various members of the Powys family, now mostly living in Dorset, and with two exceptional young Americans, Richard Little Purdy and Frederick Baldwin Adams, who had originally sought her out for her husband's sake.[25]

She worried as always about her responsibilities towards her husband's memory, towards his published and unpublished writings, and towards Max Gate itself and the study that she had kept essentially untouched. Characteristically, however, those worries never reached a point of resolution. She always stopped short of any firm or clear decision as to the future of Max Gate, and when she died—of the always dreaded cancer—in October 1937 her will left many issues unresolved. Under the terms of that will the Dorset County Museum did receive a very significant deposit of letters, manuscripts, and other papers from Hardy's study as well as of books selected from his library, but Max Gate itself, ordered to be sold, was duly put on the block by a local auction house and purchased, happily enough, by Kate Hardy.[26] Kate in her will left Max Gate to the National Trust, which was able, in 1948, to make the further and, so to speak, matching acquisition of the Higher Bockhampton birthplace.

Kate Hardy, the youngest of the Hardy siblings, was also the longest survivor. Henry Hardy's death had occurred within twelve months of his famous brother's, but Kate lived on at Talbothays until her own death in October 1940—long enough to share in the celebration of Hardy's centenary in the dark days of Dunkirk and to give a warm welcome and chatty responses to the occasional Hardy enthusiast bold enough to appear at her door.[27] With her departure the line of the Bockhampton Hardys was at an end. Hardy's own reputation, however, his unique standing as both major novelist and major poet, continues to strengthen and mature, assuring into all foreseeable futures an affirmative answer to the questions that, in 'Afterwards', he himself so diffidently posed:

> When the Present has latched its postern behind my tremulous stay,
>   And the May month flaps its glad green leaves like wings,
> Delicate-filmed as new-spun silk, will the neighbours say,
>   'He was a man who used to notice such things'?
>
> If it be in the dusk when, like an eyelid's soundless blink,
>   The dewfall-hawk comes crossing the shades to alight
> Upon the wind-warped upland thorn, a gazer may think,
>   'To him this must have been a familiar sight'.
>
> If I pass during some nocturnal blackness, mothy and warm,
>   When the hedgehog travels furtively over the lawn,
> One may say, 'He strove that such innocent creatures should come
>   to no harm,
>   But he could do little for them; and now he is gone'.
>
> If, when hearing that I have been stilled at last, they stand at the door,
>   Watching the full-starred heavens that winter sees,

Will this thought rise on those who will meet my face no more,
   'He was one who had an eye for such mysteries'?

And will any say when my bell of quittance is heard in the gloom,
   And a crossing breeze cuts a pause in its outrollings,
Till they swell again, as they were a new bell's boom,
   'He hears it not now, but used to notice such things'?[28]

GENERAL
ACKNOWLEDGEMENTS

The acknowledgements from the original edition of *Thomas Hardy: A Biography* are incorporated in what follows, and I take pleasure in reconfirming and indeed redoubling the expressions of thanks and appreciation that I originally offered. Since *Thomas Hardy: A Biography Revisited* also draws extensively on the work I have published since that first edition went to press, I also take the opportunity of warmly endorsing—though not repeating—all of the acknowledgements made in volumes iii to vii of *The Collected Letters of Thomas Hardy*, in the similarly co-edited *Thomas Hardy's 'Studies, Specimens &c.' Notebook*, and in *Thomas Hardy: Selected Letters, The Life and Work of Thomas Hardy, Letters of Emma and Florence Hardy, Thomas Hardy's Public Voice, Testamentary Acts: Browning, Tennyson, James, Hardy*, and the website (www.library.utoronto.ca/fisher/hardy/) devoted to the reconstruction of Hardy's dispersed library.

It is also a pleasure to renew my appreciation of the permissions granted by the Miss E. A. Dugdale Will Trust for my use of previously unpublished Hardy materials and of quotations from the Hardy *Collected Letters* and the *Letters of Emma and Florence Hardy*. And it is not too much to say that the production of *Thomas Hardy: A Biography Revisited*, as of much of my other work on Hardy, would scarcely have been possible without the generous and sustained support of the Social Sciences and Humanities Research Council of Canada. At various stages of my work I have also had the advantage of the relief from teaching duties offered by the award of two Killam Senior Research Scholarships and a John Simon Guggenheim Memorial Fellowship, as well as a Connaught Senior Fellowship in the Humanities from the University of Toronto.

For advice and assistance of all kinds during the preparation and composition of both the original edition and *Thomas Hardy: A Biography Revisited* I offer warmest thanks to Ellen Adams, Kathleen Alden, M. P. Alekseev,

Gertrude S. Antell, Norman Atkins, Frances Austin, John Baird, Gordon Barclay, David Baron, Nancy Bastow, A. R. G. Bax, Alan Bell, Anne Olivier Bell, Quentin Bell, Robin Biswas, Naomi Black, Caesar Blake, Claire Blunden, Mary A. Blyth, June Boose, Kristin Brady, Joan Brocklebank, Gertrude Bugler, Herbert Cahoon, James Cameron, Richard Cary, T. R. Cary, Fran Chalfont, Anthony Chambers, Maureen Clarke, Alan Clodd, J. Fraser Cocks III, Nancy Coffin, H. M. Coles, William Coles, Jane Cooper, Pierre Coustillas, Gregory Stevens Cox, Peter W. Coxon, Monica Dance, Mark Davison, Ian Dennis, Rache Lovat Dickson, Ellen Dollery, Jo Draper, Arnold Duffield, Frank Duffield, Ellen S. Dunlap, Leon Edel, Grant A. Farrow, Gillian Fenwick, Gerald M. Fitzgerald, E. M. Forster, Denton Fox, Charles Gale, Pamela Ganly, Richard Garnett, Marjorie Garson, Helen Gibson, Henry Gifford, Robert Gittings, Freda Gough, Ian Gregor, Theodore Grieder, Juliet Grindle, Phyllis Grosskurth, Viola Hall, David Hamer, Timothy Hands, Mary Hart, Alice Harvey, Montague Harvey, Nicholas Hillyard, Vanessa Hinton, Elsie Honeywell, Linda Hughes, Samuel Hynes, Heather Jackson, J. R. de J. Jackson, Hedley James, John Jenkins, Barbara Jones, Denys Kay-Robinson, E. G. H. Kempson, W. M. King, Cherry Klein, Dale Kramer, Karl Krauss, Martin Kreiswirth, J. T. Laird, Penelope Lively, April London, Desmond MacCarthy, Mrs Michael MacCarthy, Lesley Mann, David Masson, Paul Mattheisen, James B. Meriwether, Lawrence and Ruth Miller, Reginald S. Miller, Sylvère Monod, Rosemarie Morgan, W. W. Morgan, Sir Owen Morshead, Stephen Mottram, G. R. K. Moule, H. C. C. Moule, A. N. L. Munby, David Newsome, Christine Nickell, A. Nikoljukin, C. J. Norris, Christine O'Connor, Harold Oliver, May O'Rourke, Timothy O'Sullivan, Ivon Owen, Lisa Paddock, Norman Page, David Pam, Stephen Pastore, Charles P. C. Pettit, F. B. Pinion, Thomas Pinney, J. S. Pippard, Noel Polk, Christine Pouget, Stephen Poulter, E. W. Powers, Sharon Ragaz, F. Rampton, Martin Ray, Pamela Richardson, Mary Rimmer, Monica Ring, Marguerite Roberts, J. M. Robson, Barbara Rosenbaum, S. P. Rosenbaum, George Rylands, Chris and Sally Searle, Jacqueline Simms, Jim and Ruth Skilling, Ethel Skinner, Margaret Smith, Jeremy Steele, Anthony Stephenson, Barbara Sturgis, Lola L. Szladits, Dennis Taylor, Richard H. Taylor, Patrick Tolfree, Luke Tromly, Francis Warre-Cornish, Douglas Wertheimer, Stephen G. Wildman, Peter Williams, Irene' Cooper Willis, Ian Willison, Gordon Wilson, Anna Winchcombe, Murray Winer, Judith Wittenberg, Daphne Wood, and Janet Wright.

As I worked towards *Thomas Hardy: A Biography Revisited* I was often and sharply aware of the deaths of Richard Little Purdy, Hardy's bibliographer and co-editor of the *Collected Letters*, Catharine Carver, publisher's editor of genius, Albert Erskine, of Random House, the book's original co-publishers, and Henry Reed, poet, playwright, and author of an unfinished Hardy biography, all of whom read *Thomas Hardy: A Biography* in typescript and offered invaluable criticisms and suggestions. I also mourn the loss of Celia Barclay, staunch friend and devoted custodian of the papers and art work of Nathaniel Sparks junior, and of Frederick Baldwin Adams, Jr., a prince among scholar-collectors and, with Marie-Louise Adams, a magnificent host.

Michael Collie, James Stevens Cox, and John Antell, together with the late and much regretted Desmond Hawkins, Malcolm Tomkins, and John Yates, were among those who made particularly helpful contributions to the original edition of this book, while Henry Auster, Simon Gatrell, James Gibson, David Holmes, W. J. Keith, Charles Lock, Henry Lock, Robert Schweik, and Claudius and Audrey Beatty have contributed much to both editions. Among those to whom I also feel special debts of gratitude must be mentioned Roger Peers, Richard de Peyer, Judith Stinton, and Lilian Swindall at the Dorset County Museum, Elizabeth James at the British Library, Marjorie Wynne and Vincent Giroud at the Beinecke Library, Pat Burdick at Colby College, and Richard Landon and Sandra Alston at the Fisher Library of the University of Toronto. I am extremely grateful to Mary Newberry, provider of indispensable research assistance, to Peter Lennon, Michael Rabiger, and Keith Wilson, loyal friends and unfailing sources of enlivening Hardyan commentary, to Brenda Tunks, genealogist of extraordinary persistence and generosity, to Bernard Jones, devoted scholar of both Hardy and Barnes, and to Tony Bradbury, indefatigable enquirer into unexplored corners of Hardy's world. Donald Winslow is a precious friend whose memory ranges back to his visit to Kate Hardy in the 1930s, Pamela Dalziel an authoritative source of wisdom on editorial and scholarly issues, Michael Meredith an always generous and enthusiastic colleague, and I have long depended upon Ann and Anthony Thwaite for warm encouragement and informed advice and upon Bill and Vera Jesty, former tenants of Max Gate, for their extraordinary knowledge of Hardy and his family and their unwavering friendship and hospitality over the years. The proofs of the present edition received close and brilliantly perceptive readings from Ann Thwaite and Sharon Ragaz, and it has been a true pleasure and satisfaction to be publishing again with Oxford University Press under Frances Whistler's meticulous and wonderfully supportive editorial guidance. Finally, and most importantly, I have quite simply to say that this revised and enlarged edition would never have been completed without the patience, scholarly wisdom, and invariably constructive assistance of my wife Jane Millgate.

M.M.

Toronto
February 2004

ACKNOWLEDGEMENTS FOR SOURCE MATERIALS

———•◆•———

I have visited and depended upon many libraries in the course of my work on *Thomas Hardy: A Biography* and *Thomas Hardy: A Biography Revisited* and take this opportunity of expressing my particular gratitude to the following institutions for permitting access to printed and manuscript materials in their possession and to those members of their staffs from whom I have so often received assistance and advice: University of Aberdeen; Architectural Association; Albert A. and Henry W. Berg Collection, New York Public Library, Astor, Lenox, and Tilden Foundations; Berkshire Record Office; University of Birmingham; Bodleian Library; Boston Public Library; Bowdoin College; University of British Columbia; British Library; Brooks School; State University of New York at Buffalo; University of California, Berkeley, Bancroft Library; University of California, Los Angeles; University of California, Riverside; Cambridge University Library; W. & R. Chambers, Ltd.; Claremont Colleges, Honnold Library; Claybury Hospital; Colby College Library; Columbia University; Cornwall County Record Office; Dorset County Library; Dorset County Museum; Dorset County Record Office; Duchy of Cornwall Archives; English Folk Dance Society, Cecil Sharp House; Eton College Library; Family Records Centre, London; Fawcett Library (now the Women's Library, London Metropolitan University); Fitzwilliam Museum, Cambridge; Guildhall Library, London; Harvard University, Houghton Library; Hatfield House Archives; Huntington Library; King's College, Cambridge; King's College, London; University of Leeds, Brotherton Library; Library of Congress; Macmillan Press Ltd.; Magdalene College, Cambridge; Manchester Public Libraries; Marlborough College; Miami University of Ohio (the Hoffman papers); National Library of Scotland; National Portrait Gallery, Heinz Archive and Library; National Trust Archives; National Trust, Stourhead; New York Public Library, Astor, Lenox, and Tilden Foundations, Manuscripts and Archives Division; New York University, Fales Library; Pennsylvania State University, University Park; University of Pennsylvania; Pierpont Morgan Library; Princeton University Library; Public Record Office, London; Queen's College, Oxford; Rationalist Press Association; University of Reading; Royal Society for the

Encouragement of Arts, Manufactures and Commerce; Signet Library, Edinburgh; Society for the Protection of Ancient Buildings; University of Texas at Austin, Harry Ransom Humanities Research Center; The Times Archive; University of Toronto, Fisher Rare Book Library and Robarts Library; Victoria and Albert Museum; Westminster Public Libraries; West Sussex Record Office; Wiltshire Record Office; Yale University, Beinecke Library.

I am especially grateful to the many collectors and private owners who have so kindly permitted me to see and use manuscript materials in their possession: Frederick Baldwin Adams, Jr., Seymour Adelman, Gertrude S. Antell, John Antell, Celia Barclay, C. J. P. Beatty, Gertrude Bugler, Alan Clodd, Gregory Stevens Cox, James Stevens Cox, Robert S. Darby, David J. Dickinson, James Gibson, Henry Gifford, Peter Goodden, R. E. Greenland, Major R. G. Gregory, Kenneth Hince, Vanessa Hinton, David Holmes, Imogen Holst, William and Vera Jesty, Ian Kennedy, Peter Lennon, Mrs H. O. Lock, Henry Lock, Roger Lonsdale, Mrs Michael MacCarthy, Alexander Macmillan (the Earl of Stockton), William Macmillan, Elfrida Manning,, the Revd G. R. K. Moule, Peter Old, Stephen Pastore, Richard Little Purdy, F. F. Quiller-Couch, Gordon N. Ray, Pamela Richardson, Mme Romain Rolland, Carola Shephard, Robert H. Taylor, Edwin Thorne, and Daphne Wood.

I am also happy to repeat from the first edition the following acknowledgements of permissions granted in respect of material that had not at that time been previously published: Celia Barclay, for materials written and collected by Nathaniel Sparks junior; Quentin Bell, for unpublished letters by Leslie Stephen; Alan Clodd, for the diaries of Edward Clodd; Jennifer Gosse, for unpublished letters and reminiscences by Edmund Gosse; Ann Hoffman Perry, for materials written and collected by Harold Hoffman; the Countess Zamoyska, for the diary of Wynne Albert Bankes; the Master and Fellows of Magdalene College, Cambridge, for the diaries of Arthur Christopher Benson; the Miss E. A. Dugdale Will Trust, for unpublished materials by Thomas Hardy, Emma Hardy, and Florence Emily Hardy and quotations from *The Collected Letters of Thomas Hardy* and *Letters of Emma and Florence Hardy*.

ABBREVIATIONS

TH   Thomas Hardy (*TH* in titles)
ELH   Emma Lavinia Hardy (née Gifford)
FEH   Florence Emily Hardy (née Dugdale)
MH   Mary Hardy
KH   Katharine (Kate) Hardy
SCC   Sydney Carlyle Cockerell
RLP   Richard Little Purdy

Principal sources of unpublished material

Adams   Collection of Mr Frederick B. Adams, now dispersed
Berg   Berg Collection, New York Public Library
BL   British Library
Colby   Colby College, Waterville, Maine
DCM   Dorset County Museum
DCM : Lock H. E. F. Lock Collection, formerly in Dorset County Library,
            now in DCM
DCRO   Dorset County Record Office
Eton   Library of Eton College
HP   Hoffman Papers, Miami University of Ohio
Leeds   Leeds University Library, Brotherton Collection
NS   Nathaniel Sparks junior's notes and papers, now at Eton
Princeton   Princeton University Library, Princeton, NJ
RLP/FEH   Richard Little Purdy's records of conversations with FEH,
            1929–37, Beinecke Library, Yale University
SCC/TH   Sydney Cockerell's notes on meetings with TH, Beinecke
            Library, Yale University
Texas   University of Texas at Austin, Harry Ransom Humanities
            Research Center
Yale   Beinecke Library, Yale University, New Haven, Conn.

Published sources frequently cited

Career	Michael Millgate, *Thomas Hardy: His Career as a Novelist* (London, 1971; repr. Basingstoke, 1994)
CL	*The Collected Letters of Thomas Hardy*, ed. Richard Little Purdy and Michael Millgate (7 vols, Oxford, 1978–88)
Companion	N. Page (ed.), *Oxford Reader's Companion to Hardy* (Oxford, 2000)
CPW	*The Complete Poetical Works of Thomas Hardy* ed. Samuel Hynes (5 vols., Oxford, 1982–95)
DCC	*Dorset County Chronicle*
DCRO	Dorset County Record Office
Early Life	Florence Emily Hardy, *The Early Life of Thomas Hardy 1840–1891* (London, 1928)
Later Years	Florence Emily Hardy, *The Later Years of Thomas Hardy 1892–1928* (London, 1930)
LEFH	*Letters of Emma and Florence Hardy*, ed. Michael Millgate (Oxford, 1996)
LN	*The Literary Notes of Thomas Hardy*, ed. Lennart A. Björk (2 vols., London, 1985)
LW	Thomas Hardy; *The Life and Work of Thomas Hardy*, ed. Michael Millgate (London, 1984)
PN	*The Personal Notebooks of Thomas Hardy*, ed. Richard H. Taylor (London, 1978)
Purdy	Richard Little Purdy, *Thomas Hardy: A Bibliographical Study* (London, 1954; repr. 1968,1978; reissued with supplementary materials, Newcastle, Del., 2002)
PV	*Thomas Hardy's Public Voice: The Essays, Speeches, and Miscellaneous Prose*, ed. Michael Millgate (Oxford, 2001)
Studies, Specimens	*Thomas Hardy's 'Studies, Specimens &c.' Notebook*, ed. Pamela Dalziel and Michael Millgate (Oxford, 1994)
THJ	*Thomas Hardy Journal*
Wessex edn.	Wessex Edition (24 vols., London, 1912–31)

Unless otherwise indicated, all quotations of Hardy's verse are from *CPW*, and all quotations of his fiction from the prose volumes of the Wessex Edition. Interviews are by the author unless otherwise stated.

REFERENCES

———— ·•·• ————

1 Hardys and Hands

1. Elliott Felkin, 'Days with TH', *Encounter*, 18/4 (Apr 1962), 30.
2. *Letters of T. E. Lawrence*, ed. David Garnett (London, 1938), 429.
3. *LW*, 9–10; TH's copy of the 3rd edn. of Hutchins (4 vols., Westminster, 1861–73) is in DCM.
4. SCC, Notes on meetings with TH, 3 July 1916 (Yale).
5. Drawing (DCM), cf. T. O'Sullivan, *TH: An Illustrated Biography* (London, 1975), 9.
6. *CL*, i. 89.
7. NS (Eton), citing KH.
8. By Revd R. G. Bartelot, *Somerset and Dorset Notes and Queries*, 19 (Mar 1928), 106–9.
9. *CL*, iv. 37; see Brenda Tunks, 'A Re-examination of R. G. Bartelot's Version of TH's Ancestry', *Somerset and Dorset Notes and Queries*, 33 (Sept 1992), 154–6, and especially 'The John Hardys of Puddletown, Owermoigne and Tolpuddle', ibid. 33 (Mar 1993), 181–94. Mrs Tunks's extraordinary researches are brought comprehensively together in her 'Dorset Hardy Male Marriage and Family Index', accessible both in DCRO and DCM.
10. *PN*, 43–5; for paragraph as a whole, see Tunks as in preceding note.
11. *PN*, 8–9.
12. Court Rolls of the Manor of Bockhampton (DCRO).
13. B. Tunks, *Whatever Happened to the Other Hardys?* (Poole, 1990), 28–9; pp. 7–9 of this study have been superseded by the articles listed in n. 9 above.
14. Copy of lease (DCM); copy of 'Statement of Property' (DCM: Lock), and see Tunks, *Whatever Happened*, 25–7.
15. *LW*, 17; accounts submitted to William Morton Pitt (DCM: Lock), cf. Tunks, *Whatever Happened*, 22–3.
16. *LW*, 17; Stinsford churchwardens' accounts (DCRO); NS (Eton); will (DCM).
17. *LW*, 11; genealogical and other documents pertaining to the Childs family now in DCM.
18. *CL*, ii. 139; Hermann Lea, Hoffman interview, 1939 (HP).
19. *CL*, iv. 72; *LW*, 10, Purdy, 153, 155.
20. *LW*, 11–12; cf. J. Doheny, 'Biography and TH's Maternal Ancestors: The Swetmans', *THJ* 11/2 (May 1995), 46–60, esp. 55–6.
21. 'Pedigree' (DCM); *LW*, 12; church records (Melbury Osmond Church and DCRO).
22. *LW*, 11–12; J. Antell, interview, 1971; *LW*, 12. For a different estimate of G. Hand, see Doheny, 'Biography'.
23. RLP/FEH, 1936; Melbury Osmond records (DCRO).

24. *LW*, 12; *Tess*, 118–29; RLP/FEH, 1936; *CL*, ii. 8; *CPW*, i. 205.

25. R. Gittings, *Young TH* (London, 1975), 8, cf. *LW*, 12; Betty Hand to Mary Hand, 17 Jan 1842 (DCM: Lock).

26. 'Notes on Thomas Hardy's Life' (DCM); *Dorset Year Book for 1942–3*, 63; *LW*, 247.

27. *LW*, 14; *LW*, 13–14, 264.

28. *LW*, 13–17, 99; *Return of the Native*, 53–4; for negative view of church musicians, see *The Reminiscences of Lady Dorothy Nevill* ed. R. Nevill (London, 1906), 31.

29. *LW*, 17, and E. Inglis to her sister, 30 May 1916 (DCM); Stinsford Vestry Minutes, 16 June 1843 (DCRO).

30. 'Facts' notebook (DCM), cf. *Career*, 59.

31. *CPW*, i. 306.

32. NS (Eton); *LW*, 262–3.

33. *Wessex Tales*, 177–214; NS (Eton).

34. *LW*, 7.

35. SCC, letter to *The Times* (18 Oct 1932), 10; SCC, diary, 23 Aug 1925 (BL); *CL*, iv. 325, cf. W. Scott, *Guy Mannering*, ch. 22.

36. *Early Life*, 18; *LW*, 316–17, cf. 501, 530–1.

37. *LW*, 316; *LW*, 19, 21; W. Blunt, *Cockerell* (London, 1964), 212.

38. *CPW*, i. 209; *LEFH*, 228.

39. NS (Eton); Betty Hand to Mary Hand, 17 Jan 1842 (DCM: Lock), cf. J. R. Doheny, 'TH's Relatives and their Times', *TH Year Book*, no. 18 (1989), 15.

40. RLP/FEH, 1936; D. J. Winslow, 'A Call on TH's Sister', *TH Year Book*, 1 (1970), 95.

41. *LW*, 19; MH note, in Anon., *Cries of London* (DCM); SCC/TH, 3 July 1916 (Yale).

42. FEH to E. Clodd, 24 Nov 1915 (Leeds); MH to J. Sparks, 13 Dec 1904 (Eton).

43. *CPW*, iii. 474; *CPW*, iii. 232.

44. *LW*, 299; R. Gittings, *The Older Hardy* (London, 1978), 56–7, corrected on basis of St Mary's, Reading, and Chievely parish records, and Calendar of Prisoners for 1797 Quarter Sessions (Berkshire Record Office).

45. W. Scott, *The Antiquary*, ch. 40; *CPW*, i. 332.

46. *LW*, 16, and see G. Lanning, 'TH and the Bang-up Locals', *THJ* 16/2 (May 2000), 54–8; *CPW*, iii. 280.

47. *Two on a Tower*, 14.

48. TH's copy of Hullah's *The Song Book* (London, 1866) (DCM).

49. Doheny, 'Biography', 55–6; book (DCM: Lock).

50. *LW*, 26; KH, Hoffman interview, 1938 (HP).

51. *LW*, 18–19.

52. J. Antell, interview, 1971; *Daily Chronicle* (15 Nov 1911), 7.

53. SCC/TH, 25 June 1920 (Yale); *LW*, 19.

54. *LW*, 26, cf. *LW*, 501, 531.

55. NS (Eton); SCC, citing TH, MS note in Wessex edn. of *Return of the Native* (Adams).

56. Mrs Belloc Lowndes, *The Merry Wives of Westminster* (London, 1946), 148.

57. Desmond MacCarthy, Hoffman interview, 1939 (HP); *CPW*, i. 189–90.

58. SCC note in copy of *Return of the Native* (Adams), and RLP/FEH, 1936; *Return of the Native*, 44.

59. *LW*, 475; for broadside ballad, 'The Sorrowful Lamentation and Last Funeral of J. B. Rush', see A. L. Lloyd, *Folk Song in England* (London, 1967), 28.

60. *CL*, i. 259; *PN*, 6–7; *Jude*, 407.

61. RLP/FEH, 1933.
62. FEH to Rebecca Owen, 30 Dec 1915 (Colby); *LW*, 26; FEH to SCC, 24 Oct 1917 (Yale).
63. *LW*, 20; *CPW*, ii. 199–200; *Jude*, 15.
64. *LW*, 20.
65. SCC note in TH copy of *Return of the Native* (Adams), *CPW*, i. 209, *Return of the Native*, 223.
66. *LW*, 37, cf. *LW*, 408.

2   BOCKHAMPTON

1. *LW*, 7–8; E. A. Last, *TH's Neighbours* (St Peter Port, 1989), 189; see also B. Tunks, *What Happened to the Other Hardys?* (Poole, 1990), 14–27.
2. TH note (DCM); TH drawing (DCM), and see D. Morrison, *Exhibition of Hardy's Drawings & Paintings* (Dorchester, 1968), 4; Purdy, 140; see also Tunks, *Whatever Happened*, 74–7.
3. Policy (DCM); for fuller description, see F. Chalfont, 'Hardy's Residences and Lodgings: Part One,' *THJ* 8/3 (Oct 1992), 46–51, and *Hardy's Cottage* (National Trust, 1990), *passim*.
4. *LW*, 7; 'Particulars of the . . . Estate of Kingston House' (Benyon papers, Berkshire Record Office); *LW*, 7–8.
5. *PV*, 459–60; *Hardy's Cottage*, 7–8; *LW*, 20.
6. Kingston Maurward estate papers (Benyon papers, Berkshire Record Office).
7. FEH to Rebekah Owen, 30 Dec 1915 (Colby).
8. *PV*, 465.
9. TH marginal annotation in his copy of F. A. Hedgcock, *TH: penseur et artiste* (Paris, 1911), quoted *Career*, 211.
10. *CL*, i. 2, reading corrected at *CL*, vii. 171; *CL*, i. 181; MH to Mary Antell, 8 Oct 1908 (Eton).
11. NS (Eton), cf. R. Gittings, *The Older Hardy* (London, 1978), 16, and M. E. Bath, 'TH and Evangeline F. Smith', *TH Year Book*, no. 4 (1974), 44.
12. *Greenwood Tree*, e.g. 44–5; *LW*, 18.
13. From poem 'Shortening Days at the Homestead', *CPW*, iii. 133.
14. *LW*, 12.
15. Letters (DCM: Lock).
16. KH's diary, 1915–30 (DCM: Lock).
17. From 'On an Invitation to the United States', *CPW*, i. 142–3; *Woodlanders*, 146.
18. *Jude*, 274–5.
19. *Greenwood Tree*, 3; William Archer, *Real Conversations* (London, 1904), 32.
20. Murray's *Handbook for Travellers in Wiltshire, Dorsetshire, and Somersetshire* (London, 1856), 84.
21. *CL*, iv. 206, cf. N. Flower, *Just As It Happened* (London, 1950), 92. See B. Kerr, *Bound to the Soil: A Social History of Dorset 1750–1918* (London, 1968), and *Career*, esp. 98–102, 206–20, and notes.
22. Paul, 'The Condition of the Agricultural Labourer', *Theological Review*, 5 (Jan 1868), 112.
23. *PV*, 182; cf. *CL*, iv. 206.
24. *Mayor*, 293; Fordington census returns, 1841.
25. Betty Hand to Mary Hand, 17 Jan 1842 (DCM: Lock); NS (Eton); John Antell, interview, 1972.

26. 'Poetical Matter' notebook (microfilm, Yale).

27. *Greenwood Tree*, p. x.

28. *CL*, v. 269–70; Archer, *Real Conversations*, 33–6; *LW*, 26.

29. *CL*, i. 136; *CPW*, i. 255.

30. RLP/FEH, 1933; *Tess*, 23; *PN*, 12.

31. H. Child, 'Thomas Hardy', *Bookman* (London) (June 1920), 102; SCC note in his copy of *Return of the Native* (Adams); cf. J. McCabe, *Edward Clodd: A Memoir* (London, 1932), 109.

32. *LW*, 19; *LW*, 478–9, cf. 501; *LW*, 28; C. Lacey, *Memories of TH as a Schoolboy* (St Peter Port, 1968), 105.

33. *CL*, vi. 191; Purdy, 353.

34. *Tess*, 24.

35. Archer, *Real Conversations*, 37.

36. *LW*, 20.

37. RLP/FEH, 1929.

38. RLP/FEH, 1933; D. Maxwell, *The Landscape of TH* (London, 1928), 17–18; *LW*, 30; C. J. P. Beatty, *Guide to St. Michael, Stinsford* (Bridport, n.d.), [5]; *LW*, 407.

39. *LW*, 19.

40. Dr F. B. Fisher, in C. M. Fisher, *Life in TH's Dorchester 1888–1908* (Beaminster, Dorset, 1965), 21; *PV*, 207–8.

41. TH's letter mentioned in Louisa Sharpe to Jemima Hardy, 21 Sept 1859 (DCM).

42. Book (DCM); *LW*, 19.

43. Books (DCM); A. King identified by Brenda Tunks; books (DCM).

44. Gifford's *History* (Yale); other books (DCM).

45. *Companion* and *Psalter* (DCM: Lock); other books (DCM).

46. T. Dilworth, *A New Guide to the English Tongue . . . and Select Fables* (London, n.d.), 110 (DCM).

47. [Bernardin de Saint-Pierre], *Paul and Virginia* and [Sophie Cottin], *The Exiles of Siberia* (London, 1849), 94 (DCM).

48. *LW*, 21; SCC Notes on Meetings with TH, 30 June 1926 (Yale), cf. W. Blunt, *Cockerell* (London, 1964), 213–14; *CPW*, ii. 258–9; *Post Office Directory for Dorset, Hants, etc.* (London, 1848), cited in HP.

49. *CPW*, ii. 395–7; W. de la Mare, 'Meeting Thomas Hardy', *Listener* (28 Apr 1955), 756; *LW*, 447.

50. *CL*, v. 300.

51. *Early Life*, 32, cf. *LW*, 502, and see 531.

52. *CL*, v. 135.

53. R. Graves, *Good-bye to All That* (London, 1929), 375.

54. *CL*, i. 27.

55. See, however, Tunks, *Whatever Happened*, 28–32.

56. MH to N. Sparks senior, 18 Oct 1908 (Eton).

57. *LW*, 21.

58. *CL*, iv. 58.

59. Mary Hand to Betty Hand, 11 Dec 1846 (DCM); see M. Tomkins, 'TH at Hatfield', *Hertfordshire Countryside* (Feb 1976), and esp. T. Bradbury, 'TH's Hertfordshire Relatives', *THJ* 15/2 (May 1999), 49–59; Sharpe's report (Hatfield House archives, courtesy of M. Tomkins).

60. J. B. Sharpe to Christopher Hand, 18 June 1841 (DCM: Lock); A. Winchcombe, 'Mr.

Edward Sharpe from America', *Dorset* (Autumn 1971).

61. J. B. Sharpe to Lord Salisbury, [21 July 1851?], J. Bockett to Lord Salisbury, 22 July 1851 (Hatfield House archives); *Ayr Observer*, 2 Sept 1859; *PN*, 17.

62. *LW*, 21–2; M. Tomkins, 'TH at Hatfield'.

63. *LW*, 22; S. M. Ellis, 'TH: Some Personal Recollections', *Fortnightly Review*, 123 (March 1928), 395.

64. *LW*, 21; 'Notes on TH's Life' (DCM).

65. H. Lea, *TH Through the Camera's Eye* (Beaminster, 1964), 38; *CL*, vi. 299; *Jude*, 20.

66. *LW*, 27.

67. *LW*, 23; *DCC*, 22 Aug 1844.

68. *LW*, 23.

69. *LW*, 25; J. A. Martin to TH, 21 Apr [1887?] (DCM).

70. Archer, *Real Conversations*, 32; copybook (DCM).

71. *LW*, 24–5; 'The Harvest-Supper', *CPW*, iii. 95.

72. *LW*, 25; *CPW*, iii. 96; see above, p. 38.

73. *LW*, 24.

74. *LW*, 24, 43, 104–5.

75. *LW*, 105, and see *PN*, 220.

3 DORCHESTER

1. *LW*, 22–3; May O'Rourke, *TH: His Secretary Remembers* (Beaminster, 1965), 49; C. Lacey, *Memories of TH as a Schoolboy* (St Peter Port, 1968), 101–2.

2. NS (Eton).

3. *Dorset County Express* (8 Jan 1856), 3.

4. *Dorset County Express* (1 Dec 1857), 4; (15 Dec 1857), 4.

5. *LW*, 36.

6. *LW*, 26; *PV*, 289; *Career*, 242–3, and cf. *Mayor of Casterbridge*, 306–7.

7. *CL*, iii. 41; RLP/FEH 1931; cf. Lord Portman to TH, 10 Aug 1913 (DCM).

8. *LW*, 28.

9. *CL*, iii. 69–70; *Early Life*, 30, cf. *LW*, 501–2, 531, and J. M. Barrie to FEH, 26 Mar 1928 (DCM); book (DCM).

10. *CL*, vi. 3.

11. Lacey, *Memories of TH*, 101.

12. *LW*, 29; Latin receipt (DCM: Lock); book (DCM).

13. Eutropius (Colby); *Latin Grammar* (Yale), cf. *LW*, 27; *Manual* (Eton); *LW*, 29.

14. Both notebooks (DCM).

15. *Scenes & Adventures* (DCM); S. M. Ellis, 'TH: Some Personal Recollections', *Fortnightly Review*, 123 (Mar 1928) 395–6; *LW*, 30, 28–9.

16. *Novum Testamentum* (DCM); exercise book (DCM: Lock); *Popular Educator* (DCM); *LW*, 30.

17. *LW*, 457; writing desk (DCM).

18. Purdy, 325; see *Times Literary Supplement* (23 Aug 1947), 432.

19. *LW*, 37; C. Lacey, [London]*Evening Standard* (12 Jan 1928), 1; see *PV*, 1–2, and Purdy, 291–2.

20. *LW*, 31; 'Notes on TH's Life' (DCM); receipt (DCM).

21. *LW*, 31.

22. RLP/FEH, 1933; but see T. Hands, *TH: Distracted Preacher?* (Basingstoke, 1989), 9–10.

23. *LW*, 32; *CL*, vi. 27.

24. Tracings (DCM). See, for TH's architectural career: *The Architectural Notebook of TH*, ed. C. J. P. Beatty (Dorchester, 1966); C. J. P. Beatty, 'The Part Played by Architecture in the Life and Work of Thomas Hardy' (Ph.D. thesis, Univ. of London, 1963); C. J. P. Beatty, *TH: Conservation Architect* (Dorchester, 1999); and T. Hands, 'Architecture', *Companion*, 13–18.

25. Drawing (St Peter's, Dorchester); *DCC*, 19 Jan 1928; see Purdy, 293, and *PV*, 2.

26. *PV*, 251.

27. *LW*, 233; *CPW*, ii. 220–1; 'Poetical Matter' notebook (microfilm, Yale); *LW*, 30, 214.

28. *PV*, 187.

29. *CPW*, ii. 444–5.

30. *Early Life*, 33–4, cf. *LW*, 30, also 502, 531; J. M. Barrie to FEH, 26 Mar 1928 (DCM).

31. *CPW*, iii. 90, 171.

32. SCC/TH, 29 Sept 1916 (Yale); for Louisa Harding see also O'Rourke, *His Secretary Remembers*, 16–17, 49–52, and M. Rabiger, 'The Hoffman Papers', *TH Year Book*, no. 10 (1981), 16–18.

33. Rebecca Paine to Thomas and Emma Cary, 15 July 1876 (Ian Kennedy), cf. J. R. Doheny, 'TH's Relatives and their Times', *TH Year Book*, no. 18 (1989), 49.

34. *CL*, i. 1.

35. Pamela Ganly (great-granddaughter), interview, 1971; the papers (NS, Eton) of Nathaniel's son, Nathaniel Sparks the etcher (see Celia Barclay, *Nathaniel Sparks*, Greenwich, 1994), are a valuable if sometimes unreliable source of Sparks family documents and gossip.

36. Doctor's receipt (DCM: Lock).

37. *LW*, 36–7; Lacey, *Memories of TH*, 105.

38. Stinsford Church registers (DCRO).

39. *LN*, i. 100, 341.

40. TH's letter is mentioned in a letter from Louisa Sharpe to Jemima Hardy, 25 July 1870 (DCM); G. B. Sharpe to TH, 21 Sept 1859 (DCM).

41. *LW*, 40.

42. *LEFH*, 243, citing FEH to SCC, 26 May 1926 (Yale).

43. *DCC*, 10 July 1856; cf. Carl J. Weber, *Hardy and the Lady from Madison Square* (Waterville, Me., 1952), 88; and see *Far from the Madding Crowd*, 391–6.

44. *Southern Times*, 5 July 1856; cf. *CL*, iii. 109.

45. *Southern Times*, 15 Nov 1856.

46. *Dorset County Express* (17 Nov 1857), 4; *DCC*, 25 Feb 1862.

47. *LW*, 33; *DCC*, 14 Aug 1856; *CL*, vii. 5; E. Felkin, 'Days with TH', *Encounter*, 18/4 (Apr 1962), 29.

48. *LW*, 32–3; *DCC* (12 Aug 1858), 23–4.

49. *LW*, 32, 36; W. R. Rutland, *TH: A Study of his Writings and their Background* (Oxford, 1938), 21–2; book (Yale); *Jude the Obscure*, 40.

50. Photograph (John Antell); copy of hymn (DCM).

51. *LW*, 33–5; book (Yale).

52. *LW*, 34–5, 458; *Studies, Specimens*, 58–9.

53. H. Bastow to TH, 23 Dec 1863, 17 Feb 1861, 23 May 1862 (DCM); TH's letters to Bastow are not known to have survived.

54. Books (DCM).
55. H. C. G. Moule, *Memories of a Vicarage* (London, 1913), *passim*; H. Moule, *Eight Letters to His Royal Highness, Prince Albert* (London, 1855).
56. *PV*, 230; Moule, *Memories of a Vicarage*, 56; cf. *LW*, 434.
57. *LW*, 24, sketches (DCM), D. Morrison, *Exhibition of Hardy's Drawings and Paintings* (Dorchester, 1968), [1].
58. *PV*, 230.
59. Book, *Epitome of Alison's History of Europe* (DCM); *LW*, 458.
60. Book (DCM); Moule, *Memories of a Vicarage*, 35. Horace Moule matriculated at Queens' College, Cambridge, in 1854, but completed his BA only in 1867 (*Alumni Cantabrigienses*).
61. Moule, *Memories of a Vicarage*, 35.
62. *Tempora Mutantur: A Memorial of the Fordington Times Society* (London, 1859), 80.
63. *PV*, 418.
64. *LW*, 37.
65. RLP/FEH, 1931; book (Yale). See P. Ingham, 'Hardy and *The Wonders of Geology*,' *Review of English Studies*, 31 (Feb 1980), 59–64.
66. *DCC*, 18 Nov 1858.
67. Information and quotations from diary of Wynne Albert Bankes (DCRO).
68. *Jude*, 156; *CL*, vi. 30.
69. Diocesan records (Wiltshire Record Office); cf. H. Bastow to TH, 17 Feb 1861 (DCM). MH should have entered in January, was delayed, probably by illness, but then remained for the entirety of a standard two-year course.
70. Passage heavily marked, but not dated, in TH's Bible (DCM); *CL*, v. 315.
71. *DCC*, 14 Feb 1861, 30 Jan 1862, 9 June 1864.
72. Rabiger, 'The Hoffman Papers', 13–16.
73. *LW*, 37; *The Times*, 7 Aug 1862, and *DCC*, 14 Aug 1862.
74. TH, *The Excluded and Collaborative Stories*, ed. P. Dalziel (Oxford, 1992), 34; story published in *New York Times*, 4 Aug 1862.
75. *PV*, 58; *LW*, 38; *PV*, 60.
76. *Book Buyer* (May 1892), 152; cf. 'A Chronological List of Thomas Hardy's Works in verse & prose' (notebook, DCM).
77. H. Bastow to TH, 23 Dec 1863 (DCM).
78. *LW*, 35; SCC to TH, 10 Apr 1926 (Yale).
79. Drawings (DCM); *DCC*, 29 Aug 1861.
80. Coombe Keynes Churchwardens' accounts, 24 Apr 1862 (DCRO).
81. *LW*, 40.
82. Books (DCM).
83. C. M. Oliver, *TH Proposes to Mary Waight* (Beaminster, Dorset, 1964).
84. Prayerbook (DCM).
85. H. Bastow to TH, 17 Feb 1861 (DCM).
86. *DCC*, 6 Mar 1862.

4 LONDON

1. *LW*, 40; note in Keble's *The Christian Year* (DCM).
2. *PV*, 278.

3. *Early Life*, 46, cf. *LW*, 503; SCC/TH, 22 Sept 1916 (Yale).

4. *LW*, 44; *CL*, i. 1.

5. *LW*, 41.

6. *CL*, vi. 192.

7. Architectural Association Minute Book 1857–62; other information about TH and the AA derived from this and other minute books in the Association's archives or from the 'Brown Books' published by the Association in the 1860s.

8. SCC/TH, 10 Apr 1926 (Yale); *CL*, i. 2; RLP/FEH, 1931. Shaw's first name established from his signature on a photograph of TH now in DCM.

9. *CL*, i. 2.

10. *CL*, i. 3.

11. *CL*, vi. 176.

12. *LW*, 54, 43; E. Hardy, 'Hardy and the Phrenologist', *John O'London's Weekly*, 6 Feb 1954 (original report, DCM); *LW*, 53; *CL*, i. 5–6.

13. *CPW*, i. 266–7; *LW*, 44–5; *LW*, 45.

14. Executions, *The Times* (23 Feb 1864), 7; *LW*, 42.

15. *CL*, i. 1; MH to TH, 28 Nov 1862 (DCM); *CL*, i. 1; *PV*, 417–18.

16. *The Times*, 7 Aug 1862; *DCC*, 16 Aug 1883, cf. *PV*, 58–9.

17. *CL*, i. 2; Diocesan records (Wiltshire Record Office).

18. *LW*, 476; *CL*, i. 2.

19. *CL*, i. 2.

20. *CL*, i. 3.

21. *CL*, i. 4.

22. Not, however, the prestigious Sir William Tite prize of later date.

23. *PV*, 351–2; Architectural Association records.

24. *RIBA Proceedings*, Report of the Council, 4 May 1863 (where 'Colored' is so spelled).

25. Information from Dr C. J. P. Beatty, citing RIBA Council Minutes for 23 Mar 1863.

26. Sidney Heath, 'Thomas Hardy', *Teacher's World* (18 Jan 1928), 826.

27. Notebook and book (DCM); *LW*, 49.

28. H. Bastow to TH, 23 Dec 1863 (DCM).

29. Plans for All Saints' (Berkshire Record Office).

30. R. Blomfield, *Memoirs of an Architect* (London, 1932), 35–6.

31. RLP/FEH, 1935; *LW*, 42–3.

32. FEH to SCC, 15 June 1925 (Yale); *LW*, 47.

33. W. O. Milne to C. J. Blomfield, 25 May 1911 (Adams).

34. *LW*, 50; sketches (DCM and Yale respectively).

35. MH to TH, 28 Nov 1862 (DCM); MH, Denchworth reminiscences (DCM); TH sketch of school, 26 Apr 1863, *The Architectural Notebook of TH*, ed. C. J. P. Beatty (Dorchester, 1966), 113.

36. MH, Denchworth reminiscences (DCM).

37. *CL*, i. 4; KH, Hoffman interview, 1939 (HP); NS (Eton); KH diary, 25 Nov 1915 (DCM: Lock).

38. TH sketch of old church, Fawley (DCM); MH to TH, 19 May 1864 (DCM).

39. Sketch (DCM); F. Chalfont, 'Hardy's Residences and Lodgings: Part One', *THJ* 8/3 (Oct 1992), 51–2; the (unofficial) blue plaque bears an incorrect date.

40. TH annotations in prayerbook (DCM); NS (Eton).

41. T. Hands, *TH: Distracted Preacher?* (Basingstoke, 1989), 20–1.

42. For Archdeacon Hoare, friend of Wilberforce, Macaulay, and other Emancipationists, see *DNB*.

43. Information about Eliza Nicholls derived principally from her niece, Mrs Sarah Headley, interviewed by Henry Reed and RLP in 1955, and from Mrs Headley's letters to RLP (Yale).

44. TH photograph, Nicholls family photographs, etc. (Yale).

45. See I. Lees (comp.), 'Findon and Findon Valley' (typescript, West Sussex Record Office).

46. H. Bastow to TH, 20 May 1861 (DCM).

47. *Wessex Poems* (London, 1898), [30].

48. Sketches (DCM).

49. TH's prayerbook (DCM) also shows him attending a service in Brighton on the first Sunday after Easter (3 April) 1864.

50. TH drawing on back free endpaper of Alphonse Mariette, *Half-Hours of French Translation* (London, 1863), purchased 1865 (Colby). Although Nicholas Hillyard disagrees with my identification of Clavel Tower (see his 'Eliza Nicholls and Hardy Poems of 1865–7', *TH Society Review*, 1/9 (1983), 271–3), he generously drew this sketch and annotation to my attention.

51. *CL*, v. 174; Shakespeare (DCM); Neil (Yale).

52. M'Culloch (Yale); Moule letter (DCM).

53. Shorthand primers (DCM); *CL*, i. 5.

54. H. M. Moule to TH, 21 Feb 1864 (DCM).

55. Diary of Arthur Brett (DCRO).

56. Book (Yale); Hoffman interview with Revd G. H. Moule, 1939 (HP).

57. *The Excluded and Collaborative Stories*, ed. P. Dalziel (Oxford, 1992), 10–23; *PV*, 13; 'Authors Book' (W. & R. Chambers records).

58. Books (DCM); *TH's 'Studies, Specimens &c.' Notebook*, ed. P. Dalziel and M. Millgate (Oxford, 1994), *passim*; E. Murray, *Caught in the Web of Words* (London, 1977), 175.

59. *Studies, Specimens*, 50, 49; A. C. Swinburne, *Poems and Ballads* (London, 1866), 85–90, 91–3, 98–101, 178–95; *CL*, ii. 158.

60. *Studies, Specimens*, 54, 23, 32.

61. *Studies, Specimens*, 83; here as elsewhere italics indicate words underlined.

62. For this example, and for paragraph as a whole, see P. Dalziel, 'Hardy's Sexual Evasions: The Evidence of the "Studies, Specimens &c." Notebook', *Victorian Poetry*, 31/3 (Summer 1993), 143–55.

63. Extract from early pocketbook inserted into 'Poetical Matter' notebook (microfilm, Yale).

64. *Studies, Specimens*, 7, 60; italicized word underlined in notebook.

65. 'Poetical Matter' notebook (microfilm, Yale).

66. See manuscript of 'Retty's Phases', Purdy, 242, and facing illustration.

67. *LW*, 53.

68. *LW*, 52; Mariette (Colby), Stiévenard (M. Millgate); *CL*, vii. 30.

69. *LN*, i. 3–4; *LW*, 59; *PV*, 238–9; *The Times* (11 July 1865), 8; *LN*, i. 5–7.

70. Books (Yale).

71. *LW*, 53; books (DCM).

72. *CL*, i. 167; *Two on a Tower*, 255.

73. E. Felkin, 'Days with TH', *Encounter*, 18/4 (Apr 1962), 32.

74. *CPW*, i. 8–9, 285, 16–17, iii. 155, i. 10.
75. *CPW*, i. 12–13, 93–8, 197–8, 100–3 (cf. 390–3), ii. 379–80.
76. *LW*, 52.
77. R. Gittings, *Young TH* (London, 1975), 92–6; KH, interviewed by H. Hoffman (HP), identified H.A. as a friend of her mother's with first name of Henrietta; Denchworth visit dated alongside ballad of 'Auld Robin Gray' in TH's *Golden Treasury* (DCM); two drawings of Denchworth also dated (DCM).
78. Date in TH's *Christian Year*, 138 (DCM); *Architectural Notebook*, [22]; church identified from erased but still discernible 'Findon'.
79. *CPW*, i. 171, 20; for Eliza Nicholls, see n. 43 above.
80. *LW*, 56; sketch (DCM).
81. *LW*, 52–3; cf. *Career*, 37–8.
82. *CL*, i. 7; *CPW*, i. 359.
83. *LW*, 49; *LW*, 47, assigns the St Pancras episode to 'the year 1865 or thereabouts', but it belongs more precisely to 1866–7 (see *Bayswater Chronicle*, 30 June 1866).
84. For Tom Pinch, see Charles Dickens, *Martin Chuzzlewit*; *LW*, 478.
85. *Studies, Specimens*, 89.
86. *CL*, ii. 158.
87. *LW*, 415.
88. *CPW*, ii. 379, i. 284.
89. H. M. Moule to TH, Monday [June 1867?] (DCM).
90. W. O. Milne to C. J. Blomfield, 23 May 1911 (Adams).
91. *CL*, v. 174.
92. Purdy, 143; *CPW*, i. 286.
93. *LW*, 55–6, *The Times*, 27 Dec 1866, and D. Hawkins, *Hardy: Novelist and Poet* (Newton Abbot, 1976), 14–15. Ruskin, in Letter 5 of *Time and Tide by Weare and Tyne* (London, 1867), curiously asserts that all parts in the pantomime were played by women.
94. *Golden Treasury* (Yale); Wood (Chuo University, Japan).
95. *CPW*, i. 13.
96. Mrs Headley: see n. 43 above; also note at *CL*, vii. 168.
97. *LW*, 54; FEH to Lady Gosse, 5 Aug 1927 (Leeds); John Antell, interview, 1972.
98. *LW*, 54–5.

5 *The Poor Man and the Lady*

1. RLP/FEH, 1935.
2. *LW*, 58.
3. Hicks's extant drawings for the three Dorset churches are dated 1867–8, those for St Juliot 1867 (information from C. J. P. Beatty).
4. Drawing of Dogbury dated 10 Sept 1867 (DCM), cf. 'Life and Death at Sunrise (Near Dogbury Gate, 1867)', *CPW*, iii. 40; J. Digby to MH, 27 May 1867 (DCM: Lock).
5. School records, Puddletown.
6. See, e.g., Anna Winchcombe, 'Four Letters from Tryphena', *Dorset*, no. 23 (1972), 38–40, also pp. 41–2 of same issue.
7. This controversy, initiated by L. Deacon's pamphlet *Tryphena and TH* (Beaminster, 1962), amplified by L. Deacon and T. Coleman, *Providence and Mr Hardy* (London, 1966), was surveyed in G. Ford (ed.), *Victorian Fiction: A Second Guide to Research* (New York, 1978),

313–14. See also R. Gittings, *Young TH* (London, 1975), 223–9.

8. *LW*, 234; *CPW*, i. 81.

9. Information from the late Henry Reed, citing FEH; J. Antell, interview, 1972; I. Cooper Willis, 'Thomas Hardy', *Colby Library Quarterly*, 9/5 (Mar 1971), 268; NS, note dated 7 Nov 1955 (Ian Kennedy).

10. According to Deacon and Coleman, *Providence and Mr Hardy*, 42, Rebecca parted from Paine immediately after the wedding; Tryphena's son Charles Gale (interview, 1970) thought the marriage had lasted for two or three months.

11. *Providence and Mr Hardy*, 33.

12. General information about John Antell from J. Antell (great-grandson), 1970–1, although the latter's article, 'The Uncle Who Impressed Hardy', *Dorset Evening Echo*, 3 June 1983, appeared after the first edition of the present biography.

13. *An Address from the County of Dorset on the Elementary Education Bill* (Dorchester, 1870).

14. *CL*, i. 92; Gittings, *Young TH*, figs. 14a, 14b; TH note (DCM); for the Turberville portraits, see T. O'Sullivan, *TH: An Illustrated Biography* (London, 1975), 133.

15. FEH to Lady Hoare, 30 July 1915 (Wiltshire Record Office).

16. *CL*, v. 249, 253.

17. *CL*, v. 253; *CPW*, i. 177–9, iii. 110–11, 234, and Purdy, 113, 142, 258; *LW*, 59.

18. *LW*, 58.

19. For an authoritative assessment and collation of the sources for a reconstruction, see TH, *The Excluded and Collaborative Stories*, ed. Pamela Dalziel, (Oxford, 1992), 68–82; for a more detailed account, see her 'A Critical Edition of TH's Uncollected Stories' (D.Phil. thesis, Oxford Univ., 1989), 152 ff.

20. Revd G. B. Sharpe to TH, 21 Jan 1868 (DCM: Lock).

21. *LW*, 59; Macmillan & Co., 'Record of Manuscripts' (BL); *CL*, i. 7–8.

22. A. Macmillan to TH, 10 Aug 1868 (DCM), cf. slightly inaccurate text in C. Morgan, *The House of Macmillan (1843–1943)* (London, 1943), 88–91.

23. 'Macmillan Reader's Reports. Vol. I' (BL), cf. Morgan, *House of Macmillan*, 87–8.

24. *LW*, 63.

25. RLP/FEH, 1935.

26. Purdy, opp. 242; *CL*, i. 8; *LW*, 61.

27. 'Poetical Matter' notebook (microfilm, Yale); TH later wrote 'The Maid of Keinton Mandeville', *CPW*, ii. 326–7, but not, apparently, the poem here projected.

28. *CL*, i. 8.

29. Morgan, *House of Macmillan*, 92; *LW*, 60–1.

30. Prayerbook (DCM).

31. *CL*, vi. 289–90; *LW*, 61.

32. Chapman & Hall to TH, 8 Feb 1869 (DCM).

33. *LW*, 62.

34. Chapman & Hall to TH, 26 Feb and 3 Mar 1869 (DCM); TH, 'G.M.: A Reminiscence', *PV*, 469.

35. 'George Meredith, 1828–1909', *CPW*, i. 358; *PV*, 469.

36. *CL*, i. 9–10; *LW*, 64; Purdy, 275–6.

37. *CL*, iv. 130; Bible (DCM); Vulgate (Fales Library, New York Univ.); *CPW*, ii. 196.

38. *CL*, i. 10.

39. *DCC*, 18 Feb 1869.

40. *LW*, 65; C. J. P. Beatty, 'The Part Played by Architecture in the Life and Work of TH'

(Ph.D. thesis, Univ. of London, 1963), 114–27; album of photographs of Turnworth capitals (DCM).

41. *LW*, 65.
42. *Southern Times* (Weymouth), 22 May, 5 June, 10 July 1869; *Illustrated Guide to Weymouth, etc.* (Weymouth, [1865?]), 96.
43. *CPW*, ii. 245.
44. *LW*, 419.
45. *LW*, 66.
46. Leonard Patten, 'Tale of a Chimney Pot', *Society of Dorset Men in London Yearbook for 1940–41*, 78–83, where TH is said to have attended Dorcas's wedding (in 1878).
47. 'Poetical Matter' notebook (microfilm, Yale).
48. F. B. Pinion, *TH: Art and Thought* (London, 1977), 2–6.
49. *Desperate Remedies*, p. v.
50. RLP/FEH, 1936.
51. For the closeness of the two texts, see P. Dalziel, 'Exploiting the Poor Man: The Genesis of Hardy's *Desperate Remedies*', *Journal of English and Germanic Philology*, 94 (Apr 1995), 220–32.
52. *Desperate Remedies* (3 vols. London, 1871), i. 43, 45–6; Wessex edn., 23, reads 'rather humble origins'; Suleiman H. Ahmad, 'Hardy's *Desperate Remedies*: A Source', *Notes and Queries*, NS 32 (Sept 1985), 364–5.
53. *Desperate Remedies* (Wessex edn.), 278–9; *CPW*, i. 19.
54. E. Gosse, 'Thomas Hardy's Lost Novel', *Sunday Times*, 22 Jan 1928.
55. 'The Pursuit of the Well-Beloved', *Illustrated London News* (1 Oct 1892), 425; I am indebted to Nicholas Hillyard for bringing this passage to my attention.
56. *CPW*, i. 273; *CPW*, iii. 27.
57. *CPW*, i. 274.
58. Findon parish registers (West Sussex Record Office).

6 St Juliot

1. *LW*, 66; information from Dr C. J. P. Beatty.
2. G. R. Crickmay to TH, 11 Feb 1870 (DCM), see *LW*, 66; *CPW*, ii. 17; *LW*, 66.
3. *LW*, 67; ELH, *Some Recollections*, ed. E. Hardy and R. Gittings (London, 1961), 55 (original in DCM); for 'familiar appearance' ELH first wrote 'homely appearance'.
4. *Some Recollections*, 53 (reference to dentist struck through).
5. Marriage certificate.
6. ELH, *Some Recollections*, 22, 16, and see *LEFH*, 36; FEH to R. Owen, 24 Oct 1915 (Colby); Mrs Hawes to E. Gifford (ELH), 31 Oct 1872 (DCM).
7. FEH to R. Owen, 24 Oct 1915 (Colby); 'The Young Churchwarden', *CPW*, ii. 194; D. Kay-Robinson, 'The Face at the Casement', *TH Year Book*, no. 5 (1975), 34–5.
8. *LW*, 76; M. Hawes to E. Gifford (ELH), 'Wednesday' [1871?] (DCM); ELH, *Some Recollections*, 51.
9. *CL*, iv. 299.
10. *LW*, 78; *CPW*, ii. 353–4; visit to The Old Rectory, June 2003; for the bedrooms, cf. *A Pair of Blue Eyes*, 103, 108.
11. ELH, *Some Recollections*, 55–6; M. Hawes to E. Gifford (ELH), 'Wednesday' [1871?] (DCM).

12. ELH, 'The Maid on the Shore', typescript made in 1910 (DCM).
13. 'I Found Her Out There', *CPW*, ii. 51.
14. 'The Phantom Horsewoman', *CPW*, ii. 66.
15. RLP/FEH, 1929; *LW*, 78; *CPW*, ii. 165.
16. St Juliot plans (Texas), see C. J. P. Beatty, 'TH's St. Juliot Drawings', *Architectural Review* (Feb 1962), 139; copy of St Juliot restoration appeal, June 1866 (Cornwall County Record Office); *PV*, 247.
17. Letter (DCM); 'Reviews of Manuscripts', vol. 1, Macmillan archive (BL), cf. C. Morgan, *The House of Macmillan (1843–1943)* (London, 1943), 93–4.
18. *LW*, 78–9; W. Tinsley to TH, 7 Apr, 3 May, and 5 May 1870 (Princeton), and see Purdy, 329–40, and *CL*, i. 10.
19. *LW*, 79; FEH MS, 'Places where TH has lived' (DCM).
20. *LW*, 79; prayerbook (DCM).
21. *LW*, 79; *PN*, 5.
22. *LW*, 79–80; *Pair of Blue Eyes*, 141–4.
23. *Marlburian*, 30 Sept 1865, 7 June 1866, 24 June 1867, 3 Mar 1869, etc.
24. Letters (Marlborough College archives, courtesy of E. G. H. Kempson); *Saturday Review*, 26 Feb 1859.
25. *Marlburian*, 3 Mar 1869; letter (Marlborough College archives).
26. See Rabiger, 'Hoffman Papers', 13–16; Bankes diary (DCRO).
27. *LW*, 80; J. B. Harford and F. C. Macdonald, *Handley Carr Glyn Moule, Bishop of Durham* (London, 1922), 7; *CPW*, i. 22.
28. *PN*, 4.
29. *LW*, 81; 'The Voice', *CPW*, ii. 56; ELH, *Some Recollections*, 57–8.
30. Prayerbook (DCM); *CL*, vi. 29; CPW, ii. 194; Purdy, 196.
31. *CPW*, ii. 175–6; *CPW*, ii. 295–6; *Pair of Blue Eyes*, 202.
32. *LW*, 81–2; book (Yale).
33. Sketches (DCM), and see 'Under the Waterfall', *CPW*, ii. 45–6, and ELH, *Some Recollections*, between 56 and 57; ELH sketch and note (Berg).
34. *PN*, 5–6.
35. *CPW*, ii. 29.
36. RLP/FEH, 1935.
37. *CL*, iv. 260.
38. I. Cooper Willis, pocketbook (DCM).
39. *LW*, 80, 85.
40. Morgan, *House of Macmillan*, 93–4; for TH's substitution for the 'violation', see *Desperate Remedies*, 441.
41. *PN*, 6, 17; *LEFH*, 312.
42. Bible (DCM); *PN*, 6–7; Bible and Shakespeare (DCM), and see *LW*, 85.
43. Book (DCM).
44. W. Tinsley to TH, 9 and 19 Dec 1870 (Princeton), cf. Purdy, 330; *CL*, i. 10; W. Tinsley to TH, 21 Dec 1870 (Princeton).
45. Balance sheet repr. in Purdy, opp. 5; *LW*, 85–6.
46. *Athenaeum* (1 Apr 1871), 399, cf. R. G. Cox (ed.), *TH: The Critical Heritage* (London, 1970), 1–2; *Spectator* (22 Apr 1871), 481, 482, cf. Cox, *Critical Heritage*, 3–5, and see *LW*, 86–7, 507, 533.
47. *LW*, 86–7, cf. *CL*, i. 11; *PN*, 10.

48. *Architectural Notebook*, [170–2]; information from Dr C. J. P. Beatty.

49. Detached notebook fragment (DCM).

50. *LW*, 86–7; Purdy, 5; W. Tinsley to TH, 5 Oct 1871 (Princeton), cf. Purdy, 330–1.

51. *PN*, 8–10; Purdy, 7.

52. Purdy, 7, and Simon Gatrell, *Hardy the Creator: A Textual Biography* (Oxford, 1988), 12–14.

53. *Cassell's Saturday Journal* (25 June 1892), 944, cf. James Gibson (ed.), *TH: Interviews and Recollections* (Basingstoke, 1999), 36, and *PV*, 118.

54. *Greenwood Tree*, p. x.

55. *LW*, 99; *Greenwood Tree*, 7, 16, 36; E. E. T[itterington], *The Domestic Life of TH (1921–1928)* (Beaminster, 1963), 16.

56. Gatrell, *Hardy the Creator*, 127–9, and M. R. Skilling, *Hardy's Mellstock on the Map* (Dorchester, 1968); *LW*, 95; *Greenwood Tree*, 210.

57. *CL*, i. 11–12.

58. M. Macmillan to TH, 11 Sept 1871 (DCM); Morgan, *House of Macmillan*, 96–7; books (Yale).

59. *CL*, i. 13; Morgan, *House of Macmillan*, 99.

60. *CL*, i. 13–14; W. Tinsley to TH, 23 Oct 1871 (Princeton).

61. Bible (DCM).

62. *CPW*, ii. 220; the poem, subtitled 'Young Lover's Reverie', is dated 'Begun 1871: finished—'.

7 *Far from the Madding Crowd*

1. *LW*, 89–90; F. Chalfont, 'Hardy's Residences and Lodgings: Part One', *THJ* 8/3 (Oct 1992), 54–5; *CL*, i. 15.

2. *CL*, i. 16; F. Chalfont, 'Hardy's Residences', 55–6; prayerbook annotations (DCM).

3. *CL*, i. 15–16; W. Tinsley to TH, 22 Feb, 19 Mar 1872 (Princeton), cf. Purdy, 331–2.

4. George Moore, *Confessions of a Young Man* (London, 1937), 171; *LW*, 90–1.

5. *LW*, 90–1; *CL*, i. 16; W. Tinsley to TH, 15, 22 Apr 1872 (Princeton), cf. Purdy, 332.

6. *CL*, i. 16; *LW*, 91.

7. H. M. Moule to TH, 17 Apr 1872 (DCM); *LW*, 90, 91.

8. *LW*, 91–2; Purdy, 8; *Athenaeum*, 15 June 1872, cf. R. G. Cox (ed.), *TH: The Critical Heritage* (London, 1970), 9–11; *Pall Mall Gazette*, 5 July 1872; *Saturday Review*, 28 Sept 1872, cf. *Critical Heritage*, 11–14.

9. 'Coming up Oxford Street: Evening', *CPW*, iii. 25 (dated 'As seen 4 July 1872'); W. Tinsley to TH, 9 July 1872 (Princeton), cf. Purdy, 332.

10. *LW*, 92; *CL*, i. 17–18, cf. Purdy, 332, 333.

11. *LW*, 92–3.

12. *Blue Eyes* MS, fo. [1] (Berg); ELH, *Some Recollections*, ed., E. Hardy and R. Gittings (London, 1961), 28, 37, cf. R. Gittings, *Young TH* (London, 1975), 130.

13. *LEFH*, 78; 'I Rose and Went to Rou'tor Town', *CPW*, ii. 265; V. H. Collins, *Talks with TH at Max Gate, 1920–1922* (London, 1928), 26.

14. *CL*, i. 18; *LW*, 93–4; *CL*, v. 246; *CPW*, ii. 169, and see ii. 497.

15. *Blue Eyes* (London, 1873), i. 56–7 (passage absent from Wessex edn.).

16. *Tinsleys' Magazine* (Oct 1872), 259; *Blue Eyes*, 78; cf. *A Pair of Blue Eyes*, ed. P. Dalziel (London, 1998), 402–3.

17. *Blue Eyes* MS, fo. 34 (Berg); Benvill Lane references pointed out by Dr C. J. P. Beatty;

Blue Eyes, 261, cf. 1873 edn., i. 224, and see Gittings, *Young TH*, 166.

18. *Blue Eyes*, 100.

19. Information from the late Henry Reed, citing conversation with FEH.

20. R. Smith to TH, 10 Aug 1872 (DCM); *CL*, iv. 84, 83.

21. *LW*, 93–4; *PN*, 10–11; *CL*, i. 18.

22. Bible and prayerbook (DCM).

23. *PN*, 11; *CL*, i. 19; W. Tinsley to TH, 4 Oct 1872 (Princeton), cf. Purdy, 333.

24. F. Greenwood, 'The Genius of TH', *Illustrated London News* (1 Oct 1892), 431; Stephen letter (DCM), cf. Purdy, 336–7.

25. *LW*, 97–8; Stephen to TH, 4 Dec 1872 (DCM).

26. Holder letter (DCM); *LW*, 94; statement (Cornwall County Record Office).

27. *CL*, i. 20.

28. *DCC*, 20 Feb 1873, cf. *Career*, 99–100; *PV*, 52.

29. L. Stephen to TH, 7 Apr 1873 (DCM); *LW*, 94; KH, Hoffman interview, 1939 (HP); E. Smith, Hoffman interview, 1939 (HP).

30. C. W. Moule to TH, 11 May 1873 (DCM).

31. *CL*, i. 26.

32. Information about James Pole and his daughter from M. Rabiger, 'The Hoffman Papers', *TH Year Book*, no. 10 (1981), 20–4, and from Henry Reed, citing FEH.

33. Rabiger, 'Hoffman Papers', 23–4; *LW*, 284.

34. Purdy, 12; *Career*, 72–3.

35. *Spectator* (28 June 1873), 831; Hutton letter (DCM), cf. *Career*, 371.

36. H. M. Moule to TH, 21 May 1873 (DCM).

37. H. M. Moule to TH, Thursday [1870?] (DCM); 'Mr. Henry Taylor's Plays and Poems', *Fraser's*, Sept 1871; 'The Story of Alcestis', *Fraser's*, Nov 1871; 'Achilles and Lancelot', *Macmillan's Magazine*, Sept 1871.

38. *LW*, 95–6.

39. *LW*, 96, 98; RLP/FEH, 1933; *CPW*, iii. 226.

40. *LW*, 96.

41. H. Holt to TH, 29 May 1873 (DCM), and see S. Weiner, 'TH and his First American Publisher', *Princeton University Library Chronicle*, Spring 1978; *PV*, 259.

42. *LW*, 97; *CL*, iv. 58.

43. Heroine of Scott's *Rob Roy*.

44. *Madding Crowd*, 45; see R. C. Schweik, 'A First Draft Chapter of Hardy's *Far from the Madding Crowd*', *English Studies* (1972), 344–9.

45. H. C. Minchin, letter (citing FEH), *Times Literary Supplement* (9 Feb 1928), 96; RLP/FEH, 1929; FEH to SCC, 22 Apr 1918 (Yale), cf. V. Meynell (ed.), *Friends of a Lifetime* (London, 1940), 298.

46. *CL*, i. 27.

47. Annotation in J. Hullah, *The Song Book* (DCM); *LW*, 98.

48. [London] *Standard*, 23 Sept 1873, *DCC*, 25 Sept 1873, *Cambridge Chronicle*, 27 Sept 1873, *Cambridge Independent Press*, 27 Sept 1873. No official record of the inquest seems to have survived.

49. Mary Blyth (great-niece), interview, 1973; also M. Blyth, letter, *Times Literary Supplement* (13 Mar 1969), 272.

50. *Standard*, 23 Sept 1873, 3; cf. chap. 3, n. 60.

51. RLP/FEH, 1933.

52. *CPW*, i. 14, poem dated '1873' in TH's 'Chronological List' (DCM); E. Hardy, 'TH and Horace Moule', *Times Literary Supplement* (21 Jan 1969), 89; M. Blyth, letter, *Times Literary Supplement* (13 Mar 1969), 272; M. Blyth, interview, 1973.
53. Books (DCM); *London Mercury*, Oct 1922, cf. *PV*, 417–18.
54. *CPW*, iii. 226.
55. L. Stephen to TH, 6 Oct 1873 (DCM); *LW*, 98.
56. *CL*, i. 22–4; *LW*, 99.
57. *LW*, 99.
58. *LW*, 99; *PN*, 14–15.
59. *PV*, 260–1.
60. *PV*, 261.
61. The TH-designed memorial to ELH in St Juliot Church shows her residence there as terminating in 1873; *Some Recollections*, 46, 59; *LW*, 100.
62. *CL*, iii. 218; FEH to H. Bliss, 21 Apr 1936 (Adams); *PV*, 261.
63. E. McC. Fleming, *R. R. Bowker: Militant Liberal* (Norman, Okla., 1952), 150; E. Gosse, *Books on the Table* (London, 1921), 296; cf. Lady Ritchie (formerly A. Thackeray) to TH, 9 Nov 1916 (DCM).
64. *CL*, i. 30; *LW*, 103; A. Thackeray to H. Paterson, Thursday [1874?] (Colby).
65. *CL*, iii. 218; *CPW*, ii. 393.
66. *LW*, 103.
67. *Spectator* (3 Jan 1874), 22; L. Stephen to TH, 12 Mar, 13 Apr 1874 (DCM), cf. Purdy, 338, 39.
68. R. Morgan, *Cancelled Words: Rediscovering TH* (London, 1992), *passim*, cf. Simon Gatrell, *Hardy the Creator* (Oxford, 1988), 15–19; *Madding Crowd* MS, fo. 2–232 (Yale), repr. in *Cancelled Words*, 146.
69. *CL*, i. 28.
70. Purdy, 294; *CL*, i. 28.
71. *LW*, 103; *PN*, 17
72. Passport (DCM).
73. *LW*, 103; *PN*, 15–17.
74. *Madding Crowd* MS, fo. 45 (Yale).

8 MARRIAGE

1. *LW*, 103, and *CL*, i. 30–1; L. Stephen to TH, 25 Aug 1874 (DCM), cf. Purdy, 339.
2. ELH, *Some Recollections*, ed. E. Hardy and R. Gittings (London, 1961), 60; E. H. Gifford to TH, 4 and 12 Sept 1874 (DCM); E. H. Gifford in *DNB*.
3. *Some Recollections*, 60; *CL*, i. 31; marriage certificate.
4. ELH, 1874–6 diary (DCM), in *Emma Hardy Diaries*, ed. Richard H. Taylor (Ashington, 1985), 21–2, 22–3.
5. TH's copy of F. Licquet, *Rouen: Its History, Monuments, and Environs* (Rouen, 1871) (Yale); *Emma Hardy Diaries*, 24–5; *Ethelberta*, 288, 292, 296–7, etc.
6. *Emma Hardy Diaries*, 26 ff.; Murray's *Handbook* (BL); *Ethelberta*, 330.
7. *Emma Hardy Diaries*, 49, 39, 27, 40.
8. Ibid. 47.
9. *CPW*, ii. 262–4; *Emma Hardy Diaries*, 55, 56.
10. *Emma Hardy Diaries*, 54–6; information from Mrs Elsie Honeywell, 1980, and M.

Davison, *Hook Remembered Again* (Reigate, 2001), 13, 17.

11. *Emma Hardy Diaries*, 56; new information about St David's Villa from *Hook Remembered Again*, 10–15, and directly from Mark Davison, 2001.

12. *CPW*, iii. 43–4, 42–3; *PN*, 18.

13. *LW*, 104; Mrs Procter to TH, 4 Sept 1874 (DCM).

14. Mrs Macquoid's letter seems not to have survived; TH's is at *CL*, i. 33.

15. *Nation* (New York), 24 Dec 1874; *Spectator*, 19 Dec 1874; both in R. G. Cox (ed.), *TH: The Critical Heritage* (London, 1970), 21, 31; J. Hutton to TH, 23 Dec 1874 (DCM).

16. *PV*, 8–9.

17. G. Smith to TH, 15 Jan 1875 (DCM); Purdy, 18–19.

18. *CL*, i. 33–4; W. Tinsley to TH, 5 Jan 1875 (Princeton); G. Smith to TH, 19 Jan 1875 (DCM).

19. L. Stephen to TH, 2 and 7 Dec 1874 (DCM); *LW*, 106; *CL*, i. 35.

20. *CL*, i. 35; G. Smith to TH, 9 Mar 1875 (DCM); L. S. Jennings to TH, 5 Mar 1875 (DCM).

21. Letters from editors (DCM); C. Patmore to TH, 29 Mar 1875 (DCM); *LW*, 107–8.

22. *PV*, 264; *LW*, 109–10.

23. 'Poetical Matter' notebook (microfilm, Yale).

24. *LW*, 108; *The Letters of Ezra Pound 1907–1941*, ed. D. D. Paige (New York, 1950), 294; F. W. Maitland, *The Life and Letters of Leslie Stephen* (London, 1906), 450.

25. *LW*, 106, and *CL*, i. 36.

26. *PV*, 263, cf. *LW*, 108–9; the deed was recorded on Chancery roll 30 of 1875, sheet 55 (Public Record Office).

27. *CL*, v. 76.

28. *CPW*, ii. 30; *Letters of Virginia Woolf*, ed. N. Nicolson and J. Trautmann (London, 1975–80), ii. 58; ibid., i. 134; Purdy, 138; *CPW*, i. 243–7.

29. *LW*, 106; *LW*, 105.

30. These issues usefully surveyed in Tim Dolin's introduction to his Penguin Classics edition of *Ethelberta* (London, 1996); for a well-argued alternative reading, see R. Schweik, 'Hardy's "Plunge in a New and Untried Direction": Comic Detachment in *The Hand of Ethelberta*', *English Studies*, 83 (June 2002), 239–52.

31. *Ethelberta*, 158.

32. Maitland, *Leslie Stephen*, 276; cf. S. Gatrell, *Hardy the Creator: A Textual Biography* (Oxford, 1988), 19–23.

33. L. Stephen to TH, 13 and 20 May 1875 (DCM); *LW*, 106–7; *CL*, i. 37.

34. *LW*, 109, and *The Times* (11 May 1875), 10.

35. *CL*, i. 37; programme (Yale), and see F. B. Pinion, 'A Hundred Years Ago: Hardy at Oxford', *TH Society Review*, 1/1 (1975), 15–16.

36. *LW*, 110.

37. KH to ELH, [1875?, though dated '1881–3' by TH] (DCM).

38. *CPW*, ii. 161; *Moments of Vision* MS, fo. 4 (Magdalene College, Cambridge).

39. *Ethelberta*, 254, 255; see D. Lewer, 'Thomas Hardy's Winter Stay in Swanage', *TH Year Book*, no. 1 (1970), 45–9.

40. *LW*, 110–11; Maitland, *Leslie Stephen*, 276.

41. *CL*, i. 42.

42. ELH, 1874–6 diary (DCM), cf. *Emma Hardy Diaries*, 56–7, 63–4, 65–7; MH sketches (DCM); *Emma Hardy Diaries*, 211 n. 21, wrongly identifies Henry Hardy as also present.

43. *Emma Hardy Diaries*, 59–60; d'Arville letter (DCM); Purdy, 22.

44. R. Gowing to TH, 11 and 30 Sept 1875 (DCM).

45. *CL*, i. 40; *CL*, i. 39–40; *CL*, i. 37–8.

46. R. D. Blackmore to TH, 11 June 1875 (Berg); W. H. Dunne, *R. D. Blackmore: The Author of 'Lorna Doone'* (London, 1956), 164.

9 STURMINSTER NEWTON

1. *Selected Letters of Leslie Stephen*, ed. John W. Bicknell with Mark A. Reger (Basingstoke, 1996), 174–6.

2. *CL*, i. 43.

3. *CL*, i. 43, 45; C. B. Tauchnitz to TH, 22 May 1876 (DCM).

4. *CL*, i. 43; Smith, Elder to TH, 7 Mar 1876 (DCM); L. Boucher to TH, 24 Nov 1876 (DCM).

5. *Westminster Review* (July 1876), 281, and see W. J. Keith, 'TH and the Name "Wessex"', *English Language Notes*, 6 (Sept 1968), 42–4.

6. *Examiner* (15 July 1876), 793; *Madding Crowd* (London, 1895), p. vii.

7. *CL*, i. 43–4; Purdy, 23; *Spectator* (22 May 1876), 532.

8. *LW*, 113–14; *CL*, i. 45; ELH, 1874–6 diary, pages reversed (DCM), cf. *Emma Hardy Diaries*, ed. Richard H. Taylor (Ashington, 1985), 73 ff.

9. *Emma Hardy Diaries*, 76, 80, 81–2, 83.

10. *LW*, 113–14; *Emma Hardy Diaries*, 84.

11. *Emma Hardy Diaries*, 88–90.

12. Ibid. 90, 93.

13. Baedeker, dated 1875 (BL); *PV*, 89; *LW*, 114.

14. *Emma Hardy Diaries*, 103; *LW*, 111; *LW*, 115.

15. Gertrude Bugler, interview, 1974, and *TH Society Review*, 1/6 (1980), 187–8; photographs (G. Bugler and DCM); *Dorset County Magazine*, no. 111 (1985), 25.

16. *CPW*, ii. 223; *LW*, 115.

17. *LW*, 122, cf. 115; *CPW*, ii. 401.

18. R. Young ('Rabin Hill'), *Poems in the Dorset Dialect*, ed. J. C. M. Mansel-Pleydell (Dorchester, 1910); *Emma Hardy Diaries*, 103; *LW*, 120, 122.

19. *LW*, 119, 117; 'Poetical Matter' notebook (microfilm, Yale).

20. *LW*, 116; *Emma Hardy Diaries*, 103.

21. J. Antell, interview, 1972.

22. 'Poetical Matter' notebook (microfilm, Yale); book (DCM).

23. TH to J. H. Nodal, 24 Aug 1876 (DCM), cf. *PV*, 11; see also *PV*, 14, 28–9.

24. *CL*, i. 47; *CL*, i. 48. For composition of *Return of the Native*, see esp. S. Gatrell, *Hardy the Creator* (Oxford, 1988), 29–47.

25. *CL*, i. 49; F. B. Pinion, 'The Composition of *The Return of the Native*', *Times Literary Supplement* (21 Aug 1970), 931.

26. *PV*, 264.

27. *CL*, i. 50; Purdy, 25; Mrs Procter to Emma Forrest, 5 Jan 1878 (Huntington Library).

28. TH's signed receipts for monthly instalments (Adams, Yale, State Library of Victoria).

29. *The Letters of Anthony Trollope*, ed. B. A. Booth (London, 1951), 650.

30. *CL*, i. 50; *LW*, 120; SCC/TH 22 Aug 1925 (Yale); *CL*, i. 51.

31. 'Literary Notes I' notebook (DCM), see *The Literary Notes of TH*, ed. L. A. Björk (2 vols., London, 1985), i, pp. xx–xxi, 92–9.

32. On TH's classical reading see J. Steele's 'classics' entry for *Companion*, 53–9.
33. *Jude*, 331–2; *Western Gazette*, 12 Jan and 2 Feb 1877; *Sherborne Journal*, 8 Feb 1877.
34. *Western Gazette*, 25 May 1877; *LW*, 118.
35. *LW*, 117; *Western Gazette*, 8 June 1877, and see H. C. and J. Brocklebank, *Marnhull: Records and Memories* (Gillingham, 1940), 92–3; *DCC*, 5 July 1877; *LW*, 118.
36. *Emma Hardy Diaries*, 103; *LW*, 118, 119.
37. Sturminster parish records (DCRO); *Tess*, 116–23; book (DCM); John Hutchins, *The History and Antiquities of the County of Dorset* (4 vols., Westminster, 1861–73), iii. 355–8.
38. *CPW*, ii. 223; *CPW*, ii. 225, 223.
39. *CPW*, ii. 402, 401; *LW*, 119.
40. *LW*, 120; T. Hardy, sen., to KH, 13 Nov 1877 (DCM: Lock).
41. *LW*, 121.
42. *LW*, 121; RLP/FEH, 1936; I. Cooper Willis note (DCM), quoted J. O. Bailey, *The Poetry of TH* (Chapel Hill, NC, 1970), 383; RLP/FEH, 1933.
43. *LW*, 122; *DCC*, 7 Mar 1878, *Western Gazette*, 8 Mar 1878; *CPW*, iii. 326–7.
44. *LW*, 115; *LW*, 121–2

10   *The Return of the Native*

1. *LW*, 123; *CL*, i. 58; Mrs Dashwood to ELH, 6 May 1878 (DCM).
2. C. B. Tauchnitz to TH, 8 Jan 1878 (DCM); Purdy, 63, 274–5; see P. Dalziel, 'Hardy's Unforgotten "Indiscretion": The Centrality of an Uncollected Work', *Review of English Studies*, NS 43 (1992), 347–66.
3. Purdy, 25–6, and *CL*, i. 52–5, 59; Hopkins's replies (DCM), and see P. Dalziel, 'Anxieties of Representation: The Serial Illustrations to Hardy's *The Return of the Native*', *Nineteenth Century Literature*, 51 (June 1996), 84–110.
4. *CL*, i. 56; MS (Bowdoin College), cf. *PV*, 12–13. The error 'Queen's' for 'Queens'' is in the MS.
5. *LW*, 125; *LW*, 124–5; *Examiner*, 5 Dec 1874; *CL*, i. 41; *LW*, 131.
6. *LW*, 135–6.
7. '*Trumpet-Major*' notebook (DCM), cf. *PN*, 117, 120, etc.
8. *CL*, i. 52, 59; G. Smith to TH, 19 Sept 1878 (DCM).
9. *CL*, i. 40; H. Holt to TH, 8 June 1878 (DCM); H. Holt, *Garrulities of an Octogenarian Editor* (Boston, 1923), 207.
10. *CL*, i. 58; C. B. Tauchnitz to TH, 8 Jan and 2 Nov 1878 (DCM).
11. *CL*, i. 28, and see *Career*, 130–3; for the history of the manuscript, see S. Gatrell, *Hardy the Creator* (Oxford, 1988), 29–51.
12. Purdy, 27; *Athenaeum* (23 Nov 1878), 654.
13. *Athenaeum*, 30 Nov 1878, cf. *PV*, 14; *LW*, 127.
14. *Spectator*, 8 Feb 1879, cf. R. G. Cox (ed.), *TH: The Critical Heritage* (London, 1970), 55–9; E. Gosse to F. A. Hedgcock, 28 July 1909 (Adams).
15. *CL*, i. 61.
16. For sketch map, see T. O'Sullivan, *TH: An Illustrated Biography* (London, 1975), 68; J. Paterson, *The Making of 'The Return of the Native'* (Berkeley, 1963), 45–7.
17. *Return of the Native*, 440–1, cf. M. Millgate, 'Searching for Saxelby', *THJ* 19/1 (Feb 2003), 58.
18. *LW*, 126.

19. *LW*, 125; H. C. C. Moule (son of C. W. Moule), interview, 1973.

20. *CL*, i. 59–60; *Illustrated London News*, 7 and 14 Sept 1878.

21. 'Mr. Hardy's Novels', *British Quarterly Review*, 73 (Apr 1881), 342–60, cf. Cox, *Critical Heritage*, 82; *CL*, i. 89.

22. For Kegan Paul, see *Career*, 117–18, 120–3; J. Panton, *Leaves from a Life* (London, 1908), 206.

23. *LW*, 123–4; sketch (DCM), cf. J. B. Bullen, *The Expressive Eye: Fiction and Perception in the Work of TH* (Oxford, 1986), opp. 95, and see 93–7.

24. 'On an Invitation to the United States', *CPW*, i. 143; *LW*, 124.

25. *CL*, i. 73; *Return of the Native*, 197. For 'Pheidias' first edition reads 'Phidias'.

26. *Return of the Native*, 203; for Comte's influence on TH, see Lennart A. Björk, *Psychological Vision and Social Criticism in the Novels of TH* (Stockholm, 1987), esp. 94–8.

27. *LW*, 127–8; *CPW*, ii. 204–5.

28. 'Poetical Matter' notebook (microfilm, Yale).

29. *LW*, 128–9; dated sketches (DCM).

30. *LW*, 130; L. Stephen to TH, 17 Feb 1879 (DCM), cf. *LW*, 131.

31. G. A. Macmillan to TH, 20 May 1879 (DCM); *CL*, i. 65; D. Macleod to TH, 20 June 1879 (DCM); for *Good Words*, see T. R. Wright, *Hardy and his Readers* (Basingstoke, 2003), 117.

32. *CL*, vi. 333, and see Gatrell, *Hardy the Creator*, 53–5.

33. *LW*, 132–3; *PN*, 20; sketch (Gertrude Antell); *CL*, i. 92.

34. On the novel's composition, see Gatrell, *Hardy the Creator*, 52–60, and *Career*, 149–51; *CL*, i. 66–7; J. Collier to TH, 20 Nov 1879 (DCM); '*Trumpet-Major*' notebook (DCM), cf. *PN*, 177.

35. *New Quarterly Magazine*, NS no. 20 (Oct 1879), 472, 469, cf. *PV*, 24, 17.

36. *British Quarterly Review*, 73 (Apr 1881), 360, cf. Cox, *Critical Heritage*, 94.

37. W. Besant to TH, 7 Mar 1879 (DCM).

38. *CL*, i. 71; *LW*, 130; *CL*, i. 26, and *LW*, 130.

39. *LW*, 140; E. Clodd, diary, 15 Dec 1892 (Alan Clodd).

40. *LW*, 139–40; list (DCM); *LW*, 140, and see L. Edel, *Henry James: The Conquest of London, 1870–1883* (Philadelphia, 1962), 354.

41. *LN*, i. 126–7, 120, 127.

42. *LW*, 137–8; *LN*, i. 130.

43. *CL*, i. 72; *CL*, i. 73–4; H. Allingham to TH, 5 June 1880 (DCM); *CL*, i. 74–6.

44. *CL*, i. 76–7; E. McC. Fleming, *R. R. Bowker: Militant Liberal* (Norman, Okla., 1952), 146, 147.

45. *LW*, 140–2; *LW*, 142–3; *Laodicean*, 453; drawing (DCM), and see Purdy, 38.

46. *Good Words* (Dec 1880), 807; *Trumpet-Major* (London, 1880), iii. 259.

47. *PV*, 264.

48. *CL*, i. 92; *LW*, 421.

11 ILLNESS

1. *LW*, 143–4; *CL*, i. 73; *CPW*, ii. 395, dated post-1913 by D. Taylor, 'Chronological Table of TH's Poetry', *THJ* 18/1 (Feb 2002), 50, although its precise biographical relevance remains unknown.

2. F. B. Pinion, 'The Hardys and Salisbury', *TH Year Book*, no. 2 (1971), 84.

3. KH to ELH, 23 Sept 1881 and 'Thursday' [1882?] (DCM).

4. Letter, DCM.

5. *CL*, i. 84; dated presentation copies of books by Handley Moule and A. E. Moule (Yale); *LW*, 144–5; *CPW*, iii. 226.

6. *LW*, 149–50; *CL*, i. 88.

7. *CPW*, i. 189–90.

8. *LW*, 153; C. K. Paul to TH, 24 Feb 1881 (DCM).

9. E. Gosse to TH, 16 Dec 1917 (DCM); information and suggestions from Dr G. Barclay, Dr G. A. Farrow, V. Jesty, and M. Rabiger.

10. Purdy, 39–40; Harper & Brothers to TH, 24 May 1880 (copy, New York Public Library); *CL*, i. 82; *CL*, v. 237.

11. W. L. Phelps, *Autobiography with Letters* (New York, 1939), 391, 394; *CL*, i. 82; C. K. Paul to ELH, 14 Nov 1880 (DCM); G. Smith to ELH, 18 Nov 1880 (DCM); ELH to G. Smith, 19 Nov 1880 (draft, DCM).

12. MH to ELH, 28 Jan 1881 (DCM).

13. *Pall Mall Gazette* (23 Nov 1880), 11.

14. *LW*, 153.

15. *CL*, i. 87; *CL*, i. 88.

16. C. K. Paul to TH, 24 Feb and 7 Feb 1881 (DCM).

17. *LW*, 150–1; Jane S. Lock to ELH, 28 Apr 1881 (DCM), misinterpreted in D. Kay-Robinson, *The First Mrs TH* (London, 1979), 232.

18. *LW*, 153.

19. See *Career*, 174–82.

20. *LW*, 154; cf. *CL*, i, 91; the spelling 'Llanherne' occurs only at *LW*, 154, and *Early Life*, 193.

21. *CL*, i. 92; *CPW*, iii. 305.

22. Information from the late Montague Harvey, 1978.

23. *LW*, 154; B. Flint, *TH in Wimborne 1881–1883* (Wimborne, 1995), esp. 7; G. Douglas, *Gleanings in Prose and Verse*, ed. O. Hilson (Galashiels, n.d.), 28; G. Douglas, *A Love's Gamut and Other Poems* (London, 1880), 116.

24. *LW*, 156; *Blandford and Wimborne Telegram*, 6 Jan 1882.

25. *LW*, 157; *Blandford and Wimborne Telegram*, 11 May 1883, 13 Apr 1883; *LW*, 155.

26. *LW*, 164; *PN*, 21–4.

27. KH to TH and ELH, Wednesday [July 1881?] and Sunday [July 1881?] (DCM); KH to ELH, 23 Sept 1881 (DCM); M. E. Bath, 'TH and Evangeline F. Smith', *TH Year Book*, no. 4 (1974), 40–1; *DCC*, 29 Sept 1881, 6, reports TH sen.'s comic song as 'encored'.

28. For Moule's letters, see TH's 'H. J. M. Some Memories and Letters', *PV*, 229–36.

29. Douglas, *Gleanings*, 29.

30. *LW*, 150.

31. *LW*, 154–5; *CL*, i. 94.

32. T. B. Aldrich to TH, 28 Sept 1881 (DCM).

33. Noted by F. B. Pinion, *A Hardy Companion* (London, 1968), 39.

34. *Two on a Tower*, vii.

35. *CL*, i. 97; *CL*, i. 96–7; Dr Martin Beech informs me that TH is not recorded as a visitor to the Royal Observatory, cf. his 'Hardy's Astronomy: An Examination of *Two on a Tower*', *TH Year Book*, 19 (n.d.), 18–30.

36. *CL*, i. 99–101; Purdy, 28–30, but see also nn. 37 and 39 below.

37. H. T. Atkinson to TH, 31 Dec 1881 (DCM); *Daily News*, 2 Jan 1882, 2; W. Black to TH,

2 Jan 1882 (DCM); for details of the ensuing controversy, see J. F. Stottlar, 'Hardy vs. Pinero: Two Stage Versions of *Far from the Madding Crowd*', *Theatre Survey*, 18 (1977), 23–43.

38. Note copied by FEH from TH notebook subsequently destroyed (Yale).

39. Play MS (BL); *Era*, 4 Mar 1882; for textual analysis, partly correcting Purdy, see P. Dalziel, 'Whose *Mistress*? TH's Theatrical Collaboration', *Studies in Bibliography*, 48 (1995), 248–59.

40. *LW*, 158; J. Comyns Carr to TH, [1882] (DCM); *Mrs. J. Comyns Carr's Reminiscences*, ed. E. Adams (London, 1926), 78.

41. *CL*, i. 104–5; E. McC. Fleming, *R. R. Bowker: Militant Liberal* (Norman, Okla, 1952), 152.

42. *CL*, i. 105; V. Liebert, '*Far from the Madding Crowd* on the American Stage', *Colophon*, NS 3 (Summer 1938), 377–82; Suleiman M. Ahmad, '*Far from the Madding Crowd* in the British Provincial Theatre', *THJ*,16/1 (Feb. 2000), 70–81.

43. *Mrs. J. Comyns Carr's Reminiscences*, 77–8; KH to ELH, Thursday [May 1882?] (DCM).

44. *CL*, i. 103–4, and C. J. Weber, *Hardy in America* (1946; repr. New York, 1966), 62–7.

45. *CL*, i. 108–9; F. B. Adams, Jr., 'Another Man's Roses', *New Colophon*, 2/6 (1949), 107–12.

46. Montague Harvey (citing his mother), interview, 1975.

47. *CL*, i. 105; *LW*, 159–60.

48. *CL*, i. 114; Purdy, 41–4.

49. C. K. Paul to TH, 12 Nov 1882 (DCM); *Saturday Review* (18 Nov 1882), 675.

50. *CL*, i. 109, *PV*, 33, and Purdy, 44–5.

51. *St James's Gazette*, 16 and 19 Jan 1883, cf. *PV*, 35.

52. *Two on a Tower*, p. vii, cf. *Career*, 191–3.

53. W. H. Rideing, *Many Celebrities and a Few Others* (London, 1912), 286.

54. *CL*, i. 110; E. Gosse to TH, 8 Dec 1882 and 18 Jan 1883 (Adams).

55. For Gosse, see Ann Thwaite, *Edmund Gosse: A Literary Landscape 1849–1928* (London, 1984), *passim*; for Gosse and TH, see esp. 222–4.

56. *Two on a Tower* (London, 1895), p. v; H. Holder to ELH, 28 Nov 1882 (DCM); *LW*, 161–2.

57. *CL*, i. 110.

58. Mrs Dashwood to ELH, Friday [1883?] (DCM).

12 RETURN TO DORCHESTER

1. *CL*, vii. 98.

2. All notes, *LW*, 158.

3. See, for this and later periods, C. J. P. Beatty, *TH: Conservation Architect. His Work for the Society for the Protection of Ancient Buildings* (Dorchester, 1995), *passim*.

4. *CL*, i. 95, and cf. Beatty, *Conservation Architect*, 9–10; *CPW*, ii. 171–3; *CPW*, i. 197.

5. *LW*, 159.

6. *Blandford and Wimborne Telegram*, 9 Dec 1881; notebook fragment (DCM), quoted J. O. Bailey, *The Poetry of TH* (Chapel Hill, NC, 1970), 164.

7. *CL*, i. 118–19; Horace Seymour (for Mr Gladstone) to TH, 29 Oct 1883 (DCM).

8. See *Career*, 214–20.

9. *CL*, i. 121, 123–4; 'The Dorsetshire Labourer', *Longman's Magazine*, July 1883, cf. *PV*, 37–57.

10. For 'Our Exploits' see Purdy, 301–3, and TH, *The Excluded and Collaborative Stories*, ed.

Pamela Dalziel (Oxford, 1992), 155–67.

11. *Westminster Review* (Apr 1883), esp. 356, cf. R. G. Cox (ed.) *TH: The Critical Heritage* (London, 1970), 103–32.

12. *LW*, 163–4; MS (Pierpont Morgan Library).

13. *Westminster Review* (Apr 1883), 334, cf. *Critical Heritage*, 104; *CPW*, i. 289.

14. *CL*, i. 123; *Excluded and Collaborative Stories*, ed. Dalziel, 214.

15. *LW*, 165–6; RLP/FEH, 1933; *LW*, 166; signed menu card (Cambridge Univ. Library).

16. *Transatlantic Dialogue: Selected American Correspondence of Edmund Gosse*, ed. P. F. Mattheisen and M. Millgate (Austin, Tex., 1965), 115–16.

17. E. Gosse to H. Thornycroft, 23 July 1883, in E. Charteris, *The Life and Letters of Sir Edmund Gosse* (London, 1931), 156–7: E. Gosse to N. Gosse, 22 July 1883 (Cambridge Univ. Library).

18. E. Gosse to N. Gosse, 22 July 1883 (Cambridge Univ. Library).

19. L. Baxter, *The Life of William Barnes, Poet and Philologist* (London, 1887), 343; *CL*, i. 120; *LW*, 167; Charteris, *Gosse*, 157.

20. Death certificate; Daniel Defoe, *Rabinsán Krúso*, trans. into Persian by Sher Alì of Kabul, ed. in the Roman character by T. W. Tolbort (London, 1878); obituary, *DCC*, 16 Aug 1883, cf. *PV*, 57–60.

21. DCM Minute Book, AGM minutes for 13 Jan 1886 (DCM).

22. *LW*, 413; M. E. Bath, 'TH and Evangeline F. Smith', *TH Year Book*, no. 4 (1974), 42.

23. A. Everett to ELH, 14 Sept 1883 (DCM); *DCC*, 4 Oct 1883; *CL*, i. 122.

24. H. O. Lock, 'Max Gate', *Dorset Year Book, 1962–63*, 34.

25. G. Symonds to TH, 20 Aug 1884 (DCM), and see E. C. Sampson, 'TH—Justice of the Peace', *Colby Library Quarterly*, 13 (Dec 1977), 263–74, esp. 264–5; TH's library copy of Samuel Stone, *The Justices' Manual*, was 25th edn., dated 1889, but *World* (17 Feb 1886), 7, reports him as already owning a copy; *Mayor of Casterbridge*, 231–2.

26. *DCC*, 5 Nov 1885, 4.

27. *CL*, i. 272; *CL*, ii. 50.

28. *CL*, i. 127; *CL*, i. 131; *LW*, 176–7.

29. *LW*, 235.

30. *LW*, 177; *CL*, i. 131; E. H. Gifford to ELH, 6 Apr 1885 (DCM).

31. [R. N. Peers] in J. Newman and N. Pevsner, *Dorset* (Harmondsworth, 1972), 485, and see 484.

32. 'Some Romano-British Relics Found at Max Gate, Dorchester', *DCC*, 15 May 1883, cf. *PV*, 61–4; Purdy, 61.

33. *CL*, i. 73.

34. E. Clodd, diary, 27 Sept 1895 (Alan Clodd), and see *CL*, vii. 96 n.

35. *CL*, i. 73, 105; *CL*, vii. 95–6; *CL*, vii. 97–8; KH to ELH, [1883?] (DCM).

36. Estimate (DCM); *Early Life*, 226–7, cf. *LW*, 508; *LW*, 170.

37. DCM Minute Book, minutes of meeting of 5 Dec 1885 (DCM).

38. *Career*, 142–4, 174–7; *LW*, 173, 224; M. Arnold, 'Wordsworth', *Macmillan's Magazine* (July 1879), 198, and cf. *LN*, i. 122.

39. Caro and Lewes (Yale); and see W. F. Wright, *The Shaping of 'The Dynasts': A Study in TH* (Lincoln, Nebr., 1967), 38–53.

40. *CL*, i. 133–4; *CL*, i. 136–7.

41. *CL*, vii. 94.

42. *LW*, 169–70; 'Poetical Matter' notebook (microfilm, Yale).

43. *LW*, 171–6.
44. Notebook (DCM), cf. forthcoming edition by William Greenslade (Aldershot, 2004).
45. See *Career*, 237–43, and C. Winfield, 'Factual Sources of Two Episodes in *The Mayor of Casterbridge*', *Nineteenth Century Fiction*, 25 (Sept 1970), 224–31.
46. *CL*, i. 171.
47. General Preface, *Tess of the d'Urbervilles*, pp. ix, x, cf. *TH's Personal Writings*, ed. H. Orel (Lawrence, Kan., 1966), 46.
48. *Mayor of Casterbridge*, 384; *Mayor*, 385.
49. *LW*, 177, 174–5; see S. Gatrell, *Hardy the Creator* (Oxford, 1988), 75–80.
50. *LW*, 177, and see 167.

13 Max Gate

1. Drawings (DCM); Fordington Census Returns, 1851; for the tollgate cottage, see E. L. Evans, *The Homes of TH* (St Peter Port, 1968), 19.
2. *CL*, i. 217; Barbara Kerr, *Bound to the Soil: A Social History of Dorset 1750–1918* (London, 1968), 241.
3. *CPW*, ii. 243–4.
4. FEH to Mrs Belloc Lowndes, 29 Oct 1929 (Texas); *Early Life*, 226, cf. *LW*, 508.
5. NS note (Eton), cf. *CL*, vii. 95–6.
6. *CPW*, i. 100.
7. G. Gissing to A. Gissing, 22 Sept 1895, in *Yale University Library Gazette* (Jan 1943), 52.
8. List on opened-out envelope postmarked 1868 (DCM).
9. A. C. Benson, diary, 5 Sept 1912 (Magdalene College, Cambridge); Gissing letter, *Yale University Library Gazette* (Jan 1943), 52.
10. R. Tomson, 'Thomas Hardy. I', *Independent* (New York), 22 Nov 1894, 2.
11. Cf. *The Architectural Notebook of TH*, ed. C. J. P. Beatty (Dorchester, 1966), [108].
12. *LEFH*, 158; cf. A. Mitchell, *Cook at Max Gate 1913–1914* (St Peter Port, 1970), 401.
13. *World* (London) (17 Feb 1886), 6.
14. *Early Life*, 227, cf. *LW*, 509; *CL*, iii. 162.
15. *Early Life*, 32, cf. *LW*, 502.
16. *World* (London) (17 Feb 1886), 6.
17. *CL*, i. 128, and see *PV*, 131.
18. DCM Minute Book (DCM); *PV*, 36–7.
19. *PV*, 36–7; *CPW*, ii. 214; *LEFH*, 194; E. E. T[itterington], *The Domestic Life of TH (1921–1928)* (Beaminster, 1963), 10.
20. *London and the Life of Literature in Late Victorian England: The Diary of George Gissing, Novelist*, ed. P. Coustillas (Hassocks, 1978), 388; see, e.g., *CL*, i. 149, iii. 151.
21. *CL*, v. 216.
22. *CL*, iv. 6.
23. *LW*, 36; *PV*, 76.
24. *CL*, i. 69, 239–40.
25. *LW*, 179, for identification of 'Lord C—', see *LW*, 508.
26. *CL*, i. 152.
27. *CL*, i. 89.
28. *LW*, 183–4.
29. *LW*, 183.

30. *CL*, i. 142, 141.
31. *CL*, i. 156.
32. *Spectator*, 5 June 1886, cf. R. G. Cox (ed.), *TH: The Critical Heritage* (London, 1970), 137; *Saturday Review*, 29 May 1886, cf. Cox, *Critical Heritage*, 135; *Pall Mall Gazette* (9 July 1886), 5.
33. *Church of England Temperance Chronicle* (23 Jan 1886), 38.
34. Purdy, 56–7; *LW*, 182, 105, 182.
35. MS (DCM); Emma's involvement in TH's manuscripts is well treated in S. Gatrell, *Hardy the Creator* (Oxford, 1988), 47–51; for a differing view, see A. Manford, 'Emma Hardy's Helping Hand', in D. Kramer (ed.), *Critical Essays on TH: The Novels* (Boston, 1990), 100–21.
36. RLP/FEH, 1933.
37. *LW*, 181; F. Stevenson to S. Colvin, [early Sept 1885] (Yale).
38. F. Stevenson to D. Norton Williams, [Oct–Nov 1885] (Yale); on TH's nose see SCC, letter, *Times Literary Supplement* (4 Oct 1953), 2, and RLP, notes on conversations with SCC, 1948 (Yale).
39. *LW*, 186, and *CL*, i. 146–7; S. Colvin to TH, 12 June 1886 (DCM); E. Gosse to TH, 28 Aug 1887 (DCM).
40. *LW*, 185.
41. *LW*, 184–5.
42. *LW*, 213.
43. *CL*, i. 143–4, *LW*, 191, *CL*, i. 227–8; RLP, notes on conversation with D. Allhusen, 1931 (Yale); FEH to R. Owen, citing M. Jeune, 17 July 1915 (Colby), and cf. D. Kay-Robinson, *The First Mrs TH* (London, 1979), 196–7.
44. *LW*, 187, cf. *Career*, 353–8; *LW*, 187.
45. *Collected Letters of George Gissing*, ed. P. F. Mattheisen, A. C. Young, and P. Coustillas (9 vols., Athens, Oh., 1990–7), iii. 41–2.
46. *CL*, i. 151; M. E. Bath, 'TH and Evangeline F. Smith', *TH Year Book*, no. 4 (1973–4), 42; for the railway extension to Bridport harbour see J. H. Lucking, *Railways of Dorset* ([London], 1968), 32–4.
47. *CL*, i. 151; Gosse, *Critical Kit-Kats* (London, 1896), pp. v–vi; E. Gosse to N. Gosse, Tuesday [31 Aug 1889] (Cambridge Univ. Library).
48. *Athenaeum*, 16 Oct 1886, cf. *PV*, 66, 67, 70.
49. *CPW*, ii. 213.
50. FEH to Lady Hoare, 7 May 1916 (Wiltshire Record Office); *CPW*, ii.174.

14 *The Woodlanders*

1. *CL*, i. 149; *CL*, i. 147.
2. F. Macmillan to TH, 29 Mar 1886 (DCM); M. Morris to TH, 19 Sept 1886 (DCM).
3. D. Kramer, 'Revisions and Vision: TH's *The Woodlanders*, Pt. 1', *Bulletin of the New York Public Library*, 85 (Apr 1971), 213; *CL*, i. 195.
4. *New Review* (2 Jan 1890), 19, cf. *PV*, 100.
5. *Madding Crowd*, p. viii, cf. *TH's Personal Writings*, ed. H. Orel (Lawrence, Kan., 1966), 9.
6. R. R. Bowker, 'London as a Literary Centre. II', *Harper's New Monthly Magazine*, 77 (June 1888), 9.
7. RLP/FEH, 1929.

8. Drawing (DCM).

9. *CL*, iv. 212.

10. *Woodlanders*, 247; *LW*, 99.

11. *LW*, 192.

12. Purdy, 57; *The Times*, 3 Mar 1887; *LW*, 193.

13. *LW*, 194–5; *Emma Hardy Diaries*, ed. Richard H. Taylor (Ashington, 1985), 113, 117, 120–1; *CPW*, i. 132; *Emma Hardy Diaries*, 125, 160.

14. *LW*, 195; Baedeker's *Italy: Handbook for Travellers . . . Northern Italy* (Leipzig and London, 1886), TH's copy (BL).

15. *Emma Hardy Diaries*, 128, 130.

16. *LW*, 195, 198; *Emma Hardy Diaries*, 141, 138, 144; *LW*, 196.

17. *CL*, i. 163; *LW*, 196; *LN*, i. 127; *CPW*, i. 135.

18. *Emma Hardy Diaries*, 150; *LW*, 197, cf. *Emma Hardy Diaries*, 145; *CL*, i. 163.

19. *LW*, 199; *Emma Hardy Diaries*, 156, 161, 164, 166; *LW*, 199.

20. *Emma Hardy Diaries*, 169, 173; *LW*, 200–3.

21. *Emma Hardy Diaries*, 190, 191, 188; *LW*, 203–4; *Emma Hardy Diaries*, 192–3.

22. *Emma Hardy Diaries*, 193–4.

23. *The Times*, 27 Apr 1887; *Saturday Review* (2 Apr 1887), 485; E. Gosse to TH, 22 Mar 1887 (DCM); *John Bull* (7 May 1887), 302; *St. James's Gazette* (2 Apr 1887).

24. *Dublin Evening Mail*, 30 Mar 1887.

25. Purdy, 57; Lord Lytton to TH, 10 July 1887 (Univ. of California, Berkeley); *CL*, i. 165.

26. Tillotson & Son to TH, 16 Mar 1887 (DCM); 'Memorandum of an Agreement' (Bodleian Library).

27. *LW*, 192.

28. *LW*, 225–6.

29. G. Reynolds, *Painters of the Victorian Scene* (London, 1953), 77.

30. *LW*, 219; *LW*, 183.

31. W. P. Frith, *My Autobiography and Reminiscences* (3 vols., London, 1887), iii. 432.

32. *LW*, 207–10.

33. *CL*, i. 166; *LW*, 209.

34. *Career*, 299–303; *LW*, 189.

35. *LW*, 208.

36. E. Gosse to TH, 28 Aug 1887 (DCM); *CL*, i. 167, where Psalm 42: 11 is slightly misquoted; *LW*, 212.

37. L. Stephen to TH, 19 Nov 1880 (DCM).

38. Purdy, 30–1, 58–9; *LW*, 211.

39. C. J. Longman to TH, 27 Sept 1887 (DCM); *CL*, i. 168, 169, 170; W. Blackwood to TH, 30 Dec 1887 (DCM); L. Stephen to TH, 10 Jan 1888 (Berg), cf. F. W. Maitland, *The Life and Letters of Leslie Stephen* (London, 1906), 393–4.

40. *CL*, i. 174; F. Macmillan to TH, 6 Mar 1888 (DCM); *CL*, i. 175.

41. *LW*, 212.

42. *LW*, 215; *LW*, 217; 'Book of Gosse' (Cambridge Univ. Library); *LW*, 216.

43. *LW*, 217–18.

44. *LW*, 218–19; *LW*, 219–20; *LW*, 219.

45. *CL*, vii. 110; *CL*, i. 179; *CL*, i. 178–9, 180.

46. *LW*, 223; 'Memorandum of an Agreement', fo. 5 (Bodleian Library); *CL*, i. 200.

47. *CL*, vii. 111.

15 THE WRITING OF *Tess*

1. *LW*, 223–4.
2. 'Poetical Matter' notebook (microfilm, Yale); *Tess*, 299; *LW*, 223.
3. Harold Child (citing TH), interviewed by RLP (Yale).
4. *CL*, ii. 8.
5. NS (Eton); J. Stevens Cox (citing Harold Voss), interview, 1980; SCC, Notes on meetings with TH, 24 June 1920 (Yale).
6. Dorothy Van Ghent, *The English Novel: Form and Function* (New York, 1953), 201; R. Blathwayt, 'A Chat with the Author of *Tess*', *Black & White* (27 Aug 1892), 240.
7. *CL*, i. 194, 196; *The TH Archive: 1*, ed. S. Gatrell (New York, 1986), i. 1. For the development of the MS, see J. T. Laird, *The Shaping of 'Tess of the d'Urbervilles'* (Oxford, 1975), and esp. the introduction to the J. Grindle and S. Gatrell edn. (Oxford, 1983), 1–13.
8. RLP/FEH, 1933.
9. *Tess*, p. xxi; cf. Purdy, opp. 71.
10. *CL*, i. 190.
11. *LW*, 227.
12. MH and KH to ELH, 8 June 1889 (DCM).
13. *LW*, 229–30.
14. 'Max Eliot', 'Graham R. Tomson, the Poet', *Author* (Boston) (15 Sept 1890), 134. For R. Tomson see, briefly, *Companion*, 428–9, much more fully Linda Hughes, *Graham R.: Rosamund Marriott Watson, Woman of Letters*, forthcoming from Ohio Univ. Press.
15. *LW*, 221.
16. TH's copy of Graham R. Tomson, *The Bird-Bride: A Volume of Ballads and Sonnets* (London, 1889), now at Florida State Univ.; *CL*, i. 199, 200–1.
17. *CL*, ii. 24.
18. *CPW*, ii. 450–1.
19. *CL*, i. 193; for Caird, see *CL*, i. 208; for Robinson, see chap. 16, n. 8.
20. A. Thornycroft to H. Thornycroft, 3 July 1889 (Mrs E. Manning); *Career*, 401–2.
21. See esp. portrait by T. H. Wirgman, repr. on cover of *TH Journal*, Oct 1997 (Dr J. Gibson); *LW*, 230; *Tess*, 192.
22. *CL*, i. 195; C. W. Jarvis to TH, 16 Sept 1889 (DCM).
23. *CL*, i. 200.
24. M. Robinson to I. Cooper Willis, 17 Dec 1937 (DCM).
25. RLP, letter, *Times Literary Supplement* (26 June 1943), 307.
26. Purdy, 72–3; note of cancellation on memorandum (Bodleian Library).
27. E. Arnold to TH, 7 Oct 1889 (DCM); *CL*, i. 201; E. Arnold to TH, 15 Nov 1889 (DCM), cf. *Career*, 283–4.
28. M. Morris to TH, 25 Nov 1889 (DCM), cf. *Career*, 284.
29. *LW*, 232–3; *CL*, i. 170, 173–4, 201–4.
30. *LW*, 232; Purdy, 94n.
31. *LW*, 233; *CL*, i. 205.
32. *CL*, i. 206; note on verso of W. E. Henley to TH, 17 July 1890 (Texas); *CPW*, ii. 207–8.
33. *CPW*, i. 223 (cf. *LN*, ii. 7), ii. 166–7 (cf. *LW*, 226), ii. 220–1 (cf. *LW*, 233).
34. *LW*, 234.
35. L. Deacon and T. Coleman, *Providence and Mr Hardy* (London, 1966), 64–5; Tryphena's son Charles Gale recalled the occasion (interview, 1971).

36. Purdy, 65–6.
37. *LW*, 235; G. Douglas, *Gleanings in Prose and Verse*, ed. O. Hilson (Galashiels, n.d.), 30.
38. *LN*, ii. 11–12, 13–14; *LW*, 236.
39. *LW*, 268; *LW*, 251.
40. *LW*, 235–6, 239.
41. Purdy, 104; *CPW*, i. 104–5; *Globe* (24 July 1890), 6; *CL*, i. 215–16; *World*, 30 July 1890, cf. *PV*, 104.
42. W. A. Locker to TH, 25 June 1890 (DCM).
43. *CL*, i. 215–16; Purdy, 65–6.
44. W. A. Locker to TH, 25 June 1890 (DCM).
45. Purdy, 65.
46. Book (BL); *LW*, 240.
47. E. Gosse to T. Gosse, 12 Sept 1890 (Cambridge Univ. Library); photographs (Cambridge Univ. Library and DCM); E. Gosse to TH, 14 Sept 1890 (DCM).
48. *CL*, i. 217; ELH to C. K. Shorter, 23 Apr [1908] (Yale), cf. *LEFH*, 38; *LW*, 469.
49. *Early Life*, 315, cf. *LW*, 511, 536; Purdy, 70; and see J. T. Laird, 'New Light on the Evolution of *Tess of the d'Urbervilles*', *Review of English Studies*, NS 31 (Nov 1980), 414–35.
50. Purdy, 69.
51. Purdy, 71; leaves of MS (Berg, Princeton, and Texas); *PV*, 115.
52. Purdy, 63, 70.
53. *CL*, i. 218–19; *Athenaeum* (22 Nov 1890), 701, and (6 Dec 1890), 776–7, cf. *PV*, 104–5.
54. *CL*, i. 222.

16 THE PUBLICATION OF *Tess*

1. *CL*, i. 223–4; *LW*, 241.
2. *CL*, i. 230; *CL*, i. 225–6.
3. Purdy, 65–7; *LW*, 243–5.
4. *CL*, i. 230–1, 231–3.
5. *LW*, 247; *CPW*, ii. 360–2.
6. Douglas, 'TH: Some Recollections and Reflections', *Hibbert Journal*, 26 (Apr 1928), 389–91.
7. F. B. Fisher to Lady Hoare, 25 Jan 1928 (Wiltshire Record Office).
8. M. Robinson, sister of poet and biographer Mary Robinson, later Duclanx, to I. Cooper Willis, 17 Dec 1937 (DCM).
9. FEH to H. Bliss, 3 Apr 1921 (Princeton).
10. *LEFH*, 48.
11. M. Robinson to I. Cooper Willis, 17 Dec 1937 (DCM); G. Atherton, *Adventures of a Novelist* (New York, 1932), 263; T. P. O'Connor, 'TH as I Knew Him', *Living Age*, 1 Mar 1928, 456.
12. *PN*, 233.
13. *CL*, i. 232; *LW*, 246; *CL*, i. 234.
14. *DCC*, 5 Nov 1885; *CL*, i. 234; *CL*, i. 233, 236.
15. KH to TH, 15 May 1891 (DCM).
16. *CL*, vii. 110; *LW*, 246; *CL*, i. 233.
17. *LW*, 247–8, 246–7.

18. E. Clodd, diary, 20 June 1891 (Alan Clodd).

19. *LN*, ii. 28–31, 32–44, 45.

20. *PV*, 111.

21. *Pall Mall Gazette* (10 July 1891), 2; Purdy, 95.

22. *PV*, 95–102; *PV*, 106–10.

23. Purdy, 67; *CL*, i. 239–40.

24. *CL*, iii. 190; S. Heath, 'How TH Offended the County Families of Dorset', unpub. type-script (DCM).

25. *LW*, 250.

26. S. Gatrell, *TH's Vision of Wessex* (Basingstoke, 2003), 93–5; *Bookman* (London) (Oct 1891), 26; T. H. Darlow, *William Robertson Nicoll: Life and Letters* (London, 1925), 99.

27. *LW*, 51; *LW*, 250–1; G. Douglas, *Gleanings in Prose and Verse*, ed. O. Hilson (Galashiels, n.d.), 30; Douglas, 'TH: Some Recollections and Reflections', 385–6.

28. Douglas, 'Recollections and Reflections', 389–90; *CL*, ii. 32, *LW*, 244.

29. Douglas, 'Recollections and Reflections', 390.

30. *LW*, 251, *CL*, i. 243.

31. *CL*, i. 246–7; MS, fo. 1 (BL), cf. Purdy, opp. 71; *Tess*, p. xxi; cf. *CL*, i. 249.

32. Purdy, 73; W. Morris to TH, 15 Dec 1891 (DCM).

33. Purdy, 74; A. Austin, *Love's Widowhood and Other Poems* (London, 1889), 58.

34. F. Harrison to TH, 29 Dec 1891 (DCM); C. Kegan Paul to TH, 25 Dec 1891 (DCM).

35. *CL*, i. 250.

36. *Saturday Review* (16 Jan 1892), 73–4, cf. R. G. Cox (ed.), *TH: The Critical Heritage* (London, 1970), 188–91.

37. *CL*, i. 252, 253, 254.

38. W. Besant to TH, 18 Jan 1892 (Texas); E. Gosse to TH, 19 Jan 1892 (Adams).

39. *CL*, i. 255; Purdy, 74–6; *CL*, i. 253.

40. *Spectator*, 23 Jan 1892; *Tess*, 508; *New Review* (6 Feb 1892), 248, cf. Cox, *Critical Heritage*, 196.

41. *Quarterly Review*, 174 (Apr 1892), 319–26, cf. Cox, *Critical Heritage*, 214–21; *CL*, i. 268; and see *Career*, 284–8.

42. *CL*, i. 265; *LW*, 259.

43. *Tess of the d'Urbervilles* (London, 1892), p. xix; 'Tessimism' in *Daily News*, 11 Oct 1892, 4; *LW*, 265; *Longman's Magazine*, 21 (Nov 1892), 100–6, cf. Cox, *Critical Heritage*, 238–44; RLP/FEH, 1933.

44. R. Tomson, 'TH. I', *Independent* (New York) (22 Nov 1894), 2.

45. *CL*, i. 260; *Book Buyer* (New York), 9 (May 1892), opp. 151.

46. FEH to SCC, 20 Apr 1928 (Yale).

47. *CL*, i. 254; receipt for shares in name of KH, 1 Mar 1892 (DCM).

48. *CL*, i. 254; *Cassell's Saturday Journal* (25 June 1892), 944, cf. J. Gibson, *TH: Interviews and Recollections* (Basingstoke, 1999) 36; TH letters to his solicitors, Lock, Reed and Lock (DCM); additional information from Mr Henry Lock.

49. See *CL*, i. 256, 281–3, and 260, 266.

50. Blathwayt, 'A Chat with the Author of *Tess*', *Black & White* (27 Aug 1892), 238–40, cf. Gibson, *Interviews and Recollections*, 38–41.

51. *Cassell's Saturday Journal* (25 June 1892), 945.

52. F. Dugdale (FEH) to E. Clodd, 16 Jan 1913 (Leeds).

53. *CL*, i. 269–70.

54. *LW*, 258; *CL*, vii. 120; *CL*, i. 264.
55. *CL*, vii. 121; *LW*, 259.
56. *CL*, i. 268–9; 'Book of Gosse' (Cambridge Univ. Library); *LW*, 261–2; *CL*, i. 271.
57. *CL*, i. 285.
58. *LW*, 262; death certificate; *PV*, 119; prayerbook (DCM).
59. TH's MS of leaflet (G. Stevens Cox); *LW*, 262; Horace, *Part I. Odes* (London, 1855), 17 (Yale); *LW*, 262, cf. TH's copy of *Hamlet*, vol. ix of Singer edn., p. 231 (DCM).
60. Will; *CL*, iv. 72, cf. *PV*, 308–9.
61. *LEFH*, 96.
62. *LW*, 263.

17 Florence Henniker

1. For the Owen sisters see Carl J. Weber, *Hardy and the Lady from Madison Square* (Waterville, Me., 1952).
2. *DCC*, 18 Sept 1892; Weber, *Lady*, 67.
3. *Mayor*, p. vii; Purdy, 53–4; Weber, *Lady*, 64–6, 86.
4. *LW*, 264; *LW*, 13–14; *LW*, 14, and 'Notes on TH's Life' (DCM); *LW*, 264.
5. *LW*, 264.
6. Purdy, 281.
7. Annotation in TH's copy of Alden's *Oxford Guide* (BL); *LW*, 264.
8. *LW*, 244, 226, and see *Career*, 300–2; *LW*, 238.
9. *CL*, ii. 157; *PV*, 143; *LW*, 226; *CL*, ii. 169.
10. *Illustrated London News* (19 Nov 1892), 643, cf. *The Pursuit of the Well-Beloved & The Well-Beloved*, ed. P. Ingham (London, 1997), 117.
11. *LW*, 240.
12. *CPW*, ii. 329; *LW*, 37.
13. *Illustrated London News* (15 Oct 1892), 481, cf. *Pursuit*, ed. Ingham, 36, 39.
14. *Illustrated London News* (17 Dec 1892), 774, cf. *Pursuit*, ed. Ingham, 159.
15. *Illustrated London News* (17 Dec 1892), 775, cf. *Pursuit*, ed. Ingham, 168; Weber, *Lady*, 78.
16. *LW*, 265; *CL*, i. 287.
17. *CL*, i. 286; *LW*, 265.
18. Portrait, *Illustrated London News* (1 Oct 1892), 424, cf., e.g., *Illustrated London News* (17 Dec 1892), 773.
19. *LW*, 267.
20. *CL*, ii. 5–6, 13; W. M. Colles to TH, 26 June 1893 (copy, Berg).
21. W. M. Colles to TH, 5 May 1893 (copy, Berg).
22. *PV*, 94; C. W. Jarvis to TH, 1 Apr 1891 (DCM); *LW*, 231; scenario MS (DCM), and *PV*, 303.
23. *CL*, vii. 121–2; cf. *LW*, 259.
24. *CL*, ii. 7.
25. *CL*, ii. 9; Lady Jeune to TH, 4 June 1893 (DCM); Purdy, 79.
26. *LW*, 269.
27. B. Winehouse, 'TH: Some Unpublished Material', *Notes & Queries* (Oct 1977), 433–4.
28. *CPW*, iii. 108.
29. *LW*, 270; for Mrs Henniker see Purdy, 342–8, and *One Rare Fair Woman*, ed. E. Hardy

and F. B. Pinion (London, 1972), pp. xiii–xl; J. McCarthy, *Reminiscences* (New York, 1899), ii. 61.

30. I. Cooper Willis, pocketbook, citing FEH (DCM).
31. *LW*, 270.
32. *LW*, 270–1.
33. *LW*, 271–2; see, e.g., *CL*, ii. 24–5, 28, 41–2.
34. *LW*, 272; *CL*, ii. 14, where letter incorrectly dated 10 June.
35. *CL*, ii. 11, 16–17.
36. *CL*, ii. 17; *CL*, ii. 20.
37. F. Henniker, 'From the Spanish of G. Bécquer', MS inserted into TH's 'Literary Notes II' notebook (DCM), cf. *LN*, ii. 57, also 58–60, and see K. Wilson, 'TH and Florence Henniker: A Probable Source for Hardy's "Had You Wept"', *TH Year Book*, no. 6 (1977), 62–6.
38. *CL*, ii. 23–4.
39. *CL*, ii. 25.
40. 'Literary Notes II' notebook (DCM), cf. *LN*, ii. 60; book, Bertram Rota catalogue 58, item 416.
41. *CPW*, iii. 28.
42. Prayerbook annotation, Psalm 41 (DCM); Weber, *Lady*, 85.
43. Information from Henry Reed, citing FEH; *CPW*, i. 89, and cf. 'The Division', *CPW*, i. 270.
44. *CL*, ii. 28.
45. *CPW*, ii. 28; *CPW*, ii. 18; RLP/FEH, 1931; E. Clodd, diary, 18 July 1896 (Alan Clodd).
46. *CPW*, i. 172; *Poems of the Past and the Present*, MS, fo. 79 (Bodleian Library), cf. footnote, *CPW*, i. 172.
47. RLP/FEH, 1933; *CL*, ii. 32; F. Henniker to S. M. Ellis, 'Wedy' [Apr 1913?] (M. Millgate).
48. *LW*, 274–5; *LW*, 274; *LW*, 272–3.
49. *CL*, ii. 32; 'An Imaginative Woman', *Pall Mall Magazine*, 2 (Apr 1894), 952, 964, 955, cf. *Life's Little Ironies*, 4, 24, 8; MS (Aberdeen Univ.).
50. *Pall Mall Magazine*, 2 (Apr 1894), 959, 953, 952, 966, cf. *Life's Little Ironies*, 14, 5, 4, 3.
51. *LW*, 276; for an alternative suggestion, see J. Rees, *The Poetry of Dante Gabriel Rossetti: Modes of Self-Expression* (Cambridge, 1981), 197–8.
52. *LW*, 276; *CL*, ii. 38; Purdy, 60, 85.
53. *CL*, ii. 38.
54. *CL*, ii. 30.
55. Pamela Dalziel's work on 'Spectre' supersedes all previous studies, including Purdy's; see her 'Hardy as Collaborator: The Composition of "The Spectre of the Real"', *Publications of the Bibliographical Society of America*, 83 (1989), 473–501, and her edition of *The Excluded and Collaborative Stories* (Oxford, 1992), 260–98.
56. *CL*, ii. 38.
57. *CL*, ii. 39–40.
58. *CL*, ii. 40.
59. Typescript, fo. 24ᵛ (Adams); carbon typescript, fo. 1 (Adams).
60. *CL*, ii. 41, 43.

18 The Making of *Jude*

1. NS (Eton); J. Stevens Cox, citing Harold Voss, interview, 1980.
2. *Morning Post*, 19 May 1894; *Builder* (26 May 1894), 411; *The Architectural Notebook of TH*, ed. C. J. P. Beatty (Dorchester, 1966), 30–4, and cf. C. J. P. Beatty, *TH: Conservation Architect* (Dorchester, 1999).
3. *CPW*, ii. 282–3.
4. *The Times* (28 Apr 1888), 9; *LW*, 216; *Jude the Obscure* (London, 1896), p. v.
5. Cf. *CL*, i. 142, 143.
6. *CL*, i. 222; *News of the World*, 26 Oct 1890, etc. (crime); 7 Dec 1890 (trial), 28 Dec 1890 (execution); *The Times*, 1, 2, 3, 4 Dec 1890 (trial), 4 Dec 1890 (leading article).
7. Death incorrectly dated by R. Gittings, *The Older Hardy* (London, 1978), 66, 74.
8. NS (Eton); 'Poetical Matter' notebook (microfilm, Yale); cf. *LW*, 372.
9. Photograph (J. Antell); illustration, *Companion*, 213, and A. M. Jackson, *Illustration and the Novels of TH* (Totowa, NJ, 1981), plate 16; *CL*, ii. 94.
10. *Jude* (London, 1896), p. v; *CL*, ii. 38.
11. W. M. Colles to TH, 10 and 13 Nov 1893 (copies, Berg); *CL*, ii. 42; *CL*, ii. 43.
12. Purdy, 89, and entry in Harper Memorandum Book 8 (Columbia Univ.).
13. *CL*, ii. 45; *CL*, ii. 47.
14. Purdy, 89–90; J. Henry Harper, *The House of Harper* (New York, 1912), 530.
15. *CL*, ii. 48.
16. Purdy, 87 and note.
17. *Jude* MS (Fitzwilliam Museum, Cambridge); see P. Ingham, 'The Evolution of *Jude the Obscure*', *Review of English Studies*, NS 27 (1976), 27–37, 159–69.
18. Book (Univ. of British Columbia).
19. *CL*, ii. 99; *A Laodicean*, 476.
20. KH to ELH, Thursday [1883?] (DCM); MH to N. Sparks, sen., 26 Nov 1907 (Eton).
21. FEH to E. Clodd, Wednesday [24 Nov 1915] (Leeds).
22. W. Archer, *Real Conversations* (London, 1904), 40–1; *CPW*, ii. 218.
23. *CL*, v. 137; *Jude*, 352.
24. *Jude*, 276; MS, fo. 149 (Fitzwilliam Museum); *Jude*, 279.
25. E. Clodd, diary, 19 July 1896 (Alan Clodd); *CL*, ii. 99.
26. See *Career*, 320–1.
27. *CPW*, ii. 107; Purdy, 87n.
28. *CL*, ii. 24.
29. *CL*, iv. 260.
30. Carl J. Weber, *Hardy and the Lady from Madison Square* (Waterville, Me., 1952), 85.
31. A. P. Watt to ELH, 10 Jan 1894 (DCM).
32. *LEFH*, 6.
33. E. Clodd, diary, 1 Oct 1895 (Alan Clodd); D. MacCarthy, Hoffman interview (HP).
34. *LEFH*, 7–8.
35. *LEFH*, 13.
36. Book (DCM).
37. Quotations from copy of *Keynotes* annotated by both TH and Mrs Henniker (Yale).
38. *New Review*, June 1894, cf. *PV*, 132.
39. *LW*, 278; *CL*, ii. 50.
40. *LW*, 278; Weber, *Lady*, 97; *CL*, ii. 52–3..

41. *CL*, ii. 52.
42. Harper & Brothers Contract Book 6 (Columbia Univ.); *CL*, ii. 57–9; contract, Macmillan Archive (BL); *Greenwood Tree* leased from Chatto & Windus.
43. *LW*, 280–1; M. Jeune to TH, [1894] (DCM).
44. Portrait (Hardye's School, Dorchester); TH letter, e.g., *CL*, ii. 85.
45. *CL*, ii. 55; *Sketch* (30 May 1894), 219; *Illustrated London News* (18 Aug 1894), 195, cf. *PV*, 134.
46. Bible (DCM); *CL*, ii. 55–7.
47. *LW*, 280–1; E. Clodd diary, 14 May 1894 (Alan Clodd), cf. *CL*, iii, 238.
48. *LW*, 282; 'Life' TS, fo. 369 (DCM); *LW*, 283.
49. TH to E. Clodd, 2 Sept 1894 (Dr Michael Lauermann).
50. Purdy, 90 n.; drawing (DCM); *Jude* MS (Fitzwilliam Museum).
51. *LW*, 283; E. C. Sampson, 'TH—Justice of the Peace', *Colby Library Quarterly*, 13 (Dec 1977), 273; *LW*, 283–4.
52. ELH to M. Haweis, 13 Nov [1894] (Univ. of British Columbia); *CL*, ii. 64.
53. *CL*, ii. 63; Purdy, 279–81.
54. *Far from the Madding Crowd* (London, 1895), p. v; for Wessex generally, see *Career*, 95–104, and esp. S. Gatrell, *TH's Vision of Wessex* (Basingstoke, 2003), *passim*.
55. *Career*, 127–8; *Madding Crowd* (London, 1895), p. vi; Purdy, 91.
56. *Tess*, p. ix, cf. *TH's Personal Writings*, ed. H. Orel (Lawrence, Kan., 1966), 46.
57. *CL*, ii. 54.
58. *Wessex Tales* (London, 1896), pp. v–vi.
59. Shakespeare, *Henry V*, iv. iii. 50.
60. *Tess*, p. xi; *CL*, vi. 161.
61. *LW*, 284–5.
62. Notes on verso of TH letter to Macbeth-Raeburn (Adams); agreement (Pierpont Morgan Library).
63. *CL*, ii. 71–2.
64. *CL*, ii. 76; Mrs Campbell to TH, 10 July 1895 (DCM); *CL*, ii. 81.
65. *CL*, ii. 83.
66. *Daily News*, 29 July 1895; *Independent* (New York), 22 Nov 1894.
67. *CL*, ii. 66; *PV*, 135; E. Clodd diary, 27 Sept 1895 (Alan Clodd); certificate dated 29 July 1895 (Divorce Registry).
68. Book (DCM); *CPW*, ii. 450–1; 'Poetical Matter' notebook (microfilm, Yale).
69. *LW*, 286, cf. *DCC*, 12 Sept 1895, 10–11.
70. For Agnes Grove see D. Hawkins, *Concerning Agnes: TH's 'Good Little Pupil'* (Gloucester, 1982), and *The Grove Diaries: The Rise and Fall of an English Family 1809–1925*, ed. D. Hawkins (Wimborne, 1995).
71. *LW*, 286; *CPW*, iii. 215; *CL*, ii. 87.
72. W. Robertson Nicoll, *A Bookman's Letters* (London, 1913), 7; *Collected Letters of George Gissing*, ed. P. F. Mattheisen, A. C. Young, and P. Coustillas (9 vols., Athens, Oh., 1990–7), vi. 21; *CL*, ii. 86.
73. *Collected Letters of George Gissing*, vi. 27–8, 29–30; ibid. vi. 21.
74. E. Clodd, diary, 29 Sept 1895 (Alan Clodd); E. Manning, *Marble & Bronze: The Art and Life of Hamo Thornycroft* (London, 1982), 131; *CL*, ii. 106.
75. *CL*, ii. 84; *Jude the Obscure* (London, 1896), [p. vi], revised for Wessex edn.
76. *Jude the Obscure* (London, 1896), 97, 143, etc.; proofs (Signet Library, Edinburgh); *CL*, ii. 84.

19 THE PUBLICATION OF *Jude*

1. G. Douglas, 'TH: Some Recollections and Reflections', *Hibbert Journal*, 26 (Apr 1928), 396.
2. *Guardian* (13 Nov 1895), 1770; *Pall Mall Gazette* (12 Nov 1895), 4.
3. 'Pandering to Podsnap', *World*, 16 Oct 1895, see *CL*, ii. 96.
4. *World* (13 Nov 1895), 15.
5. *CL*, ii. 92–9, quotations 94, 99; cf. *LW*, 287–9.
6. *St James's Gazette* (8 Nov 1895), 4.
7. *CL*, ii. 93.
8. *CL*, ii. 99 (cf. R. G. Cox, *TH: The Critical Heritage* (London, 1970), 262–70); *CL*, ii. 105.
9. See Cox, *Critical Heritage*, 253–6, 279–83 (Wells in *Saturday Review*), 300–15.
10. Gilder, *World* (New York) (8 Dec 1895), 33, cf. *LW*, 296–7, and *CL*, ii. 103, 126.
11. See Cox, *Critical Heritage*, 256–62 (cf. *LW*, 287), 284–91.
12. A. Lang to E. Clodd, 1 May 1892, in *Journal of Rutgers Univ. Library* (Dec 1949), 4.
13. *CL*, i. 290.
14. For How's career, see *DNB*; for the text of his announcement, see L. Lerner and J. Holmstrom (eds.), *Thomas Hardy and his Readers* (London, 1968), 138; *CL*, ii. 143.
15. *LW*, 294–5.
16. *CL*, ii. 143; *LW*, 294.
17. *LW*, 295.
18. *LW*, 295.
19. *LW*, 259–60; *CL*, iv. 33.
20. *CL*, ii. 93.
21. *CL*, iii, 56.
22. *LW*, 286.
23. *LW*, 287; Pearl Craigie to TH, 15 Nov 1895, E. Terry to TH, 28 Nov 1895, 'George Egerton' to TH, 22 Nov 1895 (all DCM).
24. *LW*, 289; *CL*, ii. 100.
25. Mrs Campbell to Mrs S. Coleridge, 12 Jan 1896 (DCM).
26. *CL*, ii. 109; J. Forbes-Robertson to TH, [Jan 1896] and 14 Feb 1896 (DCM); F. Harrison to TH, 4 Mar 1896 (DCM); *CL*, ii. 113.
27. *LW*, 293; *CL*, ii. 111–12; Mrs Campbell to TH, 4 Aug 1896 (DCM); *CL*, ii. 128; see *'Tess' in the Theatre*, ed. M. Roberts (Toronto, 1950), pp. xxxiv–l, and esp. K. Wilson, *TH on Stage* (Basingstoke, 1995), 37–45.
28. *CL*, ii. 149; *The Times* (21 Feb 1900), 4, cf. *PV*, 159–60.
29. *LW*, 292; *CL*, ii. 112, 109, 108.
30. *CL*, ii. 123.
31. *CL*, ii. 116, 118; *LW*, 293.
32. D. Hawkins, *Concerning Agnes* (Gloucester, 1982), 102; *LW*, 298.
33. *Under the Greenwood Tree* (London, 1896), p. vi.
34. *CL*, ii. 124; *LW*, 298.
35. *LW*, 298–9.
36. *LW*, 299; book (DCM).
37. *LW*, 299–301; *CL*, ii. 130; *LW*, 301–2; *CL*, ii. 124.
38. *Spectator* (31 Oct 1896), 593.
39. *CL*, ii. 137, 140.

40. *LEFH*, 9.
41. *LEFH*, 10.
42. G. Gifford, letter, *Times Literary Supplement* (1 Jan 1944), 7; F. M. Ford, *Mightier Than the Sword* (London, 1938), 128–30; cf. R. Gittings, *The Older Hardy* (London, 1978), 81, and D. Kay-Robinson, *The First Mrs TH* (London, 1979), 153–6.
43. A. Sutro, *Celebrities and Simple Souls* (London, 1933), 58.
44. Carl J. Weber, *Hardy and the Lady from Madison Square* (Waterville, Me., 1952), 117.
45. *LEFH*, 65.
46. *LEFH*, 105; *CPW*, ii. 27.
47. *CPW*, i. 207, ii. 26.
48. *LW*, 302.
49. *World* (24 Mar 1897), 13–14.
50. *CL*, ii. 157.
51. *CL*, ii. 155; G. E. Buckle to TH, 10 Apr 1897 (DCM); *LW*, 303.
52. *Academy* (25 Mar 1897), 345.
53. *The Well-Beloved* (London, 1897), 88.
54. *CL*, ii. 154.
55. *Well-Beloved* (London, 1897), 388.
56. *CL*, ii. 153.
57. *CL*, i. 182.

20 KEEPING SEPARATE

1. *LW*, 302; Purdy, 121–2.
2. M. Millgate, *Testamentary Acts: Browning, Tennyson, James, Hardy* (Oxford, 1992), 156–61; and see L. Björk, 'Notebooks', in *Companion*, 290–2.
3. *CL*, ii. 166, 192–3; *DCC* (8 Apr 1897), 4.
4. *LW*, 310; *CL*, ii. 165.
5. *CL*, ii. 166; *LW*, 310–11; *Emma Hardy Diaries*, ed. Richard H. Taylor (Ashington, 1985), 200–3.
6. *LW*, 311; *Emma Hardy Diaries*, 203; *CPW*, i. 138.
7. *LW*, 313; *Emma Hardy Diaries*, 205–7; *Times* (8 July 1897), 10, cf. *PV*, 145–6; *Emma Hardy Diaries*, 208.
8. *CL*, ii. 169, 171, 170–2.
9. *CL*, ii. 171, cf. *PN*, 248, and *Daily Chronicle* (15 July 1897), 7; *LW*, 314.
10. *LW*, 314; *CL*, ii. 172; *CPW*, iii. 9.
11. Bible and prayerbook (DCM); psalter (Yale); *LW*, 315; *CPW*, i. 87–8.
12. *LW*, 315–16; *CL*, ii. 173–4; ELH letters (Mme Rolland).
13. C. M. Fisher, *Life in TH's Dorchester 1888–1908* (Beaminster, 1965), 17; invitation card (DCM).
14. *CL*, ii. 174; *Letters of Rudyard Kipling*, ed. T. Pinney (London, 1990), ii. 316–17; *LW*, 316; C. E. Carrington, *Rudyard Kipling: His Life and Work* (1955; London, 1978), 208.
15. *CL*, ii. 180; *CL*, ii. 182.
16. *CL*, ii. 182; *CL*, ii. 176–7, 178–9; cf. C. J. P. Beatty, *TH: Conservation Architect* (Dorchester, 1999), 21–6.
17. *CL*, ii. 206.

18. *CL*, ii. 193; *LW*, 317; *CL*, ii. 285.

19. W. Gifford to ELH, 7 Sept and 24 Oct 1898 (DCM); Mrs Ethel Skinner (daughter of G. Gifford), interview, 1978.

20. Ethel Skinner, interview, 1978; G. Gifford, letter, *Times Literary Supplement* (1 Jan 1944), 7.

21. K. Fisher, *Conversations with Sylvia: Sylvia Gosse, Painter, 1881–1968* (London, 1975), 27.

22. ELH to R. Owen, 24 Apr 1899 (Colby).

23. ELH to R. Owen, 24 Apr 1899 (Colby); *Animals' Friend* (Mar 1898), 108–9; ELH's copy of leaflet (DCM); *The Times* (26 Feb 1895), 3; *Daily Chronicle* (4 Sept 1899), 4, cf. *LEFH*, 16–17.

24. E. H. Begbie to ELH, 8 Mar 1898 (DCM); editor of *Temple Bar* to ELH, 8 July 1898 (DCM); *CL*, ii. 189, 190.

25. *LEFH*, 11–12.

26. *Wessex Poems* (London, 1898), 3, cf. TH's revised text at *CPW*, i. 8.

27. *CPW*, i. 106.

28. *CL*, ii. 208; *Collected Letters of George Meredith*, ed. C. L. Cline (3 vols., Oxford, 1970), iii. 1338.

29. *Saturday Review* (7 Jan 1899), 19, cf. R. G. Cox (ed.), *TH: The Critical Heritage* (London, 1970), 319, where misdated.

30. *Westminster Gazette* (11 Jan 1899), 3, cf. P. Dalziel, 'Drawings and Withdrawings: The Vicissitudes of TH's *Wessex Poems*', *Studies in Bibliography*, 50 (1997), 390–400.

31. *Athenaeum* (14 Jan 1899), 41, cf. Cox, *Critical Heritage*, 325; *Outlook* (28 Jan 1899), 823.

32. *LN*, ii. 53; *CL*, ii. 212–13.

33. *LW*, 323; L. Stephen to TH, 3 Jan 1899, T. Watts-Dunton to TH, 23 Feb 1899, A. C. Swinburne to TH, 26 Dec 1898 (all DCM); *CL*, ii. 209.

34. A. Pretor to ELH, two undated letters [1899?] (DCM).

35. ELH to R. Owen, 24 Apr 1899 (Colby).

36. Cf. ELH to Spalding Evans, 1892 (M. Millgate); prospectus for *The Pursuit of the Well-Beloved*, MS in ELH's hand (Purdy, 95 and n.); 'Saturday Night in Arcady', MS partly in ELH's hand (Purdy, 71).

37. RLP/FEH, 1913; Purdy, 38, 56.

38. *LEFH*, 26.

39. *LEFH*, 15.

40. *LEFH*, 27.

41. *CPW*, ii. 12–13.

42. B. Newcombe to N. Gosse, 8 Mar [1900] (DCM).

43. Bible (DCM); Wollstonecraft (Yale).

44. *CL*, ii. 222.

45. *LW*, 326–7; M. O'Rourke, *TH: His Secretary Remembers* (Beaminster, 1965), 7.

46. *CL*, ii. 226; *CL*, ii. 227.

47. *CL*, ii. 228

48. *Daily Chronicle* (24 Aug 1899), 3, cf. *PV*, 153–5; *CL*, ii. 229.

49. *CL*, ii. 232, and see *CL*, ii. 229.

50. *CL*, ii. 233 and n.; Ethel Skinner to RLP, 1 Jan 1973 (Yale), and interview, 1978.

51. *CPW*, i. 116; *CPW*, i. 119–20.

52. *The Times*, 11 Oct 1899; G. Gissing, 'Tyrtaeus', *Review of the Week*, 4 Nov 1899, cf. *Gissing Newsletter* (July 1974), 3; *CL*, ii. 235.

53. *CPW*, i. 122, i. 120–1; *CL*, ii. 241; *CPW*, i. 124–7.

54. *CL*, ii. 238; *CL*, ii. 240.
55. *Westminster Gazette* (23 Dec 1899), 5, cf. *CPW*, i. 121; *Daily Chronicle* (25 Dec 1899), 4.
56. *Daily Chronicle* (28 Dec 1899), 8, cf. *PV*, 156–8.
57. *LEFH*, 19.
58. *War against War* (20 Jan 1899), 21, cf. *PV*, 151; *CL*, ii. 248.
59. *CL*, ii. 248.
60. *Morning Post* (30 Nov 1900), cf. *CPW*, i. 128–9; *CL*, ii. 277.
61. *CL*, ii. 269–70.
62. *CL*, ii. 265.
63. *CL*, ii. 226; A. Grove to ELH, 20 Mar 1900 (DCM).
64. Editor of *Westminster Gazette* to ELH, 27 Mar 1900 (DCM).
65. *Sphere* (14 Apr 1900), 393; *LEFH*, 21.
66. *Academy* (27 Apr 1901), 355.
67. *CL*, ii. 251; *LEFH*, 21; *LW*, 328.
68. *PV*, 171–2; *CL*, ii. 245, 257; *CL*, ii. 257–8.
69. H. Lea, *TH Through the Camera's Eye* (Beaminster, 1964), 23.
70. *LW*, 329; *CL*, ii. 263–4; A. E. Housman to TH, 11 July 1900 (DCM); Clodd, diary, 3–7 Aug 1900 (Alan Clodd).
71. *CL*, ii. 272; *CL*, ii. 276.
72. Carl J. Weber, *Hardy and the Lady from Madison Square* (Waterville, Me., 1952), 136–7.
73. ELH to R. Owen, 31 Dec 1900 (Colby).
74. *Graphic*, 29 Dec 1900; cf. *CPW*, i. 188.

21 Pessimistic Meliorist

1. E. Gosse, 'Form in Poetry', *Literature*, 4 Mar 1899; *CL*, ii. 216–17; note (Adams).
2. W. Archer, *Real Conversations* (London, 1904), 46–7.
3. TH, 'The Darkling Thrush', *CPW*, i. 188.
4. Book (Yale); E. Clodd, diary, 3 Feb 1896 (Alan Clodd); 'Poetical Matter' notebook (microfilm, Yale).
5. *CL*, i. 235; *CL*, ii. 269.
6. *CL*, ii. 283; *CL*, ii. 282–3; *Humanity*, 4 (Aug 1901), 155–6, cf. *PV*, 166–7.
7. *CPW*, i. 115; *CL*, ii. 280, 288.
8. *CL*, ii. 282; *CL*, ii. 287.
9. *CL*, ii. 286; *LW*, 331–2; *CL*, ii. 283; Henry W. Nevinson, *More Changes More Chances* (London, 1925), 165, cf. *CL*, iii. 131.
10. *LW*, 332; information from RLP, citing FEH; photograph, see T. O'Sullivan, *TH: An Illustrated Biography* (London, 1975), 143; *Sphere* (7 Sept 1901), 288, cf. *PV*, 168–9.
11. *Later Years*, 89–90, cf. *LW*, 517, 539.
12. *PV*, 205; M. E. Bath, 'TH and Evangeline F. Smith', *TH Year Book*, no. 4 (1974), 44; MH to N. Sparks sen., Nov 1903 (Eton).
13. TH's diagram of route (Eton); MH to J. Sparks, 7 Aug 1902 (Eton); MH to N. Sparks sen., Nov 1903 (Eton).
14. NS (Eton); KH to J. Sparks, 2–12 Dec 1902 (Eton).
15. *CL*, iii. 290; J. Antell, interview, 1974.
16. KH, diary, 3, 4, 5, 9, 15 July 1916 (DCM: Lock).
17. NS (Eton).

18. NS (Eton); *CL*, iii. 38; and see C. Barclay, *Nathaniel Sparks: Memoirs of TH's Cousin, the Engraver* (Greenwich, 1994).

19. Purdy, 118–19.

20. *CPW*, i. 144–8, 149–64.

21. *CPW*, i. 206–10, 207.

22. *Bookman* (London) (Jan 1902), 131–2.

23. *CL*, iii. 11, 6, 7, 10.

24. *CL*, iii. 12–14, 15–16, 27; for Macmillan's replies, see C. Morgan, *The House of Macmillan (1843–1943)*, (London, 1943), 155–9.

25. ELH to R. Owen, 4 Mar 1902 (Colby), cf. J. O. Bailey, *The Poetry of TH* (Chapel Hill, NC, 1970), 22; *CL*, iii. 23 and n.

26. *CL*, iii. 23.

27. Annotation in prayerbook (DCM); *LW*, 340–1; *CL*, iii. 40.

28. *CL*, iii. 40; *CL*, iii. 41.

29. Purdy, 121–2.

30. *LW*, 339–40, cf. *PV*, 176–80; *LW*, 335–7, cf. Rider Haggard, *Rural England* (London, 1902), i. 283, and *PV*, 183.

31. *CL*, iii. 16.

32. *CL*, iii. 16; TH letter, *Guardian* (16 Apr 1902), 551, cf. *PV*, 173–4; *CL*, iii. 36.

33. *LW*, 350; *CL*, iii. 212.

34. See W. J. Keith, 'TH and the Literary Pilgrims', *Nineteenth-Century Fiction*, 24 (June 1969), 80–92, and S. Gatrell, *TH's Vision of Wessex* (Basingstoke, 2003), 236–8, etc.

35. *CL*, iii. 151; Nevinson, *More Changes More Chances*, 165.

36. *CL*, ii. 131–4; E. New to TH, 1 Apr 1900 (DCM); *CL*, iii. 181; *CL*, iii. 171–2, iv. 223, etc.

37. *CL*, iii. 145, 146.

38. *CL*, iii. 1; *CL*, iii. 17, cf. *PV*, 226–7.

39. *CL*, iii. 171–2.

40. *LW*, 341, *CL*, iii. 46–7.

41. *CL*, i. 50; C. J. P. Beatty, *TH: Conservation Architect* (Dorchester, 1999), 27–37.

42. E. C. Sampson, 'TH—Justice of the Peace', *Colby Library Quarterly*, 13 (Dec 1977), 273; *CL*, iii. 23.

43. *DCC* (19 Jan 1928), 4.

44. *CL*, iii. 58, cf. *PV*, 190–1.

45. *CL*, iii. 62; E. Clodd, diary, 31 May, 8 June 1903 (Alan Clodd); C. Shorter to E. Clodd, 16 Feb 1908 (Leeds).

46. *PV*, 235; M. Moule to ELH, 2 June [1903] (DCM); B. Churchill to ELH, [June 1903] (DCM); *CL*, iii. 64; *CL*, iii. 65.

47. *CL*, iii. 65; *CL*, iii. 69.

48. *CL*, iii. 74.

49. *CL*, iii. 73–4; medallion (Eton), cf. *THJ* 17/1 (Feb 2001), 14, where wrongly attributed to his brother Nathaniel; *CL*, iii. 116; *CL*, iii. 75.

50. F. Macmillan to George P. Brett, 12 Oct 1905 (MS Division, New York Public Library).

51. *CL*, iii. 85–6; *CL*, iii. 77.

52. Purdy, 122–3; *CL*, iii. 86; *CL*, iii. 94–5.

22 *The Dynasts*

1. ELH to B. Churchill, 23 Nov 1903 (M. Millgate).
2. *CL*, iii. 82–3, 83–4, 85; *CL*, iii. 86–7.
3. *CL*, iii. 90.
4. B. Churchill to ELH, 29 Nov 1903 (DCM); ELH sketch (DCM); *CL*, iii. 91–2; *CL*, iii. 95.
5. *The Dynasts*, Part First (London, 1904), p. ix.
6. *Dynasts*, Part First, Fore Scene.
7. Max Beerbohm, 'Thomas Hardy as Panoramatist', *Saturday Review* (30 Jan 1904), 137.
8. *Times Literary Supplement* (5 Feb 1904), 37, cf. *PV*, 198–200; for both sides of Hardy–Walkley exchange, see *CPW*, v. 385–96.
9. *CL*, iii. 91; *CL*, iii. 221; *LW*, 343–4.
10. *CL*, v. 130–1; see, however, David Lodge, 'TH as a Cinematic Novelist', in Lance St John Butler (ed.), *TH after Fifty Years* (London, 1977), 78–89.
11. *Times Literary Supplement* (12 Feb 1904), 46, and (19 Feb 1904), 53, cf. *PV*, 198–200.
12. *CL*, iii. 102.
13. *CL*, iii. 117; *CL*, iii. 114–16.
14. *LW*, 344–5; *CL*, iii. 120; *CL*, vii. 135; *CL*, iii. 119, and cf. iii. 115.
15. *CPW*, i. 326–7.
16. *CL*, iii. 116, 118–19; *CL*, iii. 125.
17. *CL*, iii. 123.
18. *The Times* (6 Apr 1904), 4; *DCC* (7 Apr 1904), 4; *Daily Chronicle* (9 Apr 1904), 4, cf. *PV*, 204, 205, and see 205–8.
19. *CL*, iii. 120.
20. *LW*, 345.
21. *DCC*, 7 Apr 1904, 4; prayerbook (DCM).
22. *CL*, iii. 119; Clodd, diary, 22 June 1904 (Alan Clodd).
23. 'Book of Gosse' (Cambridge Univ. Library).
24. *CL*, iii. 131–2, 132, and see *PV*, 224, and E. C. Sampson, 'TH—Justice of the Peace', *Colby Library Quarterly*, 13 (Dec 1977), 271–2.
25. *Tatler*, 25 May 1904; *CL*, iii. 98; ELH to C. Shorter, 15 Sept 1904 (Yale).
26. H. C. C. Moule (citing his father, C. W. Moule), interview, 1975; D. Stickland, *TH at Cattistock* (St Peter Port, 1968), 95; *LEFH*, 29–30; *CL*, iii. 137.
27. *Athenaeum* (29 Oct 1904), 591, cf. *PV*, 212–13, *CL*, iii. 142, 144.
28. *CL*, vii. 140; for the intended text, see *PV*, 221–4; cf. *PN*, 290.
29. Death certificate; *CL*, iii. 141.
30. Information from Dr C. J. P. Beatty, also from C. J. Norris and F. Rampton, former colleagues of G. Gifford.
31. *CL*, iii. 135.
32. *LW*, 347; *CL*, iii. 161–2.
33. *LW*, 347–8; Aberdeen *Evening Gazette* (7 Apr 1905), 2; cf. *PV*, 217, and M. Ray, 'TH in Aberdeen', *Aberdeen University Review*, 56 (Spring 1995), 58–69.
34. *LW*, 348–9.
35. *LW*, 349–50; G. H. Thring to TH, Nov 1905 (DCM); A. C. Benson, diary, 24 Jan 1902 (Magdalene College, Cambridge).
36. *Collected Letters of George Meredith*, ed. C. L. Cline (3 vols., Oxford, 1970), iii. 1529; E. Clodd, diary, 28 Sept 1905 (Alan Clodd).

37. *LW*, 351; *LEFH*, 31; E. Sharp, *Unfinished Adventure* (London, 1933), 96.
38. *LW*, 351–2; 'Poetical Matter' notebook (microfilm, Yale).
39. *PV*, 258; *CL*, iii. 183–4; *CL*, ii. 157.
40. *Morning Leader*, 1 Feb 1905, 4, cf. *PV*, 214; *The Times*, 12 Jan 1906, 15, cf. *PV*, 228; *Fortnightly Review* (Apr 1906), 638–9, cf. *PV*, 236–8, *LW*, 352–3.
41. *LEFH*, 33; *LEFH*, 34; *CL*, iii. 191.
42. F. Macmillan to G. P. Brett, 12 Oct 1905 (MS Division, New York Public Library); Purdy, 126, 128–9.
43. *CL*, iii. 185.
44. *Trumpet-Major*, 4; 'Poetical Matter' (microfilm, Yale).
45. *CPW*, i. 326.
46. Sketch (DCM).

23 After the Visit

1. Ethel Richardson (sister), MS recollections of FEH (D. Wood); *CL*, iii. 193.
2. Education Department, *Queen's Scholarship Examination, December 1897*, 44.
3. E. Richardson, recollections of FEH (D. Wood); R. Gittings and J. Manton, *The Second Mrs Hardy* (London, 1979), 22; and see entries for 'Dugdale family' and 'Hardy, Florence Emily', *Companion*, 102, 157–60.
4. E. Richardson, recollections of FEH (D. Wood); Gittings and Manton, *Second Mrs Hardy*, 25–8; Hyatt obituary, *Enfield Observer* (15 Dec 1911), 5.
5. RLP/FEH, 1935 (Yale); *CL*, iii. 179.
6. RLP/FEH, 1931 (Yale); *CPW*, ii. 15; horticultural information, Penelope Lively.
7. *CL*, iii. 179.
8. Photographs (DCM); Reading Ticket application (British Library archives), additional information, David Pam; *CL*, iii, 249; FEH to Carroll A. Wilson, 20 Mar 1937 (copy, Yale).
9. E. Gosse to TH, 26 Feb 1906, in E. Charteris, *The Life and Letters of Sir Edmund Gosse* (London, 1931), 299.
10. *CL*, iii. 199.
11. *LW*, 355; *CL*, iii. 209, 210; Henry W. Nevinson, *More Changes More Chances* (London, 1925), 165.
12. Nevinson, *More Changes More Chances*, 165; *LW*, 354, cf. M. Millgate, *Testamentary Acts: Browning, Tennyson, James, Hardy* (Oxford, 1992), 110; *CL*, iii. 212.
13. J.-É. Blanche, *Mes Modèles* (Paris, 1929), 82; *CL*, iii. 265.
14. *LW*, 357; *CL*, iii. 224.
15. *CL*, iii. 218; *CL*, iii. 233.
16. *CL*, iii. 207; *CL*, iii. 255.
17. *CL*, iii. 231; Nevinson, *More Changes More Chances*, 181.
18. Nevinson, *CL*, iii. 238–9; M. Fawcett to TH, 4 Dec 1906 (DCM).
19. *LW*, 359–60; 'Book of Gosse' (Cambridge Univ. Library); Charteris, *Gosse*, 292–3.
20. Blanche, *Mes Modèles*, 85, 84.
21. *CL*, iii. 277.
22. *CL*, iii. 287; *CL*, iii. 282.
23. *CL*, iii. 282; *CL*, iii. 288.

24. See Purdy, 130–1, esp. draft page reproduced opp. 131.

25. *CL*, iii. 253, 249.

26. Book (Adams); *CL*, iii. 261–2; *CL*, iii. 261.

27. *CL*, iii. 274; *Cornhill*, May 1908, cf. Gittings and Manton, *Second Mrs Hardy*, 32–3.

28. *CL*, iii. 270.

29. Blanche, *Mes Modèles*, 83–4; Lady Grove, *The Social Fetich* (London, 1908); *Social Fetich* proofs (Yale); *CL*, iii. 269; 'I Look into my Glass', *CPW*, i. 106.

30. *LEFH*, 36–7.

31. *CL*, iii. 273.

32. *Social Fetich* proofs (Yale).

33. *CL*, iii. 279–81; K. Wilson, *TH on Stage* (Basingstoke, 1995), 55–7; *DCC*, 7 May 1908.

34. Wilson, *TH on Stage*, 59–67; *CL*, iii. 356.

35. Wilson, *TH on Stage*, 64; *DCC*, 26 Nov 1908.

36. *CL*, iii. 322–4.

37. *CL*, vii. 147; *CL*, iii. 329; *LEFH*, 42.

38. *LEFH*, 39–41.

39. *LEFH*, 49, 53, 54; *LEFH*, 51.

40. M. Millgate, 'TH and the House of Macmillan', in E. James (ed.), *Macmillan: A Publishing Tradition* (Basingstoke, 2002), 78–9; S. Gatrell, *Hardy the Creator* (Oxford, 1988), 246–53.

41. Information from Henry Lock; *CL*, iii. 158.

42. *CL*, iii. 334; ELH to TH, 10 Sept 1908 (Eton); *CL*, iii. 334.

43. *CL*, iii. 347; *CL*, iii. 350.

44. *DCC* (31 Dec 1908), 11.

45. *LEFH*, 42–3.

46. E. C. Sampson, 'TH—Justice of the Peace', *Colby Library Quarterly*, 13 (Dec 1977), 273–4; *LW*, 370.

47. Wilson, *TH on Stage*, 99–100, 105; *CL*, iii. 337, cf. C. J. P. Beatty, *TH: Conservation Architect* (Dorchester, 1999), 41–2.

48. *CL*, iii. 245, 292; for TH's editorial procedures, see W, J. Keith, 'TH's Edition of William Barnes', *Victorian Poetry*, 15 (Summer 1977), 121–31.

49. Preface, *Select Poems of William Barnes* (London, 1908), pp. iii, xii, cf. *PV*, 292, 297.

50. *CL*, iv. 15.

51. *LW*, 372; *CL*, iv. 28.

52. *LW*, 374; Luigi Illica, *Tess: A Drama in Four Acts* (London, 1909), 50; D. Hawkins, *The Tess Opera* (Thomas Hardy Society Monograph no. 3, 1984), *passim*.

53. *CL*, iv. 30; *CL*, iv. 32; Gittings and Manton, *Second Mrs Hardy*, 49; E. Clodd, diary, 14 July 1909 (Alan Clodd); *CL*, iv. 35–6.

54. E. Clodd, diary, 5 July 1909 (Alan Clodd); *CL*, iv. 35–6.

55. E. Clodd, diary, 16 Aug 1909 (Alan Clodd); Clodd to C. Shorter, 13 Aug 1909 (Leeds); *Aldeburgh, Leiston and Saxmundham Times* (21 Aug 1909), 3.

56. E. Clodd, diary, 14, 21, and 23 Aug 1909 (Alan Clodd); F. Dugdale to E. Richardson, 18 Aug 1909 (Pamela Richardson); H. Hardy to KH, 30 Sept 1909 (M. Millgate); *LW*, 374–5.

57. Gittings and Manton, *Second Mrs Hardy*, 33.

58. For the Shorters, see Gittings and Manton, *Second Mrs Hardy*, 38–45; book, Maggs Bros. catalogue 664 (1938), item 207; K. Tynan Hinkson to F. Dugdale, re Hyatt, 17 Dec 1911 (Berg); K. Tynan, 'Dora Sigerson: A Tribute and Some Memories', *Observer*, 13 Jan 1918.

59. Postcard from 'all at home' to F. Dugdale, 31 Dec 1906 (Eton).
60. FEH to R. Owen, [17 Dec 1915?] (Colby), also *LEFH*, 66, 78–9, 110–11; Gittings and Manton, *Second Mrs Hardy*, 66.
61. *CL*, iii. 329; Gittings and Manton, *Second Mrs Hardy*, 35–7; 'Mr. Thomas Hardy. Marriage with Ex-Member of "Standard" Staff', *Standard*, 11 Feb 1919; FEH to R. Owen, [8 Mar 1916?] (Colby).
62. *CPW*, i. 243; RLP/FEH, 1936.
63. *LEFH*, 283.
64. *CPW*, i. 271, ii. 14–15; *CPW*, ii. 15–16.
65. *CPW*, ii. 15, 16, i. 271, ii. 16, 14.
66. E. Clodd, diary, 30 Oct 1909 (Alan Clodd); *CL*, iv. 61.
67. *CPW*, ii. 16.
68. *CL*, iv. 47–8.
69. *CL*, iv. 73; Purdy, 149–50.
70. *LW*, 376; *LEFH*, 152; *CPW*, ii. 31, cf. *PV*, 309–10.
71. *CL*, iv. 95; *Standard* (2 June 1910), 8, cf. *PV*, 312–16; *CL*, iv. 98.

24 A FUNERAL

1. *LW*, 356, citing ELH diary no longer extant.
2. *LW*, 377–8; *CL*, iv. 86–7.
3. *LW*, 377.
4. RLP/FEH 1935; *CL*, iv. 92.
5. F. Dugdale to ELH, 18 June, early July, 23 July 1910 (DCM).
6. F. Dugdale to ELH, 27 Oct, 11 Nov (cf. *LEFH*, 67), 20 Nov 1910 (DCM).
7. E. Clodd, diary, 23 June 1910 (Alan Clodd).
8. *CL*, iv. 128; *CL*, iv. 129.
9. *LEFH*, 66, 65.
10. *LEFH*, 68, 66; *CPW*, ii. 117.
11. *LEFH*, 64; Strang sketch (DCM); flowers (Yale).
12. *LEFH*, 68; *LEFH*, 234.
13. F. Dugdale to ELH, 20 Nov 1910 (DCM).
14. *CL*, iii. 353; *LW*, 378; E. Smith to TH, 21 July 1910 (DCM).
15. A. C. Benson, citing ELH, diary, 5 Sept 1912 (Magdalene College, Cambridge); *LW*, 378; RLP/FEH, 1936.
16. *LW*, 378–81; *LEFH*, 68; Purdy, 352, and see K. Wilson, *TH on Stage* (Basingstoke, 1995), 70–2.
17. F. Dugdale to E. Clodd, 3 June 1911 (Leeds); *LW*, 382–3; Pamela Richardson, MS, 'Florence Emily Hardy' (D. Wood); TH to the Earl Marshal, 2 Mar 1911 (draft, DCM).
18. Henry Hardy to M. Antell, 19 June 1911 (Eton); RLP, conversation with Constance Dugdale, 1948 (Yale).
19. *LW*, 383; *LEFH*, 72; joint photo in Jo Draper, *TH: A Life in Pictures* (Wimborne, 1989), 101; *LW*, 383; *CL*, iv. 168.
20. *LW*, 384; *LEFH*, 73; *CL*, iv. 195.
21. TH, *The Excluded and Collaborative Stories*, ed. P. Dalziel (Oxford, 1992), 332–47; for 'Blue Jimmy' see esp. 336–42, also *CL*, iv. 114.
22. Purdy, 314, 316, 317; *CPW*, iii. 295, 297, 304.

23. *Fifty-Seven Poems by TH*, ed. Bernard Jones (Gillingham, Dorset, 2002), 20.

24. Purdy, 316; *Fifty-Seven Poems*, p. vi.

25. *CL*, iv. 117; *CPW*, i. 243–7.

26. *CPW*, ii. 15–16, 33–4, 34–7, 11–13.

27. *CL*, iv. 287, and see C. Hassall, *Edward Marsh, Patron of the Arts: A Biography* (London, 1959), 226n.

28. *LW*, 383; *LW*, 384; Wilson, *TH on Stage*, 74–7.

29. *CL*, iv. 123–4, 198.

30. *CL*, iv. 168; *CL*, iv. 162–3.

31. *CL*, iv. 7.

32. F. Macmillan to TH, 9 Jan 1912 (Macmillan letterbooks, BL); *CL*, iv. 198; *CL*, iv. 209.

33. *CL*, i. 184–5; F. Macmillan to TH, 26 Oct 1911 (Macmillan letterbooks, BL); *CL*, iv. 209.

34. *CL*, iv. 212, cf. *LW*, 520.

35. E. Gosse, MS, 'A Visit to TH in 1912' (Princeton).

36. *LW*, 384; *CL*, iv. 178, 180–1, 184, 186–7.

37. M. Newbolt (ed.), *The Later Life and Letters of Sir Henry Newbolt* (London, 1942), 166–8, cf. *PV*, 334–6.

38. *LEFH*, 38.

39. ELH, *Some Recollections*, ed. E. Hardy and R. Gittings (London, 1961), 61.

40. List of donations (DCM); *LEFH*, 52.

41. ELH, *Alleys* (Dorchester, 1911), 2; ELH's copy, with corrections (Eton).

42. ELH, *Spaces* (Dorchester, 1912), 25–6; *Alleys* and *Spaces* both reprinted in ELH, *Poems and Religious Effusions* (St Peter Port, 1966).

43. C. H. Moule to ELH, 3 Oct 1911 (DCM).

44. *CL*, iv. 177; *Nash's Magazine* (Mar 1912), 683, cf. *PV*, 331–2.

45. A. C. Benson, diary, 5 Sept 1912 (Magdalene College, Cambridge), cf. D. Newsome, *On the Edge of Paradise. A. C. Benson: The Diarist* (London, 1980), 283–4; E. Gosse, 'Visit to TH in 1912' (Princeton).

46. A. C. Benson, diary, 5 Sept 1912 (Magdalene College, Cambridge).

47. RLP, citing Marjorie Soundy, FEH's sister; *CPW*, ii. 230, 232.

48. E. Gosse, 'Visit to TH in 1912' (Princeton Univ.); A. C. Benson, diary, 5 Sept 1912 (Magdalene College, Cambridge).

49. *Proceedings of the Dorset Natural History and Antiquarian Field Club* (1912), pp. xi, xiii; *LW*, 386.

50. D. Kay-Robinson, *The First Mrs TH* (London, 1979), 225–6, also *Fordington Monthly Messenger*, Aug 1912; Alice Harvey, née Gale, interview, 1973; *LW*, 386.

51. *LW*, 386.

52. Alice Harvey, 'I Was Emma Lavinia's Personal Maid', *TH Year Book*, 4 (1974), 6–9, and interview, 1973.

53. *CL*, iv. 246–7; *CL*, 243–4; verse MSS (Berg).

54. Carl J. Weber, *Hardy and the Lady from Madison Square* (Waterville, Me., 1952), 161–2; *CL*, iv. 246.

55. Harvey, 'Personal Maid', 9; ELH note (Berg); death certificate; *CL*, iv. 246.

56. *CL*, iv. 246; *CL*, iv. 243; C. Gifford to TH, 28 Nov 1912 (DCM).

57. Léonie Gifford to TH, 28 Oct 1912 (DCM); *DCC*, 5 Dec 1912.

25 A SECOND MARRIAGE

1. *CL*, iv. 244–5; Alice Harvey (née Gale), 'I was Emma Lavinia's Personal Maid', *TH Year Book*, no. 4 (1974), 9; *The Times*, 30 Nov 1912, 9, cf. *PV*, 338–9.
2. *CL*, iv. 239; *CL*, iv. 243.
3. *CPW*, ii. 48–9, 50–1, 53–4, 53; *CPW*, ii. 49.
4. *LEFH*, 78, 75, 78, 80, and see *CL*, iv. 260.
5. *CPW*, ii. 60.
6. *CPW*, iii. 304, and see 338.
7. *LW*, 389–90; *CL*, iv. 261, 270, and see *PV*, 478–9.
8. *LEFH*, 76; *CL*, iv. 260.
9. *CL*, iv. 267–8; E. Clodd, diary, 25 and 27 Apr 1913 (Alan Clodd); see *LEFH*, 63, 64.
10. E. Clodd, diary, 13 July 1913 (Alan Clodd).
11. Chequebook counterfoil (DCM); MH to N. Sparks, Sen., 15 Feb 1913 (Eton); MH to TH, 12 June 1913 (DCM).
12. Letters to, e.g., H. V. McArthur, [2 Aug 1910] (M. Millgate), Mackenzie Bell, 24 Dec 1912 (T. Wightman), and G. H. Thring, 26 Mar 1913 (BL).
13. *LEFH*, 88, 86.
14. *LEFH*, 86–7; L. Gifford to TH, 27 Nov 1913 (DCM).
15. *LEFH*, 87.
16. *LEFH*, 92; *PN*, 33.
17. *LW*, 390; A. C. Benson, diary, 10 June 1913 (Magdalene College, Cambridge); MH to TH, 12 June 1913 (DCM), cf. *CL*, i. 7; FEH to SCC, 9 June 1913 (Yale); *LW*, 391.
18. *CL*, iv. 397; *CL*, iv. 300; E. Gosse to TH, 7 Nov 1913 (Cambridge Univ. Library).
19. *CL*, iv. 306.
20. Mrs Sarah Headley to RLP, 7 July 1956 (Yale).
21. Flowers (Yale); *LW*, 392; *CL*, v. 10–11; *CL*, v. 13.
22. *CL*, v. 13; *CL*, v. 9; *CL*, v. 16.
23. *CL*, v. 19; *CL*, v. 15.
24. *LEFH*, 105; *LEFH*, 203–4.
25. FEH to R. Owen, 1 June 1914 (Colby).
26. *LW*, 392; 'Book of Gosse' (Cambridge Univ. Library); *CL*, v. 38.
27. FEH to R. Owen, 1 June 1914 (Colby); FEH to Lady Hoare, 7 July 1914 (Wiltshire Record Office); FEH to A. Lowell, 27 July 1914 (Houghton Library, Harvard Univ.); *CL*, 36–7.
28. *CPW*, ii. 9–10, i. 129–31.
29. FEH to SCC, 15 Aug 1914 (Yale); *CL*, v. 45.
30. FEH to Lady Hoare, 26 July 1914 (Wiltshire Record Office); FEH to R. Owen, 14 and 17 Oct 1914 (Colby).
31. Purdy, 169; 'The Voice', *CPW*, ii. 56–7.
32. *LEFH*, 104, 104–5.
33. *LEFH*, 108.
34. *LEFH*, 101–2.
35. *New Statesman*, 19 Dec 1914, 271.
36. *Bookman*, 47 (Feb 1915), 143–4; *Academy* (28 Nov 1914), 476; Purdy, 172.
37. *CPW*, ii. 290–1; *CL*, v. 43.
38. *CL*, v. 86–7; Purdy, 191–2.

39. *CPW*, ii. 289.
40. *Minutes* of Westminster House Conference, 2 Sept 1914 (copy, DCM); *PV*, 349–50; see P. Buitenhuis, *The Great War of Words: Literature as Propaganda 1914–18 and After* (London, 1989), esp.12–15, 19, and S. Hynes, *A War Imagined: The First World War and English Culture* (New York, 1991), esp. 25–9.
41. *Manchester Guardian* (7 Oct 1914), 7, *Daily News* (7 Oct 1914), 5, etc., cf. *PV*, 350–3.
42. TH to Lord Kitchener, 8 Nov 1914 (draft, DCM); H. H. Asquith to TH, 11 Nov 1914 (DCM); *CL*, vii. 157. See also *PV*, 363.
43. *CL*, v. 51, 53–6, cf. *LW*, 397, and see K. Wilson, *TH on Stage* (Basingstoke, 1995), 85–95.
44. *CPW*, ii. 294; *CL*, v. 86.
45. FEH to R. Owen, 17 Oct 1914 (Colby); *CPW*, i. 208; *LEFH*, 117.
46. *CL*, v. 87, 99; *CL*, v. 105; *CL*, v. 99.
47. *CL*, v. 104; FEH to R. Owen, [6 June 1915?] (Colby).
48. FEH to R. Owen, [1 Oct 1915?] and 1 Sept 1915 (Colby); F. George to TH, 19 May and 27 Oct 1915 (DCM); *DCC*, 9 Sept 1915; *LW*, 400.
49. FEH to R. Owen, 23 June 1915 (Colby).
50. FEH to C. W. Saleeby, 2 Oct 1915 (Adams); FEH to SCC, 3 Aug 1923 (Yale); FEH to R. Owen, 17 July 1915 (Colby).
51. FEH to R. Owen, 23 June 1915 (Colby); *LW*, 401; FEH to R. Owen, 17 July 1915 (Colby).
52. *LW*, 401.
53. *CL*, v. 121.
54. Compare the much misinterpreted allusion to 'blood-nephew or niece' at *LW*, 19.
55. *LEFH*, 109; FEH to R. Owen, 1 Sept 1915 (Colby); T. W. Jesty, interview, 1979.
56. *The Times* (3 Sept 1915), 6, cf. *PV*, 361–2; Purdy, 174; *CPW*, ii. 297–8.
57. KH, diary, 4 Apr and 9 June 1915 (DCM: Lock).
58. Information from RLP, citing M. Soundy; *CL*, iii. 196; V. Collins, *Talks with TH at Max Gate 1920–1922* (London, 1928), 58.
59. *Sphere* (25 Dec 1915), 344; *DCC* (2 Dec 1915), 8–9, cf. *PV*, 366–8; *LW*, 402.
60. KH, diary, 25 Nov 1915 (DCM: Lock); KH to E. Clodd, 26 Nov 1915 (Leeds); *LEFH*, 110.
61. FEH to R. Owen, 30 Dec 1915 (Colby); *LEFH*, 110.
62. *LEFH*, 110; FEH typed 'aimable'.
63. *LEFH*, 110, 111; FEH to R. Owen, 26, 17 Dec 1915 (Colby).
64. KH, diary, 31 Dec 1915, 10 and 18 Feb 1916 (DCM: Lock).
65. KH to N. Sparks sen., 22 Feb 1916 (Eton); KH diary, 2 Apr 1915 (DCM: Lock).

26 LIFE-WRITING

1. *CL*, v. 147; *CL*, v. 180; E. Inglis to her sister, 30 May 1916 (DCM).
2. FEH to Lady Hoare, 5 Sept 1916 (Wiltshire Record Office); *LW*, 403–4.
3. *LW*, 404; RLP/FEH, 1935; *LEFH*, 119–20.
4. *LEFH*, 115; *LEFH*, 121.
5. Purdy, 349–50
6. *CL*, v. 190; *LEFH*, 118.
7. SCC/TH, 30 June 1915 (Yale).
8. Purdy, 187; FEH to SCC, 25 July 1916 (Yale).
9. K. Wilson, *TH on Stage* (Basingstoke, 1995), 98–102, *CL*, v. 166.
10. FEH to R. Owen, 5 June 1916 (Colby)

11. *LEFH*, 126; *LW*, 404.

12. *CL*, v. 204.

13. *CL*, v. 218; *CPW*, ii. 300; *PV*, 374, cf. *LW*, 405; *CL*, v. 275.

14. *LEFH*, 117; *LW*, 408–9.

15. *CL*, v. 218, 219; *CL*, v. 220.

16. *LW*, 407; KH, diary, 25 Mar 1917 (DCM: Lock).

17. FEH to R. Owen, [29 July 1917?] (Colby).

18. RLP/FEH, 1933 (Yale); FEH to R. Owen, 24 June 1917 and 30 Dec 1915 (Colby).

19. *LEFH*, 131.

20. *LEFH*, 136.

21. FEH to R. Owen, [16 Feb 1916?] (Colby); *LEFH*, 135.

22. *LEFH*, 134; FEH to SCC, 8 Dec 1917 (Yale).

23. FEH to SCC, 19 and 22 Aug 1917 (Yale); book (DCM), cf. Purdy, 207–8.

24. *LEFH*, 135.

25. *CPW*, ii. 230–2, 168–70; Purdy, 207.

26. *LEFH*, 120–1.

27. *LW*, 408; FEH to SCC, 25 Dec 1917 (Yale), and see FEH to R. Owen, [30 Dec 1917?] (Colby).

28. *Memoir of Thomas Hardy . . . Written by Himself* (London, 1832), p. viii; for this TH (1752–1832), see *DNB*.

29. SCC/TH, 7 Dec 1915 (DCM).

30. *Early Life*, p. vii, cf. *LW*, 3.

31. Annotated copy, p. 33 (DCM); FEH to V. H. Collins, drafts, 2 and 9 July 1922 (DCM).

32. *LEFH*, 133.

33. FEH to SCC, 9 Sept 1917 (Yale).

34. *LW*, introduction, pp. xvi–xvii.

35. *Athenaeum* (12 Jan 1918), 33; *CL*, v. 250; *LW*, 414; *CPW*, ii. 481–4.

36. *Tess*, p. ix, cf. Orel, *TH's Personal Writings*, ed. H. Orel (Lawrence, Kan., 1966), 48.

37. *CL*, v. 253.

38. E. Gosse, 'Mr. Hardy's Lyrical Poems', *Edinburgh Review*, 227 (Apr 1918), cf. R. G. Cox (ed.), *TH: The Critical Heritage* (London, 1970), 459, 450; *CL*, v. 260.

39. FEH to SCC, 11, 27 June 1918 (Yale); *LEFH*, 143; FEH to SCC, 15 Nov 1918 (Yale); scrapbooks (DCM).

40. FEH to SCC, fragment only [20 Jan 1918] (Yale); FEH to R. Owen, 18 Feb 1918 (Colby); *LEFH*, 140.

41. FEH to L. Yearsley, 26 July and 25 May 1918 (Eton); *CL*, v. 283.

42. FEH to SCC, 22 Mar and 22 Apr 1918 (Yale); for sale, see *LW*, 416; KH, diary, 9 and 19 July 1918, etc. (DCM: Lock).

43. E. C. Sampson, 'TH—Justice of the Peace', *Colby Library Quarterly*, 13 (Dec 1977), 271; *LW*, 417.

44. FEH to SCC, 27 Jan 1918 (Yale), cf. V. Meynell, *Friends of a Lifetime: Letters to Sydney Carlyle Cockerell* (London, 1940), 297, where text is abbreviated and reordered.

45. T. W. Jesty, interview, 1979; L. M. Farris, *Memories of the Hardy and Hand Families* (St Peter Port, 1968); *DCC*, 14 Aug 1884.

46. FEH to L. Yearsley, 17 Sept 1922 (Eton); C. A. Baker to TH, 28 Aug 1923 (DCM).

47. Lady St Helier to TH, 7 Jan 1923 (DCM); FEH to SCC, 26 Oct 1918 (Yale).

48. *CL*, v. 338; *CL*, v. 136.

49. KH to J. Sparks, 2 Dec 1902 (Eton); Puddletown parish records (DCRO).

27 TEA AT MAX GATE

1. *LW*, 417; FEH, diary fragment, 30 Jan 1918 (Yale); *Letters of John Cowper Powys to his Brother Llewelyn*, ed. M. Elwin (London, 1975), 258–9.
2. FEH to SCC, 11 June 1918 (Yale); FEH, diary fragment, 28 Jan 1918 (Yale).
3. *CL*, v. 171; FEH to P. Lemperly, 10 Mar 1918 (Colby); *CL*, v. 201, 214; *LEFH*, 150.
4. FEH, diary fragment, 4 Dec 1918 (Yale); *LEFH*, 151–3, and see Penelope Fitzgerald, *Charlotte Mew and her Friends* (Reading, Mass., 1988), esp. 170–4.
5. E. Felkin, 'Days with TH', *Encounter*, 18/4 (Apr 1962), 32, 30.
6. FEH to SCC, 18 Feb 1919 (Yale), cf. partial text in V. Meynell (ed.), *Friends of a Lifetime* (London, 1940), 302.
7. FEH to SCC, 1 and 9 May 1919 (Yale); *LW*, 421.
8. Purdy, 287, 288.
9. Admission order for L. Gifford, stamped 26 July 1919 (Claybury Asylum Records); FEH to SCC, 7 Aug 1919 (Yale), *LEFH*, 161; FEH to Miss Dicker, n.d. (R. Greenland); FEH to SCC, 18 Apr 1921 (Yale).
10. FEH to SCC, 7 Aug 1919 (Yale), and *LEFH*, 161.
11. *CL*, v. 326, cf. *LW*, 142, where Sassoon's visit is misleadingly dated.
12. *LW*, 427–9, cf. *PV*, 398–400.
13. *LW*, 434–5; *Letters of J. M. Barrie*, ed. V. Meynell (London, 1942), 175–6.
14. *Later Years*, 209, 206, cf. *LW*, 534–5; *LW*, 528, 525; V. Meynell (ed.), *Best of Friends: Further Letters to Sydney Carlyle Cockerell* (London, 1956), 25.
15. *LW*, 435; C. Hanbury to TH, 17 Jan 1920 (DCM); *CL*, vi. 28.
16. *CL*, v. 318; F. Harrison, 'Novissima Verba', *Fortnightly*, NS 107 (Feb. 1920), 182; FEH to SCC, 24 Feb 1920 (Yale); RLP/FEH, 1933 (Yale).
17. *CL*, vi. 54, cf. *LW*, 439.
18. *LW*, 434.
19. Meynell, *Best of Friends*, 25; FEH to SCC, 27 Aug 1918 (Yale); FEH to R. Owen, 23 July 1920 (Colby).
20. FEH to SCC, 24 Apr 1918 (Yale); FEH to R. Owen, 25 May 1920 (Colby); *LEFH*, 164–5; C. Asquith, *Portrait of Barrie* (London, 1954), 108.
21. FEH to SCC, 17 Mar 1920 (Yale); *CL*, vi. 253, and see vi. 1–2, 56; FEH to SCC, 4 May 1920 (Yale).
22. *LEFH*, 167.
23. M. Lilly, 'The Mr Hardy I Knew', *TH Society Review*, 1/4 (1978), 101; Murry, script BBC Home Service broadcast, 20 Feb 1955 (M. Millgate).
24. Asquith, *Portrait of Barrie*, 110.
25. *LEFH*, 165–6; Lilly, 'The Mr Hardy I Knew', 103.
26. Purdy, 288; *CL*, vi. 6.
27. FEH to SCC, 14 Apr 1920 (Yale); *CL*, vi. 20–1.
28. For TH and Macmillan & Co., see M. Millgate, 'TH and the House of Macmillan', in E. James, ed., *Macmillan; A Publishing Tradition* (Basingstoke, 2002), 70–82, esp. 77–80, and S. Gatrell, *Hardy the Creator* (Oxford, 1988), 175–86, esp. 184–6. For TH and film, see *Companion*, 49, 517–18.
29. *CL*, vi. 35, 44–5; *CL*, vi. 57–8.

30. *CL*, vi. 49; E. Pound to F. E. Schelling, 8 July 1922, in *The Letters of Ezra Pound 1907–1941*, ed. D. D. Paige (New York, 1950), 178; *CL*, vi. 77; R. Graves, *Goodbye to All That* (London, 1929), 376, 379.

31. This font recently (2004) located by T. W. Jesty in St Luke's Church, Christchurch.

32. *The Architectural Notebook of TH*, ed. C. J. P. Beatty (Dorchester, 1966) [115–17].

33. *LW*, 442; *LEFH*, 171; for the play itself, see Purdy, 212–13, and W. Archer, *Real Conversations* (London, 1904), 34–6.

34. *LW*, introduction, pp. xvii–xix.

35. *LEFH*, 171; Gertrude Bugler, interview, 1974, and see her *Personal Recollections of TH* (Dorchester, 1964).

36. *LEFH*, 173; *CL*, vi. 81; FEH to SCC, 18 Apr 1921 (Yale).

37. FEH to SCC, 28 July and 10 Aug 1921 (Yale).

38. *DCC*, 7 Apr 1921; *LW*, 447; FEH to SCC, 12 June and 28 July 1921 (Yale); *DCC*, 21 July 1921, 5, cf. *PV*, 410–11.

39. *CL*, vi. 93.

40. V. Collins, *Talks with TH at Max Gate 1920–1922* (London, 1928); *LEFH*, 177; *Later Years*, 224–5, 221–2, cf. *LW*, 448, 445–6.

41. *CL*, vi. 93.

42. H. J. Massingham, *Remembrance: An Autobiography* (London, 1942); E. Austin Hinton, interview with TH, in J. Gibson (ed.), *TH: Interviews and Recollections* (Basingstoke, 1999), 168–70; SCC/TH, 12 Jan 1927 (Yale).

43. E. M. Forster, conversation, 1969.

44. Lilly, 'The Mr Hardy I Knew', 102.

45. *CL*, iv. 214; FEH, diary fragment, 23 Oct 1918 (Yale).

46. J. H. Morgan, letter citing TH, *The Times* (19 Jan 1928), 8; *Later Years*, 224, cf. *LW*, 448; silver box (DCM); for different TH responses, see *CL*, iii. 273, *LEFH*, 209.

47. Graves, *Good-bye to All That*, 375.

48. FEH to SCC, 28 July 1921 (Yale); 'Memoranda II' notebook (DCM), cf. *PN*, 43–4; *CPW*, ii. 395–7.

49. *CL*, vi. 104.

50. FEH to SCC, 3 Feb 1921 (Yale); *CL*, iv. 6.

51. FEH to John Lane, 15 Oct 1922 (Princeton); RLP/FEH, 1934 (Yale).

52. FEH to SCC, 11 Jan 1922 (Yale); 'Memoranda II' notebook (DCM), cf. *PN*, 55; FEH to Lady Hoare, 13 Jan 1922 (Wiltshire Record Office); *LEFH*, 190–1.

53. *CL*, vi. 131; *LEFH*, 180.

54. *CL*, vi. 116; *LEFH*, 181–2; *CL*, vi. 116–17; *CPW*, ii. 317–25.

55. *LEFH*, 181; *Sunday Times* (28 May 1922), 8; *Later Years*, 225, cf. *LW*, 448.

56. FEH to SCC, 18 June 1922 (Yale); *CPW*, ii. 317; *CPW*, ii. 326; F. Henniker to TH, 17 June 1922 (transcript, DCM).

57. *CPW*, ii. 337, 345–6, 465, 353–4.

58. *CPW*, ii. 392–3, 444–5, 326–7.

59. *LEFH*, 182.

60. FEH to SCC, 22 Oct and 25 Aug 1922 (Yale); *LEFH*, 186.

61. *CL*, vi. 132; *Later Years*, 227, cf. *LW*, 450; FEH to R. Owen, 29 Oct 1922 (Colby); FEH to SCC, 21 June 1926 (Yale).

28 PLAYS AND PLAYERS

1. E. Richardson to her family, 5 Sept 1922 (Pamela Richardson).
2. FEH to SCC, 22 Oct 1922 (Yale); *LEFH*, 192; *Later Years*, 229, cf. *LW*, 452.
3. *LEFH*, 193; *Later Years*, 229, cf. *LW* 452 and esp. *PN*, 64; *LEFH*, 194.
4. *Sunday Pictorial* (22 Aug 1915), 7; also ' "Greater Love Hath No Man . . ." ', *Sunday Pictorial* (13 June 1915), 7.
5. See, e.g., her unsigned reviews of S. C. Lethbridge's *Let Be*, in *Sphere* (1 Apr 1916), p. viii, and R. Pryce's *David Penstephen*, in *Sphere* (29 Apr 1916), p. iv, as identified in FEH to R. Owen, 9 Feb and 22 Mar 1916 (both Colby).
6. FEH, 'A Woman's Happiest Year', *Weekly Dispatch* (27 Aug 1922), 8; FEH to S. Sassoon, 30 June 1922 (Eton); *LEFH*, 193, 194.
7. FEH to L. Yearsley, 6 Jan 1923 (Eton); FEH to SCC, 7 Jan and 13 May 1923 (Yale); *Later Years*, 230, cf. *LW*, 452.
8. *CL*, vi. 120; book (DCM).
9. *Later Years*, 232–4, cf. *LW*, 453–5.
10. FEH to SCC, 30 June 1923 (Yale); RLP/FEH, 1933 (Yale).
11. *CL*, vi. 204–5; KH, diary, 20 and 21 July 1923 (DCM: Lock).
12. *CL*, vi. 197–8; M. Yearsley to TH, 14 June 1923 (DCM).
13. FEH to L. Yearsley, 11 Oct 1923 (Eton); T. E. Lawrence to FEH, 14 and 20 Nov 1923 (Texas).
14. R. Graves to TH, [21 Mar 1923?] (DCM); T. E. Lawrence to FEH, 25 Mar and 4 Apr 1923 (Texas); *Letters of T. E. Lawrence*, ed. D. Garnett (London, 1938), 429.
15. *Later Years*, 236, cf. *LW*, 457; 'Memoranda II' notebook (DCM), cf. *PN*, 77, 74, 76.
16. G. N. Ray, *H. G. Wells and Rebecca West* (New Haven, 1974), 94–5; R. Rolland, MS journal, 5 May 1923 (Mme Rolland); R. Loomis to F. B. Adams, 8 June 1953 (Adams).
17. Purdy, 228–9; *CL*, vi. 224.
18. *The Dynasts*, Part First (London, 1904), p. xii.
19. *CL*, vi. 178–9; FEH to SCC, 4 Sept 1923 (Yale).
20. H. Granville Barker to TH, 4 July and 28 Oct 1923 (DCM), cf. *Granville Barker and his Correspondents*, ed. E. Salmon (Detroit, 1986), 374–7, 378–9.
21. *CL*, vi. 221–2; *CL*, vi. 232; and see K. Wilson, *TH on Stage* (Basingstoke, 1995), 120–30.
22. Wilson, *TH on Stage*, 130–1; *CL*, vi. 232; FEH to SCC, 21 June 1924 (Yale); *Later Years*, 237–8, cf. *LW*, 459.
23. *LEFH*, 209–10, cf. Genesis 29: 17.
24. FEH to SCC, 11 Apr 1924 (Yale), cf. incomplete text in V. Meynell, *Friends of a Lifetime* (London, 1940), 310–11; RLP/FEH, 1929.
25. J. M. Murry, 'Wrap me up in my Aubusson Carpet', *Adelphi* (Apr 1924), 951–8; *CL*, vi. 246; *CL*, vi. 242–3.
26. FEH to SCC, 7 Feb and 7 Sept 1924 (Yale); *Later Years*, 239, cf. *LW*, 459.
27. TH pencil note (DCM), cf. R. Gittings, *Young TH* (London, 1975), 29 and W. Archer, *Real Conversations* (London, 1904), 38; *CL*, v. 351.
28. V. Hunt, *The Flurried Years* (London, [1926]), 69; FEH to SCC, 25 Apr 1923 (Yale).
29. FEH to R. Owen, 23 July 1920 (Colby).
30. *LEFH*, 145; May O'Rourke, *TH: His Secretary Remembers* (Beaminster, Dorset, 1967), 7, 33; O'Rourke, 'TH, O.M. 1840–1928', *The Month*, 152 (Sept 1928), 207; *LEFH*, 282–3.
31. FEH to SCC, 8 June 1924 (Yale).

32. *Later Years*, 238–9, cf. *LW*, 459; FEH to SCC, 24 June 1924 (Yale); FEH to SCC, 11 Apr 1924 (Yale), cf. abbreviated text in Meynell, *Friends of a Lifetime*, 310–11.

33. FEH to SCC, 19 Sept 1924 (Yale); 'Memoranda II' notebook (DCM), cf. *PN*, 84; J. Sherren to TH, 1 Oct 1924 (DCM); O'Rourke, *His Secretary Remembers*, 32; *CL*, vi. 277.

34. 'Memoranda II' notebook (DCM), cf. *PN*, 94; FEH to SCC, 7 July 1924 (Yale); *CL*, vi. 280; KH to TH, 5 Oct 1924 (DCM); *CPW*, iii. 55–6.

35. *Later Years*, 240, cf. *LW*, 460; Gertrude Bugler, interview, 1974; FEH to SCC, 25 Sept 1924 (Yale); *CL*, vi. 280; N. J. Atkins, *Hardy, Tess and Myself* (Beaminster, 1962), 11–16.

36. G. Bugler, interview, 1974.

37. G. Bugler, interview, 1980.

38. *CL*, vi. 297; *CL*, vi. 295–6.

39. SCC, diary (BL), cf. W. Blunt, *Cockerell* (New York, 1965), 214–16.

40. Blunt, *Cockerell*, 216; G. Bugler, *Personal Recollections of TH* (Dorchester, 1964), 9–10; G. Bugler, interview, 1974.

41. Blunt, *Cockerell*, 216; F. Harrison to G. Bugler, 4 Feb 1925 (G. Bugler); G. Bugler to TH, 4 Feb 1925 (DCM); *CL*, vi. 308; for the entire episode, see Wilson, *TH on Stage*, 132–40.

42. SCC note re FEH to SCC, 16 Jan 1925, letter itself destroyed (Yale); *LEFH*, 214–20, quotation 218.

43. *CL*, vi. 342; FEH to SCC, 20 Aug 1925 (Yale); Wilson, *TH on Stage*, 141.

44. Quoted in E. Blunden, *TH* (London, 1941), 170–1.

45. *Later Years*, 243–4, cf. *LW*, 462–3; *Daily Graphic* (11 Sept 1925), 15.

46. W. MacQueen Pope, *The Footlights Flickered: The Story of the Theatre in the 1920s* (London, 1959), 146; FEH to SCC, 22 Dec 1925 (Yale); *Daily Express*, 7 Dec 1925.

29 LAST THINGS

1. *CL*, vi. 341, 347, 341; SCC/TH, 25 Aug 1925 (DCM); *CL*, vi. 349, 358.

2. *CPW*, iii. 68–72, 146.

3. *CPW*, iii. 58–64, 9–12, 153–4, 134–5.

4. *Human Shows*, page proofs (DCM).

5. *CPW*, iii. 157.

6. RLP/FEH, 1929 (Yale).

7. Books, sketches, music books (DCM).

8. E. Felkin, 'Days with TH', *Encounter*, 18/4 (Apr 1962), 32–3; *CL*, vi. 276.

9. E. Brennecke, Jr., *The Life of TH* (New York, 1925); *LEFH*, 239–40.

10. T. E. Lawrence to FEH, 13 Feb 1926 (Texas); *LEFH*, 240; FEH to D. Macmillan, 14 July 1926 (BL).

11. 'Memoranda II' notebook (DCM), cf. *PN*, 92, 96; *Later Years*, 245, 252, cf. *LW*, 464, 470.

12. *Later Years*, 246, cf. *LW*, 465; *CPW*, ii. 289.

13. FEH to SCC, 29 Aug, 27 Oct, 7 Nov 1926 (Yale).

14. E. E. T[itterington], *The Domestic Life of TH (1921–1928)* (Beaminster, 1963), 8, 10.

15. *LEFH*, 245–59, *passim*.

16. *LEFH*, 243; J. L. Garvin to TH, 2 and 6 Mar 1926 (DCM); MS, *Winter Words* (Queen's College, Oxford), for revisions see, e.g., *CPW*, iii. 225.

17. FEH to P. Ridgeway, 11 July 1926 (DCM); *LEFH*, 242; *Later Years*, 248, cf. *LW*, 467.

18. *Later Years*, 247–8, cf. *LW*, 466; *The Diary of Virginia Woolf*, III: *1925–1930*, ed. Anne Olivier Bell and Andrew McNeillie (London, 1980), 96, 100.

19. *Diary of Virginia Woolf*, ed. Bell and McNeillie, iii. 96.

20. FEH to SCC, 13 and 16 Apr 1926 (Yale); *LEFH*, 237.

21. *CL*, vii. 31; *CPW*, iii. 225; *Later Years*, 249, cf. *LW*, 468.

22. *Later Years*, 250–1, cf. *LW*, 469–70; *LEFH*, 247.

23. S. Sassoon to E. Gosse, 15 Jan 1927 (BL); *CL*, vii. 57.

24. Purdy, 188; *CL*, vii. 59; *CL*, vii. 75; *CPW*, i. 10, 300–01, 243–7.

25. *The Times* (5 Mar 1927), 7, cf. *PV*, 457–8; *The Preservation of Ancient Cottages* (London, 1927), 13–16, cf. *PV*, 459–60; *PV*, 462–4.

26. *LEFH*, 249; FEH to SCC, 23 May 1927 (Yale); *Later Years*, 253–4, cf. *LW*, 471; FEH to E. Gosse, 12 June 1927 (Leeds); RLP/FEH, 1929 (Yale).

27. FEH to S. Sassoon, 18 June 1927 (Leeds); FEH to E. Gosse, 9 July 1927 (Leeds); *Later Years*, 254, cf. *LW*, 471–2.

28. G. Holst to TH, 4 Aug 1927 (DCM); *CL*, vii. 73; *Later Years*, 256, cf. *LW*, 473; M. Short, *Gustav Holst (1874–1934): A Centenary Documentation* (London, 1974), 36; FEH to SCC, 31 Aug 1927 (Yale).

29. *Later Years*, 257–9, cf. *LW*, 474–5; FEH to P. Lemperly, 29 Sept 1927 (Colby).

30. *DCC*, 27 Oct 1927; minute book (DCM archives).

31. *CL*, vii. 82; *CL*, vii. 86; TH's copy of *A Changed Man*, 399 (DCM), and see *Career*, 283.

32. FEH, diary (DCM), cf. *Later Years*, 261–2, and *LW*, 477, where 'melancholy' is changed to 'usual'.

33. FEH, diary (DCM), cf. *Later Years*, 260–2, and *LW*, 477–8.

34. *Later Years*, 263, cf. *LW*, 478; *CPW*, iii. 274; RLP/FEH, 1931.

35. FEH note, *PN*, 294.

36. Purdy, 261–2; *CPW*, iii. 226.

37. *CPW*, iii 199–200, 195–6, 171–2, 244–5, 211–12, 188–9, 200.

38. *CPW*, iii. 215; drawing of headstone (DCM), cf. *PV*, 482; *CPW*, iii. 176, 262–4.

39. *Later Years*, 263, cf. *LW*, 478; Purdy, 253; *CPW*, iii. 174.

40. FEH to SCC, 1 Dec 1927 (Yale); *LEFH*, 254–5; FEH to SCC, 8 Dec 1927 (Yale).

41. *Later Years*, 263–4, cf. *LW*, 479; *LEFH*, 255–6.

42. FEH to E. Gosse, 19 Dec 1927 (Leeds); *LEFH*, 256; *Later Years*, 265, cf. *LW*, 480.

43. *Later Years*, 264, cf. *LW*, 479; *CPW*, iii. 272–3; E. Gosse to TH, 24 Dec 1927 (DCM); *CL*, vii. 89.

44. *LEFH*, 258; *DCC*, 19 Jan 1928, 5; FEH to S. Sassoon, 4 Jan 1928 (Eton); *LEFH*, 261.

45. Telegram, 9 Jan 1928 (Yale); E. Dugdale, diary fragment (Yale); SCC to Mrs Cockerell, 11 Jan 1928 (Yale).

46. *Later Years*, 265, cf. *LW*, 480; photo of cheque, [London] *Evening News*, 16 Jan 1928; *Later Years*, 265, cf. *LW*, 480; Titterington, *Domestic Life of TH*, 16.

47. RLP/FEH, 1931; *CPW*, iii. 308–9, 309; *Later Years*, 266, cf. *LW*, 480–1.

48. KH, diary, 11 Jan 1928 (DCM: Lock); KH to E. Clodd, 2 Feb 1928 (Leeds); E. W. Mann, draft letter, 16 June 1963 (DCM).

49. SCC, diary, 11 Jan 1928 (BL); Titterington, *Domestic Life of TH*, 16; both contradicting Dr Mann's assertion, quoted in J. Gibson (ed.), *TH: Interviews and Recollections* (Basingstoke, 1999), 240–1, that he had never left Max Gate.

50. Eva Dugdale, diary extract, 1–17 Jan 1928 (Yale); RLP, notes on conversation with E. Dugdale, 1953 (Yale).

51. D. Allhusen, interview by H. Hoffman (HP); FEH, MS draft, chapter 38 of 'Life' (DCM); I. Cooper Willis, typescript, 'TH' (Colby), passage absent from version in *Colby Library Quarterly*, 9 (Mar 1971), 266–79.

52. FEH to E. Clodd, 18 Jan 1928 (Leeds); Titterington, *Domestic Life of TH*, 16.

30 Afterwards

1. Death certificate; KH, diary, 12 Jan 1928 (DCM: Lock); RLP, conversation with E. Dugdale, 1953 (Yale).

2. SCC to Mrs Cockerell, 12 Jan 1928 (Yale); SCC, diary, 12 Jan 1928 (BL).

3. E. E. Titterington, *Afterthoughts of Max Gate* (St Peter Port, 1969), 16; KH, diary, 12 Jan 1928 (DCM: Lock); May O'Rourke, interview, 1975; J. O'Rourke to TH, 28 Aug 1927 (DCM).

4. SCC to Mrs Cockerell, 11 Jan 1928 (Yale); RLP/FEH, 1929.

5. *CL*, iv. 23, and cf. L. Huxley (ed.), *Life and Letters of Thomas Henry Huxley* (2 vols., London, 1900), ii. 18; J. M. Barrie to SCC, 12 Jan 1928, in V. Meynell, *Friends of a Lifetime* (London, 1940), 315–16.

6. SCC, diary, 12 Jan 1928 (BL); *Daily Telegraph* (14 Jan 1928), 14.

7. *Daily Mail* (13 Jan 1928), 9; KH, diary, 12 and 13 Jan 1928 (DCM: Lock).

8. *Daily Telegraph* (14 Jan 1928), 11; E. Dugdale, diary fragment (Yale); E. W. Mann, 'TH', *Dorset Year-book 1964–65*, 95; reminiscences of Max Gate servants from T. W. Jesty.

9. G. Dru Drury, *Heart Burials and Some Purbeck Marble Heart-Shrines* (Dorchester, 1927).

10. E. Clodd to J. M. Bulloch, 14 Jan 1928 (Texas); Ann Thwaite, *Edmund Gosse: A Literary Landscape, 1849–1928* (London, 1984), 508.

11. SCC to Mrs Cockerell, 14 Jan 1928 (Yale); *DCC*, 19 Jan 1928, 2–3; *The Times*, *Daily Telegraph*, *Daily News*, etc., 12, 14, 17 Jan 1928.

12. *Later Years*, 267–8, cf. *LW*, 485–6; *The Times* (17 Jan 1928), 15; *DCC* (19 Jan 1928), 2–3.

13. KH, diary, 16 Jan 1928 (DCM: Lock); G. Bugler, interview, 1974.

14. *Later Years*, 268, cf. *LW*, 486; Order of Service (DCM).

15. Lawrence to W. Rothenstein, 14 Apr 1928, in *Letters of T. E. Lawrence*, ed. D. Garnett (London, 1938), 582.

16. G. B. Shaw to FEH, 27 Jan 1928 (Berg).

17. Drawing (Berg); tablet (St Juliot Church), cf. *PV*, 479–80.

18. *LEFH*, 266; *Punch* (18 Jan 1928), 70.

19. RLP/FEH, 1929, and see B. Willey, *Cambridge and Other Memories 1920–1953* (London, 1968), 55.

20. *LW*, 178, 276.

21. *LW*, 406, cf . *LW*, 3, 346.

22. J. M. Barrie to FEH, 3 Feb and 17 May 1928, in *Letters of J. M. Barrie*, ed. V. Meynell (London, 1942), 152, 154–5; J. M. Barrie to FEH, 26 Mar 1928 (DCM).

23. See *LEFH*, 323.

24. For a fuller treatment of these and other consequences of TH's will, see M. Millgate, *Testamentary Acts: Browning, Tennyson, James, Hardy* (Oxford, 1992), 147–68.

25. *LEFH*, 308, 327–8; *LEFH*, 336–7, 340–2; *LEFH*, 282, 323–4, etc.

26. For the provisions and consequences of FEH's will, see Millgate, *Testamentary Acts*, 168–74.

27. Notably Harold Hoffman, fragments of whose interview with KH survive (HP), and

Donald J. Winslow, author of 'A Call on Thomas Hardy's Sister', *TH Year Book*, no. 1 (1970), 93–6, and *TH's Sister Kate* (TH Society Monograph no. 2, 1982).

28. *CPW*, ii. 308–9.

INDEX